FILM
FINANCE *&*
DISTRIBUTION

FILM FINANCE & DISTRIBUTION

DISTRIBUTION

a dictionary of terms

by John W. Cones

ILMAN-JAMES PRESS
OS ANGELES

Library of Congress Cataloging-in-Publication Data

Cones, John W.
Film finance and distribution : a dictionary of terms / by John W. Cones.
p.   cm.
1. Motion picture industry—United States—Finance—Dictionaries.
2. Motion pictures—United States—Distribution—Dictionaries.
3. Motion Pictures—Production and direction—Dictionaries. I. Title.
PN1993.5.U6C635   1992   384'.83'0973—dc20   92-23667

ISBN: 1-879505-12-6

Cover design by Heidi Frieder

Printed in the United States of America

Silman-James Press
distributed by
Samuel French Trade
7623 Sunset Blvd.
Hollywood, CA 90046

for my son...

J. CHRISTOPHER CONES

Contents

Introduction

This book fills a critical gap in the literature of the motion picture industry. Many film industry books, articles and agreements include a small glossary of highly specialized terms but they do not attempt to be comprehensive. Thus, hundreds if not thousands of important terms and concepts are left undefined by such limited glossaries. There are several published dictionaries relating to film terminology (see bibliography) but these tend to stress the technical, production or marketing aspects of the film business, not the financing and distribution (business) side, which is where the emphasis is placed in this publication. In fact, most of the focus of the entire college-level educational system relating to film in the United States stresses the technical, creative or production side of this field, thus creating a situation that puts those who are involved in the independent production of feature film, the specific industry group for which this book is targeted, at a considerable disadvantage when it comes time to negotiate the terms of the production and distribution deals for any given film. If an independent producer is in a disadvantageous position as compared to the financing and/or distributing entity, then certainly private investors who may be backing the producer are also at a disadvantage; thus, this book has been written to help bridge that information gap and reduce this disparity in sophistication between the producer/investor side of many film transactions and the studio and/or distributor side of those same transactions (see "Level Playing Field").

The information contained in this volume should prove invaluable to all those concerned at one time or another with film finance and distribution, including attorneys, distributors, executive producers, producers, associate producers, studio executives, screenwriters and directors seeking to independently produce a special project, exhibitors, broker/dealers, money finders, motion picture accoun-

tants/auditors, investors, profit participants, federal and state government officials and film students.

The terms and phrases defined and discussed in this dictionary
are those of feature film finance and distribution, along with numerous other related terms from the production, marketing, music, legal,
accounting, insurance, securities (including corporate and limited
partnership) and general financial arenas. All of the principal forms of
feature film finance are covered, including studio/distributors, production companies, lending institutions, co-financing, pre-sales, grants,
foreign and passive investor financing. Some additional terms and
phrases are included, not because they commonly appear in film
finance or movie distribution agreements but because they are essential
to a well-rounded understanding of the industry and environment in
which such film finance and distribution agreements are negotiated
(see "Contract of Adhesion"). Still other terms were selected and
included by the author because they may aid in the understanding of
additional terms in this dictionary. In many instances, the definitions
also show how the defined term or phrase is specifically used in the
film industry and with respect to additional terms, certain entries
contain a comment from the author which is clearly biased in favor of
the independent producer (see "Editorial Slant" below).

Editorial Slant

As mentioned above, the examples of usage and commentary
provided for certain terms found in this book have been written
primarily with the independent film producer in mind. From that
perspective, this book is much more than a traditional dictionary, for,
with respect to certain terms, the discussion goes far beyond a mere
definition and seeks to more fully explore the film industry by also
analyzing some of the reasons why this business is dominated by the
major studio/distributors and why independent feature film producers
as a group have so little clout in the industry (see "Inferior Bargaining
Position").

Most of the ideas expressed in this book did not originate with the
author. They came from the 136 or so lecturers and panel members at
industry seminars as listed in the acknowledgements section below,
the books and articles listed in the bibliography and conversations the
author has had during the past five years with several hundred independent producers (many of whom have attended the more than 63
seminar lectures on film finance and distribution presented by the
author in Los Angeles, New York, San Francisco, Las Vegas, Dallas

and Houston during that same five year period).

Also, although the author is a practicing attorney, his background as an association executive, lobbyist and radio/television news reporter play an important role in shaping the editorial slant of this book. The author primarily would characterize his role in the publication of this book as one of a compiler of ideas and concepts relating to the business aspects of the film industry, although in the case of each term, the specific manner of expression relating to each idea or concept communicated is the author's own.

For those who do not quite understand why a book on film finance would also discuss distribution, the reason is the same or similar to the reason why film distribution cannot be adequately understood and discussed without a heavy emphasis on the anti-trust laws, i.e., neither topic can be objectively defined and discussed without the other. Film finance cannot be adequately explained if no provision is made for how invested money may or may not return to financiers and/or investors, (i.e., the financial side of distribution), just as the story of feature film distribution is in many ways an ongoing saga of competing economic factions within the industry, several of whom, from time to time have been associated with actual anti-trust law violations, investigations, allegations or lesser forms of "stacking the deck" (see "Anti-Competitive Practices"). Besides, the emphasis in this book on anti-trust issues may serve several valuable purposes. First, it may help those naive persons who are just starting out in this industry seeking fame and fortune to recognize that there are certain significant barriers to entry (see "Barriers to Entry," "Insider's Game" and "Relationship Driven Business") that may make it virtually impossible for them to get a fair hearing for their talents or ideas, thus this book may provide a most valuable service and persuade them to not waste their time. Secondly, within that segment of the film industry population that is edging up to or stepping over the line relating to what is permissible pursuant to the anti-trust laws, the editorial emphasis on anti-trust law issues herein may aid the individuals who are simply not aware of the impact of their conduct or the specific proscriptions against it, to gain a better understanding of what business practices are problematic from the viewpoint of the anti-trust laws and to possibly prevent or avoid problems for them (see "Business Practices," "Conduct Restrictions" and "Predatory Practices"). Finally, for those who were not as aware of the legal proscriptions against such conduct in the past, this book may serve to help them put such conduct into a new perspective and make them more aware of what to look for and report to the U.S. Justice Department and/or their own friendly anti-trust law litigator in the event that a civil remedy is appropriate (see "Remedy" and "RICO").

Finally, there is no question that some segments of the industry will not be as pleased about the editorial slant of the commentary portions of the term entries as other groups within the film industry. However, the author has already started a second edition of the book, and for those who wish to make suggested changes or additions, feel free to submit those suggestions relating either to specific terms, new terms, examples of usage or the commentary in letter form and the author will be happy to incorporate those that are appropriate into the second edition. In that way, the industry can come even closer to creating a reliable source for authoritative definitions, examples of usage and discussions relating to the terms used in the field of film finance and distribution.

Acknowledgements

A book of this nature will always be considered a work-in-progress—language is always evolving and there seems to be no end to the terms that relate to the topics covered in this book. On the other hand, this dictionary is still probably the most comprehensive work of its kind in the history of the film business, and it seems long overdue. A single entry may combine information from as many as six or seven sources, lecture notes, books on the industry, conversations with people who work in the industry, trade press articles, magazine articles, etc. (again, see bibliography at the back of the book). Thus, I gratefully acknowledge the many sources listed in that bibliography, most of which were relied on as authoritative sources of useful concepts and information.

I also wish to express my special thanks to feature film producer Simon Dubinsky, Los Angeles copyright attorney Greg Victoroff, screenwriter Gail McNamara, film/law school graduate Jeff Foy, international copyright attorney Dr. Rolf Auf Der Maur, actress Leigh Lombardi, producer Janeen Weiss, feature film technical consultant James Kelly Durgin, director of photography Levie Isaacks, writer/producer Tony Anselmo, Worldfest-Houston Film Festival Chariman J. Hunter Todd, actor David Charles Keeton, New York entertainment attorney Wilder Knight and writer/attorney Thomas M. Sipos for their invaluable assistance in editing this first edition.

It is also appropriate for me to acknowledge here (without suggesting that such persons are in any way directly responsible for the information or opinions expressed in this book) all of the lecturers and panelists presenting film finance and distribution related topics that I have listened to and learned from during the past several years.

At IFP/West sponsored events: Zanne Devine (Director of Acquisitions, Universal Pictures), George Jackson (Producer, "New Jack City"), Neal Jimenez (Screenwriter, "River's Edge"), Bobby Newmyer

(Producer, "sex, lies and videotape"), John Singleton (Director and Screenwriter, "Boyz N The Hood"), Courtenay Valenti (Production Executive, Warner Bros. Studios), Tom Garvin (Producer's Representative and Partner, Ervin, Cohen & Jessup), Christopher Murray (Partner in the Entertainment Department of the law firm of O'Melveny & Myers), Barbara Boyle (President of Sovereign Pictures), Douglas T. McHenry (Partner and Producer/Director with the Jackson McHenry Company at Warner Bros.), Irene Romero (Executive Vice President, Mercantile National Bank), Charles Kolstad (West Coast Entertainment Industry Tax Partner for Coopers & Lybrand), Robert Manning (Head of the Entertainment/Leisure Time Group at Oppenheimer & Co.) and Stephen Bannon (Partner at Bannon & Co., a Beverly Hills-based merchant bank).

At the 1992 UCLA Law Symposium: Peter Dekom (Partner, Bloom, Dekom & Hergott), Carrie J. Menkel-Meadow (Professor, UCLA School of Law), Ellen Peck (Judge of the State Bar of California Disciplinary Court), Dennis Perluss (Partner, Hufstedler, Miller, Kaus & Beardsley), Martin Singer (Partner, Lavely & Singer), Kenneth Ziffren (Partner, Ziffren, Brittenham & Branca), Leigh Brecheen (Partner, Bloom, Dekom & Hergott), Thomas Hansen (Partner, Hansen, Jacobson & Teller), Edward Masket (Executive Vice President-Administration, MCA Television Group), Sanford Wernick (Vice President, The Brillstein Company), Laurie Younger (Senior Vice President-Business Affairs, Walt Disney Television), Harold Vogel (First Vice President, Merrill Lynch & Co.), Stuart Glickman (Vice Chairman and Chief Executive Officer, The Carsey-Werner Company), Leonard Hill (Chairman of the Board, Allied Communications), Robert Jacquemin (President, Buena Vista Television), Art Stolnitz (Executive Vice President-Business Affairs & Finance, Lorimar Television), Ron Sunderland (Executive Vice President-Business Affairs & Contracts, Capital Cities/ABC), Valerie Cavanaugh (Executive Vice President, Gracie Films), Gary Barber (President, Morgan Creek), John Ptak (Agent, Creative Artists Agency), Strauss Zelnick (President, Chief Operating Officer, 20th Century Fox), Keith Fleer (Of Counsel, Sinclair Tenenbaum & Co.), Martin Bauer (President, United Talent Agency), Leon Brachman (Business Executive), Bertram Fields (Partner, Greenberg, Glusker, Fields, Claman & Machtinger), Barry Hirsch (Partner, Armstrong & Hirsch), Peter Hoffman (President & Chief Executive Officer, Carolco Pictures) and E. Barry Haldeman (Partner, Greenberg, Glusker, Fields, Claman & Machtinger).

At the 1992 Third Decade Council Annual Conference (not already mentioned): Peter Benedek (United Talent Agency), Preston Beckman (Vice President, Program Planning & Scheduling at NBC

Entertainment), James L. Brooks (Writer/Director/Co-Producer of "Terms of Endearment"), Stephen J. Cannell (Writer/Producer), Mark Canton (Chairman of Columbia Pictures), Caldecot Chubb (Producer of "Cherry 2000"), Carlton Cuse (Boam/Cuse Productions), Sean Daniel (President of Sean Daniel Company), Diane English (Creator/Writer/Executive Producer of "Murphy Brown"), Marc Ezralow (Producer of "Memorial Day Massacre"), Neil Alan Friedman (Executive Vice President of the Edward R. Pressman Film Corporation), Robert G. Friedman (President of Warner Bros. Worldwide Theatrical Advertising & Publicity), Ted Harbert (Executive Vice President, Prime Time, ABC Entertainment), Jerry Katzman (President, William Morris Agency), Jamie Kellner (President and CEO of Fox Broadcasting Company), Kerry McCluggage (President of Universal Television), Michael Nathanson (President, Worldwide Production at Columbia Pictures), David Nicksay (President and Head of Production of Morgan Creek Productions), Steven Roffer (The Steven Roffer Company), Tom Schulman (Writer, "Dead Poet's Society"), Tom Sherak (Executive Vice President, 20th Century-Fox), Joel Silver (Producer, the "Lethal Weapon" series), Nigel Sinclair (Managing Partner, Sinclair Tenenbaum & Co.), Gary Ross (Co-Author for "BIG"), Robert Stein (United Talent Agency), Rosalie Swedlin (Longview Entertainment), Jonathan Taplin (Producer, "Mean Streets"), Straus Zelnick (President and CEO of 20th Century-Fox) and Laura Ziskin (Producer, "Pretty Woman").

At the 1991 and 1992 UCLA Extension Class "Contractual Aspects of Producing, Financing and Distributing Film" and other UCLA Extension sponsored seminars of the author: Stephen Sills (Partner, Sills and Adelman), Deborah Dubelman (Director of Legal and Business Affairs, Republic Pictures Corporation), Mark Resnick (Senior Vice President, Legal Affairs, Columbia Pictures), Greg Victoroff (Copyright Attorney), Teri Williams (Entertainment Attorney), Gary Watson (formerly a Legal Affairs Attorney at Universal, now with the law firm of Greenberg, Glusker, Fields, Claman & Machtinger), Irene Speiser (Vice President, Entertainment Industries Division, Mercantile National Bank), Lionel Sobel (Professor, Loyola Law School), Steve Cardone (International Film Guarantors), Glenn Harvey (DAIWA Bank), Anna Bagdasarian (Bank of California), Susan Schaefer (Entertainment Attorney), Madelyn Adams (20th Century Fox Marketing), Doc Littlefield (Profit Participation Auditing Section at Deloitte-Touche) and Jonathan Dana (Triton Pictures).

At the 1991 Paul Kagan Seminar on Motion Picture Finance: Don Harris (AMC Film Marketing), Michael Mendelsohn (Banque Paribas), Mitchell Julis (Canyon Partners), John Davis (Davis Entertainment),

David Friendly (Imagine Films Entertainment), Joseph Cohen (Largo Entertainment & Inter Media Group), Lynda Obst (Lynda Obst Productions), Ken Badish (Moviestore Entertainment), Robert Shaye (New Line Cinema), Brandon Tartikoff (Paramount Pictures), William Shields (Trans Atlantic Pictures), Barry Reardon (Warner Bros. Distribution), Brian Maki (Yasuda Trust & Banking), and Paul Kagan (Kagan Seminars).

At the AFI Producers on Producing Series (1991): Renny Harlin ("Rambling Rose"), Debra Hill & Lynda Obst ("The Fisher King"), Don Phillips ("The Indian Runner") and Ron Ronholtz ("Homicide").

At other AFI seminars: Gary Prebula (Moderator, Writer/Director), and fellow panel members Bill Nestel (Rastar Productions), J. David Williams (Willsfield Productions), Robert Vince (President of Motion Picture Bond Co.), Lewis Horwitz (The Lewis Horwitz Organization), Tekla Morgan (President, International Film Guarantors), Leroy Bobbitt (Partner, Loeb & Loeb, Entertainment Division), Sam Grogg (Chief Executive Officer and Executive Producer of Apogee Productions and it's subsidiary, Magic Pictures), Jerry Leider (Chairman of the Caucus for Producers, Writers and Directors; Producer of "The Jazz Singer"), Jason Zelin (Vice President, New Business Development Liaison for The Completion Bond Company), Mitchell Cannold (Principal LillyAnna Productions and Co-Executive Producer of "Dirty Dancing"), Steve Monas (Senior Vice President for Business Affairs at Vision International), Harold Messing (Entertainment Attorney, Los Angeles and New York) and Michael Wiese (Moderator, Producer/Director).

At Cinetex '90 my fellow panel members: Michael Sherman (Jeffer, Mangels, Butler & Marmaro), John Sansone (President, Entertainment Business Services International) and Joel Koenig (Partner in Charge, Century City office of Deloitte & Touche).

At the American Academy of Independent Film Producers seminar in 1986 (with titles as of that year): Lawrence Garret (Director of Sales and Acquisitions for Arista Films), Dov S-S Simens (The Film Doctor), Lance Hool (Producer, "Missing In Action"), Hank McCann (Casting Director, "Pennies From Heaven"), Dom Spinosa (Head of MGM's Payroll Department), Susan Strasberg (Actress), Eric Epstein (Attorney), Ezra Doner (Vice President, Business Affairs, Cinema Group), Randy Gaiber (Bank of California), Wilbur Hobbs (Wells Fargo Bank), Mary Savarese (Cohen Insurance), David Rudich (Music Rights Attorney) and Roger Corman (Producer).

Again, although I have learned a great deal from my brief exposure to the above named persons, none of these individuals or entities are responsible for the definitions, usage examples or commentary contained in this book, and I take full responsibility for whatever deficiencies may exist in this publication.

Thanks also to all of the members of the 1992 Winter Quarter UCLA Extension class "Contractual Aspects of Producing, Financing and Distributing Film," the group for which this book was first drafted.

Suggestions From the Author on Alternative Ways to Use this Book

A. Of course, this publication may be used in the traditional sense that all dictionaries are used, i.e., as a reference source for helping to determine the meaning of a specific term as used in a given context.

B. Since, on the other hand, all of the terms included herein relate to the rather narrow field of film finance and distribution, it may also be useful for persons interested in gaining a fairly comprehensive understanding of the business related concepts involved in such field to read the book straight through.

C. For classroom use or independent study, it may also prove useful to take certain broad subject areas, such as those listed on the so-called "Motion Picture Production Chart" re-printed on the next page, i.e., (1) Acquisition, (2) Development, (3) Packaging, (4) Production Financing, (5) Pre-Production, (6) Principal Photography, (7) Post-Production and (8) Delivery and use the extensive cross-referencing of terms provided on that chart or within the dictionary following the definition and discussion of each term to review the definitions of a number of other terms that are related in some way to the original term. An entire reading assignment for a class can be organized in this manner.

D. For those persons who are relatively new to the field of film finance and distribution, it may be useful to review the "Motion Picture Industry Overview" to help place the terms defined in this dictionary into some general context.

Note Regarding the Order of Presentation—All entries in this book are alphabetized by letter rather than by word, i.e., multiple words are treated as single words. Also, certain abbreviations or acronyms appear as entries in the main text but generally refer to the corresponding full term as it would appear elsewhere in the text.

Capitalization and Cross-Referencing—Capitalization of defined terms and phrases within other defined terms and phrases has been avoided, since in the opinion of the author such capitalization may be distracting to the reader. The author has, instead, opted for a policy of liberal cross-referencing and the placement of such cross-referenced terms following the definition/discussion of each defined term. Review of such cross-referenced terms may aid significantly in the understanding of the referring term.

MOTION PICTURE PRODUCTION CHART
(Life of a Motion Picture Through Delivery or The Producer's Task List)
[described in major phases and terms]

(1) Acquisition

Underlying Property
Literary Work
Play
Magazine Article
Book
Original Screenplay
Copyright
Fair Use
Fixed Work
Public Domain
Plagiarism
Work Made for Hire
Submission Release
Certificate of Authorship
Chain of Title
Option Agreement
Acquisition Agreement
License

(2) Development

Development Financing
Idea/Concept
One-Line Description
Basic Story Outline
Synopsis
Treatment
Screenplay
First Draft
Polish
Rewrite
Final Screenplay
WGA Registration
Copyright Registration

(3) Packaging

Script and Breakdown
Tentative Budget
Tentative Shooting Schedule
Casting
Packaging Agent
Packaging Attorney
Packaging Service
Partial Financing
Director Commitment
Star Commitments
Producer Deferments
Director Deferments
Star Deferments
Lab Deferments
1st Draft Script Breakdown
Production Board
Distribution Agreements, if any
Pre-Sales, if any
Production Budget
Completion Bond
Producer/Director Undertakings

(4) Production Financing

Studio
P-F/D
Negative Pickup Agreement
Pre-Sales Agreements
Corporate Financing
Joint Venture
Co-Productions
Limited Partnership
Loans
Blocked Funds
Facilities Deals
Tax Shelters
Debt Capitalization
Currency Deals
Grants
Subsidies

(5) Pre-Production

Shooting Script
Annotated Script
Script Clearance
Written Releases
Director Agreement
Deal Memos
Crew/Performer Agreements
Location & Stage Agreements
Producer's Liability Insurance
Chain of Title Documents
Producer's Agreement
Music Agreements
Film/Sound Lab Agreements
Equipment Rental Agreements

(6) Principal Photography

Producer
Director
Director's Cast List
Cast/Extras
Film Stock/Sound Stock
Editing
Location List
Studio Rental
Publicity
Insurance
Fees and Taxes
Transportation
Staff
Set Design
Equipment Rentals
Lab Film Processing Letter
Dailies (Rushes)
Second Unit
Post-Production Schedule

(7) Post-Production

Editing
Dialogue Replacement
Music
Special Effects
Optical Effects
Sound Effects
Titles
Foley Stage Recording
Pick-up Photography
Pre-Mix Session
Dirty Dupes

(8) Delivery

Laboratory Access Letter
Film Credits
Delivery Schedule
Laboratory Letter
Final Screenplay
Shooting Script
Publicity Material
Credit Statement
Photographs
Final Answer Print
Original Picture Negative
Inter-Positive
Television Cover Shots
Sound Album Materials

Internegatives
Main and End Titles
Music, Dialogue and Sound Items
Film and Soundtrack Materials
Screen Credits
Dialogue
Action Continuity
MPAA Certificate
Certificate of Insurance
Residual Information
Title and Copyright Reports
Composite Optical Soundtrack
    Negative
Work Print
Out-takes (Cutouts)

Motion Picture Industry Overview

General

The theatrical motion picture industry in the United States has changed substantially over the last three decades and continues to evolve rapidly. Historically, the "major studios" financed, produced and distributed the vast majority of American-made motion pictures. During the most recent decade, many of the motion pictures released have been produced by so-called independent producers even though some of the production financing for such pictures has been provided by the major studio/distributors. In the last couple of years, fewer independently produced movies were being made.

The following general description is a simplified overview of the complex process of producing and distributing motion pictures and is intended to be an aid to investors and others in understanding the motion picture business. This overview does not describe what will necessarily occur in the case of any particular motion picture.

Production of Motion Pictures

During the filmmaking process, which may take approximately 12 to 24 months from the start of the development phase to theatrical release, a film progresses through several phases. The four general stages of motion picture production are development, pre-production, principal photography and post-production. A brief summary of each of the four general movie production stages follows:

Development

In the development stage, underlying literary material for a motion picture project is acquired, either outright, through an option to acquire such rights or by engaging a writer to create original literary material. If the literary material is not in script form, a writer must be engaged to create a script. The script must be sufficiently detailed to provide the production company and others participating in the financing of a motion picture with enough information to estimate the cost of producing the motion picture. Only a small percentage of projects in development will become completed motion pictures.

Pre-Production

During the pre-production stage, the production company usually selects (to the extent not chosen during the development stage) a director, actors and actresses, prepares a budget and secures the necessary financing. Pre-production activities are usually more extensive than the development process. In cases involving unique or desired talent, commitments must be made to keep performers available for the picture.

Principal Photography

The process of principal photography (the actual filming of a motion picture) and the creation of special effects is the most costly stage of the production of a motion picture. Principal photography generally takes from eight to twelve weeks to complete. Bad weather at locations, the illness of a cast or crew member, disputes with local authorities or labor unions, a director's or producer's decision to re-shoot scenes for artistic reasons and other often unpredictable events can seriously delay the scheduled completion of principal photography and substantially increase its costs. If a motion picture reaches the principal photography stage, it usually will be completed.

Post-Production

During the post-production stage, the editing, scoring and mixing of dialogue, music and sound effects tracks of a motion picture take place and master prints are prepared. These activities often require technically sophisticated editing, sound and effects work.

Distribution of Motion Pictures

Motion picture revenue is derived from the worldwide licensing of a motion picture: (a) for theatrical exhibition; (b) for non-theatrical exhibition (viewing in airplanes, hotels, military bases and other facilities); (c) to pay-television systems for delivery to television receivers by means of cable, over-the-air and satellite delivery systems; (d) to commercial television networks; (e) to local commercial television stations and (f) for reproduction on video cassettes (and video discs) for home video use. Revenue is also derived from licensing "ancillary rights" to a motion picture for the creation of books, published music, soundtrack albums and merchandise. A picture cannot always be sold in all of these markets or media.

The timing of revenues received from the various sources varies from film to film. Typically, theatrical receipts from United States distribution are received approximately 90% in the first twelve months after a film is first exhibited and 10% in the second twelve months. Theatrical receipts from the rest of the world are typically received 40% in the first year following initial theatrical release, 50% in the second year and 10% in the third year. Home video royalties are typically received 80% in the first year following theatrical release and 20% in later years. Pay and cable license fees are typically received 65% in the third year, 25% in the fourth year and 10% in the fifth year following theatrical release. The majority of syndicated domestic television receipts are typically received in the fourth, fifth and sixth years after theatrical release if there are no network television licenses and the sixth, seventh and eighth years if there are network licenses. The markets for film products have been undergoing rapid changes due to technological and other innovations. As a consequence, the sources of revenues available have been changing rapidly and the relative importance of the various markets as well as the timing of such revenues has also changed and can be expected to continue to change.

Expenses incurred in distributing a motion picture are substantial and vary depending on many factors. These factors include the initial response by the public to the motion picture, the nature of its advertising campaign, the pattern of its release (e.g., the number of theatres booked and the length of time that a motion picture is in release).

The following is a brief summary of each of the sources of revenue of motion pictures and the distribution/licensing process associated with such sources:

United States Theatrical Distribution

In recent years, United States theatrical exhibition has generated a declining percentage of the total income earned by most pictures, largely because of the increasing importance of cable and pay television, home video and other ancillary markets. Nevertheless, the total revenues generated in the United States theatrical market are still substantial and are still likely to account for a large percentage of revenues for a particular film. In addition, performance in the United States theatrical market generally also has a profound effect on the value of the picture in other media and markets.

Motion pictures are distributed to theatrical markets through numerous branch offices. Theatrical distribution requires the commitment of substantial funds in addition to a motion picture's negative cost. The distributor must arrange financing and personnel to: (a) create the motion picture's advertising campaign and distribution plan; (b) disseminate advertising, publicity and promotional material by means of magazines, newspapers, trailers and television; (c) duplicate and distribute prints of the motion picture; (d) "book" the motion picture in theatres; and (e) collect from exhibitors the distributor's share of the box office receipts from the motion picture. A distributor must carefully monitor the theatres to which it licenses its picture to ensure that the exhibitor keeps only the amounts to which it is entitled by contract and promptly pays all amounts due to the distributor. Distributors will sometimes reach negotiated settlements with exhibitors as to the amounts to be paid, and such settlements may relate to amounts due for several pictures.

For a picture's initial theatrical release, a United States theatre exhibitor will usually pay to a distributor a percentage of box office receipts, which is negotiated based on the expected appeal of the motion picture and the stature of the distributor. The negotiated percentage of box office receipts remitted to the distributor is generally known as "film rentals" but is more typically defined in distribution agreements to be part of "gross receipts". Such gross receipts customarily diminish during the course of a picture's theatrical run. Typically, the distributor's share of total box office receipts over the entire initial theatrical release period will average between 25% to 60% depending on the distributor; the exhibitor will retain the remaining 75% to 40%. The exhibitor will also retain all receipts from the sale of food and drinks at the theatre (concessions). Occasionally, an exhibitor will pay to the distributor a flat fee or percentage of box office receipts against a guaranteed amount. Pay television and new home entertainment equipment (such as video games, computers and video cassette players) offer competitive alternatives to motion-picture theatres.

Major film distributors are typically granted the right to license exhibition of a film in perpetuity, and normally have the responsibility for advertising and supplying prints and other materials to the exhibitors. Under some arrangements, the distributor retains a distribution fee from the gross receipts, which averages approximately 30% of the gross film rentals, and recoups the costs incurred in distributing the film. The principal costs incurred are the cost of duplicating the negative into prints for actual exhibition and advertising of the motion picture. The distribution deal usually provides that the parties providing the financing are then entitled to recover the cost of producing the film. However, bank-financed productions will typically require that the bank be paid back its principal, interest and fees out of first moneys to the distributor.

The amount major film distributors spend on prints and advertising is generally left to the discretion of the distributor. In some instances, however, the producer may negotiate minimum expenditures or ceilings on such items.

Foreign Theatrical Distribution

While the value of the foreign theatrical market varies due to currency exchange-rate fluctuations and the political conditions in the world or specific territories, it continues to provide a significant source of revenue for theatrical distribution. Due to the fact that this market is comprised of a multiplicity of countries and, in some cases, requires the making of foreign language versions, the distribution pattern stretches over a longer period of time than does exploitation of a film in the United States theatrical market. Major studio/distributors usually distribute motion pictures in foreign countries through local entities and the distribution fees for such entities usually vary between 35% and 40% depending on the territory or financial arrangements. These local entities generally will be either wholly-owned by the distributor, a joint venture between the distributor and another motion picture company or an independent agent or sub-distributor. Such local entities may also distribute motion pictures of other producers, including other major studios. Film rental agreements with foreign exhibitors take a number of different forms, but they typically provide for payment to a distributor of a fixed percentage of box office receipts or a flat amount. Risks associated with foreign distribution include fluctuations in currency values and government restrictions or quotas on the percentage of receipts which may be paid to the distributor, the remittance of funds to the United States and the importation of motion pictures into a foreign country.

Home Video Rights

The home video market in the United States has experienced substantial growth in the last decade, although it has leveled off somewhat in recent years. Certain foreign territories, particularly Europe, have seen an increased utilization of home video units due to the relative lack of diversified television programming. Consequently, sales of video cassettes have increased in such markets in recent years. Although growth in this area may be reduced because of an increase in television programming in such foreign territories, receipts from home video in these markets can be expected to continue to be significant.

Films are generally released on home video six to nine months after initial domestic theatrical release of the picture, but before the exhibition of the picture on cable/pay or network television.

United States Television Distribution

Television rights in the United States are generally licensed first to pay television for an exhibition period following home video release, thereafter to network television for an exhibition period, then to pay television again, and finally syndicated to independent stations. Therefore, the owner of a film may receive payments resulting from television licenses over a period of six years or more.

Cable and Pay Television

Pay television rights include rights granted to cable, direct broadcast satellite, microwave, pay-per-view and other services paid for by subscribers. Cable and pay television networks usually license pictures for initial exhibition commencing six to twelve months after initial domestic theatrical release, as well as for subsequent showings. Pay television services such as Home Box Office, Inc. ("HBO") and Showtime/The Movie Channel, Inc. ("Showtime") have entered into output contracts with one or more major production companies on an exclusive or non-exclusive basis to assure themselves a continuous supply of motion picture programming. Some pay-television services have required exclusivity as a precondition to such contracts.

The pay-television market is characterized by a large number of sellers and few buyers. However, the number of motion pictures utilized by these buyers is extremely large and a great majority of motion pictures that receive theatrical exhibition in the United States are, in fact, shown on pay television.

Network Television

In the United States, broadcast network rights are granted to ABC, CBS, NBC or other entities formed to distribute programming to a large group of stations. The commercial television networks in the United States license motion pictures for a limited number of exhibitions during a period that usually commences two to three years after a motion picture's initial theatrical release. During recent years, only a small percentage of motion pictures have been licensed to network television, and the fees paid for such motion pictures have declined. This decline is generally attributed to the growth of the pay television and home video markets, and the ability of commercial television networks to produce and acquire made-for-television motion pictures at a lower cost than license fees previously paid for theatrical motion pictures.

Television Syndication

Distributors also license the right to broadcast a motion picture on local, commercial television stations in the United States, usually for a period commencing five years after initial theatrical release of the motion picture, but earlier if the producer has not entered into a commercial television network license. This activity, known as "syndication," has become an important source of revenues as the number of, and competition for, programming among local television stations has increased.

Foreign Television Syndication

Motion pictures are now being licensed in the foreign television market in a manner similar to that in the United States. The number of foreign television stations as well as the modes of transmission (i.e., pay, cable, network) have been expanding rapidly, and the value of such markets has been likewise increasing and should continue to expand.

Producers may license motion pictures to foreign television stations during the same period they license such motion pictures to television stations in the United States; however, governmental restrictions and the timing of the initial foreign theatrical release of the motion pictures in the territory may delay the exhibition of such motion pictures in such territory.

Relicensing

The collective retained rights in a group of previously produced motion pictures is often a key asset, as such pictures may be relicensed in the pay and commercial television, home video and non-theatrical markets, and occasionally may be re-released for theatrical exhibition.

Although no one can be certain of the value of these rights, certain older films retain considerable popularity and may be relicensed for theatrical or television exhibition. New technologies brought about by the continuing improvements in electronics may also give rise to new forms of exhibition that will develop value in the future.

Other Ancillary Markets

A distributor may earn revenues from other ancillary sources, unless the necessary exploitation rights in the underlying literary property have been retained by writers, talent, composers or other third parties. The right to use the images of characters in a motion picture may be licensed for merchandising items such as toys, T-shirts and posters. Motion picture rights may also be licensed for novelizations of the screenplay, comic book versions of the screenplay and books about the making of the motion picture. The soundtrack of a motion picture may be separately licensed for soundtrack records and may generate revenue in the form of mechanical performance royalties, public performance royalties and sheet music publication royalties.

A BRIEF INTRODUCTORY ESSAY ON FILM FINANCE
(Or Some Advice on Cutting Through the Film Finance Jungle)

The financing of an independently produced feature film usually involves many choices. The person who generally makes most of those choices is the producer. Almost every choice that needs to be made will provide some advantages and some disadvantages. Thus, the producer must initially engage in a realistic appraisal and evaluation of which forms of film finance are actually available for a specific project (see "Availability Analysis") and then the pros and cons of those various alternatives (see "Pro and Con Analysis").

Unfortunately, many of the people who are involved in this field of film finance and have some bona fide expertise in a limited subject area tend to make self-serving presentations relating to the form of film finance he or she prefers by proclaiming that ". . . the best way to finance a feature film is (this or that specific method) . . ." or by denigrating the forms of film finance in which such person has little or no expertise. In addition, these persons often fail to provide any really useful and valuable information in their presentations, fail to provide any written handouts of value or simply indicate that those in the audience seeking to finance a film must hire a specific type of person who has a given kind of expertise, and the person speaking just happens to be one of those. The truth is that no one can stand before an audience or even write a book or an article about film finance and honestly make the statement that they know the best way to finance the films of all persons in the audience. There are too many variables that must be considered in determining such film finance choices, and unless the person with film finance expertise first determines what kind of film is being proposed, what the anticipated budget is and what resources and elements the producer group brings to the table, such self-serving statements and presentations are intellectually dishonest at best.

The next time a reader of this dictionary hears such a presentation ask the following questions: (1) How can anyone state that a specific form of film finance is the best way to finance a film without knowing what kind of film project is envisioned? (2) What are the disadvantages of the form of film finance that you recommend? (3) How many films similar to the kind of film the reader is proposing were successfully financed using this method in recent years? (4) Or if the film finance method being offered is new or different, why will it work when certain other methods may not? (5) Of what relevance is an analysis of the various advantages and disadvantages of a particular form of film finance to a producer who is foreclosed from that form of film finance due to the lack of a sufficient track record of other threshold barrier?

The Motion Picture Production Chart that precedes this essay lists some sixteen different, and in some cases related or overlapping, forms of film finance. The list can be easily expanded depending on what level of analysis and classification is used. In addition to some form of definition of these various types of film finance, this dictionary attempts to provide some discussion of the advantages or disadvantages of each while referring the reader to other terms that may help further explain the nature of a given transaction.

The other side of film finance is distribution. The method of finance may determine whether a film is produced, but the distribution deal and its implementation will almost always play an important role in determining whether and to what extent revenues will flow back to the financing source. It is thus not advisable to separate the analysis of and choices relating to film finance from the distribution approach. Almost all financing sources will share an interest in determining the probabilities for recouping their contribution at some level, and those probabilities cannot be realistically appraised without an understanding of the distribution process. In fact, the distribution side of the transaction is in most instances more important than the financing side for determining whether revenues ultimately get back to the financing source. Thus, the effects of the economic principles relating to supply and demand in the market place, the bargaining strength of the parties negotiating the distribution deal, the specific negotiated terms of the distribution deal itself, the actual implementation of the distribution deal and the effectiveness (or lack of effectiveness) of remedies available to the producer and financing groups in the event that the distribution deal is not properly administered are all important factors in determining whether any form of film finance will result in a fair sharing of film revenues among distributor, producer (including the creative side) and financing sources.

Regrettably, there appears to be more emphasis placed by film producers on finance methods as opposed to the ins and outs of distribution (at the individual deal or industry levels); thus, the actual results of distribution from a financial standpoint are seldom satisfactory to the producer and non-industry financing groups. Hopefully, the information contained in this volume will contribute to a better understanding of what is involved in distribution and how it effects the financial results of a film deal.

— A —

ABANDONMENT PROVISION. A clause in a production-financing distribution agreement which sets out under what circumstances the studio financier may be permitted to stop production and further financing of a motion picture (see "Production-Financing Distribution Agreement").

ABBREVIATED FORCE MAJEURE CLAUSE. A provision in contracts which is intended to excuse a party from performance of its obligations in the event that such performance is prevented by forces outside the control of such party and which does not specify the events or acts that excuse performance (see "Force Majeure Clause").

ABOVE-THE-LINE. The portion of a film's budget which covers major creative elements and personnel, i.e., those which are creatively unique and individually identifiable. These are primarily story acquisition, screenplay rights, script development, writer, executive producer, producer, director and principal members of the cast. The phrase "above-the-line" refers to the location on the film budget of the specific expense item/person (see "Acquisition Agreement," "Below-the-Line," "Development" and "Principal Players").

ABOVE-THE-LINE COSTS. Film production-period costs relating to acquiring the story rights, property rights associated with the screenplay, script development and signing the producer, director and principal members of the cast (see "Above-the-Line" and "Below-the-Line Costs").

ABOVE-THE-LINE DEFERRALS. The postponement of payment for some or all of the salary or other remuneration due to be paid to above-the-line personnel. Such deferrals are often negotiated in low-budget motion picture projects and sometimes are required in lender-financed pictures (see "Deferments" and "Negative Pickups").

ABOVE-THE-LINE EMPLOYMENT AGREEMENTS. Employment contracts for persons whose line-item film budget entries appear "above-the-line" in the film's budget, i.e., above the line that separates those persons whose services are considered creatively unique and individually identifiable from those that are not. Above-the-Line employment agreements are individually negotiated (see "Below-the-Line" and "Employment Agreements").

ABOVE THE REGULAR TITLE (same as "Above the Title").

ABOVE THE TITLE. A reference to the position of front credits that appear before the main title on the motion picture screen. Occasionally, the position of front credits may be a negotiating issue for certain participants in a film (see "Director," "Producer," "Star" and "Studio").

ABSORPTION (see "Absorption Arrangement").

ABSORPTION ARRANGEMENT. In feature film sub-distribution, either when an independent distributor uses a major studio/distributor for actual distribution or where the independent distributor uses other independent sub-distributors, a situation in which the independent distributor absorbs the fee of the actual distributor within its own distribution fee in order to avoid double charging the revenue stream of the film for distribution fees ("Double Distribution Fees," "Pass Through," "Override" and "Sub-Distribution").

ABSORPTION FORMULA (see "Absorption Arrangement").

ABRIDGEMENT. A shortened form of a literary work retaining the general sense and unity of the original (see "Underlying Property").

ABUSIVE TAX SHELTER. An investment transaction, often structured as a limited partnership, which is devoid of any economic purpose other than the generation of tax benefits or whose claimed tax benefits are questionable (see "Tax Shelter").

ACADEMY AWARDS. Honors presented each spring since the late 1920s by the Academy of Motion Picture Arts and Sciences. In recent years, the fact that a motion picture wins an Academy Award has added as much as $10 million to the film's gross box-office receipts during the film's continuing or subsequent runs. Thus, the ability of a distributor to influence the votes of the Academy members on such issues is extremely valuable and, to that end, many distributors have conducted expensive direct-mail promotional campaigns to Academy members in search of those votes (see "Academy of Motion Picture Arts & Sciences," "Distribution Expenses" and "Oscar").

ACADEMY OF MOTION PICTURE ARTS & SCIENCES (AMPAS). A professional honorary organization created in 1927 and now composed of more than 4,000 motion picture craftspersons. The Academy was formed for the general purpose of providing incentives for higher levels of technical and professional achievement among all branches of filmmaking. Its stated specific purposes are to advance the arts and sciences of motion pictures; foster cooperation among creative leaders for cultural, educational and technological progress; recognize outstanding achievements; cooperate on technical research and improvement of methods and equipment; provide a common forum and meeting ground for its various branches and crafts; represent the viewpoint of actual creators of the motion picture; and foster educational activities between the professional community and the public-at-large. The Academy states that it does not get involved in economic, labor or political issues. The Academy awards the Oscars, maintains a film library, and sponsors speaker programs and student film awards. Membership is by invitation of the Board of Governors and is limited to those who have achieved distinction in the arts and sciences of motion pictures. Some of the criteria for admittance are film credits of a caliber which reflect the high standards of the Academy, nomination for an Academy Award, achievement of unique distinction, earning special merit or making an outstanding contribution to film (see "Insider's Game," "Members of the Club" and "Oscars").

ACADEMY PLAYERS DIRECTORY. A multiple volume publication of the Academy of Motion Picture Arts and Sciences which contains a photographic listing of actors and actresses (see "Academy of Motion Picture Arts and Sciences").

ACCELERATED COST RECOVERY. IRS-approved methods used in depreciating (i.e., recovering the cost through tax deductions) of fixed (qualifying) assets within a shorter period than the expected useful (economic) lives of the assets, i.e., a faster recovery of such cost. Such methods of depreciation thus provide earlier tax benefits than traditional straight-line depreciation. The income forecast method of depreciation used for films is a form of accelerated cost recovery (see "Depreciation," "Income Forecast Method" and "Straight-Line Depreciation").

ACCELERATED RATE. Occurring more often during the same period or at an increased frequency, e.g., a gross participation may be paid at an accelerated rate depending on how certain the distributor is of its ability to obtain revenues which make up the distributor gross receipts out of which such participations are to be paid (see "Gross Participations," "Gross Profit Participant," "Gross Receipts" and "Participant").

ACCELERATION. The declaration by the federal Securities and Exchange Commission (SEC) that a registration statement for a public offering of securities is effective, which in turn means that the registered securities can be sold. Acceleration usually occurs the day the underwriting agreement (in an underwritten offering) is signed or after the SEC comments are complied with, and the registration statement is filed in final form (see "Effective" and "Waiting Period").

ACCOUNTABLE GROSS. A contractually defined term used in some film distribution agreements to mean something akin to distributor's film rentals minus specified off-the-top deductions (see "Adjusted Gross," "Exclusions," "Film Rentals," "Off-the-Top" and "Producer's Share").

ACCOUNTANT. One who is trained and skilled in the practice of accounting but who is not necessarily certified by a state accountancy certification agency (see "Certified Public Accountant" and "Public Accountant").

ACCOUNTANT'S OPINION. Statement signed by an independent public accountant describing the scope of the examination of the books and records of an individual or organization. Since financial reporting involves considerable discretion, the accountant's opinion may be an important consideration for a lender or investor (also called "Certificate of Accounts" and "Auditor's Certificate;" see "Limited Review" and "Qualified Opinion").

ACCOUNT EXECUTIVE. A brokerage firm employee with the legal powers of an agent who advises and executes orders for investor clients of the firm (see "Broker/Dealer" and "Registered Representative").

ACCOUNTING METHOD. The method by which a business (corporation, partnership or sole proprietorship) keeps its books and records for purposes of computing income and deductions and determining taxable income. Generally, the method of accounting affects the timing of an item of income or deduction. The two major methods of accounting are accrual and cash (see "Accrual Method of Accounting," "Cash Method of Accounting," "FASB" and "GAAP").

ACCOUNTING PERIOD. A chronological division for recording and summarizing business and financial transactions; typically, either monthly, quarterly, semi-annually or annually (see "Accounting Method").

ACCOUNTING PRINCIPLES AND PRACTICES. The rules, regulations and guides relating to a specific industry. With respect to the film industry, such principles and practices generally fall into three broad categories: cost capitalization, cost amortization and revenue recognition and reporting (see "Amortization," "Capitalization," "FASB

Statement No. 53," "GAAP," "Revenue Recognition and Reporting" and "Videocassette Revenue Reporting").

ACCOUNTING RECORDS. Written or otherwise recorded information relating to the business and financial transactions of an entity (see "Accounting Principles and Practices").

ACCOUNTING RELEASE DATE. The date on which amortization of a film begins. For television, it is the date on which the film is first telecast (see "Release Date").

ACCOUNT NUMBER. A studio accounting number assigned to a given film production at the studio and which is generally all that is required of someone to charge expenses for goods or services to the film's account at the studio. In a studio financing context, producers must carefully monitor and review studio charges to make certain they are all authorized (see "Audit," "Creative Accounting," "Over-Budget" and "Over-Budget Penalty").

ACCOUNTS RECEIVABLE. Money owed to a business for merchandise or services sold on open account ("Bad Debt").

ACCREDITED INVESTOR. Any person or entity who comes within any of eight categories of persons or entities described in Rule 501 of Regulation D, including any natural person whose individual net worth, or joint net worth with that person's spouse, at the time of the purchase of the security exceeds $1,000,000 or a natural person who had individual income exceeding $200,000 in each of the two most recent years or joint income with that person's spouse exceeding $300,000 in each of those years and who reasonably expects the same level in the current year (see "Investor Numerical Limitation," "Investor Sophistication Requirements," "Investor Suitability," "Private Placement" and "Regulation D").

ACCRUAL METHOD OF ACCOUNTING. An accounting method under which (1) income is subject to tax after all events fixing the right to receive such income have occurred and (2) deductions are allowed when the obligation to pay similarly becomes fixed, regardless of when the income is actually received or when the obligation is actually paid or met. The accrual method must be utilized by any business taxpayer which has inventory (see "Accounting Method" and "Cash Method of Accounting").

ACCRUALS. The periodic accumulation of payments that are due (see "Accounts Receivable" and "Settlement Transaction").

ACCRUE OR ACCRUED. To accumulate, to happen, to come into fact or existence; payments are said to have accrued when they have become a legally enforceable claim (see "Uncollectible Indebtedness").

A.C.E. (see "American Cinema Editors").

ACKNOWLEDGE. To admit knowledge of; recognize the rights, authority, or status of; take notice of; state that a document has been received; or recognize a document as genuine or valid (see "Certify").

ACKNOWLEDGMENT. A declaration or avowal of one's act or of a fact to give it legal validity; the thing done or given in recognition of something received. For example, an acknowledgement is used with a production/financing distribution agreement to ensure that the financier/distributor will obtain the services of a particular individual producer (see "Production-Financing/Distribution Agreement").

A.C. NIELSEN COMPANY (see "Nielsen Media Research").

"A" COUNTIES. The Nielsen Media Research designation for counties which are in the twenty-five largest metropolitan areas in the U.S. in terms of population. The largest cities and consolidated urban areas are found in these counties. Such designations are used by movie distributors in marketing their films (see "ADI Market," "B-County," "C-County," "D-County," "Key" and "Nielsen Media Research").

ACPB (see "Audited Cash Production Budget").

ACQUISITION AGREEMENT. The motion picture contract upon which all other agreements relating to the production of a film are based, i.e., the agreement through which a producer or production company acquires the right to use another's literary work or other property in producing a motion picture (see "Development," "Option or Option Contract," "Option Purchase Agreement" and "Property").

ACQUISITION DEAL (same as "Acquisition Agreement").

ACQUISITION/DISTRIBUTION AGREEMENT. The written contract between a film's producer and the distribution company which sets out the terms and conditions under which the distributor will distribute the film. The acquisition/distribution agreement differs from the production-financing/distribution agreement in that no production financing is provided by the distributor in the former. The primary difference between the acquisition/distribution agreement and the negative pickup distribution agreement is that the negative pickup commitment is negotiated and made prior to completion of the motion picture (see "In-House Production," "Production-Financing/Distribution Agreement," "Negative Pickup Distribution Agreement," "Rent-A-Distributor" and "Theatrical Distribution Contract").

ACQUISITION OF STORY RIGHTS. The first major stage in the production of a movie and with respect to the categorization of production costs. Acquisition activities (and their corresponding costs) include acquiring the rights to a concept or a license to a copyrighted literary property such as a book and/or original screenplay (see "Acquisition Agreement" and "Production Costs").

ACQUISITIONS. Films that have been independently financed and produced by independent producers for which distributors have contractually acquired the right to distribute. Technically, the term should be applied to films acquired through the acquisition/distribution agreement, but it is sometimes used in a broader sense to include the negative pickup arrangement (see "Acquisition/Distribution Agreement," "In-House Product," "Negative Pickup" and "Pickups").

ACT. One of the principal divisions of a screenplay. Generally, screenplays have three acts with some 30 to 60 scenes in each act (see "Screenplay").

ACTION. In a film sense, the term "action" refers to movement in front of the camera. On the set of a motion picture during principal photography, the word "action" is called out by the director after the cameras have started rolling to signify the start of movement and dialogue for the scene being shot. In a legal sense, the term "action" refers to a lawsuit or other judicial proceeding whereby one party pursues a remedy against another for a wrong done, for protection of a right or for prevention of a wrong (see "Action-at-Law," "Equitable Remedy," "Injunction," "Remedy or Remedies" and "Suit").

ACTION-ADVENTURE. A film genre in which the story revolves around or emphasizes danger and unknown risks and in which physical activity predominates. As a genre, such films appear to have broad international appeal, i.e., seem to travel better than other genre such as character shows, and the casting of a name star may not be as critical to its success (see "Genre").

ACTION-AT-LAW. A judicial proceeding which may only be brought before a court at law as opposed to a court of equity (contrast with "Equitable Remedy" and "Injunction").

ACTION CONTINUITY (see "Continuity").

ACTION PRODUCT (same as "Action-Adventure;" see "Product").

ACTION STILL. A photograph of an actual scene in a movie enlarged from a single frame of the motion picture film (see "Production Still").

ACTION TRACK. The exposed film depicting scenes for a movie, but without any dialogue or effects tracks (see "Sound Tracks").

ACT OF GOD. The result of the direct, immediate and exclusive operation of the forces of nature, uncontrolled and uninfluenced by human force or power, which is of such character that it could not have been prevented or avoided by foresight or prudence. Examples of so-called "acts of God" include natural floods, earthquakes, lightening, etc. (see "Force Majeure Clause").

ACTOR. Specifically in film, a person performing a role in any dramatic production, but more generally, any person, animal or product appearing in front of the camera as the subject, or one of the subjects, of the scene or shot. The term may be used generically to include the female performer (see "Actress" and "Player").

ACTOR CONTROLS. Provisions in film production and employment agreements with actors that enable such persons to exercise authority over certain specified decisions, e.g., script approval, going into production without signing the long form agreement, and, in rare instances, final cut authority (see "Approvals," "Final Cut" and "Long Form Agreement").

ACTRESS. The traditional term applied to female actors (see "Actor").

ACTUAL BREAKEVEN. The point at which revenue generated by exploitation of a motion picture equals the costs incurred in the production and/or distribution of such motion picture for the applicable entity, e.g., the film's distributor (see "Artificial Breakeven," "Breakeven," "Cash Breakeven" and "First Breakeven").

ACTUAL COMPETITORS. Genuine or real rivals in an economic context. The concept is important for anti-trust analysis purposes and forms one of the six tests making up the U.S. Department of Justice's 1984 Merger Guidelines for analyzing the competitive effects of a vertical merger (see "Anti-Trust Laws," "Merger Guidelines," "Paramount Consent Decree of 1948," "TriStar Case" and "Vertical Merger").

ACTUAL INTEREST RATE. The real interest percentage charged for the use of funds, e.g., a film production loan, as opposed to the prime interest rate (see "Interest" and "Prime Rate").

ACTUAL PRODUCTION COSTS. The amount of money actually expended in the production of a feature film as opposed to the amount projected by the film's budget (see "Audited Cash Production Budget" and "Negative Costs").

AD (see "Advertising" and "Advertisement").

ADAPTATION. A movie script which modifies a story that first appeared in another medium. Screenplays are sometimes adapted from novels, short stories and magazine articles (see "Novel" and "Screenplay").

ADDED SCENE. A scene which is inserted into a script that has already been assigned scene numbers. Such scene insertions may have significant financial implications, depending on the length and complexity of the added scene (see "Budget," "Continuity" and "Production Costs").

ADDENDUM. Something added (see "Rider").

ADDITIONAL COMPENSATION. A contractual category of remuneration paid to actors, directors and sometimes writers, over and above their basic salaries. Thus, the term would include profit participations (see "Contingent Compensation" and "Deferrals").

ADDITIONAL CREDIT. A listing on the motion picture screen in recognition of the contribution of the party listed, in the development, production or distribution of a film, aside from another credit provided to the same person, e.g., a writer who is actively involved with the production of a film may also receive an associate producer credit as an additional credit (see "Credits" and "Producers Guild of America").

ADDITIONAL INSUREDS. Persons or entities other than the primary person or entity whose interests are protected by an insurance policy (see "Insurance" and "Errors and Omissions Insurance").

"A" DEAL. The transaction and documentation associated with a major motion picture, i.e., involving the highest levels of talent and major studio/distributors (see "A Title").

ADHESION CONTRACT. A contract so heavily restrictive of one party, while so non-restrictive of another, that doubts arise as to its validity as a voluntary and uncoerced agreement; it implies a grave inequality of bargaining power. The concept often arises in the context of so-called "standard form" printed contracts prepared by one party and submitted to the other on a "take it or leave it" basis. Courts have recognized there is often no true equality of bargaining power in such contracts and have accommodated that reality in interpreting such contracts (see "Contract," "Distribution Agreement," "Negotiate," "Overreaching," "Standard Contract," "Submissions Release" and "Unconscionable Contract").

ADI MARKET. Area of dominant influence. An Arbitron audience-market classification designating a certain market area in which local television stations have partial or complete signal dominance over stations from other market areas. Commonly referred to as a television broadcast area. Similar to Nielsen DMA (designated market area). Some independent distributors use the ADI market for sub-distribution purposes as opposed to the more traditional sub-distribution areas designated by the exchanges (see "Arbitron Ratings Company," "Exchanges" and "Sub-Distribution").

ADJUDICATE. To hear a case, lawsuit, or issue and determine such matter judicially (see "Arbitration" and "Litigation").

ADJUSTED BASIS. Tax terminology referring to the base price from which to judge capital gains or losses upon the sale of an asset. During the time that a taxpayer holds an asset, such as a motion picture, certain events require that the taxpayer adjust (either up or down) his, her, or its original basis to reflect the effects of such events. The original basis adjusted by such events constitutes the adjusted basis (see "Basis").

ADJUSTED CAPITAL ACCOUNT BALANCE. A technical accounting term used in a limited partnership context which means the balance in any partner's capital account increased by an amount equal to the partner's post-payout sharing ratio multiplied by the minimum gain (see "Post-Payout Sharing Ratio" and "Minimum Gain").

ADJUSTED GROSS. A negotiated and defined term in a movie distribution deal, typically gross receipts minus certain specified deductions, which may be the basis of negotiated percentage participations in that fund, i.e., that pool of money referred to as "adjusted gross." Such deductions from gross receipts may include prints and advertising costs, taxes, residuals, advances and other specified items from first position gross. If deductions for enough different items are demanded by the distributor and accepted by the prospective adjusted gross participant, the resulting adjusted gross participation may not have any greater value than a net profit participation. Sometimes, the cost of prints and advertising alone may diminish the value of adjusted gross participation to the point that no money will ever be paid to persons or entities with rights to receive such funds (see "Accountable Gross," "First Position Gross," "Exclusions," "Net Profits," "Off-the-Top Deductions" and "Talent Participations").

ADJUSTED GROSS INCOME. The income on which a business or individual calculates his, her, or its federal income tax. For a business, adjusted gross income is determined by subtracting any unreimbursed business expenses and other deductions from gross income (see "Income Tax").

ADJUSTED RATE OF RETURN (ARR). A method of calculating the anticipated rate of return on an investment which is useful in evaluating all of the economic benefits of an investment and in comparing investments. ARR is the rate that equates the total future value of the economic benefits to the present value of the investment (see "After-Tax Real Rate of Return," "Discounted Cash Flow," "Internal Rate of Return" and "Opportunity Cost").

ADJUSTMENT. The reduction of film rentals owed by an exhibitor to a distributor pursuant to a license agreement, which occurs following a poorer-than-expected performance at the box office (see "Selling Subject to Review" and "Settlement Transactions").

ADMINISTRATIVE OVERHEAD CHARGE (see "Overhead").

ADMISSION DATE. In the context of a limited partnership offering, the date an investor (unit holder) is admitted to the limited partnership as a limited partner (see "Limited Partners" and "Unit Holder" or "Unit Purchaser").

ADMISSION PRICE DISCRIMINATION. An exhibitor business practice in which an exhibitor would charge a different amount at the box office for theatre admissions depending on which distributor provided the movie being shown. Such price differentials have, at times, been contractually or otherwise imposed on the exhibitors by the major studio/distributors (see "Anti-Trust Laws," "Price Fixing" and "Paramount Consent Decree of 1948").

ADMISSION PRICES. The amount charged at a theatre's box office for admission to see a movie (see "House Nut").

ADMISSIONS. From the perspective of motion picture analysts, either the number of ticket-buying patrons or the gross box office for a given film or group of films during a period of time (see "Box Office Gross" and "Concession Sales").

ADR (see "Automatic Dialogue Replacement" and "Dialogue Replacement").

ADVANCE OR ADVANCES. Money obtained up front in anticipation of profits, e.g., monies paid by a distributor to a producer prior to release of the producer's film. Such advances may be paid upon signing of the distribution agreement and/or upon delivery of the picture. Advances are generally recoupable and distributor advances are generally recouped by the distributor out of gross distributor rentals. Advances may be paid in relation to pre-sales, production-financing/distribution agreements, negative pickups, network production agreements, payments to talent, the sale of profit interests or an amount the exhibitor will pay the distributor prior to the film's release. Producers are paid advances on signing of the production agreement or more commonly upon delivery of materials. Arrangements for advances are negotiated and theoretically controlled by the agreements between such parties, although it is not uncommon for parties to film-industry agreements to ignore some provisions. Unfortunately, advance payments are generally taxable upon receipt (see "Deferral Structures," "Distribution Guarantee," "Guarantees," "Non-Returnable Advance," "Release Commitment," "Recoupment," "Remedy" and "Sue Us").

ADVANCE LICENSING (same as "Blind Bidding").

ADVANCE PAYMENTS (see "Advance" or "Advances" above).

ADVANCE TEASER CAMPAIGN. An advertising campaign directed to the movie-going public, consisting of a series of ads and/or commercials, begun well in advance of a film's opening and intended to stimulate the interest and curiosity of potential audiences regarding the upcoming film (see "Advertising Campaign").

ADVANTAGE. A benefit resulting from a specific course of action. Contrary to what some in the industry often suggest, there is no across-the-board "best way to finance a feature film;" each form of film finance presents certain advantages and disadvantages. In each case, the most appropriate choice may depend not only on the nature of the proposed movie, its anticipated budget level and the attached elements, but also on the special abilities and resources the producer brings to the table (see "Availability Analysis," "Disadvantage" and "Pro and Con Analysis").

ADVERTISEMENT. Any form of selling or promotional communication regarding a motion picture. Such ads may be placed in any of the various media and are generally paid for by either the film's producer, distributor, exhibitor or a combination thereof (see "Cooperative Advertising" and "Publicity").

ADVERTISING. All forms of paid media exposure, i.e., the creation and dissemination of promotional materials and the conduct of promotional activities including cooperative advertising, institutional advertising, national advertising and trade advertising in whatever form or media. The IRS defines advertising as the announcement or description of property or services in some mass communication medium (such as radio, television, newspaper, trade journals, direct mail, or billboards) and directed at all or part of the general population of actual or potential customers to induce them to buy or rent the property or service. Advertising need not be directed to the general public but may be focused toward any group of actual or potential customers. In film, advertising is responsible for the creative ad-look in the paid television and radio spots, the theatre trailers, the movie posters and other promotional materials (see "Credit," "Marketing," "National Advertising Campaign," "Positive Print," "Promotional Activities" and "Publicity").

ADVERTISING AGENCY. A business engaged in the creation of paid promotional messages and the purchase of media exposure. In some situations involving negotiations with a distributor, independent producers may want to seek certain controls or approvals over the selection of the ad agency in addition to controls and approvals relating to the creation of the film's ad campaign (see "Advertising" and "Rent-A-Distributor").

ADVERTISING APPROPRIATION. An allocation of funds from a film's total marketing budget that is used to pay for a film's advertising campaign for a stated time period. Such allocations may be made by the film's producer or distributor depending on how the film is being distributed (see "Direct Distribution Expenses," "Four-Wall or Four-Walling" and "Four-Wall Advertising").

ADVERTISING ART. The original creative art used in a film's print advertising. Ad art is combined and reproduced with title art, credits, copy and other items to create an ad to be used in the print media, typically newspapers or magazines (see "Advertising Campaign").

ADVERTISING CAMPAIGN. A planned and related series of promotional activities designed to bring about a particular result, i.e., awareness regarding a movie or motivation to go to a movie (see "Blurbs" and "Primary Advertising").

ADVERTISING CODE ADMINISTRATION. An industry organization to which all advertising for rated motion pictures must be submitted for approval prior to release of the film to the public. Such advertising includes, but is not limited to, print ads, radio and tv spots, pressbooks and theatrical trailers (see "MPAA" and "Ratings Board").

ADVERTISING COPY. The text of an ad (see "Advertising").

ADVERTISING COSTS. The direct expenses incurred in preparing and producing advertising for motion pictures. Advertising costs for opening an "A-level" motion picture in the current marketplace may be in the $15 million to $20 million range at a minimum (see "Direct Distribution Expenses").

ADVERTISING MATERIALS. All of the physical items utilized in the promotion of a film (see "Advertising").

ADVERTISING OVERHEAD. A charge imposed by all of the major studio/distributors and some independents to cover the costs of operating their internal advertising and publicity departments. Generally, the charge equals 10% of the negative cost of the movie. Net profit participants may have a reasonable basis to question this charge on the grounds that the 10% percentage has no relation to actual costs since certain pictures bear a disproportionate share of such expenses and in many instances this overhead charge will exceed the actual costs of the services provided for a given motion picture. In lieu of eliminating or limiting the amount of the advertising overhead charge, net profit participants may choose to seek to impose a ceiling on the amount that can be charged by the studio or distributor (see "Media Buys").

ADVERTISING TIE-INS (see "Promotional Tie-Ins" and "Product Placement").

ADVOCACY. The activities associated with pleading the cause of another (see "Advocacy Group," "Advocate," "Advocate Auditing," "Industry Groups," "Lobbying" and "Net Profit Participant Association").

ADVOCACY GROUP. A professional or trade association which, among other things, speaks for and/or represents the interests of its members in various forums including federal and state legislatures, governmental administrative agencies, government executives, court and the general public (see "Industry Groups" and "Lobbying").

ADVOCATE. One who pleads the cause of another (see "Advocacy Group," "Advocate Auditing," "Association Projects," "IFP," "Industry Groups," "Lobbying" and "Lobbyists").

ADVOCATE AUDITING. In the context of the motion picture business, a net profit participation auditor who not only studies a film distributor's accounting practices with respect to a given motion picture and reports to his or her net profit participation clients, but also actively negotiates with the distributor on behalf of those clients (see "Auditor" and "Net Profit Participant Association").

AFFILIATE. A person or entity that directly, or indirectly through one or more intermediaries, controls or is controlled by or is under common control with another specified person or entity; a company that owns less than a majority of the voting stock of another company; two companies which are both subsidiaries of a third company (see "Parent Corporation" and "Subsidiaries").

AFFILIATED PERSON. An individual who is in a position to exert direct influence on the actions of a business entity, including owners of 10% or more of its equity securities, corporate directors, senior elected officers and any person in a position to exert influence through them, such as members of their immediate family and other close associates; sometimes called a control person (see "Affiliate").

AFFILIATE OF AN ISSUER. A person controlling, controlled by or under common control with the issuer of securities. An individual who controls an issuer is also an affiliate of such issuer (see "Control Person" and "Issuer").

AFFIRMATIVE OBLIGATION. A duty or responsibility to do a certain thing, e.g., a contractually negotiated duty on the part of a distributor to use its best efforts to maximize the distribution of a motion picture. Producers may want to include such an affirmative obligation in their distribution agreements (see "Allocation Issues," "Conflicts of Interest" and "Settlement Transaction").

AFI (see "American Film Institute").

AFM (see "American Film Market").

AFMA (see "American Film Marketing Association").

AFTER-MARKET. In the film industry, another term for ancillary markets, i.e., the markets in which a film may be exploited following its primary market, which is usually theatrical exhibition (see "Ancillary Markets").

AFTER-TAX REAL RATE OF RETURN. The amount of money, expressed as a percentage of the investment, that an investor can keep out of the income and capital gains earned from investments and adjusted for inflation (see "Adjusted Rate of Return" and "Internal Rate of Return").

AGENCY. The fiduciary relationship created when one person, the agent, acts on behalf of another with the authority of the latter, the principal. The authority of an agent make take various forms, i.e., real, apparent, express, implied, limited, unlimited, etc., depending on the particular facts and circumstances. Individuals utilizing the services of agents should clearly set out in writing the authority of their agents (see "Fiduciary" and "Power of Attorney").

AGENT. Generally, one who, by mutual consent, acts for the benefit of another or represents the interests of another, e.g., in negotiating contracts on their behalf. In the film business, agents are licensed and regulated by the state. Actors commonly utilize the services of agents in procuring work and screenwriters often utilize the services of agents in selling their scripts to studios, producers or production companies. In film distribution, sales agents may represent producers or distributors in selling or licensing a film in certain markets (see "Conflicts of Interest" and "Packaging").

AGENT FEES. The monetary compensation paid to agents for their services, usually calculated as a percentage of some level of revenue generated by the activities of the agent's principal. The standard talent agent fee is 10% (see "Sales Agent Fees").

AGENT FOR SERVICE OF PROCESS. An individual named on behalf of a corporation or limited partnership who, as a condition of such entity's doing business in a given state, is designated to receive notices of lawsuits or court summons filed in such state against the entity represented (see "Consent to Service of Process").

AGGREGATE ADVANCES. The total amount of all advances paid in conjunction with the distribution of a motion picture, i.e., both domestic and foreign advances. Ideally, the aggregate of such advances will equal or exceed the negative cost of the picture involved (see "Advance" and "Pre-Sales").

AGGREGATE OFFERING PRICE. The sum of all cash, services, property, notes, cancellation of debt, or other consideration received by an issuer for issuance of its securities (see "Consideration and Securities").

AGREEMENT. A manifestation of mutual assent between two or more legally competent persons which ordinarily leads to a contract. In common usage, the word "agreement" is a broader term than contract, bargain or promise, since it includes executed sales, gifts and other transfers of property, as well as promises without legal obligation (see "Contract").

AGREEMENT AMONG UNDERWRITERS (AAU). Contract between participating members of an investment banking syndicate, i.e., an agreement signed by members of the underwriting syndicate empowering the managing underwriter to sign the underwriting agreement with the issuer and dividing the compensation and responsibilities among the syndicate members (contrast with "Underwriting Agreement").

AGREEMENT FOR ACQUISITION OF LITERARY MATERIAL (see "Acquisition Agreement").

AGREEMENT FOR BELOW-THE-LINE PERSONNEL (see "Below-the-Line Employment Agreements").

AICPA. Acronym for American Institute of Certified Public Accountants.

AIVF (see "Association of Independent Video and Filmmakers").

ALBUM. One or more phonograph records, tape recordings or compact discs carrying a major musical work or a group of related selections (see "Soundtrack Rights").

ALBUM COVER. The container with envelopes for phonograph records, tape recordings and compact discs (see "Jacket").

"A" LEVEL MOTION PICTURE (see "A Title").

ALIEN CORPORATION. Corporation organized under the laws of a foreign country (contrast with "Domestic Corporation" and "Foreign Corporation").

ALLIANCE OF MOTION PICTURE AND TELEVISION PRODUCERS (AMPTP). A film-industry trade organization which provides services to its member companies relating to all aspects of employment within the television and theatrical motion picture industry and other issues that affect the industry as a whole. The AMPTP acts as the bargaining agent for its member companies in industry-wide bargaining with the industry's unions and guilds and provides its members with advice regarding the administration of their industry-wide agreements. In other words, its most important issues relate to employee/ employer relations and this association represents the interests of the major studio/production company employers along with a limited number of other independent production companies. This association is also a sister-association to the MPAA (see "MPAA").

ALLIED RIGHTS. The power and authority to exploit products associated with a specific motion picture, e.g., merchandising, novelization, soundtrack recording and music publishing (see "Ancillary Markets" and "Non-Theatrical").

ALL-MEDIA DISTRIBUTION AGREEMENT. A contract between a film's producer and a distributor in which the producer grants the distributor the exclusive right to distribute the film in all media and in all languages and versions, usually in the entire world (see "World-Wide Rights").

ALLOCATION. In a film distribution context, the assignment to particular accounts or apportionment among films or entities of the revenues generated by the exploitation of a film or the costs associated with distribution, e.g., the costs of advertising several films may be allocated by the distributor among such films. Allocation issues also arise in the licensing of films in a package for television, whether for network or syndication. In foreign distribution, such issues some-times arise with respect to the allocation of a portion of film rentals to shorts and trailers. In a limited partnership context, the term allocation refers to distributions of partners' shares of partnership income or loss in a manner other than in accordance with such partners' actual percentage ownership interest (see "Creative Ac-counting" and "Syndicated Films").

ALLOCATION ISSUES. Concerns, questions or problems relating to the apportionment of a film's gross receipts. Numerous allocation issues arise in the context of film distribution accounting, partly because distributors have traditionally relied on their superior bar-gaining strength to permit themselves considerable discretionary au-thority to make such apportionment decisions (see "Allocation" and "Percentage Allocated").

ALL OR NONE. One of three arrangements under which investment banking and brokerage firms, called underwriters, may undertake to sell a stock or securities issue. In an all or none offering the entire issue must be sold or the money is returned to investors and the deal canceled, i.e., the issuer has the right to cancel the whole issue if the underwriting is not fully subscribed (see "Best Efforts Offering," "Firm Commitment" and "Underwriter").

ALLOWANCES. A share or portion allotted or granted or a sum granted as a reimbursement for expenses. Often the film distributor will grant certain allowances to the exhibitor for advertising and exploitation of a film. Profit participants must be sure that such allowances are not excessive in what amounts to a disguised attempt to cross-collateralize one movie's revenue with others the distributor is distributing or will distribute (see "Cross Collateralization" and "De Facto Cross Collateralization").

ALL TERRITORIES. Throughout the universe (see "Territory" and "Worldwide Rights").

ALTER EGO DOCTRINE. Legal doctrine under which the law disre-gards the limited personal liability one enjoys when he or she acts in a corporate capacity and attributes personal liability to such persons for their acts. To invoke the doctrine, it must be shown that the corporation is a mere conduit for the transaction of private business and that no separate identities of the individual and the corporation really exist (see "Corporation" and "Piercing the Corporate Veil").

ALTERNATE CAMPAIGN. A film advertising and promotional pro-gram which differs from the primary campaign and is used to create new interest and a fresh look for the film. The alternate campaign will often be designed to appeal to a different audience than that of the primary campaign (see "Advertising Campaign" and "Primary Campaign").

ALTERNATE DISTRIBUTOR. A film distribution company selected by a film's producer to take the place of the original distributor pursuant to a specific provision in the distribution agreement which may permit such substitution (see "Substitution Clause or Agreement").

ALTERNATIVE MINIMUM TAX (AMT). A federal tax aimed at ensuring that wealthy individuals and corporations pay at least some income tax (see "Income Tax").

ALTERNATIVE PRODUCTION FINANCING. The funding of the costs associated with producing a movie through means other than studio financing (see "Financing").

ALTERNATIVE SCENES (same as "Cover Shot").

AMERICAN ACADEMY OF INDEPENDENT FILM PRODUCERS (AAIFP). An organization which was briefly active in the late 1980s and which sponsored a seminar for independent producers covering such topics as distribution, literary rights, payroll accounting, producing, casting, financing and ultra-low-budget production, but which has not been very active since. Requests for information on the organization go unanswered (see "Association" and "IFP").

AMERICAN CINEMA EDITORS (A.C.E.). The honorary professional society of film editors whose professional designation is A.C.E. Membership in the society is by invitation only (see "Editor").

AMERICAN FILM INSTITUTE (AFI). An independent, non-profit organization founded in 1967 by the National Endowment for the Arts primarily for the purpose of increasing recognition of the moving image as an art form, to assure the preservation of the art form and to develop and encourage new talent (see "Industry Groups").

AMERICAN FILM MARKET (AFM). A motion picture marketplace devoted exclusively to the international licensing of independently produced movies in the English language. The AFM has traditionally been held in Los Angeles, in February, on an annual basis (see "Cannes Film Festival" and "MIFED").

AMERICAN FILM MARKETING ASSOCIATION (AFMA). A film-industry trade organization which states in its published literature that it represents the interests of independent producers and licensors of English language films in the international arena. However, its 100-

plus member companies are predominantly film distributors and foreign sales agents. Thus, it would be more accurate to say that the AFMA represents the interests of independent distributors, who technically may be licensees, licensors or agents, depending on the relationship between the distributor and producer (see "Industry Assessments").

AMERICAN MOTION PICTURE LABOR COOPERATIVE (AMPLC). A North Hollywood-based organization formed during the 1988 Writers Guild strike for the purpose of representing non-union workers and trying to gain benefits (such as a health plan and access to a credit union—benefits not available to freelancers) for those workers (see "Guild").

AMERICAN PLAYHOUSE. A limited source organization for production funding for films. American Playhouse is based in New York City and provides financing up to $600,000 for a film with a U.S. writer and subject (see "Grants").

AMERICAN PRODUCT. Motion pictures produced by U.S. based producers and/or production companies and distributed by U.S. distributors (see "Product").

AMERICAN STOCK EXCHANGE. The second largest (after the New York Stock Exchange) United States market maintained for the purpose of buying and selling securities (see "Stock Exchange").

AMORTIZATION. The liquidation on an installment basis of a financial obligation relating to an intangible asset. Also, recovery of cost or value over a period of time, i.e., the IRS defines amortization as the ratable deduction allowed for loss in value of intangible property due to the passage of time. It is a method of allocating the cost of an intangible asset over time for purposes of offsetting (deducting) such cost from revenues the asset helps to produce. Amortization as permitted by the IRS Code illustrates the concept of capital recovery which provides that income does not result until revenues exceed the capital expended to produce such revenues. If property is entitled only to amortization, the recovery of the cost or basis of the item may be limited to a proportionate (i.e., straight-line) deduction over the amortization period (same as "Cost Amortization;" contrast with "Depreciation;" see "Capitalization" and "FASB Statement No. 53").

AMORTIZATION OF NEGATIVE COST. The accounting procedure by which a film's negative cost is charged against the film's revenue (see "Amortization," "Cost Recovery," "Income Forecast Method" and "Negative Costs").

AMORTIZATION SCHEDULE. A written presentation in tabular form showing the amounts of principal and interest due on a loan at regular intervals and the unpaid balance of the loan after each payment is made (see "Amortization").

AMORTIZE OVERHEAD. The practice of gradually reducing or recovering the cost of an entity's indirect expenses incurred in the production and/or distribution of a film. Major studio/distributors sometimes offer their distribution facilities on a rent-a-system basis in order to amortize their overhead without incurring any additional financial risk on such motion pictures (see "Rent-A-Distributor" and "Release Slots").

"A" MOVIE (see "A Title").

AMPAS (see "Academy of Motion Picture Arts and Sciences").

AMPLC (see "American Motion Picture Labor Cooperative").

ANALYST. A person in a brokerage house who studies a number of companies and makes buy or sell recommendations on the securities of particular companies and industry groups. Most of such analysts specialize in a particular industry, e.g., the entertainment industry, and focus on corporate entities with publicly traded stock (see "Communications Industry" and "Entertainment Industry").

ANCILLARIES (see "Ancillary Markets").

ANCILLARY AGREEMENTS. Agreements that are subordinate, subsidiary, supplementary or auxiliary to a primary, preceding or original agreement. If the issue of subsequently negotiated gross participations is not negotiated and provided for in the original agreements relating to the services of a film's creative team, such ancillary agreements may alter their deal with a producer who gives away too many gross participations (see "Gross Floor" and "Gross Participants").

ANCILLARY END USERS. Those entities which exploit films in the ancillary markets, e.g., video companies (see "Ancillary Markets").

ANCILLARY MARKET RIGHTS (see "Ancillary Rights").

ANCILLARY MARKETS. Geographical or technological areas of demand for film product which are auxiliary or supplemental to the theatrical market. The ancillary markets include foreign, network and syndicated television, pay cable and home video (see "Markets," "Non-Theatrical" and "Theatrical Market").

ANCILLARY RIGHTS. The additional powers or privileges which a film's producer or distributor or other person or entity is justly entitled to exercise with respect to the original literary property and the feature film that the producer may own, i.e., additional to theatrical exhibition. Such rights may include the right to produce a remake, sequel, television series, stage play and/or soundtrack recording. The issue of whether such sources of revenue are included in the distributor's gross receipts may be negotiated in some instances. If the distributor does not include ancillary revenue in gross receipts, it may use an approach similar to that used with regard to videocassette revenues, i.e., the rights will be exploited by a third party (which is sometimes affiliated with the studio) and only a royalty is paid to the distributor. In that situation, net profit participants may want to negotiate for a separate participation in such ancillary revenues (see "Ancillary Rights," "Ancillary Markets," "Isolated Ancillary Rights," "Outside the Pot," "Retroactive Basis" and "Videocassette Revenue Reporting").

"A" NEGATIVE. The parts of a film negative which are used to print the film that is ultimately employed in the edited and completed motion picture (see "B-Negative").

ANIMAL MORTALITY INSURANCE. Insurance against the death or destruction of any specifically covered animal used in a film production. A veterinarian's certificate is usually required for this type of coverage (see "Insurance").

ANIMATION. A filmmaking process in which drawings or three-dimensional objects (e.g., models) are photographed frame by frame so that when the assembled film is projected at normal speeds, the drawings or objects appear to move (see "Genre" and "Markets").

ANNOTATED SCRIPT. A screenplay, sometimes requested by the errors and omissions insurance carrier, with notes included thereon, indicating which of the various component parts of the script are based on some existing underlying work, e.g., books, stage plays, newspaper articles and/or magazine articles (and citing such works). These notes will help the E&O carrier's attorney evaluate the risk of possible lawsuits based on the screenplay (see "Clearance" and "Errors and Omissions Insurance").

ANNOUNCEMENTS IN THE TRADES. Ads run in "Daily Variety," "Hollywood Reporter," "Village Voice" or other industry publication announcing some event relating to a film, such as the completion of principal photography. Such ads are considered useful in creating presumed value in a film (see "Daily Variety," "Hollywood Reporter" and "Trades").

ANNUAL BASIS. An accounting technique in which figures relating to a period of less than one year are extended to cover a twelve-month period. The procedure is called analyzing and it must take into account seasonal fluctuations, if any, in order to be accurate (see "Accounting Method").

ANNUAL MEETING. The once-a-year meeting at which the officers and managers of a corporation report to its stockholders on the year's results and some or all of the members of the board of directors are elected for a subsequent term (see "Corporation").

ANNUAL PERCENTAGE RATE (APR). The cost of credit that consumers pay, expressed as a simple annual percentage (see "Interest").

ANNUAL REPORT. A formal corporate financial statement issued yearly. The annual report of publicly owned corporations must comply with SEC reporting requirements, which include balance sheet, income statement, and cash-flow reports audited by an independent certified public accountant. These annual reports are filed with the SEC on Form 10K (see "Certified Public Accountant," "Form 10K" and "SEC").

ANSWER PRINT. The first positive composite print (made from the original negative) from the lab with sound, music, color (if in color), title and fades, dissolves and optical effects, i.e., color- and sound-balanced. It "answers" the question affirmatively that a viable working negative exists from which prints can be made for commercial presentation. In brief, a print potentially ready for release to its target audience. However, there are nearly always visual corrections to be made and sometimes changes in sound so that the first answer print is generally a guide to fine-tuning the prints to follow. Thus, the answer print usually precedes the first release print (see "Release Print").

ANTI-BLIND BIDDING STATUTES. State statutes which prohibit the film distribution practice of blind-bidding. Generally speaking the industry organizations that favor blind bidding are the major studio/distributors as represented by the MPAA. Ordinarily, it might be expected that the exhibitor trade group, NATO, would be opposed to the practice of blind bidding, but the existence or vigor of that opposition may depend on how many of the NATO members are owned or controlled by the major studio/distributors (see "Blind Bidding," "Lobbying," "MPAA," "NATO," "Non-Regulatory State," "Product Splitting," "State Legislatures" and "Vertical Integration").

ANTICIPATED EXPENSES. A concept often found in film distribution agreements which permits the distributor to deduct an amount adequate to cover future estimated distribution expenses from gross receipts. Such provisions often stipulate that the distributor may in

good faith retain sums necessary to pay for costs reasonably anticipated to arise in connection with the picture being distributed (see
"Creative Accounting," "Discretion" and "Good Faith").

ANTICIPATED RATING. The producer's advance judgment as to
what MPAA rating will be assigned to his or her film (see "MPAA
Rating" and "Publicity").

ANTICIPATORY BREACH OF CONTRACT. In contract law, a breach
committed before the arrival of the actual time of required performance. It occurs when one party by declaration repudiates his or her
contractual obligation before it is due. The repudiation required is a
positive statement indicating that the promisor will not or cannot
substantially perform the promised contractual duties (see "Breach of
Contract" and "Contract").

ANTI-COMPETITIVE PRACTICES. A broad term referring to all sorts
of activities which tend to reduce free competition in the marketplace. This term would include some business practices that are not
actionable under anti-trust laws, e.g., even though the MPAA rating
system might not be actionable pursuant to a given federal anti-trust
regulation, independent producers or distributors whose films are
rated in a discriminatory manner by this MPAA sponsored organization may well view this MPAA activity as anti-competitive (see "Anti-
Trust Laws," "Block Booking," "Blind Bidding," "Conduct Restrictions," "Predatory Practices" and "Reciprocal Preferences").

ANTI-FRAUD STATUTE (RULE). State and federal securities law provisions which require the written disclosure of all material aspects of
certain securities transactions in advance to prospective investors,
prohibit the omission of any material information and prohibit any
untrue or misleading representations. Non-compliance may result in
a charge of securities fraud (see "Disclosure Document" and "Fraud").

ANTI-TRUST LAWS. Federal and state statutes aimed at promoting
free competition in the marketplace, i.e., to prevent monopolies and
restraint of trade. Any agreement or cooperative effort or intent by
two or more entities that affects or restrains, or is likely to affect or
restrain, their competitors is illegal under these statutes. The two
major federal anti-trust laws are the Sherman Act and the Clayton
Act. The Sherman Act protects the right of individuals to be free to
compete and makes illegal any contract, combination or conspiracy
in restraint of trade or commerce. The Sherman Act also makes
illegal monopolies and attempts, combinations or conspiracies to
monopolize. The Clayton Act regulates price discrimination, tying
and exclusive-dealing contracts, stock acquisitions which tend to

monopolize, and certain interlocking directorates (see "Blind Bidding," "Block Booking," "Clayton Act," "Marketplace of Ideas," "Monopoly," "Price Discrimination," "Pooling Arrangements," "Pool (Industry)," "Price Fixing," "Reciprocal Preferences," "Sherman Anti-Trust Act," "Tracks" and "Tying Arrangement").

ANTI-TRUST LAW VIOLATIONS. Violations of federal and state statutes aimed at promoting free competition in the marketplace, i.e., to prevent monopolies and restraint of trade. Any agreement or cooperative effort or intent by two or more entities that affects or restrains, or is likely to affect or restrain their competitors, is illegal under these statutes. The relaxation of the federal enforcement of anti-trust laws in the years during and since the Reagan presidency may have resulted in numerous activities that may otherwise be actionable under the anti-trust laws, if such laws were being more vigorously enforced. Movie profit participants and even exhibitors must be more aware of such activities and be willing to lobby or litigate when appropriate in order to stem any potential trend toward more anti-competitive practices (see "Anti-Trust Laws," "Marketplace of Ideas," "Paramount Consent Decree of 1948," "Political Influence," "Remedy," "Sue Us" and "TriStar Case").

APPEAL. The primary theme underlying a motion picture advertisement in its effort to elicit a favorable response from a movie's prospective audience, i.e., motivate them to see the picture (see "Demand" and "Primary Audience").

APPLICATION FOR REGISTRATION OF A TAX SHELTER. IRS Form 8264 which is to be used by the organizers of certain tax shelters in registering the tax shelter with the IRS (see "Tax Shelter Registration").

APPORTION. To divide fairly or according to the parties' respective interests; proportionately, but not necessarily equally (see "Allocation," "Discretion" and "Good Faith").

APPORTIONED EXPENSE. Costs which are divided according to the parties' interests, i.e., proportionately. Many distribution agreements allow the distributor to have the discretion to apportion numerous distribution expenses relating to advertising, facilities, employees, etc. among films which are marketed in a package. A profit participant cannot make an informed judgment as to whether such apportionments are fair without having access to the information upon which such apportionments are based. Such participants should make sure the audit rights of the producer and/or profit participants include access to such documentation, i.e., try to prevent the distributor from limiting access to documents that relate to the amount of money to be received (see "Audit," "Contract of Adhesion" and "Discretion").

APPRAISAL. An estimate or opinion of value; a conclusion resulting from the analysis of relevant facts (see "Catalog").

APPRAISE. To estimate the value; to put in writing the worth of property (see "Catalog").

APPROVAL OF THE LIMITED PARTNERS. In a limited partnership context, most state limited partnership acts authorize the limited partners to vote on certain specified partnership decisions without losing their limited liability. The partnership agreement may also establish the percentage of limited partner votes required for such approval (see "Limited Partnership Agreement").

APPROVALS. The power to review certain feature film elements and exclude such elements from being part of a particular film project. For example, depending on the stature of a production company which is receiving the benefit of a production-financing/distribution agreement from a studio/distributor or a negative pickup distribution deal, the studio/distributor will typically insist on approving such elements as the budget, screenplay, director and principal cast and such approval rights will be set out in the distribution agreement (see "Creative Control" and "Controls").

APPROVED ELEMENTS. Significant aspects of a film which have been reviewed and approved by the distributor which has committed to distribute the film once it is produced, e.g., script, budget, director and lead actors. If the film as produced does not contain the elements approved in advance of production by the distributor, that distributor may be able to avoid its obligation to distribute the film. Producers and directors must not forget about those approvals as the film is produced. If the distributor does not like the film, the distributor is not likely to forget about its approval rights. If the film as produced significantly departs from the approved script, the distributor may avoid its obligation to distribute the film. The question of what is significant provides an opportunity to disagree. Some effort ought to be made in negotiating the distribution agreement to further define what departures will be allowed and to provide for some mechanism to obtain distributor approvals on changes along the way, if any (see "Approved Negative Cost," "Approved Script" and "Basic Elements").

APPROVED NEGATIVE COST. A film budget which has been reviewed and approved by a film distributor which has committed to distribute the film and provide production financing (see "Approved Elements" and "Approved Script").

APPROVED PRODUCTION BUDGET. The amount of money itemized by spending category anticipated to be required to produce a film and that has been approved by the financier, e.g., a studio/distributor (see "Production Budget" and "Production-Financing/Distribution Agreement").

APPROVED PRODUCTION SCHEDULE. A timetable and plan for conducting the principal photography of a motion picture which has been approved by the financier, e.g., the studio/distribution pursuant to a production-financing/distribution agreement. Costs resulting from changes to the approved production schedule requested in writing by the distributor may be excluded from any over-budget penalty or other provisions (see "Over-Budget Penalty").

APPROVED SCREENPLAY (same as "Approved Script").

APPROVED SCRIPT. A film screenplay which has been approved by a distributor which has committed to distribute the film with such commitment being provided prior to production of the film. If the film as produced significantly departs from the approved script, the distributor may avoid its obligation to distribute the film (see "Approved Elements").

"A" PRODUCT (see "A-Title").

ARBITRATION. The submission of a controversy, by agreement of the parties, to persons chosen by the parties for resolution. An informal, non-judicial method for resolving disputes which generally takes less time and is less expensive than litigation. Agreements sometimes provide for arbitration to resolve any disputes that arise between the parties. For example, motion picture lenders often require that disputes between a film's distributor and its producer relating to whether the film has been properly completed and delivered pursuant to the terms of the distribution agreement be submitted to arbitration to ensure a more rapid and inexpensive resolution of the dispute. In a situation where a producer signs a production-financing /distribution agreement with a studio/distributor, the producer may also want to seek an arbitration clause for the same reasons, particularly since the studio will be charging interest on the production costs of the film (see "Arbitration Clause," "Expedited Arbitration" and "Litigation").

ARBITRATION CLAUSE. A clause in a contract providing for arbitration of disputes arising under the contract as opposed to litigating the dispute in court. Before agreeing to such a clause, it is advisable to think through the implications of arbitration. For example, arbitration might be helpful with strictly technical issues, but law courts are generally more sophisticated at handling expert-witness-type evidence (see "Arbitration" and "Expedited Arbitration").

ARBITRON RATINGS COMPANY. A national media research and ratings service which uses a quarterly audience survey period to publish audience viewing and listening habits for television, cable and radio at local and national levels, showing market share for the time period covered and statistical analysis using such characteristics as sex and age of the audience (see "ADI Market" and "Nielsen Media Research").

AREA OF DOMINANT INFLUENCE (see "ADI Market").

ARM'S LENGTH. The bargaining position of two parties that are unrelated to one another and whose mutual dealings are influenced only by the independent interest of each. The term is used to describe a standard of dealing that reflects no motivation other than that normally to be expected on the part of two unconnected parties transacting in good faith in the ordinary course of business (see "Adhesion Contract," "Conflicts of Interest," "Negotiate" and "Videocassette Revenue Reporting").

ARM'S LENGTH BASIS. The manner in which negotiations are objectively and fairly conducted (see "Arm's Length" and "Videocassette Revenue Reporting").

ARRANGEMENT. The development of an existing musical composition by scoring for voices or instruments, usually for those other than the voices and instruments for which the music was originally written and including the transposition of keys and elaboration of chord structures. An arrangement must reflect substantial new matter to qualify for copyright protection, although arrangements of any work in the public domain may be freely copyrighted. Arrangements of works protected by copyright may be copyrighted, but only by the copyright owner or with such copyright owner's consent (see "Arranger" and "Copyright").

ARRANGER. A person who prepares and adapts previously written music for presentation in some form other than its original form (see "Arrangement" and "Orchestrator").

ARROGANCE. A feeling of superiority manifested in an overbearing manner or presumptuous claims (see "Code of Professional Responsibility," "Ethics" and "Market Power").

ART DIRECTOR. The film production person who works with the production designer and is responsible for planning and executing the design of the sets, including the production of all illustrations, continuity sketches, perspectives, scenery, scale models, props, surface coloration and texture, drawings and elevations. The art director also gives approval on sets, properties, set dressing and scenery, and finds and recommends, for the approval of the director and producer, locations which are visually suitable for the production (see "Production Designer").

ART FILM. A motion picture which stresses artistic qualities as opposed to more commercial elements and thus is expected to appeal to a more narrow and specialized audience (see "Art House," "Commercial," "Key Art Showcase Cities" and "Special Handling").

ART HOUSE (same as "Art Theatre").

ARTICLES OF INCORPORATION. The document or instrument which is generally filed with a state's Secretary of State as part of the process of creating a corporation and pursuant to the general corporation laws of that state. The articles determine certain basic attributes of the corporation such as the type of corporation, the amount of authorized stock and the initial directors (see "Certificate of Incorporation," "Charter" and "Ultra Vires Activities").

ARTICLE TWENTY. A controversial article of the IATSE contract which allows major studios to fully finance non-union movies and television shows so long as the studios declare they have no creative control and give the union thirty days notice before production starts. Many union supporters contend Article Twenty has helped to increase non-union movie production (see "Artificial Pickup," "IATSE" and "Industry Groups").

ARTIFICIAL BREAKEVEN. A contractually defined multiple of a film's negative cost (e.g., when gross receipts equal three times the negative cost of the motion picture) that is treated as actual breakeven (see "Actual Breakeven," "Breakeven," "Cash Breakeven," "Creative Accounting," "First Breakeven" and "Rolling Breakeven").

ARTIFICIAL PICKUP. A film project originally controlled and developed by a studio/distributor but which is farmed out pursuant to a negative pickup or anticipated acquisition distribution deal to an outside (but friendly) production company, partly to avoid the higher costs of the below-the-line union crews which the studio would have to pay if the project was produced as an in-house production at the studio (see "Acquisition Distribution Agreement," "Article Twenty," "Negative Pickup" and "Signatories").

ARTIST. A broad term referring to any person skilled in one of the fine arts; one who professes and practices an art in which conception and execution are governed by imagination and taste. In a film, artists may include the screenwriter, actors, the director, the cinematographer, the art director and others who contribute to the creative process (see "Actor" and "Artistic Control").

ARTISTIC CONTROL. The power to make decisions relating to the appearance and content of the final feature film product (see "Creative Differences" and "Final Cut").

ARTISTIC DIFFERENCES (see "Creative Differences").

ARTIST'S ADVANCE. Payment made to an actor, director or writer prior to the performance of their contractual duties, either upon the signing of the employment agreement or at other specified times (see "Advance").

ARTIST'S FEE. The amount of compensation provided for in the film's budget to be paid to the actor, writer or director, excluding any bonus or contingent compensation (see "Artist," "Contingent Compensation" and "Salary").

ART THEATRE. An exhibitor which specializes in presenting art films, generally in exclusive engagements, rather than in showing the mass-marketed and more commercial studio-distributed films (see "Art Film").

ARTWORK. Graphic, creative or otherwise aesthetic representations relating to a specific film which are used in advertising and promoting the film (see "Advertising").

ARTWORK TITLE. The name or credit to be attributed to an aesthetic representation. A distributor may seek in its distribution agreement to limit its obligations to provide credit for artwork (see "Credit").

ASPECT RATIO. The ratio of the horizontal to the vertical dimensions (i.e., width-to-height) of a motion picture frame or television screen. Most feature films are shot with 35mm negative film, using an aspect ratio of 1.85 to 1 (also written 1.85 : 1 or 1.85 x 1). A 1.85 to 1 aspect ratio means that the projected image is 1.85 times wider than it is high. Other 35mm formats include 1.33 to 1, 1.66 to 1 and 2.35 to 1. A 2.35 to 1 aspect ratio produces a very wide image and is most appropriate for pictures requiring many outdoor panoramic scenes (wide-screen). Before wide-screen, the original 35mm movie screen had an aspect ratio of 1:33 to 1, a ratio reflected approximately in TV screen images. The format for a film is generally selected by the producer, director and director of photography (see "Format" and "Pan and Scan").

ASSEMBLY. The first, rough arrangement of dailies in script order (see "Dailies").

ASSESSABLE SECURITY. A security on which a charge or assessment for the obligations of the issuing company may be made (see "Securities").

ASSET. Anything owned by a business, institution or individual that has monetary or exchange value (see "Liquid Asset").

ASSET FINANCING. The funding of a business venture by converting particular assets into working cash in exchange for a security interest in those assets, e.g., loans against accounts receivable and inventory loans (see "Collateral" and "Secured Debt").

ASSET MANAGEMENT. The control and direction of a particular individual or entity's investments by a brokerage house, bank, savings institution or other qualified financial advisor. If the assets under management by the asset manager are sufficiently large enough, a certain percentage of the assets may be available for high-risk investments such as motion pictures (see "Discretionary Funds").

ASSET VALUE. The worth of a company's collective assets; a term often used to described the worth of a motion picture company's film library [see "Catalog (Library)"].

ASSIGN. To transfer one's interest in property, a contract or other rights to another. Although often used interchangeably with pledge and hypothecate, the term "assign" implies transfer of ownership or of the right to transfer ownership at a later date. Film distribution deals often limit the rights of either or both the producer and distributor to assign their respective rights and obligations (see "Distribution Agreement," "Grant of Rights," "Hypothecate," "License," "Pledge" and "Secured Debt").

ASSIGNEE. The person to whom an assignment is made (see "Assign").

ASSIGNMENT. A written agreement which is used to transfer some or all of an owner's right, title and interest in a specific property to a purchaser. Important provisions of such an assignment include the description of the rights being transferred and the consideration to be paid. Other terms typically include owner warranties and an indemnification provision in favor of the purchaser if one of the owner warranties is breached. Distribution agreements routinely include a form of assignment as an exhibit to the distribution agreement and provide that the producer or production company agrees to sign such assignment along with any UCC-1 financing statements and the laboratory pledgeholder agreement (see "Copyright Assignment," "Laboratory Pledgeholder Agreement" and "UCC-1 Financing Statement").

ASSIGNMENT FOR THE BENEFIT OF CREDITORS. The transfer of interests to those to whom money is owed by a debtor (see "Assign").

ASSIGNOR. An individual or entity that assigns or makes an assignment (see "Assign").

ASSIGNS. Those who take from or under the assignor, whether by conveyance, devise, descent or operation of law (see "Personal Representative" and "Successor").

ASSISTANT DIRECTOR (AD). The film production-staff person who helps the film's director. An AD may serve as the director's liaison with governmental authorities and suppliers of services, may also be responsible for insuring that actors are present at the right time and place and otherwise are expected to perform whatever other useful tasks are assigned by the director (see "Director" and "Directors Guild of America").

ASSISTANT EDITOR. A person who is directly assigned to assist a film editor and whose duties may include synchronizing dailies, taking notes at screenings, obtaining cutting-room facilities, breaking down daily takes, pulling out and assembling selected takes, making trims, ordering optical and other preparatory work in film editing rooms (see "Editing Room Assistant").

ASSISTANT PRODUCER. An aide to the film's producer (see "Associate Producer," "Co-Producer Credit," "Creative Producer," "Executive Producer" and "Line Producer").

ASSOCIATE PRODUCER. A title and film credit given to a film producer's second-in-command who shares business and creative responsibilities. The associate producer is generally involved in pre-production, production and post-production as a supporting producer. The credit is sometimes given to a production manager or first assistant director for contributions that greatly exceed their routine duties. Also it is sometimes awarded to a significant financial backer or an individual who may have brought the literary property or screenplay to the producer (see "Credit Issues," "Producer" and "Producers Guild of America").

ASSOCIATION. An organization of persons who have a common interest and have joined together for a certain purpose, e.g., educational seminars, the conduct of annual conferences, the dissemination of useful information among the members and/or lobbying (see "AIVF," "AFMA," "Association Projects," "IFP," "IFP/West," "Industry Groups," "MPAA," "MPEAA," "NATO," "Professional Association," "RIPOFF" and "Trade Association").

ASSOCIATION ANTI-TRUST POLICIES. The adopted practices of professional and trade associations which relate to governmental regulations and laws on competition. The U.S. anti-trust laws apply to the membership policies of trade and professional associations such as the MPAA, MPEAA, AMPTP, AFMA, AIVF and NATO. Restrictions on which companies may become a member have particular anti-trust implications, since denial of membership, with its attendant benefits, may be held to place the applicant at an economic disadvantage. Generally speaking, trade associations must allow membership to all those in the trade if excluding them would significantly limit their opportunities to compete effectively, thereby creating a restraint on competition. Two other areas of potential concern with respect to the application of the anti-trust laws to professional and trade association policy, are (1) agreements among association members that have the effect of fixing or stabilizing prices for particular services and (2) boycotting or refusing to deal with companies that take action which is opposed by the association members (see "Anti-Competitive Practices," "Anti-Trust Laws," "Blacklist," "Blind Bidding," "Block Booking," "Insider's Game," "Member of the Club," "Predatory Practices," "Price Fixing" and "Reciprocal Preferences").

ASSOCIATION OF NET PROFIT PARTICIPANTS (see "Association Projects," "Net Profit Participant Association" and "RIPOFF").

ASSOCIATION PROJECTS. The activities a professional and/or trade association undertakes on behalf of its members. Examples of major areas of association activities may include projects of an educational nature (seminars, books, association magazines, etc.) or projects that relate to the representation of the group's interests in a legislative forum, in a court of law or before an executive branch of our governments at any level. Specific projects an association of independent feature producers may choose to undertook might include the following: (1) develop and maintain a reference library specifically to meet the special needs of independent film producers; (2) subscribe to and maintain back issues of various trade publications of interest to independent producers; (3) set up a producer anti-trust task force to study possible anti-competitive practices i.e., vertical integration, block booking, etc., which may be occurring in the film industry and report on their impact on independents; (4) specifically work to eliminate studio or other production company or distributor ownership or control of theatres; (5) lobby on behalf of the association's independent producer members with the U.S. Justice Department and the Federal Trade Commission relating to the enforcement of federal anti-trust laws in the entertainment industry; (6) study and make member producers aware of how anti-trust laws also apply to the activities of professional associations; (7) represent the interests of independent producers with respect to matters before state legislatures, Congress and the Federal Communications Commission, e.g., financial interest and syndication rules; (8) speak on behalf of the association's membership with respect to eliminating the conflicts of interest inherent in the MPAA motion picture rating program; (9) organize and maintain film distributor research files for the use of independent producer members of the association; (10) conduct seminars on matters of importance to independent producers, including the distribution deal, the status of the independent producer, performance report cards on distributors, alternative film finance methods, etc. (11) research and make available industry statistics as such statistics specifically relate to independent producers and their films; (12) maintain current referral lists of the entertainment-related professionals such as entertainment attorneys, auditing firms, anti-trust and entertainment litigating attorneys, and production accountants or payroll services; (17) monitor anti-trust litigation relating to the entertainment industry and report on developments to independent producer members (also develop a checklist of anti-competitive practices to monitor); (18) calculate/ publicize the number of theatre screens that are available or used for the exhibition of independently produced and/or independently distributed feature films on a weekly basis; (19) calculate/publicize revenue market share of independent producers vs. MPAA companies; (20) publicize instances of and work to eliminate arbitrary and unfair "blacklisting" in the industry; (21) create a producer's investment club or some similar investment vehicle to pool independent producer investments and to selectively invest in publicly held motion picture studios, production companies, distributors and exhibitors, in addition to the large public feature film limited partnerships. Such investments would permit such producer investors to participate in the economic benefits of equity ownership in entertainment entities (if any) and provide better access to information regarding the activities of such entities; (22) develop authoritative figures to substantiate and publicize among the general public and at film schools specifically, the huge disparity between the number of films that are produced each year and the films that are distributed each year, as well as the number of producers, directors, screenwriters, actors, and others who are competing for positions with the limited number of films produced and the resulting bargaining disadvantage for such groups or individuals produced by such disparity; (23) create and maintain a file describing so-called "creative accounting" practices of studios and/or distributors; (24) organize an extensive "for-credit" student intern program in cooperation with various film schools to help the association meet its person-power needs and to provide unique learning opportunities for film students interested in producing; (25) research questions relating to establishing a professional certification program for independent feature film producers; (26) publish a newsletter and magazine with articles relating to some or all of the above topics and other matters of special interest to independent producers; and (27) develop and make available a model feature film distribution agreement which provides a more balanced approach to issues as between distributors and producers (see "AIVF," "AMPTP," "IFP," "IFP/WEST," "Lobbying," "MPAA," "MPEAA," "NATO" "Political Influence," "Professional Associations" and "RIPOFF").

ASSUMPTIONS. Circumstances that are assumed to be factual for purposes of projecting the hypothetical results of an investment, such as in a partnership (see "Financial Projections").

ASYNCHRONOUS SOUND. Sound on motion picture film that is not in synch or synchronous with the image on the film (see "In Synch" and "Synchronous Sound").

"A" TITLE. A somewhat subjective term describing major motion pictures with a director, stars and/or other elements which create significant box office appeal, i.e., motion pictures with significant recognizable actors and established directors that are released by major studio/distributors in the U.S. in a wide manner. Sometimes defined as major studio product which has been released with significant print and advertising commitments or independent product which has performed well in the marketplace or had the equivalent of a major studio release (see "B-Movie" and "Commercial").

ATMOSPHERE. The extras in a movie as a group (see "Background Cast" and "Extras").

AT RISK. Exposed to the danger of loss. Investors in a limited partnership can claim tax deductions only if they can show that their investment was at risk, i.e., that there was a chance of never realizing any profit on the investment and a chance of losing their investment as well. The IRS may be able to disallow such claimed deductions if the limited partners are not exposed to economic risk, e.g., an offering where the general partner or a film distributor guaranteed the return of all capital to the investors even if the business venture lost money (see "At Risk Loss Limits").

AT RISK LIMITATION. Tax losses of certain taxpayers are limited to the amount the taxpayer has invested and which is at risk of loss. Such amounts generally include investments of cash or other property and recourse debt (see "Recourse Debt").

AT RISK LOSS LIMITS. Special tax rules which apply to most activities, including the activities of a partnership, that are engaged in as a trade or business or for the production of income. These rules limit the amount of loss a partner may deduct to the amounts for which that partner is considered at risk in the activity. A partner is considered at risk to the extent of the amount of cash and the adjusted basis of property contributed to the activity, income retained by the partnership and amounts borrowed by the partnership for use in the activity. A partner is not considered at risk for amounts borrowed by the partner or the partnership unless that partner is personally liable for the repayment or the amounts borrowed are secured by the partner's property other than property used in the activity. Also, a partner is not considered at risk for amounts which are protected against loss through guarantees, stop-loss agreements or other similar arrangements (see "At Risk" and "Basis").

ATTACHED TO THE PROJECT. Committed to play a specific role or perform certain duties in relation to a given motion picture. Such commitments may be contingent and may take the form of oral expressions of interest, letters of interest, letters of intent or contractual commitments (see "Letter of Intent," "Packaging," "Pay or Play" and "Pay and Play").

ATTACHMENT. A proceeding in law by which one's property is seized, that is, a proceeding to take a defendant's property into legal custody to satisfy a plaintiff's demand. A distribution deal may provide for certain specified remedies in the event the producer's property which is the subject of the distribution agreement, i.e., the film, or any portion thereof, is attached or levied upon (see "Levy").

ATTENDANCE CHECKING. Activities undertaken on behalf of a producer or distributor designed to verify the actual number of paid moviegoers in attendance at a showing or showings of a film. Such activities may include the hiring of checkers to go to the theatre and count those in attendance or to purchase the first and last ticket of the day at a given theatre to then compare the ticket numbers with the exhibitor's attendance reports. There are organizations that provide such checking services for producers and distributors. However, in a rent-a-distributor situation a producer may want to hire its own checking service to conduct random checks of attendance at theatres where the producer's film is being exhibited (see "Checker" and "Rent-A-Distributor").

ATTORNEY (ATTORNEY-AT-LAW). A person who has been admitted by a state's highest court or a federal court to practice law in that jurisdiction. In order to be licensed to practice, attorneys generally must pass a course of study at an accredited law school and pass an exam administered by the state bar association. Some states also now require that practicing attorneys participate in a required minimum number of hours of continuing professional-education activities (see "Code of Professional Responsibility," "Conflicts of Interest" and "Ethics").

ATTORNEY-IN-FACT. One who is an agent or representative of another given authority to act in that person's place and name. The document giving the attorney-in-fact authority is called a power of attorney (see "Power of Attorney").

"A" TYPE VEHICLE (same as "A-Title").

AUCTION. The sale of a property to the highest bidder (see "Bidding War" and "Spec Script").

AUDIENCE. The group of people who see a film or to whom a film is generally directed (see "Primary Audience" and "Secondary Audience").

AUDIENCE DEMOGRAPHICS (see "Demographics").

AUDIENCE FRACTIONALIZATION. The dividing up of movie goers and television viewers among numerous and various entertainment alternatives, thus theoretically decreasing the size of the potential audience for any given offering. The trend has caused problems for motion picture production companies and network television which had previously designed movies and programming to appeal to a mass audience (see "Homogeneous Films").

AUDIO CASSETTE (see "Cassette").

AUDIT. An inspection of the accounting records and procedures of a business, government unit or other reporting entity by a trained accountant, for the purpose of verifying the accuracy and completeness of the records. It may be conducted by a member of the organization (internal audit) or by an outsider (independent audit). An IRS audit consists of the verification of the information on the return. It is not likely that an audit on behalf of motion picture profit participants will rise to the level of a complete audit, which is so thoroughly executed that the auditor's only reservations have to do with unobtainable facts. In a complete audit, the auditor examines the system of internal control and the details of the books of account, including subsidiary records and supporting documents, while reviewing legality, mathematical accuracy, accountability and the application of accepted accounting principles. This is a technical accounting term establishing audit standards (same as unqualified audit). Producers can raise the question of a complete or unqualified audit in negotiations for audit rights although such audits are not likely to be permitted. Experienced entertainment attorneys recommend that profit participants do audit any motion picture that has any likelihood of going into profits. An audit of studio books for a domestic theatrical release may cost $15,000 or more, but few if any of such audits do not pay for themselves. Audits of major studios have uncovered millions of dollars in errors, most of which seem to be in the studio's favor (see "Audit Rights," "Broad Auditing Rights," "Limited Review," "Sub-Distributor" and "Underreported Rentals").

AUDITED CASH PRODUCTION BUDGET. An audited film budget prepared after completion of the film which excludes deferments (see "Audit").

AUDIT FEES. The compensation paid to an auditor, e.g., a motion picture net profit participation auditor for his or her services relating to a review of the books and records of a business, e.g., a motion picture distributor. The fees for a film distributor audit relating to a given film may be in the $25 to $35 thousand range, but for a "successful film" such audits will generally recover ten times that amount for net profit participants (see "Audit" and "Auditor").

AUDITION. A trial performance to appraise an actor's suitability for a specific role in a motion picture (see "Screen Test").

AUDITOR. An accountant (sometimes an attorney) who is authorized to examine and report on a business's books of account (see "Advocate Auditing," "Audit" and "Audit Rights").

AUDITOR'S CERTIFICATE (same as "Accountant's Opinion").

AUDIT RIGHTS. The power and authority to conduct an inspection of the accounting records and procedures of an entity. Such rights present an important issue with respect to the negotiation of feature film distribution agreements, since the calculations relating to gross receipts and net profits are typically very complex and rely on so many contractually defined terms, while the provisions of such agreements also very often leave a great deal of discretion in the hands of the distributor. Unfortunately, experienced motion picture profit participation auditors have reported that even on occasions where an audit has uncovered an inadvertent mistake or actual wrongdoing, the results of which tend to financially favor the distributor as opposed to any other participants, some distributors merely shrugged their shoulders and say "oh well," which is the equivalent of saying the producer's only remedy is to sue (see "Audit," "Blacklist," "Broad Audit Rights" "Contract of Adhesion," "Discretion," "Problem Producer," "Remedy" and "Sue Us").

AUDIT TRAIL. The step-by-step record by which accounting information can be traced to its source; the physical evidence of an entity's expenditures which are reviewed in an audit (see "Audit").

AUTEUR. A French concept holding that the director of a film is the true creator or author of the film, who brings together the script, actors, cinematographer and editor and molds all such contributions into a work of cinematic art with a cohesive vision (see "Collaborative Process" and "Creative Control").

AUTHOR. One who writes or composes a book or other literary work (see "Certificate of Authorship").

AUTHORITY. The permission or power delegated to another (see "Contract of Adhesion," "Discretion" and "Power").

AUTHORIZED SHARES. The maximum number of corporate shares of any class that a corporation may legally create under the terms of its articles of incorporation (see "Corporation").

AUTOMATIC DIALOGUE REPLACEMENT. The recording and synchronization of non-production, studio-recorded dialogue tracks with corresponding film images. The replacement voice may be that of an actor other than the one shown on the screen, and replacement dialogue may be in a language other than that spoken during the original production (also known as "Dubbing" and "Looping;" see "Dialogue Replacement").

AVAILABILITY. The date a motion picture can be shown commercially in a market in accordance with the offer by the distributor to the exhibitor (see "True Availability").

AVAILABILITY ANALYSIS. An objective determination as to whether a specific form of film production financing may be obtained by a producer for a given film project. As a pre-condition to the so-called "pro and con analysis," i.e., the analysis relating to advantages and disadvantages of the various forms of film finance, the producer must first make a realistic appraisal of what forms of film finance are actually available to him or her for the subject film project. For example, many producers know at the outset that their proposed film is not of interest to the major/studio distributors, that it is not adequately packaged to attract a negative pickup distribution deal, that they do not want to give up creative control or that they do not have access to prospective investors. Thus, several important traditional sources of feature film financing may be eliminated right away by using this initial level of analysis and the producer does not even have to bother with the pro and con analysis for forms of film finance that are not available (see "Advantage," "Disadvantage," "Financing," "Limited Partnerships Are Dead" and "Pro and Con Analysis").

AVERAGE GROSS PER SCREEN. The gross box office receipts per movie screen for a given motion picture per week, unless another period is stated (see "Gross Per Screen").

AVERAGE MAJOR STUDIO MARGINS. A statistical median representing the ratio of the gross profits to net sales for the major studio/distributors. Average major studio margins are closely watched by financial analysts and have reportedly been in decline in recent years, reaching the lowest point in nearly twenty years in 1991 at approximately 7%. Such margins during most of 1980s were greater than 10%, but were never higher than 17% even during the so-called "product shortage" years of the late 1970s (see "Law of Supply and Demand" and "Profitability").

AVERAGE NEGATIVE COST. An industry statistic usually calculated by the MPAA for films produced by member companies and presented as a statistical median for a given year. The average negative cost for an MPAA movie in 1991 was reportedly in the neighborhood of $28 million dollars. Studio executives and their representatives are fond of pointing to escalating advertising expenses, high labor costs and the demands of gross profit participants as the primary culprits in the escalation of negative costs while spokespersons for "A" level talent counter that if the studios would quit playing games with their books (thus making net profits virtually obsolete), there would be little need to demand gross participations (see "Creative Accounting," "Gross Participants," "Profit Participants" and "Videocassette Revenue Reporting").

AVIATION INSURANCE. Insurance protecting against the risk of loss due to the use of an airplane in the production of a movie (see "Insurance").

AWARD ADVERTISING. Promotional materials and activities used in conjunction with events designed to honor films or certain film elements (see "Advertising").

— B —

BACKEND. A film's revenues generated from exploitation of the film in all or specified markets. Percentage participations in such revenues are negotiable but are usually not paid until after distribution and/or production costs have been recouped (see "Backend Deal," "Contingent Compensation," "Gross Participant," "Net Profits," "Percentage Participation" and "Points").

BACKEND DEAL. A contractual arrangement providing for contingent compensation to be paid to a designated recipient. Such compensation may take several forms including gross participations, net profit participations, bonuses paid upon achieving gross receipts equal to specified multiples of the film's negative costs, escalations of percentage participations triggered by similar revenue levels, retroactive payments and even reductions in such compensation if certain revenue levels are not achieved (see "Backend," "Contingent Compensation" and "Percentage Participation").

BACKEND NEGOTIATIONS. The discussions relating to who will be paid monies out of a movie's revenue stream, at what point and at what level or percentage (see "Backend Deal" and "Backend Participations").

BACKEND PARTICIPATIONS. Percentage participations in the revenue stream generated by the exhibition of a movie (see "Percentage Participation," "Points," "Revenue Stream" and "Up Front Salary").

BACKGROUND CAST. The people, objects, set pieces and scenery that form the setting against which the foreground players and action are placed. An extra is also referred to as a background player (see "Atmosphere" and "Extra").

BACKLIST. [same as "Catalog (Library)"].

BACK LOT. That portion of a motion picture studio which is used for exterior filming (see "Exterior" and "Location").

BAD DEBT. An open account balance or loan receivable that has proven uncollectible and is written off; amounts earned by a specific film and owed to the distributor of the film but which the distributor will not be able to collect because the debtor is insolvent. Distributors will generally deduct such amounts before making payments to the producer. Profit participants may want to seek to limit distributor discretion to claim amounts that are uncollectible and establish some objective criteria in the distribution agreement for which "bad debts" may be written off (see "Creative Accounting" and "Uncollectible Indebtedness").

BAD FAITH. A willful failure to respond to plain, well-understood statutory or contractual obligations; the absence of good faith (see "Covenant of Good Faith and Fair Dealing" and "Good Faith").

BAD FAITH DENIAL OF CONTRACT. A relatively new tort recovery based on a defendant's bad faith conduct in asserting a stonewall ("see you in court") defense to an ordinary commercial contract. Recent cases have held that the elements of the cause of action are (1) an underlying contract, (2) which is breached by the defendant, (3) who then denies liability by asserting that the contract does not exist, (4) in bad faith and (5) without probable cause (see "Bad Faith," "Probable Cause," "Sue Us" and "Tort").

BAD TITLE. Ownership rights which are legally insufficient to convey property to a purchaser (see "Marketable Title").

BAD WEATHER INSURANCE. Insurance which provides reimbursement to a film's producer, up to the limit of insurance, for each scheduled filming day canceled due to any type of bad weather (i.e., rain, high winds, storms, clouds, etc.). This coverage can be adapted to include an automatic coverage for rescheduled shooting days (see "Insurance").

BALANCED PRINT. A copy of a motion picture that has been color corrected or graded (see "Color Corrected").

BALANCE SHEET. A financial statement that gives an accounting picture of property owned by a company and of claims against the property on a specific date. Generally, a summation of assets is listed on one side and liabilities are listed on the other side. Both sides are always in balance (contrast with "Income Statement").

BALLOON PAYMENT. Final debt payment that is substantially larger than the preceding payments. Loans with a balloon payment are sometimes referred to as partially amortized loans (see "Moratorium").

BALLPARK FIGURE. An estimate (see "Projections").

BANK. A federally or state regulated financial institution, some of which have entertainment divisions that lend funds for film production. Usually such banks will only lend against so-called "bankable" guarantees provided by pre-sale or distribution agreements, and most such banks will only lend to established producers with guarantees that in the aggregate exceed the production budget. In addition, such banks will invariably require that a completion bond be in place on the film. Banks do not generally invest in films, i.e, they do not share in the financial risk. They make money off the interest charged and, in some instances, on certain fees (see "Bank Legal Fees," "Investment Bank" or "Investment Banker" and "Merchant Bank").

BANKABLE. A descriptive adjective used in the film business to describe someone or something (e.g., actors, directors, producers, projects, distributors, etc.) whose commitments can be taken to a bank and on which the bank will lend money for film production purposes, partly because of the prior successful performances of such individuals, entities or projects, although banks will still generally require collateral (see "Bank Loan," "Bondable" and "Collateral").

BANKABLE ACTORS. Actors whose box office appeal will favorably influence entertainment lenders to be more inclined to lend monies for use in producing a given film if such actors are committed to playing a role in the film (see "Bankable").

BANKABLE DISTRIBUTION CONTRACT. A film distribution agreement, executed in advance of a film's production, which will influence entertainment lenders to be more inclined to lend money for production of the film. Most entertainment lenders will only be favorably influenced by such distribution contracts with major studio/distributors or a small number of so-called mini-majors and agreements that provide a distributor guarantee (see "Negative Pickup," "Pre-Sale Financing" and "Split Rights Deal").

BANKABLE PRE-SALE COMMITMENTS. Contractual commitments to distribute a film in a specific territory or medium made prior to completion of the film by a bank-approved distribution company and/or ancillary market entity for cable, home video, foreign markets, etc. that represent an acceptable credit-risk for the bank to lend production monies to the film's producer while contractually creating an obligation on such committing entities to repay the bank's loan (see "Guaranty," "Pre-Sale Financing" and "Secured Creditor").

BANKABLE STARS (see "Bankable Actors").

BANK BORROWINGS. Loans from banks (see "Lender Financing" and "Lender Risk Elimination").

BANK DISCOUNTING (see "Discounting").

BANK FINANCING. The funding of a film or film projects with bank loans. Banks generally make no value judgment on the quality of a film's script or the potential draw at the box office; rather its officers will look to the contracts the producer has secured from its domestic and foreign theatrical distributor(s), video cassette, television stations, etc. The bank discounts such contracts to their present value and charges a competitive business rate of interest. Banks will also ask the distributor to agree to repay the bank loan plus interest out of distributor rentals prior to distributor deductions and payments to the producer (see "Bank Loan" and "Discounting").

BANKING COMMUNITY. Entertainment banks as a group (see "Bank Financing").

BANK LEGAL FEES. The professional fees paid to attorneys representing the interests of the bank or lender in a negative pickup transaction. Such fees are generally paid by the producer/borrower out of the borrowed funds, thus the bank will receive interest on such fees. The producer may want to seek a cap on such fees (see "Conflicts of Interest" and "Negative Pickup").

BANK LINES (see "Line of Credit").

BANK LOAN. A film production loan provided by a bank. One advantage of this form of film finance is that the producer only has to repay the loan with interest, i.e., the bank usually does not take an equity ownership interest in the project. However, such loans are rarely made to producers without a track record and a bankable distribution commitment (see "Financing," "Loan" and "Negative Pickup").

BANK REQUIRED DOCUMENTS. The documents generally required by a bank (or other lending entity) in order to provide a film production loan including proof of the producer's right to film the literary property under consideration, a copy of the distribution guarantee, copy of the distribution agreement, copy of the completion guarantee, detailed budget, complete financial statement of any other investors involved, security agreement that puts the bank in a first lien position with respect to the film, the literary property upon which the film will be based and the producer's share of receipts from all sources (i.e., the bank has the first legal claim to these assets), an agreement between the bank and the distributor in which the distributor agrees to pay the producer's share of receipts directly to the bank until the loan, fees and interest are repaid, and in which the distributor agrees to pay any unpaid balance on the loan at the time of maturity or forfeit distribution rights (see "Completion Bond," "Inter-Party Agreement" and "Negative Pickup").

BANKRUPT. A person or entity which has done any of the acts that by law entitle such person or entity's creditors to have the bankrupt's estate administered for the creditors' benefit (see "Bankruptcy").

BANKRUPTCY. A state of insolvency of an individual or an organization; an inability to pay debts when they come due. The taking or acquiescing in the taking of any action seeking relief under, or advantage of, any applicable debtor relief, liquidation, receivership, conservatorship, bankruptcy, moratorium, rearrangement, insolvency, reorganization or similar law affecting the rights or remedies of creditors generally. Bankruptcy is a legal process under federal law intended not only to insure fairness and equality among creditors of a bankrupt but also to help the debtor by enabling him, her or it to start anew with property he, she or it is allowed to retain as exempt from liabilities, unhampered by creditor pressure and the discouragement of pre-existing debts. Feature film profit participants may want to make some effort to determine the financial stability of a distributor before choosing to utilize the services of such a distributor. A profit participant's share will generally not be forthcoming from a bankrupt distributor (see "Liquidation," "Mob Controlled Distribution Company," "Moratorium Statutes," "Receivership" and "Reorganization").

BANKRUPTCY CLAUSE. A provision in an agreement that provides certain rights in the event that one or the other of the parties to the contract goes into bankruptcy. In the case of a film distribution deal, the producer may seek to include a bankruptcy clause providing that in the event the distributor becomes insolvent or bankrupt, the rights to distribute the motion picture revert back to the producer (see "Bankruptcy").

BARGAINING POSITION. The various circumstances which add or detract from the strength or weakness of each of the parties involved in negotiating a transaction, e.g., distributors sometimes argue that the practice of blind bidding tends to equalize the bargaining positions as between distributors and exhibitors (see "Blind Bidding," "Leverage" and "Negotiate").

BARGAINING POWER. The relative ability to control or favorably influence negotiations between parties. Often in negotiations between film distributors and producers, the relative bargaining power of the parties plays a significant role in determining whether numerous negotiated issues are resolved in favor of one or the other. Distributors typically have the stronger position, partly because the law of supply and demand is in their favor, i.e., there are more motion pictures produced each year than there are distributors who are willing to distribute. In order to improve his or her position, the producer, on the other hand, must first assemble an attractive package and/or produce a quality picture, then seek to interest more than one distributor in its distribution. To the extent that a producer has more than one distributor interested in distributing the producer's film, the producer will theoretically, all other things being equal, increase his or her bargaining power (see "Inferior Bargaining Position").

BARGAINING STRENGTH (see "Bargaining Position" and "Bargaining Power").

BARRED. Prevented or forbidden from beginning or continuing an activity (see "Conduct Restrictions").

BARRIERS TO ENTRY. The impediments which must ordinarily be overcome in order to enter a particular kind of business or industry. For example, the barriers to entry into the distribution of major motion pictures are extremely high since substantial amounts of capital, significant expertise relating to the market place and relationships with exhibitors are required. The concept of barriers to entry and whether such barriers are natural or artificial plays a role in anti-trust law analysis relating to competition (see "Anti-Trust Laws," "Merger Guidelines" "Paramount Consent Decree of 1948," "Relationship-Driven Business," "Reciprocal Preferences," "Rising Production Costs," "Significant Barriers" and "Vertical Integration").

BASELINE. A computerized subscriber entertainment-industry information service providing information regarding above- and below-the-line film credits, box office grosses, celebrity and company contacts, information on film and TV projects in production and development, audience response and demographic data, industry news and analysis, the official Academy Awards database and pre-publication announcements of new literary properties (see "Entertainment Data, Inc").

BASIC AGREEMENT (see "WGA Agreement").

BASIC CABLE. The initial cable-television service that usually consists of twelve to twenty channels available off-the-air or via satellite and which is supported by advertising. Basic cable residuals are based on a percentage of the revenues as opposed to the flat dollar payment mandated by the guilds for the network syndication market; thus in recent years much of the off-network programming airs on cable instead of free television (see "Cable Television" and "Free Television").

BASIC ELEMENTS. The essential components of a motion picture project which are often specified in the "picture specifications" section of a distribution agreement. Such elements are generally considered to include the underlying material or screenplay, director, producer, principal cast and the approved production budget (see "Elements").

BASIC FORMULA. A phrase sometimes used to describe the method employed in calculating net profits. The basic formula is thus commonly stated as: distributor's gross receipts minus distribution fees, minus distribution expenses equals producer's gross, and producer's gross minus the production costs of the motion picture minus interest, if any, leaves net profits, if any. Another shortened version would read: receipts less fees, expenses and costs equal net profits (see "Contractually Defined Terms," "Creative Accounting," "Gross Receipts" and "Net Profits").

BASIC PAY CABLE (same as "Basic Cable").

BASIC STORY OUTLINE. A brief summary of a proposed motion picture screenplay which is sometimes used by experienced screenwriters or producers to submit a concept to studios or other production companies for development funding (see "One-Line Description," "Outline," "Synopsis" and "Treatment").

BASIS. IRS terminology for the capital invested in property; an amount that usually represents the taxpayer's cost in acquiring an asset, such as a motion picture. It is used for computing gain or loss on the sale or exchange of the asset and in calculating the depreciation deduction with respect to the asset. The taxpayer's tax basis in an asset is subject to adjustment due to depreciation and other transactions in which a taxpayer may engage (see "Adjusted Basis" and "Return of Capital").

"B" COUNTIES. The A.C. Nielsen Company designation for counties in the U.S. that have populations of more than 150,000 people, but are not "A" Counties (see "A-Counties" and "Nielsen Media Research").

BELOW-THE-LINE. Film budget items relating to the technical expenses and labor (other than above-the-line) involved in producing a film, i.e., relating to mechanical, crew, extras, art, sets, camera, electrical, wardrobe, transportation, raw-film stock, printing and post-production. Below-the-line personnel include the production manager, cinematographer, set designer, special-effects persons, wardrobe person and makeup artist. The phrase "below-the-line" refers to the location of the specific expense item/person on the film budget (see "Above-the-Line Costs," "Above-the-Line Employment Agreements and "Below-the-Line Employment Agreements").

BELOW-THE-LINE-COSTS. All costs, charges, and expenses incurred during the production of a motion picture other than the above-the-line costs and including such items as mechanical charges, crew labor, overhead, extras, art and set costs, camera, electrical, wardrobe, transportation, raw-film stock and post-production (see "Above-the-Line" and "Overhead").

BELOW-THE-LINE EMPLOYMENT AGREEMENTS. The written contract between a feature film production company and production employees who for film budget purposes are not classified as above-the-line (see "Above-the-Line").

BELOW-THE-LINE FRINGES. Compensation paid to or for the benefit of a film's crew in addition to their salaries. When such individuals are members of a guild or union, these benefits may include vacation pay and health, welfare and pension contributions. Also, such payments may be made directly to the guild or union by the film's distributor. Some distributors have reportedly overstated the cost of such benefits in determining the negative cost of a movie, thus reducing the amount of money that might flow through to the producer group in the form of net profits. A producer must determine exactly what the below-the-line fringes are and how much they cost (see "Creative Accounting" and "Unfair Business Practices").

BENEFICIAL EXCHANGE RATE. A currency exchange rate which favors a particular currency relative to the value of the currency of other countries, i.e., that is more favorable currently than previously (see "Exchange Rate").

BENEFICIAL RESULTS. Any helpful, advantageous or useful consequences. The question of whether any beneficial results would flow from a proposed merger resulting in vertical integration is part of the U.S. Justice Department's anti-trust law analysis relating to such mergers (see "Anti-Trust Laws," "Merger Guidelines," "Paramount Consent Decree of 1948," "TriStar Case" and "U.S. Justice Department").

BENEFICIARY. The party in whose favor an insurance policy or letter of credit is issued (see "Insurance Policy" and "Letter of Credit").

BEST EFFORTS. A standard of conduct in which the party performing an activity is required to put forth his, her or its maximum effort (see "Best Efforts Clause," "Conflicts of Interest," "Fiduciary" and "Reasonable Efforts Clause").

BEST EFFORTS CLAUSE. A provision in film distribution contracts which obligates the distributor to put forth its best efforts in distributing the film. In the event that a dispute arises between the producer and the distributor relating to the distributor's efforts in distributing the film, this clause would serve as a standard by which a court would determine if the distributor had met certain obligations under the agreement. Best efforts is a higher standard than reasonable efforts, so producers negotiating with distributors would be better advised to use "best efforts" in such drafting situations. If other more objective standards of conduct are available, it might be even more effective to use the more specific language in place of the best efforts clause (see "Affirmative Obligation" and "Reasonable Efforts Clause").

BEST EFFORTS OFFERING. A securities offering in which the underwriter or broker/dealer commits to use its best efforts to sell the issue but without any purchase guaranty, i.e., an underwriting agreement in which the underwriters do not assume the risk of resale and agree to sell the issue acting only as agents of the issuing company (see "All or None," "Firm Commitment," "Managing Broker/Dealer" and "Underwriter").

BIAS. A partiality toward someone or something (see "Discrimination," "Favorable Portrayal," "Marketplace of Ideas," "Nepotism," "Pattern of Bias," "Prejudice," "Reciprocal Preferences" and "Unfavorable Portrayal").

BICYCLING (PRINT). The exhibition of one print at two nearby theatres in staggered showings. The term originated with the transporting by bicycle of consecutive reels of film from one theatre to another (see "Print").

BID. A written or oral proposal (notification) from a theatre-exhibition company in response to a bid solicitation from a film distribution company to bid or negotiate the terms for exhibiting a film and stating the terms under which the exhibitor will agree to exhibit such motion picture. This, supposedly competitive, bid is the exhibitor's offer for the right to license a motion picture for showing in a given market beginning on or about a specific date. The bid usually includes commitments for minimum playing time (if applicable), the holdover figure, clearances, guarantees, an advance paid by the exhibitor to the distributor (if any), film-rental terms and advertising terms (see "Anti-Blind Bidding Statutes," "Blind Bidding" and "Negotiated Deal").

BID AND ASK. The quoted prices, generally by market makers, for a stock trading in the over-the-counter market (see "Market Makers").

BIDDING. The practice of renting, selling or licensing motion pictures through the use of bids (see "Blind Bidding").

BIDDING WAR. A vigorous competitive auction of a property or property rights. For example, screenwriters and/or their agents occasionally succeed in instigating such competitive bidding for desirable spec scripts. Independent producers also attempt to initiate such bidding contests among distributors for the distribution rights to a completed motion picture. The result in some instances is that the price paid is higher than would have been paid under other circumstances, thus bidding wars sometimes favor the sellers as opposed to the buyers. A recent round of such high prices paid for spec scripts halted rather suddenly, fueling speculation that the major studio/distributors conspired to stop such activities or were at least guilty of conscious parallelism (see "Anti-Trust Laws," "Conscious Parallelism," "Conspiracy," "Reciprocal Preferences" and "Spec Script").

BID REQUEST. A written notification from a distributor to all motion-picture exhibitors who own or operate theatres in a market area notifying them that a specific motion picture is available for showing in that area on or about a certain date and inviting them to submit an offer (a bid) to license that picture. This request may contain suggestions such as length of playing time, guarantees, advances, film-rental terms, advertising terms and deadlines for submission. Such a bid request usually specifies that bid offers must be received by a certain time and date, usually no later than ten days subsequent to its issuance (see "Blind Bidding").

BID REQUEST LETTER (see "Bid Request").

BIG-BUDGET FILMS. Motion pictures with high production costs which as of the publication date of this dictionary, routinely exceed $20 million (see "Low-Budget Films" and "Medium-Budget Films").

BIG EIGHT. An outdated reference to the largest eight U.S. accounting firms as measured by revenue. Due to mergers, acquisitions and bankruptcies, the big eight has been reduced to the big six (see "Big Six").

BIG SIX. The six largest U.S. accounting firms as measured by revenue (see "Big Eight").

BILLING. The sequence, position, and size of a performer's, crew member's, staff person's or others' credits on the screen and in movie advertisements. Billing issues may be significant negotiating points in the respective agreements of such persons. The term is also used to refer to the actual list of contractually required credits of persons involved in the production of a film (see "Credits," "Order of Appearance," "Order of Credits," "Prominence" and "Top Billing").

BILLINGS BASIS. With respect to the distributor prepared earnings statements provided to the producer, statements calculated on the basis of what the distributor has billed as opposed to what has actually been collected by the distributor (see "Collection Basis").

BILLING STATEMENT (see "Credit Statement").

BIT PLAYER. An actor who has a small speaking part, usually no more than two or three lines (see "Extras").

BLACKLIST. A list of persons with whom business is not to be conducted or who are not to be hired. The concept received a great deal of publicity in the '40s and '50s when the fear of communism allegedly prompted many studios to blacklist persons who were suspected of un-American activities. Some in the industry today still fear being openly critical of the status quo within the film industry, i.e., the dominance of the major studios, for fear of being blacklisted. Obviously, it is not necessary for a physical list actually to exist for those in control positions to effectively "blacklist" certain persons considered undesirable for any arbitrary reason (see "Discrimination," "Problem Producer" and "Sue Us").

BLACKLISTING. The listing of persons who are not to be hired. Some profit participants who are film industry professionals and hope to continue to work in the film industry suggest that one of the main reasons why most persons who feel they have legal grounds to bring a cause of action against a major studio/distributor or other distributor is this fear of being blacklisted. Further, it is suggested that one of the main reasons the lawsuits that are initiated are ultimately settled is this same fear (see "Blacklist," "Buchwald Case" and "Sue Us").

BLACK TRACK PRINT. An answer print that has no sound, just the picture (see "Answer Print").

BLANKET NETWORK BUYS. Purchases of national television advertising on the major networks, e.g., by film distributors who are opening a film in wide release (see "Media Mix").

BLIND BIDDING. The film distribution practice by which film-distribution companies (principally the major studio/distributors), through a bid request letter and without having previously screened the film for exhibitors that are invited to bid on exhibition of the film, request that interested exhibition companies submit bids to license a motion picture for showing in a given market. Blind bidding has alternatively been defined as the bidding, negotiating, offering of terms, acceptance of a bid or agreeing to terms for the purpose of entering into a license agreement prior to a trade screening of the motion picture that is the subject of the agreement. Laws that prohibit completion of exhibition contracts before exhibitors have the opportunity to view the movies on which they are bidding have been passed in a number of states. Independent distributors rarely require blind bidding and independent exhibitors consider it unethical at minimum. They ask the question, "How can any retailer in any business be expected to sell a product sight unseen?" Blind bidding provides the large theatre chains with a significant competitive advantage over their smaller independent competitors. The larger chains have greater financial resources, thus they can accept the risks inherent in blind bidding, i.e., that they will contract to exhibit a film that would have been unacceptable if it had been viewed in advance and which results in a poor performance at the box office for the theatre. The independent exhibitors are generally out-bid anyway by their larger competitors for a "can't miss" film like a sequel to a prior block-buster; but with respect to marginal films, the smaller independent exhibitor does not possess the financial resources to take a chance on the film's success. Thus, the blind bidding process effectively leaves the independent exhibitor with the leftovers, which, for many, results in financial doom. With the re-entry of the major studio/distributors into exhibition and the presumed accompanying participation in the policy decisions of the National Association of Theatre Owners, the major studio/distributors have also placed themselves in a position to oppose NATO's support for anti-blind bidding legislation at the state level and NATO may have been the only national association which might have advocated the passage of such laws on behalf of independent exhibitors (see "Anti-Trust Laws," "Anti-Blind Bidding Statutes," "Blind Selling," "Close Bidding," "Five O'Clock Look," "Lobbying," "Major Exhibition Chains," "Major Studio/Distributors," "Market Share," "Negotiated Deal," "Non-Regulatory States," "Number of Screens," "Predatory Practices" and "Trade Screening").

BLIND CHECK. The covert monitoring of the activities of a theatre's box office personnel by a checker who is posing as a regular patron and observing such activity (see "Checker" and "Open Check").

BLIND POOL. A limited partnership that has not committed its resources or offering proceeds to a specific property or project at the time of capital contributions by the limited partners, i.e., a limited partnership that does not specify the properties the general partner plans to acquire. Investors in a blind pool must more carefully evaluate and rely on the track record or prior performance of the general partner or its upper level management as opposed to a specific property. State regulations may impose limits on such offerings, e.g., the percentage of offering proceeds that may be used to acquire such unspecified properties in certain offerings (see "Pool Investments" and "Track Record").

BLIND POOL AGREEMENTS. Motion picture distribution deals which are executed before the specified films to be distributed are identified (see "Output Deal").

BLIND SELLING. A practice whereby a distributor licenses a feature before the exhibitor is afforded an opportunity to view it (the other side of the transaction described as "Blind Bidding").

BLOCK BOOKING. The film distribution practice of tying together one or more motion pictures for licensing within a market, i.e., a distributor will accept a theatre's bid on a desirable film or films contingent on the exhibitor's promise that it will also exhibit a less desirable film. This practice was addressed by the Paramount Consent Decree of 1948 in which the major distributors at that time were forbidden to employ the practice. The basic thrust of this decree was to seek to prohibit block booking, i.e., to ensure that motion pictures must be licensed picture by picture, theatre by theatre, so as to give all exhibitors equal opportunities to show a given film. In a more recent case involving the film "The Graduate," a U.S. District Court in the Central District of California held that the studio's practice of blockbooking violated the Sherman Anti-Trust Act (see "Anti-Trust Laws," "Paramount Consent Decree of 1948," "Tracks" and "Tying Arrangement").

BLOCKBUSTER. A subjective term used to describe a movie whose box office performance far surpasses the box office grosses of the average motion picture released in recent times (see "Hit" and "Successful Film").

BLOCKED CURRENCIES. Generally, monies earned by banks or corporations in a foreign country which cannot be removed from that country except under limited circumstances and, thus, generally have to be spent within its borders. In the film industry, blocked currencies may be foreign film rentals, and producers may want to negotiate a provision in the distribution deal that requires a certain portion of such funds be deposited in an account in such foreign country for the benefit of the producer (see "Blocked Funds Deals" and "Restricted Currencies").

BLOCKED FUNDS (same as "Blocked Currencies").

BLOCKED FUNDS DEALS. A variant method of motion picture financing which may be able to provide some below-the-line savings and in which a producer purchases blocked funds or currency at a discounted rate from banks or corporations doing business in a specific country. It would be even more advantageous to the producer if, instead of having to come up with the monies to purchase such blocked funds, even at the discount rate, the producer could convince the owner of the blocked funds to convert its contribution of blocked funds into an equity position in the picture (see "Blocked Currencies").

BLOCKING. The coordination and setting of movements by actors in a movie scene (under direction of the director). Blocking utilizes floor marks and other spotting devices to aid the actor or actress in being at the right place at the right time (see "Staging").

BLOWOUT. The rapid sale of all of the securities in a new offering (see "Offering").

BLOW-UP. An optical process for enlarging a film, usually in the case of feature films from 16mm to 35mm (see "Reduction Negative").

BLUE SKY FEES. The charges imposed by state securities regulatory authorities on public or private offerings of securities in their states (see "Notice Filing Fee" and "Registration Fee").

BLUE SKY LAW REPORTER. Four volume set of law books published by Commerce Clearing House, Inc. (CCH) which contains the texts of each state's blue sky laws (see "Blue Sky Laws," "Conditions and Limitations" and "Notice Filing Requirement").

BLUE SKY LAWS. Popular name given to state statutes and regulations governing the offer and sale of securities in the various states. The term signifies state securities law compliance matters as opposed to federal securities law. The phrase originated in a state court decision involving securities in which the judge reportedly justified the need for securities laws and regulations as a means of discouraging unscrupulous promoters from coming into their state and selling their good citizens so many feet of "blue sky," meaning worthless property (see "Conditions and Limitations" and "Securities Acts").

BLUE SKY MEMORANDUM. A document, usually prepared by securities counsel for the underwriters or securities issuers, that describes the conditions and limitations on the offer and sale of the securities in the states in which such offers and sales are contemplated in an offering. The memorandum is provided to the offering's issuer, the managing broker/dealer and other brokerage firms invited to join the underwriting syndicate or selling group (see "Conditions and Limitations," "Issuer" and "Managing Broker/Dealer").

BLURBS. Short, highly commendatory public notices. In feature film advertising, it is common for the publicity staff of a motion picture distributor to use a few positive words or phrases from an otherwise negative review to promote a movie, but in some cases they actually will ask movie critics to manufacture a blurb for the distributor's use in advertising a picture. Some critics reportedly will even send out a series of favorable quotes on a newly released movie hoping one will show up in the movie's ad and result in more name recognition for the critic (see "Advertising," "Conflicts of Interest," "Press Kit," "Promotional Quotes," "Puffery" and "Unethical Business Practices").

"B" MOVIE. A genre of motion pictures shot on a low budget with a short production schedule and without major stars. Most exploitation fare and art-film product are considered "B" movies (also called "B-Pictures," "B-Product" and "B-Titles;" see "A-Titles").

"B" NEGATIVE. The part of a film negative which is not used in the finished cut negative. Sometimes portions of the "B" negative may be used in the preparation of a film trailer. Also some films are re-released with scenes not used in the original theatrical release (see "A-Negative" and "Trailer").

BO (see "Box Office").

BOARD OF DIRECTORS. A group elected by a corporation's shareholders to set company policy and appoint the chief executives and operating officers (see "Corporation").

BODY COPY. The principal text of a motion picture advertisement which conveys the theme of the film (see "Copy," "Headline," "Tag Line" and "Title Treatment").

BOILERPLATE. Language found almost universally in legal documents of a given type, often in small print. In any dynamic industry such as the film industry, there is seldom any such thing as "standard" language in contracts. A producer should not be intimidated or mislead into accepting such language if it does not meet the needs of the specific parties and transaction. In addition, it is prudent to insist on comprehensible documents. They can be complex, but they must be understood by the parties involved (see "Contracts" and "Contracts of Adhesion").

BOILER ROOM (OR SHOP). A place devoted to high-pressure sales by telephone of all sorts of securities, commodities or products, some of which have questionable value. Extensive fraud is usually involved, but successful prosecution is often difficult since the operation may disband before effective legal action may be taken (see "Fraud").

BOMB. A film that fares poorly at the box office (see "Blockbuster" and "Hit").

BONA FIDE. In good faith; without fraud or deceit (see "Good Faith").

BOND. A long-term note issued under formal legal procedure and secured by some form of collateral (see "Corporate Bond," "Debt Financing" and "Sinking Fund"). Also, a written instrument with sureties, guaranteeing faithful performance of acts or duties contemplated (see "Completion Bond," "Principal" and "Surety").

BONDABLE. A descriptive adjective used in the film business to describe someone or something (e.g., producer, production company, director, actors, line producer, etc.) which, when attached to a film project, will enhance the ability of the producer to obtain a completion bond for the film. The assessment by the completion guarantor will be partly based on the success of such individuals or entities on prior film projects (see "Completion Guarantor").

BONUS. Something given in addition to what is usual or strictly due. In the case of production-financing/distribution agreements, a bonus is sometimes provided as a form of contingent compensation for the producer who brings the film in under budget and on time. Bonuses may also be awarded to producers, directors, actors and/or writers when revenues generated by the exploitation of a motion picture exceed certain specified levels (see "Contingent Compensation" and "Percentage Participations").

BOOK. As a noun, the term in its broadest sense refers to a set of written or printed sheets bound together into a volume. Books sometimes serve as the underlying material for a motion picture screenplay (see "Novel," "Play" and "Underlying Property"). As a verb in the film industry, the term refers to the activity of scheduling motion picture engagements for theatrical exhibition (see "Booker").

BOOKER. The person (usually a film distribution company employee) responsible for all aspects of monitoring and trafficking the actual motion-picture prints throughout the markets over which the booker's branch office, or other unit of distributor organization, has jurisdiction (see "Booking" and "Booking Agent").

BOOKING. The activities related to the scheduling of a motion picture for exhibition in a theatre on a given date (see "Booker," "Booking Agent," "Bookings" and "Engagement").

BOOKING AGENT. Any person or business entity, designated by an exhibitor to act on the exhibitor's behalf, who acts as the exhibitor's agent in the renting, selling or licensing of motion pictures for exhibition. A booking agent may (and usually does) represent more than one exhibitor so long as such exhibitors' theatres do not compete (see "Booker").

BOOKINGS. The contractual arrangements relating to the exhibition of a film in a given theatre (see "Booker").

BOOKS AND RECORDS. The volumes of business journals, accounts and chronicles of any of various kinds; the written evidence of a series of business transactions. In the case of a distribution deal the books and records which relate to the distribution of a film and which are of vital importance to the producer and other net profit participants (see "Creative Accounting" and "Profit Participant").

BOOKS OF ACCOUNT. The financial records of a business (see "Books and Records").

BOOK VALUE. In reference to corporations, the net worth of the corporation, i.e., the worth of the assets minus the cost of the liabilities. The various methods of computing book value vary significantly and there is no standard method for ascertaining book value (see "Corporation").

BOOTLEG. The unauthorized and therefore illegal reproduction of a film or videocassette for commercial sale (see "Piracy").

BORROW. To receive something with the implied or expressed intention of returning the same or an equivalent (see "Lender Financing").

BORROWING AGREEMENT. The written contract used by a feature film production company to employ the services of an individual director, artist, performer or crew member who utilizes a loan-out company. Borrowing agreement is the same as lending agreement except expressed from the perspective of the borrowing production company (see "Lending Agreement," "Straight Employment Agreement" and "Three-Party Agreement").

BORROWING BASE FORMULA. A banking formula used in calculating the amount of funds a bank will lend to a borrower. In film, the formula will include considerations such as the production company's assets and its distribution commitments (see "Bank Financing" and "Loan").

BOTTOM LINE. The ultimate financial result of a transaction or the operation of a business (see "Profit Margin").

BOUTIQUE. A small, specialized business firm that deals with a limited clientele and offers a limited line of products, e.g., a boutique broker/dealer firm or boutique feature film production company (see "Financial Supermarket").

BOUTIQUE STUDIO. A film production company operated under the umbrella of a major studio (see "Output Deal").

BOX (see "Jacket").

BOX OFFICE. A movie theatre's ticket booth where moviegoers pay money for the tickets which are presented at the door for admission into the theatre to see a specific movie (see "Box Office Gross" and "Checker").

BOX OFFICE APPEAL. The ability of an actor to attract an audience into a theatre which is exhibiting a movie in which such actor stars (see "Marquee Value").

BOX OFFICE COMPARABLES. A comparison of the performance of similar films that have already been produced and exhibited for the purpose of estimating a reasonable projected performance for a similar film being considered for production. Such comparisons are typically presented in tabular form and utilize the gross box office figures or reported distributor rentals for similar films that are made available through the trades or other industry publications (see "Grossing Potential," "Past Performance" and "Similar Pictures").

BOX OFFICE DOMINATION. The stronger performance at the theatrical box office of a specific film, genre of films or films distributed by a specific segment of the industry. For example, statistics originally developed by industry analyst Art Murphy and reported in "Variety," then subsequently included in the Harold Vogel book "Entertainment Industry Economics" (second edition), indicate that approximately 50% of the U.S. motion picture screens generate about 67% of the box office gross, while about 75% of the screens generate approximately 90% of the box office gross (see "Number of Screens").

BOX OFFICE GROSS. The total amount of money that has been paid by the public to an exhibitor for admission tickets to see a specific motion picture before any expenses or exhibitor percentages are deducted, i.e., the actual dollar amount taken in at the box office. Also the accumulated totals of box office gross for a single film in a market or territory or all markets or territories (see "Checker," "Concession Sales," "House Nut," "Gross," "Gross Per Screen," "Film Rentals" and "Skimming").

BOX OFFICE MAGAZINE. A motion picture trade publication which is published monthly out of Hollywood and which editorially focuses on information relating to the business side of the motion picture industry. The magazine also provides a guide to currently released and upcoming theatrical films, along with reviews (see "Trades").

BOX OFFICE RECEIPTS. The actual amount taken in at the movie box office (see "Box Office Gross" and "Rentals").

BOX OFFICE RISK. The possibility that not enough moviegoers will purchase tickets to see a given movie to justify the financial risk involved in producing the motion picture. A lender will generally not assume any of this risk and thus will require that a distributor guarantee a production loan. Thus, the only risk the lender assumes is that relating to the credit-worthiness of the distributor (see "Distributor Credit-Worthiness," "Lender Risk Elimination" and "Risk").

BOYCOTT. A concerted effort to refrain from commercial dealing with a specific business; also a refusal to work for, purchase from, or handle the products of a specific business. Although a boycott is not always illegal, a conspiracy to injure a business through intimidation or coercion may violate the Sherman Act. Specific interest groups have from time to time resorted to attempts at boycotting a given film based on the perception that the interest group is unfavorably portrayed in the film (see "Anti-Trust Laws," "Hidden Agenda," "Favorable Portrayal," "Marketplace of Ideas," "Pattern of Bias," "Sherman Act" and "Unfavorable Portrayal").

"B" PICTURE (see "B-Movie").

"B" PRODUCT (see "B-Movie").

BRANCH. The office located in a given city (usually major urban areas), staffed by employees of a film-distribution company, responsible for bidding out (licensing) the film company's motion pictures and other products (if any), servicing prints to customers and collecting film rentals that are due. Business is generally conducted with exhibitors within certain geographic regional boundaries or relative proximity to the branch office. The major distribution companies have generally maintained individual branches in twenty-five to thirty major U.S. cities. Branch staffs typically include a branch manager, sales-persons, bookers, cashiers and clerical personnel (see "Exchange" and "Settlement Transaction").

BRANCH MANAGER. The employee of a film distribution company who is responsible for supervising the activities of a given motion picture distribution branch office (see "Branch").

BREACH OF CONTRACT. A party's failure to perform some contracted-for or agreed-upon act. In drafting a film distribution agreement, vague and subjective terms or phrases should be eliminated, particularly with respect to the film's specifications or delivery requirement. Otherwise, the distributor may seek to use such vague or subjective terms or phrases as an excuse to allege breach of contract by the producer and as grounds for not performing its distributor duties pursuant to the terms of the distribution agreement, i.e., not distributing the film (see "Cure" and "Default").

BREAK (noun). A distinct stage in the release of a film within a market, i.e., the calendar date on which a film first becomes available for exhibition within a geographical area. A film's national break may not be the same as that film's break for a more limited geographical area such as major keys, ordinary keys or sub-keys. A break, whether first run break, second-run break, etc., consists of a specific combination of theatres playing a motion picture in a given availability. As a verb, to open a film in several theatres simultaneously (see "Availability," "Major Key," "Ordinary Key," "Playdate," "Run" and "Sub-Key").

BREAKAGE. The action of breaking, e.g., in the context of a production-financing/distribution agreement, the studio would take the position that a budget overage would constitute breakage of the producer's undertaking not to exceed the approved production budget. Breakage might trigger certain contractual over-budget penalty provisions (see "Bonus," "Breach of Contract" and "Over-Budget Penalty").

BREAKDOWN (see "Production Breakdown").

BREAKEVEN. The point at which sales equal costs. In film, the specific point at which an exhibited motion picture neither makes nor loses money, i.e., receipts cover all costs attributed to the picture by the individual or entity calculating breakeven. Above this point, a film begins to show a profit; below it, a loss. In other words, breakeven is the point in a movie's revenue stream at which the income to the exhibitor, distributor or producing entity is said to equal such entity's cost of producing and/or distributing the movie. Breakeven, thus, will be different for each of the different individuals or entities involved with a film, although the most commonly referred to "breakeven" is the distributor's breakeven. Generally, this is the point at which deferred compensation is paid. In many cases, the costs of distribution continue to escalate ahead of the pace at which receipts are generated. Reportedly fewer than 5% of motion pictures released in recent years and using the major studio/distributor net profits definition have earned a profit, i.e., achieved breakeven (see "Actual Breakeven," "Artificial Breakeven," "Cash Breakeven," "Creative Accounting," "First Breakeven," "Gross Floor," "Profit," "Recoupment" and "Rolling Break-Even").

BREAKEVEN FOR DISTRIBUTOR. That point in a motion picture's revenue stream after the distributor has deducted its distribution fees, at which the distributor is able to recoup its distribution expenses and advances to the producer (if any), out of the distributor's gross receipts (see "Actual Breakeven," "Artificial Breakeven," "Cash Breakeven" and "Creative Accounting").

BREAKEVEN POINT (see "Breakeven").

BREAKOUT. A significant expansion of a film's bookings after an initial period of an exclusive or limited engagement, e.g., a film that is a surprise hit (see "Crossover Film").

BREAKOUT PICTURE (same as "Breakout").

BREAKOUT POTENTIAL. The prospects that the performance of a motion picture at the box office will be so favorable that its bookings will be significantly increased (see "Breakout").

BRIBERY. The voluntary giving or receiving of a gift or something of value in an unlawful attempt to corruptly influence the performance of an official duty (see "Commercial Bribery," "Discount," "Kickback" and "Rebate").

BRIDGE FINANCING. A short-term loan made in anticipation of intermediate-term or long-term financing (similar to "Interim Credit Facility").

BRIDGE LOANS. Loans made to corporations during periods of transition (see "Corporation").

BRITISH TERRITORY. A foreign market for film distribution purposes that may be defined in the distribution agreement, typically, as the United Kingdom of Great Britain and Northern Ireland, the Republic of Ireland, the Isle of Man, the Channel Islands, Malta, Gibraltar, and ships and aircraft flying the British flag and camps wherever situated and where British forces are stationed (see "Foreign Territories").

BROAD AUDITING RIGHTS. A film producer's negotiated authority to audit the books and records of a distributor with few restrictions. Distributors typically want to limit audit rights by restricting when the audit may be started and conducted, limiting the purpose of the audit, restricting who may conduct the audit, requiring that copies of all reports made by the producer's accountant be delivered to the distributor at the same time as the producer, placing limits on the amount of time an audit may take, allowing only one audit each year, only permitting individual records to be audited once, limiting the period during which objections may be made, providing that all statements by the distributor are binding unless objected to in writing within a certain period of time, forever barring the producer from instituting any lawsuit unless timely objection is made and only permitting review of the books of the subject picture (even when the picture is marketed with other pictures as a package). Distributors will also insert language which permits them to keep records in their own unique way (see "Audit," "Audit Rights" and "Good Distributor").

BROADCAST. The act of transmitting sound or images by radio or television through the airwaves. Commercial broadcasters sell broadcast time that is used for the dissemination of information, entertainment and advertising messages (see "Radio" and "Television").

BROADCAST TELEVISION (TV). Advertising supported television including networks, independent stations and public broadcasting stations; the industry which transmits visual images and sound through the airwaves via the very-high-frequency (VHF) or ultra-high-frequency (UHF) channels (see "Broadcast," "Cable," "Free Television," "Pay," "Pay-Per-View TV" and "Television").

BROKER. Any person or entity engaged in the business of effecting securities transactions for the account of others, but not including a bank; a person who acts as an intermediary between a securities buyer and seller, usually charging a commission. A broker purchases securities on behalf of his or her customers, for which he or she is compensated solely by commissions. When a broker buys, he or she buys not for himself or herself but for his or her customers. The activities of brokers are regulated by the Securities and Exchange Commission and the National Association of Securities Dealers pursuant to the Securities and Exchange Act of 1934 as well as by the state securities regulatory agencies in each state in the U.S. (see "Broker/Dealer," "Dealer," "Finder," "Investment Adviser" and "Registered Representative").

BROKERAGE HOUSE. A firm or company of securities broker/dealers (see "Broker," "Broker/Dealer," "Finder" and "Registered Representative").

BROKER/DEALER. A commonly used term including both brokers and dealers, since most persons or entities who are either brokers or dealers typically perform or are licensed to perform the activities of both. Such persons or entities must be registered with the Securities and Exchange Commission (SEC), the National Association of Securities Dealers (NASD) and with the appropriate regulatory agency in each state in which such individuals or entities may seek to offer or sell securities including units of a film limited partnership (see "Broker," "Dealer," "Investment Adviser" and "Registered Representative").

BROKER/DEALER SALES. One of three methods for marketing securities, in this case, through broker/dealers who are paid commissions for such sales (see "Broker/Dealer," "Finder Sales" and "Issuer Sales").

BROKER/DEALER SELLING AGREEMENT. An agreement between a securities broker/dealer firm and the issuer in a securities offering setting out the terms under which the broker/dealer will sell the securities offered by the issuer (see "Managing Broker/Dealer" and "Selling Broker/Dealer").

"B" TITLE (see "B-Movie").

BUCHWALD CASE. A breach-of-contract lawsuit filed by humorist Art Buchwald and motion picture producer Alain Bernheim against Paramount Pictures relating to the Eddie Murphy film "Coming to America." The trial judge first ruled in January of 1990 that Paramount breached its option on Buchwald's treatment and that "Coming to America" was substantially based on the treatment. He later ruled that the net-profit formula used by Paramount was unconscionable. The judge characterized the profit-participation formula used by Paramount (which is similar to the net-profit formulas used by all of the major studio/distributors in the film business) as ". . . an insidious device used by the studios to perpetuate their control . . . and to create an economic caste system in Hollywood . . ." Paramount testified during the trial that the movie had grossed more than $300 million worldwide but had not yet reached net profits. Some legal experts suggest that the case (once it is finally resolved) will not serve to encourage other plaintiffs who may want to sue the major studio/distributors since an equivalent of some $2 million in attorneys fees and costs were incurred on the plaintiff's side during the trial phase of the litigation. These same experts further suggest that only rarely will anyone hoping to continue to do business in the industry seek a court fight with the major studio/distributors for fear of being blacklisted, whereas, in Buchwald's case, he did not have that same concern since he did not ordinarily rely on the motion picture business for his livelihood (see "Contract of Adhesion," "Creative Accounting," "Gross Receipts," "Inferior Bargaining Position," "Market Power," "Net Profits," "Profit Participation Litigation," "Sue Us," "Treatment" and "Unconscionable Contract").

BUDGET. Generally, a statement of the amount of money that is required for a particular purpose, i.e., an estimate of revenue and expenditure for a specified period. In film, a listing of all probable expenses anticipated to be involved in the production of a motion picture (see "Budget Overruns," "Hidden Contingency" and "Litigation Budget").

BUDGET ADMINISTRATOR. The person responsible for managing a film's budget during the film's production and for seeing that actual expenditures in the various budget categories do not exceed the budgeted amount (see "Budget" and "Production Accountant").

BUDGET FORMS. Pre-printed forms setting out typical film production expense categories with spaces for entering the dollar amounts (see "Budget").

BUDGET OVERAGES (same as "Budget Overruns" and "Penalty Free Cushion").

BUDGET OVERRUNS. The dollar amounts by which a film budget category is exceeded (see "Penalty-Free Cushion").

BURDEN OF PROOF. The duty of a party to substantiate an allegation or issue in litigation either to avoid the dismissal of that issue early in the trial or in order to convince the trier of fact as to the truth of that claim and hence to prevail in a civil suit. The term is also used in a less formal sense in business negotiations or discussions to indicate that a party making a statement has the obligation to provide some form of persuasive evidence that the statement is true before the statement need be relied on in such negotiations (see "Burden of Proof File").

BURDEN OF PROOF FILE. A collection of the written evidence which tends to show compliance with the conditions and limitations imposed on the use of a given exemption from the securities registration requirements, e.g., in a film limited partnership offering. Such evidence is compiled by the issuer (e.g., producer/general partner) of such securities and used to demonstrate compliance with the securities law requirements in the event that investors or regulators should question such compliance (see "Burden of Proof" and "Private Offering").

BURNOUT. The point in time when a tax shelter's tax benefits are exhausted and when an investor starts to receive income from the investment (see "Tax Shelter").

BUSINESS AFFAIRS DEPARTMENT. A major administrative unit of the typical motion picture studio/distributor which is primarily responsible for conducting the initial negotiations relating to the more important deal points in the studio's agreements with producers, directors, talent and writers or their respective agents. In contrast, the legal department is primarily responsible for negotiating the details of such agreements and reducing the agreements to long form contracts (see "Creative Affairs Department," "Deal Memo," "Legal Department," "Long Form Agreement," "Production Department" and "Studio").

BUSINESS AFFAIRS EXECUTIVE. A studio employee who holds a position of administrative or managerial responsibility in the business affairs department of the studio (see "Business Affairs Department").

BUSINESS MANAGER. An individual, usually a CPA, who handles the financial and business aspects of an entertainment client's career. Actors, performers, directors and some producers may have business managers in the entertainment business. A fee of 5% of the artist's gross receipts is commonly charged by the business manager for his or her services. The business manager's functions can range from simple accounting services to paying the client's bills, advising on investments, running tours and other extremely complicated functions. A business manager has strong fiduciary obligations to the client (see "Agent" and "Fiduciary").

BUSINESS PLAN. A written outline and description of a proposed commercial activity, often used in obtaining start-up financing from non-securities venture capital sources, i.e., active investors. Also a specifically mandated and major section within the much broader securities offering disclosure documents (see "Disclosure Document," "Offering Memorandum," "Plan of Business," "Producer's Package" and "Prospectus").

BUSINESS PRACTICES. The customary procedures and activities engaged in by commercial enterprises (same as "Trade Practices;" see "Anti-Trust Laws," "Anti-Competitive Practices," "Blind Bidding," "Conduct Restrictions," "Creative Accounting," "Franchise Agreements," "Predatory Practices," "Price Fixing," "Product Splitting" and "Reciprocal Preferences").

BUYER'S MARKET. A market situation in which there are more sellers than buyers; the opposite of a seller's market. Generally speaking, the film-distribution arena is a buyer's market (see "Law of Supply and Demand," "Leverage" and "Seller's Market").

BUYING A GROSS. A huge advertising and promotional campaign for a film that loses money in the domestic theatrical market. In order to prevent such an occurrence, producers may want to request some sort of cap or ceiling on the distributor's expenses for a given movie (see "Direct Distribution Expenses").

BUY/SELL AGREEMENT. A contract or contractual provision which provides that, in the event of the death, retirement or withdrawal of a corporate shareholder, the surviving shareholders have the right to purchase the stock of the deceased, retiring or withdrawing shareholder. Such agreements are sometimes referred to as cross-purchase agreements (see "Corporation" and "Shareholders").

BUZZ. The talk on the street regarding a film in progress. This early awareness of a film's initial and hopefully favorable "buzz" is considered critical to its subsequent box office performance. Creating this favorable "buzz" is so important that publicists are hired for certain movies primarily to generate such positive preliminary impressions (see "Blurbs," "Hype," "Publicist" and "Publicity").

BYLAWS. Rules adopted by the board of directors of a corporation for the regulation of the conduct of the corporation's affairs and which are subordinate to the provisions of the corporation's articles of incorporation and applicable statutory provisions (see "Articles of Incorporation" and "Charter").

—C—

CABLE (see "Cable Television").

CABLE TELEVISION. Transmission of a television signal (picture and sound) for home viewing by wire (coaxial cable) as opposed to airwave broadcast. Cable systems generally cost extra to install and a fee or monthly subscription charge is assessed for subscription to their specific multi-channel service. Many cable systems offer subscribers an opportunity to see movies, sporting events, and other special programming not available on free TV (see "Network," "Pay Cable," "Pay-Per-View," "Pay TV," "Television" and "Subscription Television").

CALENDAR HOUSE. A motion picture theatre which exhibits previously released films on a pre-scheduled basis, usually for only a few days, and which provides its patrons with a calendar of scheduled films (see "Art House" and "House").

CALL. A demand to repay a secured loan, usually made by a bank when the borrower fails to meet certain contractual obligations such as the timely payment of interest. When the loan is called, the entire principal amount becomes due immediately (see "Lender Financing").

CAMEO. A small, vivid theatrical role often limited to a single scene. A cameo appearance often involves a name actor or actress (see "Bit Player").

CAMERA OPERATOR. The film production person responsible for operating the camera at all times and maintaining the composition established by the director or, in some cases, by the director of photography (see "Director of Photography").

CAMPAIGN (see "Advertising Campaign").

CAMPAIGN CONCEPT. The basic underlying theme around which a motion picture's advertising and promotional program is developed and implemented (see "Advertising").

CAMPAIGN PACKAGE. All aspects of a film advertising and promotional program. The basic film campaign package includes the press kit (which in turn typically contains ad mats, film synopsis, cast list, running time for the film and suggested publicity articles for adaptation by the local media), a one sheet, the trailer (usually under three minutes), television ads, radio spots and black and white (8 x 10) still photos (see "Press Kit" and "One Sheet").

CAN. The round metal container in which film is stored. A completed film or scene is said to be "in the can" (see "Acquisition Distribution Agreement").

CANNES FILM FESTIVAL. A major international film festival and market held annually in May at Cannes, France. Films compete for awards, and rights to distribute films in various territories and media are bought and sold at Cannes (see "American Film Market," "Film Market" and "MIFED").

CAP. A ceiling, upper limit or maximum, e.g., a film's distributor may seek to negotiate an extension to the term of a distribution agreement if the distributor has not recouped its advances during the stated term, but the producer may want to impose a reasonable limit or a cap on such extension. Also, a producer may want to negotiate a cap on the legal fees a lending bank pays its attorneys in a production loan transaction since such fees are paid out of the producer's loan and the producer thus must pay interest on such legal fees (see "Ceiling," "Inflation Indexed Cap" and "Override").

CAPITAL. Broadly speaking, all the money and other property of a corporation or other enterprise used in transacting its business. The money invested in a business venture (for which a security may be issued) may be referred to as risk capital (see "Capital Contribution," "Capital Investment," "Return of Capital" and "Risk Capital").

CAPITAL ACCOUNTS. That part of a business's accounting records where capital assets and expenditures, and the liabilities incurred to acquire such assets and make such expenditures, are taken into account. In a limited partnership context, the accounts required by the IRS to be established for each partner in a limited partnership when special allocations are utilized, which is generally the case in a film limited partnership. The amount of the capital interest of each partner in the partnership consists of that partner's original contributions, as (1) increased by any additional contributions and by that partner's share of the partnership's profits and (2) decreased by any distribution to that partner and by that partner's share of the partnership's losses. Very detailed IRS rules regulate the creation and maintenance of partnership capital accounts and an accountant should be consulted. Capital accounts do not bear interest (see "Limited Partnership").

CAPITAL ASSETS. Long-term assets that are not bought or sold in the normal course of operating a business, e.g., land, buildings, equipment, fixtures and furniture (see "Capital" and "Capitalize").

CAPITAL CONTRIBUTION. Generally, any capital contributed to a business enterprise. In a limited partnership context, any contribution to the capital of a limited partnership made by a unit purchaser or general partner, i.e., the amount contributed by an investor to a partnership to purchase a partnership interest. Such contributions generally include cash or other property, although they may include services (contrast with "Capital" and "Capital Investment").

CAPITAL EXPENDITURE. The costs associated with acquiring or repairing property when such property or improvement has a useful life extending substantially beyond the taxable year (a capital asset). Such costs are not deductible for income tax purposes, but may be depreciated (see "Depreciation" and "Expenses").

CAPITAL GAIN. The difference between a capital asset's purchase price and selling price when the difference is positive (see "Capital Gains Rate" and "Capital Loss").

CAPITAL GAINS RATE. The tax rate required to be paid by taxpayers on capital gains. Prior to 1988, the capital gains rate was lower than the tax rate on ordinary income (see "Capital Gains Tax").

CAPITAL GAINS TAX. Federal tax on profits from the sale of capital assets. Tax law previously specified a minimum holding period after which a capital gain was taxed at a more favorable rate than ordinary income. The Tax Reform Act of 1986, however, provided that capital gains be taxed at ordinary income rates starting in 1988, although there is considerable interest in Congress for reverting to a lower capital gains rate in the future (see "Capital Gain").

CAPITAL-INTENSIVE BUSINESS. A business which requires large investments in capital assets; sometimes used to mean a high proportion of fixed assets relative to labor costs (see "Labor-Intensive" and "Money Laundering").

CAPITAL INVESTMENT. Monies paid out by an investor for an interest in a business as in the purchase of stock or other security, e.g., an interest in a film limited partnership. Also, money paid out by a business entity for acquisition of a capital asset, or something for permanent use or value in a business (contrast with "Capital," "Capital Contribution" and "Risk Capital").

CAPITALIZATION. For accounting purposes, the allocation of an item of expense to the capital account because of the relatively long life of the asset acquired by the expense (see "Amortization," "Expense" and "FASB Statement No. 53").

CAPITALIZE. To supply capital for. Also to compute the present value of anticipated income over a period of time or to record capital outlays as additions to asset accounts, not as expenses (see "Capitalization" and "Expenses"). For accounting purposes, to record capital outlays (business expenditures relating to the purchase or creation of fixed assets) as additions to asset accounts as opposed to expenses (see "Capital," "Expense" and "FASB Statement No. 34").

CAPITAL LOSS. The amount by which the proceeds from the sale of a capital asset are less than the cost of acquiring it (see "Capital Gain" and "Loss").

CAPITAL MARKETS. A general financial term referring to all markets where capital funds (debt or equity) are traded or may be raised, and including private placement sources in addition to the organized markets and exchanges. As profit margins are reduced, industry analysts report capital markets for the motion picture industry are drying up (see "Industry Profit Margins" and "Rising Production Costs").

CAPITAL REQUIREMENTS. The permanent financing needed for the normal operation of a business, that is, the long-term and working capital (see "Capital").

CAPITAL STOCK. All shares representing ownership of a corporation, including preferred stock and common stock. The number and value of issued shares are normally shown, together with the number of shares authorized, in the capital accounts section of the corporation's balance sheet. Such figures may be viewed with some skepticism since subjective considerations may be involved in the determination of such values (see "Corporation").

CAPITAL STRUCTURE. A corporation's financial framework, including long-term debt, preferred stock and net worth. Capital structure differs from a corporation's financial structure, which includes additional sources of capital such as short-term debt, accounts payable and other liabilities (see "Capital").

CAPITAL SURPLUS. A corporation's equity or net worth, not otherwise classifiable as capital stock or retained earnings (see "Corporation" and "Equity").

CAPITAL TRANSACTION. Any sale of portions of the property of a limited partnership or any interest therein (not including the sale of all or substantially all of the partnership property) and other similar transactions which in accordance with generally accepted accounting practices are attributable to capital (see "Capital").

CAP ON RETURN. In investments, a deal may sometimes be structured so as to limit the upside potential, (i.e., place a ceiling or cap on any prospective return on such investment), for investors in exchange for some downside protection. On the other hand, the fact that an investment provides no cap on the investor's return is likely to be considered desirable from an investor's point of view (see "Ceiling," "Downside Protection," "Pre-Sales" and "Upside Potential").

CAPTAIN. Teamsters union terminology for the person who is in charge of a film production company's transportation requirements. The teamster captain organizes and coordinates the transportation and driving operations of the project. The captain also arranges for the hiring of equipment and extra equipment (see "Teamsters").

CAPTIONS CLAUSE. A contractual provision usually found near the end of a written agreement (in the miscellaneous provisions section) which provides that the captions or paragraph headings in such agreement have been inserted for reference and convenience only and that such captions or paragraph headings in no way define, limit or describe the scope of the agreement or intent of any provision in such agreement (see "Contract").

CARA (see "Classification and Rating Administration," "MPAA" and "Ratings").

CARDED PREVIEW. The showing of a film before its scheduled release date where the audience is asked to answer questions about their reactions to the movie on a card. This information is then used by the producer, director and distributor to make final modifications to the movie (if any), based on the audience reaction (see "Preview" and "Test Marketing").

CARRYOVER (same as "Holdover").

CARRYOVER CLAUSE (same as "Holdover Clause").

CARRYOVER FIGURE (same as "Holdover Figure").

CARTEL. A group of independent industrial corporations, usually on an international scale, which agree to restrict trade to their mutual benefit; a group of businesses or nations that agree to influence prices by regulating production and marketing of a product. Although more prevalent outside the U.S., such groups are generally found to violate federal anti-trust laws. A number of countries, including the United States, have laws specifically prohibiting cartels. A cartel, however, has less control over an industry than a monopoly. Trust is sometimes used as a synonym for cartel (see "Anti-Trust Laws," "Conscious Parallelism," "Internationally Competitive," "Market Power," "Market Share," "Monopoly," "MPAA Cartel," "Oligopoly," "Transnational Cartelization" and "Trust").

CARTOON. An animated film short primarily designed to provide comedic entertainment. In some distributor/exhibitor deals, a percentage deduction from box office receipts is taken by the exhibitor for showing the cartoon (see "Pre-Feature Entertainment").

CARTRIDGE. A cylindrical shipping tube used by distributors in shipping film-related materials. The costs associated with cartridges are generally considered distribution expenses (see "Direct Distribution Expenses").

CASH. The asset account on a balance sheet which represents paper currency and coins, negotiable money orders and checks, and bank balances (see "Currency").

CASH BASIS. The accounting method that recognizes revenues when cash is received and recognizes expenses when cash is paid out (see "Accounting Method," "Accrual Method of Accounting" and "Cash Method of Accounting").

CASH BASIS ITEMS. IRS terminology used in a limited partnership context and meaning items of partnership deduction resulting from payments for interest, taxes, services or the use of property (see "Limited Partnership").

CASH BREAKEVEN. A concept that may be defined in several ways, but which in its most favorable form for a gross participant is defined as that point in a film's revenue stream at which gross receipts equal the film's negative cost, plus interest and distribution expenses (excluding production and advertising overhead). A more favorable definition from the studio/distributor's point of view also takes into consideration some distribution fee, although lower than normal (e.g., 17.5%), to reimburse the studio for its internal costs of distribution, plus some level of production overhead. The concept of cash breakeven is sometimes used by the studio/distributors to make sure they have recouped their real costs (as opposed to their real costs plus some profit factor) before the payment of a gross participation obligation is triggered. For example, if gross participations are to escalate at different levels of breakeven, cash breakeven is usually considered the first breakeven (see "Actual Breakeven," "Artificial Breakeven," "Breakeven," "First Breakeven," "Reduced Distribution Fee Approach" and "Rolling Breakeven").

CASH DISTRIBUTIONS. Amounts paid by a partnership to its partners in accordance with the terms of the partnership agreement. These distributions initially represent a return of investment and therefore are non-taxable to the recipient. When their cumulative total exceeds a partner's tax basis in the partnership, however, the excess normally will be taxable (also sometimes called "Distributable Cash" or "Partnership Net Receipts;" see "Tax Basis").

CASH DIVIDEND. A cash payment by a corporation to its shareholders, distributed from the corporation's current earnings or accumulated profits and taxable to the shareholder as income (see "Double Taxation" and "Stock Dividend").

CASH FLOW. Generally in business an analysis of all the changes that affect the cash account of a business during an accounting period. In investments, cash flow is the same as cash earnings, i.e., net income plus depreciation and other non-cash charges. In the film business, the term is also used to describe how a movie's revenue stream flows from its source, i.e., the box office to the investors and other net profit participants who are generally last in line, showing what deductions are taken out along the way and by whom (see "Cash Distributions," "Cash Flow Chart," "Distributor's Fee," "Negative Cash Flow," "Positive Cash Flow," "Pro Forma Cash Flow Statement," "Revenue Stream" and "When the Money's Paid").

CASH FLOW CHART. A graphic illustration of how the money earned by a motion picture travels from the box office to investors including what deductions are made along the way (see "Cash Flow").

CASH FLOW CRUNCH. A reduction either in the amount of funds returning to the financier's of motion pictures or in the rate at which invested funds return to such financiers. In the film industry today, cash comes back much more slowly than in the past, when domestic theatrical was the dominant market for the exploitation of films. Today, with ancillary markets such as home video and cable providing the bulk of film revenues, the industry actually has to wait much longer to receive its invested cash (see "Cash Flow Cycle").

CASH FLOW CYCLE. Both the route and amount of time involved for invested funds to move through the cycle of development, production, distribution, exhibition and exploitation in the ancillary markets then to return to the financiers of motion pictures (see "Cash Flow" and "Cash Flow Crunch").

CASH FLOW MARGINS. The leeway between the amount of money coming into a business and that going out (see "Cash Flow Crunch").

CASH FLOW SCHEDULE. A projection of the manner in which and the time period during which funds invested will return to the investor or financier. In the context of a production-financing/distribution agreement, a mutually approved cash flow schedule is used to establish the amount of production funds required each week in order to produce the movie, and it is used to determine the amount of installment payments to be made by the studio/distributor/financier or lender to the production company (see "Pro Forma Cash Flow Schedule").

CASH METHOD OF ACCOUNTING. An accounting method under which income is subject to tax when actually or constructively received and deductions are allowed when actually paid (see "Accrual Method of Accounting").

CASH-STRAPPED FIRM. A business entity that has so little paper currency and coins, negotiable money orders and checks, and bank balances that the company's freedom of action is restricted (see "Cash-Flow Crunch").

CASSETTE. A cartridge which houses and protects video or audio tape. Audio cassettes have two channels going in one direction and two in the other, allowing two stereo programs on one cartridge. Tape lengths may vary, e.g.,thirty minutes per side and forty-five minutes per side (see "Videocassettes").

CAST. The performers who play the roles in a film, including stars, feature players, bit and/or day players (see "Crew," "Day Player," "Extras," "Feature Player," "Production Staff" and "Staff").

CAST AND CREW INSURANCE. Insurance which promises to reimburse the production company or producer (i.e., the insured) for any extra expense necessary to complete principal photography of an insured production due to the death, injury, or sickness of any insured performer or director or crew member (see "Insurance" and "Insurance Coverages").

CAST/CREW AGREEMENT (see "Employment Agreement").

CASTING. The activity involved in interviewing, negotiating contracts with, and hiring the actors for a film. Usually commitments from some or all of the principal cast are obtained by the producer or director before the balance of the casting is conducted (see "Package").

CASTING DIRECTOR. The film production person who specializes in finding and recommending the most appropriate actors and actresses for each speaking role in a film (see "Casting").

CAST LIST. A written compilation of the actors and actresses in a given film. In addition to the names of the actors and actresses, a cast list usually includes their corresponding character name, along with their address, phone number and agent contact. A cast list submitted to the Screen Actors Guild on union films will also include salary information (see "Residuals" and "SAG").

CASUALTY INSURANCE. Insurance that protects a policyholder against property loss, damage and related liability (see "Insurance" and "Liability").

CASUALTY LOSS. Financial loss caused by damage, destruction or loss of property as the result of an identifiable event that is sudden, unexpected or unusual (see "Insurance").

CATALOG (LIBRARY). A collection of copyrighted material or recorded masters embodying performance derived from exclusive and distinctive compositions producing a unique product. Film libraries and music catalogs are often bought and sold. A film library may eventually become a valuable asset for a production or distribution company, thus the ownership rights to a film may be considered an important negotiating point in transactions between a producer and distributor (see "Asset Value" and "Backlist").

CATALOG PROMOTIONS. Advertising and publicity used for the purpose of creating demand for packages of film or video titles. Video companies commonly engage in catalog promotions to market packages of previously released titles at reduced prices. In addition to stimulating secondary sales to retailers and providing them with the opportunity to replenish rental inventories, promotions (along with reduced prices) are intended to create demand for certain titles in the consumer purchase or sell-through market (see "Backlist," "Catalog" and "Sell-Through Market").

CAUSE OF ACTION. A claim in law and fact sufficient to demand judicial attention (see "Litigation").

CAVEAT EMPTOR. A Latin phrase meaning, "let the buyer beware" and expressing the outdated principal of law that a purchaser buys at his or her own risk (see "Warranty").

"C" CORPORATION. A corporation which is not an "S" corporation for that year (see "Corporation," "Regular Corporation" and "S Corp").

"C" COUNTIES. The A.C. Nielsen Company market designation for U.S. counties with a population of more than 40,000 people but which are not "A" or "B" counties (see "A-Counties," "ADI Market," "B-Counties" and "Nielsen Media Research").

CEASE AND DESIST ORDER. An order of a court or other body having judicial authority prohibiting the person or entity to which it is directed from undertaking or continuing a particular activity or course of conduct (see "Injunction").

CEILING. An upper, usually prescribed limit, e.g., in negotiating with a bank for a loan, the producer will usually seek to establish a ceiling on the interest rate to be paid. Also, with respect to studio administrative and advertising overhead, profit participants or their representatives may want to ask that such overhead be subject to a ceiling if the overhead charges cannot be eliminated altogether or their percentages reduced (see "Cap," "Floor," "Administrative Overhead," "Advertising Overhead" and "Offering Ceiling").

CELEBRITY. A person who has received a significant amount of public acclaim, such as a movie star (see "Actor" and "Star").

CENSORABLE MATERIAL. Part of an audio or visual presentation in a film that may be considered objectionable in a given jurisdiction. This definition actually appears in some film distribution agreements as a producer warranty, i.e., the producer promises not to include any "censorable material" in the film. An effort should be made to find more suitable language to express this producer warranty, language that does not have such a chilling effect on the first amendment freedoms of producers, directors and screenwriters (see "Obscene Material," "Pornography" and "Ratings").

CENSORSHIP. The act of applying guidelines as to what can or cannot be said or shown in the performing media arts. Such criteria may differ widely among various artistic media, within the medium itself and among various communities and countries (see "Obscene Material," "Pornography" and "Ratings").

CERTIFICATE. A formal declaration that can be used to document a fact (see "Certify").

CERTIFICATE OF AUTHORSHIP. A document signed by the purported author of a screenplay or other literary work which attests as to the identity of the original creator of the work, identifies the number of pages, date of completion, title and date of delivery (if applicable) and certifies to the fact that such person wrote such literary work and that he or she owns all right, title and interest in such work throughout the world. The certificate of authorship is generally the first document in a film's chain of title and allows the purchaser to record the copyright in its own name (see "Chain of Title").

CERTIFICATE OF CODE RATING (same as "MPAA Certificate").

CERTIFICATE OF INCORPORATION. The formal document issued by the Secretary of State in the state in which a corporation is incorporated attesting to the fact of incorporation (see "Articles of Incorporation" and "Charter").

CERTIFICATE OF INSURANCE. A document provided by an insurance company which serves as evidence that a specific policy of insurance, e.g., an errors and omissions policy, is currently in effect and the premium has been paid for a specified term (see "Insurance").

CERTIFICATE OF LIMITED PARTNERSHIP. The form which is required to be executed and filed with the Secretary of State in the state in which a limited partnership is being created as part of the process of forming a limited partnership. Upon approval by the Secretary of State, the certificate is date stamped and certified as of the filing date (see "Partnership Certificate").

CERTIFIED CHECK. A check for which a bank guarantees payment. It legally becomes an obligation of the bank, and the funds to cover it are immediately withdrawn from the depositor's account (see "Bank").

CERTIFIED FINANCIAL PLANNER (CFP). A person who has passed exams given by the Institute of Certified Financial Planners, testing the person's knowledge of and ability to coordinate a client's banking, estate, insurance, investment and tax affairs. Financial planners may be compensated on a fee-only basis, making no money on the implementation of their recommended plans, or by means of a smaller fee while collecting a commission on each financial product or service their clients purchase (see "Broker/Dealer" and "Investment Advisor").

CERTIFIED PUBLIC ACCOUNTANT (CPA). An accountant who has passed certain exams, achieved a certain amount of experience, reached a certain age and met all other statutory and licensing requirements of the state where such accountant practices. CPAs provide accounting and auditing services and prepare tax returns for corporations and individuals (see "Big Six" and "Public Accountant").

CERTIFY. To attest authoritatively, e.g., a corporate officer may certify as to the authenticity of a document (see "Acknowledgement").

CHAIN OF TITLE. The successive conveyances of a certain property commencing with the original source, each being (or purporting to be) a complete conveyance of the title down to and including the conveyance to the present holder (see "Certificate of Authorship," "Chain of Title Documents," "Clear Title," "Title" and "Title Search").

CHAIN OF TITLE DOCUMENTS. The series of written instruments which demonstrate the successive conveyances of a certain property down to and including the conveyance to the present owner, i.e., documentary evidence supporting the producer's claim to the title of and right to film a literary property. Such documents may include a certificate of authorship, option and/or acquisition agreements, assignments, a title search report and opinion, WGA registration of the screenplay and copyright registration certificate. Motion picture financiers, production lenders, completion guarantors, distributors and errors-and-omissions insurance carriers will generally insist on obtaining copies of these documents prior to providing their respective services on behalf of a given motion picture (see "Chain of Title").

CHAIRMAN OF THE BOARD. A member of a corporation's board of directors who presides over its meetings and who is the highest ranking officer in the corporation, although the chairman may or may not have the most actual executive authority in a firm (see "Chief Executive Officer" and "Chief Operating Officer").

CHARACTER. The personality or part which an actor re-creates (see "Actor").

CHARACTER ACTOR. A performer who plays supporting roles and is known for playing a particular style or type of role (see "Bit Player" and "Extras").

CHARTER. After the Secretary of State approves a corporation's articles of incorporation, the state issues a certificate of incorporation and these two documents together become the charter that gives the corporation its legal existence (see "Articles of Incorporation," "Certificate of Incorporation" and "Ultra Vires Activities").

CHASING A DREAM. Pursuit of a goal. Generally, people in the United States with its free-enterprise system would not deny anyone the opportunity to pursue an important goal in life, but if that goal is more akin to a mirage, an illusion, or a fantasy, then anyone who cares about an individual has an obligation to help the "dreamer" understand how unrealistic the goal is. There is probably no other industry that attracts so many people from all corners of the world to pursue the most unrealistic of dreams as the motion picture business, which is headquartered in Los Angeles, California. For the few successes, there are thousands of shattered dreams and wasted lives. If this book can help add some balance and a modicum of reality to the perception of opportunity in motion pictures, it will have provided a valuable service (see "Free Enterprise," "Law of Supply and Demand," "Level Playing Field," "Numbers Game" and "Pied Piper").

CHECKER. A person hired by producers or distributors or by checking services on behalf of producers or distributors to verify the number of paid ticket purchasing moviegoers in attendance at showings of a given movie (see "Attendance Checking," "Checking and Collection Costs," and "Skimming").

CHECKING AND COLLECTION COSTS. Distributor expenses incurred in monitoring the activities of exhibitors to ensure that reported film attendance and receipts are accurate and in investigating the unauthorized usage of motion pictures. These are important activities that can benefit the producer too, but participants may want to audit for documentation of such costs and consider double checking with the checking services. Profit participants may also want to seek a cap on such costs, e.g., deductions of such costs shall not exceed 1% of the gross receipts for the picture (see "Cap," "Ceiling," "Kickbacks" and "Relationship-Driven Business").

CHECKLISTS. Lists of the important points that need to be negotiated and/or provided for in various entertainment industry agreements, such as for example, option agreements, literary purchase agreements, screenwriters agreements, actor agreements, loan out agreements, director's agreements, distribution agreements, etc. Most entertainment attorneys utilize such checklists to help ensure that no important provisions of such agreements are inadvertently overlooked (see "Employment Agreements").

CHECK PRINT. A composite print sent by the laboratory to the producer for approval before release prints are prepared (see "Answer Print").

CHIEF EXECUTIVE OFFICER (CEO). A corporation's executive officer principally responsible for the activities of the firm. A corporation's CEO may also be the chairman of the board, the president or an executive vice president (see "Chief Operating Officer").

CHIEF FINANCIAL OFFICER (CFO). A corporate executive officer who is responsible for handling funds, signing checks, keeping financial records and financial planning for the corporation (see "Chief Executive Officer").

CHIEF OPERATING OFFICER (COO). The officer of a firm, usually the president or an executive vice president, who is responsible for day-to-day management (see "Chief Executive Officer").

CHOOSING A DISTRIBUTOR. The method used by a producer in selecting the entity which will distribute the producer's film. The following describes a proposed system for identifying feature film distributors, a system which does not rely on the "who do you know" or "who do they know" method, but does require an organization such as a professional association of independent feature film producers to help underwrite the costs associated with research and maintaining the distributor files. [1] First the producer must identify the available distributors by obtaining a current list of all feature film distributors in the U.S. (East and West Coast). This list should have the addresses, phone numbers, names and titles of key personnel (such lists are commercially available). [2] The producer should eliminate the distributors he or she already knows will not be interested in the movie because (a) they are too big or too little, (b) the producer prefers working with a West Coast or East Coast distributor and (c) the producer knows they only handle certain types of movies and not the producer's type. [3] Then the producer should select five to ten distributors that he or she thinks are the best bets based on the producer's general knowledge of film distributors and [4] conduct a more detailed research and analysis of this limited group, i.e., determine who they are and what their track record is: (a) develop a list of the number and titles of all the movies they have distributed in the last ten years, (b) categorize each movie by genre, (c) obtain a synopsis of each movie, (d) obtain one or more reviews of each movie, (e) get the credits for each movie, (f) rent or purchase videos of some of these movies and view them, (g) evaluate the marketing and publicity campaign for the movies reviewed, (h) obtain and review press clippings for these distributors, (i) determine the box office performance of each such movie and (j) make a judgment as to whether this track record would appear to give the distributor much leverage with exhibitors. [5] Prepare a producer's package for presentation to distributors (see "Producer's Package" herein). [6] In early meetings with distributors: (a) present and discuss the producer's package, (b) discuss some or all of the issues listed in No. 4 above with the distributor representative and determine if their history is indicative of the direction they want to go in the future, (c) determine what capabilities the distributor has for distributing your movie worldwide, i.e., do they have well-established organizations with branches in many countries or do they utilize the services of sub-distributors in certain territories, (d) determine whether the distributor is in a position to contribute substantial sums of money toward prints and advertising expenditures, (e) ask about other films the distributor is currently handling (the number and what they are about) so as to determine whether they are already committed to distribute other films which may detract from your film, and (f) discuss with and make suggestions to the distributor as to a marketing strategy for your film; placement, demographics of target markets, grassroots promotions, film festivals, etc. [8] Personal chemistry—Is this somebody you want to work with for a significant period of time on a project that is important to you and others who are relying on you? Again, this system cannot, as a practical matter, be implemented without the support of an association of producers (see "AIVF," "IFP," "IFP/West," "Industry Groups," "Mob-Controlled Distribution Company" and "Relationship-Driven Business").

CHOREOGRAPHER. A performer who creates and/or stages dance numbers (see "Actor" and "Director").

CHRISTMAS SEASON. The second most important playing time of the year (after summer) for motion pictures (see "Prime Play Dates" and "Summer Season").

CHURNING. Excessive trading in a stock investment account in order to generate commissions for a broker with relatively little concern for the welfare of the customer (see "Broker/Dealer").

CINEMA. A motion picture theatre or the motion picture industry (see "Cinema Data").

CINEMA DATA. Facts, figures, information and statistics relating to the motion picture industry (see "Cinema" and "Industry Analysts").

CINEMATOGRAPHER. A person with skills relating to the art and science of motion picture photography and who serves as cameraman and photographer for a film (see "Director of Photography").

CIRCUIT. A theatre chain (same as "Exhibitor Circuit" and "Exhibitor Chain;" see "Blind Bidding," "Master Agreement," "National Circuit" and "Product Splitting").

CIVIL ACTION. A legal action maintained to protect a private, civil right, or to compel a civil remedy, as distinguished from a criminal prosecution (see "Litigation").

CIVIL LIABILITY. The vulnerability of a person or entity to a lawsuit for damages as opposed to criminal charges, i.e, liability to court actions seeking private remedies or the enforcement of personal rights, based on contract, tort, etc. In a civil action alleging securities fraud, for example, one of the civil remedies that may be available to the plaintiff is the right of rescission (see "Rescission"). In such an action involving a private placement, the plaintiff's burden is merely to show that a security was involved, that the plaintiff invested money, and that the security was not registered. Then the burden of proof shifts to the defendant, who must show that, although the security was not registered, the defendant complied with all of the conditions and limitations imposed on the use of available exemptions from the registration requirement (see "Burden of Proof," "Burden of Proof File," "Conditions and Limitations" and "Private Placement").

CLAIM OR CLAIMS. The assertion of a right to money or property (see "Litigation").

CLAIMS MADE POLICY. An insurance policy which limits the insurance company's liability to only those claims that are made against the insured and reported to the underwriters during the policy period (see "Named Perils Insurance Policy").

CLASS. Securities having similar features. The different classes in a company's capitalization are itemized on a balance sheet (see "Corporate Stock").

CLASSIC FILMS. Feature films that are considered works of enduring excellence or which are noteworthy because of special literary or historical innovations or depictions. Broadly defined, the term may also include foreign films (also see "Art Film" and "Foreign Films").

CLASSICS DEPARTMENT. A department of a major studio or production company which is responsible for the preservation and exploitation of the company's classic films (see "Classic Films").

CLASSIFICATION AND RATING ADMINISTRATION (CARA). The MPAA agency responsible for rating movies (see "MPAA" and "Ratings Board").

CLASSIFIED STOCK. Corporate common stock divided into two or more classes, e.g., a corporation may issue Class A stock to raise the bulk of equity capital while vesting voting rights in Class B stock, which is retained by management and/or the corporation's founders. Such a practice is usually confined to promotional ventures and relatively few publicly held companies have classified stock as part of their capitalization (see "Corporation").

CLAYTON ACT. A federal statutory amendment to the Sherman Anti-Trust Act which prohibits certain types of price and other discriminations, now covered by the Robinson-Patman Act. It also prohibits certain tying, exclusive dealing, total requirements agreements, mergers or acquisitions tending substantially to lessen competition in any line of commerce and interlocking directorates (see "Anti-Trust Laws," "Combination in Restraint of Trade," "Robinson-Patman Act" and "Sherman Anti-Trust Act").

CLEAR (BANKING). The collection of funds on which a check is drawn and payment of those funds to the holder of the check (see "Bank" and "Certified Check").

CLEARANCE. In exhibition, the exclusivity of a film's run within a competitive theatre area for a time certain, i.e., the period of time, usually stipulated in license contracts, which must elapse between runs of the same feature within a particular area or in specified theatres; or the relative exclusivity a theatre (exhibitor) specifies as a condition to licensing a motion picture within a market. A theatre may request an exclusive run within an entire market or may request exclusivity for exhibition of a motion picture only over those theatres that are in geographic proximity and may be considered competitive. In film production, clearance also refers to the permission needed to utilize registered and/or copyrighted material in a film or television program, e.g., music, film clips and long quotations, and to use a location. Clearance in this sense means approving, taking care of or "clearing" all legal matters or questions relating to ownership rights to a film or underlying property, obtaining individual or location releases, making contractual arrangements, etc. In studio film finance, the term "clearance" refers to the projected profit and loss statement for a film which is continually updated, i.e., before a studio releases a film, it develops a "clearance" based on its best estimate of all revenues and costs (see "Clearance Procedures," "Exclusive Engagement," "Errors and Omissions Insurance," "Licensing Terms," "Paramount Consent Decree of 1948," "Personal Release," "Financial Projections," "Release," "Right of Privacy" and "Runs").

CLEARANCE PROCEDURES. The steps to be taken, i.e., matters or questions to be investigated by the producer's entertainment attorney or the insurer's attorney prior to final cut or first exhibition or broadcast of a film, before such film can be insured. Among other things, the following are usually included: review of the script to eliminate matter which is defamatory, invades privacy or is otherwise potentially actionable; copyright report; title report; written releases for people and locations; synchronization and performance licenses; along with written agreements between the producer and all creators, authors, writers, performers and any other persons providing material (see "Errors and Omissions Insurance").

CLEAR TITLE. Title free from any encumbrance, obstruction, burden or limitation that presents a doubtful or even a reasonable question of law or fact (see "Chain of Title," "Just Title," "Title" and "Marketable Title").

CLIP. A short portion of filmed material, sometimes used for promotional purposes or in another motion picture. Examples of film clips commonly used in other motion pictures include a movie playing in the background at a drive-in or a television program or commercial playing within a scene in another movie (see "Film Clip License" and "Release").

CLOSE CORPORATION. A corporation which meets statutory requirements in some states that the number of shareholders be limited (typically to thirty-five), the shares of stock be sold privately, the close corporation election be made in the articles of incorporation and that a shareholder's agreement modifies the usual powers of the board of directors (see "Closely Held Corporation," "Public Corporation" and "S Corp").

CLOSED BIDDING. A distributor practice wherein the exhibitor bids on a film about to be released are opened by the distributor privately so that the exhibitors who did not win the bid for exhibition of such picture do not know the particulars of the bids submitted by their competitors. Distributors favor the practice, but exhibitors consider it unethical, since, as a result, losing exhibitors are unable to determine how to change their bids so that they might be successful in the future (see "Bid," "Blind Bidding," "Five O'Clock Look," "Product Splitting" and "Unethical Business Practices").

CLOSED CORPORATION. A corporation owned by a few people, usually management or family members, whose shares have no public market; also called private corporation or privately held corporation (see "Closely Held Corporation," "Public Corporation" and "S Corp").

CLOSED TOWN. A geographical area within which only one exhibitor operates theatres (see "Competitive Theatre Area").

CLOSELY HELD CORPORATION. A corporation most of whose voting stock is held by a few shareholders but with enough publicly held stock to provide a basis for trading, even though the shares held by the controlling group are not considered likely to be available for purchase (see "Close Corporation," "Closed Corporation," "Public Corporation" and "S Corp").

CLOSE-UP. A shot taken at short-range or through a telephoto lens, showing considerable detail of the subject (see "Director of Photography").

CLOSING OR CLOSING DATE. The date on which the units offered in a limited partnership or other securities offering (or at least the minimum number of units offered) are fully subscribed for and accepted by the general partners and the capital contributions made pursuant to the offering are released from the escrow account to the partnership. In an initial public offering (IPO) of a corporation's stock, the closing generally occurs one week after effectiveness and in that situation refers to the formal exchange of the issuer's securities for the proceeds of the offering (see "Initial Public Offering").

CLOUT. With respect to film-industry negotiations leading up to striking a bargain (achieving a deal), the word "clout" refers to the influence, power, pull or leverage that a party to such negotiations has, i.e., the ability of such party to obtain, in the context of such negotiations, the results desired (see "Contract of Adhesion" and "Leverage").

CODE. The Internal Revenue Code of 1954, as amended (see "Internal Revenue Service").

CODE OF PROFESSIONAL RESPONSIBILITY. The American Bar Association rules governing the ethical conduct of attorneys. The California State Bar has promulgated its own set of rules of professional conduct, which vary somewhat from the ABA ethical standards. In either case, the 1992 UCLA Entertainment Symposium presented a panel discussion relating to attorney ethics in the motion picture and television industries, only to discover that some on the panel and many in the audience appeared to express the belief that the entertainment business is significantly different than most other businesses and that bar association ethical standards cannot be applied in this industry as elsewhere (see "Arrogance" and "Conflicts of Interest").

CO-FEATURE. A film which is licensed for theatrical exhibition along with another film as a package. Such films are typically licensed on a flat rental basis for a week's engagement, thus the distributor will not know and, therefore, must estimate how much of the film rentals received for the two films is to be allocated to each film in accounting for the revenues of a given film. Distributors will often seek to negotiate a provision in the distribution agreement which allows such allocations to be made in their sole discretion and without allowing the producer of the film to review the percentage allocations made to other films (same as "Double Feature;" see "Creative Accounting" and "Discretion").

CO-INSURANCE. An insurance provision which provides that the insurer provides indemnity for only a certain percentage of the insured's loss. It reflects a relative division of the risk between the insurer and the insured, dependent upon the relative amount of the policy and the actual value of the property insured thereby (see "Insurance").

COLD CALL. A type of general solicitation in a securities offering involving direct contact, usually by telephone, with a prospective investor with whom the issuer has no pre-existing relationship (see "Conditions and Limitations," "General Solicitation" and "Limitations on Manner of Offering").

COLD READING. An audition situation in which an actor is required to read material he or she has never seen before (see "Audition" and "Screen Test").

COLLABORATIVE PROCESS. A series of actions or operations which proceed toward a particular result and in which people work jointly with others, especially in an intellectual endeavor. The production of a motion picture is a collaborative process (see "Auteur").

COLLATERAL. Assets pledged to a lender until a loan is repaid; property, including accounts, contract rights, and chattel paper which have been sold, that are subject to a security interest. To obtain a bank loan, it is almost always necessary to offer some collateral, i.e., to place within the legal control of the lender some property which may, in the event of a default, be sold and applied to the amount owed. Collateral for a film production money loan might include the physical film elements that are created during production, the underlying literary property (e.g., screenplay, treatment and/or novel), the copyright in the screenplay or film, the rights to exhibit and exploit the motion picture, and the rights to receive payments from various contracts for the exhibition and exploitation of the motion picture (also called "Collateral Security;" see "Secured Creditor" and "Security Agreement" and "Studio Security Agreement").

COLLATERALIZE. The pledging of an asset to a lender until a loan is repaid (see "Assign," "Hypothecate" and "Pledge").

COLLECTION. Conversion of accounts receivable into cash (see "Collections").

COLLECTION BASIS. With respect to the distributor-prepared earnings statements provided to the producer, a statement calculated on the basis of monies actually collected or received by the distributor as opposed to billings (see "Billings Basis").

COLLECTION RATIO. The ratio of a company's accounts receivable to its average daily sales (see "Collections").

COLLECTIONS. A distributor expense item consisting of costs incurred in connection with the collection of gross receipts, including attorney and auditor fees and costs and any liability incurred by the distributor in connection therewith (see "Direct Distribution Expense").

COLLECTION SUIT. A proceeding in a court of justice by which an individual seeks to obtain payment of monies owed or alleged to be owed (see "Litigation").

COLLECTIVE BARGAINING. In labor law, the negotiation of employment matters between employers and employees through the use of a bargaining agent designated by an uncoerced majority of the employees within the bargaining unit. It is an unfair labor practice for employers to interfere with their employees' right to bargain collectively. Employers have an obligation to bargain with their employees in good faith; that is, to meet with the representative at reasonable hours and negotiate about working conditions, hours and wages (see "Good Faith" and "Guild").

COLLECTIVE BARGAINING AGREEMENTS. Compacts relating to employment matters between employers and employees negotiated through bargaining agents designated by an uncoerced majority of the employees within the bargaining unit. The major studio/distributors are signatories to collective bargaining agreements between the studios and the various motion picture industry guilds. Recent complaints by studio spokespersons regarding the high costs of motion picture production lay part of the blame on union residual structures and the cost of below-the-line labor, both of which are issues determined through collective bargaining. However, it is difficult to expect labor rollbacks on such items in view of the high levels of compensation paid to many studio executives, the gross participations granted to certain artists, and studio accounting practices (see "Creative Accounting," "Gross Participations," "Guild Agreements," "Residuals" and "Signatories").

COLOR CORRECTED. Having conformed the chroma, hue, shade, tint and tinge of the visual images on film to a conventional or approved standard, e.g., the distribution deal delivery schedule may call for the delivery of a color corrected interpositive. The specific color values of images on a film can be altered during shooting through the use of filters or during processing at the lab (see "Balanced Print").

COLUMN ITEMS. Brief written articles suitable for presentation to the print media and designed to elicit publicity for a movie (see "Publicity Material").

COMBINATION AD. One print advertisement in which two or more films are advertised. If combination ads are used, the distributor has to allocate its costs for such ad among the applicable films. Profit participants should seek to make sure that their auditor is able to review both sides of this transaction (see "Allocation," "Creative Accounting," "Double Feature," "Good Faith," "Discretion" and "Negotiation").

COMBINATION IN RESTRAINT OF TRADE. An alliance of individuals or corporations united to achieve an economic end; in this instance, interfering with free competition in business and commercial transactions where such interference tends to restrict production, affect prices or otherwise control the market to the detriment of purchasers or consumers of goods and services (see "Idea," "Concept," "Marketplace of Ideas" and "Restraint of Trade").

COMBINED FINANCIAL STATEMENT. A financial statement that brings together the assets, liabilities, net worth and operating figures of two or more affiliated companies (see "Financial Statement").

COMBO ENGAGEMENT (see "Double Feature").

COMFORT LETTER. An independent auditor's letter required in certain securities underwriting agreements to assure that information in the registration statement and prospectus is correctly prepared and that no material changes have occurred since its preparation. Also a letter from one to another of the parties to a legal agreement stating that certain actions not clearly covered in the agreement will or will not be taken (see "Securities").

COMING ATTRACTIONS (see "Trailer").

COMMENT LETTER. The letter from the SEC describing deficiencies alleged and changes proposed by the SEC's staff in its review of a securities registration statement for a public offering of securities (see "Pricing Amendment").

COMMERCIAL (when used as an adjective) A descriptive word or concept, applied to ideas, screenplays, completed movies and in some instances television programming, indicating the power of the project to draw paying customers to view it, i.e., the sales power of the project (see "Hit").

COMMERCIAL BRIBERY. A statutory expansion of the crime of bribery which includes breach of a duty by an employee who accepts undisclosed compensation from others in exchange for exercising some discretion relating to the employee's work and granted to such employee by his or her employer (see "Bribery," "Discount," "Kickback" and "Rebate").

COMMERCIAL DISTRIBUTION. Film distribution aimed at a mass audience with a large number of theatres playing the same film simultaneously in a given area or nationally, backed by extensive advertising expenditures, usually with emphasis on television advertising (see "Wide Release").

COMMERCIAL LOAN. Short-term (typically ninety-day) renewable loan to finance the seasonal working capital needs of a business. Interest is based on the prime rate (contrast "Bridge Financing").

COMMERCIAL PAPER. A form of debt, i.e., short-term obligations with maturities ranging from two to two hundred seventy days, issued by banks, corporations and other borrowers to investors with temporarily idle cash. Such instruments are unsecured and usually discounted, although some are interest-bearing (see "Interim Credit Facility").

COMMERCIAL POTENTIAL. A prospective judgment about how well a proposed movie will do at the box office; i.e., film financiers must speculate as to whether a sufficient number of moviegoers will pay for theatre admission tickets to justify producing a given movie (see "Commercial" and "Good Film").

COMMERCIALLY ACCEPTABLE. Suitable for commerce, i.e., of a quality which would enable the rights owner to license the film for a fee in the markets for which it was created (see "Commercial Distribution").

COMMERCIAL PUBLIC EXHIBITION. The showing of a feature film to a general audience made up of paying customers (see "Public Exhibition").

COMMERCIALS. Generally, paid radio or television advertising broadcasts during breaks in programming (also called "Spots" or "Spot Announcements"). In a feature film context, however, any paid appearance of a product, commodity or service. Sometimes referred to as product placement (see "Distributor Commercials" and "Product Placement").

COMMINGLING OF FUNDS. The acts of a fiduciary or trustee who mixes his, her or its own funds with those belonging to a client or customer; generally prohibited unless the fiduciary maintains an exact accounting of the client's funds and how they have been used. A distribution deal may contractually prohibit the co-mingling of the distributor's and producer's funds, even though no fiduciary or trust relationship is established. It would be even better to require that the producer group's money be separated and deposited into a special trust account in its name (but check with the bank first to see if they will do that). This requirement would be particularly helpful if the distributor declares bankruptcy (see "Creative Accounting," "Fiduciary" and "Trustee").

COMMISSION. In contracts, a form of payment for services performed, i.e., remuneration based on a percentage of an amount collected, received or agreed to be paid for results accomplished, as distinguished from salary (see "Salary"). In securities, a fee paid to a broker/dealer for executing a trade or effecting a sale and based on the number of shares traded or the dollar amount of the sale; amounts paid to syndicators for underwriting and directing the sale of limited partnership interests. Commission expense for an offering is considered to be syndication expense for tax purposes and must be capitalized rather than deducted (see "Offering Expenses," "Royalties" and "Syndicated Expenses").

COMMISSIONED WORK. A category for "works made for hire" under U.S. copyright law including works specially ordered or commissioned for use as part of a motion picture, where the copyright is owned by the employer (see "Work Made for Hire").

COMMISSION RESTRICTIONS. Securities law limitations on the amount of transaction-related remuneration which can be paid for the sale of securities. Most state exemptions from securities registration, for example, provide that no form of transaction-related remuneration may be paid, directly or indirectly, to persons not licensed as broker/dealers. NASD guidelines on commissions also apply to public offerings (see "Blue Sky Laws," "Conditions and Limitations" and "NASD").

COMMITMENT. An agreement or pledge to do something in the future. In film, producers of independent movies may seek and acquire commitments from major studios to acquire their films once completed. They may also seek pre-sale commitments from other markets (see "Discounting," "Negative Pickups" and "Pre-Sales").

COMMITMENT FEE. A lender's charge for contracting to hold credit available. The commitment fee may be replaced by interest when the money is actually borrowed or both fees and interest may be charged (see "Bank" and "Lender Financing").

COMMODITY. An article of commerce; an economic good (see "Idea," "Intangible," "Marketplace of Ideas" and "Product").

COMMON LAW. Case made law; i.e., the system of jurisprudence which originated in England and was later adopted in the United States, Canada, and other former English colonies and is based on judicial precedent rather than statutory laws, i.e., legislative enactments (see "State Legislatures" and "Statutes").

COMMONLY UNDERSTOOD. Customarily and routinely agreed upon in the business. Many motion picture industry agreements provide that certain terms not otherwise defined within the agreement are to be defined as commonly understood in the industry. Such provisions merely provide a mechanism for determining the meaning of a term that comes into question; thus, in the context of arbitration or litigation, the fact-finder will have to entertain testimony from persons with expertise in the industry to determine whether there actually is a commonly understood meaning for such a term. Unfortunately, many terms are not commonly understood in the industry and it is likely that experts with equal authority may be produced to define such terms to favor both sides of a dispute, leaving the fact-finder to have to decide between differing interpretations of the same term. The better practice would be to negotiate a definition of the term for the purposes of the agreement and include the definition in that original agreement; otherwise, the party implementing the agreement has a certain amount of discretion in its conduct until challenged by the other party. Again unfortunately, the bargaining power of contracting parties in the motion picture industry is often vastly unequal, thus the party with the most power tends to get the definitions it wants (see "Bargaining Power," "Contract of Adhesion" and "Discretion").

COMMON STOCK. Units of ownership of a corporation; the ordinary stock of a corporation which is generally the voting stock of the corporation (see "Preferred Stock" and "Share").

COMMON STOCK EQUIVALENT. Preferred stocks or bonds that are convertible into common stock or a warrant to purchase common stock at a specified price or discount from the market price (see "Corporation").

COMMUNICATION. The process through which information is transmitted; a technique used in the effective expression of ideas. The motion picture is a form of communication and clearly one of the most effective, if not the most effective, form of communication yet devised by human beings (see "Entertainment," "Idea," "Movies With a Message" and "Propaganda").

COMMUNICATIONS INDUSTRY. A group of business enterprises engaged primarily in the dissemination of information, e.g., radio, free television, motion pictures, home video, cable television, newspapers and magazines (see "Entertainment," "Entertainment Industry," "Idea," "Movies With a Message" and "Propaganda").

COMPACT DISC. A music industry sound-reproduction and record format, i.e., an audio recording and playback device which is covered by a reflective plastic coating and uses a low-power laser beam to read the audio information encoded in a series of closely packed spiral recording grooves. The compact disc emerged in the 1980s (following cassette tapes) and, along with cassette tapes, became the dominant configuration format for the record industry replacing vinyl recordings (see "Laser Disc").

COMPANY. An organization engaged in business as a proprietorship, partnership, corporation or other form of enterprise (see "Corporation," "Joint Venture" and "Limited Partnership").

COMPARABLE FILMS. Motion pictures that are similar. It is important to producers and distributors to be able to make reasonable estimates of a proposed film's initial and long-term performance potential in all markets and such estimates begin with information about the performance of similar projects that have been released in recent years (see "Box Office Comparables" and "Project Audience" and "Profit Projections").

COMPENSATION. Pay for work done or service performed. Compensation is generally an important issue to be negotiated in motion picture industry employment agreements (same as "Remuneration;" see "Bonus," "Contingent Compensation," "Gross Participants" and "Net Profit Participation").

COMPENSATION ARRANGEMENTS. The various methods used to provide remuneration or pay for work done or service performed (see "Advance," "Compensation," "Contingent Compensation" and "Up Front Salary").

COMPENSATION SCHEDULES. Statements of the minimum compensation levels for signatories to the Writers Guild of America Theatrical and Television Film Basic Agreement as set out in such agreement (see "Minimum Wage Scales" and "WGA Agreement").

COMPETING PICTURES. Movies produced and distributed or merely distributed by a film distributor who is simultaneously distributing a movie by a producer which may vie for a portion of the same potential audience (see "Clout" and "Leverage").

COMPETITION. The effort of two or more parties to secure the business of a third party by the offer of the most favorable terms (see "Anti-Trust Laws" and "Competitor").

COMPETITIVE THEATRE AREA. A geographical area, relatively well defined by the historical practice of distributors and exhibitors and by playoff records, within which theatres compete for an audience and within which an exhibitor normally would demand an exclusive run; since a major key may have more than one competitive theatre area, the number of theatres simultaneously exhibiting a film's first run within a major key normally is equal to the number of competitive theatre areas within that major key (see "Key," "Playoff Record," "Run" and "Zone").

COMPETITOR. One selling or buying goods or services in the same market as another (see "Anti-Trust Laws" and "Competition").

COMPLETE AUDIT. An audit that is so thoroughly executed that the auditor's only reservations have to do with unobtainable facts; the auditor examines the system of internal control and the details of the books of account, including subsidiary records and supporting documents, while reviewing legality, mathematical accuracy, accountability and the application of accepted accounting principles (same as "Unqualified Audit;" see "Qualified Opinion").

COMPLETED MOTION PICTURE. A finished feature film that is ready for release (except to the extent that a distributor may require certain changes). It is axiomatic in the motion picture industry that a producer who approaches a distributor with a completed motion picture, the production funding of which was not provided by the distributor, is likely to be able to negotiate more favorable terms in the distribution agreement than a producer who has either relied on at least partial funding by the distributor or has obtained a negative pickup agreement from the distributor prior to completion of the film, assuming of course that the quality of the film is the same in either event. Even more favorable terms are presumably available to the producer who approaches the distributor with prints and ads financing available (see "Acquisition Distribution Agreement," "In the Can," "Negative Pickup," "Production-Financing/Distribution Agreement" and "Rent-a-Distributor") .

COMPLETE LIQUIDATION. The operation of winding up the corporation's affairs by settling its debts, realizing upon and distributing its assets; a status of liquidation exists when the corporation ceases to be a going concern and its activities are merely for the purpose of winding up its affairs, paying its debts, and distributing any remaining balance to its shareholders. The decisive elements are an intent to liquidate coupled with acts done to carry out that purpose (see "Dissolution," "Liquidation" and "Winding Up").

COMPLETION AND DELIVERY RISK. The possibility of loss relating to the failure of a producer to complete and deliver a motion picture to the distributor for distribution in accordance with the delivery schedule. A lender will insist that the producer obtain a completion bond so as to shift the burden of assuming this risk from the bank to the completion guarantor (see "Lender Risk Elimination" and "Risk").

COMPLETION BOND. A contractual commitment similar in form to an insurance policy (but not actually insurance) that guarantees that a film will be completed and delivered pursuant to specific requirements, that is, on schedule, within the budget and without substantial deviations from the approved script. The completion bond provides protection against overbudget costs and is supplied by a third party guarantor. It is written in the form of a surety instrument and usually authorizes the guarantor to take control over the production of the motion picture if the terms of the agreement are not met. In negotiations with the completion guarantor and the distributor, the producer may want to prevent the distributor from changing the producer's compensation, credit or continuing creative involvement in the event of takeover, particularly when the takeover is prompted by factors beyond the control of the producer. A spokesman for a completion guarantor recently estimated that completion bond companies collectively provide annual completion bond coverage for films with a total of negative costs equalling $1 billion. That is the equivalent of 100 $10 million movies or 200 $5 million movies. Thus, it may be safe to estimate that less than 200 movies a year are covered by completion bonds (see "Completion Bond Documentation," "Cut-Through Endorsement," "Guaranty," "Surety" and "Takeover Rights").

COMPLETION BOND DOCUMENTATION. Generally, before issuing a completion bond, a completion guarantor may want to review and approve of the final shooting script, production budget with detail, shooting schedule (production boards), preliminary application for completion guarantee, résumés of key personnel and principal cast, chain of title, and supporting agreements regarding the script, producer's agreement with the production entity, director's agreement with the production entity, agreements with key members of the crew, production/finance agreement, evidence of insurance coverage which includes the completion bond company as an additional loss payee, principal artist contracts, post-production schedule (not later than two weeks prior to end of principal photography), music agreements, film and sound laboratory agreements and distribution agreements (if any), in addition to signed undertakings by the producer(s) and director to cast to budget and limit expenses, by the director that the budget, shooting schedule, and post-production schedule are achievable and that the allocation of film stock in the budget is sufficient, that music and all relevant clearances thereof will be obtained within the budgeted categories, that any delivery requirements pursuant to any distribution agreements and any publicity costs that are in excess of the approved budget will be considered to be distribution costs, and that such expenses will not be chargeable to the production budget and that legal fees charged to the production budget will be limited to the amounts budgeted therein (see "Completion Guarantor").

COMPLETION BOND FEE. The consideration paid to a completion guarantor in exchange for the completion guarantee. Completion bond fees are more negotiable in the current environment due to entry in the marketplace of more completion guarantors. The fees traditionally ranged up to 6% of a film's budget, including interest (if any), and the 10% contingency, but excluding the completion guarantor's fee itself. Completion guarantors have more recently utilized various means of modifying the fee to attract customers, e.g., requiring only payment of 3% up front and the other half only if the guarantor is called upon to advance funds or by providing a bonus or rebate of its fee (i.e., 10% to 50% of the completion guarantor's fee) if the production is completed without any claims on the guarantor. Rebates above 10% have been typically reserved for the more experienced producers who have previously brought in films without calling upon the guarantee. More recently, due to an increase in competition among completion guarantors, fees have fallen to as low as 1.5% on the larger budgeted pictures or in instances where a producer can assure a guarantor the opportunity to bond multiple pictures. Such low fees may be dangerous to the bond companies in the long term. Low-budget producers must be aware that the guarantor's fee is an added cost of the film's production, although the service provided may be worth the expense. Under some circumstances, the completion guarantor may also ask for an equity position in the film, e.g., a specified percentage of net profits for every $10,000 advanced by the completion guarantor toward completion of the film and a required evaluation deposit ($500 to $2,500) will generally be applied against the completion guarantor's fee (see "Completion Guarantor").

COMPLETION FUND. A sum of money set aside by a film industry organization or governmental entity specifically for the purpose of helping to finance the completion of motion pictures. Generally, such funds are used to pay for post-production expenses on selected projects (see "Blind Pool").

COMPLETION GUARANTEE (see "Completion Bond").

COMPLETION GUARANTOR. A third party, usually an insurance or bonding company, who may agree to advance funds necessary above the final approved budget of a motion picture so that the producer will be able to guarantee delivery of a finished, commercial-quality motion picture conforming to the final approved shooting script of such picture, notwithstanding the fact that the final negative cost of the picture may exceed its final approved budget. The fee for such bond will typically range from approximately 3% to 6% of the film's production budget (see "Surety").

COMPLETION SERVICES (see "Post-Production Services").

COMPONENT PARTS. Any of the elements of a film; the constituent portions or ingredients that make up a completed film (see "Elements").

COMPOSER. The person who writes the music for a film. In the reservation of rights section of production-financing/distribution agreements (and certain other agreements), the parties may acknowledge that there may be certain composers who will wish to retain certain publishing rights in connection with the original compositions they create for use in or in connection with a motion picture (contrast with "Music Director").

COMPOSER'S ORIGINAL SCORE. The initial written arrangement of music as prepared by the person who wrote the music for a specific film (see "Score" and "Scoring").

COMPOSITE. A single piece of film on which the corresponding sound and picture images appear in synch, either for editorial, camera or projection purposes (see "Composite Print," "In Synch" and "Synchronism").

COMPOSITE DUPE NEGATIVE. A complete duplicate film with synchronized sound and picture images and with the light and dark parts in approximately inverse order to those of the original photographed scenes. A composite negative which, after exposure and processing, produces a duplicate negative picture and soundtrack image (see "Negative").

COMPOSITE MASTER POSITIVE. A complete fine-grain film print made solely for the purpose of producing composite or picture and sound dupe negatives which are in turn used for printing release prints (see "Print").

COMPOSITE NEGATIVE. A complete film which has the light and dark parts in approximately inverse order to those of the original photographed scenes and is exposed and processed to produce both soundtrack and picture negative images on the same film (see "Negative").

COMPOSITE PRINT. A processed positive film with both the visual images and soundtrack on the same film (see "Composite," "In Synch," "Print" and "Synchronism").

COMPOSITE SPLICELESS CHECK PRINT. A complete print of a film without editorial splices sent by the lab for approval to check the dupe negative. If okayed, release prints will be struck (see "Print").

COMPOUND INTEREST. Interest earned on principal plus interest that was earned earlier. Interest can be compounded on a daily, quarterly, half-yearly or annual basis (contrast with "Simple Interest").

COMPREHENSIVE LIABILITY INSURANCE. An insurance policy which protects the production company against claims for bodily injury or property damage liability arising out of filming the picture. The coverage usually includes use of all non-owned vehicles (both on and off camera), including physical damage to such vehicles. It is generally required prior to filming on any city or state roadway or at any locations requiring filming permits (see "Worker's Compensation Insurance").

COMPROMISE. To settle by mutual concession (see "Negotiate").

COMPUTER MODEL. A simulated computer-based financial forecast used by some film production and distribution companies in an effort to obtain a clear prospective view of anticipated financial results of the company's proposed plans and strategies. With a computer model, the company's executives and owners can adjust their picture mix and change the financing and distribution strategies to hopefully produce more favorable results (see "Mental Modeling" and "Picture Mix").

CONCENTRATED OWNERSHIP. A situation in which the means of production in a given industry are controlled by only a few companies, e.g., in the film industry, more than 90% of the domestic theatrical box office gross is typically generated by films distributed by the major studio/distributors (see "Market Power," "Major Exhibition Companies," "MPAA" and "Oligopoly").

CONCENTRATION OF ECONOMIC POWER. A convergence of financial and productive strength under the control of a few individuals or entities. The question as to whether the particular market is conductive to a concentration of economic power is one of the Justice Department's six tests used in analyzing proposed vertical mergers (see "Anti-Trust Laws," "Merger Guidelines" and "Vertical Integration").

CONCEPT. An abstract idea generalized from particular instances; the central theme of a movie. In the creative process, the idea precedes the concept but the concept is considered the first element of a film, as in the joke "I have an idea for a film and, if I had just a little more money, I could develop it into a concept." (see "Development," "Elements," "Idea," "Promotional Concept" and "Theme").

CONCESSION REVENUE. Gross receipts from the sale of food and drinks at a motion picture theatre (see "Concession Sales").

CONCESSIONS (see "Concession Sales").

CONCESSION SALES. Either the volume or revenue generated by the sales of popcorn, candies, drinks, etc. at a movie theatre, 100% of which is generally retained by the exhibitor, i.e., not shared with the film's distributor or others (see "House Nut").

CONCURRENCY. The near-simultaneous release of a U.S. film stateside and in one or more foreign territories. Concurrency is used to take advantage of a film's U.S. promotional campaigns and to prevent piracy (see "Foreign Territories").

CONDITIONS AND LIMITATIONS. Securities law concepts referring to the rules required to be complied with by issuers in offering or selling securities pursuant to federal or state exemptions from the securities registration requirements. Such conditions and limitations typically include numerical limitations on the number of investors, a ceiling on the amount of money to be raised, investor qualifications, commissions that may be paid and to whom, limitations on the manner of conducting the offering, limitations on resales of the securities, issuer qualifications, notice of sale requirements, disclosure requirements, required legends, the payment of filing fees, filing requirements including a consent to service of process and purchaser representation requirements (see "Limited Offering Exemption," "Limitations on Resale," "Limitations on Manner of Offering," "Regulation D" and "Blue Sky Laws").

CONDUCTING. In music, the direction of an orchestra or chorus by a leader (conductor) who employs motions of the hand and the body in order to bring about the coordination of all the players and singers (see "Arrangement" and "Instrumentation").

CONDUCT PROVISIONS. In anti-trust law, elements of court rulings or consent decrees which prohibit certain specified trade practices. For example, the Paramount Consent decrees, in addition to requiring the then five major integrated motion picture companies (Paramount, Loew's, RKO, Warners and Fox) to divorce production/distribution from exhibition, also required these companies, plus three others that did not own theatres at that time (Columbia, Universal and United Artists) to abstain from fixing admission prices and making franchise agreements (see "Anti-Trust Laws," "Franchise Agreements," "Paramount Consent Decree of 1948" and "Price Fixing").

CONDUCT RESTRICTIONS (see "Conduct Provisions").

CONFIDENCE GAME. Any scheme whereby a swindler wins the confidence of his or her victim and then cheats the victim out of money by taking advantage of the confidence reposed in the swindler. The elements of the crime of the confidence game are (1) an intentional false representation to the victim as to some present fact, (2) knowing it to be false, (3) with the intent that the victim rely on the representation and (4) the representation being made to obtain the victim's confidence and thereafter his or her money and property (see "Trust Me").

CONFIDENTIALITY AGREEMENT. A written document used by an owner of a literary property when submitting such property to others for review which provides assurances to such owner that the party to which such project has been submitted will remain confidential (see "Non-Circumvention Clause," "Non-Disclosure Agreement" and "Submission Release").

CONFIDENTIALITY PROVISION. A clause in a broader written agreement which serves the same purpose as the confidentiality agreement (see "Confidentiality Agreement").

CONFIDENTIAL PRIVATE PLACEMENT OFFERING MEMORANDUM (see "Memorandum").

CONFIRMATION LETTER. A letter commonly sent to subscribers (investors) accepted by the general partners as unit holders (limited partners) in a limited partnership, confirming such unit holders' acceptance as limited partners into the partnership and confirming the number of units purchased by such unit holders and the number of units accepted by the general partners (see "Limited Partnership").

CONFLICTING DATES. A situation that occurs when a single film distributor plans to release more than one film at or about the same time, thus dividing the time, skill and efforts of the distributor's marketing staff between such films. This is of special concern to producers who contract with a distributor on a rent-a-system basis and the distributor is not careful to allow for adequate separation in release dates between one of its own films and the independent producer's film. The independent producer's concern in such instances relates to whether his or her film will receive the marketing support it would ordinarily receive but for the conflict (see "Rent-A-Distributor").

CONFLICTS OF INTEREST. Situations in which regard for one duty leads to disregard of another or might be reasonably expected to do so. Conflicts of interest may be actual or potential. On some issues, the film producer and distributor's interests are the same or similar, whereas with regard to other issues, a distributor representing a producer's film, for example, will inevitably be confronted with numerous conflicts of interest which are inherent in the relationship. Some distributors, for example, will seek a representation from the producer in the distribution deal to the effect that the producer knows the distributor is not only distributing other films, but other films similar to the producer's film. It would seem that a distributor would not want to vigorously distribute two similar films that appeal to the same or similar target audiences at the same time and a producer should probably avoid such a conflict or allowing the distributor that freedom. Also, "Conflicts of Interest" is a required section to be disclosed in a securities offering disclosure document (see "Conflict Waivers," "Code of Professional Responsibility" and "Ethics").

CONFLICT WAIVERS. Release agreements that clients of attorneys may be asked to sign in the event the attorney represents several clients involved in the same transaction, thus raising conflict of interest issues. In such an agreement, the attorney will disclose the potential conflict, recommend that each of the client's obtain independent counsel of their own choosing, and ask for the clients' knowing consent if the client chooses to proceed without independent counsel (see "Code of Professional Responsibility" and "Ethics").

CONFORM. In filmmaking, the term "conform" means to match the film negative and all dupes to the editor's current workprint. In a legal sense, the term means to reproduce an exact copy of a document, which is often certified to by an authorized individual (see "Certify").

CONGLOMERATE. A group of corporations engaged in unrelated businesses which are controlled by a single corporate entity (see "Corporation" and "Subsidiary").

CONGRATULATORY ADVERTISING. A public announcement of sympathetic pleasure to a person or entity on account of success or good fortune expressed by means of broadcast or print media (see "Trades").

CONSCIOUS PARALLELISM. In anti-trust law analysis relating to an allegation of a conspiracy in restraint of trade, the phrase "conscious parallelism" refers to the same or similar business practices under circumstances which logically suggest joint agreement. The courts have never held that a showing of parallel business behavior alone conclusively establishes a conspiracy. Thus, in order to show conspiracy, a plaintiff has to demonstrate similar business behaviors that the parties were aware of to infer an agreement and additional circumstances which logically suggest joint agreement as distinguished from individual action. There seems to be a considerable amount of conscious parallelism in the motion picture industry, although it is difficult to prove in a court of law (see "Anti-Trust Laws," "Bidding War," "Blind Bidding," "Net Profit Participation," "Price Fixing" and "Videocassette Revenue Reporting").

CONSENT. Approval of what is done or proposed by another, e.g., certain matters covered in a distribution deal may require the written consent of the other party (see "Consent to Service of Process" and "Waiver").

CONSENT AND RELEASE. A form agreement used when a producer or production company produces a motion picture based upon or involving the life or incidents in the life of a real person and which gives the producer or production company such person's consent to portray such person in the film and releases such producer or production company from certain claims that the person may have based on such portrayal (see "Release").

CONSENT DECREE. An agreement of the parties in a litigated matter which is made under the sanction of, and approved by, the court, not as the result of a judicial determination but merely as their agreement to be bound by certain stipulated facts. A consent decree is not appealable (see "Paramount Consent Decree of 1948").

CONSENT DECREE OF 1948 (see "Paramount Consent Decree of 1948").

CONSENT TO SERVICE OF PROCESS. A legal document providing a securities issuer's consent to the filing of any notices of litigation against such issuer with a designated state official in the state where the issuer proposes to offer or sell securities instead of with the issuer, wherever such issuer is located. Such consents are typically required of an issuer of securities to be provided to the state securities regulatory authorities in each state in which such issuer proposes to offer or sell its securities (see "Conditions and Limitations").

CONSIDERATION. The inducement to a contract, something of value given in return for performance or promise of performance by another, for the purpose of forming a contract. Consideration is one element of a contract that is generally required to make a promise binding and to make the agreement of the parties enforceable as a contract. As an example, the consideration paid by a distributor for the rights to distribute a film may be in the form of advances, guarantees, participations, or royalties or a combination thereof (see "Advance," "Contract," "Contingent Compensation," "Guarantee," "Participations" and "Royalties").

CONSOLIDATED FINANCIAL STATEMENT. A financial statement that brings together all assets, liabilities and operating accounts of a parent company and its subsidiaries (see "Corporation").

CONSORTIUM. A group of companies formed to promote a common objective or engage in a project of benefit to all the members. The relationship normally entails cooperation and a sharing of resources, sometimes even common ownership (contrast with "Cartel;" see "Professional Association" and "Trade Association").

CONSPIRACY. A combination of two or more persons to commit a criminal or unlawful act or to commit a lawful act by criminal or unlawful means; or a combination of two or more persons by concerted action to accomplish an unlawful purpose or some purpose not in itself unlawful but by unlawful means. Motion picture exhibitors have generally failed in attempts to convince the courts that blind bidding is a conspiracy in restraint of trade in violation of the

Sherman Anti-Trust Law partly because of the difficulty in showing a conspiracy (see "Anti-Trust Laws," "Combination in Restraint of Trade," "Illegal Combination" and "Restraint of Trade").

CONSPIRACY IN RESTRAINT OF TRADE (see "Combination in Restraint of Trade").

CONSPIRATOR. One involved in a conspiracy; one who acts with another, or others, in furtherance of an unlawful transaction (see "Combination in Restraint of Trade").

CONSTRUCTIVE NOTICE. Notice other than actual notice which is accepted in law as a substitute for actual notice (see "Consent to Service of Process").

CONSTRUING. The interpretation of a document (see "Contract").

CONSULTANT. One who has a high level of expertise on a particular topic and provides professional advice or services relating to his or her area of expertise. Consultants are often hired by movie producers to advise on technical matters, e.g., courtroom procedure, historical details, space technology, etc. (see "Litigation").

CONSULTANT EMPLOYMENT AGREEMENT. The written contract between a motion picture producer and a person who makes his or her expertise in a certain area available for a fee or some other form of valuable consideration. From a film budgeting standpoint, consultants are generally considered above-the-line (see "Above-the-Line" and "Above-the-Line Employment Agreements").

CONSULTATION. The seeking or giving of professional advice. Many film distribution agreements provide that the distributor is obligated to consult with the film's producer regarding various matters relating to marketing the film, distributor editing and so forth. However, there is rarely any effective way for the producer to enforce such consultation rights. Producers should try to be more clear in exactly what is expected of the distributor when consulting with the producer (see "Consultation Rights").

CONSULTATION RIGHTS. The power or privilege to discuss a certain matter. In motion picture distribution agreements, provisions are commonly made for certain issues to be determined in the future by one or the other of the parties. Some of those decisions may be made in the sole discretion of specified parties. Others may require mutual approval while still others may be made by a specified party who has an obligation to at least discuss the matter with the other party. This privilege held by the non-decision making party to discuss the matter is referred to as a consultation right. As an example, a distribution agreement may provide the distributor with a right of consultation with respect to locations for the film. It may also provide the production company with a right of good faith consultation with respect to the film's distribution pattern and ad campaign for the initial U.S. theatrical release. With respect to the production company's right of consultation, however, the distributor will likely provide that its decision is final, although no such corresponding provision may be included with respect to the distributor's consultation right (see "Discretion," "Mutual Approval" and "Sole Discretion").

CONSUMER PURCHASE MARKET. Retail sales of products to the general public. The term is most used to describe the sales of video-cassettes as opposed to rental transactions (see "Sell-Through Market").

CONTACT PRINT. A positive or negative film which is made by placing a piece of exposed film in contact with unexposed film and exposing the duplicate a frame at a time in a lab printer (see "Contact Printing").

CONTACT PRINTING. The process of making a positive print directly from the working negative (see "Contact Print").

CONTACT SHEETS. The preliminary printing of multiple still photography shots for review and selection of the most desirable shots for actual use in film publicity and advertising (see "Delivery Items" and "Production Stills").

CONTINGENCIES. Pre-conditions to a contract, i.e., particular events or circumstances which must occur, before other obligations created by the contract are owed. In a production-financing/distribution agreement for example, the distributor may condition its obligations undertaken pursuant to the agreement on obtaining satisfactory clearance of the production company's chain-of-title to the rights relating to the motion picture (see "Chain-of-Title," "Clearance" and "Production-Financing/Distribution Agreement").

CONTINGENCY OR CONTINGENCY RESERVE. Money set aside in a film budget for unanticipated costs, i.e., to help prevent the film from going over-budget. Traditionally, 10% of the production budget, excluding the cost of insurance and the completion bond, although some completion guarantors may require a higher contingency reserve on some films (same as "Production Contingency").

CONTINGENT COMPENSATION. Remuneration which is not owed or paid unless and until a specified event occurs, e.g., a salary bonus paid only if a film generates a specified level of distributor gross receipts (see "Contingent Participations," "Contract of Adhesion," "Contractually Defined Profits," "Creative Accounting" and "Net Profit Participation").

CONTINGENT DEFERMENTS. All or part of salaries that are paid on a delayed basis and only upon the occurrence of a specified event, e.g., film rentals or net profits reaching a certain level (see "Deferments" or "Deferrals," "Fixed Deferments," "Percentage Participation" and "Points").

CONTINGENT LIABILITIES. Potential financial liability such as pending lawsuits, judgments under appeal and disputed claims (see "Litigation").

CONTINGENT PARTICIPATIONS. A percentage of gross or net revenues that are not due and payable unless and until a specified event occurs, e.g., gross participation may not be paid until a film's gross receipts reach a specified level of breakeven and net profit participations will not be paid unless and until the film's revenue stream actually reaches net profits (see "Contingent Compensation," "Contract of Adhesion," "Contractually Defined Profits," and "Net Profit Participation").

CONTINUITIES. Material written to link program elements but which is not written by the script's writer (see "Continuity").

CONTINUITY. The consistency of the look and sound of each shot in the film. Also, the uninterrupted and dramatically structured sequence of events in a film or tape production which maintains the continuous and seemingly uninterrupted flow of action of the story (also called "Action Continuity;" see "Sequence").

CONTINUITY BREAKDOWN SHEETS. Film production forms on which all pertinent information regarding the visual and audio requirements of each scene in a film, such as costumes, special effects, stunts, vehicles, props and special sound equipment, are recorded during the production of a film. This information is an important reference for production personnel who are concerned with the continuity of the film (see "Continuity").

CONTINUOUS SUPPLY OF PRODUCT. An uninterrupted flow of motion pictures. The ability to provide a continuous supply of quality motion pictures is an extremely important element of the leverage or bargaining power that a producer brings to the table in negotiations with a distributor and that a distributor must possess in order to effectively negotiate with exhibitors. During times when credit and capital markets are constricted, some distributors encourage producers to utilize their distribution facilities on a rent-a-system basis partly in an effort to keep enough product flow in the distributor pipeline to maintain a strong bargaining position in relation to the exhibitors (see "Product" and "Rent-A-Distributor").

CONTRACT. A promise, or set of promises, for breach of which the law gives a remedy, or the performance of which the law in some way recognizes as a duty. The essentials of a valid contract are: parties competent to contract, a proper subject-matter, consideration, mutuality of agreement, and mutuality of obligations. A contract is a transaction involving two or more individuals whereby each becomes obligated to the other, with reciprocal rights to demand performance of what is promised by each respectively. In filmmaking, contracts generally are used in acquiring the rights to a story and/or screenplay, between the producer and each of the members of the creative team, with the film's distributor and between the distributor and all other entities involved in distributing or exhibiting the film. The terms of the contract between a film's producer and distributor are critical in determining whether a producer and/or investors participate in a film's profits. Legal systems in Europe and Asia have different criteria for what makes a contract (see "Breach of Contract," "Deal Points," "Distribution Agreement," "Remedy" or "Remedies" and "Terms").

CONTRACT OF ADHESION (see "Adhesion Contract").

CONTRACT PLAYER. A player employed under a contract for a term of at least ten out of thirteen weeks and which may not specify any role, picture or series (see "Actor").

CONTRACTUAL BREAKEVEN. A point in a motion picture's revenue stream which is defined by agreement to constitute breakeven. Since there are many ways to define breakeven in film distribution agreements and certain breakeven points may never be achieved due to the effect of the so-called "rolling breakeven," it may be advantageous for all profit participants at whatever level to negotiate a contractually defined breakeven for purposes of triggering the payment of bonuses, escalations or various levels of participation (see "Artificial Breakeven," "Breakeven," "Cash Breakeven," "First Breakeven" and "Rolling Breakeven").

CONTRACTUAL INCENTIVES/DISINCENTIVES. Provisions included in the agreements between a studio or other film production company that is financing the production of a feature film and the film's producers and/or director to encourage such persons to complete the film on time and within budget (see "Double Add-Back," "Leverage" and "Penalty-Free Cushion").

CONTRACTUALLY DEFINED PROFITS. A reference to the fact that the terms "profit," "gross profit," "net profit" and other terms in a film distribution agreement are actually subjective terms and that their meaning may vary somewhat in each film deal depending on how the term is specifically defined in that contract. In other words, there is no industry standard definition for such terms since no one individual or organization has the authority to impose such definition on two individuals or entities negotiating a contract containing those terms. Producers should carefully review these definitions and reduce the overly expansive language, while also trying to keep such concepts simple so that there is less question about how to apply the terms (see "Contractually Defined Terms" and "Subjective Terms").

CONTRACTUALLY DEFINED TERMS. Words or phrases the meanings of which are agreed upon in a written agreement and whose meanings may be different than their meanings in a different context (see "Commonly Understood," "Contractually Defined Profits" and "Terms of Art").

CONTRACTUAL OVERHEAD. A motion picture distributor's expenses which cannot be directly allocated to a specific motion picture distributed, but which are deducted from gross receipts as distribution expenses for a specific film by authority of a provision in the distribution agreement which permits such deductions. Nearly all if not all major studio/distributors impose such contractually defined overhead charges on the producers of films they distribute, thus it may be fair to assume that few, if any, feature film producers have the bargaining power to eliminate such charges (see "Administrative Overhead," "Advertising Overhead," "Contract of Adhesion," "Level Playing Field" and "Overhead").

CONTRACTUAL QUAGMIRE. A phrase used to indicate that a particular transaction requires an overly burdensome and complicated amount of documentation. Some would argue that, from a contractual point of view, it is difficult to coordinate the various concerns of a bank, completion bond company, the film's producer and the various media and territories when negotiating and drafting multiple pre-sale agreements (see "Default Disaster," "Pre-Sales" and "Splits Rights Basis").

CONTRACTUAL THEATRE OVERHEAD (see "House Nut").

CONTRIBUTION. In partnerships, any money, property or services rendered, or a promissory note or other binding obligation to contribute money or property, which a partner contributes to a limited partnership as capital in that partner's capacity as a partner pursuant to an agreement between the partners, including an agreement as to value (see "Limited Partnership").

CONTROL FIGURE. The dollar amount of a theatre's gross box office receipts stipulated within the license agreement which, if not attained during a specified period of time, allows the exhibitor or the distributor to terminate the film's exhibition by that exhibitor (see "Holdover Figure").

CONTROL OF A PICTURE. The authority or power to make the final creative decisions with regard to a motion picture. A concept that may play an important role in the choice of the form of film finance, since it is generally accepted that some producers may lose creative control of their picture when it is financed by a studio (see "Creative Control").

CONTROLLED AVAILABILITY. The practice of manipulating and/or withholding the renting, selling or licensing of motion pictures to exhibitors such that a motion picture is made available to an exhibitor after that film's true availability. Distributors who choose to engage in such practices surely may be able to influence the exhibitor's choice of films that are exhibited. If an independent producer's film is being distributed by an independent distributor, such practices engaged in by the major studio/distributors would have a tendency to limit the available theatres for the independent producer's film. On the other hand, if the independent producer's film is being distributed by a major studio/distributor, the independent producer may benefit from that distributor's "special" clout, but also may be involved in an actionable conspiracy (see "Availability" and "Conspiracy").

CONTROLLED DISTRIBUTION. Securities terminology for a limited offering of securities by the owners of the securities themselves or an offering of securities by an issuer through a broker/dealer acting as an underwriter for such issuer pursuant to a formal underwriting arrangement (see "Distribution" and "Uncontrolled Distribution").

CONTROLLED THEATRE. A cinema over which a distributor has power or influence with respect to the choice of movies exhibited therein, usually due to an ownership interest held by the distributor or by virtue of such distributor's market power. The major studio/distributors have historically been able to maintain effective indirect control of production of movies through the control (and in some instances direct ownership of) first-run theatres. Harold Vogel's book "Entertainment Industry Economics" presents a very revealing chart relating to the question of domination of box-office performance by key U.S. movie theatres (the information in the chart apparently first appeared in "Variety" and was based on the work of Art Murphy).

The chart shows that 50% of the U.S. screens generate 67% of box office gross and that 75% of the U.S. screens generate 90% of box office gross. Thus, regardless of the quality of their movies (granted such movies will always meet certain minimum standards), the major studio/distributors merely have to control access to the right 75% of motion picture screens in the U.S. for their films to generate 90% of the box office gross. And, as can be seen from the information reported herein under "Market Share," the movies distributed by the major studio/distributors have consistently generated in excess of 90% of the box office gross throughout the last decade if not beyond. Experienced net profit participation auditors report that "controlled theatres" are generally more than fair in their settlements with their own exhibitors, but, on the other hand, they can afford to be since the distributor of a controlled theatre is also now participating in the "house nut" and "concessions" at such theatres (see "Anti-Trust Laws," "Blind Bidding," "Box Office Gross," "Concessions," "Day and Date," "First-Run Theatre," "House Nut," "Major Exhibition Chains," "Market Power," "Market Share," "Paramount Consent Decree of 1948" and "Settlement").

CONTROLLER OR COMPTROLLER. Chief accountant of a company who is responsible for preparing financial reports and supervising internal audits (see "Chief Financial Officer").

CONTROL PERSON. A person who is able to affect the actions or policies of the issuer or an underwriter or others in a securities offering, through the ownership of stock, position, by contract or otherwise (see "Control Stock," "Holding Company" and "Working Control").

CONTROLS. Certain required deadlines, procedures, reports or limitations imposed by a studio/distributor on a feature film production company whose film's production costs are being financed by the studio/distributor. Such controls will typically be set out in the production-financing/distribution agreement (see "Approvals").

CONTROL STOCK. Shares of a corporation owned by shareholders have a controlling interest (see "Holding Company" and "Working Control").

CONVERSION. In a tort law context, the wrongful deprivation of another's property, i.e., without his or her authorization or justification. In the context of a film distribution deal, the term "conversion" refers to a specific kind of distribution expense, i.e., costs, discounts and expenses incurred in obtaining remittances of receipts to the U.S., including costs of contesting imposition of restricted funds which are generally treated as off-the-top distribution expenses (see "Off-the-Top Expenses" and "Tort").

CONVERTIBLE SECURITIES. Corporate financial instruments that are exchangeable for a set number of another form of corporate ownership, i.e., common stock, at a pre-stated price. Convertible securities usually take the form of preferred stock or debt instruments such as bonds. They are most appropriate for investors who want higher income than is available from common stock, together with greater appreciation potential than regular bonds offer. From the issuer's standpoint, the convertible feature is usually designed as a sweetener, to enhance the marketability of the stock or bond (see "Debt").

COOLING OFF PERIOD. The interval of time (usually twenty days) between the filing of a preliminary prospectus with the SEC and the offer of the securities to the public (see "Acceleration," "Effective Date," "Public Offering," "Registration" and "Waiting Period").

CO-OP ADS (see "Cooperative Advertising").

COOPERATIVE ADVERTISING. Film advertising and promotion in which the costs are shared between the distributor and exhibitor or other entity and generally calculated on a weekly basis. The exhibitor's contribution toward the total cost of the ads is either a pre-determined fixed amount set out in the contract between the distributor and exhibitor (but decreasing from week to week) or a negotiated formula based on mutually agreed ad expenditures. The distributor's contribution may be a fixed amount or a percentage arrangement similar to that used for film rentals. Expenditures for cooperative advertising are more advantageous from a tax standpoint since such costs can usually be deducted in the year in which they are incurred, whereas national advertising may have to be capitalized and amortized over the period in which the major portion of gross revenue from the picture is recorded. Unfortunately, distributors and exhibitors commonly negotiate and settle their accounts relating to several motion pictures, thus it is often difficult to determine exactly what portion of cooperative advertising costs incurred by a distributor should be allocated to a given producer's film. The producer's auditor should have the authority to examine exhibitor/distributor contracts and the records relating to such shared expenses (see "Amortization," "Capitalization," "FASB Statement No. 53" and "Participation").

CO-PRODUCER. A person or entity joining with another to produce a motion picture or television picture (see "Co-Producer Credit").

CO-PRODUCER CREDIT. The acknowledgment or recognition on the motion picture screen awarded to producers of a film who shared producer responsibilities (see "Co-Producer" and "Produced By Credit").

CO-PRODUCTION. A film produced through the cooperation of and with substantial contributions of two or more production companies (see "International Co-Production").

CO-PRODUCTION DEAL. A film production arrangement wherein two or more production entities share in the cost of production, typically on a 50/50 basis (see "Co-Production Financing" and "Joint Venture").

CO-PRODUCTION FINANCING. A sharing between two or more entities of the responsibilities relating to the financing of a film production; distributor-financiers may make co-production deals with one or more parties for one or more territories so that the risks associated with financing the production of the film will be spread among several parties. Numerous items relating to decision-making authority on various production questions must also be negotiated in order to avoid conflicts on such issues inherent in co-production relationships (see "Financing" and "International Co-Productions").

COPY. The written selling message of an ad (see "Body Copy").

COPYRIGHT. A bundle of rights associated with the works of artists and authors giving them, among other things, the exclusive right to publish, copy, distribute or otherwise use their works or determine who may do so. Under current federal law, copyright protection for works created after 1977 is the life of the "author" plus fifty years. Copyright is governed under the federal Copyright Act of 1976, which covers copyright questions in the U.S., providing protection to original works of authorship fixed in any tangible medium of expression. The level of originality required and the degree of unauthorized use that constitutes infringement have not been precisely defined and such issues are the subject of a considerable body of case law (see "Copyright Infringement," "Fair Use," "First Sale Doctrine," "Fixed Work," "Patent," "Plagiarism," "Public Domain," "Trademark," "Transfer of Copyright Ownership" and "Work Made For Hire").

COPYRIGHT ASSIGNMENT. A written agreement which is used to transfer to a purchaser all of an owner's right, title and interest in a specific literary property that has already been copyrighted. A so-called short-form copyright assignment is usually used for recording such transfer with the U.S. Copyright Office. The short form sets out only the most basic information relating to the identity of the parties (assignor and assignee) along with a description of the literary property (see "Assignment" and "Transfer of Copyright Ownership").

COPYRIGHT CERTIFICATE. The physical documentation provided by the U.S. Copyright Office as evidence of the registration of material for copyright purposes (see "Copyright Registration").

COPYRIGHT DEPOSIT. A non-returnable submission of material to the U.S. Copyright Office for the purpose of registering such material for copyright purposes. The copyright deposit requirements vary depending on the item being copyrighted (see "Copyright").

COPYRIGHT INFRINGEMENT. The unauthorized use of copyrighted material (see "Fair Use").

COPYRIGHT LICENSE. The right granted which gives a person or entity permission to publish, copy, distribute or otherwise use their works or determine who may do so (see "Copyright" and "License").

COPYRIGHT OWNER. The holder of the exclusive right to publish a creative work or determine who may publish such work (see "Copyright").

COPYRIGHT OWNERSHIP. The possession of rights conferred by copyright registration (see "Copyright Registration").

COPYRIGHT PROPRIETOR (same as "Copyright Owner").

COPYRIGHT REGISTRATION. A formal filing for a claim to copyright protection with the U.S. Copyright Office. Copyright transfers, renewals and security interests may also be registered (see "Copyright Deposit").

COPYRIGHT REPORT. A written study, usually prepared by attorneys or copyright specialists in Washington D.C., as to the copyright status (i.e., the ownership of previously copyrighted material) of a specific literary property (book, play, motion picture, television series, rights in a character, etc.) in which someone wants to acquire rights (see "Copyright Search").

COPYRIGHT SEARCH. An examination of the copyright status (i.e., the ownership of previously copyrighted material) of a specific literary property (book, play, motion picture, television series, rights in a character, etc.) in which someone wants to acquire rights (see "Copyright").

COPYRIGHT SEARCH REPORT (same as "Copyright Report").

COPYRIGHT TRANSFER (see "Copyright Assignment").

CORPORATE BOND. A debt instrument issued by a private corporation. Corporate bonds are securities. They are typically taxable, have a par value of $1,000 and have a term maturity (i.e., they come due all at once and are paid out of a sinking fund accumulated for that purpose). If registered, they may also be traded on major exchanges, with prices published in newspapers (see "Bond," "Debenture," "Debt Instrument," "Indenture" and "Sinking Fund").

CORPORATE CONGLOMERATE (see "Conglomerate").

CORPORATE FINANCING. The raising of funds for general corporate purposes by debt or equity means, i.e., the funding of film projects through the vehicle of a corporation, e.g., by selling shares in a film production company organized as a corporation. In the film business, general corporate financing may be utilized to fund a slate of films, including acquisition, development, production and distribution (see "Financing" and "Single-Picture Financing").

CORPORATE FORMALITIES. The required activities in putting together a corporation and preserving its corporate status, including organizational and regular board meetings, annual shareholders' meetings, authorizing and issuing stock and maintaining minutes and other corporate records (see "Corporation").

CORPORATE INVESTMENT. A term used to describe situations in which a corporation or corporations make direct investments of funds in a film project, i.e., underwrite the cost of producing a film, typically because there is some sort of tie-in between the film and a product the corporation markets (see "Product Placement" and "Promotional Tie-Ins").

CORPORATE OPPORTUNITY. A situation in which a person who has a close relationship with a corporation takes advantage of the special knowledge he or she thereby acquires for personal gain. The term refers to a legal doctrine that directors or others invested with a fiduciary duty toward a corporation may not appropriate for their own benefit and advantage a business opportunity properly belonging to the corporation (see "Fiduciary" and "Insider Trading").

CORPORATE STOCK. An equity or ownership interest in a corporation usually created by a contribution to the capital of the corporation. Its unit of measurement is the share and the owner of one or more shares of stock in a corporation is entitled to participate in the corporation's management and profits and distribution of assets upon dissolution of the company (see "Security" or "Securities," "Share" and "Shareholders").

CORPORATION. An association of shareholders (or even a single shareholder) created under statute and regarded as an artificial person by courts, having a legal entity entirely separate and distinct from the individuals who compose it, with the attribute of continuous existence or succession, and having the capacity to take, hold and convey property, sue and be sued, and exercise such other powers as may be conferred on it by law, just like a natural person (see "C-Corporation," "Corporate Financing," "Perpetual Existence," "Natural Person" and "S-Corp").

CORPORATION FOR PUBLIC BROADCASTING (CPB). A source organization for limited film-production funds. The CPB may ask for a minimum number of air plays over a specified period of time on the Public Broadcasting System for a film it helps to finance (see "Free Television").

COST ACCOUNTING. The branch of accounting concerned with providing the information that enables management of a firm to evaluate production costs (see "Budget").

COST AMORTIZATION (same as "Amortization;" see "Accounting Principles and Practices").

COST BASIS. The original price of an asset, used in determining capital gains. It usually is the purchase price (see "Capital Gain").

COST CAPITALIZATION (same as "Capitalization;" see "Accounting Principles and Practices").

COST OF CAPITAL. The rate of return a business could earn if it chose another investment with equivalent risk, i.e., the opportunity cost of the funds employed as the result of an investment decision. Factors to be included in estimating or calculating the cost of capital and comparing such costs between proposed investments should include, when applicable in a given instance, all studio charges that do not directly relate to production, bank interest and commitment fees and in securities offerings: sales commissions to broker/dealers, legal and accounting fees, disclosure document costs and filing fees (see "Opportunity Cost").

COST OF MONEY (see "Cost of Capital").

COST OF OPENING. The film distribution expenses including the costs of prints and ads necessary to exhibit a film for the first week of its initial run. The costs of opening a motion picture domestically have risen from $8 million for a wide release to $11 or $12 million and higher, depending on the picture (see "Rising Production Costs").

COST RECOVERY. A procedure of allocating costs against revenue on a dollar-for-dollar basis to the point where costs are recovered. Additional proceeds would then be treated as revenue (see "Accelerated Cost Recovery" and "Depreciation").

COST REPORTS. Film production accountings prepared by the production manager or production accountant which set out the costs per budget category to the date of the report, the expenditures per category made during the most recent week, and estimates per category for finishing the film with totals. In addition to being important to the producer in controlling costs, such reports are generally required by a lender and completion guarantor when a production loan is involved (see "Cash Flow Schedule").

COST TO COMPLETE. At any given time after the start of principal photography, the amount of funds per film budget category needed to finish the motion picture (see "Projections").

COSTS TO DATE. The amount of funds that have been spent on each film budget category to the date of the cost report (see "Cost Reports" and "Cost to Complete").

COSTUME DESIGNER. The film production person responsible for the complete costume breakdown; the purchase or design and production of all costumes, color sketches or outline sketches with color samples attached, including drawings or necessary descriptions of detail and its application; all selection from existing costumes whether purchased, promoted, rented or chosen from a performer's personal wardrobe; the supervision of all necessary fittings and alteration of the costumes; the selection of all necessary fabrics and trims; the design or selection of all costume accessories; and the shopping, if necessary, for period costumes and costume accessories; all in accordance with the production design established by the director and the production designer (see "Art Director").

COSTUMER AND WARDROBE SUPERVISOR. A film production employee engaged in packing, unpacking, re-packing, sorting, hanging, cataloguing, dressing, pressing, cleaning, spot cleaning, dyeing, fitting, remodeling, repairing, sewing, altering, distributing and maintaining all the items of wardrobe and wardrobe accessories and assisting in the dressing of and making of changes for performers. The duties include any work related to the above, as well as any work related to the use, control and disposition of the wardrobe for its efficient and artistic utilization (see "Costume Designer").

COST/VALUE TREND. The tendency for the ratio between expenses and potential revenue to determine a course of action. For example, some industry analysts suggest that the cost/value trends among various markets and media in the motion picture industry argue against the fractionalization of and pre-selling of rights because, as film production and distribution costs increase, the percentage of revenue generated through a film's domestic theatrical release is reduced in relation to other media or territories and the value of cable and video rights increases, the more likely the domestic theatrical distributor will insist on including the cable and video rights as part of the domestic theatrical distribution deal (see "Fractionalizing," "Pre-Sales" and "Split Rights Basis").

COUNTER CYCLICAL. A reference to the tendency of an industry to experience economic cycles that run counter to the economic cycles of other industries (see "Cyclical Industry," "Recession-Proof" and Recession-Resistant").

COUNTER RECESSIONARY. An economic phenomenon which results in a more favorable performance for a certain business or industry during difficult economic times (see "Counter Cyclical" and "Recession Resistant").

COUNTING RULES. Securities concept commonly appearing as one of the conditions or limitations of federal or state transactional exemptions from the securities registration requirement which specifies how to count certain investors for investor numerical limitations purposes, e.g., Regulation D Rules 505 and 506 only permit thirty-five unaccredited investors but unlimited accredited investors. Pursuant to the Regulation D counting rules, however, foreign purchasers are not counted, nor are relatives, spouses or relatives of the spouse of a purchaser who has the same principal residence as the purchaser (also called "Purchaser Counting Rules;" see "Accredited Investor," "Foreign Purchasers," "Investor Numerical Limitations" and "Regulation D").

COVENANT. An agreement or promise to do or not to do a particular thing (see "Warranty" or "Warranties").

COVENANT NOT TO COMPETE. A contractual provision through which a party or the parties to a contract promise to refrain from conducting business or professional activities of a nature similar to those of the other party or parties for a reasonable period of time and in a limited geographical area (also called "Non-Compete Clause;" see "Non-Circumvention Clause" and "Non-Disclosure Agreement").

COVENANT OF GOOD FAITH AND FAIR DEALING. A contractual agreement or promise to conduct one's business dealings with another in good faith and fairly, i.e., to conduct such business dealings honestly (in fact), to observe reasonable commercial standards of fair dealing in the trade and not to deny the existence of the contract.

Some states provide that the covenant of good faith and fair dealing is implied in every contract executed in that state (see "Good Faith" and "Warranty" or "Warranties").

COVERAGE. Additional shots to augment the master shot, such as single, cutaway shots, closeups or tight two-shots. It is from the master shot and coverage (or cover shots) that the editor builds scenes. In the most general sense, coverage or cover shots are alternate depictions of portions of a film, i.e., scenes shot from different camera angles, thus providing differing points of view of the same action (see "Cover Shot").

COVERAGE (DEVELOPMENT). The process of review and comment used by most studio systems in the development of screenplays whereby a submitted screenplay is assigned to a reader who reads the screenplay and provides development notes (i.e., coverage) for evaluation by the studio's director of acquisitions and other development executives to aid them in determining whether the project should be "greenlighted" (i.e., approved) for the next stage in development or for production financing (see "Development," "Development Notes," "Reader" and "Story Analyst").

COVER SHOT. An extra take of a scene which is printed and available for use if the initially preferred take is for any reason ultimately not selected to appear in the completed film (see "Coverage" and "Take;" same as "Insurance Take").

COUNSEL. An attorney. In a film limited partnership context, an attorney may serve as the counsel for the general partner and the partnership and that counsel may be a securities attorney, tax attorney and/or an entertainment attorney ("Code of Professional Responsibility").

COUNTERPARTS CLAUSE. A contractual clause usually found in the miscellaneous clauses section of a contract which provides that two or more copies of the contract may be signed separately by individual signatories and that all of these signed contracts will be considered as one. This clause makes it more convenient for persons required to sign contracts to do so without all being physically present at the same time or actually signing the same document (see "Contract").

COUPLED FILMS. Films that are marketed together as a package (see "Allocation Issues").

COUPLED WITH AN INTEREST. A contractual phrase which provides that the authority granted in a contract is given to the agent for a consideration and that in circumstances where not recognizing such authority would result in an injustice, the courts will imply authority so as not to mislead another (see "Power of Attorney").

CRAWL. A list of credits that moves up the screen, often superimposed over a live-action background (see "Creeper Titles").

CREATIVE ACCOUNTING. A derogatory term commonly used to refer to the accounting practices of studio/distributors which may include everything from actual dishonest practices in reporting and dividing up the revenues generated by a given film at the exhibitor and distributor levels to sharp negotiating tactics used in conjunction with drafting the distribution deal. Such deals often result in agreements weighted heavily in favor of the distributor as opposed to the producer and other net profit participants. Although mistakes and misapplications of contractual terms do occur in the industry, often what is sometimes called "creative accounting" is no more than the film distributor following the terms of the negotiated distribution deal, which was clearly disadvantageous to the producer in the first place. Thus, in some instances, what producers call "creative accounting" is merely the result of their own lack of preparation for the distribution negotiation process. Independent producers must therefore work harder to improve their (or their representatives') negotiating skill and leverage and insist on broad auditing rights that are implemented (see "Account Number," "Adhesion Contract," "Allocation," "Anticipated Expenses," "Apportioned Expense," "Bad Debt," "Combination Ad," "Commingling of Funds," "Cross Collateralization," "Deal Memo," "Direct Distribution Expenses,"" Discretion," "Facilities Allocation," "Front End Load," "GAAP," "Improperly Claimed Expenses," "Kickback," "Overhead," "Rolling Breakeven," "Settlement Transactions," "Standard Contract," "Studio Accounting Practices," "Subjective Terms," "Sue Us," "Underreported Rentals" and "Usury").

CREATIVE CONTROL. The power and authority to make decisions with respect to a film being produced and with regard to significant qualitative aspects of the film, i.e., the appearance and content of the final feature film product. Creative control is often a major point of negotiation between a producer and director and sometimes between a producer and distributor. The issue comes up in the context of a distribution agreement with respect to editing rights, i.e., whether the distributor has the right to make editing changes, has final editing rights, or produces the final cut of a movie. Such rights, to some extent, depend on the parties' relative bargaining strength and the stature as well as the rights of the producer and/or director as between them. The producer may or may not be able or willing to give any editing rights to the distributor, but some editing changes may be required as per government regulation or in order to get a certain motion picture rating. If granted, such rights should be subject to a producer's right of approval, rather than just unlimited editing rights (also called "Artistic Control;" see "Creative Differences," "Creative Elements," "Editing Rights" and "Waiver of Droit Moral").

CREATIVE DECISIONS. Determinations relating to the artistic aspects of a feature film. Distribution agreements generally will make some provision for who has the authority to make creative decisions with respect to various versions of the film as between the distributor, producer and director. Such agreements may also provide a mechanism for the parties to communicate their objections to the exercise of certain cutting rights of another party (see "Editing Rights" and "Final Cut").

CREATIVE DEMANDS. The pressure to successfully compete with other films in the marketplace with respect to any and all elements of a film (see "Creative Control").

CREATIVE DEPARTMENT. A major administrative unit of the typical motion picture studio/distributor which is primarily responsible for evaluating proposed motion picture projects, reviewing and evaluating script submissions, and recommending which films the studio will develop and/or produce (see "Business Affairs Department," "Legal Department," "Production Department" and "Studio").

CREATIVE DIFFERENCES. Disagreements among producer, director, cinematographer, principal actors or other above-the-line personnel relating to elements of a film. Sometimes, such persons so strongly disagree with respect to a given motion picture element that they cannot continue to work together. Thus, "creative differences" is often cited as the reason for quitting or being fired (the same as "Artistic Differences").

CREATIVE ELEMENTS. Those aspects of a film or filmmaking that require the power or ability to produce from imaginative skill (see "Creative Talent").

CREATIVE FINANCING. Methods of funding films that involve new, different or unusual investment vehicles, techniques or combinations thereof, e.g., mixing equity from third parties with bank loans or arranging multiple pre-sales in foreign markets (see "Hybrid Security" and "Multiple Pre-Sales").

CREATIVE PRODUCER. A term used by some in the industry to distinguish between a producer who is significantly involved in artistic aspects of producing a motion picture as opposed to an executive producer who may be primarily responsible for obtaining production financing and in related business matters, and on the other hand, a line producer who is more directly involved with the logistics of actual production (see "Executive Producer," "Line Producer" and "Producer").

CREATIVE TALENT. Screenwriter, producer, director, actors, and others who participate in the creative process (see "Creative Producer").

CREDIT. Loans, bonds, charge-account obligations and open-account balances with commercial firms. Also, available but unused bank letters of credit and other standby commitments as well as a variety of consumer credit facilities (see "Distributor Credit").

CREDIT BALANCE. An account balance in the customer's favor (see "Credit").

CREDIT CONTRACTIONARY ENVIRONMENT. An economic climate in which it is difficult for businesses to obtain loans (see "Credit" and "Lender Financing").

CREDIT ISSUES. Questions relating to screen credits, e.g., where the credit will appear in relation to the film's title, whether the credit will appear on a separate card and what size type will be used (see "Credits").

CREDIT LINES. Established lending relationships in which a borrowing entity may have been pre-approved up to a specified limit or pre-qualified to obtain loans from a lender (see "Lender Financing").

CREDITOR. One to whom money is owed by the debtor; one to whom an obligation exists. A producer who borrows money from a bank for the production of a film is a debtor to that creditor bank (see "Credit").

CREDIT REQUIREMENTS. The feature film billing notices that are either mandated by an individual employment agreement or the applicable rules of a given union or guild (see "Minimum Credit Requirements").

CREDITS. The listed names and positions of the cast, crew, staff and others involved in a given film or TV production that are seen at the beginning and/or end (same as "Billing;" see "Prominence").

CREDIT STATEMENT. A written statement to be provided by the producer to the distributor setting out all main-and-end title billing, paid-advertising billing and all requirements regarding paid advertising (same as "Billing Statement").

CREDIT TITLES (see "Credits").

CREEPER TITLES. An out-of-date reference to the listing of actors, producers, directors and others involved in a film that was accomplished through the slow rotation of the listing in front of the camera with the use of a drum that was not visible (see "Crawl" and "Title").

CREW. A film's crew is composed of those who work "behind the camera" in the technical and production positions, such as soundpersons, camera people, grips and so forth. The term differentiates these people from the cast (see "Cast," "Operational Staff," "Production Staff" and "Staff").

CREW AGREEMENT. The employment contract for persons who perform the technical and production tasks, i.e., behind the camera, in the making of a feature film (see "Employment Agreement").

CREW/CAST AGREEMENT. A rather simplified form of combined employment contract used by ultra-low budget filmmakers for the employment of all production personnel, technicians and actors. Such an agreement is designed to simplify and expedite the paper work involved in contracting with such persons and may involve the use of a form agreement which numerous blanks to be filled in (see "Employment Agreement").

CRIME. Any act which the government has determined is injurious to the public and therefore prosecutable in a criminal proceeding (see "Rules" and "White Collar Crime").

CRITIC. Persons usually employed by newspapers, television stations or other media who screen newly released movies and provide their subjective views and comments on the movie for the public's information (see "Industry Critic," "Positive Review" and "Review").

CRITIC'S REVIEW. The comments and reactions of a movie critic as such appear in a newspaper column, in a television segment or other media (see "Critic").

CROSS-COLLATERALIZATION. An accounting practice used by and which benefits distributors whereby distributors offset their profits in one market against losses in another or on one film against another. In a worldwide distribution deal, the studios typically seek to cross-collateralize profits and losses among territories. With cross-collateralization, the producer can only share in the profits of one territory to the extent that the profits of that territory exceed the combined losses of all other territories worldwide. In situations where multiple films of a single producer or production company are being distributed by a single distributor, the distributor may seek authorization in the distribution agreement to cross-collateralize the financial performance of each of such films with the others. That practice should be negotiated by and between the producer and distributor. In some instances, no provision is made in the distribution agreement regarding cross-collateralization (at any level) and, thus, the distributor may choose to use its discretion with regard to this issue. In still other instances, the producer must carefully monitor the activities of the distributor to be certain that it is not effectively cross-collateralizing the financial performance of the producer's film with the performance of the films of other producers. Licensees of film packages may also cross-collateralize the results of the exhibition of such films in foreign territories (see "Allocation," "Creative Accounting," "Cross-Collateralization of Markets," "Cross-Collateralization of Slates," "De Facto Cross-Collateralization," "Discretionary Cross-Collateralization," "Overage," "Unrecouped Expenses" and "Unauthorized Cross-Collateralization").

CROSS-COLLATERALIZATION OF MARKETS. The offset of the distribution results from one market area against the results of another market area (see "Cross-Collateralization").

CROSS-COLLATERALIZATION OF MOVIE SLATES. The offsetting by the distributor of the economic results of all of the motion pictures produced by a single production company that has contracted for such pictures to be distributed by a distribution entity (see "Cross-Collateralization" and "Cross-Collateralization of Markets").

CROSS-COLLATERALIZATION PROVISIONS. The language in a film distribution agreement which authorizes the distributor to offset the profits of one movie against the profits of another movie or authorizes the distributor to offset the profits of a movie in one market against the profits of the same movie in another market. Since producers often have multiple picture arrangements with studios, their profits from one picture may be cross-collateralized against the losses of the same producer's other pictures being distributed by the same distributor, but a net profit participant other than the producer should not be subject to the distributor's cross-collateralization with the producer, i.e., the net profit participant should thus be excluded from the producer's net profit definition (see "Net Profit Participant").

CROSSOVER FILM. A feature film which was originally targeted for a narrow specialty market but which achieves acceptance in a wider market (see "Breakout" and "Crossover Potential").

CROSSOVER POTENTIAL. The prospects for a film to attract a much larger movie-going audience than originally anticipated (see "Crossover Film").

CROSS PLUGS. Promotional references to a film in several different media such as novelization of the screenplay, licensing the film's title for use by others, pre-release merchandising, etc. (see "Advertising").

CROSS PURCHASE AGREEMENT (same as "Buy/Sell Agreement").

CULTURAL DIFFERENCES. Characteristics which distinguish one society from another. Such differences may create obstacles for many forms of film finance which require international cooperation (see "Foreign Currency Deal," "Foreign Equity Investment" and "Foreign Tax Deal").

CULTURALLY BIASED. A partiality toward a specific society or segment of society. Films that are culturally biased toward U.S. society or one segment or another of U.S. society may not be received as well overseas. On the other hand, a film that provides a favorable portrayal of the culture of another country, even as a sub-theme, may facilitate the raising of funds in that country (see "Favorable Portrayal").

CULTURE PROMOTION. The promotion of a specific culture, religion or way of life through the movies; what many in the film industry recognize as an important sub-theme of movies, second only to entertainment. Foreign governments more often recognize the value of motion pictures as promoters of culture (see "Favorable Portrayal," "Hidden Agenda," "Movies With A Message," "Pattern of Bias" and "Unfavorable Portrayal").

CUMULATIVE RIGHTS. A contractual phrase which means that rights granted or created pursuant to a contract are additional to each other and not exclusive of one or the other (see "Contract").

CUMULATIVE VOTING. The corporate procedure which permits shareholders, who generally are entitled to one vote for each share held, to accumulate their votes for any one directorial candidate in corporate elections to the board of directors. The method improves minority shareholders' chances of naming representatives to a corporation's board of directors (see "Minority Interest" and "Shareholder").

CURE. To correct a legal error or defect; to free from something objectionable or harmful; to rectify or remedy. In contracts, to correct a breach. Contracts will often provide an opportunity for a defaulting party to cure the problem within a certain number of days after notice of the default (see "Breach of Contract").

CURRENCY. Something that is in circulation in a given country as a medium of exchange, including coins, paper money, government notes and bank notes (see "Currency Conversion" and "Devaluation").

CURRENCY CONVERSION. The exchanging of the monies of one country for an equivalent amount of another country's funds (see "Currency" and "Devaluation").

CURRENCY DEALS (see "Foreign Currency Deal").

CURRENCY EXCHANGE (same as "Currency Conversion").

CURRENCY EXCHANGE RATE (see "Exchange Rate" and "Exchange Rate Movements").

CURRENT ASSETS. Cash, accounts receivable, inventory and other holdings that are likely to be converted into cash, sold, exchanged or expensed in the normal course of business, usually within a year (see "Financial Statement").

CURRENT ECONOMIC REALITIES. A realistic appraisal of the present business environment. In anti-trust law, some of the major studio/ distributors subject to the Paramount Consent Decree seem to be successfully arguing that current economic realities in the entertainment industry present significantly changed circumstances and that such circumstances should be considered by the U.S. District Court judge supervising the consent decrees to allow studio ownership of theatres (see "Paramount Consent Decree of 1948" and "TriStar Case").

CURRENT LIABILITIES. Debts incurred by the reporting entity as part of normal operations and expected to be repaid during the following twelve months, e.g., accounts payable, short-term loans and that portion of long-term loans due in one year (see "Financial Statement").

CUSTODIAN. One entrusted with guarding and keeping property or records (see "Bankruptcy" and "Trustee").

CUSTOMARILY KEPT BY THE DISTRIBUTOR. A reference to the type and manner in which a film distributor maintains its books and records. Some distribution agreements will establish such a loose standard for the distributor to comply with in meeting its obligations to keep accurate books and records relating to the distribution of a film. If such language is used, and the distributor has not heretofore kept any records, such language may not impose any additional obligation on the distributor. Such language should be eliminated from distribution agreements in favor of a more responsible standard (see "Customary").

CUSTOMARY. Commonly practiced, used or observed, i.e., the provisions which are usually found in motion picture production documentation. With respect to a film distribution agreement (and other motion picture documentation), producers must recognize that the use of such vague and subjective terms are just that: "vague and subjective." Their use imposes very little on the studio/distributor and such standards of conduct can only be enforced after the fact, if at all. Such vague standards as "customary practices," "long-standing and well-established practices in the industry" or "customary terms and conditions for agreements of this nature in the motion picture industry" may often appear in so-called short-form feature film production documentation or deal memos along with a statement of the intention of the parties to negotiate, draft and sign a more complete written agreement to include such terms at a later date. However, even though there may be a certain level of unanimity regarding the type of provisions that ought to be included in the same or similar feature-film-related agreements, the specific wording, the application of such terms or their interpretation by the courts in any given circumstance is by no means standardized. In addition, some view the use of such vague standards by the major studios as a means of continuing their dominance and control over the rest of the industry. Whenever possible, such terms should be negotiated out of the agreement and replaced with a more definite standard of conduct (see "Customary Terms," "Deal Memo" and "Reasonable and Customary").

CUSTOMARY TERMS. The provisions which are usually found in motion picture production, financing and distribution documentation (see "Customary," "Deal Memo," "Letter Agreement," "Short Form Agreement" and "Standard Contract").

CUSTOM DUTIES. Fees or tolls imposed by the sovereign law of a country on imports or exports (see "Distribution Expenses").

CUSTOMS INSPECTION. The examination of goods being imported or exported into or out of a country by the agency authorized to collect duties, tolls or imposts imposed by the sovereign law of the country. Unfortunately, the customs officials of some countries are corrupt and permit the unauthorized copying of U.S. made motion pictures during the customs inspection. One producer reported that he saw videocassettes of his previously unreleased motion picture already on sale at a local bazaar while traveling from the customs offices to his hotel on a visit to a foreign country for the purpose of exhibiting his film in its world premiere at a local film festival (see "Piracy").

CUT (see "Edit").

CUTOUTS (see "Trims," "Outtakes" and "Second Take").

CUTTER (see "Editor").

CUT-THROUGH ENDORSEMENT. A provision often found in completion guarantees which allows the lender or financier to look beyond the completion bond company to the financially responsible insurance company or group which ultimately backs the completion guarantor for payment on a claim (see "Completion Guarantor").

CUTTING EDGE DEALS. Agreements drafted and negotiated by the most sophisticated attorneys and business executives in an industry incorporating the most advanced contractual provisions and taking advantage of the most current developments in the industry (see "Contract").

CUTTING RIGHTS (same as "Editing Rights;" see "Final Cut").

CUTTING ROOM. The physical room or facility where a film is edited (see "Edit").

CYCLICAL INDUSTRY. A distinct group of productive enterprises, the film industry in this case, which experiences economic cycles. The movie business is generally considered to be a cyclical industry (see "Economic Cycles" and "Out-of-Favor Indies").

CYCLICAL THEORY. A statistical theory adhered to by some in the film industry which suggests that, at some point in the future, film genre that are not currently popular will again be favored by the movie-going public (see "Genre").

— D —

DAILIES. Printed film scenes delivered daily from the laboratory of film materials shot on the preceding day. The dailies are generally reviewed and approved by the director and others before a particular set is struck (also called "Rushes").

DAILY CONTRACT FOR THEATRICAL MOTION PICTURES. A standard Screen Actors Guild contract used for the employment of performers on a daily basis. Additional clauses which are not part of the standard form may be inserted in these contracts (see "Minimum Free Lance Contract for Theatrical Motion Pictures").

DAILY VARIETY. An entertainment industry trade publication which is published daily and reports on developments in the motion picture, television, stage, home video and cable industries (see "Trades" and "Variety")

DAMAGE. A legal wrong that causes injury to another, either in his or her person, rights, reputation or property (same as "Injury;" contrast with "Damages").

DAMAGES. Monetary compensation which the law awards to one who has been injured by the action of another (contrast with "Damage;" see "Remedy" or "Remedies").

DAY AND DATE. A concept used in making a film available for exhibition which requires that one theatre's run of a film be controlled by (i.e., identical to) another theatre's run of that film. This relationship usually exists in the negative sense, i.e., forbidding the controlled theatre's exhibition of a film until the controlling theatre is able to exhibit that same film. However, "day and date" may be used in a positive sense, i.e., compelling the controlled theatre to exhibit a film simultaneously with the controlling theatre's run of that same film (see "Controlled Theatre").

DAY AND DATE RELEASE. The simultaneous (same day, same date) release of a motion picture in two or more theatres in a given market. The phrase may also be used to refer to the simultaneous opening of a movie in two or more markets (see "Day and Date").

DAY PLAYER. An actor or actress hired to work on a daily basis and who is involved in only a few scenes or has only several lines; i.e., a player employed by the day, other than an extra, stunt person, professional singer, or airline pilot (see "Actor," "Bit Player" and "Extra").

DAY PLAYER CONTRACT (see "Daily Contract for Theatrical Motion Pictures").

DBA. Acronym for "doing business as;" a phrase used to indicate that an unincorporated individual (or individuals) are conducting a business under a fictitious name (see "Fictitious Name" and "Sole Proprietorship").

"D" COUNTIES. The A.C. Nielsen Company designation for sparsely populated, mostly rural counties in the U.S., i.e., counties which do not fit within the Nielsen definitions of "A," "B" or "C" counties (see "A-Counties," "ADI Market," "B-Counties," "C-Counties" and "Nielsen Media Research").

DEAL. Slang for contract or agreement (see "Contract," "Deal Memo" and "Deal Points").

DEAL BREAKER. An issue in a contract negotiation which, if not agreed to, will prevent an agreement from being reached on the overall contract. The term is also sometimes applied to an individual, i.e., a "deal breaker" as opposed to a "deal maker" (see "Deal Points").

DEALER. A person or entity engaged in the business of buying and selling securities for his or her own account, i.e., engaged in the purchase of securities and their resale to customers. The activities of dealers are regulated by the Securities and Exchange Act of 1934 (see "Broker," "Broker/Dealer," "Investment Adviser," "NASD" and "Underwriter").

DEAL MEMO. A shortened version of a contract, i.e, a memorandum of the minimum negotiated terms between contracting parties. For example, a distribution agreement between a production company and a film distributor may initially utilize a letter agreement format, which theoretically covers the main points (deal points) agreed to by the parties, such as salary, time schedule, screen credit and percentage participation in the film's profits, if any. Deal memos may also be used in contracting with performers and others critical to the production of a movie. Deal memos are often used by the major studio business and affairs departments to get the film production process underway on a given film, with the intent that the studio's legal department will ultimately negotiate and draft a full agreement. For smaller independent producers and distributors, the deal memo may not be necessary or even desirable, since these smaller entities do not have the bureaucracy of a major studio, which often slows the negotiating and drafting process, and, in fact, a deal memo may be dangerous since the more detailed provisions of the full contract may be much more burdensome or onerous for the producer and may even conflict with the original provisions of the deal memo (see "Long Form Distribution Agreement").

DEAL MEMORANDUM. The more complete title for deal memo (see "Deal Memo").

DEAL POINTS. An informal and general reference to the most important terms of a contract, e.g., in a film distribution agreement: date, parties, term, territory, consideration, fees and expenses, identity of film, definitions of terms, provisions for production financing, ownership of picture and copyright, length, quality standard, screenplay identification, language, title clearance, MPAA rating and delivery terms (see "Deal Memo," "Distribution Agreement" and "Distribution Checklist").

DEAL TERMS. A more formal and specific reference to the provisions of an agreement. Also, the heading for a major section of some feature film distribution agreements, a section which may include provisions relating to contingencies, picture specifications, basic elements, production/delivery requirements, delivery specifications, controls/approvals/obligations, production companies right of consultation, financing, consideration, rights, notices and payments and special provisions (see "Deal Points" and "Distribution Agreement").

DEBENTURE. A general debt obligation backed only by the integrity of the borrower and documented by an agreement called an indenture. An unsecured bond is a debenture (see "Bond," "Debt" and "Indenture").

DEBT. Money, goods or services that one party is obligated to pay to another in accordance with an expressed or implied agreement. Debt may or may not be secured. Also the general name for bonds, notes, mortgages and other forms of paper evidencing amounts owed and payable on specified dates or on demand. Both the lender and the producer should be careful to ensure that what is intended to be a loan to be used for production funds for a feature film can be fairly characterized as debt and not characterized as an equity investment. If the transaction is characterized as some form of equity participation, the "lender" actually becomes an investor whose investment is at risk and thus there may be no obligation for the producer to repay the loan. Although that may sound favorable to the film's producer, it may also result in the producer having sold an unregistered security to a passive investor (thus triggering securities compliance problems), and may result in the creation of an entity (e.g., joint venture or association) which may generate unfavorable tax consequences. The factors which determine whether a transaction creates debt or equity include: (1) whether or not the loan is a non-recourse loan or a recourse loan, i.e., a non-recourse loan secured only by the film is more likely than a recourse loan to be considered an equity investment; (2) whether a fixed repayment date has been established; (3) whether the loan is secured; (4) whether the rate of interest on the "loan" is tied to the amount of profits earned by the film, i.e., if the interest rate increases with the level of profits, that increases the chances that the transaction would be characterized as an equity investment; (5) whether the "lender" exercises substantial control over the production, i.e., the more control exercised by the lender, the less likely the transaction would be characterized as a loan (on the other hand, the more control exercised by the "lender," the less likely the transaction would be characterized as a security); (6) whether the "lender" subordinates, i.e., takes a second position to third parties with respect to payments made from the film's revenues; and (7) whether another lender would have loaned funds on the same or similar basis (see "Bank," "Collateral," "Equity," "Interest" and "Lender Financing").

DEBT CAPITALIZATION (see "Foreign Debt Capitalization Programs").

DEBT FINANCING. The funding of a project or the activities of a company through the issuance of one or more debt instruments (see "Debt Instrument").

DEBT INSTRUMENT. Written promise to repay a debt; document that serves as evidence of a debt such as promissory notes, bills, corporate bonds, notes, banker's acceptances, certificates of deposit, commercial paper, debentures or indentures (see "Debt Financing").

DEBT LOADS. The burden of a company's financial obligations. If a company's debt is so great that the cash required to meet its obligations to make payments of principal and interest during any given period can only be met by siphoning off cash flow normally allocated for other important obligations, serious financial consequences may follow (see "Bankruptcy," "Debt-to-Equity Ratio," "Debt Service" and "Financial Management").

DEBTOR. One who has the obligation of paying a debt; person or business that owes money (see "Creditor" and "Debt").

DEBT RETIREMENT. Repayment of a debt (see "Debt").

DEBT SECURITY. Security representing money borrowed that must be repaid and having a fixed amount, a specific maturity or maturities and usually a specific rate of interest or an original purchase discount, e.g., a bill, bond, commercial paper or note (contrast with "Securities;" see "Collateral").

DEBT SERVICE. Cash required in a given period of time, usually one year, for payments of interest and current maturities of principal on outstanding debt (see "Debt" and "Interest").

DEBT-TO-EQUITY RATIO. In corporate finance, the total liabilities of the corporation divided by the total of shareholders' equity. The ratio may give some indication of the extent to which an owner's equity can cushion creditors' claims in the event of the corporation's liquidation (see "Debt" and "Equity").

DEBT-TO-NET-WORTH RATIO. For individuals, the total liabilities of the individual divided by such individual's net worth. These ratios are sometimes used by lenders and other prospective creditors in determining whether to make loans or extend credit to such individuals (see "Net Worth").

DECEASED PERSONS. Human beings who are no longer living. Aside from living persons, even dead persons (through their personal representatives or heirs) may have a protectable "right of publicity," especially where there is a considerable amount of fictionalization in a film being produced about such a deceased person. Releases from the proper living persons may have to be obtained in such circumstances (see "Clearance," "Defamation" or "Defamation of Character," "Libel," "Privacy, Right of" and "Releases").

DECISION-MAKING CONTINUUM. A reference to the producer and distributor decisions relating to film distribution alternatives, i.e., at one end of the spectrum, the producer merely submits a property to a studio/distributor for development and production/distribution financing, the studio/distributor obtains worldwide rights to distribute the film, bears all of the financial risk (although it significantly involved in shaping the quality of the product) and the distributor fees will be their highest at this point (approximately 30% to 40% depending on the market). On the opposite end of the spectrum, the producer approaches the distributor with an already financed completed film in addition to prints and ads money offering the distributor the opportunity to distribute the film in the domestic market only on a rent-a-system basis. There is little or no financial risk for the distributor in that situation and its distribution fees are thus the lowest under those circumstances (approximately 15%). In between are the production-financing/distribution arrangements between a distributor and an independent producer, negative pickup arrangements, the pure acquisitions and other variations of production financing, distribution funding, financial risk, creative control and distribution fees (see "Acquisition Distribution Agreement," "Distribution Alternatives," "In-House Production," "Negative Pickup," "Production-Financing/Distribution Agreement," and "Rent-A-Distributor").

DEDUCTIONS. Amounts allowed to taxpayers under the Internal Revenue Code as offsets against gross income or adjusted gross income (see "Income," "Loss" and "Proportionate Share of Deductions").

DEEM. A verb meaning to think of as true. Film distribution agreements often provide that certain things may be deemed to be so by the distributor and such provisions are examples of distributor discretion that should be examined for reasonableness. From the producer's point of view, a more objective method for determining the truth or circumstances involved in any matter dealt with in a film distribution transaction is likely to be more preferable and therefore should be negotiated where possible (see "Contract of Adhesion" and "Discretion").

DE FACTO CROSS-COLLATERALIZATION. The unauthorized arbitrary allocation of gross receipts to a motion picture marketed as part of a package either to networks, cable, syndication markets or foreign territories. Such allocations effectively cross-collateralize the profits of one movie with the profits of other movies in the package (see "Cross-Collateralization," "Cross-Collateralization of Markets," "Cross-Collateralization of Slates," "Discretionary Cross-Collateralization" and "Unauthorized Cross-Collateralization").

DE FACTO STRIKE. An unofficial and unauthorized work stoppage designed to force an employer to comply with demands (see "Guild," "Production Slowdown," "Strike" and "Union").

DEFAMATION OR DEFAMATION OF CHARACTER. The publication of anything injurious to the good name or reputation of another, or which tends to bring such person into disrepute. A defamation designed to be read is a libel; an oral defamation is a slander. There is no legal cause of action called defamation; libel and slander may be founded on defamation, but the right of action itself is libel or slander. A motion picture may defame a person (see "Clearance," "Libel," "Slander" and "Tort").

DEFAULT. A failure to discharge a duty, e.g., failure of a debtor to make timely payments of interest and principal as they come due; some omission to do that which ought to have been done by one of the parties to a contract (see "Breach of Contract" and "Interest").

DEFAULT DISASTER. A phrase used to describe the potential situation when a motion picture licensee who pre-bought rights decides to forfeit its deposit (if any), refuses to pay a promised advance, and forego exhibition of the film in its territory after seeing the completed picture and determining that it is much worse than expected. This is particularly problematic if the original pre-sales contract was used by the producer as collateral to obtain a production loan. In that event, the bank may demand that the producer repay the loan and the producer may have to seek payment from the distributor. If the producer fails to repay the loan, the bank might foreclose on the negative if it took a lien as further collateral, or attach the film and its proceeds even if it did not have an original lien (see "Bank," "Lender Financing," "Negative Pickup," "Pre-Sales" and "Split-Rights Basis").

DEFENDANT. The person defending or denying a complaint; the party against whom relief or recovery is sought in a legal action or law suit. In a civil proceeding, the defendant is one who is sued and is called upon by the complaint to make satisfaction for a wrong alleged by the plaintiff (see "Action," "Litigation," "Plaintiff," "Sue Us" and "Suit").

DEFERMENTS OR DEFERRALS. All or a portion of salaries or compensation for cast, crew or others providing property or services for the production of a movie paid (by agreement) on a delayed basis after the property and/or services have been provided and usually after the release of the film. If such deferments are to be paid out of monies generated by the exhibition of the film, they are also by definition contingent upon the film earning enough money to pay such deferments. In a studio-financed production deal, it is preferable from the producer's point of view (if possible) to have the deferments treated as distribution expenses as opposed to production overhead, since distribution expenses are not recouped until after the film is in distribution, whereas a studio's production overhead will be considered an interest-bearing production expense from the time it is incurred. Also, the distribution deal should clearly set out who pays such deferments as between the distributor and producer (see "Contingent Deferments," "Fixed Deferment," "Percentage Participation," "Producer's Share," "Production Cost Deferments" and "Points").

DEFERMENT SCHEDULE. A list, usually included as an exhibit to a film production-financing/distribution agreement, setting out the names, amounts and classes (if any) of deferred compensation to be paid to persons or entities who provided products or services in the production of a feature film (see "Deferments" or "Deferrals" and "Pari Passu").

DEFERRAL OF TAXES. Postponement of tax payments from the current year to a later year (see "Deferral Structures" and "Income Tax").

DEFERRAL STRUCTURES. A reference to the structuring of a specific transaction, such as an advance payment, so as to delay the date of payment for tax purposes while still providing access to the cash in advance. Such tax deferral techniques include the use of a refundable deposit, standby letters of credit, and payor/payee loans (see "Advances," "Deferral of Taxes" and "Refundable Deposit").

DEFICIENCY LETTER. Written notice from the SEC to a prospective issuer of securities in a public offering that the registration statement and/or preliminary prospectus needs to be revised (see "Issuer," "Prospectus," "Public Offering" and "SEC").

DELAYED REDUCTION OF NEGATIVE COSTS (see "Interest").

DELINQUENCY. Failure to make a payment on an obligation when due (see "Debt" and "Interest").

DELEVERAGING. The reduction of a company's debt in relation to equity in the firm's capital structure. The more long-term debt a company has, the greater its financial leverage (see "Financial Management" and "Leverage").

DELIVERED ANSWER PRINT (see "Answer Print" and "Delivery").

DELIVERY. In legal terminology, a voluntary transfer of title or possession from one party to another. A term defined in a film distribution agreement usually as a schedule which lists the physical items which are to be provided by the producer to the distributor (through the lab) and sets the deadlines for such items to be delivered. Delivery is usually defined as a series of objective events and does not rely on distributor approval. Producer should watch out for the distributor who tries to insert subjective approval language in the delivery mechanism. Also, examine the delivery schedule carefully with all providers of items on the list, e.g., film lab and E&O insurance carrier, to make certain that each item can be provided. Also, see that the delivery schedule is presented in chronological order for the convenience of those obligated to meet its requirements. Draft the delivery schedule so that it can be a useful and working document, not something that is signed and forgotten. Also, distributors sometimes want access to the producer's original delivery materials but the producer may want to insist that those original materials being provided through a lab remain at the producer's laboratory, assuming that the producer actually selected the film lab (see "Breach of Contract," "Laboratory Access Letter" and "Laboratory Letter").

DELIVERY COSTS. Those expenses specifically associated with delivering the required materials to the distributor. For financial planning purposes, the producer must not overlook his or her projection of the costs relating to providing the delivery materials (see "Delivery Materials").

DELIVERY DATE. The date on which all of the required elements specified in the distribution agreement are to be delivered to the distributor or made available to the distributor through the lab. Generally, delivery is defined by the specific distribution agreement which provides the producer with a means to objectively comply with his, her or its obligations under the distribution agreement (see "Delivery Schedule").

DELIVERY DATE ACCELERATION. A rarely used provision in a film distribution deal which may permit the distributor to move the date for delivery of certain items forward in the event that the producer is in breach of specified provisions of the agreement, e.g., in exercising the producer's or distributor's cutting rights, he or she does not comply with the distributor's release schedule or bidding and distribution requirements (see "Delivery Date").

DELIVERY ITEMS. The specific items slated to be delivered by the producer to the distributor pursuant to the film distribution agreement's delivery schedule (see "Delivery Materials," "Delivery Schedule" and "Major Delivery Items").

DELIVERY MATERIALS. The film-related items required to be delivered to the distributor, including the laboratory access letter, attached as an exhibit so the distributor will have access to the film materials, a delivery schedule and list of film credits. The specific items listed for delivery typically include final screenplay and shooting script, publicity material, credit statement, black and white photographs, color photographs, final answer print, original picture negative and composite optical soundtrack negative, interpositive, television cover shots and scenes, internegatives, main and end titles, music, dialogue and sound items, film and soundtrack materials, screen credits, dialogue, action continuity, laboratory letter, MPAA certificate, certificate of insurance, residual information, title and copyright reports, soundtrack album materials, work print and outtakes (see "Delivery Requirements" and "Delivery Schedule").

DELIVERY REQUIREMENTS. A provision in a film distribution agreement which sets out the actions to be taken and the items to be delivered to a film's distributor pursuant to the distribution agreement. The delivery requirements section of a film distribution agreement must be carefully drafted so that the distributor will not be able to refuse delivery of the completed film on subjective grounds. In addition, if the delivery requirements provision is not carefully drafted, a negative pickup agreement may not be acceptable to a lender, investors or other motion picture financiers (see "Delivery Materials," "Delivery Schedule" and "Negative Pickup Agreement").

DELIVERY SCHEDULE. A list (usually an exhibit to a film distribution agreement) that sets out the items to be provided by a film's producer to the distributor (much of which is provided through the lab) and provides the deadlines for such delivery (see "Delivery," "Laboratory Access Letter" and "Objective Delivery Requirements").

DEMAND. The quantity and quality of movie or movies that the general public or a projected audience wants to or will pay to see at any given time, i.e., the collective desires of the general public or projected audience to see a given movie, a specific type of movie or a unique combination of elements in a movie (see "Elements" and "Projected Audience").

DEMAND LOAN. Loan with a set maturity date, after which the lender may call for repayment at any time (see "Debt," "Interest" and "Lender Financing").

DEMAND NOTE. The loan instrument which, by its express terms, is payable immediately on an agreed-upon date of maturation without requiring any further demand. The maker of the note acknowledges his, her or its liability as of the due date; also includes those instruments payable on sight or upon presentation or for which no time for payment is stated (see "Debt" and "Interest").

DEMOGRAPHICS. The statistical characteristics of a specific human population, such as a movie audience or movie audiences generally. Such characteristics typically include (among other things) age, sex, income and level of education (see "Marketing Research," "Profile" and "Projected Audience").

DEPRECIATION. A deduction allowed to a taxpayer representing a reasonable allowance for the exhaustion, obsolescence, wear and tear of tangible property used in a trade or business, or tangible property held for the production of income. The depreciation deduction is allowed for the loss of value of tangible assets due to wear, use, etc., as well as obsolescence and passage of time. Where property is entitled to depreciation, a more rapid deduction method (more rapid than straight-line depreciation) may be permitted (see "Accelerated Cost Recovery," "Amortization," "Deduction," "Expense," "Income Forecast Method," "Straight-Line Depreciation" and "Tax Benefits").

DERIVATIVE DISTRIBUTION RIGHTS. Film distribution rights relating to remakes and sequels for both film and television (see "Ancillary Rights" and "Sequel").

DESCRIPTIVE TITLES. Titles of films that, to some extent, describe what the film is about (see "Movies With a Message" and "Title Treatment").

DESIGNATED MARKET AREA. The Nielsen audience-market classification that designates a certain market area in which local television stations have partial or complete dominance over stations from other market areas. The concept is similar to Arbitron's ADI and is sometimes used in film distribution to designate a geographical area of a film's release (see "ADI Market").

DESIGNATOR. One who designates (see "Designee").

DESIGNEE. One who is designated, i.e., appointed to serve (see "Designator").

DETAILED BUDGET BREAKDOWN. An item-by-item analysis of a film's budget, which may be some twenty-five or more pages in length (see "Budget" and "Top Sheet").

DETAILED COST REPORTS (see "Cost Reports").

DEVALUATION. The lowering of the value of a country's currency relative to gold and/or the currencies of other nations. Devaluation can also result from a rise in value of other currencies relative to the currency of a particular country (see "Currency," "Currency Conversion" and "Exchange Rate").

DEVELOPMENT. The initial stage in the preparation of a film; those activities relating specifically to taking an idea or concept and turning it into a finished screenplay. Development includes formulating and organizing the idea or concept for the movie, the acquisition of rights to the underlying literary work or screenplay, preparing an outline, synopsis and/or treatment and writing, polishing and revising the various drafts of the script (see "Development Process," "Development Stages," "Packaging," "Preliminary/Development Offering," "Pre-Production" and "Step Deal").

DEVELOPMENTAL FUNDS. The monies required to pay the expenses associated with the earliest stage in the process of making a film, the development stage (contrast with "Seed Money;" see "Development," "Investment Contract," "Preliminary Investors" and "Venture Capital").

DEVELOPMENT COMPANY. A film company which specializes in developing motion picture properties (see "Development").

DEVELOPMENT DEAL. Typically, an agreement by a studio or production entity to provide early funding for a producer during the development of a motion picture project or projects. Development funds may also be provided to directors or screenwriters. The major studios commonly fund the development costs of many screenplays that are never approved for production and those costs are recouped from the budgets of the movies that are produced as part of the studio's overhead charge (see "Creative Accounting" and "Overhead").

DEVELOPMENT EXPENSES. The costs associated with the earliest stage in the preparation of a motion picture project. Development expenses might include attorney and/or accounting fees, optioning or acquiring the screenplay or an underlying property, screenwriter compensation, research costs and budget preparation (see "Development Money Investment Agreement," "Investment Contract" and "Preliminary/Development Offering").

DEVELOPMENT FEE. A specified amount of money agreed to be paid to a producer or production company by a motion picture production financing source, e.g., a studio, for activities relating to the development of a motion picture project. If the project proceeds to production, any development fee payment may be deducted from other producing fees to be paid to the production entity ("Development").

DEVELOPMENT FINANCING. Raising the money to pay for the development activities relating to a film or films. In recent years, the major studios have used corporate funds, funds raised by means of a large public limited partnership offering or foreign equity financing for development expenses. Independent producers are more likely to use the investment contract as the developmental financing vehicle, although corporate funds (for production companies organized as a corporation), a limited partnership or even loans may provide development financing (see "Development," "Development Risk," "Investment Contract" and "Step Deal").

DEVELOPMENT HELL. A film project that enters the development process, never actually gets production funding, but is not actually placed in turnaround either (see "Development Process," "Turnaround" and "Turnaround Hell").

DEVELOPMENT MONEY INVESTMENT AGREEMENT. A written contract, which may utilize a letter format, between an investor and a feature film producer to provide funding of development activities associated with the picture (see "Investment Contract," "Investor Financing Agreement," "Preliminary/Development Funds" and "Preliminary/Development Offering").

DEVELOPMENT NOTES. A report on an review of a screenplay draft which is being developed by a film studio or production company which analyzes the script's storyline, plot structure, characters, scenes, etc., and makes suggestions on how the screenplay can be improved. This analysis will play a role in determining whether the project is approved for production (see "Coverage," "Greenlight," "Reader" and "Story Analyst").

DEVELOPMENT PROCESS. The series of activities, procedures and changes that take a script idea or concept and ultimately lead to a finished screenplay (see "Idea," "Concept," "Outline," "Synopsis," "Treatment," "First Draft," "Polish," "Revision," "Rewrite" and "Shooting Script").

DEVELOPMENT RISK. The possibilities that the investment of time, skill and money in the development of a screenplay will be lost, i.e., production funds for the film will not be forthcoming and the film will not be produced. Since hundreds of scripts are developed each year for each film that is actually produced, the development risk is considerable, therefore financiers of development costs may reasonably expect a higher rate or return on their investment, i.e., anywhere from two to five times the amount invested (see "Development Financing" and "Production Risk").

DEVELOPMENT STAGES OR STEPS. The specifically identifiable phases a motion picture script goes through during development, including idea, concept, outline, synopsis, treatment, first draft, polish, revision, rewrite, final screenplay, shooting script, etc. Few of the film projects in development actually are taken through the full series of development steps. A studio development deal, for example, may have a total possible cost of $850,000, but the first step of the deal may only cost $60,000, and the project may receive no financial commitment beyond that. In that situation, the producer may have to decide whether to continue to develop the project on his or her own or to get the project into turnaround (see "Development Process" and "Turnaround").

DGA (see "Directors Guild of America").

DGA BASIC AGREEMENT. The employment agreement for motion picture directors which has been approved by signatory production companies and the Directors Guild of America on behalf of its director members and which provides minimum standards for the employment of directors relating to compensation, benefits, residuals, working conditions and other important issues (see "Directors Guild of America" and "Signatories").

DIALOGUE. Spoken words in a film or screenplay (see "Dialogue Replacement," "Screenplay" and "Script Supervisor").

DIALOGUE DIRECTOR. The film production person responsible for reviewing lines with actors prior to a take (see "Dialogue").

DIALOGUE REPLACEMENT. The re-recording of conversation between two or more characters on the soundtrack of a motion picture. Dialogue may need to be replaced for several reasons, i.e., the

original recording on location may have produced poor sound quality or specific words or phrases may no longer be appropriate. In
replacing dialogue, the actors have to lip sync their own voices and,
in some instances, the voices of others. Actor employment agreements should provide for such contingencies (see "Automatic Dialogue Replacement," "Employment Agreement" and "Looping").

DIALOGUE TRACK(S). The audio track(s) of a motion picture
soundtrack which only contain spoken material. The dialogue tracks
exist only as separate tracks until the final mix of music, sound
effects and dialogue into a composite soundtrack (see "Music Track"
and "Sound Effects Track").

DILIGENCE. Attention to the matter at hand. Due diligence or reasonable diligence is that diligence which is required by the circumstances, the rendering of which prevents liability for negligence. This
standard of conduct is a relative one, and is determined by considering the facts of each particular case. In the context of a securities
offering, such as a film limited partnership, the phrase "due diligence" refers to the securities underwriter's or participating dealer's
obligation to verify independently the facts and representations provided by a seller or issuer of securities. The objectives of "due
diligence" are to develop confidence that the offering document
contains full and fair disclosure and that the limited partner/investor
has a shot at an economic profit (see "Due Diligence").

DILUTION. A reduction in the value of corporate shares through the
issuance of additional shares or the exercise of rights relating to
convertible securities, warrants or stock options (see "Corporation").

DIRECT ADVERTISING. Advertising, such as the mailing of flyers,
directed to individuals within a specific target group (see "Advertising" and "Projected Audience").

DIRECT CHARGES. Expenses that apply specifically to a given activity, such as production or distribution (see "Direct Distribution Expenses" and "Overhead").

DIRECT COSTS. Expenses specifically related to the production of a
given motion picture (contrast with "Indirect Costs and Expenses"
and "Production Overhead").

DIRECT DISTRIBUTION EXPENSES. All costs and expenses incurred,
paid, payable or accrued, in connection with the distribution, advertising, exploitation and turning to account of a motion picture. The
largest two items relating to the release of any picture are prints and
advertising/publicity costs. Other direct expenses may include, but

are not limited to, such things as checking and collection costs, certain taxes and freight. Items like trade-association fees and assessments, guild payments, along with market research should be considered indirect or, at most, allocated among several films that benefit from such expenditures. Generally, direct distribution expenses are specifically defined or described in some detail in a section of the distribution agreement or in an exhibit to the distribution agreement. Claimed distribution expenses often form the primary focus of producer audits. If the distribution agreement limits distributor expense deductions to direct expenses, the profit participant auditors will be concerned with ferreting out indirect expenses that are claimed by the distributor as direct expenses. Specific categories of direct expenses which the distributor may deduct should be itemized. Other "indirect expenses," such as the distributor's general administrative overhead and similar internal costs, should be regarded as a normal cost of doing business for the distributor and not recoupable from the picture's proceeds or at least the producer should negotiate for as small a percentage of such expenses to be charged to the picture as possible. It may also be useful to establish some relationship between that percentage and the number of films distributed by the distributor in the course of a year. Otherwise, the producer should be certain that the word "direct" is inserted in front of the general description of what kind of expenses are to be deducted as distribution expenses (see "Creative Accounting" and "Contractually Defined Terms").

DIRECT GOVERNMENT SUBSIDIES (see "Government Subsidies").

DIRECTOR (CORPORATE). One who sits on a board of directors of a corporation and who has the legal responsibility of exercising control over the officers and affairs of the entity. A director has a fiduciary duty to the corporation and to its stockholders to manage the affairs of the corporation in a manner which is consistent with their interests. Any breach of this fiduciary duty may subject a corporate director to personal liability to both the shareholders and the corporation (see "Fiduciary" and "Shareholders").

DIRECTOR (FILM). In the film industry, the person who is generally regarded as the primary creative force behind a motion picture and who oversees its entire artistic production. Also, the person who controls the action and dialogue in front of the camera and who is therefore responsible for interpreting and expressing in a film the intentions of the screenwriter and producer as set out in the screenplay. The director is usually hired by the producer (see "Auteur,"

"Collaborative Process," "Creative Control," "Final Cut," "Hyphenate" and "Producer").

DIRECTOR AGREEMENT (see "DGA Basic Agreement" and "Director's Employment Agreement").

DIRECTOR COMMITMENT. A promise from a motion picture director that he or she will direct a certain motion picture. Such commitments may range from informal, oral "hand-shake" deals to written director employment agreements which contain pay-and-play provisions (see "Letter of Intent," "Letter or Interest," "Nominal Payments," "Pay or Play" and "Pay and Play").

DIRECTOR DEFERMENT. A portion of a motion picture director's salary, the payment of which is delayed by agreement (see "Deferment").

DIRECTOR OF PHOTOGRAPHY (DP). The film production title and credit given to the cinematographer, who is responsible to the film's director for achieving optimum photographic images for the film, i.e., lighting, framing and shooting the film, in collaboration with the director. The DP usually does not actually run the camera (the job of the camera operator) but does oversee everything having to do with the camera and lighting, e.g., selecting the camera and lighting equipment, supervising the camera and lighting crews and determining the lighting pattern and exposure for each scene (see "Cinematographer").

DIRECTOR'S CAST LIST. The list of a film's cast prepared by the director for filing with the appropriate unions/guilds (see "Director" and "Guild").

DIRECTOR'S CUT. A completed motion picture consisting of the audio and visual elements chosen by the director. A director's cut is sometimes used as a sneak preview (see "Creative Control," "Final Cut," "Other Versions" and "Sneak Preview").

DIRECTOR'S DEVELOPMENT DEAL. A financing commitment by a studio or other production company to finance the costs of a film project being developed by a director as opposed to a producer (see "Development Deal").

DIRECTOR'S EMPLOYMENT AGREEMENT. The written contract between the feature film director and the producing entity which sets out the terms and conditions pursuant to which the director is to provide directing services for a given motion picture (see "Above-the-Line Employment Agreements," "Straight Employment Agreement" and "Three-Party Agreement").

DIRECTORS GUILD OF AMERICA (DGA). The film-industry trade union for directors, assistant directors and production managers (see "Director" and "Industry Groups").

DIRECTOR'S PROMOTIONAL BUDGET. Monies allocated for the promotion of a film by the film's director (see "Director" and "Promotional Activities").

DIRECTORS' QUESTIONNAIRES. Questionnaires circulated by a corporation's counsel to directors, officers and 10% stockholders seeking information about such individuals, the company and their relationships with the company for the purpose of gathering data which must be disclosed in a securities registration statement (see "Corporation," "Insider," "Insider Trading," "Public Offering" and "Securities").

DIRECTORY ADVERTISING. The kind of movie advertising typically run by exhibitors in newspapers every day which usually contains only the title of the films being shown, the theatre's name, address and phone number along with the times at which the film is to be exhibited (see "Display Advertising").

DIRECT PARTICIPATION PROGRAM. An investment program in which investors participate directly in the cash flow and tax benefits of the underlying investments. Such programs are usually organized as limited partnerships (see "Limited Partnership" and "Silent Partner").

DIRECT-TO-VIDEO RELEASE. A feature film produced without any intention of seeking a foreign or domestic theatrical release or which goes into video release because it was unable to attract a theatrical distribution deal. Generally, such features are low or ultra-low budget productions. Some production companies target their productions for this specific market so as to avoid the much talked about theatrical distribution accounting and business practices which tend to result in very few instances of net profit participations for producers and/or other net profit participants (see "Business Practice," "Creative Accounting," "Theatrical Release" and "Videocassette Revenue Reporting").

DIRTY DUPE. A black and white copy of the spliced, scratched and dirty work print, i.e., a work print that has not been timed (see "Workprint").

DISADVANTAGE. An unfavorable condition. Each form of film finance offers certain advantages and certain disadvantages. There is no single "best way" to finance a feature film for all motion picture producers (see "Advantage," "Availability Analysis," "Financing" and "Pro and Con Analysis").

DISBURSEMENT. The paying out of money in the discharge of a debt or an expense, as distinguished from a distribution (see "Cash Distributions").

DISBURSING AGENT. The entity or individual responsible for paying the debts or expenses out of a fund on behalf of others. The distributor usually acts as the disbursing agent for feature films (see "Creative Accounting" and "Revenue Stream").

DISCHARGED. In bankruptcy, the release of the debtor from most of his, her or its debts (see "Bankruptcy").

DISCLOSURE. The release by corporations, limited partnerships or other entities seeking to raise money through some form of securities offering of all information, positive or negative, that might bear on an investment decision, as required by the securities laws [see "Anti-Fraud Statute (Rule)" and "Securities"].

DISCLOSURE DOCUMENT. The written and bound information which is required by the federal and state securities laws to be provided in advance to prospective purchasers of securities. The securities disclosure document associated with a private placement (exempt offering) is typically called an "offering memorandum" and the securities disclosure document associated with a public/registered offering is typically referred to as a "prospectus" (see "Industry Overview," "Offering Circular," "Plan of Business, "Private Placement Offering Memorandum," "Preliminary Prospectus," "Program Highlights," "Prospectus," "Red Herring" and "Use of Proceeds").

DISCLOSURE REQUIREMENT. The information required to be provided by the issuer of a security to prospective investors in the form of a disclosure document pursuant to a specific form of registration or exemption from registration (see "Disclosure Document").

DISCOUNT. An entertainment lending institution's reduction from the stated amount provided for in a distribution or pre-sale agreement, resulting in the amount of cash such lender is willing to advance to a film producer based on the contractual commitment. Such cash advance is always less than the amount stated in the agreement (see "Bank," "Lender Financing," "Negative Pickup," "Pre-Production Financing," "Pre-Sales" and "Split Rights Deal").

DISCOUNTED CASH FLOW. The value of future expected cash receipts and expenditures at a common date, calculated using net present value or internal rate of return. Discounted cash flow is a factor in analyses of both capital investments and securities investments (same as "Present Value" and "Time Value of Money").

DISCOUNTING. In film, the practice of paying or lending a film producer an amount in cash less a certain percent against the future value of a distribution contract and/or pre-sale commitments, e.g., a lender may require that the producer provide so-called "bankable" commitments equal to 115% of a film's budget in order to lend the producer 100% of the monies required to produce the movie (see "Bankable," "Lender Financing," "Negative Pickup," "Pre-Sale Commitment" and "Split Rights Deal").

DISCOUNTS. A reduction in price. Such reductions are often negotiated and/or awarded by exhibitors and other feature film licensees to distributors on a given picture or they are sometimes based on the volume of pictures provided by the distributor. Distributors often seek to exclude the value of such discounts in profit participation calculations, arguing that the distributor's activities are responsible for earning such credits. However, without the feature film or films made available to the distributor by the producer and other profit participants, the distributor would not be in a position to either negotiate or receive such discounts. Producers may therefore want to negotiate a fair provision in the distribution agreement which includes the value of such discounts in the profit participation calculations (see "Kickback" and "Rebate").

DISCRETION. The power or right to choose between alternative courses of action or inaction. Many film distribution agreements are currently drafted so as to include numerous situations in which the distributor is allowed to exercise its discretion, sometimes even its "sole unfettered discretion," as if there is a higher level of discretion than "discretion." Such distributor discretion may relate to the manner and extent of the film's release and the markets selected, as well as the theatres in each such market, to sales methods, policies and terms, to the right of the distributor to refrain from commencing distribution or discontinuing distribution in any country or place at any time and to allocating license payments among films marketed as a package. In negotiating with distributors, independent producers may want to eliminate unnecessary, undesired or potentially troublesome distributor discretion. Producers may want to pay particular attention to the provisions which include the following words or phrases which indicate someone, usually the distributor is being allowed to exercise its discretion: "discretion," "good faith," "apportion," "allocation," "best efforts," "reasonable efforts," "latitude," "reasonably," "deem," "reasonably deem," "usual," "customary," "customarily" and "industry standards." When such a word or phrase is used, the producer may want to determine who's discretion is involved and then consider whether it is possible to negotiate and draft language which provides a more objective standard with which to comply. Some discretion will almost always be necessary, but discretion can also be an invitation for abuse (see "Creative Accounting," "Latitude" and "Trust Me").

DISCRETIONARY CROSS-COLLATERALIZATION. The offsetting of motion picture profits by a distributor between markets or films in situations where the distribution agreement does not address the practice, i.e., such cross-collateralization is left to the discretion of the distributor (see "Cross-Collateralization," "Cross-Collateralization of Markets," "Cross-Collateralization of Slates," "De Facto Cross-Collateralization" and "Unauthorized Cross-Collateralization").

DISCRETIONARY FUNDS. A small percentage of a mutual fund, trust, pension or other fund which, at the discretion of the fund manager, may be invested in a broad range of securities, even high-risk investments such as motion picture production. Some so-called Hollywood money middlemen have been known to request an up-front payment from a producer seeking production financing for the purpose of using such monies to pay what in effect might be considered a commercial bribe to an asset manager, who would then divert some of the discretionary funds under his or her management toward payment of the production costs of the motion picture (see "Asset Management," "Commercial Bribery" and "Scam").

DISCRIMINATION. The treatment of someone differently on a basis other than on merit (see "Bias," "Prejudice," "Problem Producer," "Reciprocal Preference" and "Relationship-Driven Business").

DISPLAY ADVERTISING. Advertising in newspapers and magazines which features art work or other information relating to a specific film (see "Directory Advertising").

DISPLAY ART. The illustration used in print advertising. Display art often includes title art, body copy and the billing for a movie (see "Display Advertising" and "Title Art").

DISPUTE RESOLUTION PROVISION. A clause in a contract which sets out an agreed-upon method for resolving disagreements between the parties to the contract. In film industry agreements, such provisions are extremely important for the following reasons: no single person can make a commercial feature film alone, disagreements often occur among various contributors to a film project, and such disagreements usually need to be resolved quickly in order to take advantage of the availability of certain skilled persons committed to the project or to avoid the loss of vast sums of money already invested (see "Arbitration," "Arbitration Clause" and "Expedited Arbitration").

DISQUALIFIER. One of a number of conditions typically imposed on the use of both state and federal, registered and exempt securities offerings which disqualifies the issuer from relying on a given form of registration or exemption if certain persons associated with the issuer have violated certain (mostly securities-related) rules, laws or orders in the past five years. Because of these issuer disqualifiers, it is important for any issuer of a security, e.g., a film limited partnership and its general partners, to be very familiar with the backgrounds of the people involved in raising money for the offering (also called "Issuer Disqualifier;" see "Finder" and "Issuer").

DISSOLUTION. The end of the legal existence of a corporation. The process is governed by statute in most states (see "Liquidation" and "Winding Up").

DISTANT LOCATIONS. Union terminology for out-of-town locations on which a film's production employee is required to remain away and to be lodged overnight (see "Nearby Locations").

DISTRIBUTABLE CASH. A defined term in a limited partnership offering which typically sets out what deductions, if any, will be made from partnership gross revenues before arriving at the actual cash to be distributed to the partners. For example: all funds received by the partnership from partnership activities ("gross partnership revenues") minus (a) all operating expenses of the partnership, including, if any, all remaining unreimbursed offering expenses and expenses incurred by the partnership in connection with the distribution and exploitation of the pictures and the ancillary rights thereto; (b) such reserves as the general partners deem necessary in accord with good business practice to cover future partnership expenses; (c) all costs of production of the pictures which have not been supplied by the partnership, by a completion guarantor or by any pre-sales or other similar agreements (such as, for example production funds obtained through loans); and (d) any deferments or percentage participations which are contractually committed to be paid out of gross partnership revenues. Some limited partnerships use the term "net partnership receipts" to described the same or similar concept (see "Cash Distributions," "Gross Partnership Revenues," "Partnership Expenses" and "Partnership Net Receipts").

DISTRIBUTE. The act of selling or licensing a motion picture in various markets [see "Distribution (Film)"].

DISTRIBUTING SYNDICATE. In securities offerings, a group of bro-kerage firms or investment bankers that join forces in order to facili-tate the distribution of a large block of securities (see "Selling Group").

DISTRIBUTION (FILM). The selling or licensing of a motion picture in various markets along with the advertising and promotion of the film. This process includes negotiating with exhibitors and licensees, determining the number of prints to be ordered from the lab, plan-ning and implementing the advertising and promotional campaign, transporting the prints to the theatres for exhibiting and collecting film rentals or other revenue from the exploitation of the film in all markets and media (see "Distributor" and "Sub-Distributor").

DISTRIBUTION (FINANCE). A payment in cash or in property by an entity to the owner or owners of such entity, e.g., a corporate divi-dend to its shareholders is a corporate distribution and the payment of a portion of limited partnership net receipts to its limited partners is a partnership distribution (see "Limited Partnership").

DISTRIBUTION (SECURITIES). The offer and sale of securities to prospective investors (see "Controlled Distribution" and "Uncontrolled Distribution").

DISTRIBUTION ACTIVITIES. In addition to the activities known as "distribution strategies," a film distributor is responsible for the col-lection of film rentals and other monies due, for computing all deductions from film rentals and disbursing funds to participants (see "Disbursing Agent," "Discretion" and "Distribution Strategy").

DISTRIBUTION ADVANCE. Money paid by a distributor to a film's producer as partial consideration for certain rights to distribute the film with some or all of such payments made either at the time the distribution agreement is signed and/or upon delivery pursuant to the distribution agreement delivery schedule. In either case, such advanced sums are generally recoupable from the distributor's gross receipts generated by the film (see "Advance" and "Delivery").

DISTRIBUTION AGREEMENT. The contract between a film's pro-ducer and its distributor through which the distributor commits to distribute the film in specified territories or throughout the universe, for a set period of time (sometimes in perpetuity), and which de-fines the other important terms including how and when each party is to be compensated (see "Deal Memo," "Deal Points," "Distribu-tion Checklist," "License Agreement," "Long Form Distribution Agree-ment," "Production Agreement," "Minimum Rating" and "Rent-A-Dis-tributor").

DISTRIBUTION ALTERNATIVES. The various ways which are available to release and distribute a motion picture. From a certain analytical perspective, there appear to be five major ways in which U.S. made motion pictures are distributed: (1) in-house productions (films that are developed, produced and distributed by the major studio/distributors or independent distributors with affiliated production and distribution facilities), (2) production-financing/distribution agreements (independent producers bring fully developed and packaged projects to the major studio/distributors who provide production and distribution financing for the right to distribute the film, (3) negative pickups (prior to the start of production distributors provide distribution guarantees to a producer who takes the contract or contracts to a lender for discounting and the production funds (4) acquisition distribution agreements (a distribution agreement made after the film is in the can, i.e., the independent producer obtains production financing from a third party source and makes a deal with a distributor to finance the distribution costs and distribute the film and (5) the rent-a-distributor situation in which an independent producer finances both the production and distribution costs, only using the distribution facilities of a distributor to distribute the film for a reduced distribution fee (see "Acquisition Distribution Agreement," "Four-Wall or Four-Walling," "In-House Production," "Negative Pickups," "Production-Financing/ Distribution Agreement," "Rent-A-Distributor" and "Self-Distribution").

DISTRIBUTION APPROACH. The plan and strategy of a producer for distributing a film. A discussion of a producer's distribution approach is often an integral part of the business plan in a film limited partnership's disclosure document (see "Business Plan," "Disclosure Document" and "Distribution Strategy").

DISTRIBUTION CAMPAIGN. The overall plan and strategy for distributing a film, including advertising, promotion, number of prints and the release pattern (see "Advertising" and "Release Pattern").

DISTRIBUTION CHANNELS. The worldwide combination of sub-distributors, foreign sales agents, and others involved in the distribution of a film that a given movie distributor utilizes on a regular basis (see "Sub-Distribution").

DISTRIBUTION CHECKLIST. A listing of the deal points to be negotiated and provided for in a film distribution agreement (see "Deal Memo," "Deal Points" and "Distribution Agreement").

DISTRIBUTION COMMITMENT. An agreement or pledge to provide a domestic or foreign theatrical release for a film; also agreements or pledges to provide certain specified aspects of such distribution, e.g., a specified level of expenditures for prints and ads. Producers should seek to negotiate reasonable commitments with distributors and see that they are met (see "Prints and Ads Commitment" and "Theatrical Release").

DISTRIBUTION COSTS (see "Direct Distribution Expenses" and "Distribution Expenses").

DISTRIBUTION EXPENSES. The costs involved in distributing a film. Generally included are expenses relating to advertising and publicity, conversion, checking, claims, collections, copyright and royalties, other versions of the film, insurance, trade dues, licenses, prints, taxes and transportation (see "Direct Distribution Expenses," "Pension Fund Contributions" and "Theatrical Releasing Costs").

DISTRIBUTION FEE OR DISTRIBUTOR'S FEE. The contractual amount which the company distributing a motion picture or television film charges for its distribution and related services. Such amounts are usually deducted at some defined level of gross receipts and will typically vary from 15% to 40% depending on the market and the type of distribution arrangement. The distribution fee is intended to compensate the distributor for its selling efforts and the maintenance of its home office, branch offices, worldwide sales organization and the use of monies for releasing costs. Distribution fees are usually divided into two major categories: theatrical/non-theatrical and ancillary rights (see "Decision-Making Continuum," "Gross Receipts" "Outright Sales," "Rent-A-Distributor" and "Royalty Fee Basis").

DISTRIBUTION GUARANTEE. A promise by a feature film distributor to pay a specific amount of money to or for the benefit of a film producer as consideration for the distributor's right to distribute the film. Also, a distributor commitment to pay all or part of a film's production costs (e.g., a bank loan or the capital contributions of limited partners), usually within a specified period of time, (e.g., within two years following a film's initial release) (see "Advance or Advances," "Guarantee" and "Pre-Sale Guarantee").

DISTRIBUTION PARTNERSHIPS. Limited partnerships formed and funded for the purpose of raising money to pay for the print, advertising and other expenses incurred in distributing a motion picture or motion pictures. Traditionally, such P&A investors would participate in a movie's revenue stream before production money investors and certain of the expenses incurred by the partnership might qualify as deductions in the year incurred (see "Cooperative Advertising").

DISTRIBUTION PATTERN (see "Release Pattern").

DISTRIBUTION PLAN. The strategy a producer develops for acquiring a distributor for his or her film or the method to be utilized by the distributor in releasing a film (see "Choosing a Distributor," "Release Pattern" and "Release Sequence").

DISTRIBUTION REPORTS. Monthly summaries of information relating to the distribution of a film commonly required by a production lender. Such reports typically include release dates, print and advertising budgets, an itemization of gross film rentals, distribution fees, distribution expenses and the producer's percentage participation (see "Lender Financing").

DISTRIBUTION RIGHTS. The legally enforceable interests in the distribution of a feature film which may include theatrical, ancillary and non-theatrical markets (see "Rights").

DISTRIBUTION RISK. From the point of view of the producer, investors and/or financiers, the term "distribution risk" may refer to the danger that a film will not get a distribution deal, i.e., not be distributed theatrically. From the point of view of the distributor, the term may refer to the danger that, if released theatrically, the film may not recoup its releasing costs (see "Lender Risk Elimination," "Risk," "Risk Disclosure" and "Risk Factors").

DISTRIBUTIONS. In a limited partnership context, any cash or other property distributed to partners, creative talent or third parties on account of their interest in the partnership or agreements therewith. The term "distributions" usually will not include any payments to the general partners in the form of management fees, organization fees, production fees, selling fees, or reimbursement for goods or services provided to the partnership, assuming such payments are excluded pursuant to the limited partnership agreement (see "Distributable Cash").

DISTRIBUTION STRATEGY. The overall plan employed by a film's distributor in its release. Elements of the plan usually include the advertising and publicity strategy, timing of the release, i.e., what is the optimum time during the year, in which markets or cities and in what order, how to release, i.e., single theatre exclusive engagements, multiples, wide release or saturation, along with the activities involved in preparing and handling the bidding process with exhibitors and negotiating the terms of exhibition when necessary (see "Distribution Activities" and "Distribution Approach").

DISTRIBUTION TERM. The period of time during which a film's distribution or licensee has the right to distribute the film in a given territory. Major studio/distributors often seek distribution rights in perpetuity (see "Term" and "Territory").

DISTRIBUTION TERRITORIES. The geographical areas within which a distributor organizes its sub-distribution activities in the United States and the world. Major studio/distributors will often seek distribution rights throughout the universe (see "Territory").

DISTRIBUTOR. Any person engaged in the business of renting, selling or licensing motion pictures to exhibitors; the person(s) or entities operating between the producer and exhibitor of motion pictures who obtain rights to the film, arrange for its exhibition, send such film to exhibitors (sometimes through sub-distributors), and collect film revenues and distribute such revenues to any profit participants based on their individual agreements. A distributor will typically deduct a distribution fee and distribution expenses at some pre-determined point from the revenue stream. The distributor is also generally responsible for the promotion of a film. Factors often considered important in the producer's selection of a distributor include amount of advance, extent of rights conveyed, cross-collateralization, guaranteed marketing commitment, input and veto power over artwork, theatre selection in top markets, track record, frequency of accounting statements, audit rights, producer's participation in promotion, marketing strategy, the deal, distributor's leverage with exhibitors, potential conflicts with other films the distributor is handling, turnaround provision and personal chemistry (see "Creative Accounting," "Choosing a Distributor," "Direct Distribution Expenses," "Sub-Distributor" and "Track Record").

DISTRIBUTOR COMMERCIAL. A promotional message, e.g., previews of other films to be released by the same distributor or any paid appearance of a product, commodity or service, as in product placements arranged by the distributor. The distribution agreement provision relating to distributor commercials should limit such commercials to before or after the exhibition of the film, unless product placements arranged by the distributor are approved by the producer and the distributor's product placement fee is included in the distributor's gross receipts for purposes of calculations involving the producer and other participants (see "Commercials" and "Product Placement").

DISTRIBUTOR COMMITMENTS (see "Distribution Commitment" and "Financing").

DISTRIBUTOR CREDIT. Any extension of payment terms offered by the distributor to sub-distributors and/or exhibitors or indebtedness owed to the distributor by such entities. An abuse of such extension delays payment to the producer (see "Settlement Transaction").

DISTRIBUTOR CREDIT-WORTHINESS. The ability and willingness of a distribution company to pay its debts and other financial obligations in a timely manner. The credit-worthiness of a distributor who provides a negative pickup distribution agreement and distributor guarantee to a producer is a major consideration for the lender in the determination of whether to lend motion picture production funds to that producer using the distributor guarantee as collateral. From the lender's point of view, the risk relating to the credit-worthiness of the distributor is the only risk the lender is willing to assume in a negative pickup deal (see "Lender Financing," "Lender Risk Elimination" and "Negative Pickup").

DISTRIBUTOR/EXHIBITOR SPLIT. A reference to the ratio of sharing as between the film distribution company and the theatre in net box office after overhead (see "Box Office Gross," "Film Rentals," "House Nut," "Ninety/Ten Deal" and "Sliding Scale").

DISTRIBUTOR FINANCING. Production financing for a film either partially or wholly provided by the film's distributor (see "Financing").

DISTRIBUTOR GUARANTEE (see "Distribution Guarantee").

DISTRIBUTOR INCENTIVES. Provisions in a motion picture distribution agreement which tend to stimulate the distributor to more aggressively distribute a motion picture, i.e., to open the picture in the better theatres and to provide ample prints and ads expenditures. Production lenders sometimes require such incentives, e.g., having the distributor put up at least 1/4 to 1/2 of the film's production budget, letting the distributor keep the higher distribution fees in the deal (e.g., approximately 32% as opposed to 22%) and/or having the distributor keep other rights to exploit besides domestic theatrical (see "Distribution Commitment").

DISTRIBUTOR RELEASE CAMPAIGN. The film distributor's strategy relating to the exhibition of a film and its implementation. The release campaign may include plans relating to advertising and publicity, the release date, the distributor's prints and ads commitment, the film's release pattern and its release sequence in all markets and media (see "Advertising," "Publicity," "Release Date," "Release Pattern" and "Release Sequence").

DISTRIBUTOR RENTALS (see "Film Rentals," "Gross Receipts" and "Rentals").

DISTRIBUTOR REVENUE. The total income (money or value received by a motion picture distributor) generated by the exploitation of a given film or received by distributors collectively for all films distributed during a given period, e.g., in recent years distributor revenue has exceeded $15 billion annually (see "Revenue Recognition and Reporting").

DISTRIBUTOR'S ASSUMPTION AGREEMENT. A provision in the distribution agreement through which a film distributor takes possession of or lays claim to a feature film while also providing that the producer takes on the responsibility for certain liabilities of the distributor which are incurred by the distributor as a result of its distribution of the producer's film (see "Leverage").

DISTRIBUTOR'S FILM RENTALS (see "Film Rentals" and "Gross Receipts").

DISTRIBUTOR'S GROSS RECEIPTS. A term which is usually defined in the distribution agreement and which typically refers to the total amount of money received by the distributor from all sources for the exploitation of a film (see "Film Rentals").

DIVERSIFICATION. The spreading of investment risk by putting assets into several categories of investments, e.g., stocks, bonds, money market instruments and precious metals, or into several industries, or into a mutual fund, with its broad range of stocks in one portfolio; at the corporate level, by entering into different business areas, as conglomerates do and in film by investing in more than one film (same as "Spreading Risk;" see "Exotic Investment Product," "Portfolio" and "Risk Factors").

DIVEST OR DIVESTITURE. To deprive or dispossess, especially of property, authority or title. In a legal sense, divestiture is a remedy, by virtue of which a court of law may order an offending party to rid itself of property or assets before that party would normally have done so. The purpose of divestiture is to deprive a defendant of the gains of his, her or its wrongful conduct, and it is commonly used to enforce anti-trust laws. A court, however, will generally not invoke this rather extreme remedy unless it finds divestiture to be both necessary and practicable in preventing monopoly or restraint of trade. In 1948, after ten years of litigation, the major studio/distributors at that time were ordered to divest themselves of their theatre holdings. The term divestiture may also refer to a corporation's orderly distribution of large blocks of another corporation's stock, which were held as an investment (see "Anti-Trust Laws," "Combination in Restraint of Trade," "Monopoly," "Paramount Consent Decree of 1948," "Restraint of Trade" and "TriStar Case").

DIVIDEND. Distribution of corporate profits or earnings to the corporation's shareholders, prorated by class of security and paid in the form of money, stock or company products or property. The amount is decided by the board of directors and is usually paid quarterly. Dividends must be declared as income by the recipient and thus are taxable in the year they are received (see "Double Taxation" and "Limits on Dividends").

DIVISION. An administrative or operating unit of a business, e.g., a corporation. In the film industry, a studio may be a division of a larger corporate organization which has other divisions relating to feature film production, film distribution, a video company, publishing, cable television interests, a record company, etc. (see "Corporate Conglomerate").

DIVISION OF GROSS RECEIPTS. The heading of a provision typically found in feature film distribution agreements which sets out what deductions the distributor will take from its gross receipts (e.g., distribution fees and distribution expenses), what the distribution fee percentages will be in each market, at what point any producer advance will be recouped and whether the distributor will participate in the balance (see "Direct Distribution Expenses" and "Net Profits").

DMA (see "Designated Market Area").

DOCUDRAMA. A film that uses actors to re-create events that supposedly actually occurred (see "Documentary").

DOCUMENTARY. A film or video presentation of actual events using the real people involved and not actors (see "Docudrama").

DOCUMENTATION (see "Loan Documentation").

DOCUMENT-INTENSIVE BUSINESS. A commercial activity requiring extensive contract negotiations and drafting between many related parties. The motion picture business is a document-intensive business (see "Entertainment Industry").

DOG AND PONY SHOW. A somewhat irreverent reference to the sales presentation made by representatives of securities issuers to prospective investors or in other business related presentations (see "Road Show").

DOLBY NOISE REDUCTION. Any of a series of licensed noise suppression formats that yield an improved signal-to-noise ratio, i.e., a film sound system which minimizes noise level and allows for cleaner recording and greater fidelity (see "Dolby Stereo" and "Sound Tracks").

DOLBY SOUND (see "Dolby Noise Reduction" and "Dolby Stereo").

DOLBY STEREO. A licensed, release print format in which four tracks of sound are derived through a process of encoding and decoding of the audio material contained on stereo optical tracks (see "Dolby Noise Reduction").

DOMESTIC CONTRACTS. The written agreements between U.S. distributors and film producers which U.S. banks may consider lending against (see "Foreign Contracts").

DOMESTIC CORPORATION. A corporation doing business in the state in which it was incorporated. In all other states in the U.S., its legal status is that of a foreign corporation (see "Alien Corporation" and "Foreign Corporation").

DOMESTIC DISTRIBUTOR. A film distribution company which distributes films in the U.S. and Canada (see "Distributor").

DOMESTIC NUMBER ONE HIT. The top grossing film compared to other films during at least one week, which is a traditional time period used for comparing the exhibition performances of feature films (see "Hit").

DOMESTIC PICKUP. A feature film, the distribution rights to which are acquired after the film is completed, through the means of an acquisition distribution agreement and which is only to be distributed pursuant to such agreement in the domestic theatrical marketplace (contrast with "Negative Pickup;" see "Acquisition Distribution Agreement," "Decision-Making Continuum," "Distribution Alternatives" and "Worldwide Pickup").

DOMESTIC RECEIVABLES. Monies owed to a producer or distributor from domestic sources. Both domestic and foreign receivables from approved obligors are included in the borrowing base formulas used by entertainment lending banks (see "Borrowing Base Formula" and "Lender Financing").

DOMESTIC RIGHTS. The authority to distribute a feature film in the U.S. and Canada (see "Theatrical Distribution").

DOMESTIC THEATRICAL ADMISSIONS. The number of people who buy tickets to see feature films exhibited at theatres in the U.S. and Canada during a given period of time, e.g., a year (see "Box Office Gross" and "Theatrical Admissions").

DOMESTIC THEATRICAL DISTRIBUTION CONTRACT. The agreement between a film's producer and distributor relating to the distribution of the film in U.S. and Canadian theatres (see "Theatrical Distribution").

DOMESTIC THEATRICAL MARKET. For U.S. produced films, the United States of America, the District of Columbia and Canada and their territories and possessions including Bermuda, the Bahamas and Puerto Rico (see "Domestic Rights").

DOMESTIC THEATRICAL RELEASE. A motion picture exhibition pattern encompassing the U.S. and Canada (see "Release Pattern").

DOMESTIC VERSION. A reference to the cut of a film that is released in the U.S. and Canada as contrasted with a version that may differ and which is released in foreign markets or which is prepared for television (see "Cultural Differences" and "Over Versions").

DOMICILE. The place where an individual or entity has his, her or its permanent home or principal establishment, to where, whenever he or she is absent, he or she has the intention of returning (see "Foreign Banks" and "Foreign Corporation").

DOMINANT MEDIA CONGLOMERATES. The largest and most influential corporations in the communications industries including feature film production, distribution and exhibition, network television, cable television, radio, newspaper, magazines, book publishing, etc. When the Reagan administration eased regulatory restraints, i.e., adopted a policy of less government regulation (specifically a relaxation of the enforcement of the U.S. anti-trust laws in the entertainment industry), the dominant media conglomerates, including the major U.S. studio/distributors, regained control over some of the most important theatre chains. These exhibitor circuits are not only the largest in terms of the total number of theatres and screens, but are also the most strategically located in the leading film markets (see "Anti-Trust Laws," "Communications Industry," "Entertainment Industry," "Number of Screens," "Major Exhibition Chains," "Paramount Consent Decree of 1948" and "TriStar Case").

DOUBLE ADD-BACK. A commonly used over-budget penalty included in agreements for studio production financing of a film which permits the studio to recoup from the film's producer or director twice the amount of the overage prior to breakeven on the film. Notwithstanding the fact that unreasonable contractual penalties may not be enforceable, this studio overbudget policy raises a question as to whether such overbudget costs, when added twice, bear interest and overhead charges the second time around. Also, a determination has to be made as to whether the increased costs are due to certain factors excluded from the calculations relating to the question "was the overbudget threshold exceeded." Distribution agreements sometimes exclude such costs as losses covered by insurance, losses caused by events of force majeure, changes initiated by or approved by the studio, third-party breaches, currency fluctuations, union increases and/or lab increases (see "Budget Overages," "Force Majeure Clause," "Interest-Bearing," "Over-Budget Penalty," "Overhead," "Penalty-Free Cushion" and "Withholding").

DOUBLE BILL OR DOUBLE BILLING (see "Double Feature").

DOUBLE BOOKING. An exhibitor's renting, purchasing, licensing and/or scheduling for exhibition on a certain date more films at its theatre than the theatre has screens on which to exhibit the films. Occasionally the exhibitor will not even exhibit the extra film (i.e., does not split the screen) but rather postpones the extra film's run to a later date, and sometimes this postponement occurs too late in time for the exhibitor's competitors, who have been contractually prohibited by the distributor from exhibiting the film until after the exhibition at the preferred theatre, to exhibit the postponed film on or after the date of postponement (see "Day and Date" and "Exhibitor").

DOUBLE DISTRIBUTION FEES. In situations in which a film's distributor utilizes the services of a sub-distributor in certain markets or territories, the film's producer and other profit participants may be subjected to distribution fees from both entities, portions of which are redundant. The producer should seek to have the primary distributor absorb some or all of the distribution fee of the sub-distributor within its own distribution fee, retaining the balance as a supervision fee or have the fees of the sub-distributor passed through without markup. In the alternative, the producer may seek to negotiate a minimal override for the primary distributor on the distribution fees of sub-distributors (see "Override," "Pass-Through," "Supervision Fee," "Sub-Distributor" and "Sub-Distribution").

DOUBLE FEATURE. The exhibition of two motion pictures in the same theatre (one after another) for which patrons are only charged the price of a single ticket. During the Great Depression, motion picture theatre ticket sales fell significantly and the "double-feature" was created by independent exhibitors in an effort to re-attract audiences. The distributor of such a pairing must allocate (based on a pre-determined formula, at the distributor's discretion or otherwise) the film rentals generated by the joint exhibition of the films between the two films for purposes of calculating payments due to profit participants, if any (see "Allocation Issues," "Combo Engagement," "Creative Accounting," "Discretion," "Double Feature" and "Settlement Transaction").

DOUBLE SCALE. The payment of twice the union minimum salaries established for film cast or crew members by the applicable union or guild (see "Scale").

DOUBLE TAXATION. Taxation of earnings at the corporate level, then again as stockholder dividends (see "Corporation" and "Limited Partnership").

DOUBLE WEEK. A variation on the distributor/exhibitor deal referred to as the 90/10 split in which the distributor reduction in its percentage share is effected every two weeks instead of every week (see "Ninety/Ten Deal").

DOWNSIDE EXPOSURE (same as "Downside Risk" and "Downside Protection").

DOWNSIDE PROTECTION. Elements of a film finance package which are designed to reduce the risk of loss for the film's investors or financiers, e.g., well-known actors, a completion guarantee, pre-sales and/or a domestic theatrical distribution commitment may be considered downside protection (see "Downside Risk" and "Safety Hedges").

DOWNSIDE RISK. The dangers of an investment producing negative results; an estimate that a security will decline in value (also called "Downside Exposure;" see "Downside Protection" and "Upside Potential").

DRAFT SCRIPT OR SCREENPLAY. A preliminary version of a completed screenplay. Union definitions call for a complete draft of a script in a mutually agreed form to a length to be specified by the producer (see "Polish" and "Revision").

DRAMA-LOGUE. A casting newspaper which regularly publishes announcements that describe producers' casting requirements and information about how actors may apply for those roles (see "Casting").

DRAMATIC. Relating to a composition involving interesting or intense conflict of forces, intended to portray life or characters or to tell a story through action and dialogue and designed for film, radio, television or theatrical performance (see "Docudrama" and "Screenplay").

DREAM. A goal or purpose ardently desired (see "Chasing a Dream" and "Pied Piper").

DROIT MORAL. French for moral right (see "Moral Rights").

DRY MORTGAGE. An arrangement whereby a motion picture is the sole collateral for a production loan and the loan is repayable only from the proceeds of distribution of the motion picture. Production lenders usually require secondary sources of loan and interest repayment (see "Collateral" and "Lender Financing").

DUAL LISTING. A security that is listed on more than one exchange, thus increasing the competition for bid and offer prices as well as the liquidity of the securities (see "Broker/Dealer" and "Securities").

DUAL REGULATION. Securities law requirement that the offer and sale of securities must comply with both federal and state laws and regulations (in each state in which securities are to be offered or sold) and to the extent that such regulatory provisions conflict, the more burdensome standard must be adhered to (see "Blue Sky Laws" and "Securities").

DUB. To copy a film, videotape or audio recording (see "Dupe," "Looping" and "Mix").

DUBBING. The act of synchronizing the lip movements of an actor with a voice not originally recorded in synch for a motion picture. The voice may be that of another actor and it may be speaking another language (see "Automatic Dialogue Replacement," "Dub" and "Looping").

DUE DILIGENCE. In the offering of securities, such as corporate stock or limited partnership interests, the investigation conducted by counsel, the managing underwriter in an underwritten securities offering, a managing broker/dealer, selling broker/dealer firms and accountants, for the purpose of demonstrating a reasonable basis for believing that the statements contained in the registration statement, prospectus or other securities disclosure document (e.g., a private placement offering memorandum) are true and that no material facts have been omitted. Sufficient due diligence at the start of such an offering may help such persons avoid liability if in fact it is subsequently established (e.g., by a disgruntled investor) that the issuer of such securities engaged in securities fraud in the conduct of such offering. The publication and general availability of this dictionary of film finance and distribution may even make it more essential that producers, attorneys, accountants, broker/dealers and others involved in the financing of motion pictures through some form of securities offering exercise a greater level of diligence and specifically investigate or inquire as to whether any of the illegal or inappropriate practices described here are actually being engaged in by the proposed distributor for the project being funded (see "Creative Accounting," "Diligence," "Initial Public Offering," "Stock Fraud" and "Underwriter's Questionnaire").

DUE DILIGENCE KIT. A notebook, typically in the form of a three-ring binder with index tabs, containing information developed by an issuer of securities for review by a prospective selling broker/dealer firm which is conducting a due diligence investigation of the issuer of the securities to determine whether such broker/dealer will participate in the issuer's securities offering. The information is designed to aid the broker/dealer in its investigation of the issuer and the offering and some of the information in the due diligence kit will overlap disclosures ultimately found in the offering disclosure document (see "Due Diligence").

DUE DILIGENCE MEETING. A meeting conducted by the underwriter of a new offering at which brokers can ask representatives of the issuer about the issuer's background and financial reliability and the intended use of the proceeds of the offering. Brokers who recommend new offerings without very careful due diligence work may find it more difficult to successfully defend lawsuits if the issuer is subsequently sued by disgruntled investors (see "Due Diligence").

DUES AND ASSESSMENTS. The charges levied by the Motion Picture Association of America (MPAA), the Association of Motion Picture and Theatrical Producers (AMPTP) and other industry groups for their work in representing the interests of their respective segments of the motion picture industry. These dues payments are allocated to each film based on a percentage of the gross receipts generated by the film. Thus, such payments are considered a distribution expense and are paid prior to any payments to net profit participants. The MPAA distribution companies reportedly extract these dues allocations from theatrical revenues generated by MPAA-distributed films whereas the percentage used is based on the anticipated revenues from television, video and theatrical distribution. Thus, producers should seek to negotiate a cap on the amount of dues charged to a given film (see "Professional Association," "Trade Association" and "Residuals or Residual Payments").

DUMMY. A straw person, a sham. For example, a dummy corporation is a corporation which has no business purpose other than to provide protection from liability or from the disclosure of the principal behind its activities. In some instances, a general partner of a limited partnership may be no more than a "dummy" for the limited partners (see "Limited Partnership" and "Piercing the Corporate Veil").

DUPE. A duplicate. As a verb, dupe means to copy a film or tape recording (see "Dub" and "Optical Dupe").

DUPE NEGATIVE. Copy of a film with the light and dark parts in approximately inverse order to those of the original photographic subject. A dupe negative is produced by printing from a positive film, i.e., it is made from a fine grain master positive or interpositive and is used to strike release prints (see "Internegative").

DURESS. Action by a person which compels another to do what he or she would not otherwise do. Duress is a recognized defense to any act, such as a crime, contractual breach or tort, which must be voluntary in order to create liability for the person committing the act (see "Blacklisting" and "Contract of Adhesion").

DUTY. Obligatory conduct owed by a person to another person (see "Tort").

— E —

EARNINGS AND PROFITS. Generally, a tax term referring to the income of a corporation or limited partnership which, if distributed to its shareholders or limited partners respectively, would constitute a dividend (or cash distribution) to the distributee shareholder or investor (see "Corporation" and "Limited Partnership").

EARNINGS BEFORE TAXES. Corporate profits after interest has been paid to bondholders but before taxes have been paid (see "Corporation").

EARNINGS PER SHARE. That portion of a corporation's profit allocated to each outstanding share of common stock. The figure is calculated after paying taxes and after paying preferred shareholders and bondholders, if any (see "Corporate Stock" and "Corporation").

EARNINGS-PRICE RATIO. The relationship of earnings per share to a corporation's current stock price. It is used in comparing the relative attractiveness of stocks, bond and money-market instruments (also called "Earnings Yield;" see "Corporate Stock").

EARNINGS STATEMENT (see "Income Statement").

EARNINGS YIELD (see "Earnings-Price Ratio").

EASE OF INTEGRATION. The relative difficulty of achieving vertical integration in an industry. Another component of the U.S. Justice Department's six-part test relating to vertical mergers (see "Anti-Trust Laws," "Merger Guidelines," "Paramount Consent Decree of 1948" and "TriStar Case").

ECONOMIC ABUSES. Unfair, exploitative or offensive business practices. A state has a legitimate interest in eliminating economic abuses which are harmful to its citizens (see "Anti-Trust Laws," "Anti-Competitive Practices," "Blind Bidding" and "Business Practices").

ECONOMIC CYCLE. The interval of time during which a recurring succession of economic events or phenomena is completed. World and national economies as well as the movie business are said to be cyclical in nature, i.e., trends tend to repeat themselves (see "Cyclical Industry" and "Out-of-Favor Indies").

ECONOMIC LIFE. The period over which a property will yield a return on investment (see "Economic Cycle" and "Rate of Return").

ECONOMIC MICROCOSM. A smaller unit of a larger industry, e.g., the feature film industry is a smaller unit of the larger communications and entertainment industries, or, on an even smaller scale, it may be said that the so-called "A" level deals and those involved in such transactions in one way or another exist in their own microcosm of the feature film industry (see "A-Level Motion Picture").

ECONOMIC REPRISAL. A retaliatory act by a business or industry segment. In response to the passage of anti-blind bidding statutes in various states, some of the major studio/distributors have reportedly threatened from time to time to take their lucrative location filming to non-regulatory states (see "Anti-Blind Bidding Statutes," "Blind Bidding," "Economic Abuses," "Location Filming" and "Non-Regulatory States").

ECONOMIC WAR ZONE. An industry in which various factions are battling for dominance and/or survival. It would appear that some in the film industry will use whatever tactics are necessary to win their war (see "Anti-Trust Laws," "Blind Bidding," "Creative Accounting," "Industry Groups," "Market Power," "Number of Screens," "Predatory Practices," "Reciprocal Preferences" and "Unethical Business Practices").

EDIT. To select, arrange and assemble film, videotape or audio tracks, i.e., prepare for projection or playback or to make the film ready for its final sound mix. Also, to creatively arrange the elements of a motion picture for presentation in the most desirable sequence based on the subjective opinion of the editor, director, producer or whoever has ultimate creative control over the project at the time the film is being edited (see "Creative Control," "Cut," "Final Cut" and "Pan and Scan").

EDITING RIGHTS. A negotiated provision in feature film distribution agreements which sets out the authority of the distributor to edit a picture after it is delivered to the distributor by the producer (see "Creative Control," "Final Cut" and "Droit Moral").

EDITING ROOM ASSISTANT. A person engaged in and about the editing room, film library and vault, whose duties may include splicing, patching, rewinding, coding film and carrying materials to and from the editing room, library and splicing machines (see "Assistant Editor" and "Editor").

EDITOR. The person responsible for assembling the raw material of a motion picture into a coherent whole. An editor will take the film through several stages: from an assembly to a rough cut and then to a fine cut, while typically delegating the preparation of music and sound effects tracks to a specialist in sound editing (see "Cutter" and "Supervising Editor").

EDITOR'S WORKTRACK. A sound print that usually contains all of the sound tracks (including sound effects, original sound and dubbed sound), but generally does not include the final musical score, which in many situations is added to the finished film [see "Work Print (Sound)"].

EFFECTIVE. The declaration by the SEC that a registration statement in a public securities offering is complete and that the offering to prospective investors can commence (see "Acceleration").

EFFECTIVE DATE. The date on which a securities public offering is approved by the SEC for sale to the public (see "Quiet Period" and "Waiting Period").

EFFECTS TRACK(S) [see "Sound Effects Track(s)"].

ELECTRICAL REPRODUCTION. The reproduction of an image or sound by means which utilize electricity (see "Mechanical Reproduction").

ELECTRICAL TRANSCRIPTION. A recording (as on magnetic tape or phonograph record) made for later broadcast (see "Cassette").

ELECTRONIC MEDIA BUYS. Purchases of advertising time on radio and television. Industry analysts report that the total cost of electronic media buys has increased 30% to 40% in the last several years and threatens to climb further. Such price increases make it increasingly more difficult to open a feature film on a wide basis because of the high cost of national electronic media support (see "Advertising" and "Distribution Costs").

ELECTRONIC PRESS KIT. An audio and/or video version of motion picture promotional materials that is sent out to radio or television stations in the market in which a movie is being promoted. An electronic press kit may contain audio or video taped presentations of stories for possible inclusion in news programming, interviews and any other information that might interest the press regarding the movie being promoted (see "Press Kit").

ELEMENTS. The various components that go together to make a movie, e.g., the concept, the screenplay, producer, director, director of photography, cast and crew, the distribution deal or distributor, and publicist. Also, units of original edited reversal or negative film, as well as sound tracks that are used to make the composite print (see "Concept," "Idea," "Investment Letter of Intent" and "Package").

EMBARGO. A legal prohibition upon commerce, i.e., a common carrier or public regulatory agency order prohibiting or restricting freight transportation (see "Restricted Currencies").

EMPLOYEE. One who works for and under the supervision of another, usually for a salary and in a position below the executive level; a hired person who is subject to the control of the hirer as to the means, method and details of performance. Film producers, for example may be considered employees on studio in-house productions, whereas, in production-financing, negative pickup, acquisition and rent-a-distributor distribution deals, the producer would be considered an independent contractor (see "Distribution Alternatives," "Freelance Employee," "Independent Contractor" and "Producers Guild of America").

EMPLOYER. One who hires, uses or engages the services of other persons for pay. An employer need not actually exercise the right of control over the means, the method and the details of an employee's performance. The AMPTP represents the major studio and certain other production company employers with respect to guild issues (see "Alliance of Motion Picture and Television Producers," "Employee" and "Guild").

EMPLOYMENT AGREEMENT. A contract which governs the hiring and work of an employee. With respect to motion pictures, employment agreements may be used for both above-the-line and below-the-line personnel ("Above-the-Line Employment Agreements," "Below-the-Line Employment Agreements" and "Deal Memo").

EMPLOYMENT VERIFICATION. A requirement in employment agreements that makes any offer of employment contingent upon the prospective employee's ability to prove his or her identity and employment eligibility as required by the Immigration Reform and Control Act of 1986 and obligates the prospective employee to complete, execute and deliver certain forms relating to employment eligibility verification along with documentation of the prospective employee's employment eligibility (see "Employment Agreement").

ENCUMBERED. Owned by one party but subject to another party's valid claim (see "Claim," "Clearance" and "Title").

ENCUMBRANCE. A burden on title or a charge on property; a third party's lawful interest in property that diminishes the value of that property and impairs the transfer of marketable title (see "Chain of Title" and "Clearance").

END CREDITS (see "End Titles").

END-TITLE BILLING (same as "End Titles").

END TITLES. The list of cast and crew who worked on a motion picture that runs at the conclusion of a film or tape (see "Main and End Titles").

END USERS IN THE FOREIGN MARKETPLACE. A term referring to foreign entities, such as television networks, entertainment consortiums, foreign conglomerates or foreign theatrical and home video distributors who purchase rights to exploit U.S. made films in foreign markets. Some of these entities are capable of financing a domestic film production and/or distribution company and may do so in exchange for product flow and participation in worldwide revenues (see "Foreign Distribution").

ENGAGEMENT. The exhibiting of a film in a movie theatre where admission is charged and film rentals are paid to the film's distributor (see "Exclusive Engagement" and "Run").

ENJOIN. To command or instruct another, with appropriate authority, either to do a specific act or to refrain from doing a certain act (see "Injunction").

ENTERPRISE. A business firm; a term often applied to a newly formed venture (see "Business Plan" and "Venture Capital").

ENTERTAINMENT. Something diverting or engaging, particularly a public performance which is designed to be amusing or to cause the time to pass agreeably (see "Communications," "Communications Industry," "Entertainment Industry," "Idea," "Movies With a Message," "Multi-Cultural Society" and "Propaganda").

ENTERTAINMENT ATTORNEY. A lawyer who has expertise in the field of entertainment law. The entertainment industry generally includes movies, radio/television, live theatre, music and print publishing. Common areas of law involved include anti-trust, copyright, contract, defamation, labor, music, obscenity, tort and trademark (see "Securities Attorney").

ENTERTAINMENT BANKER. A banker or bank with specialized knowledge of the entertainment industry and which holds itself out as being interested in making loans for entertainment-related projects, including feature film production (see "Bank," "Interest" and "Lender Financing").

ENTERTAINMENT DATA, INC.. An on-line computerized data gathering and data base service for the motion picture industry which tracks box office performance, lists films in release with release dates, stars, genre and box office grosses to date, the pictures released in a single month coupled with a display of releases and grosses for the same month in the prior year, provides information on scheduled releases including title, stars, major credits and synopses, and permits comparisons of genres in the marketplace, release patterns and market share (see "Baseline").

ENTERTAINMENT INDUSTRY. A distinct group of productive enterprises involved in the creation of programs primarily for the amusement and diversion of the public. The entertainment industry includes motion pictures, television, theatre, recording, music publishing, video and literary publishing (see "Communications Industry," "Marketplace of Ideas" and "Propaganda").

ENTERTAINMENT INVESTMENT BANKER. An investment bank which specializes in or has a department providing banking services relating to the funding of entertainment projects (see "Investment Bank" or "Investment Banker").

ENTERTAINMENT PORTFOLIO. The combined holdings of a bank involved in entertainment lending or the similar holdings of a corporate conglomerate or investor (see "Bank," "Corporate Conglomerate" and "Lender Financing").

ENTERTAINMENT STOCKS. The shares of corporations which are significantly involved in the entertainment industry and which may be traded on the New York Stock Exchange, the American Stock Exchange, the NASDAQ Stock Exchange and/or over-the-counter. Current information relating to such stocks is regularly reported in the trades (see "Entertainment Industry," "Exchange," "Over-the-Counter (OTC)" and "Trades").

ENTIRE AGREEMENT CLAUSE. A provision included in many contracts, including film distribution agreements, which provides that the agreement constitutes the entire agreement and supersedes and cancels all prior negotiations, undertakings and agreements, both written and oral, between the parties with respect to the subject matter of the agreement. The clause may provide further that no officer, employee or representative of either party has any authority to make any representations or promises not contained in the agreement and that neither party has signed the agreement in reliance on any such representations or promises. Producers negotiating with various representatives of distributors should make notes of any oral representations made by such persons and systematically see that such representations are incorporated into the distribution agreement, otherwise, they are likely to be worthless (same as "Entire Understanding Clause;" see "Deal Memo" and "Oral Representations").

ENTIRE UNDERSTANDING CLAUSE (same as "Entire Agreement Clause").

ENTITY. Generally in commerce, a term meaning a business which is in a form that has a distinct existence separate from its owners. Thus, under this definition a corporation and a limited partnership are entities but a sole proprietorship is not. For accounting purposes an entity is more broadly defined as any unit, existing or to be formed, for which financial statements could be prepared in accordance with generally accepted accounting principles or another comprehensive basis of accounting. Pursuant to this definition, an entity can be an individual, partnership, corporation, trust, estate, association or governmental unit (see "Corporation," "Joint Venture," "Person," "Partnership" and "Proprietorship").

ENTREPRENEUR. A person who takes on the risks of starting a new business. Often, venture capital is used to finance the start-up in return for a piece of the equity. Once an entrepreneur's business is established and organized as a corporation, shares may be sold to the public as an initial public offering, assuming favorable market conditions (see "Business Plan," "Enterprise" and "Venture Capital").

EQUAL LIKENESS. A clause in actor employment agreements which provides that if anyone else's photograph or likeness appears in paid advertisements relating to the motion picture, a photograph of the actor of equal size and prominence must also appear in such advertisement (see "Employment Agreement" and "Perks").

EQUIPMENT INSURANCE. Insurance covering all risks of direct physical loss, damage or destruction to company owned or leased miscellaneous equipment, including cameras, camera equipment, sound, lighting, editing equipment, grip equipment and projectors. Coverage can be extended to mobile equipment vans and studio location units (see "Insurance" and "Miscellaneous Equipment Insurance").

EQUIPMENT RENTAL. The hiring or leasing for a fee of various motion picture production machinery, tools or gear during the period of production for which it is needed. Renting movie production equipment eliminates the need for many production companies to purchase and maintain such equipment during times when films are not being produced (see "Equipment Rental Houses").

EQUIPMENT RENTAL AGREEMENT. The contract between a film production company and a motion picture equipment rental facility which sets forth the terms and conditions under which the rental facility will permit the production company to use motion picture production equipment owned by the rental facility in the production of a motion picture (see "Equipment Rental" and "Equipment Rental Houses").

EQUIPMENT RENTAL HOUSES. Businesses which specialize in providing all sorts of film production equipment to production companies on a rental basis (see "Equipment Rental Agreement").

EQUITABLE REMEDY. The means employed to enforce or redress an injury other than remedies at law; (see "Action," "Action-At-Law," "Injunction" and "Specific Performance").

EQUITY. The interest or value that an owner has in property, over and above any liens against it. For corporations, the ownership interest possessed by shareholders, i.e., stock as opposed to bonds, for limited partnerships, the profit sharing interests of the partners and, for a direct investment in a film project, the percentage participation interest in the backend (contrast with "Debt;" see "Backend," "Limited Partnership," "Ownership," "Percentage Participation," "Share" and "Shareholder"). In law, the term means fairness, i.e., that equity will derive a means to achieve a just result when legal procedure or remedies are inadequate (see "Equitable Remedy," "Action-At-Law," "Injunction" and "Litigation").

EQUITY FINANCING. Raising money by offering ownership interests in an entity, e.g., shares of common or preferred stock for a corporation, limited partnership interests for a limited partnership or percentage participations in a film's revenue. Equity financing of a feature film enables the producer to finance the film unhampered by studio executives or the oversight of a completion guarantor's representative (if the producer so chooses) but will likely permit a higher level of participation in the film's revenue stream by investors, when compared with lender financing (see "Creative Control," "Equity," "Investor Financing," "Lender Financing," "Studio Financing" and "Risk Capital").

EQUITY FINANCING CONTRACT. A funding agreement through which investors provide monies for a project or for a company's use in exchange for an ownership interest in the entity, typically through corporate stock, limited partnership interests or a direct investment in the project (see "Equity" and "Equity Financing").

EQUITY INVESTMENT. A direct investment for an ownership stake in a single film, package of films or company, as opposed to debt that requires pre-arranged repayment with interest, but without profit or losses participation for the lender (see "Debt," "Equity" and "Interest").

EQUITY INVESTMENT FUND. A sum of money set aside for a specific purpose, e.g., to help finance the completion of feature motion pictures, wherein the fund's contribution to a picture allows the fund to gain an ownership interest in the picture (see "Completion Fund" and "Loan").

EQUITY KICKER. Offer of an ownership position in a deal that involves loans. In return for that equity kicker, the lender is likely to charge a lower interest rate on the loan. Convertible features and warrants are offered as equity kickers to make securities attractive to investors (see "Sweetener").

EQUITY PARTICIPANTS. Individuals or entities which contribute funds for the production of a movie and/or toward its theatrical releasing costs in exchange for an ownership position in the producing and/or distributing entity (see "Equity" and "Investor").

EQUITY SECURITY. Any security which provides an equity ownership interest (see "Equity" and "Security").

ERRORS AND OMISSIONS INSURANCE. Financial protection which covers legal liability and defense for a film production company and other named insureds against lawsuits alleging unauthorized use of titles, format, ideas, characters or plots; plagiarism, unfair competition or breach of contract and failure to obtain requisite releases. E&O coverage also commonly protects against alleged libel, slander, defamation of character or invasion of privacy. The producer usually pays for such coverage, at least initially, but if the coverage is expanded to include possible distributor error, the distributor should pay for some or all of the coverage for the distribution period. Also, when errors and omissions insurance is provided, there is no longer any need for the distributor to withhold sums of money from distribution proceeds to cover such claims, unless there is a possibility that such claims may exceed the limits of the insurance coverage. The producer should discuss the E&O requirements as set out in the distribution deal with his or her insurance agent or carrier to make sure the distributor is not obligating the producer to provide coverage that is not available in the current marketplace (see "Excess Insurance Coverage," "Insurance" and "Privacy, Right of").

ERRORS AND OMISSIONS POLICY. The insurance agreement relating to errors and omissions risks (see "Errors and Omissions Insurance").

ERRORS AND OMISSIONS RENEWALS. The extension of the coverage period for an existing errors and omissions insurance policy through the payment of the premium. In the context of a film distribution deal, the distributor often provides that it is not responsible for such renewal, but in the event the producer does not renew, the distributor may renew and can deduct the premium cost as a distribution expense. Some suggest that if the errors and omissions of the distributor are also covered by the policy, the distributor should pay a portion of the premium (see "Distribution Expenses" and "Errors and Omissions Insurance").

ESCALATING CONTINGENT COMPENSATION. Remuneration to be paid to persons who provide products or services for use in the production of a motion picture which is paid in progressively higher percentages or amounts following receipt of specified levels of distributor gross receipts or any other specified triggering mechanism (see "Bonus," "Contingent Compensation" and "Front-End Compensation").

ESCALATION. Language in employment agreements which provide for an increase in a participant's net or gross profit participation in the event that the box office gross or the distributor's gross receipts rise to certain pre-designated levels. Also, clauses in distribution agreements which permit the distributor's distribution fees to escalate under certain circumstances (see "Escalating Contingent Compensation").

ESCALATION POINT. That place in a motion picture's revenue stream at which a participant's participation percentage increases or a distributor's distribution fees increase (see "Distribution Fee," "Escalating Contingent Compensation").

ESCROW. Money, securities or other property or instruments held by one who is not a party to a transaction (third party) for future delivery to a party upon the occurrence or non-occurrence of a specific event or events. Escrows are commonly used by independent producers to provide assurances to the agents for actors that the agreed upon compensation will be paid when due. Escrows are also used when raising production monies through the vehicle of a limited partnership to hold investor funds until the minimum offering amount is achieved (see "Impound," "Third-Party Escrow" and "Trustee").

ESCROW ACCOUNT. An accounting relationship with a financial institution under a particular name usually evidenced by a deposit against which withdrawals may be made under certain circumstances (see "Escrow").

ESCROW AGENT. The financial institution through which an escrow account is established. Some such institutions prefer to be referred to in the documents which establish the relationship as escrow holders, thus ostensibly avoiding the implications of an agency relationship (see "Escrow Holder").

ESCROW AGREEMENT AND INSTRUCTIONS. The written contract between the party that is placing money in escrow and the escrow holder which sets out the terms and conditions under which the escrow holder agrees to act as such and provides instructions to the escrow holder for the maintenance and closing of the escrow account (see "Escrow" and "Escrow Holder").

ESCROW HOLDER. A financial institution which maintains the escrow account but which prefers not to be referred to as an escrow agent (see "Escrow Agent").

ESCROW OF FIXED COMPENSATION. A common requirement for obtaining a firm commitment from an important actor or director to work in a proposed motion picture which means that their agreed-upon salary has to be deposited into an escrow account before they will commit to the picture. The agents representing actors and directors who are in demand will insist on this provision before taking their principals off the market for the time period during which their services are to be required (see "Escrow Account").

ETHICAL. Conduct that is consistent with the standards followed in a business or profession (see "Ethics").

ETHICS. The discipline dealing with what is good and bad and with moral duties and obligations; the principals of conduct governing an individual or a group; the standards followed in a business or a profession (see "Code of Professional Responsibility," "Conflicts of Interest" and "Unethical").

EVIDENCE OF INSURANCE COVERAGE. A certificate of insurance provided by the insurance carrier which serves to demonstrate that a specific policy of insurance, e.g., producer's liability, is currently in effect and the premium has been paid for a specified term. Such evidence of insurance is generally a perquisite to obtaining a motion picture completion bond (see "Certificate of Insurance," "Completion Bond" and "Insurance").

EXACT INTEREST. Interest calculated on a 365-day year. Studio/distributors providing production financing often prefer to use ordinary interest since it results in higher interest payments on the negative cost of the picture in the final accounting period (see "Interest" and "Ordinary Interest").

EXCERPTS. Passages or film clips selected or copied for use in another film (see "License of Stills/Excerpts").

EXCESS INSURANCE COVERAGE. Insurance protection above the limits of the basic policy for which an additional premium will be charged (see "Errors and Omissions Insurance," "Insurance," "Primary Insurance" and "Reinsurance").

EXCESSIVE INTEREST RATES (see "Interest").

EXCHANGE. A regional office of the larger film distributors. These offices are responsible for supplying the distributor's motion pictures to exhibitors in the region where the exchange is located (see "Major Studio/Distributors" and "Sub-Distribution").

EXCHANGE CONTROLS. A country's regulations relating to the exchange of foreign currencies (see "Currency Conversion").

EXCHANGE RATE. The measure or value of currencies traded between various countries (see "Beneficial Exchange Rate").

EXCHANGE RATE FLUCTUATIONS (see "Currency Conversion" and "Exchange Rate Movements").

EXCHANGE RATE MOVEMENTS. Changes in the value of a country's currency relative to the currency of other countries. Such changes may significantly affect the value of foreign film rentals (see "Currency Conversion" and "Floating Exchange Rate").

EXCLUSIONS. A term used and defined in some distribution agreements to be the amounts of all adjustments, credits, allowances (other than advertising allowances), rebates and refunds, given or made to sub-distributors, exhibitors and licensees which are excluded from accountable gross. Also, monies in the nature of security deposits, advances or periodic payments are not included in accountable gross until they have actually been earned (such as by the exhibition of the film) or forfeited. In other words, some distribution deals will allow the distributor to not count and therefore not be obligated to include in its net calculations, certain items that otherwise might be included in gross receipts. Such exclusions must be carefully reviewed for reasonableness. The term may also be used in describing what costs are to be excluded in determining whether or not the cost of a production has exceeded a specified percentage e.g., 110% of the approved production budget (see "Accountable Gross," "Adjusted Gross," "Approved Production Budget" and "Gross Receipts").

EXCLUSIVE ENGAGEMENT. A method of releasing a feature film in which the film is opened in a single theatre (or possibly more than one screen in a given theatre complex) in any given major city or market. The contractual arrangement with the exhibitor usually provides the distributor with an option after a specified period of time to keep the film at that theatre for a long exclusive run or to widen the release of the film in that city based on the film's performance (see "Engagement," "Mini-Multiple," "Run" and "Special Handling").

EXCLUSIVE GROUND TRANSPORTATION. A provision sometimes requested in the employment agreements for actors and others which requires the production company to provide a vehicle and a driver for the sole use of that artist in getting to and from the set of a motion picture in production or to and from the airport when the artist is required to fly to an out-of-town location (see "Perk").

EXCLUSIVE OPENING (see "Exclusive Engagement").

EXCLUSIVE RUN (see "Engagement," "Exclusive Engagement" and "Run").

EXECUTE OR EXECUTION. The signing, dating and sealing (if applicable) of a contract or agreement making it valid (see "Acknowledge" and "Certify").

EXECUTIVE OFFICER. The president, any vice president in charge of a principal business unit, division or function (such as sales, administration or finance), any other officer who performs a policy-making function, or any other person who performs similar policy-making functions for the issuer of a security (see "Chief Executive Officer").

EXECUTIVE PRODUCER. For independent productions, an individual or individuals who provide something very important to the production of the motion picture, such as providing or obtaining production funding, obtaining a commitment from a big-name star or director or packaging some or all of the project. At the major studio lots, the executive producer is often the producer in charge of the logistics of production, a staff producer working for the studio and keeping track of schedules, budgets and all general production areas. In a feature film limited partnership context, the executive producer is the person designated by the general partners to receive the executive producer screen credit for services rendered in the organization and funding of the partnership, preparation of the offering memorandum, conduct of the offering and/or in otherwise arranging for the production of a film or films. The term also refers to such person's screen credit (see "Employee," "Line Producer," "Packaging" and "Producer").

EXECUTIVE PRODUCER FEE. A payment or payments made to the executive producers out of a film's budget for services rendered in the organization and funding of a film limited partnership, in the preparation and execution of a feature film limited partnership offering, in otherwise arranging for the production of a film or films and/ or for other administrative duties associated with a given film (see "Executive Producer").

EXEMPTED SECURITY. A security which is not required to be registered under the provisions of the Securities Exchange Act. This term may include both exempt securities and exempt transactions (see "Exempt Security" and "Exempt Transaction").

EXEMPTION. A deduction allowed to a taxpayer because of his, her or its status as a taxpayer rather than because of specific economic costs or expenses incurred during the taxable year (see "Income Tax").

EXEMPT OFFERING (see "Private Offering").

EXEMPT SECURITY. A security which is not required to be registered under the provisions of the Securities Exchange Act because of the type of security it is, as opposed to the type of transaction in which such security is offered or sold, e.g., securities listed on a national securities exchange, securities issued or guaranteed by the U.S., any state, any political subdivision of a state, or any agency of such governmental entity or any security issued by and representing an interest in or a debt of any bank organized under the laws of the U.S. (see "Transactional Exemption").

EXEMPT TRANSACTION. A securities offering which is exempt from the securities registration requirements because of the manner in which the securities are offered or sold as opposed to the type of securities involved, e.g., Regulation D offerings do not permit advertising or general solicitation. Regulation D is a federal transactional exemption, and most states provide compatible exemptions as limited offering or small offering exemptions (also called "Transactional Exemption;" see "Exempt Security" and "Private Offering").

EXHIBIT. To show a motion picture to the public for a charge (see "Exhibitor").

EXHIBITION. A public showing of a feature film for a charge (see "Exhibitor" and "Major Exhibition Chains").

EXHIBITION CONTRACT. The agreement between a film's distributor (or producer who is self-distributing) and the theatre or theatre chain which sets out the terms of a film's exhibition at such theatres (see "Distributor/Exhibitor Split").

EXHIBITOR. The owners or operators of movie theatres or the actual theatres which exhibit feature films; also any person engaged in the business of operating a theatre (see "Major Exhibition Chain").

EXHIBITOR CHAIN. Motion picture exhibition companies which own and operate theatres at multiple locations. Major exhibitor chains include American Multi-Cinema, Cineplex Odeon, General Cinema and United Artists (see "Exhibitor" and "Major Exhibition Chains").

EXHIBITOR CIRCUIT (same as "Exhibitor Chain").

EXHIBITOR FINANCING. The partial or complete funding of the production costs of a motion picture by a theatrical exhibitor. Although exhibitors often complain about the quality of the films that are made available to them for exhibition, they seldom risk their own capital in the effort to improve on that quality. Occasionally, however, a theatre circuit may involve itself in production financing (see "Major Exhibitor Chains" and "NATO").

EXHIBITOR'S BID (see "Bid").

EXIT POLL. A market-research technique in which moviegoers are interviewed after they have seen a motion picture and as they leave the theatre in an effort to gauge the audience's reaction to the picture (see "Focus Groups").

EXOTIC INVESTMENT PRODUCT. A strikingly different, unusual or high-risk investment vehicle or opportunity. Relative to other financial or investment products ordinarily handled by securities broker/dealer firms, a feature film limited partnership is considered exotic (see "Investor Financing" and "Risk Factors").

EXOTICS (same as "Exotic Investment Product").

EXPEDITED ARBITRATION. An even quicker resolution of a dispute than that normally provided by regular arbitration. Lenders sometimes require a provision for expedited arbitration in the inter-party agreement, specifically with respect to disputes over whether delivery has been effected. The lender wants a quick resolution as to whether completion and delivery have been properly made so that it can collect from the either the distributor or the completion guarantor (if it is determined that completion and delivery have not been properly made (see "Arbitration," "Completion Guarantor," "Inter-Party Agreement," "Lender Financing" and "Negative Pickup").

EXPEND. To pay out or spend (see "Expenses").

EXPENSE. As a verb, to deduct a cost item in order to reduce tax liability (see "Capitalize" and "Expenses").

EXPENSE ALLOWANCE. A pre-paid stipend or reimbursement privilege for out of pocket expenses incurred by an employee, such as an actor or director, while involved in the production of a film (see "Perk").

EXPENSES. Costs that are currently deductible as opposed to capital expenditures which may not be currently deducted but which either must be depreciated or amortized over the useful life of the property or may not be deducted at all (see "Amortization," "Capital Expenditure," "Capitalization" and "Depreciation").

EXPLOIT. In the motion picture business, to manipulate and/or capitalize on a given feature film (see "Maximum Exploitation" and "Traffic In").

EXPLOITATION. All of the advertising, publicity, merchandising, licensing and promotion of a motion picture, and, in a broader sense, any use of a film, soundtrack album or other product for one's own profit or advantage (see "Maximum Exploitation").

EXPLOITATION FILM. A feature motion picture which contains obligatory or gratuitous sex, violence, horror, catastrophic events or a combination of any or all of such themes and which has little socially redeeming value. The exploitation film blatantly advertises and uses these themes to attract audiences. Such films typically enter and exit the theatrical market more quickly than other feature films (see "Genre," "Production Value" and "Theme").

EXPLOITATIVE APPROACH. A film advertising campaign designed to appeal to the traditional themes of exploitation films (see "Exploitation Film").

EXPORT CAPABILITIES. The ability of a country or an industry within a country to sell goods in other countries. Some entertainment industry analysts expect the export capabilities of the U.S. film and television industries to experience a steady decline in the years ahead (see "Foreign Market").

EXPOSED FILM. The acetate-based, emulsion-coated strip of plastic with perforations on the edges (which is used to make photographic images) that has been subjected to light but not yet processed (see "Film").

EXPRESS REPRESENTATION. A statement set out in words (see "Implied Representation" and "Representation").

EXTERIOR. Any motion picture scene shot out of doors (see "Back Lot" and "Location").

EXTERNAL FINANCING. Funds brought in from outside the corporation, e.g., a bank loan, proceeds from a bond offering or cash from venture capitalists. External funds supplement internally generated cash flow and are used for business expansion, as well as for seasonal working capital needs (see "Internal Financing").

EXTORTION. The illegal taking of money by anyone who employs threats or other illegal use of fear or coercion in order to obtain the money, and whose conduct falls short of the threat to personal safety required for robbery, e.g., the use of the threat to use violence in order to collect interest or the debt itself. For example, if a distributor's representative suggested or implied that a profit participant might be "blacklisted" if such profit participant did not forego a lawsuit or settle a lawsuit for less money than is owed, that threat might be considered a form of extortion (see "Loan Sharking" and "Racketeering").

EXTRA DIVIDEND. Corporate dividend paid to shareholders in addition to the regular dividend (see "Corporation").

EXTRA EXPENSE INSURANCE. An insurance policy which will reimburse a production company or producer (the insured) for any extra expense necessary to complete principal photography of an insured production due to the damage or destruction of property or facilities (props, sets or equipment) used in connection with the production (contrast with "Completion Bond;" see "Insurance").

EXTRA RELEASE. An agreement between feature film producers and persons who may appear in a recognizable manner in a film (and who have not otherwise provided their authorization for such appearance) which authorizes the appearance and thus eliminates the risk of future claims against the production company or its assigns (see "Release").

EXTRAS. Non-speaking atmosphere talent; actors who have no spoken lines in a movie (unless as part of a group) and who are generally not called upon to make any gesture which would set such actors apart from the other extras (see "Atmosphere," "Background Cast," "Bit Player" and "Screen Extras Guild").

EXTRINSIC EVENT. Outside of or not a part of an occurrence or happening. For example, pursuant to the terms of some film distribution agreements, costs caused by an extrinsic event may be excluded from the determination as to whether the production costs of a motion picture have exceeded the specified percentage (e.g., 110%) of the approved production budget (see "Force Majeure Clause").

— F —

FACILITIES ALLOCATION. The apportionment of studio or distributor operating expenses among the studio's various components for the purpose of charging such expenses against a given film's costs. In studio/distributor financed films, the producer should consider negotiating to exclude such indirect costs from the permissible distribution expense deductions or to place a limit on the percentage of such allocations or in the alternative, carefully review such allocations to make certain they are reasonable. If facilities allocations are made by an independent distributor, such expense allocations are no different than studio overhead (see "Contract of Adhesion," "Creative Accounting," "Inferior Bargaining Position," "Market Power" and "Overhead" or "Overhead Costs").

FACILITIES ARRANGEMENTS AND AGREEMENTS. Film production deals which make locations and/or studios available for shooting films in a certain locale, either at no cost or at significantly reduced rates (see "Facilities Subsidies").

FACILITIES DEALS. Film finance transactions in which crews, locations, local cast, studio facilities, cameras or some combination thereof are offered to cover a certain percentage of a film's below-the-line costs. Such deals are sometimes offered by local studios trying to stimulate business for their facility (see "Foreign Below-the-Line Deals").

FACILITIES LESSOR. The person or entity who leases his, her or its facilities (e.g., a studio sound stage) to a film production company. As well as sometimes serving as financiers and distributors, the major studio/distributors sometimes also serve as facilities lessors (see "Major Studio/Distributor" and "Studio").

FACILITIES SUBSIDIES. Film production deals offered by governments (usually foreign) which make locations and/or studios available in their jurisdiction either at no cost or significantly reduced rates (see "Facilities Arrangements" and "Foreign Government Grants and Subsidies").

FAIR COMPETITION. The conduct of rival businesses in an impartial, unbiased and equitable manner. The court in the Paramount case determined that the only means of promoting fair competition within the motion picture industry was to order divestiture of the ownership of theatrical exhibition from the production/distribution side of the business. Although some in the film industry feel such prohibitions against vertical integration should remain in place, the federal government has apparently backed away from its earlier position (see "Anti-Trust Laws," "Blind Bidding," "Major Exhibition Chains," "Merger Guidelines," "Paramount Consent Decree of 1948," "Political Influence," "TriStar Case" and "Unfair Competition").

FAIR MARKET VALUE. The price at which an asset or service passes from a willing seller to a willing buyer, assuming that both are rational and have a reasonable knowledge of all relevant facts relating to such sale (see "Law of Supply and Demand" and "Market Value").

FAIR USE. In federal copyright law, the use of copyrighted materials in a manner that does not constitute an infringement of copyright and without payment of royalties; a permitted use by copying and acknowledgment. The fair use exception to copyright infringement is a privilege in others than the owner of the copyright to use the copyrighted material in a reasonable manner without the owner's consent, not withstanding the exclusive rights granted to the owner by the copyright. Whether a use is considered a fair use depends upon the purpose and character of the use, the nature of the copyrighted work, the amount and substantiality of the portion used, and the effect of the use upon the market value of the copyright. Important factors include whether the copied material was creative or research-oriented; the status of the user (reviewer, scholar, critic, journalist, compiler, parodist, etc.); extent of use (both qualitatively and quantitatively); the absence of an intent to plagiarize as evidenced by proper acknowledgment and the original contribution of the user (see "Copyright" and "Plagiarism").

FASB (see "Financial Accounting Standards Board").

FASB STATEMENT NO. 34. A set of accounting principles and guidelines promulgated in 1980 by the Financial Accounting Standards

Board for use by the film industry and relating to the capitalization of interest costs. FASB Statement No. 34 requires that interest costs be capitalized as part of the historical cost of acquiring certain assets. To qualify for interest capitalization, assets must require a period of time to get them ready for their intended use, e.g., assets intended for sale or lease that are constructed as discrete projects (such as motion pictures). Interest capitalization is required for those assets if its effect, compared with the effect of expensing interest, is material. If the net effect is not material, interest capitalization is not required. Prior to 1980, interest costs of a motion picture studio were written off as incurred, i.e., deducted in the year incurred, but under FASB Statement 34, such costs must be capitalized and then charged in the studio's accounting as part of the negative cost (see "Capitalization," "Expense," "Interest" and "FASB Statement No. 53").

FASB STATEMENT NO. 53. A set of accounting principles and guidelines promulgated by the Financial Accounting Standards Board which relate to financial reporting by producers and distributors of motion picture films. Such guidelines cover three key areas: (1) expense versus capitalization policies, (2) product availability and revenue recognition concepts and (3) estimation procedures and profit or loss determination. FASB Statement No. 53 provides that producers and distributors who license film exhibition rights to movie theatres generally must recognize revenue when the films are shown, i.e., that all film exploitation costs (for prints, advertising, sub-distribution fees, rents, salaries and other distribution expenses) that are clearly to benefit future periods should be capitalized as film-cost inventory and amortized over a period in which the major portion of gross revenue from the picture is recorded. This method of accounting must be applied to national advertising but local and co-operative advertising expenditures are generally closely tied to local grosses and are thus normally taken as a deductible expense in the year incurred because they usually do not provide any benefits in future periods (see "Capitalize," "Expense," "Interest" and "Revenue Recognition and Reporting").

FASB STATEMENT NO. 96. A set of accounting principles and guidelines promulgated by the Financial Accounting Standards Board which relate to financial reporting by producers and distributors of motion picture films and more specifically to the difference between what a company records in its books as a tax liability and what it actually has to pay in taxes. Previously, a company could record a column called "deferred taxes," but that option is no longer available. Now, tax liability is only recognized when it actually takes effect. These rules are designed to prevent film companies from carrying an excessive value on their movies (see "Creative Accounting," "Financial Accounting Standards Board" and "Tax").

FAULTY STOCK, CAMERA AND PROCESSING INSURANCE. An insurance policy that covers loss, damage or destruction of raw film or tape stock, exposed film (developed or undeveloped), recorded videotape, soundtracks and tapes caused by or resulting from fogging or the use of faulty developing, faulty editing or faulty processing and accidental erasure of videotape recordings (see "Exposed Film" and "Insurance").

FAVORABLE PORTRAYAL. A positive depiction in a motion picture (see "Bias," "Hidden Agenda," "Marketplace of Ideas," "Pattern of Bias" and "Unfavorable Portrayal").

FAVORED NATIONS CLAUSE. A provision in a contract meaning the contracting party will be given treatment on a par with that provided others with whom the other party deals. In entertainment agreements, the clause may be used to denote a level of profit participation, the size and placement of billing, the calibre of dressing rooms or motor homes on location, and other such matters (see "Pari Passu," "Perks" and "Percentage Participation").

FEATURE. The principal attraction playing in a movie theatre; a full-length dramatic film (not documentaries or film shorts) made for entertainment and commercial theatrical release. Feature-length made-for-television films or tapes are often referred to as TV films, movies-of-the-week or TV specials and may have a slightly longer running time than the typical ninety minutes of a feature film. Some in the industry define a feature as any motion picture, regardless of topic, which is longer than 4,000 feet (see "Feature Length" and "Pre-Feature Entertainment").

FEATURED PLAYER. A principal actor who does not have a starring role in a motion picture but is a main character. The featured player will generally have higher billing and will receive greater compensation than a day player (see "Actor," "Bit Player" and "Star").

FEATURE FILM (see "Feature" and "Feature Length").

FEATURE FILM FUND. Private or government monies set aside for the purpose of financing some or all of the production costs of certain feature films that meet the requirements of the fund (see "Completion Fund" and "Telefilm Canada").

FEATURE FILM LIMITED PARTNERSHIP. A film financing vehicle through which passive investors (the limited partners) typically provide some or all of the production monies for producing one or more motion pictures. Like corporate stock, interests in limited partnerships are securities; thus, the federal and state securities laws, including the anti-fraud provisions, apply to the sale and offer of limited partnership interests. In recent years, the film limited partnership has often been portrayed in a negative light by many broker/dealers, financial commentators, investment advisors and certainly film industry professionals who have expertise in other forms of film finance, ostensibly because investors have not fared well with their investments in such film-financing vehicles. In some specific instances, it is entirely possible that greedy general partners or others help to create a situation in which excessive up-front fees or expenses are deducted from the offering proceeds, i.e., the monies raised through such limited partnership offerings, thus not leaving enough of such funds to actually produce the movie promised or envisioned. It is also possible that such excessive up-front payments to key people do not leave enough profit participation incentive to provide adequate motivation for the producer to negotiate a distribution deal that treats such passive investors fairly, i.e., the producer has a conflict of interest with such investors. It might just as accurately be pointed out, however, that the industry and distributor practices cited elsewhere in this book probably play an even more significant role (in most feature film limited partnership situations) in actually determining whether such investors recoup or see a reasonable profit on their investment. If, in fact, any feature film distributor engages in very many of the practices described herein, it is not likely that any profit participant including limited partnership investors are going to see any share of such profits (see "Business Practice," "Creative Accounting," "Disclosure Document" and "Stock Fraud").

FEATURE LENGTH. A full-length motion picture which is seventy-plus minutes. Feature films today generally do not run less than ninety minutes and are typically between ninety to one hundred twenty minutes. Exhibitors do not like longer motion pictures because they want to bring in a new ticket-buying audience which will spend more money on popcorn and other concessions (see "Feature" and "Running Time").

FEATURE MOTION PICTURE OR FEATURE FILM (see "Feature").

FEATURETTE. A behind-the-scenes look at the making of a given movie presented on film. Movie featurettes are made primarily for use on television for the purpose of promoting the movie on which it is based (see "Feature Length" and "Film Short").

FEDERAL I.D. NUMBER. An identification number which pursuant to IRS rules must be obtained by every business that pays wages to one or more employees. Such number must be used on the business' income tax return (see "Employer" and "Internal Revenue Service").

FEDERAL TAX DISCUSSION (same as "Tax Aspects").

FEDERAL TRADE COMMISSION (FTC). Federal administrative agency established in 1914 for the purposes of preventing misrepresentation and fraud in advertising, protecting consumers against unfair methods of competition and deceptive business practices and investigating and curbing violations of the anti-trust laws. The agency's Bureau of Competition is responsible for the enforcement of the anti-trust laws and it generally accomplishes its goals through civil remedies, i.e., its authority to order the offender to "cease and desist" from a prohibited practice. If its order is disobeyed, the FTC must then go to federal court to seek enforcement (see "Blurbs," "Business Practices," "Conduct Restrictions," "Fraud" and "U.S. Justice Department").

FEES. A charge for a service. One of the categories of feature film distribution expenses which is typically deductible from the distributor's gross receipts (see "Distribution Expenses," "Location Fee," "Location Permit," "Permits" and "Taxes").

FESTIVALS (see "Film Festivals").

FICTIONALIZATION. The act, process or product of converting a literary work into fiction, i.e., a story invented by imagination, e.g., taking a story based on an actual incident and writing a screenplay by changing the characters, the plot and details enough to justify its status as an original work of fiction (see "Clearance," "Docudrama," "Novelization" and "Release").

FICTITIOUS NAME. The name of a business that is different than the name of the business' owner (see "DBA," "Fictitious Name Filing" and "Sole Proprietorship").

FICTITIOUS NAME FILING. An application that is to be completed and placed among the records of the county courthouse of the county in which an unincorporated business is conducting its operations under a name other than the name of the business' owner. Corporations and limited partnerships, two other common forms of doing business besides the sole proprietorship, must clear their proposed names with the Secretary of State in the state of formation (see "DBA," "Fictitious Name" and "Sole Proprietorship").

FIDUCIARY. A person or entity having a legal duty, created by his, her or its undertaking, to act primarily for the benefit of another in matters connected with an undertaking, i.e., a person in a position of trust and confidence. General partners of limited partnerships are considered fiduciaries in their relationship with the limited partner investors. Under certain circumstances, feature film distributors may also be considered fiduciaries on behalf of all net profit participants (see "Conflicts of Interest," "General Partner," "Good Faith" and "Limited Partnership").

FIFTY/FIFTY FIRST DOLLAR SPLIT. A feature film distribution deal which consists of an equal 50/50 split of the distributor's gross receipts from the first dollar with no advance paid to the producer. This is a rare but desirable variation of the feature film distribution agreement from the producer's standpoint. The theory here is that since the producer financed the film and the distributor is financing the distribution, they are taking an approximately equal risk and should therefore share equally from first dollar (see "Fifty/Fifty Net Deal" and "First Dollar").

FIFTY/FIFTY NET DEAL. One of the negotiated divisions of net profits between a film producer and distributor. Such a division of revenue is generally made after distribution expenses have been recouped by the distributor and is rarely seen today (see "Fifty/Fifty First Dollar Split," "First Dollar Gross Deal," "Modified Gross Deal," "Seventy/Thirty Deal" and "Sliding Scale").

FILING FEES. Payments required to be made to state and federal securities regulatory authorities in public or private securities offerings. In public offerings, fees are generally required to be paid to the SEC, the NASD and to each state in which such securities are to be offered. In private placements, pursuant to Regulation D, for example, no filing fee is required to be paid to the SEC (with the Form D), but many states will require a filing fee be submitted along with other documents which are part of the required notice filing (see "Blue Sky Laws," "Conditions and Limitations," "Form D," "NASD," "Notice Filing," "Private Placement," "Public Offering," "Regulation D" and "SEC").

FILM. Raw stock used either for negative or positive prints, or, in a larger sense, a portion of or the total finished motion picture production (in this latter sense, the same as "Motion Picture;" see "Exposed Film").

FILM BUYER. A representative of an end user of feature films in the foreign marketplace who is responsible for negotiating the purchase of licensing rights to feature films for exploitation in the foreign territories and/or media represented (see "Booking Agent," "End

Users in the Foreign Markeplace," "Foreign Distribution" and "Foreign Sales Agent").

FILM CLIP (see "Clip").

FILM CLIP LICENSE. An agreement between one party (usually a production company) and the owner of the copyright to a motion picture or television program permitting the use of a brief segment of the motion picture or television program in a subsequent film or program. Such agreement grants permission to use the film clip in the second film (see "Clip," "License of Stills/Excerpts" and "Release").

FILM COMMISSIONS. Governmental agencies created primarily for the purpose of attracting film production activity to their jurisdiction (whether it be at the national, regional, state, county or local level) and in assisting filmmakers with the logistics of their local shoot, partly by acting as a liaison between the film company and the local community. Film commissions commonly promote the suitable film production locations within their jurisdiction to the film community, provide free location-scouting services and publish or promote directories of local production facilities and services. Such film commissions seldom engage in the more meaningful activities relating to facilitating financing of the production and/or distribution costs associated with feature films, which, in the long term, may tend to generate films that provide more favorable portrayals of the local area than those produced by outside financing sources and production entities with few if any local personal ties. Such governmental or quasi-governmental agencies are also generally not permitted to become involved in the issue of anti-blind bidding legislation (see "Anti-Blind Bidding Statutes," "Blind Bidding," "Economic Reprisal," "Film Festivals," "Lobbying," "Location Filming" and "Regulatory States").

FILM CREDITS (see "Credits").

FILM EXCHANGES. Regional film distribution centers from which many films are distributed to individual movie theatres in the region. Also companies which purchase leftover, unopened cans of raw stock from the major studios and, in turn, sell to producers for less than the manufacturer's charges (see "Distributor," "Exchange" and "Sub-Distributor").

FILM ELEMENTS (see "Elements").

FILM FESTIVALS. Special commercial, social and cultural events featuring the showings of numerous films which may be based on a specific theme, such as comedy or politics. Such festivals ordinarily take place in one city or location over a period of several days, may include film-related seminars, workshops, dinner programs and are usually climaxed by the presentation of commendations, awards and prizes (see "Cannes Film Festival").

FILM LABORATORY (see "Lab").

FILM LABORATORY AGREEMENT (see "Laboratory Film Processing Agreement").

FILM LIBRARY [see "Catalog (Library)"].

FILM LIBRARY VALUES (see "Library Values").

FILM LICENSING TERMS (see "Licensing Terms").

FILMMAKER. One who directly and individually handles and/or supervises all of the production steps necessary to create and produce a complete motion picture (see "Collaborative Process," "Director" and "Producer").

FILMMAKER'S RETURN. Another term for producer's net or producer's net profits, i.e., what is left for the filmmaker or the filmmaker's share of net film rentals after deferrals, investor obligations and other debts are paid (see "Gross Receipts," "Net Profits" and "Producer's Share").

FILM MARKET. A gathering of motion picture producers and distributors for the purpose of buying, selling and/or licensing film product (see "American Film Market," "MIFED" and "Cannes Film Festival").

FILM PACKAGE. A group of films that are being financed together or films being sold as a group to various media, e.g., independent television stations or foreign territories (see "Allocation Issues," "Packaging" and "Television Syndication").

FILM PACKAGE FINANCING. The funding of a multiple-film package or the activities relating to the packaging of a given film or the packaging of films for television syndication purposes (see "Packaging").

FILM RATING SYSTEM (see "MPAA" and "Ratings").

FILM RENTALS. The money owed and/or paid by an exhibitor to a distributor under a film's lease agreement, i.e., the monies paid by the exhibitor and/or earned and due to be paid to the distributor as rental fees for the right to license a film for public showing. Authorities do not seem to agree on this issue of "owed" versus "paid," thus most film distribution agreements do not even use the term "rentals" but instead use and contractually define the broader concept of "gross receipts." Film rentals are generally computed weekly on a consecutive seven-day basis (Wednesday through Tuesday or Friday through Thursday, depending on the day on which the film first opens in the market). Film rentals, as between the distributor and exhibitor, are negotiable and may be determined by several different methods, including a 90/10 basis, sliding scale, fixed percentage, minimums (floors) that relate specifically to the gross box-office receipts and a flat-fee basis that is a predetermined, unchanging amount. In many distributor/exhibitor contracts, the film rentals earned will change from week to week, with the distributor's relative share generally decreasing and the exhibitor's share increasing from the first through subsequent weeks. Quite often the exhibitor and distributor will negotiate a settlement amount for film rentals which is actually less than the actual amount owed by the exhibitor. The term also refers to the accumulated film rentals for a given film from all theatres in a market or all markets (also called "Distributor Film Rentals," "Fiduciary," "Gross Film Rentals" and "Gross Rentals;" contrast with "Gross Receipts;" see "Percentage Rentals," "Selling Subject to Review" and "Settlement Transaction").

FILM RENTAL PERCENTAGES. The division of box office receipts between the exhibitor and distributor following deductions for a second feature and cartoon, if any, for the exhibitor's expenses (contractual theatre overhead) and expressed as a percentage of the remaining box office net. While the major studio/distributors are able to extract distribution terms for a major motion picture which calls for the payment of 70% and more of the box office receipts (in a film's initial weeks of release), the industry average for all pictures is pegged at about 35% to 45% of box office receipts, depending on the type of motion picture and its distributor (see "Collection," "House Nut," "Gross Receipts," "Rentals," "Selling Subject to Review" and "Settlement Transactions").

FILM SCHOOLS. Colleges and universities which offer a degree program in film. Some of the better known film schools include New York University, the University of Southern California and the University of California at Los Angeles. Recent reports indicate film-study programs across the U.S. graduate some 26,000 students each year, but that only 5% to 10% of those graduates actually end up making a living in their chosen field. It may be possible that both the industry and the film schools are actively misrepresenting the promise of career opportunities in the film industry, that they are misleading some 23,400 individuals annually and persuading them to pretty much waste their undergraduate studies on subjects which are not likely to be of much value in their lives. The film industry, college and university administrations, and their professors all have a self-serving reason for actively or passively encouraging this fraud on unsuspecting students (see "Chasing a Dream," "Law of Supply and Demand" and "Pied Piper").

FILM SHORT. The DGA defines a short as any motion picture which when released is 2,700 linear feet or less in length on 35mm, or 1,080 linear feet or less in length on 16mm film. The WGA defines a short as a motion picture which, when released, is 3,600 linear feet or less in length. In some distributor/exhibitor deals, a percentage deduction from box office receipts is taken by the exhibitor for showing the film short (see "Feature Length").

FILM SPLITTING (see "Product Splitting").

FILM STARTS. The number of films for which principal photography has begun in a given geographical area, i.e., in a city, county, state, region or country (see "Film Commissions").

FILM STOCK. Unexposed and unprocessed rolls of film which come in standard roll-lengths of 100, 200, 400, 1000 and 2000 feet (see "Film").

FILM SUBSIDIES. A grant by a government to a film producer or production company to assist in the production of a film, i.e., for a film project deemed advantageous to the public (see "Foreign Subsidies," "Government Subsidies" and "Grants").

FINAL ANSWER PRINT (see "Answer Print").

FINAL COST STATEMENT. In the context of a production-financing/distribution agreement, the last accounting of expenses associated with the production of a motion picture as determined after all of the studio's departments and the production company have reported their costs on the picture to the studio's comptroller. The final cost statement is submitted by the studio to the production company and any bonus due the production company or others based on the size of the remaining balance in the production account is paid (see "Bonus," "Production Account" and "Rising Production Costs").

FINAL CUT. The last fine-tuning of a motion picture immediately following acceptance of the fine cut version, wherein the sound is mixed and the picture conformed and made ready for the lab to run off the answer print. The final cut is the finished version of the work print to which the negative is conformed in order to strike the release prints that are to be exhibited in theatres. Who has the ultimate authority to approve this version of a film is a significant negotiating point between producers and directors and also between producers and distributors. Many film distribution agreements provide that the distributor has sole discretion to edit the film as it sees fit. Producers generally want to limit the rights of distributors to edit the film without the producer's approval to certain situations, i.e., to meet censorship and MPAA rating requirements (see "Answer Print," "Creative Control," "Discretion," "Editing Rights" and "Marketplace of Ideas").

FINAL CUT DIRECTOR. A motion picture director who has the ability to negotiate a provision in a distribution agreement authorizing him or her to control the final editing of the film for all or certain specified versions of the picture, e.g., for the domestic theatrical release (see "Editing Rights" and "Final Cut").

FINAL DRAFT. The last version of a completed screenplay prepared by the screenwriter(s) prior to the shooting script and any directorial changes (see "Draft Script or Screenplay," "Polish," "Revision" and "Shooting Script").

FINAL JUDGMENT. The decision of a trial court which prevents the relitigation of a matter. The finality of a judgment may be overturned on appeal, and the matter is then returned to a trial court for redetermination. Many feature film distribution agreements require the producer to reimburse the distributor for legal fees if the producer files a lawsuit against the distributor but fails to obtain a final judgment against the distributor. The producer may want to consider making such a requirement reciprocal, but even more important, if possible, the producer may want to eliminate the "final judgment" requirement altogether since most lawsuits are settled prior to "final judgment" and substantial legal fees may have been incurred (see "Litigation" and "Sue Us").

FINAL MARKETING OUTLET. The retail level of a business. In the feature film theatrical business, exhibition is the final marketing outlet. From 1940 to 1948 (most of the years during which the Paramount case was being litigated) the major studio/distributors of that period produced about 62% of the films and distributed approximately 71% of the domestic films released. The major studio/distributors gained effective indirect control of feature film production through their control of first run theatres. By monopolizing the final marketing outlet, they successfully curtailed entry by independent producers. The Paramount Consent Decree was partly intended to weaken the market dominance of the major studio/distributors. But, in the last ten years or so (a period which has witnessed relaxed U.S.

Justice Department enforcement of anti-trust laws in the entertainment industry), the feature films distributed by the current group of major studio/distributors generate about 93% of the domestic box office gross in any given year (see "Barriers to Entry," "MPAA Cartel," "Major Exhibition Chains," "Merger Guidelines," "Number of Screens," "Paramount Consent Decree of 1948" and "TriStar Case").

FINAL PRINT (same as "Release Print").

FINAL PROSPECTUS. The portion of the effective registration statement delivered in advance to all prospective purchasers of securities in a public offering (see "Disclosure Document," "Prospectus" and "Red Herring").

FINAL SCREENPLAY (same as "Shooting Script;" see "First Draft," "Polish" and "Revision").

FINAL SHOOTING SCRIPT. A completed film script which has been broken down and re-organized in accordance with the manner in which the film will be shot (same as "Shooting Script").

FINANCE CHARGES. Any charge for an extension of credit including interest, service or carrying charges, loan fees or finders fees, fees for credit investigations and charges protecting the creditor against default. Finance charges are also subject to state prohibitions against usury (see "Interest" and "Usury").

FINANCIAL ACCOUNTING STANDARDS BOARD (FASB). An independent, Connecticut-based entity or board, formed in 1973, which makes the rules for accountants relating to establishing and interpreting generally accepted accounting principles. The FASB succeeded and continued the activities of the Accounting Principles Board (see "Creative Accounting," "FASB Statement No. 34," "FASB Statement No. 53," "FASB Statement 96" and "GAAP").

FINANCIAL CONDITION (see "Financial Position").

FINANCIAL FORECASTS. Prospective financial statements that present, to the best of the responsible party's knowledge and belief, an entity's expected financial position, results of operations, and changes in financial position. A financial forecast is based on the responsible party's assumptions reflecting conditions it expects to exist and the course of action it expects to take. A financial forecast may be expressed in specific monetary amounts as a single-point estimate of forecasted results or as a range, where the responsible party selects key assumptions to form a range within which it reasonably expects, to the best of its knowledge and belief, the item or items subject to the assumptions to actually fall. When a forecast contains a range, the range should not be selected in a biased or misleading manner, e.g., a range in which one end is significantly less expected than the other (see "Assumptions," "Computer Model," "Financial Projections," "Limited Use," "Partial Presentations," "Profit Projections," "Pro Forma Financial Statements," "Prospective Financial Statements" and "Responsible Party").

FINANCIAL INSTITUTION. An organization that collects funds from the public to place in financial assets such as stocks, bonds, money market instruments, bank deposits or loans (see "Bank" and "Lender Financing").

FINANCIAL LEVERAGE (see "Leverage").

FINANCIAL MANAGEMENT. The direction of the fiscal aspects of a business. Some financial analysts say that a commonly held notion about the film industry is false, i.e., that the primary reason for most of the recent film production company bankruptcies is the failure of their motion pictures to perform at the box office. Instead, such analysts point to improper financial management (e.g., increasing rather than decreasing debt during good times) as one of several reasons for such failures. Other reasons cited include the failure to use sophisticated computerized financial modeling on a continuous basis and the abandonment of successful actions (while substituting new, untried ideas without first piloting them with limited financial commitments). Other industry observers suggest that improper financial management may be irrelevant in an industry that is so dominated by a few major players who have long-standing reputations for engaging in numerous questionable business practices (see "Anti-Competitive Practices," "Barriers to Entry," "Business Practices," "Computer Model," "Conscious Parallelism," "Creative Accounting," "Debt," "Financial Modeling" and "Reciprocal Preferences").

FINANCIAL MODELING. The design and manipulation of mathematical representations of an economic system or corporate financial applications so that the effect of various proposed changes can be studied and forecast (see "Computer Model," "Financial Forecasts," "Financial Projections" and "Mental Modeling").

FINANCIAL PERFORMANCE. The effectiveness and achievements of an individual or entity in the business world, specifically as such performance relates to fiscal matters (see "Bottom Line" and "Profit Margin").

FINANCIAL POSITION. The status of a firm's assets, liabilities and equity accounts as of a certain time, as shown on such firm's financial statement (also called "Financial Condition").

FINANCIAL PROJECTIONS. The hypothetical results of an investment in a film (structured as a limited partnership offering or otherwise) in the event that certain stated assumptions prove accurate. Financial projections are estimates (based on reasonable assumptions) of the future financial results of an investment and its activities relating to the production, distribution and exploitation of a film or films. Financial projections are prospective financial statements presenting one or more hypothetical courses of action for evaluation based on the responsible party's assumptions reflecting conditions it expects would exist and the course of action it expects would be taken, given one or more hypothetical assumptions. The estimate of financial results may be based on assumptions that are not necessarily the most likely. In a film offering, such assumptions may include, among other items, assumed numbers for domestic theatrical box office gross, exhibitor's take, distribution fees and expenses, projected revenues from all other markets, partnership expenses including deferments, if any, along with the various percentage participations of the partners and others. The SEC provides guidelines for financial projections used in conjunction with a public/registered offering (see "Financial Forecasts," "Limited Use," "Partial Presentations," "Profit Projections," "Pro Forma Financial Statements," "Prospective Financial Statements" and "Responsible Party").

FINANCIAL RESOURCES. Available means to capitalize the activities of a business. The major studio/distributors have traditionally possessed the financial resources to distribute a sufficient number of films each year to satisfy the exhibition needs of the most important theatre chains, to fund their films' costly advertising and promotional campaigns, to maintain nation-wide distribution networks and to bear the large losses which films sometimes generate (see "Barriers to Entry," "Capital-Intensive Business" and "Major Exhibition Chains" and "Major Studio/Distributors").

FINANCIAL RISKS. The possibilities associated with the investment of funds in a business activity that such funds will not be recouped or will not be returned in sufficient amount to justify the original investment (see "Lender Risk Elimination" and "Risk Factors").

FINANCIAL STANDINGS. The rankings of corporate fiscal attributes by industry analysts including total revenue, operating margins, net income, long-term debt, return on investment, current assets, current liabilities and cash flow margins (see "Industry Analysts" and "Paul Kagan Associates, Inc.").

FINANCIAL STATEMENT. A written record of the financial status of an individual, association or business organization, including a balance sheet and an income statement (operating statement or profit and loss statement). The financial statement may also include a statement of changes in working capital and net worth (see "Balance Sheet" and "Net Worth").

FINANCIAL SUPERMARKET. A large brokerage firm that offers a wide variety of financial services and investments to a wide variety of clients (see "Boutique").

FINANCIERS OR FINANCING SOURCE. Persons or entities which raise or provide development, production and/or distribution monies or financing for a given movie or movies. A movie financier or financing source may be active or passive with respect to his, her or its involvement in the project. Financiers may be investors. The use of financing from a passive financier or investor usually indicates that a securities offering is involved, and thus compliance with the federal and state securities laws is mandated. Major motion picture studio/distributors may serve as facilities lessors and distributors as well as financiers (see "Investor," "Broker/Dealer," "Finder," "Securities" and "Studio").

FINANCING. The techniques or activities involved in obtaining or raising the monies required to pay the expenses incurred in the various phases of a business, e.g., the stages of motion picture development, production and/or distribution. The most substantial blocks of feature film financing are typically provided through [1] studio financing, which in a broader sense is distributor (or, as some prefer, "employer") financing, [2] bank loans (which usually require bankable pre-sale and/or distributor commitments; also some production money lenders are not banks), [3] co-production or joint venture financing in which two or more industry individuals or entities combine funds to finance the production of a film in which the co-production or joint venture parties are actively involved, [4] passive investor financing provided through various securities vehicles such as corporations, limited partnerships or investment contracts offered to the investing public either through public/registered or private/exempt offerings, or [5] various forms of international financing. A limited number of grants are also made available through some organizations but are generally not significant dollars relative to the costs of producing a feature film for theatrical release (see "Bank Loan," "Co-Production Financing," "Corporation," "Distributor Commitments," "Distributor Financing," "Investment Contract," "Joint

Venture Financing," "Limited Partnership," "Outside Investors," "Passive Investor Financing," "Pre-Sales," "Public Offering" and "Private Offering," "Production-Financing/Distribution Agreement," "Single Picture Financing," "Split Rights Deals" and "Studio Financing").

FINANCING DATE. The date upon which the producer receives its requisite production financing for a given picture. Sometimes this date is used in calculating the producer's delivery date in a distribution agreement (see "Delivery" and "Start Date").

FINANCING ENTITY. The individual or firm that is putting up the production costs for a motion picture. A financing entity rarely commits to production financing without a substantially developed package, i.e., a completed screenplay (or the rights to an existing literary property) and commitments from stars and director, along with a detailed production budget and shooting schedule (see "Financing" and "Package").

FINANCING FEES. Monies paid to the financing entity which provided or arranged for the production financing for a motion picture (see "Financing," "Financing Entity," "Finder's Fee" and "Executive Producer Fee").

FINANCING OPTIONS. The alternative forms of film finance (see "Financing").

FINANCING UNIT. A separate entity, typically a subsidiary corporation, created primarily for the purpose of raising capital for the production of the movies of the parent corporate film production company. Such a separate corporation may be able to sell its stock (thus raising production funds) and participate in a joint venture with the parent producing entity without diluting the ownership interests of the parent's shareholders (see "Corporate Stock," "Dilution" and "Equity").

FINDER. A person who brings together the buyer and seller in a transaction. Many state securities laws place severe restrictions on the payment of any form of transaction-related remuneration to persons who are not licensed as securities broker/dealers, i.e., finders, in certain transactions involving the offer or sale of securities. No such restrictions are involved in active investor transactions (see "Active Investor Vehicle," "Business Plan, "Finder's Fee," "Passive Investor Vehicle," "Private Offering" and "Securities").

FINDER AGREEMENT. The written contract between a feature film producer (or production company) and a person (or entity) who is not licensed as a securities broker/dealer which sets out the terms and conditions under which such person/entity may participate in the finding of funds for a film project or film production entity (see "Finder").

FINDER SALES. A method of raising funds relating to film finance and one of three methods of marketing securities, although a misnomer since the actual sale in securities transactions must be conducted through the issuer, i.e., the finder's activities should be limited to merely bringing the buyer and seller together (see "Active Investor Vehicle," "Broker/Dealer Sales," "Finder," "Issuer Sales," "Passive Investor Vehicle" and "Securities).

FINDER'S FEE. A negotiated fee or commission paid to an individual or organization for "finding" what the other party needs or desires. In the film industry, such a fee may be paid for finding a buyer for the purchase of a literary property or finding a financier for the production of a film. If a security is involved (i.e., passive investors), many state laws severely limit the activities of such finders and/or the payment of such fees to persons who are not licensed as securities broker/dealers (see "Active Investor Vehicle," "Finder," "Finder Agreement" and "Passive Investor Vehicle").

FINE CUT. A more refined version of the work print and the version which follows the rough cut. At each successive stage in the editing of a film, the cutting is refined and unnecessary footage is eliminated (see "Workprint").

FINE-GRAIN. Film emulsions in which the grain size is smaller or finer than the older-type emulsions commonly employed prior to the mid-'30s. Fine-grain film is usually slower (requiring more exposure) than other films (see "Film" and "Film Stock").

FINE-GRAIN DUPE. A dupe negative made from a master positive which was taken from the original black and white negative. Also a dupe negative made directly by using the contact reversal-printing process from the original black and white negative (see "Fine-Grain," "Negative" and "Print").

FINE-GRAIN MASTER POSITIVE. The film processing step (in black and white) that comes after the original black and white negative. This processing step both protects the original and allows printing of optical effects (see "Fine-Grain" and "Optical Effects").

FIRM. A broad term describing a business entity and including a corporation, partnership or proprietorship (see "Corporation," "Entity," "Person" and "Natural Person").

FIRM COMMITMENT. A securities offering in which the underwriter agrees to purchase the entire offering and resell it to the public (see

"All or None," "Best Efforts Offering," "Broker/Dealer," "Selling Concession" and "Underwriting Spread").

FIRM LEASE AGREEMENT. A film lease agreement which is not subject to adjustment (see "Selling Subject to Review" and "Settlement Transaction").

FIRST-ANSWER PRINT. The first conformed and sound-mixed composite print prepared by the film laboratory. This print is checked by the lab timer and the film's producer and/or director for correct and satisfactory color timings, sound-printing and synchronization (see "Collaborative Process" and "Print").

FIRST ASSISTANT CAMERAPERSON. The film production person responsible for maintaining and cleaning all elements in the camera package, setting up the camera with the appropriate lens and filters for each shot, and setting the lens stop and focus for each shot (see "Cinematographer" and "Director of Photography").

FIRST ASSISTANT DIRECTOR. The person whose work on a film involves specifically managing the pre-production preparation, including organizing the crew, securing equipment, breaking down the script (or storyboard) and preparing the strip-board and shooting schedule. During production, he or she assists the director with respect to the on-set production details, coordinates and supervises crew and cast activities, organizes and facilitates the flow of production activity [see "Director (Film)" and "Second Assistant Director"].

FIRST DOLLAR. The earliest monies that a film generates following its release, i.e., the first monies received by the distributor. Distributors will seek to draft a distribution deal which will allow them to deduct their fees and expenses from these first monies. Also, gross profit participants, if any, by definition will have a right to take their percentage from these earliest funds (subject to contractually defined deductions). Others who may seek to negotiate for a participation in such first monies include investors (possibly until recoupment), deferred salaried talent, lenders and film labs (see "Adjusted Gross," "Fifty/Fifty First Dollar Split," "Gross Receipts" and "Net Profit").

FIRST DOLLAR DEAL. Generally, a type of distribution agreement which provides that revenues generated from the exploitation of a film are divided amongst the participants starting with the very first dollars returned to the distributor, i.e., after settlement with the exhibitors but before any distributor fees or expenses are deducted. In the current marketplace, first dollar deals occur rarely, if ever (see "First Dollar Gross Deal" and "Net Deal").

FIRST DOLLAR GROSS (see "First Dollar," "First Dollar Deal" and "First Position Gross").

FIRST DOLLAR GROSS DEAL. A specific and rare distribution deal which provides that the producer gets approximately 25% to 30% of the distributor's gross until a multiple of print and ad expenditures is reached, at which point the producer's share escalates to approximately 65% (see "Modified Gross Deal" and "Net Deal").

FIRST DRAFT. The first complete version of a motion picture screenplay in continuity form including full dialogue. A first draft is usually longer than the final draft (see "Polish" and "Shooting Script").

FIRST DRAFT SCRIPT BREAKDOWN (see "First Draft," "Production Board," "Production Breakdown" and "Shooting Script").

FIRST-GENERATION DUPE. A reversal print made from a reversal-stock original or master tape, often for the purpose of producing further prints or tapes, which are known as second-generation dupes (see "Print").

FIRST LOOK DEAL. A studio development deal in which the studio provides development financing or other assistance to a producer on a film project or projects in exchange for the studio having the right of first refusal on further development, production and/or distribution of the film (see "Overall Deal" and "Right of First Refusal").

FIRST MONIES (see "First Dollar" and "First Dollar Deal").

FIRST NEGOTIATION RIGHT (see "Right of First Negotiation").

FIRST OPTION (same as "First Look Deal").

FIRST POSITION GROSS. A share of the gross receipts or total revenues from a given source or stage in a movie's revenue stream, such as film rentals or home video, which is accounted for before distribution fees, distribution expenses, negative costs or other gross participations are deducted. First position is generally considered to be the most sought-after participation in a movie deal, but it is seldom awarded by movie studio/distributors, except to a handful of the most-recognized talent in the industry. To the extent that anyone other than the distributor is participating in distributor gross receipts in a first position, chances for that film generating net profits are substantially diminished (also called "First Dollar Gross;" see "Gross Receipts" and "Video Corridor").

FIRST-RUN. The initial exhibition of a motion picture in a designated geographic area for a specified period of time, i.e., the opening cycle in the exhibition of a motion picture or the first release of a film in a major market area. The "first run" of a motion picture usually is booked as a single feature (except at drive-ins), and as the release of the movie continues (or earlier if the picture does not perform well), it may be double-billed in so-called sub-run markets (see "Booking," "Double-Bill," "First-Run Date" and "First-Run Theatre").

FIRST-RUN DATE. The specific period of time during which a motion picture is initially exhibited in major market areas (see "First-Run" and "First-Run Theatre").

FIRST-RUN SYNDICATION. The initial showing of a motion picture in the off-network market (see "Off-Network" and "Television Syndication").

FIRST-RUN THEATRE. A theatre that primarily exhibits films on those films' first run, i.e., the better theatres in the major market areas (see "Final Marketing Outlet," "First-Run" and "First-Run Date).

FIRST-RUN ZONING. Arbitrary, fixed rankings of exhibitors for film releases. In other words, not all theatre owners have the same opportunity to show movies at their theatres on the first run of certain motion pictures. The major studio/distributors have resorted to what in effect is "tier releasing," i.e., the categorization of exhibitors based on the arbitrary judgment of the distributors and the releasing of the distributors' films only to the "more desirable" theatres first while denying the less desirable theatres an opportunity to exhibit such films until later in the film's release schedule, if at all. First-run zoning was one of the conduct restrictions of the Paramount Consent Decree (see "Admission Price Discrimination," "Blind Bidding," "Block Booking," "Conduct Restrictions," "Five O'Clock Look," "Paramount Consent Decree of 1948" and "TriStar Case").

FIRST SALE DOCTRINE. A legal doctrine which imposes a limit on a copyright owner's exclusive distribution rights of a literary property that has been copyrighted. The doctrine states that the lawful owner of a copy or the literary property itself may sell, rent or otherwise dispose of that copy or property without the authority of the copyright owner and that, in the absence of any contrary contractual restrictions, this owner (e.g., a video rental store which contracted with the copyright owner for a videocassette of a movie) may resell it or rent it without any further financial obligation to the copyright owner, e.g., the producer or distributor. This doctrine has permitted the video stores to rent film videos repeatedly without paying further compensation to the video distributor/wholesaler (see "Copyright," "Pay-Per-Transaction" and "Video Rights Agreement").

FIRST THEATRICAL RELEASE. The initial distribution of a feature film to theatres (see "Theatrical Release").

FISCAL. Of or pertaining to financial transactions (see "Fiscal Year").

FISCAL YEAR. Any twelve-month period used by business as its fiscal accounting period (see "Fiscal").

FIVE O'CLOCK LOOK. An unethical business practice allegedly engaged in by some distributors who wait until the exhibitor bids for the first-run of an about-to-be-released film are in, then the distributor calls an exhibitor to whom the distributor would like to award the movie and reports the highest bid received for the film to that point from the favored exhibitor's competitors. The distributor then allows that exhibitor to come in late with a higher bid and awards the first-run of the movie to the late (and highest) bidder. Such a practice obviously favors the financially stronger theatre chains (see "Bid," "Blind Bidding," "Closed Bidding," "Conduct Restrictions," "Predatory Practices," "Selling Subject to Review" and "Unethical Business Practices").

FIXED ASSET. Tangible property used in the operations of a business but not expected to be consumed or converted into cash in the ordinary course of events; normally represented on a company's balance sheet at the fixed asset's net depreciated value (see "Asset" and "Capitalize").

FIXED BONUS. A specific and negotiated amount of compensation which is awarded to a person who provides services in the production of a motion picture, if the film generates a specified level of gross revenues at the domestic theatrical box office or achieves a specified level of distributor gross receipts (see "Contingent Compensation" and "Escalating Contingent Compensation").

FIXED CAPITAL. The amount of capital permanently invested in a business (see "Capital").

FIXED COSTS. Expenses that remain constant regardless of sales volume, e.g., executive salaries, interest expense, rent, depreciation and insurance costs (see "Direct Distribution Expenses" and "Overhead").

FIXED DEFERMENT. A specified amount of all or some of agreed upon compensation, i.e., not based on a percentage, which is to be paid after the services for which the payment is being made have been performed and after the time at which such compensation might otherwise be paid (see "Contingent Compensation," "Contingent Deferments," "Deferments" or "Deferrals" and "Percentage Participation" or "Points").

FIXED INSTALLMENTS. Periodic payments of a specific amount of money. Pursuant to the terms of a production-financing/distribution agreement, a studio/distributor may advance funds to the production company for the production of a picture up to the total of the approved production budget, and, if required thereafter, up to and including the contingency, in fixed installments and consistent with a cash flow schedule mutually approved by the production company and the studio/distributor (see "Approved Production Budget," "Cash Flow Schedule," "Contingency" and "Mutual Approval").

FIXED PRICE. In a public offering of new securities, the price at which investment bankers in the underwriting syndicate agree to sell the issue to the public. In contract law, a type of contract where the price is preset and invariable regardless of the actual costs of production (see "Price Fixing," "Public Offering" and "Securities").

FIXED RATE LOAN. A loan in which the interest rate does not fluctuate with general market conditions (see "Lender Financing").

FIXED WORK. In copyright terminology, a work is fixed in a tangible medium of expression and therefore is copyrightable when its embodiment in a copy or phonorecord, by or under the authority of the author, is sufficiently permanent or stable to permit it to be perceived, reproduced or otherwise communicated for a period of more than transitory duration (see "Copyright" and "Fair Use").

FLAT DOLLAR PAYMENTS. Disbursement of a specific amount of money. Some executives of the major studio/distributors and other industry spokespersons who consistently champion the studio view on industry issues complain that union and guild requirements calling for flat dollar payments as residuals on syndicated programming (as opposed to the percentage residuals paid for the same programs carried on basic pay cable) have contributed to a declining syndication market. These spokespersons suggest that the unions and guilds should bring this component of their required residual payments into alignment with current economic realities by modifying their residual packages and converting their flat dollar payment requirements into payments based on percentages of revenue (see "Collective Bargaining Agreements," "Guild," "Residuals" and "Syndicated Films").

FLAT FEE OR FLAT RATE. A set and unchanging amount of money or fee paid for services rendered or a product. In a film context, a flat rate most often appears in the negotiations between producers and cast or crew. No overtime is paid on a flat rate as opposed to weekly or hourly rates (see "Flat Rentals" and "Outright Sale").

FLAT RENTALS. Compensation paid by a film's exhibitor to the distributor on a weekly basis at a pre-determined amount, i.e., not based on a percentage of the film's box office (see "Film Rentals" and "Percentage Rentals").

FLAT SALE. A term used in certain feature film distribution agreements which is contractually defined to refer to a license for theatrical exhibition of a motion picture for a period in excess of two years for a territory or area in consideration of the payment of a specified amount of money not fixed by a percentage of the buyer's receipts. As thus defined, flat sale does not apply to the customary manner in which motion pictures are licensed to most exhibitors in the U.S. and Canada but is more typical of motion picture rights sales in most of the foreign markets, although not necessarily the top foreign markets (see "Outright Sale").

FLAT WORLDWIDE DISTRIBUTION FEE. A fixed percentage charged by a feature film distributor for distributing a film in all media throughout the world. Such fees are associated with rent-a-system transactions and the percentages tend to fall in the 15% to 20% range (see "Rent-A-Distributor").

FLIP-FLOP. That point when special allocations of tax attributes between general and limited partners in a limited partnership terminate. Thereafter, the sharing of tax attributes reflects a new relationship between the general and limited partners in which the general partners' profit-sharing percentage usually is increased substantially (see "Limited Partnership" and "Payout").

FLOAT. Amount of unrestricted securities of a given issuer publicly available for trading (see "Public Offering").

FLOATING EXCHANGE RATE. The movement of a foreign currency exchange rate in response to changes in the market forces of supply and demand. Currencies strengthen or weaken based on a nation's reserves of hard currency and gold, its international trade balance, its rate of inflation and interest rates and the general strength of its economy (see "Exchange Rate Movements").

FLOOR. A lower limit. In the context of a distributor/exhibitor agreement, the minimum percentage of box office gross the distributor is entitled to receive, regardless of the exhibitor's operating expenses, i.e., a minimum weekly percentage of a film's gross box office receipts which the film's lease agreement guarantees the distributor will receive as film rental regardless of the theatre's house allowance. Floors may be subject to adjustment, i.e., reduced over the course of the film's engagement, and may range from 70% to 25%. Also, in negotiating with a bank for a loan, a producer may seek a floor and a ceiling on interest rates to fix the financing costs within a certain range. Producers may also seek to negotiate a gross floor in the distribution agreement or, if third-party participations are being deducted from net profits (or the producer's share), the producer may want to insert a floor to keep such participations from falling below a specified percentage (see "Box Office Gross," "Ceiling," "Film Rentals," "Gross Floor," "Hard Floor," "House Nut" and "Soft Floor").

FLYERS. Advertising circulars for mass distribution (see "Advertising" and "Direct Advertising").

FOCUS GROUPS. A gathering of people for the purpose of reviewing and discussing their reactions to a motion picture or its proposed advertising campaign, e.g., focus groups are sometimes used to determine which feature film poster design is more appealing or best represents the film being marketed (see "Advertising Campaign").

FOLEY STAGE RECORDING. The registering of artificially created motion picture sounds on tape in a specially designed recording studio that has facilities to project picture and sound simultaneously while recording new sounds which are being created by the so-called foley artists. The foley stage is a large room with various types of floor surfaces and other objects used to create most of the sound effects for a motion picture (see "Sound Effects").

FORCE MAJEURE CLAUSE. A provision in contracts which is intended to excuse a party from performance of its obligations in the event that such performance is prevented by forces outside the control of such party. Typically, such events or forces are partially specified and may include strikes, labor disturbances, acts of God, etc., and then will include a catchall phrase at the end e.g., ". . . or other force majeure." The provision may provide for the suspension, extension or termination of the agreement if the event of force majeure continues beyond a specified period of time (see "Abbreviated Force Majeure Clause").

FORECASTING. Projecting current trends using existing data (see "Computer Modeling," Financial Forecasts," "Financial Projections" and "Pro Forma").

FOREIGN BANKS. Banks headquartered outside the U.S. (see "Lender Financing" and "Split Rights Deals").

FOREIGN BELOW-THE-LINE DEALS. Film finance transactions in which a foreign government offers to provide the crew, locations, local cast, studio facilities, cameras or some combination thereof to cover a certain percentage of a film's below-the-line costs. In exchange, the foreign government will typically ask for distribution rights in their own country (and sometimes in neighboring countries) and that a significant portion of the film be shot in the host country. U.S. producers who have taken advantage of these programs report that the film stock is generally not included, the cameras are generally not that good, and it is best for producers to take their own lighting (see "Facilities Subsidies").

FOREIGN COMPETITION. Business rivals based outside the United States. The experience of other U.S. industries in recent years has convinced some observers that the motion picture industry is not immune from the impact of reduced productivity and foreign competition (see "Reduced Productivity").

FOREIGN CONTRACTS. The written agreements between foreign theatrical distributors or representatives of other foreign film markets and movie producers which banks may consider lending against. Generally, U.S. banks are not as willing to lend against such foreign contracts because it is more difficult to determine the credit-worthiness of such foreign businesses and more difficult to perfect the U.S. banks' security interest in the foreign collateral (see "Domestic Contracts").

FOREIGN CORPORATION. A corporation chartered under the laws of a state other than the one in which it is conducting business (also called "Out of State Corporation").

FOREIGN CURRENCY DEAL. Film financing arrangement in which a foreign country, e.g., an Eastern European nation, will offer to provide goods and production services for below-the-line costs for a small amount of so-called hard currency (i.e., U.S. dollars). Such deals, however, usually mean that the film's producer will have to successfully negotiate through a difficult and archaic bureaucratic system, that the technical production expertise and equipment made available is not up to par, that living standards may be unacceptable to many of the film's above-the-line personnel, and that extraordinary logistical problems will be created. Producers experienced with these sorts of arrangements suggest that location desirability must be the more important consideration over saving money (see "Exchange Rate" and "Facilities Subsidies").

FOREIGN DEBT CAPITALIZATION PROGRAMS. Financial arrangements formally adopted by numerous third-world countries that owe large amounts of debt to foreign banks which encourage the purchase of the foreign country's debt at a significant discount and exchanging it for foreign currency to be used for film production activities in the foreign country. A U.S. producer seeking to take advantage of such programs must contact the U.S. office of an official representative of such foreign country and complete an application. Once approved, the foreign currency is contributed to a corporation incorporated in that foreign country, the stock of which is owned by the U.S. producer (see "Debt").

FOREIGN DISTRIBUTION. The theatrical licensing, exploitation and/ or sales of a film in markets outside the market in which the film was produced. For U.S. produced films, foreign distribution involves theatrical exhibition and/or sales outside the U.S. and Canada (see "Domestic Theatrical Release," "Foreign Markets" and "Foreign Sales Agents").

FOREIGN EQUITY FINANCING. Film funding provided by foreign sources (non-U.S.) in exchange for an ownership interest or profit participation in the film or films financed or in the entity producing such film(s). In addition to requiring an equity participation in the film's receipts, foreign equity investors may also require that the rights relating to the exploitation of the film in certain territories be reserved for them (see "Financing").

FOREIGN EQUITY INVESTMENT. A movie financing arrangement in which the motion picture producer actually co-ventures the production with a foreign partner, i.e., the foreign investor becomes the financial and/or creative partner of the domestic producer. When such foreign partners are industry insiders in their home market, they often can provide expertise in exploiting the film or films in that territory and in guiding a particular film production through complex governmental bureaucracy. Thus, movies that are at least considered a part domestic production in such foreign countries may be accorded some favoritism when such a foreign partner is aboard (see "Financing" and "International Co-Production").

FOREIGN EXCHANGE SERVICES. Banking services relating to the exchange of foreign currencies (see "Currency Conversion").

FOREIGN FACILITIES DEALS (see "Foreign Below-the-Line Deals").

FOREIGN FILM. From the perspective of someone who is primarily involved in the U.S. film business, films produced by a production entity based outside the U.S. (see "Foreign Corporation" and "Production Company").

FOREIGN FILM RENTAL. The money owed and/or paid to a film's distributor under the various film licensing agreements relating to the exploitation of the motion picture in foreign territories (see "Film Rentals" and "Restricted Currencies").

FOREIGN FINANCING. Film funding of all types (debt and equity) originating from foreign (non-U.S.) sources (see "Financing").

FOREIGN GOVERNMENT GRANTS OR SUBSIDIES. Specific donations by non-U.S. governments to filmmakers to assist in the production of a film which is deemed advantageous to the country or a given locale within the country that is served by that government, e.g., production of the movie will provide jobs and help the economy in a given area or the movie will provide favorable publicity for the locale (see "Facilities Subsidies").

FOREIGN LICENSING DEAL. A movie distribution agreement with a foreign entity and providing for the exhibition of a movie in a foreign territory (see "Foreign Market").

FOREIGN MARKET. Non-domestic geographical area of demand for films. Films are usually sold on a country-by-country basis outside the U.S. and Canada and all rights, i.e., television, video, etc. are included (see "Domestic Theatrical Market").

FOREIGN OWNERSHIP. Possession and title held by non-U.S. based individuals or entities; in a business context, top-level management and title to a company's assets held by persons or entities based in a non-U.S. country. Major U.S. studio/distributors have been purchased in recent years by Italian, Australian and Japanese interests (see "Corporate Stock" and "Equity").

FOREIGN POTENTIAL. The prospects of a film with regard to its appeal to foreign audiences. Certain types of films do better in foreign markets than others (see "Action/Adventure," "Genre" and "Physical Comedy").

FOREIGN PRE-SALES AND AGREEMENTS. Contracts to provide cash advances or commitments (hopefully bankable or lendable commitments) to purchase a film for distribution in a given foreign market provided prior to the film's completion (see "Foreign Sales Agents" and "Pre-Sales").

FOREIGN PRODUCTION PROBLEMS. Common difficulties that arise in the production of a feature film at non-U.S. locations, e.g., restrictive regulations relating to cast, crew and the script, language barriers, frequent delays, unstable governments, riots, civil war and less-than-adequate housing facilities for the cast and crew (see "International Co-Production" and "Pro and Con Analysis").

FOREIGN PURCHASERS. For purposes of compliance with the federal Regulation D securities registration exemption, offers and sales of securities to foreign persons made outside the U.S. effected in a manner that will result in the securities coming to rest abroad may be excluded from the Regulation D numerical limitation on the number of investors (see "Counting Rules" and "Regulation D").

FOREIGN RECEIPTS. Monies earned by exploitation of a film outside the U.S. and received by the distributor. It is important for the producer and other profit participants to clarify at what point foreign receipts are to be included as part of the distributor's gross receipts, i.e., when profit participants will receive the benefit of the collection of foreign receipts which could but have not been remitted to the U.S. (see "Foreign Tax Credits" and "Remitted or Remittable").

FOREIGN RECEIVABLES. Monies owed to a producer or distributor from non-domestic sources (see "Domestic Receivables").

FOREIGN REVENUES. The total income produced by the exploitation of feature films outside the domestic marketplace. Although foreign revenues have grown in recent years, that growth appears to be leveling off ("Revenue Sources").

FOREIGN SALES (see "Foreign Distribution").

FOREIGN SALES AGENTS. Persons or entities authorized to sell rights and to exploit a film on behalf of the producer on a country-by-country or market by market basis in the non-domestic territories. Most foreign sales agents do not cross-collateralize the profits of a single film between markets. However, any group of films sold as a package to a foreign territory may raise allocation issues which are effectively the same as cross-collateralization. Typically foreign sales agents will charge a 25% fee if an advance is given to the producer but a 15% fee if no advance is provided (see "Cross-Collateralization," "Foreign Distribution" and "Foreign Sales Representative").

FOREIGN SALES REPRESENTATIVE. The person or entity authorized by a film's distributor or producer to sell rights to the film and exploit the film in foreign markets; a broader term than "foreign sales agent" including both "foreign sales agents" and "foreign distributors" (see "Cross-Collateralization," "Foreign Distribution" and "Foreign Sales Agents").

FOREIGN SUBSIDIES. Film subsidies granted by foreign governments, i.e., not any governmental unit within the U.S. Such subsidies usually require that most of the film be shot in the subsidizing country, using almost exclusively native technicians, facilities and actors (see "Film Subsidies," "Foreign Tax Shelters," "Government Subsidies," "Grants," "International Co-Productions" and "Pro and Con Analysis").

FOREIGN TAX CREDITS. Dollar-for-dollar deductions from an individual or entity's U.S. income tax for the payment of foreign taxes levied by countries as a remittance or gross receipts tax. Foreign taxes generally represent the largest part of the distribution expense item "taxes." Distributors often pay such taxes, then deduct such payments from their gross receipts as a distribution expense (meaning that the producer and other net profit participants have actually paid the taxes) while the distributors still claim the foreign tax credit against their U.S. tax liability. Producers should insist that the distribution agreement provide that the distributor should not deduct the payment from gross receipts. ("Creative Accounting," "Fraud" and "Unethical Business Practices").

FOREIGN TAX DEALS. Tax benefits offered by a foreign country to filmmakers from other countries as an incentive to shoot the movie in that country; such deals usually require that the majority of the film be shot in the offering country and, in some cases, that the key actors, creative personnel and the producer must be from that country (see "Foreign Production Problems," "International Co-Productions" and "Tax Shelters").

FOREIGN TAXES. An assessment levied pursuant to the authority of a non-U.S. governmental entity on a person or property for public purposes including support of the government (see "Foreign Tax Credit").

FOREIGN TAX SHELTERS. A transaction based on foreign law (i.e., non-U.S.) and structured so that foreign taxpayers reduce their tax liability by engaging in activities that provide deductions or tax credits to apply against their tax liability (see "Abusive Tax Shelter," "International Tax Attorney" and "Tax Shelter").

FOREIGN TELEVISION LICENSE FEES. Payments made for the rights to show U.S. made television programming in non-U.S. territories (see "Foreign Territories").

FOREIGN TERRITORIES. All portions of the territory not included in domestic, i.e., from the perspective of a U.S. filmmaker, outside the U.S. and Canada (see "Foreign Market").

FOREIGN THEATRICAL. The market for films exploited through exhibition in theatres located in countries other than the U.S. and Canada (see "Foreign Territories").

FOREIGN VERSION. A motion picture that has been changed in some way for release in foreign markets. Generally, the change consists of adding sub-titles or dubbing in the foreign language, but may also include other changes, e.g., to meet local governmental censorship requirements (see "Cultural Differences" and "Other Versions").

FORMAT. The width-to-height ratio of a motion picture as it is projected on the screen (see "Aspect Ratio" and "Pan and Scan").

FORM D. The federal Regulation D notice filing form which provides notice to the SEC that an offering claiming a Regulation D exemption from securities registration is being claimed by the issuer. The form must be filed with the SEC within fifteen days of the first sale in the offering and at other times, pursuant to Regulation D. Some states will also accept the SEC's Form D to meet the state's notice filing requirement pursuant to the state's limited offering exemption which is considered compatible with the federal Regulation D, although many states require notice filings to be effected prior to the offer or sale of securities in their state (see "Notice Filing Requirement" and "Regulation D").

FORM S-1. The general purpose form of registration statement (for public offerings) prescribed by the SEC under the Securities Act of 1933. An unlimited amount of money can be raised pursuant to an S-1 offering, extensive disclosure is prescribed and the prospectus and registration statement must be filed with the SEC in Washington D.C. (see "Form S-18," "Prospectus," "Public Offering," "Registration Statement" and "Regulation A").

FORM S-18. A form of federal securities registration which may be used for public offerings of securities in cash amounts up to $5 million per year. An S-18 registration requires less disclosure than an S-1 offering and can be filed with the regional office of the SEC, which presumably speeds the review process (see "Form S-1," "Prospectus," "Public Offering," "Registration Statement" and "Regulation A").

FORM 10-K. The annual report required by the SEC of every issuer of a registered security, every exchange-listed company and any company with 500 or more shareholders or $1 million or more in gross assets (see "Publicly Held" and "Public Offering").

FORMULA DEAL. A film licensing agreement between a distributor and a circuit of theatres in which the license fee of a given feature is

determined, for the theatres covered by the agreement, by a specified percentage of that feature's national box office gross. This in
effect cross-collateralizes the financial performance of the film among
the various theatres at which it is exhibited. The results of film
formula deals have been found to be an unreasonable restraint of
trade. If the major studio/distributors also own certain exhibitors,
there is nothing to keep them from effectively utilizing formula deals
as between their internally controlled distributor and exhibitor (see
"Anti-Trust Laws," "Cross-Collateralization," "Major Exhibition Chains,"
"Paramount Consent Decree of 1948," "TriStar Case" and "Vertical
Integration").

FORMULA FOR COMPUTING NET PROFITS. A negotiated provision
which often appears as an exhibit to a production-financing/distribu-
tion agreement and sets out the manner in which net profits on a
film are calculated (also called "Net Profits Formula").

FOUNDER. One who organizes or begins an entity (see "Corporate
Stock," "Corporation," "Founder's Shares" and "Shareholders").

FOUNDER'S SHARES. Corporate stock issued to the corporation's
organizers, and often carrying special privileges (see "Corporate Stock,"
"Corporation," "Founder" and "Shareholders").

FOUR-RUN BREAK. A film's break being available for no more than
four theatres within the break's geographical area (see "Two-Run
Break" and "Three-Run Break").

FOUR-WALL OR FOUR-WALLING. A technique used by some distribution companies and/or producers for exhibiting their film or films
in which the distributor or producer handling his, her or its own
distribution offers the theatre(s) a pre-set negotiated price or flat
weekly rental fee for the use of the theatre. The rental fee is thus
guaranteed to the exhibitor regardless of the film's revenue intake at
the box office. This fee is for the use of the "four walls" of the
theatre. The distributor or producer pays all advertising expenses
and usually hires personnel to be at each theatre for supervision and
nightly collection of all monies taken in at the box office. Through
this method, the exhibitor has eliminated certain risks in that rental
income is guaranteed; however, the exhibitor is foregoing the opportunity to show other movies during that same period. The distributor
or producer incurs a greater risk but is also in the position, should
the film be successful, of reaping the benefits of 100% of the monies
taken in at the box office, less advertising, administrative and rental
costs. Concession sales may be negotiable (see "Distribution Alternatives" and "Self-Distribution").

FOUR-WALL ADVERTISING. A specific advertising approach used to support a film's four-wall engagement which consists entirely of local advertising, the purpose of which is to achieve a high frequency of impressions among the film's potential audience in the local market (see "Four-Wall" and "Four-Walling").

FOUR-WALL ENGAGEMENTS (see "Four-Wall").

FOUR-WALL EXHIBITION AGREEMENT. The contract between the theatre owner and the distributor or producer in which the theatre owner agrees to allow the distributor or producer to exhibit a film in the theatre based on a pre-set negotiated price or flat weekly rental fee to be paid for the use of the theatre. The rental fee is thus guaranteed to the exhibitor regardless of the film's revenue intake at the box office. This fee is for the use of the "four walls" of the theatre (see "Four-Wall").

FRACTIONALIZED RIGHTS. In film distribution, the stripping or separating out of various markets or media from the domestic theatrical distribution, i.e., not making some or all of the ancillary rights available to the domestic theatrical distributor (see "Fractionalizing" and "Split-Rights Basis").

FRACTIONALIZED SALES (see "Fractionalized Rights," "Fractionalizing" and "Split-Rights Basis").

FRACTIONALIZING. The separate selling of the various distribution rights to a film, e.g., domestic theatrical, video and cable (see "Multiple Pre-Sales" and "Split-Rights Basis").

FRACTURED RIGHTS (see "Fractured Rights Deal").

FRACTURED-RIGHTS DEAL. A film finance and distribution transaction, commonly utilized in the 1980s, in which the film's producer pre-sold domestic video and international rights, then engaged a distributor to distribute in the domestic theatrical marketplace for a fee. Sometimes the producer also retained all domestic television rights. The pre-sales would typically cover all of the production and some or all of the domestic releasing costs for the picture, leaving the producer's share of theatrical revenues and television rights for potential net profits. Fractured rights deals worked (1) before video became a significant revenue source for the major studio/distributors (thus the studios did not demand to participate in the video revenue stream at that time); (2) independent video companies were still paying substantial fees for video rights, (3) more banks were prepared to loan money to support these deals and fund production, (4) the funds supplied by independent video companies and outside banks were sufficient to cover production costs and a significant portion of domestic releasing costs. The fractured rights deals of the 1980s have now been replaced by the split rights deals (see "Lender Financing," "Pre-Sales," "Rising Production Costs" and "Split Rights Deal").

FRANCHISE. A special privilege granted to an individual, entity or group; also the right given to a private person or corporation to market another's product within a certain area. Thus, motion picture theatres that have an exclusive contractual arrangement to show the pictures of a single distributor are operating through a franchise granted by that distributor (see "Franchise Agreements").

FRANCHISE AGREEMENTS. A film licensing agreement, or series of licensing agreements, entered into as part of the same transaction, in effect for more than one motion picture season and covering the exhibition of features released by one distributor during the entire period of the agreement. Such agreements typically protect the exhibitor by prohibiting the exhibition of that distributor's films within the geographical market of the exhibitor and protect the distributor by committing the exhibitor to book the distributor's films. In recent court hearings relating to the requests of certain distributors to be relieved of the Paramount Consent Decree conduct provisions in dealings with exhibitors, the U.S. Justice Department has taken the position that franchise agreements are not necessarily anti-competitive in the current marketplace (see "Anti-Trust Laws," "Conduct Restrictions," "Paramount Consent Decree of 1948" and "TriStar Case").

FRANCHISED SUB-DISTRIBUTOR. A defined term in some film distribution agreements referring to a person or entity, other than the distributor, who is licensed by the distributor to distribute or sub-license a film for exhibition in a particular geographic area outside of the domestic territory with an obligation for such person or entity to account for or report to the distributor the amount of any income or expense of such distribution or sub-licensing, regardless of whether any amounts payable to the distributor by such person or entity for such licenses are fixed, on a percentage, guaranteed or other basis, or computed or determined in any other manner or by any combination of any of the foregoing. The major studio/distributors usually do not use such sub-distributors in the domestic territory (see "Outright Sale" and "Sub-Distributor").

FRANCHISE TAX. A tax generally imposed by the states upon corporations as a tax upon the net income of the corporation attributable to activities within the state or on the net worth of the corporation located in the state (see "Corporation").

FRAUD. Intentional deception resulting in injury to another. Elements of fraud are (1) a false and material misrepresentation made by one who either knows it is false or is ignorant of its truth, (2) the maker's intent that the representation be relied on by another and in a manner reasonably contemplated, (3) the recipient's ignorance of the falsity of the representation, (4) the recipient's rightful or justified reliance on the representation and (5) proximate injury to the recipient. Fraud usually consists of misrepresentation, concealment or non-disclosure of a material fact, or at least misleading conduct, devices or contrivance. If in fact, a given feature film distributor actually engaged in a significant amount of the unethical or predatory business practice described in this book, it is likely that such distributor has intentionally deceived and caused an injury to all of the profit participants involved in the deal; thus, such distributor may well have committed some form of actionable fraud (see "Creative Accounting," "Overreaching," "Predatory Practices," "Racketeering," "RICO," "Scam" and "White Collar Crime").

FREE AND CLEAR. Unencumbered title to property (see "Title").

FREE ENTERPRISE SYSTEM. An economy structured around unfettered choice, i.e., businesses are free to choose what products they will make, consumers are free to choose what they will buy and prices are generally left to fluctuate with supply and demand in an openly competitive market. Free enterprise has traditionally been one of the basic underlying economic principles of the U.S. economy. Unfortunately, some businesses, if not limited by government, will use predatory practices, unfair business practices, anti-competitive practices, unethical practices, etc., to gain a competitive edge over some competitors, often to the detriment of the consuming public (see "Anti-Competitive Practices," "Anti-Trust Laws," "Greed," "Combination in Restraint of Trade," "Law of Supply and Demand," "Marketplace of Ideas," "Predatory Practices," "Role of Government," "Unethical Business Practices" and "Unfair Competition").

FREELANCE EMPLOYEE. A person who is not regularly employed by a business but who agrees to perform film-related duties for compensation. For film union purposes, those who are employed for a period of less than sixteen weeks (see "Employment Agreement" and "Independent Contractor").

FREE TELEVISION. Broadcast television programming which is supported by television commercial sponsors, i.e., the exhibition of a program on home-type television receivers without any specific charge, either for the program or for the channel on which the program is received and without originating the program on a cable facility (see "Basic Pay Cable," "Pay Cable" and "Pay-Per-View").

FREQUENCY OF PAYMENTS. How often compensation is disbursed. Frequency of payments can be an important issue as between producers and distributors when the distributor or its studio affiliate provides financing for a motion picture project and is thus charging interest on the negative cost of the film, particularly since the distributors typically deduct their distribution fees and distribution expenses from gross receipts, then deduct interest payments from the revenue stream before the negative costs start to be recouped (see "Interest").

FRINGE BENEFITS. Compensation other than salary paid to persons who work on the production of film. Fringe benefits generally are not paid in the form of cash but may include life insurance, vacation pay, health, welfare and pension benefits, free screenings of a movie, Christmas bonuses, car-pooling, etc. Some distributors have reportedly over-stated the amount of fringe benefits paid to unions or guilds and then deducted the inflated amount from the distributor's gross receipts as distribution expenses or film production costs on which interest charges accumulate (see "Creative Accounting" and "Unethical Business Practices").

FRINGE PLAYER. A person who does not actively participate in the activities of the entertainment community's mainstream (see "A-Title," "Bankable Actors," "Economic Microcosm," "Independent Producer," "Major Exhibition Chains," "Major Studio/Distributors" and "Star").

FRONTEND CASH COMPENSATION. Money paid for services to be performed and either paid upon the signing of a written agreement or as of the start of the services. Similar to an advance except that frontend cash compensation may or may not be recoupable (see "Contingent Compensation").

FRONTEND LOAD. The sales charge applied to an investment at the time of initial purchase; that portion of the capital contributed by investors in a film limited partnership that is absorbed by certain costs or fees such as management fees, syndication costs (offering selling costs), legal fees, accounting fees, disclosure document printing and binding, etc. As a general rule of thumb, such costs should not exceed approximately 15% of the offering proceeds, since the larger frontend load reduces the amount that ultimately may be available to produce the film, i.e., the asset that may result in income or gain. The concept of frontend loading also describes the efforts of stars, directors, producers and other creative personnel, in-studio, bank or investor-financed films, who demand higher compensation to be paid at earlier stages of production or at earlier stages of the revenue stream, thus making less revenue available for subsequent profit participants (see "Creative Accounting," "Gross Participations," "Leverage," "Net Profits," "Participant" and "Up Front").

FULL AUDIT (see "Audit").

FULL DISCLOSURE. The requirement to disclose all material facts relating to a securities transaction [see "Anti-Fraud Statutes (Rule)," "Disclosure Document" and "Securities"].

FULLY DISTRIBUTED. A new securities issue that has been completely resold to the investing public, i.e., to institutions, individuals and/or other investors as opposed to broker/dealers (see "Securities").

FULLY NEGOTIATED AGREEMENT. A contract the terms and provisions of which have all been considered and treated by the parties (also sometimes referred to as a "Long Form Agreement" although a long form agreement may not have been fully negotiated; see "Deal Memo," "Letter Agreement," "Player Agreement" and "Short Form Agreement").

FUND. To provide monies to finance the production and/or distribution activities of a feature film. As a noun, a pool of money, some of which may be available for use in meeting the production/distribution costs of a film (see "Financing" and "Venture Capital").

FUNDAMENTAL ANALYSIS. Analysis of the balance sheet and income statements of companies in order to forecast their future stock-price movements (see "Corporate Stock" and "Fundamentals").

FUNDAMENTALS. The basic characteristics of a company considered by financial analysts in determining investment prospects. Among other things, fundamentals include past records of assets, earnings, sales, products, management and markets. A statement that the fundamentals of the movie business have never been better suggests that such companies are strong and the climate for investing in such firms is favorable, although a distinction must be made about which segment of the industry is favored since, for example, there can be a significant difference among the conditions of the major studio/distributors, independent producers, independent distributors and individual entities within each such segment of the industry (see "Corporate Stock," "Fundamental Analysis," "Paul Kagan Associates, Inc." and "Publicly Held").

FUNDING. The raising or providing of monies to finance a film project (see "Financing").

FUNDING SOURCES. All of the places where feature film producers may go to find financing for the development, production and/or distribution of motion pictures. Such sources have traditionally included the major studio/distributors, other established film production companies, independent distributors, film, television and cable organizations, other ancillary market entities, banks and other lenders, private investors, joint venture investors, family and friends, etc. In the course of any given year, there may be some 400 to 500 motion pictures released theatrically in the United States. There may be a couple of hundred more feature films that were actually produced but did not get a theatrical release. All of these were financed in some manner. No one has apparently been able to take the time or make the effort to do what would be necessary to determine what financing methods were used by each of these production companies and for several reasons: (1) there are so many films produced each year, (2) many are produced by small companies that come together just to produce that one film and then their principals go on to other things and may be hard to find, (3) even if located and they were willing to be questioned about their film's financing, many film production company executives, both large and small, have been known to mislead others about their actual costs and funding sources and (4) some of these entities would not disclose their method of financing even if subpoenaed before a Congressional investigating committee. Thus, no one really knows how many films were financed in a given year as in-house studio productions, through the use of a production-financing distribution agreements, as negative pickups, as fractured rights deals, as split rights deals, with collateralized bank loans, using foreign territorial pre-sales, as joint ventures (domestic or formal international co-productions), with corporate stock or debt offerings, through public or private limited partnerships, with investment contracts or investor financing agreements, with domestic facilities deals, through grants, using foreign below-the-line deals, through foreign tax shelters, as foreign equity financing or foreign currency deals, through self-financing techniques, family and friends and money laundering schemes (see "Financing").

FUNDRAISING PROCESS. The activities associated with arranging for the production financing of a motion picture, i.e., the manner, means and procedures involved in acquiring capital (see "Financing," "Offering" and "Venture Capital").

FUNDRAISING PROPOSALS. Propositions relating to the acquisition of financing for a project, e.g., production financing for a motion picture (see "Business Plan," "Development Financing," "Disclosure

Document," "Investment Contract," "Investor Financing Agreement," "Financing," "Joint Venture Agreement" and "Limited Partnership Offering").

FUNDS FOR RELEASING COSTS. The money required to pay for the expenses associated with the release of a motion picture, principally for prints and advertising costs. All other things being equal, a producer who approaches a distributor with a completed motion picture including well-known talent, with funds for releasing costs and with worldwide rights still available should be in the best possible bargaining position with respect to negotiating the terms of a distribution deal (see "Advertising," "Decision-Making Continuum," "Prints," "Releasing Costs" and "Rent-A-Distributor").

— G —

GAAP. Acronym for generally accepted accounting principles (see "Creative Accounting," "Generally Accepted Accounting Principles").

GAFFER. The chief electrician in a film production. The film production person responsible to the director of photography for the safe and efficient execution of the lighting patterns outlined by the director of photography (see "Director of Photography" and "Gaffer's Best Boy").

GAFFER'S BEST BOY (OR BEST GIRL). The first assistant electrician. The film production person responsible for assisting the gaffer in the performance of his or her duties and for supervising the operation of the lighting and electrical equipment (see "Gaffer").

GAUGE. A measurement term used to describe the width of positive film. For feature films, the gauge is usually 35mm and sometimes 70mm. Also, some low-budget feature films are shot in 16mm and blown-up to 35mm (see "Film" and "Thirty-Five Millimeter").

GENERALLY ACCEPTED ACCOUNTING PRINCIPLES (GAAP). Conventions, rules and procedures that define accepted accounting practice. Financial statements included in a securities registration statement must be prepared in accordance with GAAP, as well as the SEC's own accounting standards. Major studio/distributors generally do not restrict themselves to the use of generally accepted accounting principles (see "Contractually Defined Terms," "Creative Accounting," "FASB" and "Regulation S-X").

GENERAL PARTNER. In a limited partnership, the person or entity named as the general partner in the opening recital of the partnership agreement, together with any other person who becomes a general partner of such partnership pursuant to the limited partnership agreement. In a limited partnership, an individual general partner's liability to partnership creditors is not limited. In a film partnership the general partner is generally the producer or the person who put the deal together (or an entity controlled by such person) and is responsible for control and management of the partnership's activities. A general partner of a limited partnership may be an individual or a corporation (see "Corporation" and "Limited Partnership").

GENERAL PARTNERSHIP. A partnership without limited partners, i.e., an unincorporated association of two or more persons doing business as co-owners for profit. A general partnership is a contract of two or more competent persons to place their money, effects, labor and skill, or some or all of them, in lawful commerce or business and to divide the profit and bear the loss in certain proportions. Partners in a general partnership are individually liable for the debts of the partnership and assets individually owned will be subject to execution to satisfy any such debt when partnership assets are insufficient. A general partnership (like a limited partnership) is not subject to income taxes; rather, its partners are directly taxed individually on the income, taking into account their share of partnership gains and losses. A joint venture is a specialized form of general partnership (see "Partnership," "Investor Financing," "Joint Venture" and "Limited Partnership").

GENERAL RELEASE. A motion picture that is exhibited in a large number of theatres (some consider 500 theatres as a general release) and throughout the country, i.e., in most of the major U.S. markets (see "Limited Engagement," "Mini-Multiple," "Print," "Release Pattern" and "Wide Release").

GENERAL SOLICITATION. Activities relating to the offer and sale of securities, by whatever means, which involve contact by an issuer or its representatives with prospective purchasers with whom the issuer has no pre-existing relationship, e.g., mass-mailings and cold calls. A general solicitation is prohibited pursuant to both state and federal exemptions from the securities registration requirements but is permitted in a public/registered offering (see "Cold Calls," "Limitations on Manner of Offering," "Private Placement," "Public Offering" and "Solicitation").

GENERAL THEATRICAL RELEASE (see "General Release" and "Theatrical Release").

GENERAL USE. With respect to prospective financial statements in accounting, a reference to the use of such statements by a person with whom the responsible party is not negotiating directly, e.g., in an offering statement of an entity's debt or equity interests. Because recipients of prospective financial statements distributed for general use are unable to question the responsible party directly, the presentation most useful to them is one that portrays, to the best of the responsible party's knowledge and belief, the expected results. Thus, technically, only a financial forecast is appropriate for general use (see "Financial Forecasts," "Financial Projections" and "Limited Use").

GENERATION. Each progressive step in the film preparation process starting from an original negative going through a release print. As the process moves away from the original, each generation will typically show some slight loss in quality (see "Answer Print," "Release Print" and "Workprint").

GENRE. A distinctive type or category of literary composition and a particular type of motion picture, for example, action/adventure, love story, comedy, romantic comedy, western, science fiction (sci-fi), horror/fantasy or murder/mystery (see "Exploitation Film," "Movies with a Message" and "Theme").

GEOGRAPHIC MARKET. The area where a particular product is sold. Film licensing agreements between a film distributor and an exhibitor will typically describe the geographic market which will be exclusive to the exhibitor (see "Foreign Market" and "Territory").

GLAMOUR INDUSTRY. A business which is considered to be fascinating and exciting to the public. The film industry is such a business and this factor is often cited as an underlying reason for investor interest in the industry, at least for individual investors, i.e., some of these investors are partially motivated to invest in movies because of the so-called "cocktail chatter" value of such investments (see "Investor Motivation").

GLOBAL ENVIRONMENT. A reference to the trend toward more international financing of the production and distribution of feature films based partly on the realization that films are often produced for a worldwide audience ("Global Integration," "Internationally Competitive" and "Transnational Cartelization").

GLOBAL INTEGRATION. The combining of businesses on an international scale (see "Horizontal Integration" and "Vertical Integration")

GLOBAL MEDIA PRESENCE. Communications industry interests throughout the world (see "Communications Industry," "Entertainment Industry" and "Internationally Competitive").

GLOBAL RECESSION. A worldwide economic downturn (see "Global Environment").

GO AHEAD. The approval of a motion picture project for production (see "Greenlight" and "Pass").

GOING PRIVATE. Changing public ownership of a corporation to private ownership either by the company's repurchase of shares or through purchases by an outside private investor (see "Corporate Stock," "Private Placement" and "Publicly Held").

GOING PUBLIC. The process of offering a corporation's shares to the public through a public/registered offering for the first time, thus shifting the company's ownership from one or a few private stockholders to a base that includes public shareholders. Such an offering is referred to as an initial public offering (IPO) and the shares are said to have market value (see "Corporate Stock," "Initial Public Offering," "Market Value," "Public Offering" and "Publicly Held").

GOOD DISTRIBUTOR. A subjective term which, from an independent producer's point of view, suggests at least some of the following: a feature film distributor who does not abuse the disparity in bargaining power as between the producer and distributor at the negotiating table, i.e., does not offer unconscionable distribution terms on a take-it-or-leave-it basis, is enthusiastic about distributing the motion picture it has committed to distribute, develops a credible marketing plan for the film, can afford the expense of adequately promoting the motion picture, will make reasonable prints and ads commitments, will honor in good faith the consultation rights of the producer, does not unreasonably interfere with or limit the audit rights of the producer and other net profit participants, will fairly respond to the discovery of accounting discrepancies, does not engage in unethical business practices and otherwise has a good track record with other producers ("see "Allocation Issues," "Anti-Competitive Practices," "Audit Rights," "Blacklisting," "Conduct Restrictions," "Contract of Adhesion," "Creative Accounting," "Paramount Consent Decree of 1948," "Problem Producer," "Sue Us," "TriStar Case," "Unconscionable Contract" and "Unethical Business Practices").

GOOD FAITH. Being faithful to one's duty or obligation, i.e., a total absence of any intention to seek an unfair advantage or to defraud another party; an honest and sincere intention to fulfill one's obligations. Film distribution agreements often turn to this rather vague standard which can only be applied after the fact. When possible, such terms should be replaced in the distribution agreement with a more precisely defined standard of conduct (contrast with "Bad Faith;" see "Covenant of Good Fair and Fair Dealing").

GOOD FAITH CONSIDERATION. Something of value given by one party in return for a performance or a promise of performance by another, for the purpose of forming a contract without any intention to seek an unfair advantage or to defraud the other party (see "Consideration" and "Good Faith").

GOOD FILM. A subjective term which, in the final analysis, means a film that its intended audience enjoyed and appreciated. From the standpoint of distributors and film financiers, a good film is a film people will pay money to see (see "Blockbuster," "Bomb" and "Hit").

GOOD TITLE (see "Clearance," "Clear Title," "Just Title" and "Title").

GOODWILL. An intangible but recognized business asset which is the result of such features of an ongoing enterprise as the production or sale of reputable brand-name products, a good relationship with customers and suppliers, and the standing of the business in its community. Goodwill can become a balance sheet asset when a going business is acquired through a purchase transaction in which the price paid exceeds the net asset value. A distributor's reputation for providing a continuous flow of quality films is an important aspect of its goodwill with exhibitors. Also, the preservation of a feature film production and/or distribution company's goodwill is an important concern in selecting merchandising partners (see "Asset," "Merchandising Agreement," "Merchandising Rights," "Mergers and Acquisitions" and "Rent-A-Distributor").

GOVERNING LAW CLAUSE. A contractual provision usually found in the miscellaneous provisions section of a contract which names the state under whose laws any dispute arising pursuant to the contract is to be resolved (see "Arbitration Clause," "Contract" and "Dispute Resolution Provision").

GOVERNMENT SUBSIDIES. Grants by a government (state, federal or foreign) to filmmakers to assist in the production of a film which is deemed advantageous to the community served by that government, e.g., production of the movie will provide jobs and help the economy in a given area or the movie will provide favorable publicity. In contrast to foreign governments, the U.S. government has tended to avoid such subsidies and has not recognized the value of motion pictures for cultural promotion purposes, choosing instead to leave the pursuit of such "hidden agendas" to the private sector (see "Film Subsidies," "Foreign Subsidies," "Grants," "Hidden Agenda" and "Marketplace of Ideas").

GRACE PERIOD. The period of time provided in most loan contracts and insurance policies during which default or cancellation will not occur, even though a payment is past due. Also a negotiated provision in some long-term loans whereby repayment of principal does not begin until some point well into the life of the loan. A borrower will sometimes accept a higher interest rate for a longer grace period (see "Debt," "Insurance" and "Lender Financing").

GRANTEE. One to whom a grant is made. The grantee in a film distribution agreement is the distributor (see "Grant of Rights" and "Grantor").

GRANT OF RIGHTS. The awarding of power or privilege to which one is justly entitled. In a motion picture context, grant of rights refers to the power or privilege of developing, producing and exploiting a literary property, screenplay and/or movie. Such rights are granted to producers in the acquisition of literary properties, to distributors by producers through the distribution agreement and to sub-distributors and others through various licensing agreements. The phrase "grant of rights" also refers to the provision in such agreement which sets out what rights are being granted. Generally, in a film distribution deal, such rights will cover markets, changes to the title, the use of music on a soundtrack, dubbed versions and trailers, re-editing, advertising and publicizing the picture, use of excerpts, use of the names and likenesses of cast members, commercials, publishing a novelization, adding the name and trademark of the distributor, merchandising, music, publishing and radio rights, remakes and sequels, assignment of producer's rights, and warranties from the producer not to encumber the rights granted nor grant the same rights to others. The producer must confirm that this provision accurately sets out the grant actually being made (see "Grant of Rights Provision" and "License").

GRANT OF RIGHTS PROVISION. The paragraph (or paragraphs) in a film distribution or licensing agreement which provides for the grant of rights (see "Grant of Rights").

GRANTOR. One who makes a grant. The grantor in the film distribution agreement is generally the film's producer or the production entity (see "Grantee" and "Grant of Rights").

GRANTS. Motion picture production funds, generally provided for only a portion of a feature film's budget, made available through government agencies, private foundations, special interest groups, educational research organizations or the media. Each grant source may impose unique requirements and restrictions regarding the awarding of its grant, e.g., only to individuals, only to non-profit organizations or only in a specific field of interest (see "Film Subsidies," "Foreign Subsidies" and "Government Subsidies").

GRAPHICS. The visual components of a print advertisement including the type styles used, logos, drawings and the ad's border (see "Logo").

GRASS ROOTS CAMPAIGN. Advertising campaign which uses flyers, posters, stickers, etc. to promote special screenings which in turn seek to build word-of-mouth for a specific film in the local community (see "Word-of-Mouth" and "Outreach Campaign").

"G" RATING. An MPAA rating indicating that a motion picture has been approved by the MPAA's Classification and Rating Administration for general audiences, i.e., in the MPAA's opinion, there is nothing contained in the film that would offend parents if the film were viewed by children (see "MPAA" and "Ratings").

GRAYLISTING. A form of discrimination based on age, i.e., age bias. Screenwriters have recently complained about the youth-driven agents and executives who run the U.S. television and film companies saying such persons have an obsession with youth and that it has become a factor in deciding whether a scriptwriter can write (see "Bias," "Blacklist," "Discrimination," "Pattern of Bias" and "Prejudice").

GREED. Inordinate or reprehensible acquisitiveness. Although no scientifically conducted study is cited to support the statement, it would appear that there is adequate informal evidence to support a conclusion that greed is a motivation which seems to occur frequently in the film business. When a motion picture like "Coming to America" grosses more than $300 million worldwide but does not reach net profits, it may be fair to assume that "greed" was involved in the negotiation or implementation of that distribution deal somewhere along the line. When the number-one box-office hit of all time for Warner Bros. ("Batman") achieves $253.4 million in distributor gross receipts as of September, 1990 but, based on the distributor accounting, still shows a deficit of $35.8 million, it may be fair to conclude that someone taking off-the-top was being greedy in that deal. In that specific situation, the movie's star, Jack Nicholson, reportedly received $50 million. Now for the poor and working people of this country, that may appear obscene. It would not be unreasonable for them to boycott every movie Jack Nicholson makes in the future because his $50 million is enough for a lifetime, and it came out of somebody's else's share. In the meantime, the moviegoers have to pay for all of this greed. The motion picture "Rain Man" reportedly grossed more than $400 million, but, according to an MGM/Pathe accounting statement for the period from November 1990 to February 1991, it was still more than $27 million away from breaking even (see "Boycott," "Breakeven," "Buchwald Case," "Creative Accounting," "Gross Receipts," "Inferior Bargaining Position," "Leverage," "Market Power" and "Net Profits").

GREEN BAND TRAILER. A movie trailer that has been edited for showing to general audiences (see "Red Band Trailer" and "Trailer").

GREENLIGHT. Authority or permission to undertake a project (see "Go Ahead," "Greenlighting Films" and "Pass").

GREENLIGHTING FILMS. Granting approval for a film project to proceed to the next stage in its development and/or production (see "Greenlight").

GRIP. A general term for a crew member who provides labor on the set of a motion picture (see "Key Grip").

GROSS (see "Box Office Gross").

GROSS AUDIENCE. The total audience that combined media advertising generates for a movie (see "Advertising").

GROSS BOX OFFICE AND GROSS BOX OFFICE RECEIPTS (see "Box Office Gross").

GROSS CORRIDORS. Percentage participations in the gross receipts of a specific market or medium as opposed to an across-the-board gross participation in all of the distributor's gross receipts (see "Gross Receipts," "Percentage Participation" and "Video Corridor").

GROSS DEAL. In the context of a film distribution contract, a profit participation for the producer or others in the distributor's gross receipts as opposed to a participation in net profits (see "Adjusted Gross," "Film Rentals," "Gross" and "Net Profits").

GROSS FILM RENTALS. The distributor's share of the gross box office before distribution fee and costs (advertising, prints and promotion expenses) are deducted by the distributor (also called "Gross Rentals;" see "Gross Receipts").

GROSS FLOOR. A negotiated minimum level of backend participation in a movie's revenue stream regardless of the number or amount of distributor or other deductions from gross rentals. This device permits a producer or other person relying on a percentage participation in net profits to receive at least this minimum, i.e., gross floor, regardless of how many gross points are awarded to others or distributor deductions are otherwise made from gross receipts. It may be necessary to include such a gross floor to preserve some profit participation for the producer and others participating in the producer's share. In light of the reported figure that only about 5% of movies using the major studio/distributor net profits formula ever reach breakeven, i.e., generate net profits, it would seem to be quite essential for every producer to insist on at least some small percentage of a gross floor until distribution deals begin resulting in more films that generate net profits (see "Floor," "Gross Participants" and "Gross Receipts").

GROSSING POTENTIAL. A theatre's historical ability, with films comparable to the film whose exhibition at that theatre is being considered, to produce box-office receipts and, consequently, film rental; also the prospective box office gross for a given film (see "Box Office Comparables" and "Financial Projections").

GROSS INCOME. In general terms, the total amount of income generated by a property before deduction of any expenses (see "Box Office Gross," "Distributor's Film Rentals" and "Gross Receipts").

GROSS PARTICIPANTS. Persons or entities who are able to negotiate a percentage interest in a motion picture distributor's gross receipts. Generally, only a very few high-powered actors, directors and producers have the kind of leverage which will permit such participations. Without a gross floor being negotiated by a net profit participant, too many gross participants may eliminate the possibility of a movie's revenue stream ever generating net profits. It would be better for the producer to stand up for the interests of all net profit participants at the time of negotiating for high-priced star talent and refuse to grant gross points. For example, it would be difficult to believe that every net profit participant on the all-time box office champ for Warner Bros., "Batman," would not resent the fact that Jack Nicholson, in addition to a reported up-front fee advance of $6 million, was successful in negotiating one of the richest deals in Hollywood history: 15% of the gross with an escalator clause that boosted his take to as high as 20% the more money the film took in. Thus, Nicholson's earnings alone accounted for more than $50 million of "Batman's" production costs, according to industry sources, and, along with the distributor's fees and expense reimbursement provisions, pretty well eliminated all possibilities that net profit participants on that film will ever see another dime. In another example, when Richard Dreyfuss and his agent reportedly asked for gross points in the film "Close Encounters of the Third Kind," producer Julia Phillips reportedly refused to cave in and thus gave all net profit participants on that film a better shot at realizing additional compensation. Also, in the context of split-rights deals (where the domestic and international markets are separate transactions for the producer), the question arises with respect to what happens to the interests of gross participants in such situations? Domestically in such deals, the producer will collect gross revenues minus the distributor's fee, so presumably the gross participants will participate in the producer's gross. But, in the international market, licensing rights are often sold for a minimum guarantee against fees in the territories, thus the producer would either have to negotiate with gross participants to limit their international participations in return for larger up-front cash compensation or in the alternative, structure the deal with international buyers so that they are responsible for accounting to the producer and other gross participants and for covering such participations, but this latter approach is unlikely (see "Average Negative Cost," "Gross Participations" and "Split Rights Deals").

GROSS PARTICIPATIONS. Percentage interests in the distributor's gross receipts on a motion picture (see "Gross Participants," "Gross Receipts," "Minimum Guarantee" and "Net Profit Participation").

GROSS PARTNERSHIP REVENUES (see "Partnership Gross Revenues").

GROSS PER SCREEN. A commonly used standard of motion picture performance which measures, for comparison purposes, the amount of box office gross generated by a given movie over the course of a specific period of time. Unless specifically stated, the time period is one week (see "Box Office Gross").

GROSS PLAYER (see "Gross Participants").

GROSS POINTS. Percentage participations in film rentals as opposed to net profits (see "Points").

GROSS POSITIONS (see "Gross Participations").

GROSS PROCEEDS (see "Gross Rentals").

GROSS PROCEEDS AFTER BREAKEVEN. A defined stage in a motion picture's revenue stream (in this case the distributor's gross receipts) which may trigger a bonus or escalation as soon as the gross receipts reach a specified form of breakeven (see "Actual Breakeven," "Bonus," "Breakeven," "Cash Breakeven," "Escalation," "First Breakeven," "Gross Receipts" and "Second Breakeven").

GROSS PROCEEDS AT FIRST BREAKEVEN (see "Gross Proceeds After Breakeven").

GROSS PROCEEDS OF THE OFFERING. The aggregate total of the original invested capital of the partners, i.e., the total amount of money to be raised in a limited partnership offering (also called "Offering Proceeds" or "Proceeds of the Offering").

GROSS PROFIT. Generally, net sales less the cost of goods sold (see "Gross Receipts").

GROSS PROFIT PARTICIPANT. One who has a right to participate on a percentage basis in the gross profits to the distributor generated by a movie (see "First Dollar" and "Gross Points").

GROSS RECEIPTS. A contractually defined term in motion picture distribution agreements, generally referring to all monies actually received by the distributor (or its subsidiaries or affiliates) from the exploitation of any rights granted pursuant to the distribution agreement, from all sources, stated in U. S. dollars, and not subject to forfeiture or return, including non-returnable advances and guarantees. The major areas from which gross receipts are derived include home video, theatrical revenue or "film rental," non-theatrical, pay television, network television, television syndication and ancillary rights. Producers must be careful to clarify whether and to what extent any advance and/or guarantee is to be included in gross receipts. The studio/distributors will generally take the position that advances should not be included in gross receipts until earned, in other words, the distributor will want to deduct an amount equal to any advance that has been paid to the producer from monies received by the distributor and will not want to consider such amounts as part of gross receipts for any calculations based on gross receipts (contrast with "Film Rentals" and "Gross Rentals;" see "Contractually Defined Term").

GROSS RECEIPTS TAX. A government levy based on total sales (see "Foreign Tax Credit").

GROSS RENTALS. The aggregate amount of the film distributor's share of monies paid at theatre box offices computed on the basis of negotiated agreements between the distributor and the exhibitor. Note that gross receipts refers to amounts actually received and from all markets and media, whereas gross rentals is sometimes defined to refer to amounts earned from theatrical exhibition only, regardless of whether received by the distributor (also called "Gross Proceeds;" see "Gross Receipts").

GROSS REVENUES TO THE PARTNERSHIP (see "Partnership Gross Revenues").

GROSS TO DISTRIBUTOR BASIS. A manner of reporting film earnings that is the equivalent to distributor's gross receipts; film earnings are sometimes reported on this basis in the trades (see "Box Office Gross" and "Gross Rentals").

GUARANTEE. Agreement that a specific sum of money will be paid when conditions specified in the contract are met. In film, a guarantee is a sum of money which is payable regardless of a film's performance in the marketplace. It most typically appears as a dollar amount of minimum film rental that the exhibitor promises to pay the distributor regardless of the amount of film rental earned by the distributor under the film's lease agreement. Generally, a guarantee is paid prior to the film's exhibition (payable up front in installments or in a lump sum at a specific date). Such sums are advance payments against the producer's or distributor's share of any profits but are not refundable (contrast with "Guaranty" and "Guaranty Agreement;" see "Advance" or "Advances," "Distributor Guarantee," "Pay or Play," "Personal Guarantee," "Pre-Sale Guarantee" and "Release Commitment").

GUARANTEE CLAUSE. A provision in a contract, note or other agreement which creates an obligation of some kind, that commits the guarantor to perform the obligation, pay the debt, etc. in the event of a failure to do so by the original obligor (see "Guaranty," "Completion Bond" and "Surety").

GUARANTEE DEAL (see "Distribution Guarantee" and "Guarantee").

GUARANTOR REINSURANCE. The spreading of risk and sharing of insurance premiums between insurance companies relating to a motion picture completion guarantee (see "Completion Guarantor," "Cut-Through Endorsement" and "Reinsurance").

GUARANTOR'S FEE. The fee charged by the completion bond company for providing its over-budget protection. Such fees generally range from 2.5% to 6% and sometimes include a share in the film's profits. Due to a more competitive environment, some completion bond fees as low as 1.5% have been reported in recent times (see "Completion Guarantor").

GUARANTY. An agreement or promise to answer for the debt, default of miscarriage of another. One giving a guaranty agrees to perform the act promised to be done or properly done by another person if that person does not fulfill his, her or its obligation (see "Completion Bond" and "Surety").

GUARANTY AGREEMENT. An undertaking by any person to pay the debt or perform the contract or duty of another even when that person remains liable on the underlying obligation. The agreement sets forth the parties' rights and duties, in conditional or absolute form. For example, a film lab may require a guarantee from the principal owner or owners of its customer, particularly if such customer is a small independent film production company (see "Guaranty" and "Surety").

GUILD. Labor organization, i.e., association of workers who do the same or similar kinds of work. The word guild is used in the names of most of the performing arts unions, e.g., Screen Actors Guild, Directors Guild of America, American Guild of Variety Artists and the American Guild of Musical Artists, but other guilds include the American Federation of Television and Radio Artists and the American Federation of Musicians. Trade unions are generally limited to skilled or semi-skilled workers who have learned crafts. The organization bargains collectively on behalf of its members with single employers, business firms, or associations of employers. Then the guild will restrict the rights of its members to work for companies that have not signed the union's basic agreement. The unions set up working rules relating to work standards, wages, hours and credits and other matters, arrange for membership meetings and social functions, call strikes when deemed necessary, issue bulletins, and in some cases offer legal advice and apprenticeship/intern openings for those starting in the particular discipline of the union. The craftspeople and artists working at the major studios are nearly all union members, and thus their salaries are typically higher than those paid non-union craftspeople. In independent, "off-the-major-studio-lot" film and tape productions, the employees are often a mix of union and non-union. The unions are supported financially primarily through membership dues (see "Professional Association" and "Trade Association").

GUILD AGREEMENTS. The film union contracts between film producers and the various unions representing different segments of motion picture labor which set out working rules relating to work standards, wages, hours and credits and other matters for the members of such guilds (see "Guild").

GUILD REQUIREMENTS. Film union rules relating to work standards, wages, hours, credits and other matters which producers must comply with in order for the members of specific guilds to properly be employed on such producer's film (see "Guild").

GUILD/UNION FLIGHT ACCIDENT INSURANCE. A type of insurance which provides motion picture/television guild or union contract requirements for aircraft accidental-death insurance to all production company cast or crew members (see "Insurance").

— H —

HARD FLOOR. A percentage that is not subject to further reduction, e.g., a minimum percentage gross participation of 20%. As a variation of the concept, a hard floor might be negotiated for net profit participations while a soft floor is used for gross participations (see "Floor" and "Soft Floor").

HARD TO AUDIT EXPENSES. Costs that are difficult to verify. Many of the film distributor distribution expenses deducted from the distributor's gross receipts in order to arrive at net profits are difficult to verify or judge as to reasonableness. For this reason alone, it might better serve the overall film community for the entire system relating to the deduction of distribution expenses to be abandoned in favor of negotiated across-the-board gross participations for all participants (see "Direct Distribution Expenses").

HDTV. High definition television, a television transmission standard which may replace the systems currently in use. HDTV is a developing technology which promises improved video images, a new format for producing films and potentially a new market for films. HDTV proponents claim that it offers images equal in quality to 35mm film. The U.S. TV system (NTSC) presently uses 525 lines of resolution. HDTV would use no less than 1,000 lines. The Japanese have adopted a 1,125-line standard or format (see "Video Format").

HEADLINE. A catchy phrase or word, usually set in boldface and larger type and placed above the body copy of an ad. Headlines are designed to grab the attention of the reader (see "Advertising," "Body Copy" and "Sub-Head").

HEIRS. Technically, those to whom statutory law appoints to inherit an estate should the ancestor die without a will, however, as commonly used, the term often includes those who inherit by will or deed as well as by operation of law (see "Assigns," "Personal Representative" and "Successor").

HERTZ. A unit of frequency equal to one cycle per second; abbreviated Hz. (see "Sound").

HIATUS. A break in an activity or a lapse in continuity (see "Gross Participants").

HIDDEN AGENDA. Plans of things to be done or intentions that are not apparent or divulged. Filmmakers make movies for many reasons. Making money, becoming famous, earning the respect of professional peers, providing entertainment and communicating important ideas would seem to be high on anyone's list of the typical reasons why movies are made, although the order of importance certainly may differ amongst individuals. The feature film, as a communications medium, with its large screen, color technology, special effects, lighting techniques, exquisite photography, incredible sound, and excellent talent on and off the screen is also, without question, one of the most effective forms of communicating ideas that the world has yet devised. It would indeed be naive for anyone to assume that the communication of ideas is not an important motive for any serious filmmaker or filmmaking concern. A feature film also affords a unique opportunity for those who control or dominate the process of decision-making as to which movies or ideas are included in motion pictures, to insert such ideas or select and actively promote the movies which best express the views held by those decision-makers (see "Bias," "Favorable Portrayal," "Government Subsidies," "Marketplace of Ideas," "Pattern of Bias" and "Unfavorable Portrayal").

HIDDEN CONTINGENCY. A budgeting technique which incorporates an extra 10% into each and every budget category of a film budget (see "Budget Overruns," "Completion Guarantor" and "Contingency").

HIGH CONCEPT. A film idea, concept or plot that can be described in a very few words (see "Hype-Worthy").

HIGHEST LEVERAGE POSITION. Circumstances which provide an individual or entity with the maximum amount of bargaining strength. For example, a producer who approaches a distributor with a quality motion picture in the can along with prints and ads money is likely to be able to negotiate more favorable terms for the distribution deal than a producer who approaches a distributor seeking production and distribution funds for a movie yet to be produced. The producer in the first situation above also eliminates some of the opportunities for the distributor's so-called "creative accounting" (see "Creative Accounting," "Decision-Making Continuum," "Funds for Releasing Costs" and "Rent-A-Distributor").

HIGH NET-WORTH INDIVIDUALS. Persons whose assets significantly exceed their liabilities. Banks are usually quite willing to make loans to such individuals (see "Lender Financing" and "Net Worth").

HIT. A subjective term for which no precise definition is available but which is applied to motion pictures that are well received by the general public and do well at the box office. A "hit" film does not necessarily mean that all persons who participated in the production or distribution of the film (and receive screen credit therefor) either made significant contributions to the film or participated in the financial success of the film. Also, in the view of some industry analysts, poor financial management is a more significant contributing factor to the many recent film production company failures than the lack of so-called "hit" motion pictures (see "Blockbuster," "Bomb," "Creative Accounting," "Domestic Number One Hit," "Financial Management," "Gross Receipts," "Net Profits" and "Successful Film").

HOBBY LOSSES. A loss incurred by a taxpayer in an activity not engaged in for profit. In general, hobby losses are deductible only against income generated by the hobby (see "Tax Deduction").

HOLDBACK PERIODS. A time frame within which a film cannot be released in a given media or market. If the distributor is given a broad grant of rights in the distribution agreement, the distributor will want to make its own internal decisions regarding appropriate sequential distribution in various media in the territory. The producer, on the other hand, may want to seek a holdback schedule in order to ensure that the picture has an opportunity for maximum revenues in each medium of exploitation. If the producer has reserved certain rights, the distributor may seek holdback provisions. Typical holdback periods might include: videocassette rights: nine to twelve months after initial theatrical release; cable and pay tv: three months after start of videocassette distribution; free television: two years after initial theatrical release (see "Release Sequence").

HOLD HARMLESS. Protect from loss or liability; indemnify; guaranty. In contract law, the phrase is used to signify a commitment by one party to make good or repay another party to an agreement in the event of a specified loss (see "Indemnify").

HOLDING COMPANY. A corporation that owns enough voting stock in another corporation to influence its board of directors and therefore to control its policies and management. A holding company need not own a majority of the shares of its subsidiaries or be engaged in similar activities ("Control Stock," "Parent Corporation" and "Subsidiary Corporation").

HOLDOVER. An exhibitor's keeping of a film for exhibition beyond the minimum period of exhibition time stipulated in the license agreement. A holdover may occur either by reason of the exhibitor's voluntary action with the distributor's consent or by operation of the license agreement's holdover clause (same as "Carryover").

HOLDOVER CLAUSE. A clause within a license agreement which requires the exhibitor to continue exhibiting a film beyond the film's minimum period of exhibition time, such requirement being triggered by the film achieving its holdover figure. A holdover clause may provide that the exhibiting theatre's clearance is reduced during the holdover (same as "Carryover Clause;" see "Clearance" and "Exclusive Engagement").

HOLDOVER FIGURE. The negotiated weekly minimum dollar amount of money taken in at a theatre's box office that a film must reach in order to be held over for the next week, i.e., a dollar amount of a theatre's gross box office receipts which, if equaled or exceeded from the exhibitions during a specific period of time, requires the exhibitor to continue to exhibit that film for an additional week. This figure is mutually agreed on by the exhibitor and distributor when the terms under which the film will be played are originally established and set out in the distributor/exhibitor agreement. The holdover figure is an objective standard and provides a means for either the distributor or exhibitor to insist that the picture continue if the figure was achieved or, if not, cease to be shown in that specific theatre (same as "Carryover Figure;" see "Control Figure").

HOLLYWOOD ACCOUNTING (see "Creative Accounting").

HOLLYWOOD REPORTER. A daily (except weekends) entertainment-industry trade publication (published in Hollywood) reporting on developments in the motion picture, television, stage, home video and cable segments of the industry (see "Trades" and "Variety").

HOME VIDEO. The presentation of a film in private homes on a television screen by means of rented or purchased video cassettes or discs (see "Video" and "Videocassette Revenue Reporting").

HOME VIDEO RIGHTS. The rights associated with the exploitation of a film in the home video market (see "Home Video Royalty" and "Videocassette Revenue Reporting").

HOME VIDEO ROYALTY. A share of the proceeds from the sale or rental of motion picture videocassettes paid by the video wholesaler to the distributor. In contrast to feature film sub-distribution in other media, film distributors handling the distribution of motion pictures on videocassettes accept mere royalties from the wholesalers instead of the balance of the wholesale proceeds minus a modest sub-distribution fee. Royalty payments are traditionally much smaller than other forms of percentage participations. Before this rapidly diminishing revenue stream generated by home video reaches the producer, the distributor will also typically deduct its negotiated distribution fee. This system was designed by the major studio/ distributors who, in many instances, own significant and/or controlling interests in the video wholesalers or manufacturers, thus these major studio/distributors get to participate twice in the videocassette revenue stream and are able to minimize the dollars that ultimately flow past the distributors to the producer and other net profit participants (also called "Royalty on Home Video;" see "Conflicts of Interest," "Fiduciary," "Twenty Percent Rule," "Unethical Business Practices" and "Videocassette Revenue Reporting").

HOMOGENEOUS FILMS. Motion pictures that are the same or similar. During the early years of the motion picture industry, the major studio/distributors produced a large volume of films that were very similar, i.e., they were designed to and did appeal to the same mass audience, thus exhibitors had little need to pre-screen each motion picture offered. With today's more fractionalized audiences and film's of widely varying quality which appeal to separate but more narrow audiences, there is a greater need for exhibitors to pre-screen the product they are asked to exhibit (see "Anti-Blind Bidding Statutes," "Audience Fractionalization," "Blind Bidding," "Heterogeneous Product" and "Mass Audience").

HOOK. Something unique that will set a project apart, attract the attention or gain the interest of a target audience. In a motion picture context, a "hook" may be utilized by a writer, producer or director pitching a project in search of production financing, a "hook" may be emphasized by a producer who seeks a distributor, and the distributor's marketing department will utilize a "hook" to help make the film stand out from the other movies competing for attention, to get prospective moviegoers into the theatre and to stimulate favorable word-of-mouth. In these situations, the "hook" for a movie may be a unique storyline, someone's first film, an ultra-low-budget production, great special effects, a major star, etc. (see "Advertising," "Marketing Department," "Pitch" and "Primary Audience").

HORIZONTAL INTEGRATION. A consolidation of business entities at the same level within an industry, e.g., the motion picture business basically has three levels: production, distribution and exhibition.

Thus, if two production companies merge, that is an example of horizontal integration. On the other hand, if a production company and a distribution entity merge, that is an example of vertical integration (see "Merger Guidelines," "Paramount Consent Decree of 1948," "TriStar Case" and "Vertical Integration").

HORIZONTAL MERGER. The combination of two or more companies at the same level within an industry. Mergers typically occur in three ways (1) through a pooling of interests, where the accounts of the respective companies are combined; (2) through a purchase, where the amount paid over and above the acquired company's book value is carried on the books of the purchaser as goodwill; or (3) through a consolidation where a new company is formed to acquire the net assets of the combining companies (see "Goodwill," "Horizontal Integration," "Merger Guidelines" and Vertical Integration").

HORIZONTAL PRICE FIXING. Price fixing engaged in by those in competition with each other at the same level in an industry. For example, if exhibitors conspired to fix prices at a certain level, that would be an example of horizontal price fixing. On the other hand, if an exhibitor and a distributor conspired to fix prices, that would be an example of vertical price fixing (see "Anti-Trust Laws," "Price Fixing" and "Vertical Price Fixing").

HOT ISSUE. A public offering of securities where the securities, after their initial sale to the public, are resold in the open market at prices substantially higher than the original public offering price. The NASD defines a hot issue as a securities issue in which the aftermarket price is 10% or higher than the original price. The SEC definition, on the other hand, requires that the market be looked at thirty to sixty days later and that factors leading to the rise in price be examined (see "Corporate Stock," "Public Offering" and "Publicly Held").

HOUSE. A motion picture theatre (see "House Manager" and "House Nut").

HOUSE ALLOWANCE. A negotiated dollar amount as between a film's distributor and its exhibitor which represents the estimated expenses during the course of a week for the film exhibitor, i.e., the amount it supposedly costs an exhibitor to operate a theatre for a week. In a typical exhibitor/distributor agreement, the distributor would split the balance of the box-office gross (in accordance with the agreed-upon percentages between them) after the "house nut" has been deducted by the exhibitor, i.e., the exhibitor deducts the amount of the "house nut" before the distributor/exhibitor split of the balance. This negotiated figure may range from $5,000 a week to

$35,000 a week depending on the theatre (same as "Contractual Theatre Overhead," "Weekly House Allowance" and "Weekly House Expense;" see "Box Office Gross," "Concession Sales," "Controlled Theatre," "Distributor's Film Rentals" and "House Nut").

HOUSE EXPENSE (see "House Nut").

HOUSEKEEPING DEAL. A motion picture development deal between a production company and a major studio/distributor in which the studio agrees to pay the overhead expenses of the production company in exchange for the first opportunity to acquire the right to produce and distribute any projects developed by the production company (see "First Look Deal," "Independent Producer" and "Overall Deal").

HOUSE MANAGER. The person in charge of a movie theatre ("house") who manages the operation of the theatre, runs the theatre's logistics and supervises ticket sales. Sometimes the house manager also owns or is a co-owner of the theatre (see "House Nut").

HOUSE NUT. Actual theatre expenses for a week (see "House Nut").

HOUSE OVERHEAD ALLOWANCE (same as "House Allowance").

HYBRID SECURITY. A security which combines features of debt and equity, e.g., of both bonds and stocks (see "Bond" and "Stock").

HYPE. Publicity and advertising, including personal and television talk-show appearances along with newspaper and magazine articles, designed to promote and publicize a film. Film producers often hire publicists to create hype within the film industry in an effort to add value to a film in production when it comes time to negotiate a distribution deal (see "Buzz," "Publicist" and "Publicity").

HYPE-WORTHY. A film concept or project which can be effectively advertised and publicized (see "High Concept").

HYPHENATE. A single individual who performs the work and obtains the screen credit for two positions in the production of a film, e.g., producer-director or writer-director (see "Actor," "Director," "Producer" and "Screenwriter").

HYPOTHECATE. To pledge something as security without turning over possession of it (see "Pledge").

HYPOTHECATION. In banking, the pledging of property to secure a loan. Hypothecation does not transfer title, but does transfer the right to sell the hypothecated property in the event of default. In the securities field, hypothecation is the pledging of securities to brokers as collateral for loans made to purchase securities or to cover short sales (see "Collateral," "Lender Financing," "Pledge" and "Secured Debt").

HYPOTHETICAL ASSUMPTIONS. Facts or statements taken for granted and upon which a financial projection may be based, i.e., the assumption is used in a financial projection to present a condition or course of action that is not necessarily expected to occur, but is consistent with the purpose of the projection (see "Financial Projections" and "Key Factors").

HZ. The abbreviation for hertz (see "Hertz").

— I —

IATSE (see "International Alliance of Theatrical and Stage Employees").

IDEA. A formulated thought or opinion; a mental image or formulation of something seen or known or imagined; a pure abstraction, or something assumed or vaguely sensed. In theory and in filmmaking, the idea is more narrow in scope than a concept, thus the concept is considered the initial step in creating a movie. Many persons both in and out of the film business recognize that ideas are the film industry's most important article of commerce and that the motion picture is one of the most powerful methods for communicating ideas that human beings have yet to devise (see "Concept," "Culture Promotion," "Marketplace of Ideas" and "Theme").

IDEAS ORIGINATING WITH PRODUCER. Language in a development deal between a studio/distributor and an independent production company which provides a mechanism for dividing film projects (at their earliest stages) between the entities at the end of the present contractual relationship, i.e., those ideas or motion picture concepts that originated with the production company as opposed to the studio/distributor can be retained by the production company to the exclusion of the studio/distributor (see "Development Deal," "First Look Deal," "Housekeeping Deal," "Overall Deal" and "Term Deal").

IFIDA. Acronym for International Film Importers and Distributors of America (see "Industry Groups").

IFP/WEST. The West coast chapter of the Independent Feature Project. One of five IFP chapters (see "Independent Feature Project").

ILLEGAL. Behavior that is against the law, i.e, that can result in either criminal or civil sanctions. Criminal sanctions include prison sentences and fines. Civil sanctions include damages, liability and injunctions (see "Remedy").

ILLEGAL COMBINATION. Two or more persons or entities who join together to commit an illegal act, e.g., the joining together of two competing companies in an industry to alter the competitive balance in their favor is an illegal combination in restraint of trade (see "Combination in Restraint of Trade").

ILLEGAL TRADE PRACTICE. A custom in a business that is against the law, e.g., the fixing as between competitors of film licensing terms, runs, clearances and minimum admission prices (see "Anti-Trust Laws," "Price Fixing," "Reciprocal Preferences" and "Splitting Arrangements").

ILLEGAL USE OF MOTION PICTURE. A broad concept referring to any unauthorized exhibition of a film by exhibitors or individuals, including piracy (see "Copyright" and "Piracy").

ILLIQUID. A reference to a firm that lacks sufficient cash flow to meet current and maturing obligations. With respect to investments, illiquid means not readily convertible into cash, i.e., assets for which there is no ready market and which therefore may take some time to sell (see "Cash" and "Liquid Asset").

ILLUSORY PROMISE. A promise so indefinite that it cannot be enforced or which, by virtue of provisions or conditions contained in the promise itself, is one whose fulfillment is optional or entirely discretionary on the part of the promisor. Since such a promise does not constitute a legally binding obligation, it is not sufficient as consideration for a reciprocal promise and thus cannot create a valid contract (see "Contract" and "Contract of Adhesion").

IMMEDIATE WINDOW. The opportunity to exhibit a film in one medium shortly after it is exhibited in another medium, e.g., on basic cable following the network airing (see "Window").

IMPLIED REPRESENTATION. A statement which is not explicitly written or made but which is determined by deduction or inference from known facts and circumstances (see "Express Representation" and "Representation").

IMPORT PERMITS. Written authorizations provided by sovereign governments allowing an individual or entity to bring in a product from a foreign or external source. Motion picture distributors generally must obtain import permits in order to bring a film into a given country for exhibition in that country (see "Foreign Distribution").

IMPOUND. A condition required in certain securities offerings in which the investor funds received are placed in an escrow account, i.e., impounded and not released to the issuer of the securities until the amount needed has been raised. If the minimum amount is not received, all impounded funds are returned to the subscribers (see "Escrow").

IMPROPERLY CLAIMED EXPENSES. A distributor accounting practice in which the distributor wrongfully or unfairly allocates certain of its incidental expenses or costs to a film, or completely fabricates distribution expenses that are allocated to a film (see "Creative Accounting," "Overreported Travel," "Studio Accounting Practices" and "Unethical Business Practices").

INCENTIVE PAYMENTS. Compensation awarded to persons or entities for helping to produce above-average or better-than-expected results (see "Contingent Compensation").

INCESTUOUS SHARE DEALING. The buying and selling of the corporate stock of one company by another company and vice versa for the purpose of creating tax or other financial advantages (see "Reciprocal Preferences").

INCOME. An economic benefit; money or value received (see "Net Income").

INCOME FORECAST METHOD. An accounting procedure, i.e., a method of depreciation (the recovery of cost through tax deductions), generally used for films which helps to ensure acceleration of deductions against film revenues. It is computed by multiplying the capitalized cost of the film by a fraction with a numerator equal to the net receipts (gross receipts less current deductible costs and distribution fees) from the film for the taxable year in question and a denominator equal to the total estimated net receipts from the film. Such estimates must be reasonable or they may be challenged by the IRS (see "Accelerated Cost Recovery," "Net Receipts," "Straight-Line Depreciation" and "Tax Benefits").

INCOME STATEMENT. A financial statement that gives operating results for a specific period; also referred to as earnings report, operating statement and profit-and-loss statement. Such statements normally cover twelve months of operations with interim statements at quarterly periods in current fiscal or calendar years (see "Profit and Loss Statement").

INCOME TAX. An annual tax imposed upon income received, reduced by the allowable deductions and credits (see "Foreign Tax Credits" and "Internal Revenue Service").

INCOME TAX EFFECTS. The results of a transaction with regard to federal income taxes (see "Income Tax").

INCORPORATE. To form a corporation; to organize and be granted status as a corporation by following procedures prescribed by law (see "Corporation").

INDEMNIFICATION. An agreement between two parties whereby one agrees to pay the other if the other incurs certain expenses. In a securities offering, a form of intended reimbursement to an underwriter by an issuer for payment by the underwriter to a customer/investor who successfully litigates issues relating to the purchased securities sold by such underwriter. Also, the process of protecting or compensating someone or an entity against hurt, loss or damage and/or compensating them for any incurred hurt, loss or damage, i.e., an exemption from incurred penalties or liabilities (see "Insurance" and "Liability").

INDEMNIFICATION PROVISION. A contractual provision for the indemnification of one or both parties to an agreement (see "Indemnification").

INDEMNIFY. To secure against loss or damage which may occur in the future, or to provide compensation for or to repair loss or damage already suffered; also to insure or to save harmless (see "Hold Harmless").

INDEMNITY. The obligation or duty resting on one person to make good any loss or damage another has incurred or may incur by acting at his, her or its request or for his, her or its benefit. Typically a film distribution agreement will require that the producer or production company provide such an indemnity, i.e., agree to indemnify the distributor for any breach of the producer's warranties and representations. In addition, there is usually no reciprocal indemnification provision in favor of the producer nor are there extensive distributor warranties (see "Warranty" and "Representations").

INDENTURE. A written agreement which sets out the terms under which bonds or debentures may be issued. Terms include the amount of the issue, the interest rate, the maturity, the property pledged as collateral, if any, and certain covenants including any provision for a sinking fund. An independent trustee, usually a bank or trust company, is named to oversee the issue of the bonds, to collect and pay interest and principal and to protect the bondholder's rights as specified in the indenture (see "Bond," "Debenture" and "Sinking Fund").

INDEPENDENT AUDIT RIGHTS. The authority to conduct an examination of the books and records separate from an authorized entity, e.g., in a film distribution agreement, the distributor will undertake the responsibility for paying directly to third-party participants any portion of the production company's share of gross or net proceeds as assigned by the production company, provided that no such third party has an audit right other than that granted to the production company (see "Audit," "Audit Rights" and "Broad Audit Rights").

INDEPENDENT CHECKING COMPANY. A business that can be hired by a producer or distributor to verify the number of paid ticket purchasing moviegoers in attendance at showings of a given movie and which is not the checking service normally used by the major studio/distributors (see "Attendance Checking," "Checker," "Checking and Collection Costs," "Puffed Numbers" and "Skimming").

INDEPENDENT CONTRACTOR. One who makes an agreement with another to do a piece of work while retaining control of the means, method and manner of producing the result (see "Employee," "Freelance Employee").

INDEPENDENT CONTRACTOR AGREEMENT. The written contract between a feature film producer and a person providing services in the production of a motion picture when such services are being rendered on an independent contract basis as opposed to on an employee basis pursuant to an employment agreement (see "Independent Contractor").

INDEPENDENT DISTRIBUTOR. A motion picture distributor not affiliated with one of the major studio/distributors (see "American Film Marketing Association," "Independent Producer" and "Major Studio/ Distributors").

INDEPENDENT FEATURE FILM. Any feature motion picture production that is not made by one of the major studios (see "Independent Producer" and "Major Studio/Distributors").

INDEPENDENT FEATURE PROJECT (IFP). A non-profit, membership organization dedicated to promoting quality American independent feature filmmaking and supporting the efforts of individual filmmakers through educational programs, publications, services and awards. Members include producers, directors, writers, craftspeople, distributors and movie industry executives. The IFP is not an advocacy group and, even if it modified its charter and status as a not-for-profit educational organization, it would probably have difficulty obtaining a consensus relating to a single important advocacy issue from its diverse membership and corporate sponsors (see "AIVF," "Conflicts of Interest," "IFP/West" and "Producers Guild of America").

INDEPENDENT FILM (see "Independent Production").

INDEPENDENT FILMMAKER. One who has an idea for a film (or obtains the rights to an existing literary property), raises the funds with which to make the film, maintains substantial creative control throughout the making of the film, and ultimately arranges for marketing and distribution (see "Filmmaker" and "Producer").

INDEPENDENTLY DISTRIBUTED FILM. A film which is produced by a company that does not rent, sell or license its films through a major motion picture distributor (see "Independent Distributor," "Independent Feature Film," "Market Power" and "Market Share").

INDEPENDENT MARKET SHARE. The percentage of theatrical box office-gross garnered by the films distributed by independent distributors collectively as opposed to the percentage of box office gross of the films distributed by the major studio/distributors. The independent distributor market share has only averaged about 7% of the box office gross in the last ten years or so (see "Market Share").

INDEPENDENT PRODUCER. In the narrowest sense, individual producers or film production companies that do not work for the major studios, i.e., are not studio employees. Some make the further distinction that independent producers or production companies generally do not own their own production studios and are not likely to be a continual source of motion pictures for exhibitors. However, many producers who qualify as independent producers using these criteria have contractual relationships with the studios which provide for the studio financing of these independent producers' feature film projects and provide substantial authority for the studio to approve certain significant elements of the film. Since 1971, independent producers have produced more than half of the films made in the United States. Unfortunately, of the 600 to 700 feature films that are produced each year in the U.S., only 400 to 500 get any kind of theatrical release, about half of those are self-distributed (i.e., each was the only film distributed by the same company that produced it), and only about 150 of the others are distributed by the major studio/distributors (the MPAA companies). While some of the MPAA company releases are produced by independent producers, the MPAA releases generate more than 90% of the domestic theatrical box-office gross each year. On the other hand, profit participation auditors who work in the field on a daily basis estimate that only 5% of the MPAA films released each year achieve net profits [see "Acquisition," "Financing," "Housekeeping Deal," "Output Deal," "Overall Deal," "Producer," "Production-Financing/Distribution Agreement," "Right of First Refusal" and "Spec (Speculation)"].

INDEPENDENT PRODUCTION. Technically, TV or film production not financed by a major studio. However, studios today often finance all of a so-called independent producer's overhead, research and development, production and distribution costs in exchange for owning the rights to distribute the film throughout the world in all media, and, in that context, "independent" is used to indicate the producer is not on the studio's permanent payroll. Independent productions not financed by studios or other production companies that are not signatories to the various guild agreements may involve non-union cast and crew. Generally, films produced as independent productions are lower budgeted films than studio-produced films (see "Independent Feature Film").

INDEPENDENT PRODUCTION COMPANY. A company which specializes in producing feature films and is not associated with a major studio except contractually (see "Major Studio/Distributors").

INDEPENDENT PRODUCTION PARTNERSHIPS. A reference to several joint venture feature-film production entities, not directly associated with the major U.S. studio/distributors that have been created in recent years with massive funding from foreign sources. The term could also apply to any feature film limited partnership that is not closely affiliated with a major/studio distributor (see "Foreign Equity Financing," "Joint Venture" and "Limited Partnership").

INDEPENDENTS (see "Independent Distributor," "Independent Producer" and "Independent Production Company").

INDEPENDENT SPECIALTY DISTRIBUTORS. Small entrepreneurial film distributors who specialize in distributing the lower-budgeted, so-called "B" projects (see "Art Film," Art Theatre," "B-Movies" and "Calendar House").

INDEPENDENT THEATRE. A theatre not owned or operated by a large theatre chain (see "Blind Bidding" and "Major Exhibition Chains").

INDIRECT COSTS AND EXPENSES (see "Direct Distribution Expenses," "Overhead," "Overhead Costs" and "Production Overhead").

INDIVIDUAL FILM FORECAST METHOD (see "Income Forecast Method").

INDUCEMENT AGREEMENT (same as "Inducement Letter").

INDUCEMENT LETTER. An informal written agreement in letter form signed by an individual artist/performer, stating that such artist/performer has a binding agreement with his or her loan out company and agrees to be bound by and perform all provisions of the loan out (or lending) agreement executed as between the loan out company and the motion picture production company which is hiring the artist through the use of a loan out agreement (see "Lending Agreement," "Loan Out Arrangement" and "Loan Out Company").

INDUSTRY ANALYSTS. Persons, usually specialists in financial matters or in the news media, who observe, collect data, study and report on trends in the entertainment field (see "Broker/Dealer," "Paul Kagan Associates, Inc." and "Trades").

INDUSTRY ASSESSMENTS. The prorated dues, fees or other costs required of member companies to support the activities of industry trade groups such as the MPAA, MPEAA, AFMA, etc. Such costs are typically included in the definition of distribution expenses in a distribution agreement (see "Distribution Expenses," "Dues and Assessments" and "Industry Groups").

INDUSTRY CRITIC. An individual who provides analysis and information which is critical of the film industry or a segment of the industry (see "Critic" and "Industry Analysts").

INDUSTRY GROUPS. A broad term including all film or entertainment-related organizations such as trade associations, professional associations, union and guilds. Industry groups include the MPAA, the MPEAA, the Academy of Arts and Sciences, AMPTP, AFI, AFMA, IFP, and the numerous guilds (see "Association Projects," "Lobbyists" and "Professional Association").

INDUSTRY OVERVIEW. A section of a securities offering disclosure document which is required to be included in some circumstances. The overview relates to the industry generally and not to the specific project(s) being funded. Typically, a motion picture industry overview will include an explanation of the various stages of film production (development, pre-production, principal photography and distribution) and a description of the route the money, if any, will take in getting back to the investors, including the ranges of fees or percentages typically deducted along the way and by whom (see "Disclosure Document" and "Investor Financing").

INDUSTRY PROFIT MARGINS. The average difference between gross sales and net profits for an industry as a whole or a significant portion of an industry, e.g., the major studio/distributors in the motion picture business. Industry analysts have pegged industry profit margins for the "majors" at below 10% for the first several years of the '90s (see "Profit Margin" and "Profitability").

INDUSTRY TRADES (see "Trades").

INFERIOR BARGAINING POSITION. Economic and other circumstances that result in less leverage for one party when negotiating a transaction. With few exceptions, independent feature film producers in the current industry environment have little or no real negotiating power when it comes to determining the terms of the distribution deal. In the first place, the basic economic law of supply and demand is working against the independent producers, i.e., there are too many films being produced each year. More films are being produced than there are available distributors who are willing to distribute, and, even though many of the films being produced arguably do not deserve to be released, there are still too few distributors that are both capable and willing to distribute the worthy films. Thus, even though the available distributors may be willing to negotiate on certain aspects of the distribution deal as to any given issue, distributors pretty much have the power to say "take it or leave it." Of course, many independent producers foolishly believe that by producing a "great" film, all of their problems associated with their inherent "inferior bargaining position" will go away. Unfortunately, by concentrating most if not all of their time, energy and skill on the creative side of the film-business equation as opposed to the business side of the business, many independent producers end up winning the "film" but losing the "deal" (see "Arm's Length," "Creative Accounting," "Contract of Adhesion," "Law of Supply and Demand" and "Leverage").

INFLATION. An increase in the volume of money and credit relative to available goods resulting in a substantial and continuing rise in the general level of prices (see "Inflation Indexed Cap").

INFLATION INDEXED CAP. A ceiling on payments that may move up or down with the rate of inflation (see "Inflation").

IN-FLIGHT VERSION. A feature film edited so as to make it suitable for exhibition on airplanes, specifically with respect to the exhibitor's time and rating requirements (see "Non-Theatrical" and "Other Versions").

INFORMATION REQUIREMENTS. Securities disclosure regulations relating to the type of information required to be furnished to prospective purchasers of securities under an exemption from registration such as Regulation D or a specific form of registration, e.g., Regulation A, Form S-1 or Form S-18 (see "Disclosure Document," "Regulation D" and "Securities").

INFRINGEMENT OF COPYRIGHT (see "Copyright Infringement," "Fair Use" and "Plagiarism").

INFRINGEMENT SUIT. A federal court lawsuit brought against someone who is alleged to have used copyrighted material in an unauthorized manner (see "Copyright" and "Plagiarism").

IN-HOUSE PRODUCT. A motion picture developed and produced by and within the organization of a producer/distributor as opposed to a film produced by an independent producer and acquired by the distributor for distribution (see "Acquisitions," "Distribution Alternatives," "Negative Pickup," "Production-Financing/Distribution Agreement" and "Rent-A-Distributor").

INITIAL ACTUAL BREAKEVEN. Another contractually defined breakeven point in the revenue stream of a motion picture, which commonly means that point at which net proceeds are reached (see "Actual Breakeven," "Artificial Breakeven," "Breakeven," "Cash Breakeven" and "Rolling Breakeven").

INITIAL DISTRIBUTION. The first release of a completed motion picture for viewing by the general public; also the first release of a video (see "Release," "Re-Release" and "Re-Issuing Costs").

INITIAL PUBLIC OFFERING (IPO). A corporation's first offering of stock to the public through a registered/public stock offering (contrast with "Primary Distribution;" see "Corporate Stock," "Penny Stock," "Pricing Amendment," "Publicly Held" and "Public Offering").

INITIAL RELEASE (see "Initial Distribution").

INITIAL RELEASE BUDGET. The planned and categorized expenditures associated with a film's first distribution (see "Initial Distribution").

INITIAL U.S. THEATRICAL RELEASE. The first distribution of a motion picture in the United States. Some distribution agreements provide that the distributor will consult in good faith with the production company regarding the distribution pattern and ad campaign for the initial U.S. theatrical release, provided, however that the distributor's decisions with respect thereto will be final (see "Advertising Campaign," "Release Pattern" and "Right of Consultation").

INJUNCTION. A judicial remedy granted for the purpose of requiring a party to do or refrain from doing or continuing to do a particular act or activity. The injunction is a preventative measure which guards against future injuries rather than affording a remedy for past injuries (see "Enjoin," "Equitable Remedy," "Litigation" and "Remedy or Remedies").

INJURY. Any wrong or damage done to the person, rights, reputation or property of another (see "Crime," "Damage" and "Tort").

IN KIND. To return something of the same or similar type or quality to that which was received, though not necessarily the identical article (see "Restitution").

IN PERPETUITY. To exist forever; perpetually (see "Term").

INSERT. A close-up of short duration edited into a film sequence to help explain some part of the action or to assist in the film's continuity (see "Action," "Close-Up," "Continuity" and "Sequence").

INSIDE INFORMATION. Corporate affairs that have not yet been made public. SEC rules restricts the ability of an insider to trade on the basis of such information (see "Insider" and "Insider Trading").

INSIDER. In the corporate world, a person with access to key corporate information before it is announced to the public; every officer and director of a corporation and any person who owns more than 10% of the stock of that corporation is an insider. In a more general sense, a person who is in a position of power in a business or industry (see "Control Person" and "Principal Stockholder").

INSIDER'S GAME. A competitive industry viewed as a contest between rival factions and run by a restricted inner circle of people, admission into which may be limited by arbitrary considerations. These so-called "insiders" in the film industry are also sometimes referred to as being "members of the club." Although different people may use varying criteria for defining who or how many people are actually "members of the club," in a general sense these "club members" are the top level owner/executives of the major studio/distributors and the top actors, producers and directors in the industry along with their agents and attorneys (see "Economic War Zone," "Level Playing Field," "Member of the Club," "Reciprocal Preferences" and "Relationship-Driven Business").

INSIDER TRADING. The illegal buying or selling of corporate stock by a corporate officer or other corporate insider who profits by his or her access to information not available to the general public (see "Corporate Opportunity," "Fiduciary," "Inside Information," "Insider" and "Securities").

INSOLVENCY. A financial condition in which one is unable to meet his, her or its obligations as they mature in the ordinary course of business or has liabilities that exceed his, her or its assets at any given time (see "Bankruptcy").

INSTALLMENT SALE. A sale made with the agreement that the purchased goods or services will be paid for in fractional amounts over a specified period of time (see "Interest").

INSTITUTIONAL ADVERTISING. Advertising sponsored by or carried on behalf of large or significant organizations in a given society or culture, e.g., banks, insurance companies, labor unions, universities, etc. (see "Advertising").

INSTITUTIONAL INVESTOR. An organization that trades large volumes of securities, usually an insurance company, investment company or bank (see "Bank" and "Investor").

INSTRUMENTATION. In music, the theory and practice of composing, arranging or adapting music for a group of instruments of different kinds. Also, the term is sometimes used to refer to the list of instruments for which a work is scored (see "Conducting" and "Orchestration").

INSTRUMENT OF TRANSFER. The legal document which conveys the title of property and/or rights to the new owner (see "Chain of Title" and "Title").

INSTRUMENTS. Legal documents in which some contractual relationship is given formal expression or by which some right is granted (see "Contract").

INSURABLE INTEREST. That relationship with a person or thing that will support the issuance of an insurance policy. A person or entity is usually regarded as having an insurable interest in the subject matter insured when such person or entity will derive pecuniary benefit or advantage from its preservation, or will suffer pecuniary loss or damage from its destruction (see "Insurance," "Insured" and "Insured Risk").

INSURABLE RISK. Any possibility of loss relating to the production of a motion picture that may be insured against. Production lenders and completion guarantors will not assume responsibility for such risks and will require that the producer obtain available insurance to protect against loss (see "Insurance," "Insurance Coverages" and "Lender Risk Elimination").

INSURANCE. A financial arrangement or agreement (insurance policy) between an individual or company (the insured) and a financial institution (insurance company, insurance carrier or insurer) whereby the insurer agrees to compensate the owner of the insurance policy in the event of the destruction, or loss of, or injury to, a specified person or thing in which the policy owner has an insurable interest. The policy owner pays premiums as consideration for the insurer's commitment. In a broad economic sense, insurance transfers risk from individuals to a larger group. Motion picture insurance premiums for various coverages, excluding the completion bond, generally equal about 3% of a film's budget (see "Claims Made Policy," "Completion Bond," "Insurance Policy," "Policy," "Premium" and "Reinsurance").

INSURANCE CARRIER. An insurance company (see "Insurance").

INSURANCE COVERAGES. The various kinds of insurance policies and occurrences for which insurance is designed to provide financial protection. Motion picture insurance may include coverage for the camera and processing; cast; comprehensive liability; completion guaranty; errors and omissions; extra expense; faulty stock, props, sets and wardrobe; guild/union flight accident; miscellaneous equipment; negative film and videotape; property damage liability and worker's compensation. A producer's insurance policy may incorporate all or some combination of these coverages (see "Insurable Risk" and "Producer's Insurance Policy").

INSURANCE POLICY. The actual document which is the contract between the insurance company and the insured that states the agreement terms (see "Certificate of Insurance" and "Claims Made Policy").

INSURANCE PREMIUM. The consideration paid by the insured to the insurance company for the insurance policy and the coverages it provides (see "Insurance Coverages").

INSURANCE TAKE (see "Cover Shot").

INSURED. The person or entity protected by an insurance policy; usually, the person who contracts for a policy of insurance that indemnifies him, her or it against loss, although the policyholder (owner) may not be the same as the insured in some cases (see "Additional Insureds" and "Insurance").

IN SYNCH. A technical phrase stating that the sound and the picture in a film are synchronously joined, i.e., properly timed (see "Composite" and "Synchronism").

INTANGIBLE. Abstract; having no physical material body. In its intangible form, a motion picture is viewed as a collection of rights that may be sold or licensed in their entirety or piece by piece (see "Commodity," "Intangible Assets," "Product" and "Tangible Asset").

INTANGIBLE ASSETS. Rights or non-physical resources that are presumed to represent an advantage to the firm's position in the marketplace. Such assets include copyrights, patents, trademarks, goodwill, computer programs, capitalized advertising costs, organization costs, licenses, leases and import and export permits (contrast with "Tangible Assets").

INTEGRATION. In securities law, a concept used for determining whether a given offering is a separate offering, and thus may qualify for an available exemption from registration, or whether it is part of a larger offering and must be treated as such for regulatory purposes. The Regulation D integration provision requires that all sales which are part of the same Regulation D offering must meet all of the terms and conditions of Regulation D. However, offers and sales that are made more than six months before the start of a Regulation D offering or are made more than six months after completion of a Regulation D offering will not be considered part of that Regulation D offering, so long as during those six month periods there are not offers or sales of securities by or for the issuer that are of the same or a similar class as those offered or sold under Regulation D, except for other specified exempt offers or sales. The SEC considers the following factors in determining whether offerings should be integrated for regulatory purposes: whether the offerings (1) are part of a single plan of financing, (2) involve the same class of security, (3) are made at or about the same time, (4) involve the same type of consideration and (5) are made for the same general purpose (see "Offering" and "Regulation D").

INTER-CLIENT CONFIDENTIALITY. Attorney ethics require that a lawyer not reveal information relating to representation of a client unless the client consents after consultation, except for disclosures that are impliedly authorized in order to carry out the representation. This ethical prohibition sometimes presents problems for the entertainment attorney who represents several clients, all of whom may be involved in the same film production (see "Code of Professional Responsibility," "Conflicts of Interest," "Ethics" and "Representation of Multiple Clients").

INTERCUT. A film editing technique in which different sequences of action are alternated between each other to make them appear to be happening concurrently in the movie (see "Edit").

INTEREST. Consideration or compensation paid for the use of money loaned; the cost of using money, expressed as a rate per period of time, usually one year, in which case it is called an annual rate of interest. In studio financing, interest is typically deducted as part of the net profit calculation. The interest issue creates problems for independent producers at several levels: (a) **Interest Plus Profit Participation**. Distribution agreements involving at least partial studio or distributor financing of the negative cost of a film often allow the distributor to charge interest on its unrecouped negative cost in addition to permitting the studio or affiliated distributor to retain a substantial if not overwhelming interest in any profit participation. If a distributor is being paid a fair rate of interest on its borrowed funds, it should not also be permitted to participate in a motion picture's net profits or other defined level of the film's revenue stream beyond the deduction of its distribution fee and direct expenses; (b) **Interest Rates That Are Excessive**. The interest rate charged by the studio is often not in proportion to the actual cost of funds. Studios have been known to charge interest rates of 20% to 30%. If anything, since the studio affiliated distribution company is also able to obtain compensation in the form of its distribution fees, the affiliated studio acting as a financier should charge less than the market rate for interest on the borrowed funds; (c) **Interest on Advances**. The studio/distributors may take the position that advances should not be included in gross receipts until earned, in other words, the distributor will want to deduct an amount equal to any advance that has been paid to the producer from monies received by the distributor and will not want to consider such amounts as part of gross receipts for any profit participation calculations which start with a gross receipts figure. At the same time, the studio/distributor may seek to charge interest on such advances. The producer and other profit participants may want to take the position that if advances are excluded from gross receipts, no interest should be charged on such amounts; (d) **Interest on Monies Not Spent**. Interest is sometimes charged on monies not yet spent by the distributor, e.g., in preparing an earnings statement for a film, the distributor may accrue the print and advertising costs incurred but not yet paid so that an interim participation statement will not show a profit. This accrual of expenses also reduces gross receipts which could be used to reduce negative costs and thereby also reduce interest charges. In other words, the studio may seek to calculate interest on negative costs from the point at which such expenses are incurred (as an accounting entry), whereas the producer may prefer to have such interest calculated as of the time such expenses are actually paid by the studio; (e) **When Interest Charges Stop**. Studios may also seek to continue charging interest on the negative costs of a film until the end of the accounting period in which payments reducing the negative cost total and/or interest are received by the studio, whereas the producer and other net profit participants may insist that interest charges stop when such payments are actually received by the studio and not wait until the end of the accounting period, however many months that might involve; (f) **Interest on Negative Cost Balances**. In calculating this interest on the studio's unrecouped negative costs, all direct distribution costs and fees are typically first deducted from gross receipts as expenses of distribution, thus significantly decreasing the amount of gross receipts, if any, which may apply toward recoupment of the studio's contribution toward production costs. Thus, at many early stages of earnings statements, no recoupment of negative costs is achieved and the interest charges simply continue to accrue. In contrast, with a bank-financed motion picture production, the bank will recoup its loaned amount (including the negative cost, plus interest and fees) before the distributor deducts its distribution fee and expenses. If a studio wants to act like a bank and charge interest on borrowed funds, then it ought to also allow a priority position for the recoupment of negative costs so as not to unfairly extend the repayment of the loaned amount thus increasing the total interest charges. In such situations, the studio/bank is guilty of self-dealing; (g) **Interest on Overhead**. In many instances, even some or all of the indirect distribution costs, the normal costs of doing business as a distributor which are not specifically tied to a particular film being distributed (overhead), are also deducted from gross receipts as distribution expenses and again, are not available for recoupment of the negative cost. Other items of overhead may be inappropriately characterized as production costs, thus interest may also be charged by a studio or distributor on some of these indirect distribution expenses; (h) **Simple vs. Exact Interest**. Studio/distributors also may use a form of simple interest, based on a 360-day year, instead of exact interest (based on a 365-day year), and that practice, particularly when dealing with substantial amounts of money in the form of negative costs, will result in the payment of a greater amount of interest to the studio/distributor for that final partial-interest-bearing term and (i) **Interest on Gross Participations**. A variation on the practice of charging interest on monies not actually spent in which the distributor for a distributor-financed motion picture categorizes gross participations as production costs (as opposed to distribution expenses) and thus charges interest and overhead on such participations (see "Actual Interest," "Contract of Adhesion,"

"Creative Accounting," "Exact Interest," "FASB Statement No. 53," "Greed," "Loan," "Overhead," "Overhead Costs," "Prime Rate," "Production Overhead" and "Usury").

INTEREST BEARING. An account or charge that yields interest. In film, the term usually refers to the studio's practice of charging interest on the studio's overhead surcharge and treating such interest as a production expense of the film. With respect to distribution and production expenses, it is important that a clear distinction be made between the two since, if an expense is categorized as a production cost, it will bear interest and overhead on studio financed films (see "Creative Accounting," "Interest" and "Production Costs").

INTEREST ON ADVANCES (see "Interest").

INTEREST ON GROSS PARTICIPATIONS (see "Interest").

INTEREST ON MONIES NOT SPENT (see "Interest").

INTEREST ON NEGATIVE COSTS BALANCES (see "Interest").

INTEREST ON OVERHEAD (see "Interest").

INTEREST ON PRODUCTION COSTS (see "Interest").

INTEREST ON THE SURCHARGE. Interest charged by a studio on the overhead fee it extracts from a studio financed production (same as "Interest on Overhead;" see "Interest Bearing," "Overhead," "Overhead Costs" and "Overhead Surcharge").

INTEREST PLUS PROFIT PARTICIPATION (see "Interest").

INTEREST RATE RISK. The possibility that a fixed-rate debt instrument will decline in value as a result of a rise in interest rates (see "Lender Risk Elimination").

INTERESTS OF LIMITED PARTNERS. The aggregate interests of all limited partners in their respective capacities as limited partners in the current profits derived from business operations of the partnership (see "Majority-in-Interest" and "Unit").

INTERIM CREDIT FACILITY. A loan or some form of credit extended to an organization during a period of transition, i.e., until the organization's permanent financing for its primary activity is obtained (similar to "Bridge Financing;" see "Commercial Paper").

INTERIM DIVIDEND. A corporate dividend declared and paid before annual earnings have been determined, generally on a quarterly basis (see "Corporate Stock" and "Dividend").

INTERIM RELIEF. A temporary interruption of court imposed restrictions. In recent years, distributors and theatre owners have sought interim relief from the application of the Paramount Consent Decrees (see "Conduct Restrictions," "Merger Guidelines," "Paramount Consent Decree of 1948," "TriStar Case" and "Vertical Merger").

INTERIM STATEMENT. A financial report covering only a portion of a fiscal year. Public corporations supplement the annual report with quarterly statements informing shareholders of changes in the balance sheet and income statement, as well as other corporate developments of interest to shareholders, the business community and the public (see "Annual Report").

INTERLOCKING DIRECTORATES. Corporate boards of directors whose members serve as directors on more than one corporate board (see "Corporate Conglomerate" and "Corporation").

INTERNAL FINANCING. Funds produced by the normal operations of a firm (see "External Financing").

INTERNAL RATE OF RETURN (IRR). A method of calculating the return on an investment, i.e., the discount rate which equates the yearly economic benefits to the present value of the investment; the rate that will discount future cash flows from an investment to an amount that equals the amount invested. Thus, it results in a net present value of zero (see "Adjusted Rated of Return," "Discounted Cash Flow," "Rate of Return" and "Required Rate of Return").

INTERNAL REVENUE SERVICE (IRS). The U.S. government agency responsible for collecting nearly all federal taxes, including personal and corporate income taxes, social security taxes and excise and gift taxes. The IRS administers the rules and regulations of the U.S. Department of the Treasury and investigates and prosecutes tax illegalities (see "Income Tax").

INTERNATIONAL ALLIANCE OF THEATRICAL AND STAGE EMPLOYEES (IATSE). The parent organization of some 1,000-plus local unions in North America representing every branch of film production, including stagehands, makeup artists and wardrobe handlers, as well as employees in film distribution and exhibition (see "Guild").

INTERNATIONAL BUYERS. Individuals or entities who acquire licensing rights to motion pictures for exploitation in foreign territories (see "Territory").

INTERNATIONAL CO-PRODUCTION AND AGREEMENTS. A source of film financing in which two or more entities from different countries contribute a portion of production financing and in exchange receive a share of profits from exploitation of the film. Most European countries, as well as Canada and Australia, have formal co-production treaties relating to financing and producing films. Often in such transactions, facilities such as studios, scenery, staff, etc., are provided in order to obtain foreign currency. Satisfaction of the requirements of an international co-production may yield financing benefits, such as subsidies, television quota benefits, tax benefits, and certain in-kind investments (see "Co-Production Financing," "Foreign Production Problems" and "Nationality Test").

INTERNATIONAL FILM IMPORTERS AND DISTRIBUTORS OF AMERICA (IFIDA). An assembly of independent producers and distributors which was listed in the MPAA publication about the history of the MPAA Ratings Board, as one of the three industry organization partners in the creation of the movie rating system. The rating system replaced its predecessor the Production Code Administration in November of 1968. Unfortunately, after numerous inquires, this author has been unable to find anyone at the MPAA, MPEAA or NATO who knows anything about this organization. It is also not listed in the Los Angeles or area telephone listings. Thus, it appears likely that the organization no longer exists, in which case its current status should be noted in the above referenced MPAA publication, because otherwise it is misleading to suggest that any association of independent producers is currently supporting the MPAA Ratings Board (see "Industry Groups," "MPAA" and "Production Code Administration").

INTERNATIONALLY COMPETITIVE. Able to vie for business throughout the world. On the one hand it appears reasonable for the major studio/distributors to use their political influence to persuade the U.S. government to relax its enforcement of the anti-trust laws in the entertainment industry in an effort to free these entities from restrictions that impair their ability to compete in a global marketplace. On the other hand, if such relaxed enforcement increases the competitive stranglehold of the major studio/distributors on the domestic industry and makes it even more difficult for the many thousands of independent, small business persons to survive (whether they be production companies, distributors, exhibitors or otherwise), then there needs to be a better balancing of interests in this industry. Also, certain domestic film-industry organizations have traditionally worked together in the foreign distribution of films anyway, thus there may be no need to permit vertical integration in the domestic marketplace in order to create more strength for U.S. companies in the foreign marketplace (see "Anti-Trust Laws," "Paramount Consent Decree of 1948" and "TriStar Case").

INTERNATIONAL PARTICIPATIONS. Percentage interests in some level of a motion picture's revenue stream generated through a film's foreign exhibition (see "Foreign Equity Financing" and "Gross Participations").

INTERNATIONAL TAX ATTORNEY. A lawyer with expertise relating to the tax laws of foreign countries (see "Entertainment Attorney" and "Securities Attorney").

INTERNATIONAL TAX SHELTER/INCENTIVES (see "Foreign Tax Shelters" and "Foreign Subsidies").

INTERNEGATIVE. A negative made from the original film negative and using reversal film stock (see "Dupe Negative" and "Reversal Film Stock").

INTER-PARTY AGREEMENT. An agreement among the lending entity, the film distributor and the producer which, among other things, provides that the distributor's interest in the revenues generated from the exploitation of the film is subordinated to the interest of the bank in repayment of the bank's loan and the payment of its interest charges (see "Lender Financing" and "Negative Pickup").

INTERPOLATING. Inserting between other things or parts, e.g., interpolating additional film footage (see "Edit" and "Final Cut").

INTERPOSITIVE. A positive print of a film produced from the original negative which is used to produce dupe negatives. An interpositive is not used for projection (see "Print").

INTERSTATE OFFERING. A securities offering made or which may be made to residents of more than one state (see "Intra-State Offering").

IN THE CAN. The exposed film, ready to go to the lab; or that filming is completed (see "Acquisition Distribution Agreement," "Can" and "Rent-A-Distributor").

INTRA-STATE OFFERING. A federal exemption from the SEC securities registration requirement which may be made by an issuer organized under the laws of a given state, doing its principal business in such state, and offered solely to bona fide residents of such state with substantially all of the proceeds of the offering remaining in the state. Such an offering would still need to comply with the applicable state registration or exemption requirements. This federal exemption is primarily used to fund local businesses such as restaurants. It would not be appropriate for financing a film since the market for a film generally includes the entire universe (see "Blue Sky Laws," "Interstate Offering," "Private Offering," "Public Offering" and "Securities").

IN TURNAROUND. The film development status in which the developing studio or production company decides not to continue developing the property or decides not to go into production on the film, thus making the property available for acquisition by others (see "Turnaround").

INVASION OF PRIVACY. The wrongful intrusion into a person's private activities by other individuals or by the government including the unauthorized use of a person's name or likeness, the unauthorized disclosure of private facts and false depiction of the voice of a person (see "Right of Publicity" and "Tort").

INVESTMENT. The use of capital to create more money, either through income-producing vehicles or through more risk-oriented ventures designed to result in capital gains (contrast with "Loan;" see "Debt," "Investor Financing" and "Securities").

INVESTMENT ADVISER. A person or entity who, for compensation, engages in the business of advising others regarding investing in, purchasing or selling securities. The activities of such persons are regulated by the Investment Advisers Act of 1940. It is generally illegal for the sellers of securities to provide compensation to investment advisors unless the investment advisor is also licensed as a broker/dealer and the compensation is fully disclosed to all parties (see "Broker," "Broker/Dealer," "Dealer" and "Finder").

INVESTMENT BANK OR INVESTMENT BANKER. A broker who acts as an underwriter of securities. The investment banker can act as principal by buying the entire issue from the issuer or as agent by selling the offering on a "best-efforts" basis. In either case, the investment banker sells the issue to other dealers who, together with the lead banker, have formed an underwriting syndicate. Members of the syndicate in turn sell the shares to the investing public and to institutional investors (see "Broker," "Broker/Dealer" and "Selling Group").

INVESTMENT CLUB. A group of people who pool their assets in order to make joint investment decisions. Choices of which investments to make are made by a vote of members. Pursuant to Regulation D, an investment club investment in a Regulation D offering would be counted as one investor so long as such entity was not organized for the specific purpose of acquiring the securities offered (see "National Association of Investment Clubs" and "Regulation D").

INVESTMENT COMMUNITY. Individuals and/or entities who invest or may invest in a given industry such as the entertainment industry (see "Investor Financing").

INVESTMENT CONTRACT. A form of investor financing which does not involve the creation of an entity (like a joint venture, limited partnership or corporation) but which does involve a contractual relationship between the so-called "contract administrator" and the investor group. An investment contract is otherwise defined as an investment in a common enterprise in which the investors hope to make a profit primarily off the managerial efforts of others. An investment contract may be suitable for all sorts of small securities offerings, however, in the context of feature film financing, it may work best as a contractual financing vehicle between a producer (contract administrator) and a passive investor or investors used to raise funds by means of a preliminary/developmental securities offering to pay for a film's development costs, along with the up-front costs associated with a subsequent "main offering" (e.g., limited partnership offering) or the costs associated with marketing the developed property to a major studio/distributor or other production company/distributor. This financing vehicle might also be useful in financing the production costs of an ultra-low budget film, video or television pilot project. An investment contract is a security and a direct investment, thus compliance with federal and state securities laws is required and the investors do not enjoy the limited liability of the investor/owners of limited partnership interests or of corporate stock. A limited partnership is a form of investment contract and thus also a security (see "Financing," "Investor Financing," "Investor Financing Agreement," "Preliminary/Development Disclosure Document," "Preliminary/Development Offering," "Preliminary/Development Funds" and "Security" or "Securities").

INVESTMENT GRADE BONDS. Corporate bonds with high ratings (see "Bond" and "Junk Bonds").

INVESTMENT GROUP. An association of individuals or entities brought together for the purpose of investing in a project or venture. The term "investment group" is more commonly applied to higher levels of investment than the term "investment club," e.g., several companies may go together to form an investment group and, in the process, create a new entity such as a corporation or joint venture, but the original group may be referred to as an investment group (see "Foreign Equity Investment" and "Investment Club").

INVESTMENT INCOME. Income from securities and other non-business investments, e.g., dividends, interest, royalty income and capital gains on stocks. Under the Tax Reform Act of 1986, investment income earned by passive activities, such as a limited partnership, must be treated separately from other passive income; also called portfolio income (see "Passive Income" and "Passive Loss").

INVESTMENT LETTER OF INTENT. A letter from a financial backer of a motion picture stating the intention of the financier to provide production funding for the picture which the producer can use to help in assembling the various elements required to produce a film. An investment letter of intent is also used in the private placement of new securities between the issuer of the securities and the purchaser establishing that the securities are being bought as an investment and not for resale. This purchaser representation is often included in the subscription agreement which the investor signs. Under SEC Rule 144A, a purchaser of such restricted securities may eventually resell them to the public if certain specific conditions are met including a minimum holding period of at least two years (see "Elements" and "Private Offering").

INVESTMENT MEMORANDUM (same as "Offering Memorandum").

INVESTMENT TAX CREDIT (ITC). A federal U.S. tax credit provided by the tax code which allowed feature films to be recognized as capital assets having a useful life of over three years, thus making films eligible for a 6 2/3% credit (based on the total negative investment) assuming that more than 80% of the picture was produced in the U.S. The ITC was considered to be a significant form of government subsidy for the film industry, i.e., the ITC had been a major selling point for film financing deals structured as limited partnerships. However, the ITC was repealed as part of the Tax Reform Act of 1986. In repealing the ITC, it would appear that any advantage a U.S.-based film industry had in producing movies in the U.S., i.e., keeping production dollars at home, was severely limited. A producing entity's decision to incur negative costs abroad may now make more economic sense because of lower foreign production costs and particularly if other governments offer tax incentives or other accommodations to attract the film production business. There has been some mention in Congress regarding the possibility of bringing back the ITC (see "Selling Point," "Tax Benefits" and "Tax Credit").

INVESTOR. A person or entity which provides development, production and/or distribution funding for a given movie project or projects, generally, and at least partly, for the purpose of earning a return (profit) on such investment. Unlike financiers, investors do not generally raise funds but only invest. The same active/passive distinction which applies to financiers also applies to investors. Generally, the raising of funds from passive investors involves the sale of a security and thus requires compliance with the federal and state securities laws (see "Financiers" or "Financing Source" and "Financing").

INVESTOR DAY ON THE SET. A special day set aside on the set of a motion picture during principal photography in which the investors are invited to visit the set. An often-used technique in low-budget filmmaking for films financed through the vehicle of a limited partnership which helps to glamorize the investment for the limited partners (see "Investor Financing").

INVESTOR FINANCING. A broad category of film finance, i.e., the funding of a motion picture project or projects through an investment vehicle, i.e., the placement of capital in an endeavor with the hope of making a profit. Generally, the distinction between active and passive investors forms the basis for distinguishing between a non-securities and securities investment offering, respectively. Interests in investor financing agreements and joint ventures, whose investors are generally actively involved in the management of the endeavor are typically not considered securities. Corporations, limited partnerships and investment contracts, whose investors are generally not actively involved in the management of the endeavor, are typically considered securities and thus must be offered in compliance with applicable federal and state securities laws (see "Financing," "Preliminary/Development Funds" and "Financiers" or "Financing Source").

INVESTOR FINANCING AGREEMENT. A written contract between a project manager, e.g., a feature film producer and a financing source. If the financing source is an active investor or a so-called industry partner who provides production monies in addition to some other service, such as distribution in a given medium or territory, such an arrangement probably does not involve a security. However, if such investors provide their financing and otherwise play a passive role with respect to the project, the federal and state securities laws probably apply to the transaction which then would more properly be characterized as an investment contract (see "Preliminary/Development Offering," "Investment Contract," "Development Money Investment Agreement," "Joint Venture" and "Limited Partnership").

INVESTOR MOTIVATION. The underlying incentives which prompt individuals or entities to contribute to the financing of certain business activities such as the development, production and/or distribution of feature films (see "Adjusted Rate of Return," "Glamour Industry," "Internal Rate of Return," "Profit Margin," "Profit Motive," "Rate of Return," "Return of Capital" and "Return on Invested Capital").

INVESTOR NUMERICAL LIMITATIONS. Federal and state securities law limitations imposed on the use of exemptions from the securities registration requirements to limit the number of investors who may purchase securities in such offerings, e.g., Regulation D Rules 505 and 506 limit sales to no more than thirty-five non-accredited investors (see "Accredited Investor," "Counting Rules" and "Regulation D").

INVESTOR RELATIONS ACTIVITIES. Activities conducted by an issuer of securities relating to keeping the investors informed about their investment (see "Investor Day on the Set" and "Investor Financing").

INVESTOR SOPHISTICATION REQUIREMENTS. Federal and/or state securities offering investor suitability requirements relating to the background, experience and education of a prospective investor, e.g., Regulation D Rule 506 requires that immediately prior to the sale, the issuer must reasonably believe that each non-accredited investor, either alone or with his or her purchaser representative, must have such knowledge and experience in financial and business matters that he or she is capable of evaluating the merits and risks of the prospective investment (see "Accredited Investor," "Investor Suitability Standards," "Purchaser Representative" and "Regulation D").

INVESTOR SUITABILITY STANDARDS. Federal and state securities rules that those selling sophisticated and potentially risky financial products, such as limited partnerships, must follow to ensure that investors have the financial means to assume the risks involved (also called "Investor Sophistication Requirements;" see "Purchaser Representations," "Suitability Questionnaires" and "Suitability Rules").

INVITATION TO BID. A written or oral solicitation or invitation by a distributor to one or more exhibitors to bid or negotiate for the right to exhibit a motion picture (see "Bid" and "Blind Bidding").

IPO. Initial public offering by a corporation of its stock (see "Initial Public Offering," "Mezzanine Level" and "Securities").

IRREVOCABLE. Incapable of being revoked; unalterable (see "Irrevocable Letter of Credit").

IRREVOCABLE LETTER OF CREDIT. A financing transaction in which a bank issues to a borrower a letter authorizing the borrower to draw on the bank for a stated amount for a specified period, guaranteeing to accept the drafts on the bank if they are made and providing that such authority cannot be revoked (see "Letter of Credit" and "Standby Letter of Credit").

IRREVOCABILITY. The quality or state of being irrevocable (see "Irrevocable").

IRREVOCABLY APPOINTED. An appointment that is not revocable (see "Power of Attorney").

IRS (see "Internal Revenue Service").

ISOLATED ANCILLARY RIGHTS. The rights to exploit a film in any single geographical or technological market other than theatrical distribution in the domestic market. Any such ancillary right that is likely to be worth a significant sum of money will probably be demanded by the domestic theatrical distributor as a pre-requisite for its commitment to distribute a film (see "Ancillary Rights," "Fractured Rights Deals" and "Split Rights Deals").

ISSUE. To authorize, execute and deliver shares of stock or other securities for sale to the public; the securities themselves (see "Issuer" and "Issuer Sales").

ISSUED AND OUTSTANDING. Shares of a corporation, authorized in the corporate charter, which have been physically delivered to and are being held by the corporation's shareholders (see "Corporation" and "Stock").

ISSUER. The entity which is issuing the securities, i.e., corporate stock or limited partnership interests, pre-formation limited partnership interests or units in a limited partnership offering. In a limited partnership context, the general partner as well as the limited partnership may be considered part of the issuer organization (see "Issuer Sales").

ISSUER DISQUALIFIER (see "Disqualifier").

ISSUER SALES. An offering of securities conducted directly by the issuer without the use of underwriters or broker/dealers. Persons conducting such sales on behalf of an issuer (1) must not be subject to a statutory disqualification, (2) cannot be compensated in connection with their participation by the payment of commissions or other remuneration based either directly or indirectly on transactions in securities, (3) cannot, at the time of their participation, be an associated person of a broker or dealer, (4) must primarily perform, or intend to perform at the end of the offering, substantial duties for or on behalf of the issuer otherwise than in connection with transactions in securities, (5) cannot have been brokers or dealers, or associated persons of a broker or dealer, within the preceding twelve months and (6) cannot participate in selling an offering of securities for any issuer more than once every twelve months (see "Broker/ Dealer," "Broker/Dealer Sales," "Broker/Dealer Selling Agreement," "Disqualifier," "Finder Sales," "Issuer" and "Underwriter").

IT'S ONLY MONEY. A rationalization that some distributors use when excusing some of the unethical business practices described herein. They're expressing the view that the film business is merely a game, that many of the disputes that occur only relate to money, and that's not important. The truth is that, in most instances, the money being squabbled over represents several years of people's lives, expertise and efforts as well as their dreams and that many of the film industry professionals whose rights are trampled because "it's only money" end up with a drinking problem or some other dysfunction due to the dilemma in which they find themselves, i.e., they don't feel they can sue the distributor and still be able to get another job in this town. Again, it is extremely important for producers and others to check the credits on other films distributed by a prospective distributor and inquire as to the distributor's attitude toward such things as fairness and honesty in business transactions (see "Blacklisting," "Business Practice," "Creative Accounting," "Insider's Game" and "Sue Us").

—J—

JACKET (OR BOX). The carton or covering of an album, videocassette or audio tape package used to protect and market such mechanical reproductions (see "Cassette").

JAMAICAN TAX INCENTIVES (see "Motion Picture Industry Encouragement Act").

JAPANESE MONEY. In recent years, many billions of dollars have been invested in the American film industry by Japanese owned concerns. A great deal of speculation has occurred relating to the questions of how such investments might impact on the domestic film industry and how such investments might turn out for the investors. If the distributor and/or industry practices described herein become or continue to be prevalent, it would be surprising if the investment of Japanese monies in the domestic film industry had any significant impact whatsoever on the domestic industry and equally surprising for the Japanese investors to fare any more favorably than other groups which have invested in the American entertainment industry in the past (see "Creative Accounting" and "Insider's Game").

JOINT VENTURE. A business undertaking by two or more parties in which profits, losses, and control are shared. A joint venture is a combination of two or more persons who jointly seek a profit from some specific business venture without designating themselves as an actual partnership or corporation. Although technically a form of general partnership, a joint venture usually connotes an enterprise of a more limited scope and duration. Investors in both joint ventures and general partnerships have joint liability for debts and torts. In film joint ventures, the parties may contribute various elements, financing, e.g., or non-monetary contributions such as the screenplay, an underlying property or a fully packaged project (see "Corporation," "Financing," "General Partnership," "Liability," Limited Liability" and "Limited Partnership").

JOINT VENTURE AGREEMENT. The written contract between individuals or business entities engaged in a joint venture which sets out the terms of their joint business endeavor (see "Joint Venture").

JOINT VENTURE FINANCING (see "Financing," "Investor Financing" and "Joint Venture").

JUDGMENTS. The determinations of courts of competent jurisdiction on matters submitted to such courts, i.e., for a final determination of the rights of the parties to lawsuits (see "Final Judgment" and "Litigation").

JUNK BONDS. Corporate debt instruments with a low credit rating issued by companies without extensive track records of sales and earnings, or by companies with questionable credit strength. Junk bonds are more risky and pay higher returns than investment grade bonds (see "Bond" and "Investment Grade Bonds").

JUNKET. A trip to the location of a film during principal photography sponsored by the film's producing entity and/or distributor for the working entertainment press and during which key cast and crew of the film are made available for photo sessions and interviews. Such film production junkets are designed to generate publicity for the film (see "Press Tour" and "Publicity").

JUNKING COSTS. Expenses incurred in discarding the accumulated scrap associated with the production or distribution of a film. Such costs are generally included in the list of distribution expenses in film distribution agreements (see "Distribution Expenses" and "Scrapping Prints").

JURISDICTION. A geographical territory in which there is a sovereign power or a governmental authority to govern or legislate. Thus, a jurisdiction may be a country, state, county or city. Also, in film labor matters, the term jurisdiction may relate to whether a particular union or guild has the authority to deal with a given matter (see "Collective Bargaining Agreement" and "Guild").

JUSTICE DEPARTMENT (see "U.S. Justice Department").

JUST TITLE. An ownership claim to property that is supportable against all other legal claims (also called "Clear Title," "Good Title" and "Proper Title;" see "Clearance" and "Title").

— K —

K-1 (see "Schedule K-1" and "Taxable Year").

KAGAN ASSOCIATES (see Paul Kagan Associates, Inc.).

KEY. In film distribution and exhibition, a geographical area in which a film is released for theatrical exhibition. Keys are further classified on the basis of population as major keys, ordinary keys or sub-keys (see "Break," "Key Cities," "Major Key," "Ordinary Key" and "Sub-Key").

KEY ART. Art work used in posters and ads for a motion picture (see "Advertising").

KEY ART-SHOWCASE CITIES. The major markets for art films in the U.S., including Los Angeles, Washington D.C., San Francisco, Seattle, Boston, Chicago, Toronto and New York (see "Art Film").

KEY CITIES. Cities which are cultural and media centers, larger and generally more lucrative film exhibition markets (see "Key").

KEY CREW AGREEMENTS. The employment contracts for the most important members of a film's production crew. Copies of such agreements are often part of the documentation required for review by a completion guarantor (see "Completion Bond" and "Crew").

KEY FACTORS. Accounting terminology for the significant matters on which an entity's future results are expected to depend. Such factors are basic to the entity's operations and thus encompass matters that affect, among other things, the entity's sales, production, service and financing activities. Key factors serve as a foundation for prospective financial statements and are the bases for the assumptions (see "Hypothetical Assumptions" and "Prospective Financial Statements").

KEY GRIP. The film production person responsible to the director of photography for supervising all grip crews who assist the gaffer during lighting procedures and to maneuver the camera unit during moving shots. Grips also aid various production departments such as sound, electrical, wardrobe and property in the moving and handling of their equipment (see "Crew" and "Grip").

KEY PERSONNEL. Other than the cast, the most important people involved in the production of a film are generally considered to be the producer, director, line producer, director of photography and production accountant (see "Cast" and "Crew").

KEY TRENDS. Where an industry seems to be heading on important issues (see "Trend").

KICKBACK. A form of bribery; a practice in which the seller of goods or services gives back to the purchasing agent of those goods or services a portion of the purchase price in order to induce the agent to enter into the transaction. In most commercial transactions, kickbacks are illegal and prohibited by criminal commercial bribery statutes. The principal of the purchasing agent may also have a cause of action against the agent to recover the amount of the bribe. Also, for tax purposes, amounts paid as kickbacks or bribes generally are not deductible. Producers and their auditors have to watch for indications of such arrangements in all of the distributor's relationships with the providers of services which the distributor pays for and deducts the cost as distribution expenses, e.g., outside advertising agencies, film labs, trailer production firms, exhibitors in co-operative advertising arrangements, distributor employees and facilities, distributor editing, censorship approvals, checking services, screening expenses, industry assessments, residuals and banking costs. It may also be difficult to distinguish between kickbacks and discounts or rebates in some situations (see "Creative Accounting," "Discount" and "Rebate").

— L —

LAB (LABORATORY). A company specializing in developing exposed motion picture stock, for both image and optical sound. Film laboratories make, process or develop the camera negative, positive work prints from the negative, black and white dupes from the work print, interpositive prints from the original negative and internegative prints from the interpositive, color-reversal internegatives from which release prints are made, the optical soundtrack, color and density corrections from scene to scene within the film (timing) and release prints for distribution. Many of the labs also have full post-production videotaping facilities for tape-to-tape, film-to-tape or tape-to-film transfers (see "Lab Charges" and "Laboratory Access Letter").

LAB CHARGES. The fees and expenses imposed by the film laboratory for developing the exposed film, making prints and performing the other services provided by the lab (see "Laboratory" and "Laboratory Deferments").

LAB EFFECTS. Optical images that can be added to film during lab processing and printing, e.g., pushing light, printing for night effect and sepia-toning black-and-white stock (see "Lab").

LABELS. Brands of commercial recordings issued under a name which is usually trademarked (see "Soundtrack Albums").

LABORATORY ACCESS AGREEMENT (same as "Laboratory Access Letter").

LABORATORY ACCESS LETTER. A letter signed by a film's producer authorizing the film laboratory to deliver to the distributor or its designee at any time during the term covered by the applicable distribution agreement any of the items described in the distribution agreement's delivery schedule (see "Delivery Schedule" and "Lab").

LABORATORY ACKNOWLEDGEMENT. A provision commonly found in laboratory access letters which provides that, by signing the laboratory access letter, the laboratory agrees to be bound by the instructions and directions contained in that letter and acknowledges that it has received negative and sound materials of at least standard commercial quality which are suitable for making commercially acceptable release prints and dubbed and subtitled versions of such prints (see "Laboratory Access Letter").

LABORATORY DEFERMENTS. The delayed payment (by agreement) of some or all of the compensation due to a film lab for its work in processing film (see "Deferments" and "Lab").

LABORATORY FILM PROCESSING AGREEMENT. A contract between the depositor of film elements with the film laboratory (the production company, owner or distributor) and the lab which contains the terms relating to processing the film and for compensating the lab (see "Lab" and "Lab Charges").

LABORATORY LETTER. A letter issued by a film laboratory upon completion of a film stating that the finished film is of acceptable commercial quality, that the script was substantially adhered to and that the agreed-upon cast members appeared in their proper roles. Upon receipt of the film and this laboratory letter, the distribution advance, if any, will be released to the producer or lending institution to pay back some or all of a production loan (see "Lab" and "Negative Pickup").

LABORATORY PLEDGEHOLDER AGREEMENT. An agreement between a lending bank and a film lab, which is often used in film financing situations involving bank loans, to minimize the laboratory's ability to interfere with the bank's right to enforce its security interest in the film negative. The agreement typically provides that the laboratory holds the negative as a trustee for the lender and includes language that protects the bank against the laboratory's creditors. It may also limit or waive the common-law or statutory lien a laboratory might impose on a film negative in the event that the film production company does not pay for lab services on other films of the same production company at the same lab (see "Lab").

LABOR-INTENSIVE BUSINESS. A business which requires a large pool of workers; an industry in which labor costs are more important than capital costs (see "Capital-Intensive Business").

LARCENY. The taking of another's property unlawfully with the intention of depriving the owner of its use (same as "Theft;" see "Racketeering" and "RICO").

LASER DISC. A video recording and playback device which is covered by a reflective plastic coating and uses a low-power laser beam to read audio and/or video information encoded in a series of microscopic depressions or tracks on the disc. Such discs can only be played on one side, but the tracks on a laser disc are spaced much more closely than those found on an audio record (see "Compact Disc," "Record" and "Technological Developments").

LATIN. A source language for English, French, Spanish and other languages. Some Latin phrases are still used in legal documents, although it would be preferable to eliminate their use and focus on making such documents more understandable to those who read them (see "Caveat Emptor").

LATITUDE. Freedom of action or choice. Most of the film distribution agreements offered in the current marketplace give the distributor a great deal of latitude with respect to matters relating to the distribution of the film and in the distributor's handling of monies resulting from the exploitation of such film (see "Creative Accounting," "Contract of Adhesion," "Contractually Defined Terms" and "Discretion").

LAUNCH. The commencement of a motion picture release (see "Release").

LAUNCH WINDOWS. Periods of times during which a film may be exhibited in a given market, e.g., theatrical, foreign, video, pay-tv, television network and syndication (see "Optimum Release Pattern" and "Release Sequence").

LAW OF SUPPLY AND DEMAND. A basic economic principle which provides that, to the extent the supply of goods or services is greater than the demand for such goods and services, and all other things are equal, the market price for such goods and services will be lower than if the demand was greater than the supply. In the film industry, this law is always at work. For example, there are clearly more talented actors and directors available for work on motion pictures than there are motion pictures produced in a given year, thus without the support of their respective unions, the compensation for the working actors and directors would likely be significantly less than it is. In addition, since there are more motion pictures produced each year than there are capable distributors willing to distribute such films, the distributors are in the stronger bargaining position with respect to the terms of the distribution agreements. In the U.S., the exhibitors have also built so many theatre screens that the distributors tend to have the advantage in negotiating the terms of their exhibition agreements, although a significant fluctuation in the number of films distributed in any given year may have an impact on the bargaining power between such parties. Also, as mentioned elsewhere in this book, some distributors are entering or re-entering the exhibition arena, thus eliminating any question of arm's length negotiation, disparity of bargaining power or the impact of the law of supply and demand as between the distributor and exhibitor in such situations. This presentation of the concept is, of course, an oversimplification, but the law of supply and demand does underlie and influence most of the negotiations between the parties named in this paragraph and many others in the film industry. It would also appear, however, that, based on the compilation of reported industry and distributor practices contained herein, certain distributors may have leveraged this basic economic advantage into an abusive dominance which could, under certain circumstances, be criminal. As indicated above, the disparity in bargaining power between distributors and others in the industry is partly based on this law of supply and demand; however, industry interest groups, such as unions, guilds, professional or trade associations—or even film schools— seem to be either unaware of the critical need to take steps to reduce this great disparity and unaware of the impact such legitimate action might have on the economic fortunes of the smaller numbers remaining in the field, or, in the alternative, they are unwilling to take such actions. It is important to note that the anti-trust laws may apply to the activities of such groups and that any measures taken to reduce the numbers of available suppliers of specified services in given field must comply with such laws (see "Anti-Trust Laws," "Buyer's Market," "Inferior Bargaining Position," "Market Value," "Negotiate," "Predatory Practices" and "Soft Market").

LAWSUIT (see "Action," "Litigation" and "Suit").

LAZINESS. A human affliction described as a disinclination to work. When it comes to negotiating a custom film distribution agreement that actually fits the interests and needs of two individual parties (the distributor and producer), laziness sometimes plays a part, particularly with the smaller, understaffed film distribution companies. Working through a twenty- or thirty-page film distribution agreement and making changes requested by a producer is quite tedious. As with the production of any lengthy and complicated document distribution agreements are often primarily based on some prior distribution agreement either previously used by the present distributor or some other distributor, and, as such, may contain numerous provisions that simply do not apply to the transaction being currently negotiated. The term laziness may also apply to producers who allow the financial prospects of their film and all who share in the transactions as profit participants to be controlled by a document whose provisions went largely unnegotiated (see "Contract of Adhesion" and "Negotiate").

LEAD. The primary acting role in a screenplay or teleplay. There can be two leads—the male and the female (see "Principals" or "Principal Player").

LEAD BANK (see "Participation Loan").

LEAD LENDER (see "Participation Loan").

LEAD LINE. A descriptive phrase or sentence used in the advertising and promotion of a film which elaborates on the title of the film (see "Hook").

LEASE. A contract through which one party called the lessor relinquishes his, her or its right to immediate possession of property while retaining ultimate legal ownership or title (see "Lessee," "Lessor" and "Title").

LEGAL DEPARTMENT. A major administrative unit of the typical motion picture studio/distributor which is primarily responsible for negotiating the details of and drafting the long form agreements on behalf of the studio with producers, directors, talent and writers or their respective agents (see "Business Affairs Department," Creative Affairs Department," "Deal Memo," "Long Form Agreement," "Production Department" and "Studio").

LEGAL OPINION. Although there may be many types of legal opinions, in film finance the term may refer to a statement provided by an attorney relating to the legality of the issuance of securities in a public/registered offering (see "Corporate Stock," "Federal Tax Discussion," "Limited Partnership," "Public Offering" and "Tax Opinion").

LEGAL PROCEEDINGS. A required disclosure in securities offerings through which the issuer provides information regarding any material pending legal proceedings, other than ordinary routine litigation incidental to the business of the issuer, to which the issuer is a party or to which any of its property is subject (see "Disclosure Document" and "Securities").

LEGEND. In securities terminology, an all-caps, bold face statement or paragraph (usually some sort of disclaimer) required to be prominently displayed in a required disclosure document (prospectus or offering memorandum) as a condition of relying on an available federal or state exemption from the securities registration requirement or in the use of a specific form of registration (see "Conditions and Limitations," "Investor Suitability Requirements," "Private Placement," "Public Offering" and "Purchaser Representations").

LEGS. An attribute of a film in release meaning it has strong audience appeal and that its positive word-of-mouth assures a long play in theatres (see "Word-of-Mouth").

LENDER. Individual or firm that extends money to a borrower with the expectation of being repaid, usually with interest. In the event of a corporate liquidation, lenders are paid before stockholders receive distributions (see "Debt" and "Lender Financing").

LENDER FINANCING. The funding of the production costs of a motion picture through loans. Some lending organizations which regularly lend movie production funds are not organized as banks (see "Bank Loans" and "Inter-Party Agreement").

LENDER LEGAL FEES. Compensation paid out of the loaned funds to attorneys who represent the bank or lender in a production loan transaction, thus adding to the principal the producer has borrowed and increasing the amount of interest earned by the bank. It is in the producer's interest to seek a cap on such fees, although some banks will not permit the imposition of a ceiling (see "Cap," "Cost of Capital," "Lender Financing" and "Negative Pickup").

LENDER RISK ELIMINATION. Banks and other lenders who regularly lend monies to motion picture producers for the production costs of a movie or movies generally attempt to assign, neutralize or eliminate all of their non-credit risks in the transaction including title risk, insurable risks, completion and delivery risk, box-office risk, cash-flow risk and currency risk. Thus, the only remaining risk for the lender in such transaction relates to the credit-worthiness of the distributor furnishing the distribution guarantee (see "Bank Loans" and "Insurable Risk" and "Interest Rate Risk").

LENDING AGREEMENT (see "Loan Out Agreement").

LENDING STANDARDS. The criteria a bank establishes and follows in making film production loans, e.g., a certain percentage of a film's budget must be secured by distribution and other contracts and/or other collateral, the producer and director must have a successful track record and a completion bond must be in place (see "Completion Bond" and "Track Record").

LESSEE. One who holds an interest in property by virtue of a lease (see "Lease" and "Lessor").

LESSOR. One who grants a lease to another, thereby transferring an exclusive right of possession and use of certain property which is subject to the lease and subject only to the rights expressly retained by the lessor in the lease agreement (see "Lease" and "Lessee").

LETTER AGREEMENT (see "Letter of Agreement").

LETTER OF AGREEMENT. A short, written agreement in letter form. This shorter form of agreement, i.e., more brief than a so-called fully negotiated or long-form agreement, does not usually contain all of the terms and provisions of the more complete agreement and is used to shorten the negotiation process so that pre-production or production on a motion picture may begin. Such agreements usually recite that other terms and provisions will be negotiated and added to or incorporated within the short-form agreement at some time in the future. It may be important to set a specific deadline for completing and signing the long-form agreement, because if a dispute arises before the longer agreement is in effect, the dispute will have to be resolved based on the provisions of the shorter agreement. In contrast, some argue that it is better to forego the more detailed agreement since many parties in the film industry do not have the bargaining power to actually conduct arm's length negotiations resulting in a fully negotiated agreement with the other party anyway (similar to "Short Form Agreement;" see "Contract of Adhesion," "Deal Memo," "Letter of Intent," "Long Form Agreement" and "Standard Contract").

LETTER OF CREDIT (LC). A financing transaction in which a bank issues to a borrower a letter authorizing the borrower to draw on the bank for a stated amount for a specified period and guaranteeing to accept the drafts on the bank if they are made. A letter of credit is not a standby letter of credit if it may be drawn upon in the absence of default in payment of the underlying evidence of indebtedness. Limited partners in some film partnerships are asked to obtain such letters which may be used as security for partnership loans. Also, some foreign distributors offering pre-sale contracts may be required to put up U.S. dollar-denominated letters of credit before their contracts will be discounted by U.S. banks (see "Irrevocable Letter of Credit," "Negative Pickup," "Split Rights Deal," "Standby Letter of Credit" and "U.S. Dollar-Denominated Letters of Credit").

LETTER OF INTENT (COMPLETION GUARANTOR). A letter of intent issued by a feature-film completion guarantor confirming that it is prepared, in principle, to grant a guarantee of completion, subject to certain conditions. The following conditions are generally included: that the completion guarantor is satisfied with the budget, script, shooting schedule and delivery requirements; that the financing for the approved budget (including an agreed-upon contingency reserve) is in place; that all agreements for the acquisition of rights, and the employment of all creative elements and key personnel are available; and that other items including but not limited to insurance, studio, and location agreements, etc., are satisfactory (see "Pre-Production").

LETTER OF INTENT (FILM). A written communication from a director, actor, or other person (or company) who has been invited to be involved in the production or distribution of a film, expressing the intent of such person (or company) to perform whatever services he, she or it has been asked to perform on that movie contingent upon certain specified conditions being met, e.g., agreement on mutually acceptable compensation, production monies being raised and/or no contractual commitments that would interfere with such person's or company's availability at the time they are needed to work on the film. A letter of intent expresses a higher level of commitment than a letter of interest but may or may not be legally binding depending on the language used [see "Letter of Intent (General Legal)," "Letter of Interest" and "Pre-Production"].

LETTER OF INTENT (GENERAL LEGAL). A written communication setting out a preliminary understanding of the parties. Such a letter is generally not considered a contract, i.e., does not constitute a binding agreement and creates no liability as between the parties. Rather, it is an expression of the tentative intentions of the parties; an agreement to agree, in other words, a contract to make a contract is not a contract. However, if a formal writing is contemplated by the parties and the letter of intent is properly drafted, a binding contract may arise between the parties before this latter writing is executed as long as there has been a meeting of the minds concerning the essential elements of the writing (see "Contract").

LETTER OF INTENT (SECURITIES). A negotiated agreement between an underwriter and a corporation seeking a public offering of its securities which sets out the amount of the issue, calls for preparation of a registration statement and formation of an underwriting group, states the proposed maximum and minimum offering price and the maximum percentage for underwriting discounts and determines how expenses will be allocated (see "Broker/Dealer," "Corporate Stock," "Public Offering," "Securities" and "Underwriter").

LETTER OF INTENT TO ACQUIRE LITERARY PROPERTY. A party's statement of his, her or its intention to purchase a literary work under certain stated circumstances. Such letters are often given or requested to indicate the purchasing party's level of interest in the property (see "Letter of Intent/Film" and "Letter of Intent/General Legal").

LETTER OF INTEREST. A written communication from a person who has been approached regarding the possibility that they might play some role or perform some function relating to the production of a motion picture, that expresses their interest in participating in the project pending its further development, funding of the film and/or after further talks at a later date. A producer, for example, may want to obtain letters of interest or so-called letters of support from a distributor while seeking funding for a project. Although some in the industry suggest that such letters are "worthless," it would be more accurate to say that such letters are not intended to be binding, but they do show that the producer has identified certain film distributors, that the producer has presented the film project to such distributors and the distributors were at least interested enough to say in writing (if this is what they said) that, when the project is funded and produced, they would like to see it to determine at that time whether they would have any interest in distributing the film (also sometimes called "Letters of Support;" see "Letter of Intent").

LETTER OF SUPPORT (same as "Letter of Interest").

LEVEL PLAYING FIELD. An expression which, when used with respect to a particular industry, such as the film industry, refers to whether the rules of the game are the same for all of the players, or whether the environment ("field") in which the business is conducted provides a fair opportunity for all to participate on an equal basis. Some industry observers suggest that the primary reason for most of the failures of the independent production and distribution companies in recent years relates to this issue of the "level playing field" and not "lack of hits" or "poor financial management" (see "Anti-Competitive Practices," "Anti-Trust Laws," "Blind Bidding," "Contract of Adhesion," "Creative Accounting," "Financial Management," "Hit," "Leverage," "Reciprocal Preferences" and "Unethical Business Practices").

LEVERAGE. In the context of film industry negotiations, the power to control or influence others. The concept is extremely important in determining the outcome of negotiations as between film distributors and producers. A different form of leverage, financial leverage refers to the amount of debt a company has in relation to its equity. The more long-term debt the company has, the greater the financial leverage. Some industry observers point out that the extensive use of financial leverage was not part of the business culture prior to the 1970s and suggest that most failures of feature film production companies are associated with excessive use of financial leverage (see "Clout," "Computer Modeling," "Contract of Adhesion," "Debt," "Equity," "Financial Management," "Law of Supply and Demand," "Level Playing Field," "Most Favored Nations Clause," "Pari Passu" and "Power").

LEVY. To raise or collect; to seize or assess. Also an amount levied (see "Dues and Assessments," "Foreign Tax Credits" and "Tax").

LIABLE. The state of being obligated according to law (see "Liability" and "Limited Liability").

LIABILITY. An obligation to do or refrain from doing something; a duty which eventually must be performed; an obligation to pay money; signifies money owed, as opposed to an asset. The term is also used to refer to one's responsibility for his, her or its conduct, such as in contractual liability or tort liability (see "Corporation," "Joint Venture," "Limited Liability," "Limited Partnership" and "Tort").

LIABILITY INSURANCE. Insurance which protects a film producer against the risks involved in engaging in various activities which may generate pecuniary obligations (see "Errors and Omissions Insurance," "Insurance" and "Property Damage Liability Insurance").

LIABILITY LIMITATION. A contractual provision which limits the responsibility or exposure of a given party for certain risks or obligations. If, for example, a film distributor assumes the burden of protecting a film's copyright against infringement, it may also incur some potential liability if it fails to act conscientiously in the protection of such copyright. Thus, the distributor may seek a provision in the distribution agreement which limits its liability for its own conduct in attempting to protect the film's copyright. The producer, particularly if the distribution rights granted are limited, may want to negotiate to see that such limits do not protect the distributor against willful misconduct or gross negligence and possibly even negligent conduct, because such limits may not provide enough incentive for the distributor to act conscientiously to protect the copyright (see "Copyright Infringement," "Errors and Omissions Insurance" and "Liability").

LIBEL. A tort consisting of a false and malicious publication made or printed for the purpose of defaming one who is living (see "Defamation," "Defamation of Character," "Public Figure," "Slander" and "Tort").

LIBRARY [see "Catalog (Library)"].

LIBRARY VALUES. The monetary worth of a collection of films owned by a movie studio or production company (see "Asset Value").

LICENSE. A right granted which gives a person or entity permission to do something which he, she or it could not legally do absent such permission, i.e., a grant of permission by the licensor for the licensee to do a particular thing, to exercise a certain privilege or to carry on a particular business. In film, license agreements typically include the agreement between a film's producer and distributor and the agreements between the distributor and other parties which outlines the rights and limitations relating to the use of the film and the profit split or consideration. Film license agreements are thus used for granting film distribution, theatrical exhibition, home video, television, merchandising and other rights. A film license is generally characterized by a time limitation and conveys control but not ownership of such rights (see "Assign," "Copyright License," "Distribution Agreement," "Grant of Rights," "Licensee," "Mechanical License" and "Release").

LICENSE AGREEMENT. The contract between a distributor and an exhibitor for the exhibition of a motion picture by the exhibitor. Also, any of the agreements as between the distributor of a film and sub-distributors, territorial distributors and others (such as video companies) who obtain rights to exploit a feature film from the distributor. Although technically the distribution agreement itself, as between the production company and the film's distributor is a license agreement, it is more commonly referred to as a "distribution agreement" (see "Distribution Agreement" and "License").

LICENSED MEDIA. A provision in a film distribution agreement which sets out the specific forms of communication vehicles in which the motion picture may be distributed and/or exploited, e.g., theatrical, non-theatrical, free and pay television and home video (see "Licensed Term" and "Licensed Territory").

LICENSED TERM. The number of years that a distributor, sub-distributor, or territorial distributor has to exploit a film, e.g., seven years commencing from the delivery of the picture (see "Licensed Media," "Licensed Territory" and "Perpetual Rights").

LICENSED TERRITORY. The geographical area in which a distributor or sub-distributor is authorized to distribute a film, e.g., in the United States and Canada, including their territories and possessions, the military installations of such countries wherever situated, and on ships and airlines flying the flag of the U.S. or Canada (see "Licensed Media," "Licensed Term" and "Sub-Distributor").

LICENSEE. One to whom a license has been granted. A film distributor, sub-distributor, exhibitor and other parties who are licensed to exploit a film in any manner may all be licensees (see "Distributor," "Exhibitor," "Sub-Distributor" and "Video Companies").

LICENSE FEES. The compensation paid to a licensor for the grant of rights provided in a licensing agreement (see "Licensed Territory" and "Licensee").

LICENSE FOR MERCHANDISING AGREEMENT (see "Merchandising Agreement").

LICENSE OF STILLS/EXCERPTS. A written agreement between a feature film producer and the owner of a prior motion picture which provides the producer with the owner's permission to use excerpts or stills from the earlier movie, primarily for the purpose of avoiding the possibility of future claims, e.g., copyright infringement (see "Clip," "Excerpts," "Film Clip License" and "Production Still").

LICENSE PERIOD (see "Licensed Term").

LICENSING AGREEMENT. Any of the written agreements executed by and between a film's producer and distributor as well as between the distributor and other parties granting the producer's or distributor's permission for such parties to exploit the film in a specified manner and for consideration (see "License" and "Merchandising Agreement").

LICENSING PROCESS. The activities engaged in, the procedures used and the negotiations involved while a feature film distributor is contracting with exhibitor's and sub-distributors for the exploitation of a film. Typically, the final print of a film is not available for screening at the beginning of this process (as between the distributor and exhibitor); thus, the exhibitors often have to make their offers based on a very sketchy information provided by a distributor. Such information usually only includes the names of the principals involved in the film and a brief synopsis of the plot. Some exhibitors complain that such a small amount of disclosure relating to a film does not allow them to adequately assess a film's potential profitability or its suitability for their particular patrons (see "Anti-Blind Bidding Statutes," "Blind Bidding," "Licensing Terms," "Locked Picture" and "Trade Screening").

LICENSING TERMS. The typical provisions of feature film agreements authorizing the exploitation of a film, including in a distribution deal, contingencies, picture specifications, consideration, rights, financing arrangements, credit provisions, representations and warranties, indemnification, etc. In the licensing agreements between the distributor and exhibitors or sub-distributors, such terms might include the length of the run (term), territory, media, rights and fees. Film rental fees are usually calculated on a weekly basis and a floor, if any, declines each week during the run until it reaches a specified minimum. Consequently, it is generally to the advantage of the exhibitor to secure successful films with longer runs since the exhibitor typically retains a larger percentage of the box office gross as the run is extended ("Floor," "Long-Run Engagement" and "Run").

LICENSOR. One who grants a license, e.g., a producer who retains ownership rights in a film may grant a license to a distributor. A distributor may in turn grant a license to a sub-distributor or exhibitor (see "Licensee").

LIE, CHEAT AND STEAL SYNDROME. The signs and symptoms of a pattern of business practices and behavior which seem to occur regularly in the film industry and can be characterized by a lack of basic honesty or ethics and motivated by greed. Producers should always check with other producers that have done business with a distributor in the past before going forward with a distribution agreement (see "Business Practices," "Contract of Adhesion," "Creative Accounting," "Greed," "Insider's Game," "Predatory Practices," "Reciprocal Preferences" and "Unethical Business Practices").

LIEN. A charge, hold, claim or encumbrance upon the property of another as security for some debt or charge; not title to property but a charge upon it. The term connotes the right which the law gives to have a debt satisfied out of such property (see "Claim," "Clearance," "Encumbrance" and "Title").

LIMITATION OF LIABILITY. A ceiling on the amount of money an investor in a corporation or limited partnership is responsible for paying as a result of a lawsuit against the entity. Generally such investor liability is limited to the amount of the investor's investment (see "Cap," "Ceiling," "Liability" and "Limited Liability").

LIMITATIONS ON MANNER OF OFFERING. Securities restrictions typically imposed pursuant to federal and state exemptions from securities registration requirements, e.g., that neither the issuer nor any person acting on its behalf may offer or sell such securities by any form of general solicitation or general advertising, including but not limited to (1) any advertisement, article, notice or other communication published in any newspaper, magazine, or similar media or broadcast over television or radio and (2) any seminar or meeting whose attendees have been invited by any general solicitation or general advertising (see "Broker/Dealer Sales," "Cold Call," "Conditions and Limitations," "Finder Sales," "General Solicitation," "Issuer Sales" and "Regulation D").

LIMITATIONS ON RESALE. A securities limitation typically imposed pursuant to federal and state exemptions from the securities registration requirements which provides that, following the initial sale, such securities cannot be resold unless they are registered with the SEC and in each state where sales are anticipated or, in the alternative, are separately qualified for available exemptions from registration (see "Conditions and Limitations").

LIMITED ENGAGEMENT. A phrase used in conjunction with a film's exhibition which suggests that a motion picture is to be exhibited at that theatre for a shorter time than usual (see "General Release," "Mini-Multiple" and "Wide Release").

LIMITED LIABILITY. The limitation placed on the amount an investor can lose resulting from a lawsuit against the entity invested in or other loss suffered by such entity. Liability for corporate shareholders and limited partnership investors is generally limited to the amount such investors invested (see "Corporation," "Liability," "Limitation of Liability" and "Limited Partnership").

LIMITED OFFERING EXEMPTION (LOE). The term generally applied to the state transactional exemptions from the securities registration requirement that are somewhat compatible with the federal Regulation D exemption (see "Conditions and Limitations," "Small Offering Exemption," "Regulation D" and "ULOE").

LIMITED PARTNERS. Purchasers of interests or units in a limited partnership offering who are accepted as unit holders by the partnership's general partner(s), i.e., a partner in a limited partnership whose liability to partnership creditors is limited to the amount of his, her or its investment in the partnership, any additional amounts such partner may be obligated to contribute under terms of the partnership agreement and such partner's share of undistributed partnership earnings. A limited partner may lose his, her or its limited liability status by participating beyond a permitted level in the control of the partnership (same as "Unit Holders" in many partnerships, although it is possible to be a unit holder and not be a limited partner in situations where a unit is subsequently transferred and the general partner has not yet approved the new unit holder as a limited partner; see "Unit Holder" or "Unit Purchaser" and "Silent Partner").

LIMITED PARTNERSHIP. A state-regulated form of doing business which is a special form of partnership that has both general and limited (or silent partners), i.e., an entity created by two or more persons and having one or more general partners and one or more limited partners. The activities of the limited partnership are controlled primarily by the partnership agreement between the general partners and the limited partners and pursuant to the state's limited partnership act. A limited partnership is an entity in which one or more persons, with unlimited liability (the general partners) manage the partnership, while one or more other persons only contribute money, property or their past services for interests in the limited partnership (the limited partners). The limited partners have no right to participate in the day-to-day management and operation of the business and assume no liability beyond their contribution. Interests in limited partnerships are securities, therefore the federal and state securities laws must be complied with in raising funding for a film using the financing vehicle of a limited partnership. The various state partnership acts provide a producer/general partner with more flexibility in structuring the deal as between the general and limited partners than corporate statutes provide (see "Corporation," "Creative Control," "Financing," "General Partner," "Joint Venture," "Lender Financing," "Offering," "Passive Investor Financing," "Securities" and "Syndication").

LIMITED PARTNERSHIP AGREEMENT. The written agreement between the general partner(s) and limited partner(s) in the creation of a limited partnership. A written limited partnership agreement is generally required by state law as part of the process of forming a limited partnership. Such agreement also defines and controls the relationship as between the parties. To the extent an issue is not provided for in the limited partnership agreement, the applicable state's limited partnership act will typically control. A common misconception held by some independent feature film producers is that a limited partnership agreement is all that is needed to raise money by means of a film limited partnership. The limited partnership agreement by itself is not enough to either create a limited partnership or to make offers and sell interests in the limited partnership. The creation of the limited partnership entity requires a filing with the Secretary of State in the state in which the limited partnership is being organized and compliance with other provisions of that state's limited partnership act. In addition, the offer and sale of interests in limited partnerships requires compliance with both the federal and state securities laws, which in turn mandate, among other things, the written disclosure of all material aspects of the transaction to prospective investors (see "Anti-Fraud Statute," "Disclosure Document," "Limited Partnerships," "Offering Memorandum," "Prospectus" and "Security or Securities").

LIMITED PARTNERSHIP INVESTMENT AGREEMENT (see "Limited Partnership Agreement").

LIMITED PARTNERSHIPS ARE DEAD. A fairly common sentiment regarding feature film limited partnerships expressed by some attorneys and others in the film industry who either (1) feel there are no longer any tax benefits available for use with a limited partnership, (2) recognize that historically, feature film limited partnerships have not performed well as investment vehicles for investors (and consequently, it is difficult to interest securities broker/dealers in the sales of film limited partnerships), or (3) do not have the required securities-law compliance expertise to do film limited partnerships and thus are promoting other forms of film finance. When the U.S. Congress (in its wisdom) repealed the investment tax credit and imposed the passive loss rules, those tax decisions made it more difficult to sell limited partnership interests. However, it is misleading to say that there are "no" tax benefits associated with limited partnerships since the very nature of the vehicle itself (limited partnerships are non-taxable entities) is a major tax benefit as compared to the "double taxation" aspects of the regular corporation. Also, the lack of reasonable investment returns for the large publicly offered film limited partnerships of the 1980s do not reflect so much on the appropriateness of using limited partnerships as film finance vehicles as on the much discussed (although not discussed enough) business practices of the motion picture distributors who distribute the films and are responsible for collecting and disbursing revenues. As further evidence that there is nothing inherently wrong with the limited partnership as a financing vehicle for the right projects, the Investment Program Association reports that individuals investing in cable television partnerships more than doubled their money in 1991 with an average return of $2,584 for each $1,000 invested. Finally, using the "availability analysis" suggested herein, for many low-budget independent producers seeking single-picture financing, other forms of film financing are simply not available, thus the advantages-versus-disadvantages analysis relating to film finance options may be irrelevant in those situations. Thus, for those projects, the small, private offering of film limited partnership interests may be the only available film finance option (see "Adhesion Contract," "Availability Analysis," "Creative Accounting," "Double Taxation," "Funding Sources," "Investment Tax Credit," "Passive Activity Loss," "Pro and Con Analysis," "Security or Securities," "Tax Shelter Opinion" and "When the Money's Paid").

LIMITED RELEASE. The exhibition of a motion picture in a small, specific area or nationally with a limited number of prints, e.g., fifty or less. Sometimes the limited release is used for test marketing, i.e., to sample audience reaction to a film, to limit the risk of financial loss on a given film or as part of a regional release pattern (see "General Release," "Mini-Multiple," "Print," "Release Pattern" and "Wide Release").

LIMITED REVIEW. An accountant's review of financial statements which does not rise to the level of a full audit. In certain circumstances, a limited review, which is less expensive than a full audit, may be sufficient to provide a financier, investor group, producer or net profit participants with an adequate level of comfort (see "Accountant's Opinion" and "Audit").

LIMITED USE. With respect to prospective financial statements in accounting, a reference to use of such statements by the responsible party alone or by the responsible party and third parties with whom the responsible party is negotiating directly, e.g., negotiations for a bank loan, submission to a regulatory agency and use solely within the entity. Third-party recipients of prospective financial statements intended for limited use can ask questions of the responsible party and negotiate terms directly with it. Any type of prospective financial statements that would be useful in the circumstances would normally be appropriate for limited use. Thus, the presentation may be a financial forecast or a financial projection (see "General Use," "Financial Forecasts," "Financial Projections," "Prospective Financial Statements" and "Responsible Party").

LIMITS ON DIVIDENDS. In bank lending, barriers imposed by the lending bank on a corporation's ability to pay dividends to its shareholders. However, such a limit or barrier on dividends in a loan agreement may help a company avoid an IRS tax imposed on the unreasonable accumulation of retained earnings (see "Corporation" and "Lender Financing").

LINE OF CREDIT. A bank's moral commitment, as opposed to its contractual commitment, to make loans to a particular borrower up to a specified maximum during a specified period. Bank lines of credit may be based solely on the financial statements and quality of the people associated with a film production or distribution company, and such funds may provide working capital to buy scripts, turn novels into screenplays and scout site locations, among other things (also called "Bank Lines" and "Lender Financing").

LINE PRODUCER. The supervisor of below-the-line elements of a film during its production. The line producer is generally an employee of the production company and is primarily responsible for seeing that the film is completed on time and within the prescribed budget. In some situations, a line producer may report to a production manager, but on other pictures, particularly lower-budgeted projects, the responsibilities of the production manager and line producer may be combined into one job. A completion guarantor may insist that a line producer with an excellent track record be hired for a certain film before it will approve the bond for that picture (see "Completion Guarantor," "Creative Producer," "Executive Producer," "Producer," "Production Manager" and "Unit Production Manager").

LIQUID ASSET. Cash or something that is easily convertible into cash. A corporation's liquid assets may include cash, marketable securities and accounts receivable. An investor in an illiquid investment such as a privately placed limited partnership is required to have substantial liquid assets which would serve as a financial cushion if the illiquid investment does not work out favorably (see "Illiquid" and "Investor Suitability Standards").

LIQUIDATE. To settle; to determine the amount due, and to whom due, and, having done so, to extinguish the indebtedness. Also, to sell; to reduce the value of an object or an asset to its cash value. To liquidate a business means to assemble and mobilize the assets, settle with the creditors and debtors, and apportion the remaining assets, if any, among the owners (see "Asset Value" and "Bankruptcy").

LIQUIDATING DIVIDEND. A distribution of assets in the form of dividends from a corporation that is going out of business, i.e., in the process of liquidating (see "Corporate Stock" and "Liquidate").

LIQUIDATING VALUE. Projected price for an asset of a company that is going out of business (also called "Auction Value;" see "Liquidate").

LIQUIDATION. The dismantling of a business, paying off debts in order of priority and distributing the remaining assets in cash to the owners. Involuntary liquidation is covered under Chapter 7 of the federal bankruptcy law (see "Bankruptcy," "Corporate Stock," "Dissolution" and "Winding Up").

LIQUIDATOR. In a limited partnership context, the person or persons who liquidate the partnership pursuant to the partnership agreement (see "Limited Partnership" and "Liquidation").

LISTED SECURITY. A security which has been listed for trading on one of the stock exchanges or which has been listed with the SEC (see "Publicly Held" and "Stock Exchange").

LISTED STOCK. Corporate stock which is traded on an organized stock exchange. Such companies must satisfy the requirements of the exchange on which their stock is traded in addition to those of the SEC (see "Publicly Held," "Securities and Exchange Commission" and "Stock Exchange").

LISTING. A paid entry in a regular list of movies playing locally that is published in a newspaper or magazine (see "Advertising").

LISTING REQUIREMENTS. Rules that must be met before a stock is listed for trading on an exchange (see "Listed Stock").

LITERARY MATERIAL. Writings which may be used as the basis for a feature film, including stories, adaptations, books, treatments, scenarios, continuities, teleplays, screenplays, dialogues, scripts, sketches, plots, outlines, narrative synopses, routines and narrations (see "Literary Property" and "Property").

LITERARY PROPERTY. A literary work upon which a motion picture may be based. The term is more narrow than underlying property since the latter may include literary as well as other material on which a motion picture may be based (see "Literary Materials," "Literary Works," "Novel," "Option," "Purchase" and "Underlying Property").

LITERARY WORKS (see "Literary Material").

LITIGANTS. The parties involved in a lawsuit or litigation (see "Action" and "Litigation").

LITIGATION. Lawsuit, a controversy which is presented to a court, at least through the initial filings (see "Action," "Arbitration," "Final Judgment" and "Mediation").

LITIGATION BUDGET. The monies required to initiate, maintain and pursue a lawsuit. Such budget may include filing fees and other court costs, investigatory expenses and attorney fees. In addition to auditing funds, an independent producer may need to set aside some funds to cover litigation costs in the event a dispute arises with respect to a film's distribution (see "Audit" and "Litigation").

LITIGATION DISCLAIMER. A contractual clause, usually found among the producer warranties in the film distribution agreement, which is a general disclaimer by the producer that there is any litigation pending that could impair distribution of the picture. The producer may want to obtain corresponding representations and warranties from the distributor along with indemnification (see "Indemnification" and "Warranty").

LIVE STAGE PRODUCTION. A theatrical presentation involving live performers (see "Live Stage Rights").

LIVE STAGE RIGHTS. The authority to exploit a version of a film presented as a theatrical presentation involving live performers (see "Live Stage Production").

LIVING EXPENSES. The ordinary costs of maintaining a person away from his or her home while on location or other assignment relating to the production of a motion picture (see "Budget," "Exclusive Ground Transportation," "Perks," "Rising Production Costs" and "Transportation Costs").

LOAN. The delivery of a sum of money to another under contract to return an equivalent amount at some future time with or without an additional sum agreed upon for its use. The characterization of a transaction as a loan or some other type of borrowing has significance in ascertaining whether usury laws apply to the amount of interest being charged, or in the alternative in ascertaining whether the transaction should be more properly characterized as some form of equity investment that may also involve the securities laws (contrast with "Investment" and "Security" or "Securities;" see "Bank Loan," "Debt" and "Interest").

LOAN DOCUMENTATION. All of the documents prepared by the lending institution relating to a loan and the documents required to be provided by the producer in obtaining a loan (see "Loan").

LOAN OUT AGREEMENT. The written contract between an individual artist and a company which sets out the terms and conditions of the relationship which has been created for the purpose of hiring out the services of the artist to third parties through the company (also called "Lending Agreement;" see "Inducement Letter," "Loan Out Arrangement," "Loan Out Company" and "Straight Employment Agreement").

LOAN OUT ARRANGEMENT. The agreement between an individual artist and a corporation owned by such artist whereby such company provides the artist for employment through the company to third-party employers. The concept originally developed to take advantage of certain tax laws which favored such arrangements; however, not all of those tax benefits are still in effect, thus the desirability of creating such an arrangement for a given artist depends on an analysis of the impact of the current tax laws on the special circumstances of a specific individual (see "Inducement Letter," "Loan Out Agreement" and "Loan Out Company").

LOAN OUT COMPANY. A corporation owned by an individual artist which contractually furnishes the services of such individual to a third party, e.g., a motion picture production company (see "Loan Out Agreement" and "Loan Out Arrangement").

LOAN OUT CORPORATION (see "Loan Out Company").

LOAN SHARKING. The practice of lending money at usurious rates of interest. Many states have laws that render usurious interest, and in some instances even the underlying debt, uncollectible (see "Extortion" and "Usury").

LOBBY CARD. A standard size poster used for display in a movie theatre lobby or outside the theatre. A lobby card is smaller than a one-sheet (see "One-Sheet," "Poster" and "Sell-Sheet").

LOBBYISTS. Persons engaged in the business of seeking to persuade public officials, especially legislators, to pass laws that are favorable and to defeat those that are unfavorable to their interests or the interests of their clients, or to assist in the drafting of acceptable provisions in such legislation. Lobbyists usually work for professional or trade associations, labor groups, corporations or other organizations whose interests may be affected by a given piece of legislation. The activities of lobbyists are regulated by statute in most jurisdictions (see "Association Projects," "Industry Groups," "MPAA," "Paramount Consent Decree of 1948," "Political Influence," "Professional Association" and "TriStar Case").

LOBBYING. Activities engaged in by persons (lobbyists) in an attempt to persuade legislators (and in some cases government regulators) to pass or vigorously enforce laws or regulations that are favorable to their interests or the interests of their clients, or to defeat, amend or not vigorously enforce those laws or regulations that are unfavorable. The activities of lobbyists are generally regulated by statute, and, contrary to what is often suggested in the press, there is nothing wrong with lobbying per se. Lobbyists merely represent the interests of organized interest groups and most significant interests are represented by lobbyists. If a significant interest is not represented by lobbyists, it should be. Some segments of the motion picture industry (e.g., major motion-picture producers and distributors) are well represented by their trade associations, which vigorously lobby on behalf of the interests of their member companies, while other segments of the same industry (e.g., independent producers) are not organized at the industry level in a manner which will permit the effective advocacy of their interests with respect to important issues. Thus, certain laws, government regulations and/or the enforcement of such laws and regulations are not likely to be favorable to the interests of the unrepresented group. That, in fact, may be the case with respect to questions relating to the enforcement of the federal anti-trust laws (specifically vertical integration), blind bidding, block booking, the motion-picture rating system, the membership policies of certain industry associations, controlled theatres, etc. Some in the industry consider it foolish for independent producers to try to function in an industry without an effective advocacy group representing their interests at the industry level and that the circumstances for the independent producer will continue to deteriorate without such representation (see "Anti-Trust Laws," "Association Projects," "Contract of Adhesion," "Creative Accounting," "Industry Groups," "Lobbyists," "Major Exhibition Chains," "Marketplace of Ideas," "Market Share," "MPAA," "Number of Screens" and "Political Influence").

LOCAL STATIONS. Television stations which broadcast programming within a limited geographical area (see "Syndication").

LOCOMOTIVES. High profile, "A-level" motion pictures that are part of a package of films sold in syndication or in foreign territories. These "locomotives" drive the package, i.e., motivate buyers to purchase the package of films just to get access to these few good pictures (see "Allocation Issues," "Package" and "Syndication").

LOCATION. Any place, other than the studio lot, where films may be shot. The term is also used to refer to the geographical site of a motion picture theatre (see "Right of Consultation" and "Set").

LOCATION ACCOUNTANT. A person hired by a studio on a studio-financed film, a producer or a payroll-service company and assigned to work on the film's location and to generate regular written reports which account for all the money spent while the film is being shot on location (see "Completion Guarantor," "Production Accountant" and "Production-Financing/Distribution Agreement").

LOCATION AGREEMENT. The written contract between a feature film production company and the owner of a specifically identifiable site or building which is to be used in or portrayed in a movie (see "Stage Agreement").

LOCATION FEE. The consideration or compensation paid for the use of a site and the facilities thereon in the process of shooting a motion picture (see "Location Permit").

LOCATION FILMING. The shooting of scenes for a motion picture at any place other than on a studio lot or in a studio soundstage. Many states in the United States have established film commissions which aggressively compete to attract location filming and the accompanying expenditure of funds for their state. In reaction to the passage of anti-blind bidding statutes in some states, certain major studio/distributors have reportedly threatened to (and may have in some instances) restricted their location filming to states that have not passed such legislation (see "Anti-Blind Bidding Statutes," "Blind Bidding," "Economic Reprisal," "Film Commission," "Lobbying," "Location," "Location List," "Location Permit" and "State Legislatures").

LOCATION LIST. A record or inventory of sites that are suitable for shooting scenes for a film (see "Location Manager").

LOCATION MANAGER. The film production person responsible for all film logistical matters relating to the use of film shooting sites other than the studio lot. Generally, the location manager will help to identify the locations that are called for by a given script, scout the locations, take or acquire location photographs, analyze and evaluate the suitability of various locations, budget the cost of using the prospective locations, consult with the film's director, producer and production designer regarding the use of such locations, and then, after locations are chosen, arrange for needed releases and negotiate the terms for the use of such locations. The location manager also is responsible for making the arrangements for location permits, parking, catering, necessary police and fire personnel and other matters relating to the specific locations (see "Location List" and "Location Permit").

LOCATION PERMIT. Licenses often required and granted (usually for a fee) by local governmental units for the privilege of going onto private or government owned property to shoot scenes for a movie (see "Location Filming" and "Location Manager").

LOCKED PICTURE. A work print of a finished film of such quality that screening prints may be made therefrom for viewing by potential exhibitors (see "Blind Bidding," "Licensing Process," "Trade Screening" and "Work Print").

LOE. Acronym for limited offering exemption (see "Limited Offering Exemption" and "Securities").

LOGISTICS. The procurement, maintenance and transportation of material, facilities and personnel (see "Location Filming" and "Location Manager").

LOGO. A signature design or device which is unique and identifiable with a certain product or company. Logos may appear on literature, letterhead, in advertising and in a film. Logos may also include trademarks or service marks (see "Service Mark" and "Trademark").

LONG FORM AGREEMENT. Contracts which are fully negotiated and contain all of the terms and provisions intended by the parties thereto. Long form film distribution agreements, for example, relating to the licensing of feature films, are negotiated by and between the film's producer and a distributor (or their legal representatives) and usually include long lists of delivery items, detailed lists of what will be considered distribution expenses, extensive producer warranties, the laboratory access letter, and an instrument of transfer. Sometimes negotiators will opt for a letter agreement, deal memo or short-form agreement in order to save time, although such a tactic involves certain risks if a dispute on a question not covered by the shorter form of agreement arises before the long-form agreement is signed (see "Deal Memo," "Distribution Agreement," "Fully Negotiated Agreement," "Letter of Agreement" and "Short Form Agreement").

LONG FORM DISTRIBUTION AGREEMENT. A motion picture distribution agreement which has been fully negotiated (see "Distribution Agreement" and "Long Form Agreement").

LONG-RUN ENGAGEMENT. An extended exhibition of a motion picture at a theatre. The run of most feature films exhibited in the domestic theatrical market do not extend beyond one or two weeks. The very successful films may run as long as ten weeks or more. The distributor of the motion picture "Hook" reportedly extracted a twelve-week minimum guarantee from exhibitors as part of its licensing terms (see "Licensing Process," "Licensing Terms" and "Run").

LONG-TERM DEBT. A liability that is not due for more than a year. Generally, interest payments will come due on long-term debt periodically, typically on a quarterly, semi-annual or annual basis (see "Long-Term Financing").

LONG-TERM FINANCING. Liabilities not repayable within one year and of an equity nature (see "Debt," "Equity" and "Long-Term Debt").

LOOPING. The synchronization of separately recorded film dialogue with its corresponding film image (see "Automatic Dialogue Replacement," "Dub" and "Synchronization").

LOSS. Tax term for the excess of expenses over income in a tax year. An individual can deduct only those losses which are incurred in his, her or its trade or business, in a transaction entered into for profit (as opposed to a hobby), or as a result of a casualty or theft (see "Capital Loss," "Deductions," "Net Operating Loss" and "Passive Investment Losses").

LOT. The grounds of a studio, including administration buildings, production offices, standing sets, soundstages, dressing rooms and all structures, streets and fencing associated therewith (see "Studio").

LOW-BUDGET FILMS. Generally, feature films in the $1 to $3 million range, however, SAG defines a low-budget feature, for purposes of its low-budget features agreement, to be a feature-length motion picture, intended for theatrical exhibition, at a total production cost not exceeding $800,000 or $2,000,000 in the case of affirmative-action motion pictures (see "Big-Budget Films" and "Medium-Budget Films").

LYRICIST. One who writes the words to a song (see "Music").

LYRICS. The words of a song (see "Lyricist" and "Music").

— M —

MADE-FOR-TELEVISION PRODUCT. Feature films made specifically for showing on television and without a theatrical release (see "Movie of the Week").

MADE-FOR-VIDEO. Feature film specifically produced for release to video markets only, i.e., without a theatrical or television release (see "Direct to Video Release" and "Video Companies").

MAFIA. Originally, a Sicilian secret criminal society, but a term which is sometimes currently used to describe a secret organization composed chiefly of criminal elements engaged in controlling racketeering, peddling of narcotics, gambling, prostitution and other typically illicit activities throughout the world. Some writer/researchers have alleged that significant Mafia connections and influence have long existed in the capital-intensive motion picture industry, but, as with anti-trust law violations, such allegations have been difficult to prove (see "Anti-Trust Laws," "Extortion," "Mob Controlled Distribution Company," "Money Laundering," "Movies With a Message," "Organized Crime," "Political Influence," "Racketeering," "RICO," "Theft" and "White Collar Crime").

MAGAZINE ARTICLE. A periodical containing miscellaneous prose compositions, usually forming an independent part of the publication. Magazine articles may serve as the basis of a motion picture screenplay (see "Clearance" and "Underlying Property").

MAGNETIC FILM. An iron-oxide-coated (light sensitive) strip of plastic perforated with sprocket holes and containing a thin magnetized audio track which is used for recording sound material in synch with the visual film images, all of which are used to produce negative and positive motion picture prints with sound (see "Film").

MAG-OPTICAL TRACK. Film with multiple sound tracks, one or more of which is magnetic and at least one of which is optical. At the time it was first introduced, the mag-optical track permitted virtually all theatres to exhibit such films regardless of the playback technology the theatres were using. However, the system is no longer in common use (see "Optical Sound Track").

MAIN AND END TITLES. The titles and credits at the beginning and end of a film (see "End Titles").

MAIN ELEMENTS (see "Elements").

MAINSTREAM AUDIENCE. A broad, general audience, targeted by most commercial film releases (see "Projected Audience").

MAINTAINING A MARKET. The making of a market by a securities broker/dealer over a long period of time (see "Making A Market" and "Market Makers").

MAIN-TITLE BILLING. All credits appearing at the beginning of a film (see "Main and End Titles").

MAJOR DISTRIBUTORS (same as "Major Studio/Distributors").

MAJOR EXHIBITION CHAINS. The largest theatre owners who control the most theatres and screens in the best locations. Although ownership interests have changed often in the last several years, one recent report (source: Paul Kagan Associates, Inc. Motion Picture Investor) listed the top ten exhibitors (with the number of sites and screens shown after) as: (1) UA Communications—543/2,517, (2) AMC Entertainment—263/1,604, (3) General Cinema—312/1,504, (4) Cineplex Odeon—277/1,120, (5) Carmike—260/960, (6) Loews—203/835, (7) Cinemark—135/839, (8) National Amusements—75/568, (9) Act III—122/544 and (10) Cineamerica—112/488. Following the Reagan administration easing of regulatory restraints, the major studio/distributors have regained a certain level of control over these major exhibition chains, e.g., MCA, the parent of Universal, has a substantial ownership interest in Cineplex Odeon, Columbia and TriStar have an ownership affiliation with the Loews theatre chain, and Paramount and Warner have ownership interests in Cinemerica. Paramount also operates Famous Players, one of the largest Canadian exhibition circuits (see "Number of Screens," "Paramount Consent Decree of 1948," "TriStar Case" and "Vertical Integration").

MAJOR FOREIGN MARKETS. The countries outside the U.S. which currently provide the greatest demand for domestic theatrical entertainment product, i.e., Japan, Germany, Italy, United Kingdom, France, Spain, Canada and Australia (similar to "Prime Foreign Territories;" see "Foreign Market").

MAJORITY. The status of a person who has reached the age established by state law for such person to be held legally responsible for his or her actions. The required age may differ among jurisdictions and even within a jurisdiction for different purposes (see "Minor" and "Minority").

MAJORITY-IN-INTEREST. In film and other limited partnerships, more than 50% of the interests of limited partners (see "Interests of Limited Partners," "Limited Partnership" and "Unit").

MAJORITY SHAREHOLDER. A corporate shareholder who controls more than half the outstanding shares of a corporation (see "Principal Stockholder," "Sole Shareholder" and "Working Control").

MAJOR KEY. A geographical area, relatively well-defined and denoted by a concentrated population (generally of approximately 100,000 or more) within a metropolitan setting, by the geographical area's historical ability to produce film rental income for distributors and by the geographical area's media advertising umbrella. An exchange area's major keys generally break a first-run simultaneously (see "First-Run," "First-Run Theatre" and "Key").

MAJOR MARKETS (U.S.). New York, Chicago and Los Angeles (see "Markets").

MAJOR-OWNED SCREENS. Exhibition outlets, i.e., theatrical screens owned by the major studio/distributors (see "Major Exhibition Chains" and "Number of Screens").

MAJORS (see "Major Studio/Distributors" and "Major Exhibition Chains").

MAJOR STUDIO/DISTRIBUTORS. An unofficial entertainment industry designation which may change from time to time and which refers to the largest and most powerful film studio, producer/distributor entities. From an exhibitor's perspective, a "major" is any distributor that can provide long-term, consistent output of predictably high-quality feature films. Generally these so-called "majors" maintain distribution sales offices in the major exchanges in the U.S. and operate sub-depots which function as shipping offices for prints and related promotional materials in the remaining territories. Some industry analysts also include ownership of production studios as an integral part of the definition of "major." In recent years, the "majors" have been generally considered to be the MPAA companies Columbia Pictures, TriStar, Walt Disney, MGM/Pathe, Orion, Paramount, 20th Century-Fox, MCA/Universal and Warner Bros., although MGM/Pathe and Orion have been struggling of late. New Line may ultimately merge with Orion and, in the process, become a "major." Some of the majors are also entering or re-entering the exhibition arena during this period of relaxed U.S. Justice Department policy toward certain possible anti-trust law violations (see "Insider's Game," "Lobbying," "Major Exhibition Chains," "Market Share," "Member of the Club," "Mini-Majors," "MPAA," "Number of Screens," "Political Influence," "Studio," "Studio Financing," "Studio Lots" and "Vertical Integration").

MAKE-UP ARTISTS/HAIR STYLISTS. Film persons who prepare, style, mix and/or apply all facial, body or hair cosmetics; style and/or apply all head, body and facial wigs, hair pieces and transformations and, in consultation with the producer, order the same where such work is required; style, cut and/or color hair; perform prosthetic work, including preparation, styling, lab work and application; and consult when the producer elects to engage a consultant for an unusual effect in make-up and/or in hair style (see "Cast," "Crew," "Operational Staff," "Production Staff" and "Staff").

MAKING A MARKET. The maintaining of a firm bid and offer price by a securities broker/dealer on a given security by standing ready to buy or sell round lots at publicly quoted prices. A managing underwriter typically makes a market for its client's stock (see "Market Maker," "Maintaining a Market" and "Round Lot").

MANAGEMENT. The combined areas of policy and administration for a business. Also the people who make the decisions and provide the supervision necessary to implement the business owners' objectives. In some instances when a major studio/distributor has been acquired by a corporate conglomerate in recent years, the studio's management team has pretty much stayed in place (see "Corporation," "Mergers and Acquisitions," "Officers" and "Shareholders").

MANAGEMENT FEE. A fee or compensation paid for services rendered in connection with the management of a business activity. In film limited partnerships, such fees may be paid to the general partner/producer or to others and may be based on a percentage of offering proceeds during the first year and on a percentage of partnership gross receipts in subsequent years. Such fees may also be waived by the general partner (see "Limited Partnership").

MANAGING BROKER/DEALER. Another less-formal term for managing underwriter used to describe a broker/dealer firm which takes the lead in organizing a selling group of broker/dealers put together for the distribution of a security in a best-efforts offering (see "Best Efforts," "Managing Underwriter" and "Selling Broker/Dealer").

MANAGING BROKER/DEALER AGREEMENT. The contract between the issuer of securities and the managing broker/dealer setting out the terms under which the managing broker/dealer will organize a selling group of broker/dealers and distribute such securities (see

"Managing Broker/Dealer," "Selling Broker/Dealer" and "Underwriting Agreement").

MANAGING UNDERWRITER. The leading and originating investment banking firm of an underwriting group organized for the purchase and distribution of a new issue of securities (also called "Syndicate Manager;" see "Managing Broker/Dealer" and "Underwriter").

MANIPULATION. The buying or selling of a security to create a false appearance of active trading and thus influence other investors to buy or sell shares. Both civil and criminal penalties may apply to this activity (see "Corporation," "Insider Trading," "Publicly Held," "Securities" and "Stock Exchange").

MANNER OF OFFERING LIMITATION (see "Limitations on Manner of Offering").

MARGINAL PICTURES. A subjective term used to describe feature films that are not necessarily expected to be major successes at the box office but still could be financially successful for a distributor (see "Blockbuster" and "Hit").

MARKETABILITY. The speed and ease with which a particular security may be bought and sold (see "Securities").

MARKETABLE SECURITY. Security that is of reasonable investment caliber and can be easily sold on the market, i.e., any security for which, as of the date of disposition, there was a market on an established securities market or otherwise (see "Securities").

MARKETABLE TITLE. Ownership rights which a reasonably well-informed purchaser would, in the exercise of ordinary business prudence, be willing to accept (see "Bad Title," "Clearance" and "Title").

MARKETING. In film distribution, the combined activities of the sales and advertising departments of the film distributor. The sales department books pictures into theatres, determines when a film will open, what the release pattern will be and upon what terms the film will be exhibited. The advertising and publicity departments seek to increase the awareness of a film among prospective moviegoers and their interest in seeing a film (see "Advertising" and "Publicity").

MARKETING CAMPAIGN. A specific plan or strategy designed to promote awareness of a motion picture and to motivate the general public to go see it (see "Advertising Campaign," "Marketing Strategy," "Publicity" and "Release Strategy").

MARKETING DEPARTMENT. The major administrative division of the typical film industry studio/distributor which is primarily responsible for planning and implementing the distribution of motion pictures (see "Advertising," "Business Affairs Department," "Creative Affairs Department," "Distributor Release Campaign," "Legal Department," "Marketing," "Production Department," "Release Pattern," "Release Sequence" and "Studio").

MARKETING RESEARCH. The systematic collection and analysis of demographic and other information relating to potential movie-going audiences used in making motion picture marketing decisions (see "Demographics").

MARKETING STRATEGY. This term may apply to several different situations, including a producer's plan for promoting a film to distributors, the distributor's plan or method used in advertising and promoting a film to exhibitors, the plans of sales agents in marketing to prospective licensees in the ancillary markets and the concepts and plan for selling a movie to the public, i.e., advertising and promoting a motion picture so as to create demand among filmgoers to see the film (see "Marketing," "Marketing Campaign" and "Release Strategy").

MARKET MAKER. Securities broker/dealers who make a market for a given security (see "Making A Market," "Maintaining A Market" and "Underwriting").

MARKETPLACE OF IDEAS. The worldwide environment in which formulated thoughts or opinions may be expressed. Because of the presumed (or well-established) importance of the motion picture as a vehicle for the expression of ideas, the obvious power of this form of communication and the fact that movies are often exhibited worldwide, it is vitally important that all significant human interests whether based on racial, cultural, religious, socioeconomic, political or other factors be concerned about the use and abuse of the motion picture medium as a means for advocating any of such interests. In other words, all of these interest groups should be concerned as to whether their views are consistently portrayed in a positive or negative fashion through feature films. Thus, to the extent that an industry such as the motion picture business might be dominated by a particular interest group that consistently espouses a biased point of view on numerous issues that are presented in films, and to the extent that such an interest group utilizes the practices described in this book to perpetuate its dominance of the industry, other interest groups, including government, may justifiably take action which is both designed to "level the playing field" and to broaden the points of view expressed through the motion picture medium (see "Anti-Trust Laws,"

"Hidden Agendas," "Insider's Game," "Level Playing Field," "Market Share" and "Movies With a Message").

MARKET POWER. The ability to control or dominate a specific level of an industry (e.g., wholesale or retail). Generally, in the application of the anti-trust laws to the film business, market power may be presumed from the fact that the product involved, i.e., motion pictures is copyrighted. However, in recent years, the U.S. Justice Department has taken the position that if a market is not otherwise susceptible to market power wielded by a single firm or a coordinated group of companies, even significant increases in barriers to entry in that market are unlikely to adversely affect competition in the marketplace (see "Anti-Trust Laws," "Barriers to Entry," "Merger Guidelines," "MPAA," "Paramount Consent Decree of 1948," "Political Influence," "TriStar Case" and "Vertical Merger").

MARKETS. Geographical or technological areas of demand for film product, including theatrical and ancillary markets (see "Ancillary Markets," "Foreign Territories" and "Theatrical Market").

MARKET SHARE. The percentage of industry sales of a particular company, product or segment of an industry, e.g., for the period from 1984 through 1990, independently distributed feature films only generated a yearly average of approximately 8.1% of the domestic theatrical box-office gross. That means the MPAA company distributed films (some of which were produced by independent producers) generated an average of 91.9% of the domestic box-office gross. One of the more puzzling of motion-picture-industry phenomena is the rather common occurrence at the annual Academy Awards for independently produced films to win a disproportionate share of the more important awards, e.g., best picture, best director, best actor, best actress, best screenplay, etc., particularly since many of those same award-winning films are not as commercially successful as many of the films produced by the major studio/distributors. Some industry observers would quickly dismiss that anomaly as the result of differences between movies that are targeted for the mass audience (commercial product) and those that are designed to be small films tailored for a limited but more discriminating audience (not commercial). Another factor in how well these two categories of films are received at the box office may have nothing to do with whether such pictures are quality award-winners or merely commercial, but have more to do with which distributors have the market power to get their films shown at theatres, to spend the money to advertise and promote their pictures and the leverage to collect film rentals from exhibitors. Besides, the more artistic, award-winning, independently produced films, after receiving all of the free publicity and promotion associated with the Academy Awards, are suddenly now more "commercial" and those distributed by the major/studio distributors before the awards can be re-released (or continued in release) to take advantage of their new profit-making potential (see "Academy Awards," "Blind Bidding," "Cartel," "Controlled Theatre," "Major Exhibition Chains," "Market Power," "Oligopoly," "Political Influence," "Prints and Ads Commitment" and "Settlement").

MARKET VALUE. The price that goods or a property would bring in a market of willing buyers and willing sellers, in the ordinary course of trade (see "Law of Supply and Demand").

MARQUEE. The signboard, usually cantilevered and often lighted, which is most commonly situated in front of a theatre, typically above the entrance and box office. It has movable letters that spell out the names of the current and/or coming attractions and the featured performers (see "Marquee Value" and "Star").

MARQUEE VALUE. Actors and actresses who have names which are recognizable to the theatre-going public and who have some level of drawing power or so-called "box office appeal" (see "Box Office Appeal," "Marquee Value" and "Star").

MASS ADVERTISING CAMPAIGN. A film marketing and promotion program which is directed to the general public primarily through radio, television and newspapers (see "Advertising" and "Advertising Campaign").

MASS AUDIENCE. A large cross section of society (see "Blind Bidding," "Homogeneous Films" and "Projected Audience").

MASS MARKETING. A commercial marketing approach for films which provides high visibility in all media and in many theatres (see "Direct Advertising," "Homogeneous Films" and "Projected Audience").

MASTER AGREEMENT. A licensing agreement or "blanket deal" covering the exhibition of features in a number of theatres, usually comprising a circuit (see "Circuit" and "Formula Deal").

MASTER LIMITED PARTNERSHIP (MLP). A limited partnership formed under state partnership law where the limited partnership interests are publicly traded, e.g., on the New York Stock Exchange or "over the counter." Unless a securities registration exemption applies, interests in MLPs are required to be registered. The term "master limited partnership" originates from the structure of the entity. Partnership interests are issued to a "master" limited partner who then arranges for the sale of the units to the public (also called "Publicly Traded Partnership;" see "Limited Partnership").

MASTER POSITIVE. A positive film with special photographic characteristics that make it suitable for serving as a master from which a series of dupe negatives can be printed while minimizing any loss of quality (see "Print").

MASTER SCENE. A primary dialogue or action scene in a motion picture in which the characters are developed or the plot is advanced (see "Master Shot" and "Scene").

MASTER SCRIPT. The final shooting script from which all others are duplicated (see "Screenplay" and "Shooting Script").

MASTER SHOT (OR MASTER SCENE). A complete movie scene covering all dialogue and action in the widest and longest shot. Into this scene are added cutaway shots, close-ups, medium shots, etc. All of these shots are called coverage or cover shots. Sometimes the problem of matching physical action is handled by simultaneous multi-camera filming/taping. However, the master shot is the scene to which all else is referenced in editing and to which all other action must be synchronized or matched (see "Scene").

MATERIAL. Important, necessary or substantial (see "Anti-Fraud Statute," "Breach of Contract," "Material Breach" and "Material Tax Issue").

MATERIAL BREACH. In contract law, a breach that is substantial and operates to excuse further performance by the aggrieved party. A material breach impairs the value of the contract and gives rise to an action for breach of contract (see "Breach of Contract" and "Material").

MATERIAL FACT. Securities terminology for information of reasonably sufficient importance to be disclosed to investors in a securities offering, i.e., a fact which, if called to the attention of a reasonably prudent investor, would tend to influence, either positively or negatively, the investor's judgment relative to buying or selling the securities of an issuer [see "Anti-Fraud Statute (Rule)" and "Disclosure Document"].

MATERIAL TAX ISSUE. Any federal income-tax issue relating to a tax shelter that would make a significant contribution toward sheltering, from federal taxes, income from other sources by providing deductions in excess of the income from the tax shelter investment in any year, or making available tax credits to offset tax liabilities in excess of the tax attributable to the tax shelter investment in any year (see "Tax Shelter," "Tax Opinion" and "Tax Shelter Registration").

MAXIMUM EXPLOITATION. The highest level of profit or advantage that may be gained from the exhibition or related activities and products associated with a motion picture (see "Exploitation," "Foreign Distribution," "Live Stage Rights," "Merchandising," "Product Placement," "Tie-Ins," "Video Rights Agreement" and "Wide Release").

MAXIMUM INTEREST ALLOWED BY LAW. The highest percentage of interest which is permitted to be charged by lenders pursuant to state usury laws (see "Actual Interest," "Interest," "Prime Rate" and "Usury").

MAXIMUM OFFERING. The greatest amount of money being sought in a mini-maxi securities offering (see "Mini-Maxi Offering").

MECHANICAL LICENSE. Written authority granted by the owner of a copyright, or such owner's agent, to reproduce copyrighted material for a designated consideration. Copyright law provides that any composition may be mechanically reproduced once the owner of the copyrights has used or permitted the use of the composition for mechanical reproduction (see "License Agreement").

MECHANICAL REPRODUCTION. Reproduction by machine or tools as opposed to reproduction by electrical means (see "Compact Disc," "Electrical Reproduction" and "Phonograph").

MECHANICAL RIGHTS (ROYALTIES). The rights to reproduce and to distribute to the public copyrighted materials. Mechanical royalties are paid to obtain such rights, usually on a per-copy basis (see "Copyright" and "Royalties").

MEDIA. The means of communication that reach the general public, such as radio or television; the plural form of medium. Media is a generic word that includes the specific medium of the press (see "Communications Industry" and "Entertainment Industry").

MEDIA BUYS. The purchase of motion picture advertising time and space on television and radio and in newspapers and magazines. Advertising is generally the single largest expenditure incurred in the distribution of a motion picture. Independent producers who use the facilities of unaffiliated distribution entities must carefully monitor and vigorously audit distributor practices relating to media buys to make sure the distributor is not simply charging off its most expensive media buys in time or space on the independently produced picture, as opposed to other movies it may be distributing at the same time or while recording the less expensive time for its own motion pictures (regardless of which advertising cost was actually tied to which movie). Also, independent producers must be very careful as to which distribution personnel, if any, gets charged against the costs of such advertising and which personnel are simply absorbed into the distributor's fee. Generally, the time of distributor marketing department employees should not be separately charged to a motion picture, particularly if an advertising overhead charge is imposed (see "Advertising," "Advertising Overhead" and "Creative Accounting").

MEDIA MIX. The combination of communication outlets chosen to advertise a given film (see "Advertising").

MEDIATION. A form of alternative dispute resolution, i.e., a method of settling disputes without going to court and through the use of a neutral third party who serves as mediator between the parties (see "Arbitration," "Litigation" and "Negotiation").

MEDIUM (see "Media").

MEDIUM-BUDGET FILMS. As of the publication date of this dictionary, motion pictures with budgets in the neighborhood of $8 to $15 million, although these figures may vary from year to year (see "Big-Budget Films" and "Low-Budget Films").

MEMBER OF THE CLUB. Another reference to the point that the motion picture industry is an insider's game. However, the "club" must be a fairly limited group of people since the producer who actually made this statement had been involved in the production and financing of a fairly significant number of feature films, some of which had been very successful and he indicated he did not consider himself a "member of the club" (see "Insider's Game," "MPAA" and "Relationship-Driven Business").

MEMORANDUM. The securities disclosure document associated with a private placement limited partnership offering. This is the document that is created for a securities offering pursuant to the general disclosure requirements of the anti-fraud statute and the more specific disclosure requirements relating to the type of offering being conducted [same as "Confidential Private Placement Offering Memorandum," "Offering Memorandum" and "Private Placement Offering Memorandum;" see"Anti-Fraud Statute (Rule)"].

MEMORANDUM OF AGREEMENT. A written outline of some intended agreement or an instrument drawn up in brief form. The phrase is sometimes used as the title of a complete agreement which has been memorialized in writing, i.e., the term is often used as the title of entertainment industry contracts, e.g., memorandum of agreement to co-finance theatrical motion pictures (see "Contract" and "Deal Memo").

MENTAL MODELING. Projecting the financial results of a company without the aid of a computer (see "Computer Model" and "Financial Management").

MERCHANDISE AND PUBLISHING ROYALTIES. Percentages of revenue paid for the authority to use and exploit property rights relating to products, names and events appearing in or used in connection with a motion picture as well as property rights relating to published materials (see "Maximum Exploitation" and "Merchandising").

MERCHANDISING. The manufacture, distribution, licensing, selling or other exploitation of characters, names and events appearing in or used in connection with a motion picture, e.g., in the form of T-Shirts, books, posters, jewelry, games, dolls and/or toys (see "Allied Rights" and "Goodwill").

MERCHANDISING AGREEMENT. The licensing contract between a production company, as the owner of the property rights associated with a feature film, and a manufacturer and/or distributor which has the capability of producing and distributing licensed products based on the characters or objects portrayed in a motion picture (same as "License for Merchandising Agreement").

MERCHANDISING RIGHTS. The rights to manufacture, distribute, license, sell or otherwise exploit characters, names and events appearing in or used in connection with films beyond the motion picture market, e.g., in the form of T-Shirts, books, posters, jewelry, games, dolls and/or toys. Such rights on certain movies may be very valuable (see "Merchandising").

MERCHANDISING TIE-INS. Cooperative promotional campaigns connecting specific merchandise with a given film (contrast with "Product Placement;" see "Promotional Tie-Ins").

MERCHANTABLE. An item fit for sale in the usual course of trade, at usual selling prices. A merchantable item must be of ordinary marketable quality, bring the average price, be lawful merchandise, be good and sufficient of its kind and be free from any remarkable defects (see "Sale of Goods Statutes").

MERCHANT BANK. A financial institution that engages in investment banking, counseling and negotiating in mergers and acquisitions and a variety of other services, including securities portfolio management, the acceptance of foreign bills of exchange, etc. (see "Bank," "Investment Bank" and "Investment Banker").

MERGER. The combining of two or more companies (see "Mergers and Acquisitions," "Merger Guidelines" and "Vertical Integration").

MERGER GUIDELINES. A six-part analytical framework set forth by the U.S. Justice Department in 1984 for use as a guide in analyzing the competitive effects of a proposed vertical merger in the motion picture business which is based on the U.S. Justice Department's analysis of Clayton Act cases. The guidelines are summarized below: (1) Does the contemplated merger significantly foreclose other competitors (e.g., exhibitors) from access to motion pictures or access on competitive terms? (2) Does the proposed merger significantly foreclose other competitors (e.g., distributors) from access to theatres or a substantial portion of theatres? (3) If actual competitors are not likely to be foreclosed from access to motion pictures on competitive terms, does the proposed action nonetheless effectively force actual or potential competitors to enter or continue in the distribution or exhibition business on a vertically integrated basis? (4) If vertical integration is effectively required in order to enter or continue in the business, how difficult is to it to achieve vertical integration? (5) If vertical integration is required, and if there are significant barriers to such integration, is the market otherwise conducive to (i.e., will it allow) non-competitive performance? and (6) Does the proposed vertical merger have offsetting positive benefits for the economy by creating efficiencies? (see "Anti-Trust Laws," "Barriers to Entry," "Clayton Act," "Internationally Competitive," "Market Share," "Paramount Consent Decree of 1948," "Political Influence," "TriStar Case" and "Vertical Integration").

MERGERS AND ACQUISITIONS. Activities relating to the combining of two or more companies and/or the purchase of companies. Such activities often involve and therefore must be conducted in compliance with the securities laws since corporate shares are securities. Some attorneys and investment bankers specialize in the very complex transactions relating to mergers and acquisitions. Also, since mergers or acquisitions could result in an illegal restraint of trade, proposed mergers or acquisitions of certain companies in the same or related industries may have to first be approved by the U.S. Justice Department anti-trust law division (see "Anti-Trust Laws," "Merger Guidelines," "Securities and Exchange Commission" and "U.S. Justice Department").

MESSAGE MOVIE (see "Culture Promotion," "Marketplace of Ideas" and "Movies With A Message").

MEZZANINE LEVEL. Stage of a company's development just prior to its going public, in venture-capital terminology. Venture capitalists investing at this point generally have a lower risk of loss than at previous financing stages and can hopefully look forward to earlier capital appreciation as a result of the market value gained through a subsequent initial public offering (see "IPO," "Second Round" and "Venture Capital").

MICRO-BUDGET FILM (see "Ultra-Low Budget").

MICRO-MAJORS. A fairly recently coined category of motion picture production companies which may or may not have their own distribution capabilities, but which do have independent lines of bank or financing credit to finance their production slates and possibly even releasing costs (see "Independent Distributor," "Independent Producer," "Major Studio/Distributors," "Mini-Majors" and "Rent-A-Distributor").

MID-WEEK BOX OFFICE. The Mondays, Tuesdays and Wednesdays of each week, which traditionally have generated the lowest number of theatre admissions. A major studio/distributor recently proposed that the nation's movie theatre operators offer their releases at a discount on Tuesdays in an effort to boost mid-week attendance at the theatres. The proposal was reportedly greeted with reluctance by many of the largest exhibitors (see "Box Office Gross").

MIFED. An international film market held in Milan, Italy, each fall. At this market, representatives of various entities in the film industry meet to exhibit and view films, to promote proposed films, and to discuss the possible financing, acquisition and/or distribution of such films (see "American Film Market," "Cannes Film Festival" and "Film Market").

MIME. To act a part with mimic gesture and action usually without words (see "Actor" and "Bit Player").

MINI-MAJORS. An arbitrary, unofficial and probably outdated term used to describe a second tier of feature film producer/distributors. Some analysts use the lack of production studio facilities as a criterion for separating "mini-majors" from "majors." The list changes from time to time depending upon how such entities fare in the movie marketplace. Such labels are often used by investment analysts and the trade press in describing various entertainment companies. In recent years, the mini-majors included Atlantic, Wientraub, De Laurentiis, Lorimar, Cannon, New Line, Vestron, Island, Alive, New World, Cineplex-Odeon, Carolco, Hemdale, Miramax and Cinecom, many of which are no longer functioning entities. Also in recent years, "Variety" has discontinued the use of the term as a category for statistical reporting purposes in its annual list of films distributed by major studio/distributors and independents (see "Independent Distributor," "Independent Producer," "Major Studio/Distributors," "Micro-Majors," "Studio Lots" and "Trades").

MINI-MAXI OFFERING. An underwriting arrangement with a broker/dealer requiring the broker/dealer to sell a stated minimum of securities on an all-or-none basis and the balance on a best-efforts basis, e.g, a mini-maxi offering might permit a filmmaker to seek a minimum (enough to produce one film) and a maximum (enough to produce several films) in a multiple film offering. Issuer sales, i.e., without the participation of broker/dealers or finders may also raise funds through a mini-maxi offering. The required estimated use of proceeds section of a mini-maxi offering must disclose the estimated use of proceeds for both a minimum and maximum column, as well as explain how a level of offering proceeds somewhere in between the two will be handled (see "Disclosure Document" and "Use of Proceeds").

MINI-MULTIPLE. A feature film release pattern in which the film is exhibited at a number (more than an exclusive engagement and less than a wide release) of quality theatres in strategic geographic locations (see "Exclusive Engagement," "General Release," "Limited Engagement" and "Wide Release").

MINIMUM. In film exhibition, the lowest acceptable weekly rental payment to be paid by a film's exhibitor to the distributor as a percentage of such film's box-office gross at a theatre (same as "Floor").

MINIMUM ADMISSION PRICES. A specified amount below which motion picture theatre ticket prices may not fall. One of the conduct restrictions of the Paramount Consent Decree was designed to prevent the major studio/distributors from conspiring to fix minimum admission prices among the theatres they either owned or controlled (see "Controlled Theatre," "Paramount Consent Decree of 1948" and "Price Fixing").

MINIMUM ADVANCE (see "Advance").

MINIMUM CREDIT REQUIREMENTS. The feature-film billing notices specified in the applicable union or guild basic agreement for its members or in an individual employment agreement. The credit should be specified in the employment agreement if a union/guild agreement does not apply or if the individual being hired is to receive credit beyond the union/guild minimum (see "Credit Requirement" and "Guild").

MINIMUM FILM RENTAL. A reference to what is probably the most common film rental split between distributors and exhibitors, i.e., the 90/10 deal. Pursuant to this arrangement, the distributor would be paid 90% of the box office receipts after the theatre's overhead has been deducted, but not less than an agreed upon minimum percentage of the total box office (a floor) (see "Ninety/Ten Deal" and "Sliding Scale").

MINIMUM FREELANCE CONTRACT FOR THEATRICAL MOTION PICTURES. The Screen Actors Guild standardized contract to be used by producer signatories to the Producer-SAG agreement in hiring performers on a weekly basis. Additional clauses which are not part of the standard form may be inserted in such contracts (see "Daily Contract for Theatrical Motion Pictures").

MINIMUM GAIN. A technical accounting concept used in a limited partnership context, meaning the excess of the outstanding principal balance of any non-recourse debt of the partnership over the partnership's allocable share of the adjusted basis of the project for federal income-tax purposes (see "Limited Partnership").

MINIMUM GUARANTEE. A commitment to pay no less than a specified amount out of revenues generated. Motion picture licensing arrangements for the major foreign territories typically utilize this method of compensation, although fee advances paid, if any, would be deducted from the minimum guarantee (see "Outright Sale").

MINIMUM RATING. A commitment made by a feature film producer to a distributor and/or financiers that the film being produced will receive an MPAA rating not worse than a specific rating, e.g., an "R" rating. Such commitments are often required in film distribution agreements and if the producer fails to deliver the agreed-upon rating, the distributor may be relieved of its obligation to pay monies or release the picture. Such situations which involve an MPAA member distributor and an independent producer may raise the question relating to the inherent conflict of interest involved in rating films through the facilities of an MPAA sponsored organization (see "CARA," "Distribution Agreement," "Financing," "Independent Producer," "MPAA" and "Ratings").

MINIMUM REQUIREMENTS. A phrase and provision associated with an output distribution agreement which establishes certain standards or conditions (e.g., relating to budget, rating, running time, subject matter, etc.) for the motion pictures to comply with before the distributor will be obligated to distribute films under the agreement (see "Output Deal" and "Output Distribution Agreement").

MINIMUM WAGE SCALES. Salary minimums set by the various film-related unions and guilds (see "Compensation Schedules," "Double Scale" and "Scale").

MINOR. A person who is not old enough to be held legally responsible for all of his or her actions, e.g., entering into contracts, and/or who is not legally entitled to the rights held by citizens generally, e.g., voting. In most states, a minor is a person who has not yet achieved his or her eighteenth birthday but many states have set a higher legal age for the purchase of alcoholic beverages. Feature film producers must give special consideration to performers who are minors and, since laws relating to the employment of minors are generally promulgated by the states, must be aware of what the specific requirements are in the state in which some or a portion of a motion picture is being shot. Such state laws typically impose a ceiling on the number of hours each day that a minor may work, provide educational or schooling requirements, and, in some cases, require court approval of the minor's contract (see "Location Filming," "Majority," "Minority" and "State Legislatures").

MINORITY. The status of a person who has not yet reached majority, i.e., legal age; a person who is not old enough to be held legally responsible for all of his or her actions, e.g., entering into contracts or voting. In most states the age of majority is now eigthteen; however, some states have set a higher legal age for the consumption and purchase of alcoholic beverages (see "Minor" and "Majority").

MINORITY INTEREST. The interests of shareholders who, in the aggregate, own less than half of the shares of a corporation (see "Corporate Stock," "Corporation," "Shareholders" and "Working Control").

MISCELLANEOUS EQUIPMENT INSURANCE. An insurance policy which covers against all risks of direct physical loss, damage or destruction to cameras, camera equipment, sound, lighting and grip equipment, owned by or rented to the production company. Coverage can sometimes be extended to mobile equipment vans, studio location units or similar units upon payment of an additional premium (see "Equipment Insurance").

MIX (MIXING). The process of combining a number of separate sound tracks of dialogue, music or sound effects onto a single track with optimum balance. "Mixing" is also sometimes referred to as "re-recording" and "dubbing" (see "Dubbing").

MIXED DIALOGUE. The spoken words of two or more actors and/

or actresses blended together on a single track. The term also applies to mixed music and mixed sound effects (see "Mix").

MIXING [see "Mix (Mixing)"].

MIXING FACILITY. The physical plant where the mixing of movie sounds occurs [see "Mix (Mixing)"].

MOB (see "Mafia").

MOB-CONTROLLED DISTRIBUTION COMPANY. A film distribution company controlled by organized crime. An independent production company once reportedly licensed a small, independent distributor to distribute its film, but shortly after exploitation of the film was completed in the primary markets, the distributor filed for bankruptcy and the production company was never paid its portion of the film's revenues. Subsequent investigations revealed that the distributor had been set up specifically for that purpose. Even the possibility that this may occur makes it imperative that producers investigate the distributors with whom they do business (see "Choosing A Distributor," "Mafia," "Money Laundering," "Racketeering," "RICO," "Track Record" and "White Collar Crime").

MODIFIED GROSS DEAL. A film distribution deal in which the producer gets an advance and the distributor recoups some negotiated multiple of that advance plus its distribution fees and expenses off the top before splitting the remainder with the producer (see "First Dollar Gross Deal" and "Net Deal").

MODEL AGREEMENT. A sample contract which may be drafted by an industry organization for educational purposes. Unlike the unions and guilds, professional and trade association are not allowed to bargain collectively on behalf of their members, but there is no reason that seminars and other educational programs cannot be properly conducted (in compliance with the anti-trust laws that apply to such association activities) so as to meet the needs of association members with respect to the study and understanding of certain key industry agreements which significantly effect their livelihood. For example, the AFMA reportedly has model distribution agreements with terms and provisions from which its members may choose when drafting their own distribution agreements for the distribution of feature films. It has also long been recognized in the film industry that the terms and provisions of the film distribution agreements used by the major studio/distributors are remarkably similar regardless of whether their association (the MPAA) was actively involved in that phenomenon or not. Since many of the terms and provisions of the feature film distribution agreements being used today are not favorable to the independent feature film producers, there may be some value for such producers to organize their own association and include the development of a model distribution agreement, the terms of which are more favorable to independent producers, among the projects which such association undertakes (see "Association Projects," "Conscious Parallelism," "Contract of Adhesion," "Industry Groups," "Lobbying," "Producers Guild of America," "Professional Association," "RIPOFF," "Squeaky Wheel Gets the Grease" and "Standard Contract").

MODELING. The envisioning of the future operation of a company (see "Computer Model" and "Mental Modeling").

MODELING SERVICES. Financial management consultants who specialize in or offer computerized financial modeling assistance (see "Computer Model," "Financial Management," "Mental Modeling," "Modeling" and "Real Model").

MONETARY ADVANCES. With respect to motion picture pre-sales, the consideration paid to a feature film producer by an entity acquiring distribution rights in a given medium or territory may take a form that is readily convertible into cash, i.e., monetary advances or bankable commitments which may be used by the producer as collateral for a discounted bank loan (see "Collateral," "Pre-Sales" and "Split-Rights Deal").

MONETARY DAMAGES. Compensation, in the form of money, awarded by a court of law to one who has been injured by the action of another (contrast with "Damage;" see "Injury" and "Remedy" or "Remedies").

MONETIZED TRADE SURPLUSES. The excess of goods and services provided by one country to another converted into money. The monetized trade surplus of Japan in recent years has permitted Japanese business entities to purchase significant ownership interests in U.S. based companies, including major studio/distributors (see "Global Integration" and "Japanese Money").

MONEY LAUNDERING. The funneling of money obtained by illegal means through an apparently or previously legitimate operation. For example, consider this reported scenario in the film industry: A drug dealer agrees to pay the production costs of a feature film in exchange for the rights to distribute that film in a single foreign territory where that drug dealer controls a chain of theatres. It is then possible for the drug dealer and his exhibitor associates to inflate the theatrical box-office admission figures and send what appears to be a legitimate but inflated distributor's share of the box office gross back into the U.S. as laundered money. In any given year in which 400 to 500 feature films are distributed in the U.S., with the source of the production financing for many of such films unknown or difficult to determine, it is quite likely that such practices are occurring (see "Capital-Intensive Business," "Mafia," "Mob Controlled Distribution Company," "Movies With a Message," "Racketeering," "Relationship-Driven Business," "RICO" and "White Collar Crime").

MONOPOLIZE. To obtain or create a monopoly of the production and distribution of a product or service (see "Anti-Trust Laws" and "Monopoly").

MONOPOLY. Control of the production and distribution of a product or service by one firm or a group of firms acting in concert; a market condition where all or nearly all of an article of trade or commerce within a community or district is brought within the control of one person or company, thereby excluding competition or free traffic in that article. Monopolization is prohibited by the federal U.S. statute called the Sherman Act. Conviction can lead to criminal penalties and divestiture. The offense of monopoly has two elements: (1) the possession of monopoly power in the relevant market, and (2) the willful acquisition or maintenance of that power as distinguished from growth or development as a consequence of a superior product, business acumen or historical accident (see "Anti-Trust Laws," "Cartel," "Oligopoly" and "Transnational Cartelization").

MORAL RIGHTS. The right of an author or artist to object to or prevent the distortion, mutilation or other alteration of his or her work, which is detrimental to the author or artist's honor or reputation. Although the term is widely recognized in civil law countries, as currently codified in the U.S. Copyright Act, federal moral-rights legislation covers only certain works of the visual arts, and specifically excludes protection for motion pictures. Nevertheless, a right analogous to a moral right has been recognized in this country in several situations in which the integrity and reputation of an artistic creator were protected by the courts. The express grounds on which common-law protection has been given include libel, unfair competition, copyright and the right of privacy. Several states also have their own state statutes relating to moral rights. Feature film distributors often include a provision in the distribution agreement which results in the waiver of such rights by the producer (see "Common Law," "Droit Moral," "Editing Rights," "Moral Rights Waiver," "Lobbying" and "Tort").

MORAL RIGHTS WAIVER (see "Waiver of Moral Rights").

MORATORIUM. A legally authorized period of delay in the performance of a legal obligation or the payment of a debt, i.e., a waiting
period set by an authority, e.g., a moratorium on principal and/or
interest for a period of time (see "Balloon Payment" and "Moratorium
Statutes").

MORATORIUM STATUTES. A law enacted by the legislative branch
of government which authorizes periods of delay in the performance
of a legal obligation or the payment of a debt (see "Bankruptcy,"
"Moratorium" and "Restricted Currencies").

MOST FAVORED NATIONS CLAUSE. A contractual clause by which
each signatory grants to the other the broadest rights and privileges
which it accords to any other entity with which it deals. In film
contracts with multiple percentage participants, this provision en-
sures that one participant's terms will be no less favorable than those
of any other participant of like standing. Thus, this clause is crucial
to those participants who find themselves in the same category, e.g.,
net profit participants. If two such participants are supposed to be
paid a specified percentage of net profits but the definitions of net
profits in their respective agreements differ, without the most favored nations clause, one may prevent the other from being paid at
that level or at all (see "Leverage," "Pari Passu," "Profit" and "Percentage Participation").

MOST FAVORED NATIONS TREATMENT. To be dealt with in a
manner that is just as favorable as others in the same position (see
"Most Favored Nations Clause" and "Pari Passu").

MOTION PICTURE. A series of pictures projected on a screen in
rapid succession with people and objects shown in successive positions slightly changed so as to produce the optical effect of a continuous picture in which the objects move. For purposes of delivery,
this term is often a defined term in film distribution agreements, for
example: each picture will be between ninety and one hundred
twenty minutes in length. Each picture, when delivered, will be
completely finished, fully edited and titled and fully synchronized
with language dialogue, sound and music and in all respects ready
and of a quality, both artistic and technical, adequate for general
theatrical release and commercial public exhibition. Each picture will
consist of a continuous and connected series of scenes based on the
above described screenplays of the same name and shall be suitable
for exhibition to the general public in any and all domestic and
foreign markets. Such pictures will be produced utilizing the English

language on 35mm film in color. To the extent that the above described version of each picture is not suitable for U.S. network broadcast or does not comply with such network standards and practices, cover shots, alternate scenes or another version of each picture suitable for such broadcast shall be delivered to the distributor (same as "Film").

MOTION PICTURE ACCOUNTANTS. Accountants or accounting firms which specialize in or have expertise in areas relating to the movie industry, e.g., auditing, corporate finance for motion picture companies, etc. (see "Production Accountant").

MOTION PICTURE ACQUISITION/DISTRIBUTION AGREEMENT (see "Acquisition/Distribution Agreement").

MOTION PICTURE ASSOCIATION OF AMERICA (MPAA). A movie industry association organized to promote the international dissemination of American films and to upgrade imported films. The organization was founded in 1922 as the trade association for the American film industry but has evolved into an advocate for major producers and distributors as opposed to the independent producers and distributors. Its members include Columbia Pictures (now Sony Pictures), the Walt Disney Company, MGM/Pathe (formerly MGM/UA), Orion, Paramount, 20th Century-Fox, MCA/Universal and Warner Bros. One of the MPAA's functions is the assigning of audience ratings. The MPAA also maintains a strong lobbying arm which constantly monitors both the federal and state legislative branches for proposed bills or provisions in bills that are considered unfavorable to the interests of the MPAA companies. The MPAA also monitors and works to eliminate certain alleged exhibitor practices, e.g., product splitting, piracy and the illegal use of motion pictures (see "Illegal Use of Motion Picture," "Lobbying," "MPEAA," "NATO, "Piracy," "Product Splitting" and "Ratings").

MOTION PICTURE EXHIBITOR (see "Exhibitor").

MOTION PICTURE EXPORT ASSOCIATION OF AMERICA (MPEAA). The Motion Picture Export Association of America is the international counterpart of the MPAA. It was formed in 1945 by MPAA companies to respond to the rising tide of protectionism resulting in barriers aimed at the importation of American films into other countries. The President and Chief Executive Officer of the MPAA is also the Chairman and Chief Executive Officer of the MPEAA. The MPAA is also a sister association of the AMPTP (see "Alliance of Motion Picture and Television Producers" and "MPAA").

MOTION PICTURE INDUSTRY ENCOURAGEMENT ACT. A Jamaican statute passed in September, 1991, which grants film companies set up to film in Jamaica nine years of income tax exemption on profits or gains earned in the production of a motion picture. The entire production need not be filmed in Jamaica. U.S. stockholders of such film companies would not be subjected to U.S. tax under terms of a previous treaty between the two countries that precludes double taxation. The act also grants relief from customs duties on equipment, machinery and materials for the building of studios or for use in motion picture production, so long as those items are not available locally in Jamaica (see "Government Subsidies" and "Tax Benefits").

MOTION PICTURE INSURANCE. Customized packages of insurance policies covering risks associated with movie production, including insurance for the cast, negative film and videotape, props, sets and wardrobe, animal mortality, equipment, bad weather, extra expense, property damage liability, errors and omissions, non-owned aircraft, watercraft, worker's compensation, comprehensive general liability, auto liability and union and guild flight accidents. Insurance costs usually account for approximately 3% of a film's budget, and that does not include the completion bond fee, which does not technically relate to insurance (see "Completion Bond," "Insurance" and "Surety").

MOTION PICTURE LABORATORIES (see "Laboratory").

MOTION PICTURE MARKETPLACE (see "Film Market").

MOVE-OVER. A movie exhibitor/distributor term meaning to move a film out of one theatre into another, i.e., to transfer a film's showing from a theatre to another theatre within the same competitive theatre area, for that film's subsequent run within that competitive theatre area, without that film's subsequent run having been available to any other theatre. A move-over right is a privilege given by a distributor to an exhibitor/licensee to move a picture from one theatre to another as a continuation of the run at the licensee's first theatre (see "Move-Over Clause").

MOVE-OVER CLAUSE. A provision in a distributor/exhibitor agreement which permits the exhibitor to exhibit a film at another theatre under certain specified circumstances (see "Move-Over").

MOVIE. Another name for motion picture and feature film (see "Motion Picture").

MOVIE HOUSE. Another name for motion picture theatre (see "Exhibitor").

MOVIE LENDER. A bank that lends production and/or distribution funds to movie studios and/or production companies (see "Financing" and "Lender Financing").

MOVIE OF THE WEEK. A made-for-television movie produced specifically for a slot in an ongoing series of movie presentations on television or a motion picture selection aired as part of such an ongoing series (see "Made-for-Television Product" and "Pilot").

MOVIES WITH A MESSAGE. Motion pictures in which a moral, social or other statement predominates over the entertainment value of the movie. All movies have one or more messages, and financiers, producers, screenwriters, directors, actors and others in the industry have long recognized and used the medium as one of the most effective means yet devised by humanity for the communication of all sorts of ideas. However, if the message is too strong or seems out of place, it may be resented by and distracting to the audience which generally goes to the movies primarily to be entertained. The Oliver Stone movie "JFK" could be considered an example of a strong "message movie." Some might even suggest that the real message coming out of that motion picture was not designed to convince the moviegoing audiences that a conspiracy was involved in the assassination of a U.S. President (which many people already believed anyway), but instead to divert attention from one suspect group (the mob) and direct it toward others (the CIA and the highest levels of the U.S. government), while simultaneously suggesting that the same conspiracy was also involved in the killings of Bobby Kennedy and Martin Luther King. If allegations that elements of the mob were really the moving force behind the killings of the Kennedy brothers and that the mob has connections with the motion picture industry are true, this might help to explain why the motion picture took that particular editorial slant (see "Approvals," "Controls," "Creative Control," "Culture Promotion," "Favorable Portrayal," "Final Cut," "Funding Sources," "Hidden Agenda," "In-House Production," "Mafia," "Marketplace of Ideas," "Negative Pickup," "Pattern of Bias," "Production-Financing Distribution Agreement" and "Unfavorable Portrayal").

MOW (see "Movie of the Week").

MPAA (see "Motion Picture Association of America").

MPAA CARTEL. A tongue-in-cheek reference to the extraordinary influence that the member companies of the Motion Picture Association of America exert over the film industry, in addition to their dominance of the industry in terms of market share (see "Anti-Trust Laws," "Barriers to Entry," "Bidding War," "Cartel," "Conscious Parallelism," "Major Exhibition Chains," "Market Power," "Market Share," "MPAA," "Paramount Consent Decree of 1948," "Transnational Cartelization," "TriStar Case" and "Vertical Integration").

MPAA CERTIFICATE. The certificate for a film's designated rating issued by the MPAA's Code and Rating Administration (same as "MPAA Code Seal;" also called "Certificate of Code Rating").

MPAA CODE SEAL. A certification that a film, its trailers and advertising have been made and rated in conformity with the regulations and standards of the MPAA (same as "MPAA Certificate").

MPAA RATING (see "Ratings").

MPAA RATING ADMINISTRATION. The MPAA department that classifies completed motion pictures as being suitable for different audiences (see "Motion Picture Association of America" and "Ratings").

MPAA RATING AND CERTIFICATE. The certificate for a film's designated rating issued by the MPAA's Code and Rating Administration. The rating of a movie may significantly affect the number of people who may see a given movie. Since the MPAA rating is provided by a board of MPAA employees, there is an unethical built-in conflict of interest in the rating of films produced by non-MPAA member production companies. This conflict of interest should not be tolerated by independent producers. A professional association of independent feature film producers and the existing AFMA, which represents independent distributors, should start an alternative and improved movie rating system or become partners with the MPAA in sponsoring the movie rating system. Also, a movie's distribution agreement may provide for a specified MPAA rating, and if that rating is not obtained, the obligation on the part of the distributor to distribute the film may have been eliminated. Thus, the producer must be careful not to commit to producing a movie that cannot achieve the rating called for in the distribution agreement (see "Independent Producer," "MPAA" and "MPAA Code Seal").

MPEAA (see "Motion Picture Export Association of America").

MULTI-CULTURAL SOCIETY. A community, nation or other broadly defined group of people in which a variety of distinctive traditions, institutions, relationship patterns, collective activities and interests co-exist. The United States is clearly a multi-cultural society. Given that ideas are the most important commodity of the motion picture business and that the feature film is one of the most effective, if not the most effective means of communication yet devised by human beings, it is of critical importance to a multi-cultural society that all significant cultural and other interest groups within that society have a fair opportunity to express their most important commodity (their ideas) through our most effective means of communication (the feature film). To this end, both the federal and state governments in the U.S. have an obligation to its multi-cultural citizenry to assure such fairness and equal opportunity in the marketplace of ideas (see "Communication," "Communications Industry," "Culture Promotion," "Entertainment," "Entertainment Industry," "Idea," "Marketplace of Ideas," "Movies With a Message" and "Propaganda").

MULTI-NATIONAL CORPORATION. A corporation that has production facilities or other fixed assets in at least one foreign country and makes its major management decisions in a global context (see "Corporate Conglomerate").

MULTI-PART SERIES. A succession of television presentations which are all portions of the same overall program (see "Television Series").

MULTI-PICTURE FINANCING. The funding of the production and possibly distribution expenses associated with more than one film. Corporate financing for a studio or film production company is generally multi-picture financing. Limited partnerships or lender financing may also be used to raise funds for multiple pictures (see "Single-Picture Financing" and "Slate of Pictures").

MULTIPLE. In film exhibition, the situation in which more than one exhibitor or theatre is involved in the simultaneous showing of a film in a given market (for an explanation of the way the same term is used in corporate finance (see "Price/Earnings Ratio").

MULTIPLE FILM OFFERING. A securities offering which seeks to raise enough money to produce and/or distribute more than one motion picture (see "Mini-Maxi Offering" and "Slate of Pictures").

MULTIPLE PICTURE DISTRIBUTION AGREEMENT. A feature film licensing contract that covers more than one movie (see "Output Deal" and "Overall Deal").

MULTIPLE-PICTURE SLATE. A film production company's planned program of film production involving more than one film (see "Output Deal" and "Slate of Pictures").

MULTIPLE PRE-SALES. Pre-production commitments to license a film in more than one market, e.g., several foreign markets, video and pay cable (see "Creative Financing," "Fractionalizing," "Negative Pickup," "Pre-Sales" and "Split Rights Basis").

MULTIPLE REPRESENTATION (see "Conflicts of Interest," "Inter-Client Confidentiality" and "Representation of Multiple Clients").

MULTIPLE SCREEN MOVIE HOUSE (see "Multiplex").

MULTIPLEX. A motion picture entertainment facility at which two or more theatres under the same ownership are housed in one structure utilizing a common lobby, ticket sales booth and concession counter (see "Major Exhibition Chains," "Number of Screens" and "Overflow").

MULTI-SCREEN COMPLEX (see "Multiplex").

MULTI-TIERED AUDIENCE. A film audience of different types of people who are attracted to the film for different reasons. It may sometimes be necessary to reach such an audience through differing forms of advertising, promotion and publicity (see "Advertising" and "Projected Audience").

MUSIC. Vocal or instrumental sounds having rhythm, melody or harmony (see "Lyrics").

MUSIC AGREEMENTS. Contracts relating to the music and music rights associated with a motion picture. On pictures which are being bonded, copies of all existing music agreements must be furnished to the completion guarantor for its review (see "Completion Bond" and "Music").

MUSICAL SCORE (see "Score" and "Scoring").

MUSIC CUE. Music written to accompany a specific portion of a film (see "Music Cue Sheets").

MUSIC CUE SHEETS. Listings by film reel of the places on the film where various musical contributions begin and end, also showing the composer and publisher. The music cue sheets are used in licensing and in determining royalties (see "Music" and "Music Cue Sheets").

MUSIC DIRECTOR. The person responsible for seeing that music is composed and/or selected for a motion picture and is orchestrated and copied. The music director also supervises the actual scoring sessions, and in some cases may conduct them (see "Music").

MUSIC EDITOR. A film post-production person engaged in assembling and synchronizing music film tracks for the purpose of re-recording (see "Editing").

MUSIC MIXER. The person responsible for controlling, balancing and combining a number of separate music sound tracks and achieving the best musical sound for a given film. The music mixer is typically a member of a team of re-recording mixers who prepare the final sound for a film during its post-production. Except in the case of the lowest of budgeted films, the music is not mixed to a single sound track (see "Mix").

MUSIC PUBLISHER. One who controls the rights in a musical composition to license for performances, mechanical reproductions and synchronizations and to print, publish and sell sheet music (see "Publish").

MUSIC RIGHTS. The power and authority to use and otherwise exploit the music associated with a movie. Such rights are sometimes referred to as music publishing rights (see "Synchronization License" and "Synchronization Rights").

MUSIC TRACK(S). The audio tracks containing only music. These tracks only exist as separate tracks until the final mix of music, sound effects and dialogue into a composite soundtrack (see "Dialogue Track" and "Sound Effects Track").

MUTUAL APPROVAL. The sanction of one or more parties to a transaction or with respect to specific issues which arise as part of a given transaction. For example, a production-financing/distribution agreement may call for the mutual approval of the production company and the distributor in selecting the actors and actresses engaged to play roles set forth in the distribution agreement if persons already pre-approved are not ultimately used for any reason (see "Approvals," "Discretion" and "Right of Consultation").

MUTUAL PARTICIPATION. Language in an agreement which sets out the circumstances under which parties to the agreement (and possibly others) will take part in a specified common activity in the future. For example, in a production-financing/distribution agreement the distributor may provide that if it determines to exercise its theatrical derivative distribution rights granted in the distribution agreement, the distributor, the production company and certain associated artists must then negotiate with each other for their mutual participation in the theatrical production and the terms of such participation will be no less favorable to the production company and the associated artists than those contained in the distribution agreement (see "Production-Financing/Distribution Agreement").

— N —

NAME-ACTORS. On-the-screen talent whose names are recognizable by much of the movie-going public and whose inclusion in a film may tend to provide some level of box-office draw for the film (see "Marquee Value" and "Star").

NAMED PERILS INSURANCE POLICY. An insurance policy which limits coverage to the risks specified in the policy (see "Claims Made Policy" and "Insurance").

NAME-DROPPING. Including the names of very important people in a conversation or other communication for the purpose of impressing the person receiving the communication. A technique financial analysts suggest has been successfully used by the large public feature-film limited partnership offerings in recent years to raise monies for films produced and distributed by major studio/distributors with well-known stars. Investors appeared to be more willing to invest in such vehicles, even though the performance record of such large major-studio offerings has not been impressive from an investment perspective. The disappointing performance of such film partnerships from the investor perspective has also contributed to the more general perception that feature-film limited partnerships are not useful financing vehicles for motion pictures (see "Investor Motivation," "Limited Partnership" and "Limited Partnerships Are Dead").

NARRATION. The reciting of the details of a story (see "Narrative" and "Novel").

NARRATIVE. The story itself (see "Narration," "Novel," "Story Line" and "Treatment").

NARROW RELEASE. A platformed distribution of a motion picture, i.e., begun in a few theatres in the hope that favorable word-of-mouth will allow a wider distribution in the weeks ahead. The risks of such a release pattern are high, since, if the picture does not make it initially, it will generally not be booked into other theatres, which calls for a more expensive advertising campaign, which in turn adds value to the ancillary rights, particularly pay television and video (see "Platformed" and "Release Pattern").

NASAA. Acronym for North American Securities Administrators Association (see "Blue Sky Laws," "Securities" and "Uniform Limited Offering Exemption").

NASD. Acronym for National Association of Securities Dealers (see "Broker/Dealer" and "National Association of Securities Dealers").

NASDAQ. The acronym for National Association of Securities Dealers Automated Quotations, a national automated quotation service for over-the-counter securities. Operation is supervised by the NASD and input is provided by hundreds of over-the-counter market makers (see "Market Makers," "NASD" and "Securities").

NATIONAL ADVERTISING CAMPAIGN. A movie marketing and promotional strategy and plan which is implemented on a national basis, particularly in the U.S. It may involve television, radio, newspaper and possibly other media advertising buys. Such campaigns take time to plan and implement and have to be timed to coordinate with the release of the motion picture. Distributors feel that this coordination of timing is critical because national advertising campaigns may also involve numerous tie-ins which stimulate maximum exploitation of a motion picture's profit potential during the first few weeks of its exhibition in the domestic theatrical marketplace (see "Advertising," "Blind Bidding," "Merchandising," "Tie-Ins" and "Trade Screening").

NATIONAL ASSOCIATION OF INVESTMENT CLUBS. An association based in Royal Oak, Michigan, that helps investment clubs get established (see "Investment Club" and "Investment Group").

NATIONAL ASSOCIATION OF SECURITIES DEALERS (NASD). The national professional/trade association which is authorized and partly responsible for enforcing the SEC rules and regulations relating to investment banking and securities broker/dealer activities. In an IPO or other public/registered securities offering, the NASD reviews copies of the registration statements and underwriting agreements to determine whether the underwriting compensation fits within the NASD's guidelines as to what is fair and reasonable (see "Broker/Dealer," "Over-the-Counter Market," "Private Securities Transaction" and "SEC").

NATIONAL ASSOCIATION OF THEATRE OWNERS (NATO). The trade association of feature film exhibitors. NATO headquarters is in North Hollywood (see "Exhibitor" and "Major Exhibition Chains").

NATIONAL CIRCUITS. Motion picture theatre chains with theatres generally across the U.S. Included among the national circuits are Cineplex-Odeon, Columbia Pictures Entertainment (owner of Loews), United Artists Entertainment, AMC Entertainment, General Cinema and Hoyts Cinemas (see "Major Exhibition Chains").

NATIONALITY TEST. Requirements of the formal international co-production treaties which relate to the content of a film, where it is shot and who is involved. Under such tests, films will typically be required to use a local director, script, writer and source material, local stars, local crews and, in some cases, the film will have to be shot in the local language. Also, creative and financial contributions from each of the countries involved will generally have to be more than 30%, studio shooting and lab work will have to be carried out in one of the countries, local producers must be credited on screen and all the actors and creative elements must come from one of the two countries (see "Foriegn Production Problems" and "International Co-Productions and Agreements").

NATIONAL MARKETING STRATEGY. A motion picture advertising and publicity campaign that involves media buys throughout the country. The advent of television has provided feature film distributors with an efficient, although increasingly expensive, medium for promoting a wide release (see "Narrow Release," "Releasing Costs" and "Wide Release").

NATIONAL RELEASE. Distribution of a film for exhibition in theatres throughout the U.S. (see "Regional Release Pattern" and "Wide Release").

NATIONAL REVIEWERS. Film critics who are read or listened to by a national audience (see "Blurbs," "Industry Critic" and "Critics").

NATO (see "National Association of Theatre Owners").

NATO/SHOWEST. An international convention and trade show of film exhibitors, distributors, suppliers and vendors which is held annually, usually in February in Las Vegas (see "Trade Association").

NATURAL PERSON. A human being, as opposed to artificial or fictitious "persons" or things such as corporations and limited partnerships (see "Corporation" and "Entity").

NC-17. The relatively new, copyrighted MPAA rating established in September of 1990 to replace the "X" rating (which was not copyrighted by the MPAA and was therefore available for use by anyone) and indicating that no children under the age of 17 should be admitted. The NC-17 rating does solve the problem of unauthorized use of the "X" rating by pornographers, but some states or local communities will still not admit persons under twenty-one to such films and some newspapers will still not carry advertising for an NC-17 rated film. This rating change also does not address the concerns of parents and independent producers relating to a more detailed rating system which distinguishes between violence, sex and language. Nor does this rating deal with the inherent conflicts of interest in having an MPAA sponsored organization rating the films produced by non-MPAA member production companies (see "Independent Producer," "MPAA," "MPAA Rating" and "Certificate").

NEARBY LOCATIONS. Union terminology for film locations on which employees are not lodged overnight but return to the studio or home at the end of a day's work. All work performed away from a studio is considered on location (see "Distant Locations" and "Location Filming").

NECESSARY EXPENSE. For tax purposes, an expense is necessary if it is appropriate and helpful rather than necessarily essential to the taxpayer's business. To be deductible as a trade or business expense, an expenditure must be both ordinary and necessary in relation to the taxpayer's trade or business (see "Deductions," "Ordinary Expense" and "Tax Benefits").

NEGATIVE. Film with the light and dark parts in approximately inverse order to those of the original photographic subject. The term is used to designate any of the following: raw film stock specifically designed for a negative image, the negative image itself, the negative raw film stock that has been exposed but not yet processed and film that has been processed and which bears a negative image (see "Exposed Film," "Original Picture Negative," "Original Sound Negative" and "Picture Negative").

NEGATIVE CASH FLOW. The business situation in which a business spends more cash than it receives through earnings or other transactions in an accounting period (see "Cash Flow," "Cash Flow Cycle" and "Positive Cash Flow").

NEGATIVE COSTS. The total of all of the various costs, charges, and expenses incurred in the acquisition and production of a motion picture, in all its aspects prior to release, i.e., to produce the final negative. These include such items as facilities (soundstage, film lab, editing room, etc.) and raw material (set construction, raw film stock, etc.). Typically segregated as pre-production, above-the-line production-period costs and below-the-line costs and post-production-period costs. Negative costs are also distinguished from distribution, sub-distribution and exhibition costs. When a studio/distributor finances the production costs of a film, there may be a tendency for the distributor to characterize some of what are actually distribution costs as production costs, with the result that interest being incurred by the production cost side is inflated. The term "negative cost" for a studio/distributor not only may include the out-of-pocket production expenses but also a non-allocated overhead percentage charge which may range from 10% to 15% (see "Distribution Expenses," "Interest," "Overhead," "Production Costs" and "Rising Production Costs").

NEGATIVE CUTTING (OR NEGATIVE MATCHING). The cutting of the original negative of a film to match the edited positive, shot-by-shot and frame-by-frame (see "Edit").

NEGATIVE FILM AND VIDEOTAPE INSURANCE. An insurance policy which covers against all risks of direct physical loss, damage or destruction of raw film or tape stock, exposed film (developed or undeveloped), recorded videotape, sound tracks and tapes up to the amount of insured production cost (see "Insurance").

NEGATIVE INSURANCE (see "Negative Film and Videotape Insurance").

NEGATIVE PICKUP. The term "negative pickup" usually refers to the contractual commitment made by a distributor to a producer to purchase or license feature film distribution rights from the producer and to pay an agreed upon purchase price ("pickup price") when the distributor picks up the negative after delivery of the completed picture. The commitment is usually made prior to the completion of the film. The money is usually not paid to the producer until the film is finished, but if the negative pickup deal is with a distributor that meets the criteria of entertainment lenders, e.g., a major studio, and sometimes a mini-major, the producer may be able to take the agreement to such a bank where it can be discounted, i.e., for a fee paid to the bank, converted into an amount of cash less than the face value of the distributor's guarantee. Such funds may then be used to pay for some or all of the production costs of the film. Sometimes, the term "negative pickup" is used to refer to a sale or license of distribution rights at any time, even after completion of the film. However, that transaction is more accurately referred to as an "acquisition" or "pure acquisition" which is documented by an acquisition/distribution agreement (see "Acquisitions," "Pickups," "Pickup Price," "Production-Financing/Distribution Agreement" and "Split-Rights Basis").

NEGATIVE PICKUP DEAL (see "Negative Pickup" and "Negative Pickup Distribution Agreement").

NEGATIVE PICKUP AGREEMENT. A contract between a film's producer and a distributor in which the distributor commits to distribute the film and provides such commitment prior to the completion of the film (see "Negative Pickup Distribution Agreement" and "Acquisition/Distribution Agreement").

NEGATIVE PICKUP DISTRIBUTION AGREEMENT. Technically a misnomer, since there is no significant difference between an acquisition/distribution agreement and this so-called negative pickup distribution agreement except that the negative pickup transaction takes place prior to completion of the film. Thus, a negative pickup actually refers to a form of film finance as opposed to a separate type of distribution agreement (see "Acquisition/Distribution Agreement," "Negative Pickup," "Production-Financing/Distribution Agreement" and "Theatrical Distribution Contract").

NEGLIGENCE. Failure to exercise that degree of care which a person of ordinary prudence (a reasonable person) would exercise under the same or similar circumstances (see "Liability" and "Tort").

NEGOTIATE. To confer with another party to a proposed agreement for the purpose of arriving at a settlement as between the parties with regard to the issue or issues of concern. In film exhibition, to rent, sell or license motion pictures without bidding (see "Arm's Length," "Bid," "Contract of Adhesion," "Good Faith," "Leverage," "Market Power" and "Overreaching").

NEGOTIATED CONTRACTUAL DEFINITIONS. A phrase which refers to terms used in certain motion picture industry agreements, such as film distribution contracts, whose meanings have been specifically bargained for or settled on after some discussion between the parties to the contract. Some spokespersons for the major studio/ distributors are fond of explaining that most if not all of these alleged "creative accounting" practices are really the result of disappointed net profit participants who did not understand the effect of the contractually defined terms in their agreement. It is probably more accurate to observe that most of these terms, whose defined meanings in film industry contracts sometimes vary considerably from the meanings of the same terms as used in the agreements of other industries, are not negotiated at all, and if they are negotiated, the negotiations are between parties with such a disparity in bargaining power that there is an absence of any meaningful choice on the part of the weaker party (see "Contract of Adhesion," "Contractually Defined Terms," "Contractually Defined Profits," "Creative Accounting," "Inferior Bargaining Position" and "Unconscionable Contract").

NEGOTIATED CUSHION. A provision in a production-financing/distribution agreement which sets an upper limit (i.e., an amount over and above the film's approved production budget) which has to be exceeded before the film will be considered overbudget and any over-budget penalties kick in, e.g., 10% of a film's budget or 10% of below-the-line costs (see "Double Add-Back," "Over-Budget Penalty" and "Penalty-Free Cushion").

NEGOTIATED DEAL. As between exhibitors and distributors, an agreement which is negotiated as opposed to one which was accepted on bid. In the event that a distributor rejects all bid offers submitted by exhibitors for the right to license a film for exhibition within a market, the branch office of the distributor will in turn either re-bid the picture suggesting different terms or send out a notice to all exhibitors by which it offers to negotiate openly in an effort to award the film to the theatre that offers the most attractive negotiated terms. Such negotiations between film distributors and exhibitors may have the same negative results on prospective net profit participants as the settlement transactions between the same distributors and exhibitors (see "Bid," "Blind Bidding," "Five O'Clock Look" and "Settlement Transactions").

NEGOTIATED OFFER (see "Negotiated Deal").

NEGOTIATED UNDERWRITING. An underwriting of a new securities issue in which the spread between the purchase price paid to the issuer and the public offering price is determined through negotiation rather than multiple competitive bidding. This spread represents the compensation to the investment bankers participating in the underwriting (see "Purchase Group," "Syndicate" and "Underwriter").

NEGOTIATION. The discussions with others relating to the settlement of or agreement on a matter. Also, the practice of renting, selling or licensing motion pictures in the absence of bidding (see "Bid," "Blind Bidding," "Boilerplate," "Contract of Adhesion," "Standard Contract" and "Unfair Negotiating Tactics").

NEPOTISM. Favoritism shown to a relative or in the broadest sense, on the basis of some other relationship, e.g., hiring an employee because of his or her relationship to the employer instead of purely on the merits (see "Bias," "Discrimination," "Insider's Game," "Member of the Club," "Prejudice," "Reciprocal Preferences" and "Relationship-Driven Business").

NET. Generally, the figure remaining after all relevant deductions have been made from the gross amount (see "Net Assets," "Net Profit" and "Net Worth").

NET ASSETS. The difference between a company's total assets and liabilities (also called "Owner's Equity" or "Net Worth").

NET BOX OFFICE AFTER OVERHEAD. In calculations relating to the distributor/exhibitor deal, the balance of box office gross following deductions by the exhibitor for a second feature, cartoon or other pre-feature entertainment, if any, and deduction for the negotiated house nut (see "Film Rentals," "Gross Receipts," "House Nut" and "Net Box Office Receipts").

NET BOX OFFICE RECEIPTS. In calculations relating to the distributor/exhibitor deal, the balance of box office gross following deductions by the exhibitor for a second feature, cartoon or other pre-feature entertainment, if any, but before deduction for the negotiated house nut (see "Gross Receipts," "House Nut" and "Net Box Office After Overhead").

NET CURRENT ASSETS. The difference between current assets and current liabilities (also called "Working Capital").

NET DEAL. A film distribution deal in which the distributor recoups all its costs and collects all distribution fees before giving the producer all or a specified percentage of the remainder of the film's revenues or net profits. If distributor fees are deducted first and calculated as a percentage of distributor gross receipts, those distributor fee percentages should be lower than the percentages charged when and if distributor expenses are deducted prior to the distributor fee calculation. Also, if a studio/distributor which finances the production cost of a film inflates its distribution fees, includes its overhead as part of the negative cost of a film, takes its distribution fees and expenses prior to deducting interest on the negative cost and applying any revenues toward the reduction of the negative cost charges, while also permitting an actor or director to participate in some form of the film's gross receipts, it is very unlikely that the film will ever generate any net profits for anyone else to participate in (see "Adhesion Contract," "Creative Accounting," "First-Dollar Gross Deal," "Modified Gross Deal," "Net Profits" and "Overreaching").

NET FILM RENTAL. Revenue from theatrical release after distribution costs and fees are deducted from gross film rental, i.e., what remains of gross film rental after distribution and merchandising costs (usually prints and advertising) as well as the distributor fee percentages in various media and markets are deducted (see "Net").

NET INCOME. Generally, the sum remaining after all expenses have been met or deducted; the income in excess of costs. The term is synonymous with net earnings and with net profit or net loss, depending on whether the figure is positive or negative (see "Income," "Profit," "Receipts" and "Revenue").

NET INCOME AND NET LOSSES. IRS terminology for all income or losses of a limited partnership for any taxable year determined before taking into account any depreciation and not including any income, gain or loss realized in connection with a capital transaction or upon termination of such partnership (see "Income Tax").

NET OPERATING LOSS (NOLS). Tax term for the excess of business expenses over income in a tax year. Under the tax-loss carry-back, carry-forward provisions, NOLs can (if desired) be carried back or forward for a certain number of years (see "Loss").

NET POINTS (see "Net Profits," "Net Profit Participant," "Points" and "Talent Participations").

NET PROCEEDS. Generally, the amount (usually cash) received from the sale or disposition of property, from a loan, or from the sale or issuance of securities after deduction of all costs incurred in the transaction. In computing the gain or loss on a securities transaction for tax purposes, the amount of the sale is the amount of the net proceeds. The term "net proceeds" is also sometimes used as a contractually defined term to mean the same as the more commonly used phrase "net profits" (see "Gross Receipts," "Breakeven," "Initial Actual Breakeven" and "Net Profits").

NET PROCEEDS OF THE OFFERING. Gross proceeds of a limited partnership offering minus expenses incurred and to be paid by the partnership in connection with organizing the partnership and in offering units to prospective purchasers, so long as the deduction and payment of such expenses are authorized and to the extent such expenses are not limited by the partnership agreement (see "Gross Proceeds of the Offering").

NET PROCEEDS TO PARTICIPANT. Assuming this is the deal and the specific film distribution agreement uses this terminology, the term "net proceeds to participant" refers to the balance of the motion picture's revenue stream remaining after deducting off-the-top expenses, distribution fees and other distribution expenses. Such a participant may be considered a gross participant since he or she is getting the balance of gross receipts minus the specified deductions, or in the alternative, a net profit participant since the described calculations come pretty close to being the same as the calculations for determining what net profits are in a lender financed transaction (negative pickup). On the other hand, in a studio-financed production-financing/distribution arrangement and in investor-financed productions, the interest and negative costs of the picture still have to be deducted before arriving at net profits (see "Gross Participant," "Net Profits" and "Off-the-Top Expenses").

NET PROFIT BEFORE PARTICIPATIONS. Another variation on the term "net profit" which may imply that there have been no gross participations in the deal and that "net profits" are being determined before any participations are to be paid. Generally speaking, percentage participations may be paid out of gross receipts, net profits, the producer's share or some other defined portion of the revenue stream (see "Producer's Share").

NET PROFIT DEFINITION. The manner in which the term "net profit" is defined in a film distribution agreement (see "Net Profits").

NET PROFIT FORMULA. The method for arriving at net profits, typically taking into consideration such concepts as gross receipts (or distributor gross rentals), distribution fees, distribution expenses, adjusted gross and the net profits definition (also called "Formula for Computing Net Profits;" see "Net Profits").

NET PROFIT(S). This term is generally defined in the distribution agreement, i.e., its definition is contractual. Generally speaking, in a net deal, net profits are the amount of gross receipts remaining after deducting distribution fees, distribution expenses, interest on negative costs, negative costs (plus overhead) and specified deferments and gross participations, if any. Net profits is not a static concept and is continually subject to recalculation from one accounting period to another to take into consideration additional distribution fees and expenses even after net profits were first achieved (see "Gross Receipts," "Net Points," "Rolling Breakeven" and "Talent Participations").

NET PROFIT PARTICIPANT. Any party who has a right to be paid a percentage of a film's net profits (see "First Dollar," "Gross Receipts," "Net Points," "Net Profits" and "Profit Participation").

NET PROFIT PARTICIPANT ASSOCIATION. A proposed association of net profit participants formed for the purpose of protecting the interests of all net profit participants, including producers, executive producers, directors, screenwriters, actors, actresses, financiers, investors, etc. with a particular focus on accounting practices of the feature film distributors as such practices effect contingent compensation (see "Association Projects," "Business Practices," "Contract of Adhesion," "Creative Accounting," "Industry Groups," "MPAA," "Professional Association" and "RIPOFF").

NET PROFIT PARTICIPATION. A form of percentage participation in a motion picture's revenue stream that has been characterized by some as "the customary form of participation," although it has not always been so, nor is it likely to continue to be, since more and more prospective net profit participants within the industry understand how unlikely it is for a film to generate net profits (see "First Dollar Gross Deal," Fifty/Fifty Split," "Modified Gross Deal," Seventy/Thirty Split," "Fifty/Fifty Net Deal" and "Net Deal").

NET PROFIT PARTICIPATION SCHEDULE. A list, usually accompanying a distribution agreement as an exhibit, which sets out the names and percentage participations of persons who are to receive net profit participation payments (see "Participant" and "Participation").

NET RECEIPTS. Sometimes used in place of net profits and also contractually defined, e.g., an amount equal to the sum remaining after deducting from gross receipts, first, the distributor's fees, and, second, all distribution expenses. In each distribution agreement in which distribution expenses are being deducted, careful attention should be given to what constitutes a distribution expense. Sometimes this definition appears as an exhibit to the distribution agreement. Net receipts in a limited partnership context may be the same as distributable cash (see "Distributable Cash," "Limited Partnership" and "Net Profits").

NETWORK. National television corporation which owns and operates or affiliates with independently owned television stations across the country and transmits through such stations regularly scheduled series, news, drama, sports and other programming commissioned to be produced by others or produced by the network itself. The network sells air time and programming to sponsors and pays compensation to its affiliate stations to carry its scheduled national programming. The television networks in the U.S. include ABC, CBS, NBC, PBS and Fox (see "Cable," "Network Television" and "Public Broadcasting System").

NETWORK BROADCAST. A television program transmitted over the airwaves and originated by one of the television networks in the U.S. such as ABC, CBS, NBC, PBS or Fox (see "Network").

NETWORK STANDARDS AND PRACTICES (see "Standards and Practices").

NETWORK TELEVISION. The market for films on the ABC, NBC, CBS, PBS and Fox affiliated broadcast stations (see "Public Broadcasting System").

NETWORK TELEVISION FILM LICENSE AGREEMENT. The contract between a film's producer or distributor and a television network for the broadcast of a film on free television (see "Network" and "Network Television").

NET WORTH. The excess of assets over liabilities (same as "Net Assets" and "Owner's Equity").

NEW DELIVERY TECHNOLOGIES. Newly developed forms of presenting a motion picture for viewing. Over the years, new technologies have included cable television, satellite delivery, pay-per-view capability, laser discs, video recorders and videocassette (see "Technological Developments").

NEW EQUITY. Capital raised by selling additional ownership interests in a business. Based on the fairly common references appearing from time to time in the film-industry trade press regarding various creative forms of financing resorted to at one time or another by major studio/distributors, certain segments of the film industry and its deal-makers seem to take special pride in putting such deals together. On the other hand, it is quite possible that if the financiers or investors involved in the creative film-financing deals of several years ago (or of the last decade for that matter) had received reasonable returns, there probably would be no need to be so creative, for the capital needs of the film industry would be met by those same financiers and investors coming back to invest again (see "Creative Accounting," "Equity," "Profit Margin" and "Rising Production Costs").

NEWSPAPER. A paper that is printed and distributed usually on a daily or weekly basis and which contains news, articles of opinion, features and advertising. The concepts upon which motion pictures are based have sometimes come from newspaper articles (see "Idea," "Clearance," "Concept" and "Underlying Material").

NEWS RELEASE. A misnomer since only the press can determine whether, on any given day, an item is of sufficient interest to be considered news (see "Media" and "Press Release").

NEW TECHNOLOGIES. A reference to all sorts of new technological developments which may have an impact on the entertainment industry, not just those relating to the delivery of such entertainment (see "New Delivery Technologies" and "Technological Developments").

NIELSEN MEDIA RESEARCH. A television ratings service (same as "A.C. Nielsen Company;" see "Arbitron Ratings Company").

NINETY/TEN DEAL. A distributor/exhibitor split of box office revenue. In one variation of the 90/10 deal, after the theatre's nut (weekly operating expense) is deducted from gross box office, the distributor receives 90% of the remaining box-office receipts and the exhibitor 10% for the first week of a film's exhibition and then the distributor's share is reduced by 10% each week for the remainder of the run until a minimum distributor percentage is achieved, e.g., 35%. In another variation, the minimum starts out at 70% (although the distributor percentage share is still 90%), and the minimum is reduced proportionately along with the distributor's share each week until the lowest floor level is achieved (see "Double Week," "Floor," "Minimum Film Rental" and "Sliding Scale").

NO-ACTION LETTER. A letter requested from the SEC in which the SEC agrees to take no civil or criminal action with respect to a proposed securities related activity as factually described in a letter to the SEC asking for the SEC staff's opinion (see "Securities and Exchange Commission").

NOMINAL PAYMENTS. The disbursement of small or modest amounts of money. A compromise tactic used by some independent feature film producers in obtaining contingent commitments from directors or actors which then can be used in demonstrating to prospective financiers and/or investors that a substantial movie package is in place, i.e., only awaiting financing. Depending on the specific agreement, such payments would probably not be recouped by the producer if financing fell through (see "Letter of Intent," "Letter of Interest," "Pay and Play" and "Pay or Play").

NON-ALLOCATED OVERHEAD PERCENTAGE CHARGE (see "Overhead").

NON-ASSESSABLE STOCK. Corporate stock purchased from the issuer at full par value or more per share. Fully paid stock cannot be assessed to pay debts of the issuer in the event of bankruptcy or liquidation and is, therefore, non-assessable (see "Corporate Stock" and "Corporation").

NON-CIRCUMVENTION CLAUSE. A provision in a contract designed to prevent one or the other party, or both, from utilizing information gained or relationships developed as a result of their original agreement in pursuing other business opportunities without the other party (see "Covenant not to Compete" and "Non-Disclosure Agreement").

NON-COMPETE CLAUSE (see "Covenant not to Compete").

NON-DISCLOSURE AGREEMENT (OR PROVISION). An agreement or provision in a larger contract by one party not to reveal information presented to such party by another (see "Covenant not to Compete," "Non-Circumvention Clause," "Submission Release" and "Trade Secret").

NON-EXCLUSIVE ELECTION. Securities concept referring to the fact that an issuer choosing to avail itself of one of the Regulation D exemptions from securities registration (Rule 504, 505 or 506) does not preclude itself from also relying on other available exemptions, such as Sections 4(2) or 4(6) of the Securities Act of 1933, if the conditions and limitations imposed on the use of those exemptions are complied with (see "Limited Partnership," "Regulation D" and "Securities").

NON-MARKETABLE SECURITY. A security which cannot be sold on the market such as certain government bonds and notes. It can only be redeemed by the holder. Also, a security which is not of investment quality (see "Marketable Security").

NON-OWNED AIRCRAFT LIABILITY INSURANCE. Insurance providing coverage when aircraft are used in connection with a film's production (see "Insurance").

NON-PERFORMANCE. In contract law, the failure to fulfill an obligation. The non-performance must be material and substantial to justify suspension of another's return performance (see "Breach of Contract," Consideration" and "Material Breach").

NON-PUBLIC OFFERING (same as "Private Offering").

NON-RECOURSE. Without personal liability. An obligation that is non-recourse does not provide a tax basis for federal taxation purposes for individuals or partnerships except in limited cases (see "Basis," "Lender Financing" and "Limited Partnership").

NON-RECOURSE DEBT. In a limited partnership context, any debt secured by a film (being funded by a limited partnership), with respect to which none of the partners have any personal liability as determined under Treasury Regulations issued under Section 752 of the Code (see "Non-Recourse" and "Recourse Debt").

NON-RECOURSE LOAN. A loan for which the borrower has no personal liability. Such loans, however, may be secured by specific assets of the borrower (see "Recourse Loan").

NON-REFUNDABLE GUARANTEE. A contractual promise that a specific sum of money will be paid when certain conditions are met and once that sum is paid, the person or entity which makes the payment does not have the right to recoup such payment out of subsequent revenues (see "Advance" and "Guarantee").

NON-REGULATORY STATES. States within the United States which have not adopted anti-blind bidding statutes (see "Anti-Blind Bidding Statutes," "Blind Bidding," "Economic Reprisal," "Lobbying" and "Trade Screening").

NON-RESIDENT ALIENS. Persons who are not citizens of the United States who also do not reside within the borders of this country. A non-resident alien may not be a shareholder in an "S" corporation (see "S Corp").

NON-RETURNABLE ADVANCE. A payment made prior to a specified event and which may or may not be recoupable. If recoupable, such a payment can only be recovered from future earnings. In either case, the recipient of the payment is under no obligation to return the payment. Studios often obtain advances or guarantees from exhibitors, thus issues arise relating to whether and to what extent an advance or guarantee is included in the distributor's gross receipts (since advances, even if labeled "non-returnable," are subject to certain adjustments as between the exhibitor and distributor). The major studio/distributors prefer not to include advances in gross receipts until they are earned (see "Advance" or "Advances," "Distribution Guarantee," "Guarantee," "Non-Refundable Guarantee" and "Recoupment").

NON-THEATRICAL. The term does not mean all distribution other than theatrical but refers instead to a relatively specialized market of institutionalized users as opposed to the general public. The market includes in-flight airplanes, hotels, the Red Cross, trains and ships, schools, colleges and other educational institutions, libraries, governmental agency facilities, military installations, business and service organization clubs, shut-in institutions, retirement centers, prisons, museums, film society facilities, churches, offshore drilling rigs, logging camps, and remote forestry and construction camps. The non-theatrical market may also be divided into domestic and foreign (see "Allied Rights," "Ancillary Markets" and "Theatrical Release").

NON-THEATRICAL DISTRIBUTION RIGHTS. The authority to sell and/or license a film in the ancillary markets (see "Distribution Rights" and "Non-Theatrical").

NON-THEATRICAL DISTRIBUTION LICENSE AGREEMENT. A contract between a film's producer and a specialized distributor for distribution of the film in the specialized market of institutional users as opposed to the general public (see "License Agreement" and "Non-Theatrical").

NON-UNION FILM. A feature film production which does not fall within the jurisdiction of any applicable guild agreements. The term is also sometimes used to refer to films that are being produced with SAG actors (pursuant to SAG rules) but with non-union below-the-line personnel (see "Artificial Pickup," "Development," "Guild," "Negative Pickup," "Screen Actors Guild" and "Union").

NON-UNION PRODUCTION (see "Non-Union Film").

NON-THEATRICAL FILM RENTAL. Motion picture distributor receipts generated by the exploitation of a movie in the non-theatrical markets (see "Non-Theatrical").

NON-VOTING STOCK. Corporate stock that does not empower the shareholder to vote on corporate resolutions or the election of directors. Preferred stock is usually non-voting stock (see "Common Stock").

NO-PAR STOCK. Corporate stock issued with no stated value on the stock certificate. New issues of stock used to be commonly issued as par value stock but this practice has generally been abandoned since states started taxing corporations based on par values. Today, par value is more likely to be arbitrarily set as a low value or the stock will be issued as no-par stock when allowed by state law. In accounting for stock issues, the par value is carried as a separate item with the balance of stock issue proceeds carried as capital surplus (see "Corporate Stock" and "Corporation").

NO-PAR VALUE STOCK (see "No-Par Stock" above).

NORTH AMERICAN SECURITIES ADMINISTRATORS ASSOCIATION. An organization made up of state securities regulators who meet periodically and promulgate model state securities laws, industry disclosure guides and regulations designed to provide uniformity in the implementation of state securities laws and to achieve the consumer protection goals of securities regulation at the state level (see "Blue Sky Laws," "SEC" and "ULOE").

NO STRIKE, NO LOCKOUT CLAUSE. A provision in certain guild basic agreements which provides that the guild agrees (on behalf of its members) that during the term of the basic agreement, the guild will not call or engage in any strike, slowdown or stoppage of work affecting theatrical or television motion picture production against the production company signatories to the basic agreement (see "Guild" and "Strike").

NOTE (same as "Promissory Note").

NOTICE AND CURE PERIOD. A negotiated period of time, e.g., ten days, during which a breaching party to a contract has to correct the breach following notice by the non-breaching party (see "Notice and Cure Provision").

NOTICE AND CURE PROVISION. A clause in an agreement which provides in the event that a breach of a contractual provision occurs, the breaching party may have a specified period of time to correct the breach, following written notice by the non-breaching party (see "Notice and Cure Period").

NOTICE FILING. With respect to securities offerings, the presentation of the document or documents prescribed by law with the appropriate securities regulatory authorities for the purpose of notifying such authorities that a security is to be or has been offered or sold in the regulated jurisdiction. The SEC's Regulation D requirement that five copies of a completed Form D be filed with the SEC within fifteen days of the first sale of a security in a Regulation D offering is a form of notice filing. Most states which make available a private placement-type exemption (limited offering exemption) from the state securities registration requirements typically require some form of notice filing either before or after the sale of such securities (see "Blue Sky Laws," "Limited Partnership," "Registration" and "Securities").

NOTICE FILING FEE. The charges imposed by the state securities regulatory authorities which must accompany the notice filing in a private placement offering (see "Blue Sky Fees" and "Registration Fee").

NOTICE FILING REQUIREMENT. Federal and state securities law requirements that a notice be filed with the appropriate securities regulatory authority of the offer or sale of a security within the applicable jurisdiction, e.g., the federal Regulation D exemption from securities registration requires that a notice on Form D be filed with the SEC within fifteen days of the first sale in the offering. Some state notice filings for exempt offerings are required to be filed in advance of any offer in the state (see "Form D," "Blue Sky Law Reporter" and "Regulation D").

NOTICE OF ASSIGNMENT. A form used by a secured party (e.g., a lending bank) to give notice to the payor (i.e., the person or entity obligated to make payments) to make such payments directly to the secured party. The notice of assignment is used when the proceeds of a specific contract (e.g., a film distribution agreement) are assigned as security for an obligation, i.e., the obligation of a feature film producer who borrows production money from a bank to repay the loan (see "Security Agreement").

NOTICE OF SALE. The form or document required to be filed with the SEC at the federal level and with many state securities regulatory authorities at the state level before or after offering or selling a security in such jurisdictions. The event that triggers the notice filing and the timing of the filing will vary from jurisdiction to jurisdiction (see "Notice Filing Requirement").

NOTICE OF TENTATIVE WRITING CREDITS. A Writers Guild of America form used by producers in notifying all writers who participated in the writing of a screenplay for a motion picture of the statement of credits proposed to be used by the producer, i.e., the tentative credits for "story by" and "screenplay by" are listed on the form. Each participating writer then has a specified number of days (usually ten) to object to the proposed credits if such writer is not satisfied with the credit assigned to him or her. The notice is usually provided at the same time the writers are provided with a copy of the "shooting script" (see "Writers Guild of America").

NOTICE PROVISION. A common clause in contracts which sets out the addresses of the parties to the agreement and provides instructions for sending important written communications to such parties (see "Contract").

NOVEL. A literary form characterized by a long and complex original prose narrative that deals with human experiences as related through a connected series of events (see "Literary Property").

NOVELIZATION OF A SCREENPLAY. The converting of a motion picture script into a novel. The novelization of a screenplay provides another possible avenue for exploitation of a motion picture to a film's producer/distributor, i.e., the licensing of such rights may generate additional revenue from a motion picture project (see "Merchandising" and "Novel").

NOVELIZATION RIGHTS. The authority to convert a motion picture script into a long and complex original prose narrative, i.e., novel (see "Novel" and "Novelization of a Screenplay").

NUDITY CLAUSE. A negotiated provision in actor/actress employment agreements which specifies when, if, and under what circumstances an actor may be filmed in the nude (see "Nudity Rider").

NUDITY RIDER. An amendment or addition attached to a performer's employment agreement for the purpose of obtaining the prior approval of the actor in situations where such performers are appearing in a feature film which calls for such actor to be nude or seminude (see "Nudity Clause" and "Rider").

NUDITY/SEX SCENES. A typical heading for the paragraph in a performer's employment agreement that sets out the contractual provisions relating to nudity and/or the performer's appearance in sex scenes. If the producer intends to obtain a nudity waiver, the contract should be drafted to limit allowable nudity and/or sex scenes (or to provide for the use of a double where appropriate) according to the performer's requirements. The contract should also prohibit the use of nude scenes in trailers, music videos, still photographs, etc. unless the performer provides his or her written consent (see "Nudity Rider" and "Nudity Waiver").

NUDITY WAIVER. A full or partial release signed by an actor which provides that such person intentionally and voluntarily has given up, relinquished or surrendered his or her right to object to being photographed in the nude (see "Nudity Rider").

NUMBER OF SCREENS. The total count of the whitish, matte, beaded or metallic surfaces on which the motion picture is projected in theatres in the United States or other jurisdictions. The number of screens in the United States in 1980 was approximately 17,600. The U.S. screen count has now increased to approximately 23,600 (or slightly more). Thus, hypothetically assuming the major studio/distributors in the aggregate have twenty films in release (on average) in any given week and average 866 prints per film, that means those films being distributed by the major studio/distributors would take up 17,320 screens in the U.S. or 73.38% of the available screens), thus preventing the films being distributed by independent distributors from exhibiting their films on those same screens. Also, interestingly enough, this hypothetical 73.38% of screens is very close to the percentage of screens reported at the entry "Market Share" herein which points out that it only takes a selected 75% of the theatres in the U.S. to generate more than 90% of the box office gross. In addition, as also pointed out at the entry "Market Share" herein, for the last decade or so, the MPAA companies (i.e., the major studio/distributors) have succeeded in grabbing off a 92%-plus market share of U.S. theatrical box office receipts (see "Blind Bidding," "Controlled Theatre," "Major Exhibition Chains," "Market Power," "Market Share" and "Relationship-Driven Business").

NUMBERS GAME. A term referring to the fact that certain transactions are predominantly influenced by the applicable numerical variables and that persons involved in such transactions must be aware of such variables, i.e., must play the odds. For example, if a film producer were to conduct a general solicitation of prospective investors, in the context of a public/registered securities offering and used cold calls (i.e., telephone calls to prospective investors with which the producer had no pre-existing relationship), experienced telephone solicitors suggest that eventually such telephone calls will settle into a fairly dependable ratio of calls to sales, which then makes such a calling operation a numbers game, i.e., if the producer calls enough people, he or she will raise the money needed. In addition, the concept is relevant to the producer's choice between available forms of film finance, e.g., a banking executive recently indicated that only about 1 in 200 of the producers who approach the bank seeking production financing succeeded in getting a loan. A spokesman for an international bank, active in financing films on a splits-rights basis, estimates that approximately 65 out of 400-500 U.S.-made films each year are financed in this manner. On the other hand, not even the studio executives responsible for reviewing submitted screenplays know how many such scripts are considered by the studios in the course of a given year, thus determining the odds against obtaining studio financing on a project are simply not known, although clearly enormous. One major studio/distributor has indicated that it acquires some six or seven films each year by virtue of the negative pickup deal (three others are purely in-house productions and twelve or thirteen more are production-financing/distribution deals). Thus, if the other seven majors also pick up seven films a year, that would mean the majors acquire approximately fifty-six films a year by means of the negative pickup (or pure acquisition deals). If these same majors utilize the production-financing/distribution arrangement to finance ten films each, that's another eighty films a year. If each then also produces three films apiece as purely in-house product, that's another twenty-four films and that would account for approximately 160 films. According to "Variety," the major studio/distributors distributed 157 films in 1990 and 150 in 1991 (see "Availability Analysis," "Number of Screens" and "Pro and Con Analysis").

NUMERICAL LIMITATION ON INVESTORS (see "Investor Numerical Limitations").

NUT (see "House Nut").

— O —

OBJECTIVE DELIVERY REQUIREMENTS. Quantifiable and time-specific standards which must be met by a film's producer in delivering various elements of a completed feature film to a distributor. Such delivery requirements should not be based on some subjective approval of the distributor, thus producers should avoid language in the distribution agreement that calls for an artistic judgment by the distributor (see "Delivery Schedule").

OBLIGOR. Generally, one who has an obligation, such as an issuer of bonds, a borrower of money from a bank or another source or a credit customer of a business supplier or retailer. In a loan situation, an obligor is legally bound to repay the debt (to the obligee), including interest, when due (see "Debt" and "Lender Financing").

OBSCENE MATERIAL. Material which, taken as a whole, appeals to the prurient interest and lacks serious literary, artistic, political or scientific value. Matter so classified is not protected by the "free speech" guarantee of the First Amendment to the U.S. Constitution. Material is considered "obscene" when (1) the subject as a whole appeals to the prurient interest of the average person, using contemporary community standards, (2) the work depicts or describes in a patently offensive way sexual conduct proscribed by state statute, and (3) the work as a whole lacks serious literary, artistic, political or scientific value. The issues of how "local" the community must be and by whose standards obscenity is to be determined are set out in statutes but it has been held that "contemporary community standards" is a sufficient jury instruction without specifying the geographical extent of the community (see "Censorship," "Pornography" and "Prurient").

OBSTRUCTION OF JUSTICE. The impeding of those who seek justice in a court of law, or those who have duties or powers of administering justice. The offense includes attempting to influence, intimidate or impede any juror, witness or officer in any court regarding the discharge of his or her duty, as well as the actual impeding of the due administration of justice (see "Racketeering" and "RICO").

OFF-BALANCE SHEET PARTNERSHIPS. Film financing vehicles, such as limited partnerships, which raise money that is not reflected on the balance sheets of the controlling production company or studio (see "Corporation" and "Limited Partnership").

OFFER. A manifestation of willingness to enter into a bargain, so made as to justify another person in understanding that his, her or its assent to that bargain is invited and will conclude it. The offer creates a power of acceptance permitting the offeree by accepting the offer to transform the offeror's promise into a contractual obligation (see "Contract").

OFFER FOR SALE (see "Sell").

OFFERING. In a limited partnership context, the offer and sale of limited partnership interests or units in the partnership made in reliance on available exemptions from registration under the 1933 Act and compatible state securities laws (private offering), or in a public offering, i.e., registered with the SEC and in each state in which offers or sales are to be made (see "Limited Partnership").

OFFERING CEILING. A limit on the total amount of money that can be raised pursuant to a specific type of securities registration or exemption (see "Ceiling," "Private Placement" and "Registration").

OFFERING CIRCULAR. An alternative phrase used in describing securities disclosure documents. The SEC's Regulation A disclosure document is specifically referred to as an offering circular (also see "Disclosure Document," "Offering Memorandum," "Prospectus," "Regulation A" and "Preliminary Offering Circular").

OFFERING DATE. The date on which a distribution of securities is first made available for sale to the public (see "Limited Partnership" and "Securities").

OFFERING EXPENSES. The organizational and syndication expenses incurred in organizing the entity and selling the securities in a securities offering, such as a corporate stock or limited partnership offering. As a rule of thumb, the offering expenses in a private placement should not exceed approximately 15% of the aggregate offering proceeds. Some states impose a ceiling on such amounts in private offerings. NASD guidelines limit broker/dealer commissions in a public offering to 10% plus .5% for bona fide due diligence expenses and limits offering expenses to 15% of the offering (see "Commission," "Gross Offering Proceeds," "Organizational Expenses," "Proceeds of the Offering" and "Syndication Expenses").

OFFERING MEMORANDUM. A securities disclosure document (e.g., in limited partnership, corporate stock or investment contract offerings) usually associated with a private placement offering, i.e., an offering which is being conducted in reliance on available exemptions from the federal and state securities registration requirements. This is the document provided to potential investors in a film limited partnership. It normally contains information on the proposed investment, the terms and conditions under which it is offered, the risks involved, the federal tax consequences of the investment, financial projections, various information concerning the general partner and the general partner's relationship to the venture, certain required legends and purchaser representations, etc. Also sometimes referred to as a "prospectus," although most securities practitioners reserve the term "prospectus" for the disclosure document used in a public/registered securities offering (see "Private Placement Offering Memorandum," "Offering Circular," "Memorandum" and "Prospectus").

OFFERING PRICE. The price per unit at which a new or secondary distribution of securities is offered for sale to the public (also called "Public Offering Price"' see "Offering").

OFFERING PROCEEDS (see "Proceeds of the Offering").

OFFICERS. Persons empowered by a corporation's bylaws and by statute to perform the duties of their offices and to execute contracts and other instruments on behalf of the corporation. A corporation's day-to-day operations are supervised and conducted by its officers and employees [see "Corporate Stock," "Corporation," "Director (Corporate)" and "Shareholders"].

OFFICIAL NATIONALITY (see "Nationality Test").

OFF-NETWORK. Other than on the three major free-television organizations: CBS, ABC and NBC. The phrase is sometimes used to refer to television syndication as in the "off-network syndication market" (see "Syndication").

OFF-NETWORK SYNDICATION MARKET (same as "Television Syndication").

OFF-NETWORK TELEVISION PRODUCTIONS. Television programming produced especially to be shown on local television stations or cable (see "Off-Network," "Off-Network Syndication Market" and "Syndication").

OFFSET RIGHTS. The authority to adjust accounting records to compensate for a credit or loss incurred by a second party. In the film distribution agreement, the distributor may seek offset rights to adjust the accounts as between the producer and distributor. Also, if a distributor/exhibitor agreement provides for offset rights, the exhibitor is able to deduct co-op advertising or other expenses owed to the exhibitor by the distributor from distributor rentals which would have otherwise been paid to the distributor. Lending banks will typically require that the distributor's offset rights be waived so as to better ensure more rapid payment to the bank. It would make sense for any entity providing production funds (e.g., a film limited partnership) to also request that the distributor's offset rights be waived until the financing entity has recouped its investment (see "Distribution Agreement," "Lender Financing," "License Agreement," "Limited Partnership" and "Negative Pickup").

OFFSHORE (as used in the U.S.) any financial organization with headquarters outside the country (see "Offshore Banks").

OFFSHORE BANKS. Banks headquarters outside the U.S (see "Offshore").

OFFSHORE COMPANIES. Business organizations with headquarters outside the U.S. (see "Offshore Banks").

OFFSHORE ENTITY. Any business organization that is headquartered outside the U.S. (see "Offshore").

OFFSHORE TERRITORIES (see "Foreign Market").

OFF-THE-BOTTOM EXPENSES. Another contractually defined term sometimes used in feature film distribution agreements to describe another category of distributor expense deductions that are taken by the distributor after payment of gross participations, if any, but before net profits. For example, in a distribution arrangement where production costs are provided by a limited partnership or a third-party financier (other than a bank/lender), the distributor may want to first deduct from gross receipts its distribution fee, then any off-the-top expenses, then gross participations (if any), then off-the-bottom expenses and remit all of the balance to the producer's group. The producer's group then is responsible for providing the partnership or financier with recoupment of the negative costs plus whatever return they contracted for and is responsible for dividing up the balance of the net profits as between deferrals, net profit participations and the producer's share. On the other hand, if a bank or lender were involved in a negative pickup situation, the negative costs plus interest and fees would be paid to the bank or lender first out of the distributor's gross receipts, then the distributor might take its distribution fees, off-the-top expenses, pay gross participations (if any), take off-the-bottom costs and remit the balance to the producer's group as net profits. In the studio-financed production-financing/distribution arrangement, the distributor typically takes its distribution fees first, then off-the-top expenses, pays gross participants (if any), takes off-the-bottom costs, deducts interest payments, then recoups the negative costs and finally, if anything is left, remits the balance to the producer group as net profits (see "Lender Financing," "Limited Partnership," "Negative Pickup," "Off-the-Top Expenses," "Production-Financing/Distribution Agreement" and "When the Money's Paid").

OFF-THE-TOP DEDUCTIONS (see "Off-the-Top Expenses").

OFF-THE-TOP EXPENSES. Contractually defined feature film distribution costs that represent the first group of expenses deducted by the distributor from the distributor's gross receipts. Off-the-top expenses typically may include licenses and taxes, checking and collection costs, any expenses associated with converting foreign currency into U.S. dollars, residual payments, trade dues, assessments and local advertising. The major studio/distributors rather uniformly deduct their distribution fees first, i.e., they base the percentage calculation on the largest pool of money received by the distributor, 100% of the distributor's gross receipts, then they deduct off-the-top expenses, if any, before paying any contractual gross participations out of this remaining fund which may be labeled "accountable gross" or "adjusted gross." Some independent distributors may deduct certain distribution expenses off-the-top before computing their distribution fee. Note that a lower distribution-fee percentage is most likely to result in higher distribution fees if the fee calculation is applied to the larger pool of money, i.e., before the off-the-top expenses are deducted. Other distributors may want to deduct all distribution expenses off-the-top and then divide up the balance between participants pursuant to pre-agreed percentages (see "Accountable Gross," "Adjusted Gross" and "Fifty/Fifty Net Deal").

OLIGOPOLISTIC INDUSTRY. A business which is dominated by a few large sellers of products (see "Cartel" and "Oligopoly").

OLIGOPOLY. An industry in which a few large sellers of substantially identical products dominate the market; a market situation in which a small number of selling firms control the market supply of a particular good or service and are therefore able to control the market price. An oligopolistic industry is more concentrated than a competitive one but is less concentrated than a monopoly (see "Anti-Trust," "Cartel," "Market Share" and "Monopoly").

OMISSIONS. Things neglected or left undone (see "Errors and Omissions Insurance").

OMNIES. Extras who speak only atmospheric words as part of a group (see "Bit Player" and "Extras").

ONE-LINE DESCRIPTION. The briefest possible written representation of a proposed motion picture screenplay which is sometimes used by experienced screenwriters or producers to submit a concept to studio or other production companies for development funding (see "Basic Story Outline," "Synopsis" and "Treatment").

ONE-PICTURE LICENSE (see "Single-Picture License").

ONE SHEET. A standard size (27" by 41") color movie poster which is used for display at theatres and in other locations. The one sheet usually contains the basic elements from which a film's newspaper ads are made, including a graphic design such as a photograph or drawing, a custom title treatment, a lead line to accompany the title, credits for principal cast and crew and any outstanding quotes from critical reviews (see "Lobby Card" and "Sell-Sheet").

ONGOING COSTS. Expenses that continue to accrue. For example, in the context of a film distribution deal, any of the distributor expenses that are based on some percentage of a defined portion of the film's revenue stream would be considered ongoing costs, so long as there was no ceiling on such expenses. Thus, residuals, taxes, trade association dues, gross profit participations and even interest up to a point all might be considered ongoing costs. This concept helps to explain why after a motion picture achieves net profits for one accounting period, it may not be in net profits as of the next accounting statement, i.e., these ongoing costs may have increased substantially during the next accounting period (see "Gross Receipts" and "Net Profits").

ON SPEC (SPECULATION). The production of a motion picture with no negative pickup or distribution deal in place, i.e., the producer is speculating that the film will be good enough to attract a distribution deal. Producers without funds often seek the assistance of writers, attorneys, accountants and others in the development or financing of a film project and ask that such services be provided on spec, i.e., without being compensated on a current basis. Also, screenwriters sometimes write screenplays on spec (see "Bidding War," "Independent Producers" and "Spec").

OPEN CHECK. The monitoring of ticket sales at a motion picture box office in which the person doing the checking (i.e., the checker) identifies himself or herself to the theatre manager and asks permission to monitor the conduct of the theatre's box office personnel. Such observation enables the checking entity, usually the film's distributor, to compare box office receipts on the day checked with a day in which ticket sales were not observed (see "Blind Check," "Checker" and "Distribution Expense").

OPENING. The commencement of public exhibition for a film. A film's producer and distributor will typically want to create a special event for a film's opening with the film's director and stars present. As the old film industry joke goes: "Movies are like parachutes—if they don't open, you die." (see "Distribution Expenses," "Premiere" and "Promotional Activities").

OPENING DATE. The day on which a film's public exhibition commences (see "Release Date").

OPERATING MARGIN. The difference between the revenues of a business and expenses of operating the business, excluding income derived from sources other than the business' regular activities and before income deductions. Reportedly the major studio/distributor operating margins reached an eighteen-year low point in 1991 (see "Profitability," "Profit Margin" and "Rising Production Costs").

OPERATING PERFORMANCE. An analytical and judgmental term used in evaluating the overall accomplishments and behavior of a business. A business' operating performance is usually evaluated with respect to its financial results (see "Bottom Line" and "Financial Standings").

OPERATING PROFIT (OR LOSS). The difference between the revenues of a business and the related costs and expenses, excluding income derived from sources other than its regular activities and before income deductions [also called "Net Operating Profit (or Loss)," "Operating Income (or Loss)" and Net Operating Income (or Loss)"].

OPERATING STATISTICS (see "Financial Standings").

OPERATIONAL STAFF. Those hired to work on a film where the worked performed in relation to the production of a motion picture is considered practical as opposed to creative. Operational staff includes camera, sound and stunt persons, grips, drivers and others. Sometimes these categories are simply referred to as production staff and/or crew (see "Cast," "Crew," "Production Staff" and "Staff").

OPINION MAKERS. Influential people from various walks of life (arts, media, politics, etc.) who may be available to help spread favorable word-of-mouth about a film prior to its opening. The term does not include film critics and feature writers (see "Critic," "Industry Critic" and "Sneak Preview").

OPM. Other people's money (see "Investor Financing," "Lender Financing" and "Studio Financing").

OPPORTUNITY COST. Generally, the highest price or rate of return an alternative course of action would provide (see "Adjusted Rate of Return" and "Cost of Capital").

OPTICAL DUPE. A duplicate film negative printed in an optical printer and typically containing optical effects (see "Dupe").

OPTICAL EFFECTS. Modifications of the photographic image as filmed in a motion picture camera, produced in an optical printer (see "Optical Printer").

OPTICAL HOUSE. A company that specializes in customized optical printing and/or special effects for film (see "Optical Effects").

OPTICAL PRINT. A film with positive images produced on an optical printer, i.e., other than by contact printing (see "Optical House" and "Optical Effects").

OPTICAL PRINTER. A film camera and projector that operate in combination to reproduce photographic images on film that has already been processed. The optical printer is used to add images or to enlarge or reduce the existing images (see "Optical Effects").

OPTICAL SOUNDTRACK. A sound track optically recorded onto photographic film. It is read (played back) on an optical sound reader (see "Mag Optical Sound Track").

OPTIMUM RELEASE PATTERN. A movie distribution plan which produces the most favorable results in terms of attendance (see "Launch Windows" and "Release Pattern").

OPTION OR OPTION CONTRACT. Generally, a binding promise by which the owner of property agrees that someone else has the privilege of buying the property at a fixed price within a stated period of time. In film, a negotiated written agreement which provides to the option purchaser who pays an option fee the exclusive right to develop or sell the property during a specified period of time. The option contract typically specifies a given date by which the property is in production, funding is secured, the outright purchase takes place or the option is renewed for an option renewal fee. Otherwise, the option and associated rights will expire and the rights to the property will revert to the original owner. The option agreement is typically one of the first steps in the development of a property into a motion picture (also referred to as "Option Agreement;" see "Acquisition Agreement," "Acquisition of Story Rights," "Clearance" and "Development").

OPTION AGREEMENT (see "Option").

OPTION PERIOD. With respect to a literary property, the period of time provided by contract within which the party holding the option right has to exercise that right, i.e., the length of time (usually six months or a year) during which a producer who has optioned a literary property has to secure financing to produce the property, to find a purchaser, to purchase rights to the property or renew the option as per the option agreement (see "Option/Purchase Agreement").

OPTION/PURCHASE AGREEMENT. A contract between a producer or production company and a writer which sets out the terms and conditions for the holding of an option right or specified right to make a motion picture based on the literary property and, if specified contingencies are met, the outright purchase of the property (see "Option Period").

ORAL REPRESENTATIONS. Spoken statements as opposed to written. A common problem in the negotiation of all contracts. In film distribution situations, statements regarding the manner in which the distributor intends to distribute a given film are often made orally in various conversations between a film producer and representatives of the distributor. The problem occurs when such statements are not included in the written memorialization of the parties' negotiations, i.e., the written distribution agreement. The problem is made worse because most film distribution agreements contain a so-called "entire agreement" clause (see "Contract of Adhesion," "Distribution Agreement," "Entire Agreement Clause," "Good Faith" and "Negotiate").

ORCHESTRA. A large ensemble of musicians who perform on a collection of instruments in which strings are prominent, thereby distinguishing it from the band or wind ensemble (see "Conducting" and "Symphony Orchestra").

ORCHESTRATION. The art of scoring for different instruments from a musical sketch (see "Instrumentation," "Orchestra" and "Scoring").

ORCHESTRATOR. The person who takes the composer's or arranger's sketch and assigns parts to the various voices and/or instruments (see "Arranger" and "Orchestra").

ORDER OF APPEARANCE. A method of listing the screen credits of the performers in a film in which the performers' names are listed in the order that they appeared on screen, i.e., chronological order as opposed to alphabetical or some other order (see "Credits" and "Order of Credits").

ORDER OF CREDITS. How screen billing is organized. The front credits sometimes run as follows: distributor, producer/production company presents a (name of director) film, followed by the name or names of the principal stars, then the film title (see "Billing," "Order of Appearance" and "Top Billing").

ORDINARY COURSE OF BUSINESS. According to the common practices and customs of commercial transactions; the usual and necessary activity that is normal and incidental to a business. Occasional isolated or casual transactions are not frequent or continuous enough to constitute the ordinary course of business. A phrase which is commonly seen in feature film distribution agreements when the parties have failed to negotiate more specific language. The phrase "ordinary course of business" is a very vague standard of conduct for business practices. It is not a precise standard that can be applied in advance. It is merely a standard that can be applied after the fact, in arbitration or litigation, by bringing in various persons with expertise in the industry to explain what is usual and customary with respect to such practices. Thus, the distributor using this language in its distribution agreement has a lot of leeway pursuant to such language to do whatever it desires, on a given issue, knowing that it may take a complaint from the other party and either an arbitration proceeding or a trial and court judgment to firm up the standard of conduct. The distributor knows that the producer is not likely to sue anyway and, if the producer sues, the distributor will most likely settle out of court for a smaller amount. Producers may want to consider negotiating such language out of the distribution deal wherever possible and replacing it with a more clear standard of conduct (see "Contract of Adhesion," "Inferior Bargaining Position," "Market Power," "Subjective Terms" and "Sue Us").

ORDINARY EXPENSE. For tax purposes, an expense which is customary or usual within the experience of a particular trade, industry or community. To be deductible as a trade or business expense, an expenditure must be both ordinary and necessary in relation to the taxpayer's trade or business (see "Necessary Expense" and "Tax Benefits").

ORDINARY INCOME. Income from the normal activities of an individual or business, as distinguished from capital gains from the sale of assets. For tax purposes, the income subject to being taxed at the highest rates as opposed to capital gains which may be taxed at lower rates. Generally, only capital losses may be deducted against capital gains and only ordinary income may be offset by the other deductions (see "Capital Gain" and "Income").

ORDINARY INTEREST. Simple interest based on a 360-day year, unlike exact interest, which is calculated using a 365-day year. Film distributors charging simple interest on the negative cost of a film will collect more interest for that final partial accounting period than if exact interest were being charged. Such amounts could be substantial in light of the recent increases in film production costs (see "Exact Interest" and "Interest").

ORDINARY KEY. A geographical area with the attributes of a major key but with a metropolitan population of approximately 50,000 to 80,000 (see "Key" and "Major Key").

ORGANIZED CRIME. A syndicate of professional criminals who primarily rely on unlawful activities as a way of life (see "Extortion," "Fraud," "Larceny," "Mafia," "Racketeering," "RICO" and "White Collar Crime").

ORGANIZATIONAL EXPENSES. Expenses paid or incurred in connection with the organization of a limited partnership or other new business. Such expenses are not deductible but must be amortized over a sixty-month period beginning with the commencement of the business. They are costs which are incident to the creation of the partnership, are chargeable to a capital account, and are of a character which, if spent incident to the creation of a partnership having an ascertainable life, would be amortized over that life. They must be incurred during the period beginning at a point which is a reasonable time before the partnership begins business and ending on the date prescribed by law for filing the partnership return (determined without regard to extensions) for the taxable year the partnership begins business. Included are legal fees for services incidental to the organization of the partnership, such as negotiation and preparation of the limited partnership agreement and preparation and filing of the certificate of limited partnership, accounting fees for establishing the partnership accounting system and necessary partnership filing fees (see "Amortization," "Start-Up Costs" and "Syndication Expenses").

ORGANIZATION FEES (same as "Organizational Expenses").

ORIGINAL. With respect to a screenplay, one that has not been adapted from an article, book, play, existing movie or other source material (see "Certificate of Authorship," "Chain of Title," "Clearance" and "Screenplay").

ORIGINAL COST. All costs associated with the acquisition of an asset (see "Asset").

ORIGINAL INVESTED CAPITAL. The amount in cash contributed to the capital of a limited partnership by the unit holders and the general partners, if any such general partner cash contributions are made (see "Capital").

ORIGINAL ISSUE. The initial sale or issue of a security (see "Issuer" and "Securities").

ORIGINAL PARAMOUNT DEFENDANTS. The film industry companies that were sued for anti-trust law violations by the U.S. Justice Department in 1938 resulting in the Paramount Consent Decree of 1948. The defendants fall into three groups: (1) the producer/distributor/exhibitor defendants (Paramount, Loews, RKO, Warner Bros. and 20th Century Fox), all of which produced motion pictures but distributed and exhibited their own films through subsidiary or affiliate companies, (2) the producer/distributor defendants (Columbia and Universal), both of which produced films and distributed their own films through subsidiaries and (3) a single distributor defendant (United Artists), which was engaged only in distribution (see "Controlled Theatre," "Major Exhibition Chains," "Market Share," "Number of Screens," "Paramount Consent Decree of 1948," "Political Influence" and "TriStar Case").

ORIGINAL PICTURE NEGATIVE. The film that is initially exposed in the camera and subsequently processed (see "Exposed Film" and "Negative").

ORIGINAL SCREENPLAY. The film script that is created by a writer or writers from his or her or their or others' concept and story and not adapted from a book, play or other literary work (also see "Original" and "Screenplay").

ORIGINAL SCORE (see "Composer's Original Score," "Score" and "Scoring").

ORIGINAL SOUND NEGATIVE. Film that is initially exposed in a film recorder (see "Negative" and "Original Picture Negative").

OSCARS. The nickname given to the copyrighted statuettes awarded annually through the Academy Awards ceremonies for outstanding achievement in numerous areas of expertise in the film industry (see "Academy Awards," "Academy of Motion Picture Arts and Sciences," "Insider's Game," "Market Share" and "Member of the Club").

OTHER PEOPLE'S MONEY (see "OPM").

OTHER VERSIONS. Different edited copies of a feature film for use in various markets or territories; also sub-section in certain feature film distribution agreements which specifically sets out the requirements relating to different edited copies of a film either for the purpose of protecting a producer or distributor's cutting rights or to establish the distributor's requirements for different copies of the same film. For example, besides the domestic theatrical version of a movie, other versions may be edited for U.S. free television, airline in-flight use, syndication, pay and cable television and the United Kingdom (see "Creative Control," "Delivery Requirements" and "Final Cut").

OUTLINE. A preliminary treatment of an idea for a film, i.e., a rough sketch of the filmmaker's intended approach to the film's subject including some description of the principal characters and basic story elements in 5,000 words or less (see "Synopsis" and "Treatment").

OUT-OF-FAVOR INDIES. A phrase used by industry analysts to refer to independent producers who as a group may be less favored than the major studios for film finance purposes during certain parts of the industry's economic cycles. The industry is currently so dominated by the major studio/distributors that it is difficult to foresee when and if independent distributors and/or producers will ever be back in favor regardless of any so-called economic cycles. Thus, the phrase "out-of-favor indies" may describe a permanent state of affairs for independent filmmakers in the U.S. (see "Cyclical Industry," "Economic Cycle" and "Market Power").

OUT-OF-STATE CORPORATION (see "Foreign Corporation").

OUTPUT ARRANGEMENTS (see "Output Deal").

OUTPUT DEAL. A contract through which one entity promises to deliver its entire output to another and the other party promises to accept the entire output supplied, e.g., a distribution arrangement between a production company and a distributor in which the distributor commits in advance to distribute the films produced by the producer. The term also refers to a licensing agreement in which a pay television entity commits to present whatever films a studio produces (see "Independent Producers" and "Output Distribution Agreement").

OUTPUT DISTRIBUTION AGREEMENT. A contract between a feature film production company and a film distributor which provides that, so long as the films produced by the production company meet certain specified minimum requirements, the distributor agrees to distribute all of such films (see "Minimum Requirements" and "Output Deal").

OUTREACH CAMPAIGN (see "Grass Roots Campaign").

OUTRIGHT SALE. A term defined in some distribution agreements as a license to any person, by the distributor or any franchised sub-distributor, to distribute the film for theatrical exhibition, in a particular geographic area and for a particular period of time (other than any such license for a period of less than one year for theatrical exhibition in a part of any country), without any obligation of such person to account for or report to the distributor or such franchised sub-distributor the amount of any proceeds or expenses of such distribution or sub-licensing. Thus, in the motion picture industry, an "outright sale" does not refer to a true sale, but instead to the license of a right for a flat fee instead of a percentage. Flat fee arrangements are commonly employed with certain territories and particular media, e.g., some foreign territories. The outright sale provides a lump-sum payment or payments and minimizes the distributor's expenses since it will not have to monitor sub-distribution and provide periodic accounting statements for those territories. However, there can be a significant difference between what a distributor is paid by a foreign sub-distributor for the rights to exploit a motion picture in a given territory on an outright sale basis and what the distributor may have been able to earn on the film if it distributed the film in such territory through its own facilities (in the event that such facilities existed). The producer may want to seek limits on the distributor as to the territories and media in which such types of sales may be made, i.e., the producer may want to insert language in the distribution agreement which prohibits outright sales by the distributor in the major foreign territories including France, the United Kingdom, Germany, Australia, Japan, Spain and Italy (see "Flat Sale," "Franchised Sub-Distributor" and "Receipts").

OUTS (see "Outtakes").

OUTSIDE DIRECTOR. A member of a corporation's board of directors who is not an employee of the company. Such directors are usually paid on a per-meeting basis for such service (see "Corporation," "Officers" and "Shareholders").

OUTSIDE INVESTORS. Individuals or entities who invest money for the production of films on a project basis or through limited partnerships and who are not shareholders, directors, officers or employees of the producing entity (see "Financing").

OUTSIDE OFFERED PROJECTS. In the context of a film distribution agreement in which the distributor has a right of first negotiation for an individual artist's next theatrical film, the term "outside offered projects" refers to proposed motion pictures not developed by the artist but with respect to which the artist is offered employment in the capacity of producer, director, player and/or writer. The distribution agreement may provide that the artist negotiate exclusively with the distributor in good faith with respect to their mutual participation in the production and distribution of the artist's next theatrical motion picture project. The agreement may further provide that if no agreement is reached within thirty days after such negotiations have commenced, neither party shall have any further obligations to the other with respect thereto (see "Right of First Negotiation").

OUTSIDE PRODUCTION COMPANY. A feature film producer or producing entity that is independent from a major studio affiliated production company (see "Independent Producer").

OUTSIDE THE POT. Ancillary revenue that is not included in the distributor's gross receipts. In some feature film distribution agreements, the distributor will separate out certain ancillary revenues from the gross receipts revenue stream that is subject to participations. In those situations, participants may want to negotiate a participation in that separate revenue stream (see "Ancillary Rights," "Gross Receipts" and "Retroactive Basis").

OUTSIDER'S VIEWPOINT. The perspective of someone who is not from the same country, region or a particular group in control of a given business or industry. The U.S. film industry, for example, has from time to time, produced motion pictures focusing on purely American social phenomenon or events with directors from other countries, pointing out that it is sometimes most revealing to look at ourselves as others see us. This book represents another example of this approach to the search for truth (see "Insider's Game," "Marketplace of Ideas" and "Member of the Club").

OUTSTANDING. Unpaid; not yet presented for payment; also stock held by shareholders and shown on the corporation's balance sheets under the heading of capital stock issued and outstanding (see "Accounts Receivable" and "Settlement Transaction").

OUTSTANDINGS. Among film distributors and exhibitors, the money for advertising expenses or film rentals that the distributor owes the exhibitor or the exhibitor owes the distributor. If the distributor and exhibitor disagree as to the correct amount due on a given film or several films from the same distributor, such amounts may remain unsettled for a period of time and may have to be settled on the basis of a compromise figure relating to more than one film. This practice can have an adverse impact on a movie's other profit participants (see "Creative Accounting" and "Settlement").

OUTSTANDING SECURITY. A security which is held by an investor and which has not been redeemed or purchased back by the issuing corporation (see "Corporate Stock" and "Corporation").

OUTTAKES. Rejected takes of the same basic film shots which are not used in the completed version of the film; i.e., footage shot but not selected for the final cut of a film (see "Cutouts" and "Take").

OVERAGE. The amount an exhibitor exceeds a film rental commitment to a distributor on a given film. Exhibitors sometimes use excess film rental earned in one circuit theatre to fulfill a rental commitment defaulted by another. Also, foreign distributors usually retain a distribution fee computed from the first dollar of film rental in the foreign territory and recoup their guarantees and distribution costs before any additional amounts, known as overages, are payable to the sales agents (see "Creative Accounting," "Foreign Distribution," "Foreign Sales Agent," "Split Rights Deal" and "Underage").

OVERAGES. Film production costs that exceed the amount provided in the prepared budget (see "Over-Budget").

OVERALL DEAL. An arrangement with a studio/distributor entered into by an independent producer in which the studio supplies funds to finance the development of the independent producer's film projects and to cover the independent producer's overhead for a specific period of time. In exchange, the studio/distributor gets a right of first refusal on the projects developed by the independent producer (same as "Housekeeping Deal" and "First Look Deal").

OVERALL TERM DEAL (see "Overall Deal").

OVER-BUDGET. Exceeding the planned expenditures for a film (see "Budget" and "Over-Budget Penalty").

OVER-BUDGET PENALTY. A form of financial punishment or forfeiture imposed by a studio when a producer of a studio-financed film goes over budget. While the terms forfeiture and penalty are often used interchangeably, the generic term "penalty" includes forfeiture and the term "forfeiture" in a more narrow sense relates to a loss of real or personal property, while a penalty most often relates to the loss of money. In either case, the major studio/distributors will try to avoid the use of these particular words in describing their over-budget policy relating to the production of a motion picture, since contract law may not allow unreasonable penalties to be enforced in commercial transactions (see "Double Add-Back," "Negotiated Cushion," "Over-Budget Policy," "Penalty-Free Cushion" and "Withholding").

OVER-BUDGET POLICY. The established practice and procedures of a motion picture studio acting as a film financier for a picture with regard to the production costs of the picture exceeding the approved production budget (see "Double Add-Back," "Negotiated Cushion," "Over-Budget Penalty," "Penalty-Free Cushion" and "Withholding").

OVERFLOW. Moviegoers who choose to see a movie other than their first choice because the movie they came to see is sold out. Such a phenomenon occurs most commonly at multiplex theatres (see "Multiplex").

OVERHEAD OR OVERHEAD COSTS. Generally, the costs of operating a business that are not directly associated with the production or sale of goods or services; also called indirect costs and expenses or production overhead; i.e., a charge typically levied by a motion picture studio, generally within the range of 10% to 25% of the movie's production costs or budget, which is designed to cover the studio's overhead. Such overhead costs are attributed to accountants, lawyers, studio executive salaries and their expenses, rental of sound stages or other studio facilities such as dressing facilities, vehicles, telephones, office space and equipment, secretaries salaries, story-abandonment costs and general administrative costs relating to the production area or other costs of doing business which are all absorbed by the production. The actual accounting entry for such costs is referred to as the overhead surcharge. Since it is expressed as a flat percentage, it has no relation to actual costs. Interest is usually charged on the overhead surcharge, and the overhead surcharge amount is generally deducted prior to the calculation of net profit participations, thus adding significantly to the amount that must be recouped by the studio before a motion picture can realize net profits. Studios have also been known to charge an overhead fee on other expenses which are in themselves overhead. Producers may be able to avoid some overhead costs by avoiding the studio/distributors or by negotiating a smaller percentage for such charges, by specifically listing the deductible charges or in the alternative, by closely monitoring such charges for reasonableness (same as "Production Overhead" and "Non-Allocated Overhead Percentage Charge;" see "Creative Accounting," "Interest," "Production Overhead" and "Overhead Surcharge").

OVERHEAD SURCHARGE. The actual accounting entry made by the studio in studio financing of the production of a film that covers the studio's overhead costs (see "Distribution Expenses," "Overhead" or "Overhead Costs" and "Production Overhead").

OVERPAYMENT. An amount of money either paid to the producer by the distributor or credited to the producer's account and reflected on the earnings statement which is in excess of the proper amount. A provision is often found in film distribution agreements which allows the distributor to deduct equivalent amounts from future producer payments or demand repayment of overpayments already paid to the producer (see "Distribution Agreement").

OVERREACHING. In commercial law, taking an unfair advantage over another through fraudulent practices or abuse of superior bargaining power; synonymous with fraud. Contracts that are the product of overreaching in an unequal bargaining context may be unenforceable today under modern concepts of fraud or the unconscionability doctrine (see "Contract of Adhesion," "Negotiate," "Submission Release" and "Unconscionable Contract").

OVERREPORTED TRAVEL. Another of the wrongful studio accounting practices sometimes complained about by producers in which the studio inflates the travel expenses associated with the production of a film being produced in conjunction with the studio (see "Improperly Claimed Expenses," "Kickbacks" and "Studio Accounting Practices").

OVERRIDE. A commission taken by a film's primary distributor on the distribution fee charged by a sub-distributor. In a situation where an independent distributor utilizes the distribution services of a major studio/distributor for actual distribution (sub-distribution in this case), instead of an absorption or "pass through" arrangement, some independent distributors will charge an "override," e.g., 10% to 15%, of the amounts received from the actual theatrical distributor (see "Absorption Approach," "Double Distribution Fees," "Pass-Through," "Supervision Fee" and "Sub-Distribution").

OVERRIDE APPROACH (see "Override").

OVER SCALE. Salaries that are paid to actors and others that exceed the union minimums (see "Guild" and "Union").

OVERSEAS RECEPTIVITY. The manner in which U.S. produced films are received by the movie-going public or television viewers in foreign countries (see "Culturally Biased," "Culture Promotion" and "Marketplace of Ideas").

OVER SUPPLY OF PRODUCT. More production or output of items destined for a commercial market than demand for the same item. In the motion picture industry, for example, there are more feature films produced each year than there are willing and capable distributors to distribute such films. That over supply of films is partly responsible for a market condition that puts producers (generally) at a disadvantage when it comes time to negotiate the terms of a distribution deal (see "Inferior Bargaining Position" and "Law of Supply and Demand").

OVER-THE-COUNTER (OTC). A method or mechanism for trading securities that are not listed and traded on an organized exchange (see "Corporate Stock," "Over-the-Counter Market," "Penny Stock" and "Pink Sheets").

OVER-THE-COUNTER-MARKET. A securities market created by dealers who primarily handle trading in securities that are not listed stocks on an organized exchange. OTC trading differs from exchange trading in that transactions are carried out through a telephone/computer network and negotiations with a number of dealers, called market makers, as compared to the single specialist, single-location auction market mechanism used for listed securities trading, and the market maker acts as principal in the transaction which involves the dealer as buyer and seller from his or her own inventory (see "Broker/Dealer," "Market Makers," "National Association of Securities Dealers" and "Stock Exchange").

OWNER. The person who has legal title to property (see "Clearance" and "Title").

OWNER'S EQUITY (same as "Net Assets" and "Net Worth").

OWNERSHIP. One's exclusive right of possessing, enjoying and disposing of a thing, e.g., all or a percentage equity interest in the copyright, gross receipts and expenses of a motion picture (see "Equity").

OWNERSHIP INTEREST. In a limited partnership context, the interest of each partner in the partnership (see "Equity" and "Limited Partnership").

— P —

P&A (see "Prints and Ads").

PACKAGE. As a noun, the total presentation of the basic elements needed to do a film or TV series or special. Such a film package minimally consists of a script, a budget, a shooting schedule and often commitments by a star or stars and a director. It can also be enhanced by including agreed-upon deferments from the lab, performers or director, and having part of the funding already raised or agreed upon. As a verb, package means to put together the various elements of a film (script, director, actors, producer, etc.) which make a film project marketable to potential financiers, producers and/or distributors. In the broadest sense, packaging is inherent in the process of producing and financing a motion picture. However, some agents, talent agencies, entertainment attorneys and others engage in packaging activities and utilize some of their own clients, with the intent of maximizing their own fees on the packaged film project. In this more narrow sense, packaging may be considered somewhat unethical and have a negative connotation in that these "packaged" films are not "cast;" rather, they are "packaged" for the benefit of the packaging entity instead of "cast" for the purpose of bringing together the most desirable combination of elements which are likely to result in the best motion picture. Certain "packaged" elements of a film may also prove to be unacceptable to a financing source and may thus become a detriment to the production of a given film. As a verb, package means to fully develop and bring together all of the commercial elements of a film (see "Casting," "Elements," "Financing Entity," "Pay or Play" and Syndicated Films").

PACKAGE FEE. The compensation paid by a buyer and received by the person responsible for assembling a group of films for sale as a package or a film project with assembled elements (see "Elements" and "Package").

PACKAGE SALES. More than one film sold as a group for a lump sum. Distributors sometimes will seek to make outright sales of a picture in certain territories as part of a package of several films for a fixed price. Films may also be licensed as part of a package for television (network or syndication). The producer may want to seek to impose reasonable limits on the distributor's ability to sell or license a producer's picture as a package unless a mechanism is established for providing a fair valuation of such picture compared to the others in the package (see "Allocation," "Outright Sales," "Sub-Distributor" and "Syndication").

PACKAGING. The activities relating to putting together a film package (see "Package," "Package Fee" and Packaging Agent").

PACKAGING AGENT. A motion picture talent agent who goes beyond the traditional services relating to representing the interests of his or her talent clients and puts together a film package specifically with roles for the talent represented (see "Package" and "Package Fee").

PACKAGING ATTORNEY. Entertainment lawyers who bring together the various elements of a film project and assist in obtaining either production financing for the project and/or attaching the elements to the project (see "Elements," "Executive Producer," "Package," "Packaging" and "Producer's Representative").

PACKAGING SERVICE. A person or entity (not an agent or attorney) who holds themselves out as having expertise relating to the assembling of feature film elements for the purpose of obtaining production financing and provides such services (see "Package," "Packaging Agent" and "Packaging Attorney").

PACKAGING SERVICES AGREEMENT. An agreement between a film's producer and a packaging services company through which the packaging services company agrees to perform certain services relating to the packaging of the film project (see "Package" and "Packaging Service").

PAGE. A means of time measurement for a screenplay. A screenplay page, in running time, averages about sixty seconds. For principal photography, a given number of pages are scheduled on a specified shooting (see "Screenplay").

PAID ADS (see "Advertisement" and "Advertising").

PAID ADVERTISING (see "Advertisement" and "Advertising").

PAID-IN CAPITAL. The capital received by a corporation from investors in exchange for stock, as distinguished from capital generated from earnings or donated (see "Capital").

PAID MEDIA. All forms of paid advertising (see "Advertising").

PAN AND SCAN. A process used in presenting feature films on television in which the film's wide-screen dimensions are pared down to fit the smaller ones of the TV screen. The process involves cutting off some of the wide-screen film images on the edges or editing back and forth between subjects that would have appeared together in the frame on the larger movie screen. Many filmmakers are opposed to the technique, saying it distorts the original film's intent. However, the vast majority of films released on videotape and subsequently to pay-TV, basic cable and free-TV outlets use the process (see "Edit" and "Moral Rights").

PANNING/SCANNING (see "Pan and Scan").

PAPER PROFIT (OR LOSS). Unrealized capital gain or capital loss in an investment or portfolio; calculated by comparing the current market prices to the prices at which those assets were originally bought. Such profits and losses become realized only when the securities are sold [see "Realized Profit (or Loss)"].

PAR. Equal to the nominal or face value of a security. Par value for a corporation's common stock is set by the company issuing the stock. Par value generally does not have any relation to market value (see "No-Par Stock" and "Stated Value").

PARALLEL BUSINESS BEHAVIOR. The similar conduct of businesses with respect to specific business practices. In the film business, for example, exhibitors have sometimes alleged that the practice of blind bidding, which is engaged in by most of the major studio/ distributors, is a conspiracy in restraint of trade, a violation of the federal Sherman Anti-Trust Act. However, U.S. courts have never held that a showing of parallel business behavior alone conclusively establishes a conspiracy. In order to prove conspiracy, the plaintiff exhibitors would have to show conscious parallel business behavior to infer an agreement, but they need to show additional circumstances which logically suggest joint agreement, as distinguished from individual action which happens to be the same (see "Bidding War," "Blind Bidding," "Conscious Parallelism" and "Twenty Percent Rule").

PARAMOUNT CASE (see "Paramount Consent Decree of 1948").

PARAMOUNT CONSENT DECREE OF 1948. The popular name for the final judgments handed down by the U.S. District Court for the Southern District of New York, with respect to each studio/distributor or motion picture related defendant (Loew's, Paramount, Columbia Pictures, United Artists, Universal, American Theatres, Warner Bros., 20th Century Fox and RKO) in the U.S. v. Paramount Pictures case. A separate judgment was issued for each of the nine defendants, and although similar, the judgments were not identical. Generally, the decrees prohibited certain trade practices (e.g., block booking, unreasonable clearances), and with respect to some of the defendants, but not all, the decrees mandated that the defendants divest themselves of all motion-picture theatre holdings and prohibited the acquisition of theatres in the future. The decrees sought to put an end to so-called vertical integration, through which the motion-picture companies produced, distributed, and exhibited their film products to the public. The intention was to provide competing theatres an equal opportunity to license motion pictures for commercial presentation. Since the Reagan Presidency, however, and partly due to the effective lobbying effort of the MPAA, the U.S. Justice Department has relaxed its enforcement of the anti-trust laws as applied to the major movie studios and vertical integration is once again on the rise. This trend does not favor independent producers, and, in order to combat the resulting increased control of the major studio/distributors over all levels of the industry, independent producers must organize a permanent professional association and seek to protect their long-term economic interests by making sure the current administration, the Justice Department and Congress is aware of the effects of the major studio/distributors' re-entry into movie exhibition, i.e., the effects vertical integration has on independent producers (see "Anti-Trust Law Violations," "Block Booking," "Clearance," "Lobbying," "Market Power," "Market Share," "Merger Guidelines," "Number of Screens," "Original Paramount Defendants," "Political Influence," "Tracks," "TriStar Case" and "Vertical Integration").

PARAMOUNT DECREES (see "Paramount Consent Decree of 1948").

PARENT CORPORATION (see "Affiliate," "Corporation," "Holding Company" and "Subsidiary").

PARI PASSU. A Latin phrase meaning pro rata and concurrent. The phrase is used most often to describe the relationship between investors and/or profit participants in a film and when such persons are to recoup their investment or receive their contracted for payments of deferments or profits (see "Latin" and "Profit").

PARKING. A temporary placement of securities, in a public offering, by a broker/dealer, with favored customers who buy at the offering price but resell in the aftermarket at prices generally higher than the initial offering price (see "Broker/Dealer," "Public Offering" and "Securities").

PARTIAL FINANCING. A portion of the production funds for a feature film have been raised, are in place or are committed. In the current marketplace for the financing of feature films, it is often helpful to spread the risk, i.e., to use more than one source for the high-risk production financing, and, of course, it is generally helpful when approaching a prospective financing source if at least part of the financing is already in place (see "Financing," "Investor Financing," "Lender Financing" and "Studio Financing").

PARTIALLY AMORTIZED LOANS (see "Balloon Payment").

PARTIAL PRESENTATIONS. An accounting term for financial presentations that do not meet the minimum presentation guidelines of the AICPA or other authoritative accounting organization (see "Prospective Financial Statements," "Financial Forecasts," "Financial Projections" and "Pro Form Financial Statements").

PARTIAL SECONDARY OFFERING. An offering of securities by both the company and stockholders (see "Corporate Stock," "Corporation," "Offering" and "Securities").

PARTICIPANT. A term defined in some distribution agreements as any person entitled to receive contingent compensation, as distinguished from fixed compensation (see "Contingent Compensation," "Gross Receipts," "Net Profits" and "Profit Participation").

PARTICIPATION. A share in the profits of a film; contingent compensation as distinguished from fixed compensation. Also, as between a film's distributor and exhibitor, the weekly dollar sharing on the part of each for cooperative advertising expenditures on a film in a given market (see "Profit Participation" and "Cooperative Advertising").

PARTICIPATION LOAN. A loan made by more than one lender and serviced (administered) by one of the participants, called the lead bank or lead lender (see "Debt" and "Lender Financing").

PARTICIPATION RATE. The percentage of a specified portion of a motion picture's revenue stream, i.e., gross receipts or net profits, that an individual or entity is to receive as some or all of his, her or its contribution to the project (see "Gross Receipts," "Net Profits" and "Participation").

PARTICIPATIONS IN GROSS RECEIPTS. A percentage interest held by an individual or entity in that portion of a motion picture's revenue stream defined as distributor's gross receipts (see "Gross Receipts," "Interest" and "Participation").

PARTICIPATORY DEBT INSTRUMENT. A hybrid security which, in addition to debt features, also provides equity participation, i.e., the right to participate with common stockholders in additional distributions of earnings under specified conditions (see "Corporate Stock," "Debt," "Equity" and "Security or Securities").

PARTIES (TO THE CONTRACT). Those individuals or entities who negotiate and sign an agreement, e.g., the distributor and producer who sign a film distribution agreement. In some such agreements, the producer is referred to as the grantor or the licensor and the distributor referred to by a shortened form of its name or as grantee or licensee. Use of the terms distributor and producer helps make it easier for all persons who may review a distribution deal to keep the parties straight (see "Grantee," "Grantor," "Licensee" and "Grantee").

PARTNERS. Typically defined in a limited partnership context to include the general partners and all unit holders in the limited partnership. Reference to a partner in such a limited partnership refers to any one of the above (see "General Partners," "Limited Partnership" and "Profit-Sharing Ratio").

PARTNERSHIP. A general term which may include both general and limited partnerships; a legal but unincorporated relationship and form of doing business that has been created between two or more persons who contractually associate in the conduct of a trade or business and agree to share in the profits and losses of the enterprise. For tax purposes, the term "partnership" includes any syndicate, group, pool, joint venture or other unincorporated organization through or by means of which any business, financial operation or venture is carried on and which is not, within the meaning of the tax code, a corporation, trust or estate (see "Corporation,"

"General Partnership," "Joint Venture," "Profit Sharing Ratio" and "Limited Partnership").

PARTNERSHIP AGREEMENT. An agreement, generally prepared by the general partner's securities attorney, which serves as the basic underlying legal document relating to and regulating the relationship between a limited partnership's general partners and limited partners, i.e., any valid written agreement of the partners as to the affairs of a limited partnership and the conduct of its business, including all amendments thereto. Such agreements must be drafted in accordance with the specific provisions of the state limited partnership act of the state in which the partnership is being created (also called "Articles of Partnership;" see "Joint Venture Agreement" and "Limited Partnership").

PARTNERSHIP CERTIFICATE. Documentary evidence of the ownership of an interest in a limited partnership, setting out the number of units owned. Partnership certificates are not commonly used in marketing limited partnerships (see "Certificate of Limited Partnership" and "Stock Certificate").

PARTNERSHIP CONTRIBUTION TO NEGATIVE COST. A concept relating to films financed partially by funds provided by a limited partnership that refers to what percentage of a film or films' production and/or distribution costs the partnership has provided. Such percentage will be used in determining what profits, if any, will be paid to the partnership. Such deals are usually structured as joint ventures between the limited partnership and a studio/distributor or production company (see "Joint Venture," "Limited Partnership" and "When the Money's Paid").

PARTNERSHIP EXPENSES. The costs incurred in organizing, maintaining and selling the interests in a partnership. Generally, in a film limited partnership, the general partners will be authorized in the partnership agreement to deduct monies to pay for on-going partnership expenses such as the annual preparation of the partnership K-1's, from partnership gross receipts before arriving at distributable cash (see "Distributable Cash," "Offering Expenses," "Schedule K-1" and "Syndication Expenses").

PARTNERSHIP NET (see "Partnership Net Receipts").

PARTNERSHIP NET RECEIPTS. The remaining portion of partnership receipts after specified deductions are taken from partnership gross revenues. Some limited partnerships use the term "distributable cash" to mean the same thing. Partnership net receipts are the funds distributed among the partners pursuant to the pre-recoupment and post-recoupment profit-sharing ratios (see "Cash Distributions," "Distributable Cash," "Profit-Sharing Ratio" and "Payout").

PARTNERSHIP GROSS REVENUES. The total amount of revenue received by the partnership from all sources for partnership activities including with respect to a film limited partnership the distribution, exhibition and exploitation of the partnership's films (same as "Gross Partnership Revenues" or "Gross Revenues to the Partnership;" see "Limited Partnership").

PASS. A declination, e.g., an indication from a studio or other production company that they do not wish to participate in the production, financing or development of a given motion picture project submitted to them (see "Go Ahead" and "Greenlight").

PASSIVE ACTIVITY. Any activity that involves the conduct of a trade or business and in which the taxpayer does not materially participate. Losses and credits from passive activities are limited by the tax laws, e.g., passive losses can only be deducted from passive income. In a limited partnership context, the passive activity limitations apply to each partner's share of any loss or credit attributable to passive activity of the partnership. Such limitations do not apply to the partnership entity itself (see "Internal Revenue Service," "Investor Financing," "Passive Investors," "Securities" and "Tax Shelter Opinion").

PASSIVE ACTIVITY LOSS. The amount by which the aggregate losses from all passive activities exceed the aggregate income from all passive activities for the tax year (see "Passive Activity" and "Passive Income").

PASSIVE INCOME. Income from activities in which a taxpayer does not materially participate, such as a limited partnership, as distinguished from income from (1) wages and active trade or (2) business and investment income, such as dividends and interest. Pursuant to the Tax Reform Act of 1986, losses and credits from such passive activities are deductible only against income and tax from passive activities, although one passive activity can offset another and unused passive losses can be carried forward from year to year (see "Deductions," "Passive Activity" and "Passive Loss").

PASSIVE INVESTMENT LOSSES. Expenses that exceed annual income from an investment in which the investor is not actively involved, e.g., limited partnership (see "Limited Partnership" and "Loss").

PASSIVE INVESTOR FINANCING (see "Financing," "Limited Partnership" and "Passive Investors").

PASSIVE INVESTORS. Persons who invest in trade or business activities in which such investors do not materially participate, e.g., limited partners (see "Investor Financing" and "Securities").

PASSIVE INVESTOR VEHICLES. A business financing instrument or structure involving contributors of funds who are not active in any significant way in the management of the business. Passive investor vehicles include limited partnerships, corporations and investment contracts (see "Passive Income" and "Securities").

PASSIVE LOSS (same as "Passive Activity Loss").

PASS-THROUGH. In sub-distribution situations, the charging of the sub-distributor's fee against a film's rentals without a markup or override by the primary distributor (see "Absorption Arrangement," "Double Distribution Fees," "Override," "Sub-Distribution" and "Supervision Fee").

PASS-THROUGH ARRANGEMENT (see "Pass-Through").

PAST PERFORMANCE. A concept used by producers to illustrate to prospective distributors and/or investors how well a proposed film may perform at the box office by comparing such future performance with the actual performance of similar films that have already been distributed (see "Box Office Comparables," "Similar Pictures" and "Track Record").

PATENT. A government grant of a right to exclude others from the making, using or selling of an invention during a specified time. Thus, a patent constitutes a legitimate monopoly (see "Anti-Trust Laws," "Copyright," "Monopoly" and "Trademark").

PATRON. In art circles generally, a wealthy or influential supporter of an artist or writer, but in a film context, anyone who purchases a movie ticket and thus supports its production and exhibition with a small contribution (see "Boycott" and "Investor").

PATTERN OF BIAS. The consistent repetition of an outlook or prejudice (see "Favorable Portrayal," "Hidden Agenda," "Prejudice" and "Unfavorable Portrayal").

PAUL KAGAN ASSOCIATES, INC.. Media analysts specializing in financial and investment research who present seminars and publish newsletters, studies and reference books for cable tv, pay tv, broadcasting, motion pictures, tv program syndication, home video and home shopping (see "Industry Analysts," "Major Exhibition Chains" and "Show Biz News").

PAY AND CABLE TELEVISION VERSION. An edited copy of a feature film that is suitable for exhibiting on pay cable and basic cable (see "Other Versions").

PAY AND PLAY. A contractual commitment from a motion picture production company or studio to not only pay the agreed upon compensation to an artist (producer, director, actor, etc.) but to actually produce the picture and utilize the services of the artist therein. The pay and play arrangement is particularly important for the artist who takes a developed project to a production company and for situations in which the artist's compensation is principally contingent compensation (contrast with "Pay or Play;" see "Nominal Payments").

PAYBACK. The method and manner of returning money loaned to or invested in a venture (see "Interest" and "Rate of Return").

PAYBACK PERIOD. The length of time needed to recoup the cost of a capital investment (see "Payback").

PAY CABLE. The system for transmitting television signals and programming by wire to the homes of fee paying subscribers (see "Cable TV").

PAYEE. Any person to whom a debt should be paid; one to whose order a negotiable instrument, such as a bill of exchange, note or check, is made payable (see "Payer").

PAYER (or PAYOR). One who pays a debt or is obligated to pay a debt under a promissory note or other financial instrument (see "Payee").

PAY OR PLAY. A contractual obligation between the producer and generally actors or directors which provides that the producer will pay a stated amount whether or not the services of the actor or director are performed or required. Such commitments are made by producers in order to obtain corresponding commitments from talent in packaging a film which in turn helps to procure production funding for the project. Such commitments from talent may also be obtained in some circumstances with nominal non-returnable payments that do not rise to the level of a pay or play commitment or other arrangements. The "pay or play" arrangement does not commit the producer to utilize the services of the artist; thus, if the project falls through, the artist may not only incur some down-time in his or her career and lose a specific opportunity to appear in what was obviously a desirable vehicle but also is cutoff from receiving any contingent compensation related to the project (see "Financing," "Nominal Payments," "Packaging" and "Pay and Play").

PAY-OR-PLAY COMMITMENTS (see "Pay or Play").

PAYOUT. That point in time when an amount invested in a limited partnership has been recouped through cash distributions, i.e., the point in time when the aggregate unreturned capital contributions of the limited partners in a limited partnership have become $0. Payout generally is accompanied by a reallocation of the rights to income or cash flow among the participants in an investment (same as "Recoupment;" see "Post Payout Sharing Ratio" and "Pre-Payout Sharing Ratio").

PAY-PER-TRANSACTION. An experimental videocassette distribution system that holds out the promise that movie distributors will be paid a portion of video cassette rental income (contrast with "Pay-Per-View;" see "First Sale Doctrine").

PAY-PER-VIEW. A cable-television delivery method wherein the subscriber is billed only for specific programs, i.e., a cable service that makes available to a subscriber an individual movie, sporting event or concert on payment of a fee for that single event (contrast with "Pay-Per-Transaction;" see "Cable Television" and "Subscription Television").

PAY-PER-VIEW RIGHTS. The authority to exhibit a motion picture or other program on a pay-per-view basis (see "Pay-Per-View").

PAYROLL MANAGEMENT (see "Payroll and Production Accounting").

PAYROLL AND PRODUCTION ACCOUNTING. Accounting services relating specifically to movie cast and crew payrolls and production expenses. Such services may include pre-production budgeting, auditing services, preparation of final cast lists, payroll job-cost data, final job cost reports and federal and state tax reports along with the computation and payment of residuals and the coordination of union contracts (see "Production Accountant").

PAYROLL SERVICE (see "Payroll and Production Accounting").

PAY TELEVISION. Subscriber-paid-for television, generally the first pay television window (time period during which a film may be exhibited on pay television) which is presented in an uncut and uncensored format. Pay television includes satellite-delivered pay cable, over-the-air-subscription TV and standard cable (see "Cable Television").

PAY TELEVISION LICENSE AGREEMENT. The contract between a film's producer or distributor and a provider of television programming paid for by subscribers (see "Pay Television Revenue").

PAY TELEVISION OUTPUT ARRANGEMENT. An agreement between a production company or studio and a subscriber-paid-for-television service such as HBO or Showtime for the pay television service to purchase all of the programming produced by the production company or studio, so long as certain requirements are met (see "Output Deal").

PAY TELEVISION REVENUE. Income generated through subscriber-paid-for television (see "Free Television").

PECUNIARY. Relating to money and monetary affairs; consisting of money or that which can be valued in money (see "Monetary Advances" and "Monetary Damages").

PENALTY CLAUSE. A provision commonly found in contracts, borrowing agreements and savings instruments which provides for penalties in the event a contractual promise is not kept, a loan payment is late or a withdrawal is made prematurely (see "Prepayment Penalty").

PENALTY FORMULA. A predetermined formula for reducing the producer's profit participation if the production goes over budget (see "Over-Budget Policy" and "Penalty-Free Cushion").

PENALTY-FREE CUSHION. A percentage of a film's budget (negotiated by the producer with a studio providing production financing) that would have to be surpassed before the film would be considered over-budget and penalties (typically in the range of 5% to 10%), are imposed (see "Budget Overages," "Double Add-Back," "Penalty Formula" and "Withholding").

PENNY STOCK. Corporate shares that generally sell for less than $1 per share, although the price may rise to as high as $10 per share after the initial public offering. Penny stocks are traded over-the-counter (see "Corporate Stock," "Initial Public Offering," "Over-the-Counter" and "Security or Securities").

PENNY STOCK OFFERING. The offer and sale of securities relating to low-priced corporate stock (see "Penny Stock" and "Securities").

PENSION FUND CONTRIBUTIONS. Payments made by a film producer or distributor out of a film's budget or from the revenues generated by a film to the retirement funds of the various unions or guilds whose members were involved in the production of the film (see "Distribution Expenses" and "Guild").

PER ANNUM. With respect to a year. The major studio/distributors in the film business generally will distribute about twenty to twenty-five motion pictures per year (see "Number of Screens," "Rent-A-Distributor" and "Release Slots").

PERCENTAGE ALLOCATED. That portion of a specific fund which is to be apportioned among two or more participants (see "Allocation Issues," "Block Booking" and "Double Bill").

PERCENTAGE INTEREST. In limited partnership terminology, the respective interests of each partner in the partnership which interests are set forth for each partner in the disclosure document and the limited partnership agreement (see "Limited Partnership" and "Percentage Participation").

PERCENTAGE PARTICIPATION OR POINTS. The percentage or fraction thereof of any of several defined levels of a movie's revenue stream (film rentals, gross receipts, adjusted gross, accountable gross, net receipts, net profits, general partner's net receipts, etc.), i.e., the financial interests of persons or entities in a film's revenues, receipts or profits, expressed as percentages and designated by the person or entities authorized to award such participations (an executive producer or producer and in the context of a film limited partnership, possibly the general partner). Thus, a person making a contribution to the production or distribution of a given film may negotiate for a percentage of such specified level. A percentage participation may or may not represent deferred compensation in a given situation (see "Contingent Compensation," "Contingent Deferment," "Deferment" or Deferrals," "Fixed Deferment," "Points," "Profit Participation" and "Talent Participations").

PERCENTAGE RENTALS. Film rentals paid by a film's exhibitor to the distributor based on a negotiated percentage of the film's box office (see "Film Rentals" and "Flat Rentals").

PERCENTAGE SALE. A film rental agreement between a motion picture distributor and an exhibitor which is based on a negotiated percentage of the film's performance at the box office (see "Film Rentals" and "Percentage Rentals").

PERFECTIONIST DIRECTOR. An overly fussy director who wastes film and the time of cast and crew trying to make every shot perfect. Such directors can be responsible for time and budget overruns and should be avoided by producers (see "Budget," "Collaborative Process," "Director" and "Prima Donna").

PERFORMANCE. The fulfillment of an obligation; a promise kept; refers especially to completion of one's obligation under a contract (see "Duty" and "Contract").

PERFORMANCE RECORD. In the context of limited partnerships, e.g., feature film limited partnerships, the results of operations of such partnerships from an investment perspective (see "Past Performance," "Prior Performance" and "Track Record").

PERFORMER EMPLOYMENT AGREEMENT. A general term referring to written contracts by and between feature film production companies and actors (see "Employment Agreement" and "Player Agreement").

PERFORMERS. Actors in film productions who have speaking, dancing or singing parts. Extras and walk-ons are not considered performers (see "Featured Player" and "Supporting Player").

PERK. A fringe benefit or privilege or profit over and above a salary. The word is an abbreviation for perquisite. Perks often are important negotiating points in employment agreements for the services of actors. Such negotiated perks may include exclusive ground transportation, the right to retain the artist's wardrobe at the end of the shoot (or to purchase at a negotiated percentage of the producer's cost), for the production company to cover the actor and loan-out company (if any), on the errors and omissions, general liability and worker's compensation insurance policies for the film, to receive invitations to film festivals and celebrity premieres for the film (with a guest), a complimentary copy of the film on videocassette (or laser disc), a "workout" trainer during principal photography (or before if important for the role), use of the studio's corporate jet, for the studio to rent the actor's own motor home (if he or she owns one) and hire a driver to get it to the location, employment of the artist's assistant(s) (providing per diem, airfare and credit, if appropriate), provide a nanny for the artist's children and/or provide a security person, dialogue coach and/or translator (see "Rising Production Costs").

PERMANENT FINANCING. Long term corporate financing by means of either debt (bonds or long-term notes) or equity (common or preferred stock) (see "Corporation," "Financing," "Investor Financing" and "Lender Financing").

PERMITS. Governmental licenses granting permission for a film production company to shoot a portion of a film within the governmental unit's jurisdiction (see "Location Permit").

PERPETUAL EXISTENCE. An important corporate characteristic which permits the corporation to continue in existence forever as opposed to a sole proprietorship which is limited by the natural lifetime of its owner and a partnership which can exist only so long as the contractual relationship remains in effect among the parties (see "Corporation," "Partnership" and "Sole Proprietorship").

PERPETUAL RIGHTS. The legal power and authority to exploit a film without limit in terms of time, i.e., for an infinite period; forever (see "Distribution Term" and "Term").

PERPETUITY. Until the end of time, i.e., forever. Feature film distributors, particularly in situations where a studio/distributor provides funding for both the production costs of a motion picture and the distribution expenses will want to obtain a grant of distribution rights in perpetuity, effectively adding that film to its library of films even though copyright ownership stays with an independent production company (see "Distribution Term").

PER SE VIOLATIONS. An infraction of the law which does not require extraneous evidence or support to establish the existence of the infraction. In anti-trust law, certain types of business practices are considered per se restraints of trade. Since proof of the conduct alone proves a violation of the Sherman Anti-Trust Act, there is no need to prove any injury to competitors, which would otherwise be a necessary element in an anti-trust action. Price fixing, for example, is a per se violation of the federal anti-trust laws (see "Anti-Trust Laws," "Conduct Restrictions," "Minimum Admission Prices," "Paramount Consent Decree of 1948," "Price Fixing" and "Sherman Anti-Trust Act").

PERSON. In law, an individual or incorporated group having certain legal rights and responsibilities, thus, an individual, partnership, limited partnership (domestic or foreign), trust, estate, association, corporation or other entity may be referred to as a person (see "Natural Person").

PERSONAL APPEARANCE TOURS. Publicity appearances by actors and directors, a certain number of which are commonly contracted for between the producer and distributor (see "Promotional Activities").

PERSONAL GUARANTEE. A guarantee for which the guarantor is personally liable (see "Guarantee" and "Guaranty").

PERSONAL LIABILITY PROVISION. Language in an agreement, e.g., a loan, which provides that an individual may be held personally responsible for repayment of the debt or other obligation. A producer will seek to set a limit on his or her personal liability and/or exempt specific assets (see "Liability" and "Limited Liability").

PERSONAL MANAGER. A person who manages the affairs of another. In the entertainment industry, the personal manager is generally intimately involved with career development and the creation of a favorable public perception for their clients. Their activities are generally more directed toward the day-to-day activities of their clients than those of agents. Some personal managers combine several roles such as that of lawyer, personal manager and film and television producer (see "Agent," "Business Manager," "Entertainment Attorney," "Personal Representative" and "Producer's Representative").

PERSONAL RELEASE. A written document signed by an individual whereby such individual gives up some claim, right or interest to the person against whom the claim, right or interest could have been enforced. In film, personal releases are generally obtained from all persons whose names or likenesses may appear in a movie (see "Clearance," "Release" and "Title").

PERSONAL REPRESENTATIVE. A person who represents another in the affairs of that other person, under a power of attorney or due to the incapacity of the principal through death, incompetency or infancy (see "Assigns," "Heirs," "Personal Manager," "Producer's Representative" and "Successor").

PERSONAL SECURITY. An obligation to repay a debt evidenced by a pledge, note or bond in contrast to collateral security. Evidences of debt which bind the creditor to the debtor, not the debtor's collateral (see "Collateral," "Debt" and "Recourse Loan").

P-F/D AGREEMENT (see "Production-Financing/Distribution Agreement").

PGA (see "Producers Guild of America").

"PG" RATING. An MPAA rating indicating that a motion picture has been reviewed by the MPAA's Classification and Rating Administration, and that parental guidance is suggested, i.e., in the MPAA's opinion, the film may contain some material parents might not like for their young children (see "Ratings").

"PG-13" RATING. An MPAA rating indicating that a motion picture has been reviewed by the MPAA's Classification and Rating Administration and that parents are urged to be cautious since the film may contain some material that may be inappropriate for pre-teenagers (see "Ratings").

PHANTOM INCOME/GAIN. Taxable income or gain that exceeds cash flow or distributable cash in a limited partnership (see "Income Tax" and "Limited Partnership").

PHONOGRAPH. An instrument by means of which sounds can be mechanically recorded and reproduced (see "Compact Disc" and "Music").

PHONOGRAPH RECORD. A disc with spiral grooves carrying recorded sound for phonograph reproduction (see "Phonograph").

PHOTOGRAPH. A picture or likeness obtained through the art or process of producing images on a sensitized surface by the action of light or other radiant energy (see "Film" and "Photoplay").

PHOTOPLAY. Another name for screenplay or script, although seldom used anymore (see "Screenplay").

PHYSICAL COMEDY. A genre of film of a light, amusing or humorous character which utilizes facial expression, bodily action or gestures and/or other prop, scenery or action based humor as opposed to mental humor. Such comedies have tended to fare better in foreign markets in recent years as opposed to the more subtle forms of comedy or e.g., so-called relationship movies (see "Foreign Potential" and "Overseas Receptivity").

PHYSICAL PRODUCTION DEPARTMENT. A somewhat redundant phrase most commonly used by film industry personnel who are associated with the major studio/distributors to refer to the studio's production department and to clearly distinguish that department from the studio's creative department (see "Creative Department" and "Production Department").

PHYSICAL PROPERTIES. Tangible possessions or effects. The phrase is sometimes used as a catchall phrase in the "security interest" paragraph of a studio distribution agreement which indicates that in order to secure the studio's advance of production funds to an independent production company for the production of a film, the production company assigns to the studio as security all of its right, title and interest in the picture, all associated copyrights, all negatives, film, tape and other physical properties created or acquired for the picture (see "Security Agreement" and "Security Interest").

PICKUP. Scenes or shots filmed after the completion of a film's principal photography in order to fill in any gaps in the film's continuity (see "Pickups").

PICKUP DEAL (see "Pickups").

PICKUP DISTRIBUTION DEAL (see "Acquisition Distribution Agreement" and "Pickups").

PICKUP PHOTOGRAPHY (see "Pickup").

PICKUP PRICE. The consideration agreed to be paid by a motion picture distributor to a film's producer upon completion and satisfactory delivery of the film to the distributor pursuant to the terms of a negative pickup distribution agreement. The term is also used by some in the industry to indicate the price paid for a film purchased pursuant to an acquisition distribution agreement. Sometimes the pickup price will approximate the negative cost of the picture (see "Acquisition Distribution Agreement" and "Negative Pickup").

PICKUPS. Sometimes the term "pickup" is used alone to refer to partially completed or completed film projects presented to studio-financiers or distributors for further funding or distribution. To avoid confusion, it would be more appropriate to distinguish between negative pickup and acquisition deals, using the term "negative pickup" when the distributor commitment is made prior to completion of the film and the term "acquisition" when the distributor commitment is made after completion of the film (same as "Negative Pickup;" see "Acquisition Distribution Agreement" and "Pickup Price").

PICTURE(S) (see "Motion Picture").

PICTURE EDITOR. The film production person actually engaged in the editing and/or cutting of positive prints of a motion picture into proper sequence and story form (see "Sound Editor" and "Supervising Editor").

PICTURE MIX. The combination of feature films that make up the production slate of a motion picture production company. From a financial management point of view, the varying combinations of low, medium and high budget pictures in different genres provide varying financial risks and opportunities which need to be analyzed using financial modeling techniques (see "Computer Model," "Financial Management" and "Mental Modeling").

PICTURE NEGATIVE. Film which, after exposure to a subject or positive image and subsequent processing, produces a negative picture image on the film (see "Exposed Film" and "Negative").

PICTURE PRINT. Processed film with a positive image and no sound track (see "Print").

PICTURE RELEASE NEGATIVE. A film negative which has been conformed to the work print and from which release prints are struck (see "Answer Print" and "Release Print").

PICTURE SPECIFICATIONS. The required characteristics and elements of a motion picture to be delivered to a financing studio or distributor pursuant to a production-financing/distribution agreement. Such specifications may include the requirement that the approved basic elements be used in the film, such as the specifically identified underlying material or screenplay and specified director, producer and principal cast members. Also, such specifications will require that the final budget not exceed the approved production budget. Production specifications generally also include a start date, production schedule, locations, along with the identification of the production company's attorney and the studio's production executive(s). Delivery specifications will include a delivery date and a specified film lab. In addition, certain controls, approvals and obligations may be set out in the agreement along with the production company's right of consultation relating to the film's distribution pattern and ad campaign for the initial U.S. theatrical release (see "Delivery Requirements").

PIECE OF THE ACTION. Equity participation in an economic endeavor (see "Equity" and "Investor Financing").

PIED PIPER. In the context of the motion picture business, a reference to the allure of the much publicized glamour, fame and fortune associated with the industry. Just as the "Pied Piper" of the children's fairy tale, films which are exhibited in almost every community in the country and in many across the globe entice the "children" of the world to come to the center of American filmmaking, Los Angeles (see "Chasing a Dream" and "Film Schools").

PIERCING THE CORPORATE VEIL. The process of imposing liability for corporate activity, in disregard of the corporate entity, on a person or entity other than the offending corporation itself. Generally, the corporate form of doing business isolates both individuals and parent corporations from liability for corporate misdeeds. However, the courts will ignore the corporate entity and strip organizers and managers of the corporation of limited liability in certain circumstances, e.g., under capitalization, commingling or misappropriation of funds and other assets, failure to obtain authority to issue stock, disregarding legal formalities, etc. In so doing, the court is said to be piercing or lifting the corporate veil (see "Corporation," "Ultra Vires Activities" and "Undercapitalization").

PILOT. Typically a ninety-minute or two-hour Movie of the Week (MOW) that is produced as a hopeful forerunner to a television series (see "Television Series" and "Television Special").

PINK SHEETS. Daily publications of the National Quotation Bureau that detail the bid and asked prices of thousands of over-the-counter equity stocks. Brokerage firms subscribe to the pink sheets, named for their color, because the sheets not only give current prices but list market makers who trade each stock (see "Broker/Dealer," "Market Maker," "Over-the-Counter" and "Securities").

PIPELINE. A reference to the established relationships and the film distributor's organization which takes a film from the producer and lab to its exhibitors (see "Distribution Channels," "Reciprocal Preferences" and "Relationship-Driven Business").

PIRACY. The commercial appropriation, reproduction and distribution of property in contravention of the protections provided by copyright, patent, trademark or trade secret law. Piracy is often committed in foreign territories, i.e., beyond the reach of the owner's jurisdiction. The MPAA takes a lead role in the prevention of piracy. Domestic exhibitors have occasionally been accused of engaging in such activities (see "Jurisdiction," "MPAA" and "NATO").

PITCH. A brief oral presentation made to a studio, production company or other source of development or production financing in order to persuade such financing source to become involved in the production of the movie (see "Pitch Meeting").

PITCH MEETING. A conference between a person who has an idea or concept for a motion picture (which may or may not exist in any written form) for the purpose of presenting that idea to a representative of a development or production financing source, e.g., a production company or studio (see "Idea," "Concept," "Copyright Infringement," "Outline," "Pitch," "Screenplay," "Synopsis," "Treatment" and "Submission Release").

PLAGIARISM. Appropriation of the literary composition of another and passing off as one's own the product of the mind and language of another. The offense of plagiarism is known in the law as infringement of copyright and usually only occurs when the work allegedly copied is protected by copyright. The offense may also refer to copying uncopyrighted or "public domain" works without giving credit to the work being copied (see "Copyright," "Fair Use" and "Public Domain").

PLAINTIFF. The one who initiates a civil lawsuit (see "Defendant," "Litigation" and "Original Paramount Defendants").

PLAN OF BUSINESS. In venture capital fundings, the document prepared by the entity seeking funding and presented to prospective providers of capital which contains a description of the intended business, the principal products to be produced and the principal markets for and methods used in distributing such products. The use of a business plan alone may be adequate for non-securities financing vehicles. In a securities offering, more than a business plan is required, i.e., the business plan forms only one of many required sections of the disclosure document and its contents are determined by the disclosure guidelines which apply to the specific offering contemplated. The plan of business for a feature film limited partnership usually covers proposed activities, significant current statistics regarding the movie industry, partnership management including narrative biographies of key people involved, information on the film or films including history of rights acquisition, screenplay synopsis, production information, marketing and promotion plans, distribution approach, box office comparables, completion bond arrangements, if any, and other financing arrangements, if any (same as "Business Plan;" see "Disclosure Document" and "Venture Capital").

PLAN OF DISTRIBUTION OF UNITS. A required section of the disclosure document in a securities offering which discusses how the securities will be marketed, i.e., through issuer sales, broker/dealer sales and/or finders (see "Corporate Stock," "Limited Partnership" and "Securities").

PLATFORMED. A motion picture that has been exhibited in a few theatres for the purpose of building an audience for the picture before expanding its exhibition to more theatres (see "Platforming," "Release Pattern" and "Rollout").

PLATFORMING. A method of releasing a film in which the film is opened in a single theatre or a small group of key theatres in a major territory with the specific intention of widening the run to numerous theatres either in one step or in phases after the film has established itself (see "Platformed" and "Wide Release").

PLATFORM RELEASE (see "Platformed" and "Platforming").

PLAY. When used as a verb and in the context of motion picture exhibition, the term "play" has the same meaning as "exhibit." A play, as in "live stage play," may form the basis of a screenplay (see "Exhibit," "Live Stage Play" and "Underlying Property").

PLAYDATE. The actual calendar date on which a motion picture opens in a market or nationwide; the actual full-length public showing of a film in its domestic theatrical release (see "Break," "Engagement" and "Prime Theatrical Playdates").

PLAYER. Another term used for actor, actress or performer (see "Actor," "Actress" and "Bit Player").

PLAYER AGREEMENT OR PLAYER DEAL MEMO. A short-form contract for a performer which serves as the memorandum of the minimum negotiated terms between the production company and performer concerning provisions usually most essential to the performer, i.e., compensation, credit and reimbursement of expenses. The form is often used to establish the central deal points when production is about to be commenced and the production company needs the performer to provide his or her services right away. It may also serve as the basis for the preparation of a long form performer agreement (see "Deal Memo," "Fully Negotiated Agreement," "Performer Employment Agreement" and "Short Form Agreement").

PLAYING TIME (same as "Playtime").

PLAYOFF. The distribution of a film after key openings (see "Release Pattern").

PLAYOFF RECORD. A record of the dates and locations at which a film has been exhibited (see "Playoff").

PLAYTIME. The same as the length of a run, i.e., the amount of time, expressed in days, that a film is shown or is expected to be exhibited in a given theatre or market from its opening in that market. Playtime may also mean a particular period of the calendar year such as "Christmas playtime" or "summer playtime" (see "Run").

PLEDGE. A deposit or transfer of personal property (such as securities or the cash surrender value of life insurance) to a lender or creditor as security (collateral) for an obligation or debt. The terms pledge and hypothecate are similar since neither involves the transfer of title (contrast with "Assign;" see "Hypothecate").

PLEDGE AGREEMENT. An agreement relating to a pledge of personal property to a lender or creditor as security (or collateral) for an obligation or debt (see "Collateral," "Debt" and "Pledge").

PLOT. The main story line of a screenplay. If the plot can be described in a very few words, it is considered high concept (see "Hidden Agenda," "High Concept," "One-Line Description," "Synopsis," Sub-plot and "Theme").

PLOT POINT. A turning point in the action of a film's screenplay (see "Plot").

POINTS. The percentage of a film's anticipated profits negotiated or awarded to a participant in the production of the film. For clarity's sake, points must be expressed as a percentage of a specified level of a film's revenue stream, e.g., gross receipts or net profits (see "Gross Receipts," "Net Profits," "Percentage Participation" or "Points," "Profit Participation" and "Revenue Stream").

POLARIZATION. A separation of parts into opposite extremes. Some film industry observers have expressed concern that the industry has become more polarized in recent years, meaning that the differences between the "haves" and the "have nots" have widened. For producers and production companies, this means that, as compared to independent producers, the resources, capabilities, leverage, market power and market share of the major studios has increased, i.e., the barriers to entry in that level of the industry have increased. It also appears that the same is true for the distribution level of the industry as well as exhibition, i.e., the larger organizations have distanced themselves from their competitors (see "Barriers to Entry," "Independent Producer," "Market Power," "Major Exhibition Chains," "Major Studio/ Distributors," "Paramount Consent Decree of 1948" and "TriStar Case").

POLICY. The written contract of insurance (see "Insurable Interest," "Insurance" and "Insured").

POLICY HOLDER. One granted an insurance policy (also called "Policy Owner").

POLICY LOAN. A loan from an insurance company secured by the cash surrender value of a life insurance policy (see "Insurance").

POLISH. Revisions of specific scenes in a movie script, but not a complete rewrite; a special stage in the scriptwriting process between drafts that is recognized by the Writers Guild of America and for which separate compensation is paid, i.e., a polish is a slight revision of a script. A more extensive polish would constitute a revision and a substantial revision would create the next draft. A polish is the writing of changes in dialogue, narration or action in a script, not including a rewrite (see "Development," "Draft," "First Draft," "Final Screenplay," "Revision," "Rewrite," "Script" or "Screenplay" and "Shooting Script").

POLITICAL INFLUENCE. The ability to persuade governmental decision-makers. The most powerful group of companies in the motion picture business, the MPAA, finally realized a long-term goal with the installation of its friend, Ronald Reagan, in the U.S. Presidency during the decade of the 1980s. Reagan did not disappoint the MPAA when he adopted a policy of relaxed federal anti-trust law enforcement for the entertainment industry. That policy change made it possible for some of the MPAA companies to re-enter the exhibition arena, become even more vertically integrated than they had been since the 1940s and regain the additional clout in the market place that would allow them to exert even greater control over the exhibition, distribution and production of feature films and generally at the expense of the independent producers and independent distributors (see "AFMA," "Anti-Trust Laws," "Association Projects," "Lobbying,"

"Market Power," "MPAA," "Paramount Consent Decree of 1948" and "TriStar Case").

POOL (INDUSTRY). A group or combination of individuals or entities organized for the purpose of eliminating competition among the members and combining their resources in order to achieve benefits for themselves. A pool of sufficient size or power to restrict competition throughout a particular trade or industry is illegal under the Sherman Anti-Trust Act (see "Anti-Trust Laws," "Cartel," "MPAA" and "Oligopoly").

POOL (INVESTMENTS). The combination of resources for a common purpose or benefit (see "Blind Pool" and "Limited Partnership").

POOLING AGREEMENTS. Exhibitor agreements with each other and their affiliates by which theatres of two or more of them, normally competitive, are operated as a unit or managed by a joint committee or by one of the exhibitors, the profits being shared according to prearranged percentages. Some of these agreements state that the parties cannot acquire other competitive theatres without first offering them for inclusion in the pool (see "Anti-Trust Laws" and "Product Splitting").

PORNOGRAPHY. Books, magazines, films, pictures and other such material depicting sexual acts that appeal to one's prurient interests (see "Censorable Material" and "Obscene Material").

PORTFOLIO. The combined investment holdings of an individual or institutional investor. Investors seek to diversify their portfolios in order to spread the risk (see "Corporation," "Investor Financing," "Securities" and "Stock").

POSITIVE. A film print made from a negative (or stock shot in the camera with reversal film) with the colors appearing in the appropriate places (see "Negative" and "Print").

POSITIVE CASH FLOW. A business situation in which more cash comes in than goes out in a given accounting period (see "Cash Flow" and "Negative Cash Flow").

POSITIVE PRINT. The phrase "positive print" can be used to mean the raw stock specifically designed for producing a positive image, the positive image itself, positive raw stock that has been exposed but not processed or processed film bearing a positive image (see "Paid Advertising").

POSITIVE REVIEW. A favorable evaluation of a motion picture by a movie critic (see "Blurbs," "Critic" and "Industry Critic").

POSTER. The generic term used to describe printed motion picture display advertisements which are usually in color and which typically contain the basic elements from which movie newspaper ads are made, including a graphic design such as a photograph or drawing, a custom title treatment, a lead line to accompany the title, credits for principal cast and crew, and any outstanding quotes from critical reviews. A movie poster may range in size from the 8 1/2" by 11" sell-sheet to outdoor billboards (see "Lobby Card," "One Sheet," "Print" and "Sell-Sheet").

POSTER SERVICE. A firm which offers guaranteed delivery of movie advertising material to exhibitors (see "Poster").

POST-BREAK PARTICIPATION. Contractual percentage participations due to be paid after reaching a specified form of breakeven, i.e., net profits (see "Actual Breakeven," "Breakeven," "Cash Breakeven," "Gross Participations," "Net Profits" and "Pre-Break Participation").

POST-PAYOUT SHARING RATIO. The percentage ownership interest of a partner in a limited partnership following payout or recoupment (see "Recoupment," "Payout" and "Pre-Payout Sharing Ratio").

POST-PRODUCTION. The final stage in the preparation of a film prior to delivery to the lab on behalf of a distributor. Post-production activities include editing, looping, the application of music, special effects and titles. The post-production process brings all the elements together to form the finished feature film (see "Development," "Delivery," "Pre-Production" and "Principal Photography").

POST-PRODUCTION COSTS. The expenses incurred in the production of a motion picture in the final stage of production, i.e., following principal photography (see "Post-Production").

POST-PRODUCTION SCHEDULE. A listing of the amount of time (usually expressed in terms of weeks) that the various component tasks or stages relating to the production of a film following principal photography will take. For example, the tasks or stages may include laboratory processing, final dubbing, recording sound, scoring and recording music, final cut, director's cut and assemblage or rough cut. This schedule may appear as an exhibit to the director's employment agreement (see "Post-Production").

POST-PRODUCTION SERVICES (OR COMPLETION SERVICES). Feature film production services provided by post-production companies following principal photography. Such services include looping, sound transfers, lab printing, conforming of original picture, graphics and sound mixing (see "Post-Production Sounds").

POST-PRODUCTION SOUNDS. The sounds added to a movie during post-production, including dialogue, sound effects and music added by the dialogue editor, sound effects editor, composer and music editor, respectively (see "Post-Production").

POST-SYNCHING OR SYNCHRONIZATION. The re-recording of film dialogue or sound in an acoustically proper environment. This post-production technique is used when sound has been recorded unsatisfactorily at the time of shooting or when it was impossible or difficult to record the actual sounds or dialogue while shooting. Post-synchronization is also used to translate a film's dialogue from one language to another (see "Automatic Dialogue Replacement").

POTENTIAL COMPETITORS. Prospective business rivals. The U.S. Justice Department merger guidelines suggest that if a proposed vertical merger effectively forces actual or potential competitors to enter or continue in the distribution or exhibition business on a vertically integrated basis, then such proposed vertical merger is less likely to meet with the approval of the Justice Department (see "Actual Competitors," "Merger Guidelines," "Paramount Consent Decree of 1948," "TriStar Case," "Vertical Integration" and "Vertical Merger").

POTENTIAL DOWNSIDE (see "Downside Exposure").

POTENTIAL UPSIDE (see "Upside Potential").

POWER. The possession of control or influence over others (see "Major Exhibition Chains," "Major Studio/Distributors," "Market Power," "Market Share," "Merger Guidelines," "Number of Screens," "Predatory Practices" and "Reciprocal Preference").

POWER OF ATTORNEY. A written instrument by which one person, as principal, appoints another as his or her agent and confers upon such agent the authority to perform certain specified acts or kinds of acts on behalf of the principal. Such powers of attorney may be made irrevocable. Often, the subscription agreement in a film limited partnership will include a power of attorney which, among other things, authorizes the general partner to sign the limited partnership agreement on behalf of the investors, i.e., subscribers (see "Agency," "Attorney-in-Fact" and "Proxy").

POWER COUPLED WITH AN INTEREST. A power over property that is accompanied by or connected with an interest in the property subject to the power. Under the law of agency, when an agent has a power over property and also has a beneficial interest in that property, the principal may not revoke the agent's power until the interest has expired or unless the principal and agent have agreed otherwise (see "Agent" and "Power of Attorney").

PRE-BREAK PARTICIPATION. Contractual percentage participations due to be paid prior to achieving a specified form of breakeven in a motion picture's revenue stream, i.e., a gross participation. Since gross participations are deducted from gross receipts earlier in the revenue stream, they effectively reduce (and in many instances eliminate altogether) all net profit participations. Anyone negotiating for a net profit participation with a studio on a studio financed film would be wise to inquire as to whether the studio has or intends to award any gross participations on the project. A studio may play a game of semantics and contend that net profits are not being reduced by gross participations since the concept of net profits inherently contemplates certain deductions from gross receipts. Prospective net profit participants (or their representatives) should counter that after the applicable breakeven point there should be no separate treatment for gross participants since the gross participation is merely another form of net profit participation expressed in a different way, especially in the case of gross participations which only begin after a specified form of breakeven is achieved and which are calculated on a rolling breakeven basis (see "Actual Breakeven," "Artificial Breakeven," "Cash Breakeven," "Gross Participations," "Net Profits," "Post-Break Participation" and "Rolling Breakeven").

PRE-CONDITIONS. Requirements that must be met in advance. For example, in a distribution agreement awarding final cutting rights to the director, the distributor may impose certain pre-conditions upon such rights, i.e., the cost of production must not exceed 110% of the approved production budget and contingency, the picture as delivered must substantially and materially conform to the approved screenplay, the picture must have a running time of not less than 95 nor more than 110 minutes with a rating no more restrictive than "R," the picture and all major delivery items must be fully delivered on the dates required in the distribution agreement and the director's final cutting rights must be exercised so as not to conflict with the picture's planned release schedule and the distributor's bidding practices (see "Approved Production Budget," "Blind Bidding," "Final Cut" and "Running Time").

PREDATORY PRACTICES. An aggressive manner of conducting business which is designed to exploit or destroy others for the gain of the business (see "Adhesion Contract," "Cartel," "Conduct Restrictions," "Inferior Bargaining Position," "Mini-Majors," "Polarization" and "Reciprocal Preferences").

PREEMPTIVE RIGHT. A right giving existing stockholders the opportunity to purchase shares of a new issue before it is offered to others. Its purpose is to protect shareholders from dilution of value and control when new corporate shares are issued (see "Offering" and "Rights Offering").

PRE-EXISTING RELATIONSHIP. One of the conditions directly or indirectly required for compliance with the federal and state transactional exemptions from the securities registration requirement in order to avoid a prohibited general solicitation. Generally, a pre-existing relationship includes any relationship consisting of personal or business contacts of a nature and duration such as would enable a reasonably prudent purchaser to be aware of the character, business acumen and general business and financial circumstances of the person with whom such relationship exists (see "Finder," "Regulation D" and "Subscription Application and Agreement").

PRE-FEATURE ENTERTAINMENT. Programs exhibited at theatres prior to the feature film, i.e., film shorts, cartoons, newsreels, reports on the music industry, "ask a celebrity" presentations, etc. (see "Cartoon" and "Short").

PREFERRED STOCK. A class of capital stock that pays dividends at a specified rate and that has preference over common stock in the payment of dividends and the liquidation of assets. Generally, preferred stock does not carry voting rights (see "Common Stock," "Dividends" and "Stock").

PRE-FORMATION INTERESTS. Interests (units) in a film limited partnership that are being offered prior to the formation of the limited partnership, i.e., a limited partnership to be formed (see "Limited Partnership" and "Unit").

PRE-FORMATION LIMITED PARTNERSHIP INTERESTS. Units of a limited partnership offered prior to the actual formation of the limited partnership. Generally, in such instances, the partnership is formed shortly after the minimum offering is funded (see "Limited Partnership" and "Unit").

PREJUDICE. Preconceived judgment or opinion; an irrational attitude of hostility directed against an individual, a group, a race or their supposed characteristics (see "Bias," "Discrimination," "Insider's Game," "Member of the Club," "Nepotism," "Pattern of Bias," "Regional Prejudice" and "Relationship-Driven Business").

PRELIMINARY/DEVELOPMENT DISCLOSURE DOCUMENT. The written information which is required to be disclosed to prospective passive investors in a preliminary/development offering (see "Development Financing," "Disclosure Document" and "Investment Contract").

PRELIMINARY/DEVELOPMENT FUNDS. A term similar in meaning to the venture-capital concepts of start-up monies and seed capital but more typically associated with feature film investment contract offerings raising something in the neighborhood of $50,000 to $150,000 to fund the development of a film or films along with the up front costs associated with preparing a subsequent "main offering" feature film limited partnership offering (see "Development Money Investment Agreement," "Investment Contract," "Investor Financing Agreement," "Preliminary Investors" and "Preliminary/Development Offering").

PRELIMINARY/DEVELOPMENT OFFERING. A film financing transaction specifically designed to raise funds from passive investors and to pay for the costs associated with the development phase of a film project as well as any expenses incurred in seeking production financing, e.g., through a studio/distributor or a subsequent film limited partnership offering. A preliminary/development offering structured as an investment contract for passive investors would generally be considered a securities offering and investment interests sold in such an offering would have to be offered and sold in compliance with the federal and state securities laws (see "Development," "Development Money Investment Agreement" and "Preliminary Investors").

PRELIMINARY FUNDING (see "Development Funds").

PRELIMINARY INVESTORS. Individuals or entities who provide development funds for a motion picture project through an investment vehicle such as an investment contract (see "Development Funds," "Preliminary/Development Funds," "Preliminary/Development Agreement" and "Seed Money").

PRELIMINARY OFFERING CIRCULAR. A securities disclosure document which is permitted to be used pursuant to the SEC's Regulation A to allow the solicitation of indications of interest from prospective purchasers prior to the SEC clearance date (see "Prospectus" and "Regulation A").

PRELIMINARY PROSPECTUS. The initial securities disclosure document provided to prospective investors by an underwriter or broker/dealer relating to a new issue of securities in a public/registered offering (see "Disclosure Document" and "Red Herring").

PREMIERE. The first official public showing of a theatrical film in a specific theatre, the first airing of a film on television or the screening of the first segment of a new TV series (see "Opening" and "Premiere Benefit").

PREMIERE BENEFIT. The first official public showing of a theatrical film, all or a portion of the proceeds of which are to be donated to a designated charity (see "Premiere").

PREMIUM. The fee paid to an insurance company for insurance protection (see "Insurance").

PRE-MIX SESSION. The combining of several soundtracks at an early stage in the creation of a composite soundtrack which is designed to make the eventual final mix less complicated (see "Soundtracks").

PRE-OPENING ADVERTISING. Film advertising carried prior to the opening of a film (see "Advertising").

PRE-PACKAGED. A feature film project that already has significant elements attached before its producer approaches either a prospective financier or distributor (see "Elements" and "Package").

PREPAYMENT CLAUSE. A provision in loan agreements that permits prepayment of the loan at any time without penalty. If such a provision is not contained in the agreement, the lender may charge a fee if the loan is paid off before it is due (see "Debt," "Lender Financing" and "Prepayment Penalty").

PREPAYMENT PENALTY. A fee paid by a borrower to a bank when a loan that does not have a prepayment clause is repaid before its scheduled maturity (see "Prepayment Clause" and "Right of Prepayment").

PRE-PAYOUT SHARING RATIO. The percentage ownership interest of a partner in a limited partnership prior to payout or recoupment (see "Payout," "Recoupment" and "Post-Payout Sharing Ratio").

PRE-PRINT LABORATORY WORK. Activities relating to the preparation of a specific film at the film laboratory and prior to the printing of the camera negative or positive work prints (see "Laboratory").

PRE-PRODUCTION. The earliest phase of film production (as opposed to development), although there may be some overlap between the two phases. Pre-production, for example, may encompass polishing and breaking down the script for budgeting purposes, preparing story boards, hiring or obtaining letters of intent from creative personnel (including the director and principal cast), establishing shooting locations and shooting schedules, preparing the budgets, casting, the finalization of creative decisions and such other steps as are necessary to prepare for the actual commencement of photography. The pre-production stage of the film will generally extend from two to three months, although this time period may vary widely from film to film. Principal photography follows the pre-production stage [see "Development," "Letter of Intent (Film)" and "Letter of Intent (Completion Guarantor)"].

PRE-PRODUCTION FINANCING (see "Development Financing," "Negative Pickup," "Pre-Production" and "Pre-Sale Financing").

PREQUEL. A feature film that is released after the original but which actually tells a related story that occurred before the story depicted in the earlier released film (see "Remake" and "Sequel").

PRE-SALE AGREEMENT. A contract relating to the licensing of motion pictures which is negotiated and signed prior to the completion of the film and sometimes before the start of principal photography. Such agreements sometimes result in monetary advances or otherwise may be used by independent feature film producers as a form of security or collateral for a discounted bank loan or to aid in obtaining production financing from financiers or investors. Generally, in order to be "bankable" or "lendable," such agreements must guarantee a specific amount of money by a certain date and the payment of such sum should not be dependent on too many contingencies (see "Debt," "Lender Financing," "Monetary Advances," "Multiple Pre-Sales," "Negative Pickup," "Pre-Sale Financing" and "Split-Rights Basis").

PRE-SALE COMMITMENT (see "Pre-Sale Financing").

PRE-SALE DISTRIBUTION GUARANTEES (see "Pre-Sale Financing").

PRE-SALE FINANCING. The funding of a film's production costs through the granting of a license for film rights by a producer in a particular media or territory prior to completion of the film. Pre-sales may take the form of funds, guarantees or commitments which may be obtained or used to obtain funds, in addition to other available production financing in the form of cash advances or guarantees paid by domestic or foreign distributors, pay or cable television systems, video cassette producers, television syndicators, and/or bank loans obtained by using such cash advances or guarantees as collateral. For example, if a producer had a contract for the pre-sale of a movie to a U.S. or foreign distributor, a home video company, a pay TV service or a TV syndicator, the producer might be able to present those contractual commitments to a bank and walk away with cash (for a fee). However, pre-sales are based on contingencies, e.g., the actual collection of moneys due from movie theatres and international distributors has generally turned out to be much more difficult than anticipated (see "Monetary Advances," "Pre-Production Financing," "Pre-Sale Agreement" and "Split-Rights Deal").

PRE-SALE GUARANTEE (see "Distribution Guarantee," "Guarantee" and "Pre-Sale Financing").

PRE-SALES (see "Pre-Sale Financing").

PRE-SCREENING. Exhibitions of a motion picture or components of the movie conducted in order to get preliminary audience reaction to help the producer and distributor make decisions about what to or what not to include in the final version (see "Focus Group," "Preview" and "Screening").

PRESENT VALUE. The value today of a future payment, or stream of payments, discounted at some appropriate compound interest or discount rate, e.g., the present value of $1,000 to be received ten years from today would be approximately $385.50, using a discount rate equal to 10% interest compounded annually. The present value method is used to measure the return on investment (same as "Discounted Cash Flow," "Rate of Return" and "Time Value of Money").

PRESS AGENT (see "Publicist").

PRESS KIT. Part of the basic film advertising campaign package designed to be offered to the media; it generally consists of a portfolio type case containing ad mats, synopsis of the film's story, cast and crew list, narrative biographies of the director and stars, copies of the film's critical reviews, 8 x 10 stills from the film, running time for the film and suggested publicity articles for adaptation by the local media. The press book is sent by the distributor to sub-distributors and exhibitors and is designed to give them a feeling for what the film is about and provide them with the information that reporters and critics may request (see "Campaign Package," "Publicity Articles" and "Support Materials").

PRESS PACKET (see "Press Kit").

PRESS RELEASE. A prepared statement released to the news media for their use and consideration in preparing their news reports. Generally, press releases are issued by a company's management regarding events or occurrences it considers noteworthy (see "Promotional Activities" and "Trades").

PRESS TOUR. An important part of motion picture publicity campaigns in which a film's director and/or stars are made available for local newspaper, magazine and radio/television talk show interviews in the major cities in which the film opens. Generally, the participation of such persons, the number of appearances or the amount of time required are negotiable items in the contractual agreements which commit the director and actors to a movie (contrast with "Junket").

PREVIEW. An advance showing of a film before its scheduled release date, usually to invited groups, like the press or industry executives to help spread good word-of-mouth or to the paying public as part of a test marketing program. Editing changes are sometimes made after such tests (see "Screening," "Sneak Preview," "Test Marketing" and "Word-of-Mouth").

PRICE CASE. A lawsuit in which the plaintiff has the burden of showing that the terms of the litigated agreement are so disparate from market prices that the contract is unconscionable (see "Contract of Adhesion," "Market Power" and "Unconscionable").

PRICE DISCRIMINATION. The practice of charging different persons different prices for the same goods or services. When price discrimination is engaged in for the purpose of lessening competition, for instance, through tying the lower prices to the purchase of goods or services, it constitutes a violation of the Sherman Anti-Trust Act. Unlawful price discrimination is also specifically covered by the Clayton Act and by the Robinson-Patman Act (see "Anti-Trust Laws" and "Price Fixing").

PRICE/EARNINGS RATIO (P/E). The current market price of a share of a corporation's stock divided by its earnings per share over a twelve-month period. The P/E ratio gives investors an idea of how much they are paying for a company's earning power (same as "Multiple;" see "Corporate Stock").

PRICE FIXING. Under the federal anti-trust laws, a combination or conspiracy formed for the purpose and with the effect of raising, depressing, fixing, pegging or stabilizing the price of a commodity in interstate commerce. The test is not what the actual effect is on prices but whether such agreements interfere with the freedom of traders and thereby restrains their ability to sell in accordance with their own judgment (see "Anti-Trust Laws," "Horizontal Price Fixing" and "Vertical Price Fixing").

PRICING AMENDMENT. The amendment to the registration statement in a securities public offering which includes information regarding the price of the offering, underwriters' compensation, the list of underwriters in the syndicate and the issuer's latest responses to the SEC's comment letter (see "Comment Letter," "IPO" and "Public Offering").

PRIMA DONNA. An extremely sensitive, vain or undisciplined performer. In the case of a film, a prima donna is more likely to be an actor or director and may cause delays or other problems for a production which may translate into higher production costs (see "Auteur," "Collaborative Process," "Completion Guarantor," "Director," "Final Cut," "Perfectionist Director," "Perks" and "Star").

PRIMARY AUDIENCE. A specific demographic population to which a movie is believed to have the most appeal and at which such movie is primarily aimed (same as "Target Audience;" see "Appeal," Audience," "Projected Audience" and "Test Marketing").

PRIMARY CAMPAIGN. The initial film advertising and promotional program which is designed around a specific theme and to attract a given audience segment (see "Advertising Campaign" and "Alternate Campaign").

PRIMARY DISTRIBUTION. The sale of a new issue of securities, as distinguished from a secondary distribution, which involves previously issued securities (same as "Primary Offering," but contrast with "Initial Public Offering;" see "Underwrite").

PRIMARY LOCATIONS. The most important locations to be used for a film. In location scouting, generally the primary locations are sought first, then nearby secondary locations are acquired (see "Location").

PRIMARY INSURANCE. The basic insurance coverage provided by a policy with its initial ceiling on the amount which will be paid out on any claim or claims under such policy (see "Errors and Omissions Insurance," "Excess Insurance Coverage" and "Reinsurance").

PRIMARY OFFERING (same as "Primary Distribution;" see "Underwriting").

PRIME FOREIGN TERRITORIES. The United Kingdom, the Scandinavian countries, France, Germany, Italy, Spain, Japan, Turkey and Australia (similar to "Major Foreign Markets").

PRIME PLAYDATE. The best calendar date on which to open a motion picture (see "Christmas Season" and "Playdate").

PRIME RATE. The interest rate banks charge their most credit-worthy customers. Loans to less credit-worthy borrowers are often tied to the prime rate, i.e., a few percentage points above prime (see "Actual Interest" and "Interest").

PRIME RELEASE DATE. The most advantageous date on which to first open a motion picture, in a particular market and/or nationally (see "Release Date" and "Summer Season").

PRIME SCHEDULES (see "Prime Theatrical Playdates").

PRIME THEATRICAL PLAYDATES. The actual calendar dates or periods which, based on past performance, tend to produce the largest movie-going audiences for feature films, e.g., Christmas holidays and summer. Successful independent distributors have commonly used the strategy of not releasing their movies during such periods so as to avoid direct competition with motion pictures released by the major/studio distributors (see "Anti-Trust Laws," "Competition," "Market Power," "Market Share" and "Playdate").

PRINCIPAL. In general, the major party to a transaction or the owner of a privately held business. In the law of agency, a principal is one who has permitted or directed another to act for such principal and subject to his or her direction or control. With respect to investments, the principal is the basic amount invested, exclusive of earnings. In banking and finance, the term refers to (1) the face amount of a debt instrument or deposit on which interest is either owed or earned and (2) the balance of a debt, separate from interest (see "Debt," "Interest," "Lender Financing" and "Surety").

PRINCIPAL ARTISTS' CONTRACTS. Employment agreements relating to the services of the major feature actors (see "Employment Agreements").

PRINCIPAL ASSETS. The most important property of a company (see "Asset").

PRINCIPAL CAST MEMBERS (see "Principals" and "Principal Players").

PRINCIPAL PHOTOGRAPHY. The actual filming of all scripted material covering most of the speaking parts in a film and the time period during which such filming occurs (see "Development," "Post-Production," "Pre-Production" and "Second Unit").

PRINCIPALS OR PRINCIPAL PLAYERS. The main featured actors in a film who have major speaking parts. Some union definitions specify that a principal player is a performer engaged to speak or mime eleven or more lines of dialogue, or an actor engaged to perform a major role without dialogue (see "Guild" and "Lead").

PRINCIPAL STOCKHOLDER. Corporate stockholder who owns a significant number of shares in a corporation. SEC rules specify that a principal stockholder is a person who owns 10% or more of the voting stock of a publicly held corporation (see "Corporation," "Insider," "Majority Shareholder" and "Sole Shareholder").

PRINCIPAL SUM (same as "Principal").

PRINT. Copies of a film which are distributed to theatres; the print is a positive made from an original (or dupe) negative which is used for projection. A print is a copy made from the master for the purpose of motion-picture presentation, i.e., the specific motion-picture release. The master is preserved for additional duplication. A distribution company may make only a few copies or some 2,000-plus prints depending on the coverage desired for a particular motion picture. The term "print" also refers to movie advertising placed in newspapers and magazines and by means of posters (see "General Release," "Limited Release," "Poster" and "Wide Release").

PRINT COSTS. The expenses incurred in making a film's release prints for theatrical exhibition. The cost of a single print may be in the $2,000 range; thus, if a distributor were to effect a 2,000-print release, its print costs would equal $4,000,000. Clearly, then, print costs are one of the major distribution expenses (advertising being the other) and present a significant opportunity for overstating the amount or for possible kickback arrangements (see "Audit," "Discounts," "Kickbacks," "Prints and Ads," "Rebates" and "Release Print").

PRINTS AND ADS. The film prints actually distributed to theatres for exhibition and the advertising which promotes the film. The number of prints actually made and used in the release of films varies widely from only a few to more than 2,000 or more and as such can be a major expense in the distribution of a film (see "Direct Distribution Expenses" and "Print Costs").

PRINTS AND ADS BUDGET. The funds allocated to be spent on the costs associated with printing copies of the film for exhibition and the advertising for such film (see "Advertising," "Print" and "Print Costs").

PRINTS AND ADS COMMITMENT. The promise by a film distributor or others to expend a certain amount on prints and advertising for a movie. Minimum levels of prints and advertising in the theatrical release may also be required by home video companies in order to trigger a particular deal with such companies. In some circumstances, it may also be to the advantage of a film's producer and other net profit participants to place a ceiling on the amount of prints and ads expenses that a distributor may incur in the distribution of the producer's film without the producer's approval (see "Distribution Commitment" and "Print Costs").

PRINTS AND ADS FINANCING AGREEMENT. A contract between an independent feature film producer or production company and a financier in which the financier agrees to provide the monies necessary to pay for the prints and advertising of a film in return for a specified payback. Such an agreement with active industry parties, e.g., film labs or distributors may be structured as a joint venture agreement. On the other hand, if the financier is a passive investor, compliance with the federal and state securities laws may be required (see "Prints and Ads Budget" and "Rent-A-Distributor").

PRIORITY OF RUN (same as "Clearance").

PRIORITY RECOUPMENT. An earlier position in a revenue stream for the recovery of invested or expended funds than another or other positions. Generally, in the current marketplace, distributor-paid prints and ads expenditures have a priority recoupment position, i.e., such costs are recovered by the distributor before almost all other deductions from the revenue stream (except for the distributor's fees and possibly the limited off-the-top expenses). On the other hand, in a lender-financed motion picture transaction, the lender will contractually impose a priority recoupment position for its principal, interest and fees over all other parties. In a film limited partnership, unless the producer/general partner successfully negotiates a priority recoupment position on behalf of the partnership's investors, the limited partners will have to rely on net profit participations or some similar specified portion of the revenue stream to recoup their investment (see "Inter-Party Agreement," "Negative Pickup" and "When the Money's Paid").

PRIOR PERFORMANCE. The past results of similar movies. In the context of limited partnerships, the past results of operations of prior partnerships operated by the same general partner (see "Box Office Comparables" and "Limited Partnership").

PRIVACY, RIGHT OF. A general right to be left alone; a right to live life free from unwarranted publicity; a generic term encompassing various rights recognized to be inherent in the concept of ordered liberty. Invasions of one's privacy constitute a tort for which remedies are available. The four different types of torts are (1) appropriation, or the use of a person's name, picture, or likeness as a symbol of his or her identity without compensation; (2) an intrusion upon a person's physical solitude or seclusion; (3) the public disclosure of private facts; and (4) placing a person in a false light in the public eye by associating this person with beliefs or activities with which this person has no connection (contrast with "Publicity Rights;" see "Clearance," "Errors and Omissions Insurance" and "Tort").

PRIVATE CORPORATION (see "Closed Corporation").

PRIVATE LIMITED PARTNERSHIP. A limited partnership which did not register the offering of limited partnership interests with the SEC or with the state securities regulators in each state in which such securities were to be offered and sold but instead relied on available exemptions from such securities registration requirement (see "Private Placement" and "Regulation D").

PRIVATE LITIGATION. A lawsuit that does not involve the government, i.e., the parties are civil litigants. In addition to both criminal and civil sanctions that may be pursued in court by the U.S. Justice Department, the federal anti-trust laws provide civil remedies for private citizens and/or businesses (see "Anti-Trust Laws" and "Damages").

PRIVATELY HELD CORPORATION (see "Closed Corporation").

PRIVATE OFFERING (same as "Private Placement").

PRIVATE PLACEMENT. Generally, any offer or sale of a security (e.g., limited partnership interests or corporate stock) that is not required to be registered with either the state or federal securities regulatory authorities because such offers or sales comply with all of the conditions and limitations imposed on the use of specific federal and state exemptions from the securities registration requirements. The issuer in a private offering is not allowed to advertise or generally solicit. The offering costs associated with a private placement are generally much lower than in a public offering and the offering can generally be "on the street" (i.e., sales can start) sooner (same as "Exempt Offering" or "Private Offering;" see "Public Limited Partnership," "Public Offering," "Registered Offering," "Small Offering Exemption" and "Regulation D").

PRIVATE PLACEMENT OFFERING MEMORANDUM. The securities disclosure document provided to prospective purchasers which must fully disclose all material aspects of the transaction and not omit any information which would be an important consideration in a prospective investor's decision as to whether to invest or not (see "Disclosure Document," "Memorandum," "Offering Memorandum" and "Prospectus").

PRIVATE SECURITIES TRANSACTION. A securities transaction in which an associated person (i.e., a person associated with an NASD member broker/dealer firm, e.g., a registered representative) sells a security to an investor on behalf of another party (e.g., as part of a private offering of limited partnership interests) without the prescribed participation of the associated person's employer broker/ dealer firm. Such transactions are prohibited by the NASD (see "Broker/Dealer," "NASD" and "Registered Representative").

PRIVATIZATION. The conversion from government control to nongovernment, i.e., public ownership and control, for example as in the ownership and control of television in many European countries in recent years (see "Foreign Market").

PRO AND CON ANALYSIS. An objective evaluation of the advantages and disadvantages of the various forms of film finance available to a producer for a given film project. In the world of film finance, producers are confronted with a bewildering array of production funding choices and unfortunately in their written, panel and lecture presentations relating to film finance, many industry professionals with bona fide expertise in a narrow area of film finance tend to stress the advantages of the form of film finance he or she favors without objectively discussing the disadvantages. The producer, on the other hand, must look beyond such self-serving presentations and demand a realistic appraisal of the disadvantages associated with the particular form of film finance being discussed. As the producer's research progresses, he or she will eventually want to be in a position to objectively analyze the pros and cons of several available forms of film finance as applied to a specific film project (see "Advantage," "Availability Analysis," "Disadvantage" and "Financing").

PROBABLE CAUSE. Facts and circumstances within one's knowledge and of which one has reasonably trustworthy information, sufficient in themselves to warrant a person of reasonable caution to believe the assertion that has been made (see "Bad Faith Denial of Contract").

PROBLEM PRODUCER. A term used to describe a producer considered by the person applying the label to be difficult to work with as a film producer or who does not play along with some of the inequities in the studio/distributor dominated U.S. film industry (see "Blacklist," "Completion Guarantor" and "Discrimination").

PROCEEDS. In a loan context, funds given to a borrower after all costs and fees have been deducted (see "Debt" and "Lender Financing").

PROCEEDS OF THE OFFERING. Funds raised by means of a securities offering (see "Gross Proceeds of the Offering" and "Net Proceeds of the Offering").

PRODUCED BY CREDIT. The acknowledgment which appears on the motion picture screen and sets forth the name of the film's producer (see "Co-Production Credit" and "Producer").

PRODUCER. The person who carries ultimate responsibility for the original shaping and final outcome of a film, although the distributor may insist on certain editing rights which may allow such distributor considerable discretion in changing the film once delivered to such distributor. The producer generally finds and develops a film project, hires the writer or writers, develops the script, hires the director and actors, arranges for financing and oversees the production of the film. For the purposes of anti-trust law analysis, the producer or production company is the manufacturer of a product (the film) and the distributor is a wholesaler (there may be different levels of wholesaling involved, e.g., sub-distribution) and the exhibitor is the retailer (see "Collaborative Process," "Creative Producer," "Director," "Editing Rights," "Executive Producer," "Filmmaker," "Independent Producer," "Line Producer," "Producers Guild of America" and "Studio Producer").

PRODUCER AGREEMENTS. All motion picture documentation, i.e., contracts or employment agreements relating to feature film producers, including executive producers and line producers. Such agreements are usually executed as between the studio or production company and the producer (see "Independent Producer," "Producer Employment Agreement" and "Production Company").

PRODUCER CREDITS. The on-screen acknowledgment of the persons who performed certain production or financing related functions with respect to a motion picture. Producer credits may include executive producer, producer, line producer, associate producer, co-producer, assistant producer, supervising producer, "a production of" and "produced by." Unfortunately, since no guild or association has jurisdiction to control the granting of producer credits, the producer credit is sometimes used to reward persons who are not really producers at all and has reportedly been used to help some otherwise undeserving persons to become members of the Academy. This aspect of the credits problem, of course, raises questions about the entire membership selection process at the Academy and the credibility of its Oscar winning selections (see "Academy of Motion Picture Arts & Sciences," "Academy Awards," "Member of the Club," "PGA," "Reciprocal Preferences" and "Relationship-Driven Business").

PRODUCER DEFERMENT. The agreed upon delayed payment of compensation due a producer. Low-budget producers often find it helpful to defer some or all of their fee when seeking financing for their project (see "Deferrals" and "Producer").

PRODUCER/DIRECTOR UNDERTAKINGS. Written promises by a film's producer and director, required by a completion guarantor as a prerequisite to the issuance of a completion bond, (1) providing assurances that the full financing necessary to fund the budgeted cost of the picture (including a contingency amount of usually 10% and the completion guarantor's fee) is available to the producer to be spent on the picture, (2) to stay within the budget in casting the film and to limit expenses, (3) by the director that the budget, shooting schedule and post-production schedule are achievable and that the allocation of film stock in the budget is sufficient, (4) that the film's music and related clearances will be obtained within the budgeted amounts, (5) that any delivery requirements pursuant to any distribution agreements and any publicity costs that are in excess of the approved budget will be considered to be distribution costs and expenses and will not be chargeable to the production budget and (6) that legal fees charged to the production budget will be limited to the amounts budgeted (see "Completion Bond").

PRODUCER EMPLOYMENT AGREEMENT. A contract between the producing entity or production company and the producer which includes provisions relating to the producer's compensation and credit, the producer's rights with respect to the basic property and the producer's responsibility for ensuring that the motion picture is completed (see "Independent Producer" and "Production Company").

PRODUCER PARTICIPATION ALTERNATIVES. Other ways for a film's producer to be compensated for his or her services in producing a film besides participating in the distributor's gross receipts. Such alternatives may include the payment of a specified bonus for every increment of distributor gross receipts or box office gross the film generates above a certain level, the payment of a bonus on the sale of a certain number of videocassettes, letting the producer retain the rights to exploit a film in a certain territory or medium (e.g., television syndication) or paying the producer with options to purchase stock in the distribution company (see "Net Profit Participant" and "Video Corridor").

PRODUCER'S ADVANCE. Money paid by a film's distributor to its producer prior to release of the producer's film. Such advances may be paid upon signing of the distribution agreement and/or upon delivery of the picture (see "Advance" or "Advances" and "Up-Front Distribution Money").

PRODUCER'S APPROVALS AND CONTROLS. Language negotiated for inclusion in some feature film distribution agreements which provides that the producer of a film has mutual approval (with the distributor) over certain matters relating to distribution, e.g., advertising, marketing and publicity, campaign strategy, release plan and the pricing strategy and advertising campaign for the home video release. This section of the distribution agreement may also provide that the distributor does not have any right to edit, alter or change the picture after the director's final cut, except to add the distributor's logo and releasing credit, and except as legally required for government censorship or time slot requirements, in which event the agreement may provide that the director will have the right to perform the necessary editing to comply with the censorship or time slot requirements (see "Collaborative Process" and "Final Cut").

PRODUCER'S DEVELOPMENT DEAL. A financing arrangement provided to a producer for covering the costs associated with the earliest stage in the production of a motion picture, i.e., the development of the screenplay. The phrase "producer's development deal" is sometimes used to distinguish such transactions from development deals awarded to writers or directors (see "Development" and "Development Deal").

PRODUCER'S ERRORS AND OMISSIONS INSURANCE (see "Errors and Omissions").

PRODUCER'S FEE. Compensation paid to a film's producer out of the budget of the film. Also the up-front payment to the person who has developed a film project and sells it to a studio for production and distribution. In most situations, the producer's fee is the only compensation a feature film producer will receive for the production of a film, since net profits are rarely generated (see "Contingent Compensation," "Gross Receipts," "Independent Producer" and "Net Profits").

PRODUCERS GUILD OF AMERICA (PGA). An organization created partly for the purpose of correcting the use of inappropriate screen credits for executive producers, producers and associate producers. However, the PGA, unlike the Writers Guild or the Directors Guild, is not recognized as a collective-bargaining agency and has no specific legal jurisdiction over the dispensation of credits. In 1983, when the PGA tried to gain such status, the National Labor Relations Board ruled that producers cannot be a union because their jobs are essentially managerial. That appears to be true for independent producers but not necessarily the case with producers who are employees of the major/studio distributors. As a result of the NLRB's decision and the PGA's own narrow focus, independent producers are left without any industry organization which is exclusively devoted to the vigorous advocacy of the interests of independent producers in whatever forum such interests arise. Independent producers must organize some form of association of independent feature-film producers (much like the American Film Marketing Association—the trade group representing the interests of independent distributors) in order to protect their interests at the industry level (see "AFMA," AIVF," "American Academy of Independent Film Producers," "Association Projects," "IFP," "IFP/West," "Model Agreement" and "RIPOFF").

PRODUCER'S INSURANCE POLICY. A special type of insurance contract which incorporates most or all of the various kinds of insurance coverages that relate to the production of motion pictures (see "Insurance" and "Insurance Coverages").

PRODUCER'S LIABILITY INSURANCE (see "Insurance Coverages" and "Producer's Insurance Policy").

PRODUCER'S NET OR PRODUCER'S NET PROFITS. Monies received by the producer for the exploitation of a film over and above the producer's expenses in producing such film (see "Net Profits," "Producer's Fee" and "Producer's Share").

PRODUCER'S PACKAGE. The written presentation prepared by a film producer which describes or otherwise represents the elements of a planned film project and is used in obtaining financing and/or distribution arrangements. Depending on at what stage it is presented to prospective financiers and/or distributors, the package may include some or all of the following items: title report, copyright search report, chain of title documents including certificate of authorship for the screenplay, a copy of the copyright registration(s) (some register the screenplay, the music and the film), corporate resolution authorizing the producer to negotiate and sign a distribution deal, final screenplay and shooting script, proposed cast and production credits, synopsis of the script, biographies of key people, feature stories on lead actors and director, production stills, casual cast photos, agreements relating to the film's music, MPAA certificate (if available) and the E&O certificate of insurance (see "Choosing a Distributor," "Distribution Alternatives," "Financing" and "Package").

PRODUCER'S REPRESENTATIVE. A person who is authorized by a motion picture producer to act on behalf of the producer in the conduct of the producer's business affairs, e.g., in negotiating script option or acquisition agreements, development deals, personnel agreements, production financing arrangements and distribution agreements. Although not required, many producer's representatives are attorneys. A producer's attorney, on the other hand, does not become a producer's representative, unless such attorney goes beyond advising the client and the drafting of documents and actually becomes involved in the direct negotiation of the producer's deals with the parties on the other side of the transaction (see "Agent," "Executive Producer," "Entertainment Attorney," "Packaging Attorney," "Personal Manager" and "Personal Representative").

PRODUCER'S ROYALTY. Payments to a feature film producer or production company for the rights to exploit certain of the ancillary rights associated with a motion picture, e.g., for the soundtrack album. As an example, the film distribution agreement may provide with respect to producer royalties on the film's soundtrack album that two-thirds of the amount of any advance from the record company acquiring the soundtrack distribution rights in excess of the cost of production of the soundtrack and soundtrack album for the picture (including, but not limited to, producer advances, artist's advances, third-party costs and all other costs which are customarily recognized in the phonograph record industry) is payable to the production company for its own account with the remaining one-third payable to the film distributor (see "Royalties" and "Soundtrack Albums").

PRODUCER'S SHARE. A term defined in some distribution agreements as the accountable gross remaining after the deduction, on a continuing basis, of the aggregate of the distributor's distribution fees, distribution expenses and gross participations, if any. Some distribution agreements provide that third-party participations, if any, be deducted from the producer's share. The reasoning used to support this position is that the producer, to a greater or lesser extent, is responsible for the production of the motion picture, including all of the associated costs, i.e., the producer is responsible for negotiating and allowing such third-party participations (which include talent participations since talent is not a party to the distribution agreement between the producer and distributor). Thus, logically (from the distributor's point of view) the producer should pay the costs of these contingent commitments to talent out of the producer's portion of the film's revenue stream, i.e., out of net profits. The producer may readily agree with this analysis since the producer and all other net profit participants are likely to fare better if they are paid on a pari passu basis with the talent as opposed to allowing talent to receive gross participations. On the other hand, in the studio/distributor financed films, gross participations are sometimes also defined as a production cost and thus the studio/distributor collects interest and overhead charges on these "expenses" which were never actually paid out by the studio/distributor (see "Accountable Gross," "Creative Accounting," "Gross Participations," "Interest" and "Pari Passu").

PRODUCING ENTITY. In instances where a film is produced by a production company or other entity as opposed to an individual producer, the production company is said to be the producing entity, although one or more individual principals of the company may receive the producer or executive producer screen credits (see "Independent Producer" and "Production Company").

PRODUCING FOR HIRE. Performing the services of a feature film producer as an employee of a studio or other production company (see "Independent Producer," "Producer" and "Producers Guild of America").

PRODUCT. Something produced. In film, the result of the combined efforts of all of those persons involved in the production of a motion picture, i.e., the motion picture or finished film itself (see "Collaborative Process," "Commodity," "Idea," "Intangible" and "Tangible Asset").

PRODUCT COSTS (same as "Negative Costs").

PRODUCT FLOW. The continuing or uninterrupted movement of motion pictures week after week at movie houses. The ability of a distributor to provide a consistent flow of quality motion pictures to exhibitors gives such distributors greater leverage with the exhibitors in booking films in their theatres and negotiating the terms of the deal (see "Major Studio/Distributors" and "Product Source").

PRODUCT GLUT. An unusually high number of motion picture films produced and/or available for distribution in a given year (see "Law of Supply and Demand" and "Product Shortage").

PRODUCTION. A presentation of a story or exposition on film or videotape which has continuity and direction, complete in itself. The general term used to describe the processes involved in making all the original materials that are the basis for the finished motion picture. Also a film in the process of being produced (see "Product" and "Motion Picture").

PRODUCTION ACCOUNT. The bank account into which funds designated to be spent on the production of a motion picture are deposited (see "Production" and "Production Accountant").

PRODUCTION ACCOUNTANT. The person who sets up and maintains the books and payroll system throughout the making of a film (same as "Production Auditor").

PRODUCTION ACCOUNTING SERVICES (see "Payroll" and "Production Accounting").

PRODUCTION AGREEMENT. A contract between a feature film financier or financing source and a production company setting out the terms under which the production company will produce a motion picture being financed by the financier or financing source. When such agreements are made with an integrated organization such as a studio, they are often combined with distribution agreements, e.g., the production-financing/distribution agreement (see "Distribution Agreement," "Financing Agreement" and "Production-Financing/Distribution Agreement").

PRODUCTION AUDITOR. A member of a film production staff who maintains up-to-date, accurate financial records of the costs of producing a film. The production auditor works closely with the production manager and may report to the financing entity. He or she will set up an auditing office, open production bank accounts, review the budget, furnish cost reports, pay all bills incurred by the production, pay the salaries of the cast and crew and handle insurance claims, if any (see "Production Accountant").

PRODUCTION BOARD. A board with several panels on which separate strips containing sketches of each scene of a film script are placed to aid in scheduling and budgeting (see "Shooting Schedule").

PRODUCTION BREAKDOWN. A detailed system of separating each and every element of a film script and then re-arranging them in the most efficient and least expensive manner for filming. The term also refers to a detailed analysis prepared by a film's script supervisor for the purpose of timing the script (see "Production Board").

PRODUCTION BUDGET. The amount of money itemized by spending category anticipated to be required to produce a film. The production budget will generally include pre-production, principal photography and post-production costs but not development. Other film-related costs such as insurance, contingency reserves and completion bond fees are usually not included in the production budget (see "Budget" and "Development").

PRODUCTION CODE ADMINISTRATION. An entertainment industry organization which operated from the 1930s until 1968 and which approved or disapproved of the content of films until the system was abandoned in 1968 in favor of the so-called MPAA rating system (see "MPAA," "IFIDA" and "Ratings").

PRODUCTION COMPANY. An organization or business entity which develops and produces feature films (see "Distributor," "Independent Producer," "Major Studio/Distributors" and "Studio").

PRODUCTION COMPTROLLER (see "Production Accountant").

PRODUCTION CONTINGENCY. An amount of money, typically 10% percent of the production budget, which is set aside to cover unexpected expenses or budget overages. The percentage might be raised for a low-budget picture being shot without a completion bond. Also, a completion guarantor may require a higher percentage on certain films before agreeing to provide the completion bond (same as "Contingency or Contingency Reserve").

PRODUCTION CONTRACTS. The written agreements negotiated and signed between a film's producer and all persons or entities providing products or services in the production of a film, e.g., director, cinematographer, actors catering and transportation services, etc. (see "Contract" and "Production").

PRODUCTION COSTS. The costs of producing a film, i.e., the expenses incurred in the production of a film negative. Such costs are generally incurred in four stages: story rights acquisition, pre-production, principal photography and post-production, and the complete production process can take a year to eighteen months. Production expenses may include the cost of the story, salaries of cast, directors, producers, etc., set construction and operations, wardrobe, sound synchronization, editing and any other costs necessary to create a finished film negative. Other components of movie production costs might include (depending on the form of film finance used) residuals, participations, allocated studio overhead, abandonment costs and capitalized interest. Production costs may also include contractual overheads and contractual facility and equipment charges in excess of actual costs, rebates and receipts from sales of props and sets, provision for self-insurance, a completion bond charge, participations before breakeven, and overhead thereon, and deferments, along with actual or imputed interest. The production cost for studio-financed films does not mean the studio's cost in providing a certain service or product but what it arbitrarily decides to charge the film for such service or product and the studio markup for such items is often extremely high. It is also very important to clearly define in any production-financing/distribution agreement the distinction between production costs and distribution expenses (and to vigorously monitor the studio's classification of expenses), since a studio financier will typically seek to charge interest on the cost of producing the negative (production expenses) as well as apply the overhead percentage against the production cost total. The producer and other profit participants, therefore, must insist that no expenses which are actually distribution costs be classified by the studio as production costs since such a practice would tend to delay any net profit participation (see "Creative Accounting," "Direct Distribution Expenses," "Gross Participations," "Interest," "Negative Costs" and "Rising Production Costs").

PRODUCTION COST DEFERMENTS. Arrangements for the deferral of some or all of the costs of goods and/or services provided by the suppliers of such goods and/or services so that the payments are not a production cost but rather are paid out of specified receipts before or after investor or financier recoupment (see "Deferments" or "Deferrals").

PRODUCTION DEFERMENTS (same as "Production Cost Deferments").

PRODUCTION DEPARTMENT. A major administrative unit of the typical studio/distributor which is primarily responsible for the physical production of a motion picture being produced by the studio on an in-house basis (see "Business Affairs Department," "Creative Department," "Legal Department," "Major/Studio Distributors," "Marketing Department" and "Studio").

PRODUCTION DESIGNER. The film production person who works closely with the director and who is responsible for conceiving, planning and supervising the overall visual design of a film (see "Art Director" and "Set Designer").

PRODUCTION/DISTRIBUTION AGREEMENT (see "Production-Financing/Distribution Agreement").

PRODUCTION ENTITY. The company responsible for the production of a motion picture. The term is used to make a distinction between the production company and the producer which is an individual. Production entities usually take the form of a corporation, but may also be limited partnerships or joint ventures (see "Corporation," "Joint Venture," "Limited Partnership" and "Producer").

PRODUCTION EXECUTIVE. An administrative manager employee of the major studio/distributors who is responsible for overseeing the interests of the studio when it acts as a financier in the production of a motion picture. The studio's production executive will sometimes be named in the production-financing/distribution agreement (see "Production-Financing/Distribution Agreement").

PRODUCTION EXPENSES (see "Production Costs").

PRODUCTION FINANCING. Funding provided for the production of a film as opposed to development or distribution financing (see "Development," "Direct Distribution Expenses" and "Distribution Alternatives").

PRODUCTION-FINANCING/DISTRIBUTION AGREEMENT. A contract between a studio/distributor (or other distributor) and a feature film producer which sets out the terms and conditions under which the distributor will provide production financing for a motion picture in exchange for the right to distribute the film in some or all markets; one of the principal forms of motion picture production financing. Such distributors will usually exercise certain controls and approvals over the production process (also called "Production/Distribution Agreement;" see "Acquisition/Distribution Agreement," "Financing," "In-House Product," "Negative Pickup Distribution Agreement," "Studio Financing" and "Theatrical Distribution Contract").

PRODUCTION FUND. A sum of money set aside either by governmental or private interests for the purpose of contributing some or all of the monies needed to produce feature films (see "Completion Fund" and "Production Financing").

PRODUCTION FUNDS. The monies deposited into a feature film production account to be used in the production of a motion picture. With respect to a studio-financed project (i.e., production-financing/distribution agreement), the studio/distributor will typically advance funds to the production company for the production of the picture up to the total amount of the approved production budget, and, if required thereafter, up to and including the contingency, in fixed installments and consistent with a cash-flow schedule which has been mutually approved by the production company and the studio/distributor (see "Production-Financing/Distribution Agreement").

PRODUCTION LOANS. Funds that are borrowed from a bank or other lending source for the purpose of producing a motion picture (see "Collateral," "Completion Guarantor," "Inter-Party Agreement," "Negative Pickup," "Security Agreement" and "Split-Rights Deal").

PRODUCTION MANAGER. The film production person responsible to the producer for assembling the budget, organizing the shooting schedule, expediting all aspects of the production and authorizing all expenditures. The production manager supervises the daily production of a film, working directly with the assistant director, producer, and director. He or she relays orders from the director and producer to the assistant director and oversees the signing of contracts, scouting of locations, permit arrangements for all non-studio shoots, catering and daily accounting. The work of the production manager is similar to and overlaps the responsibility of the assistant director. On some movie sets, the production manager is the same as the line producer (see "Line Producer" and "Unit Production Manager").

PRODUCTION NOTES. Notes and/or reports made during the filming or taping of all aspects of a film or video production including camera and sound reports, production manager's reports, script clerk's notes, and other similar reports. Such notes are useful during production and in post-production, particularly in editing the film. Production notes are also referred to as production reports (see "Production Reports").

PRODUCTION OFFICE COORDINATOR. The person on a film production who serves as a liaison among the producer, production manager, assistant directors and script supervisor and who is responsible for the set-up and efficient running of the production office for a specific film production (see "Production Reports").

PRODUCTION OVERHEAD. Those costs and expenses incurred by a studio/distributor in the business of producing and distributing motion pictures that cannot be directly charged to specific pictures, regardless of whether or not such facilities or staff are actually used on a given picture. They include such things as rental of soundstages or other studio facilities such as dressing facilities, vehicles, telephones, office space and equipment, secretaries' salaries, studio executives salaries and their expenses, development and story-abandonment costs and general administrative costs relating to the production area. In view of the fact that distributors are generally permitted to recoup at least 100% of their direct distribution expenses and distribution fees for distributing a film in various media and markets, some take the position that such indirect distribution or other expenses should not be charged against a specific film, either on an actual cost or percentage basis, but rather such studio/distributors should cover such costs as most businesses do with their earned fees. It is particularly troublesome for some to have a studio/distributor finance the production costs of a film, then add such overhead to the negative cost of the film and charge interest on that overhead while delaying recoupment of the negative cost until after distribution fees are collected and distribution expenses are recovered, if ever (see "Gross Participations," "Interest," "Leverage," "Overhead," "Overhead Surcharge" and "Overreaching").

PRODUCTION PAYROLL SERVICE. An accounting service which may provide above and below-the-line film production related accounting services (see "Payroll" and "Production Accounting").

PRODUCTION REPORTS. Regular written documentation (usually daily), in production ledgers or on special pads, which indicate acceptable and non-acceptable takes and additional relevant information relating to the specific movie in production. Such pads are pre-printed in a special long, rectangular form with multiple carbons to facilitate the making and distribution of notations relating to each take. Examples of such reports include sound and camera reports. The script supervisor's notes are also generally considered production reports. Production reports are prepared by line producers and unit managers. They contain the work hours for each member of the cast and crew, amount of film stock shot, costs of the shooting day, number of pages filmed, balance of script pages yet to be shot, location and scouting data in brief, i.e., everything essential to the logistics of a movie shoot (see "Production Manager" and "Production Notes").

PRODUCTION RISK. The danger that a planned feature film production will not be completed, that it will not be completed on time or that it will go over budget (see "Completion Bond" and "Lender Risk Elimination").

PRODUCTION SCHEDULE. The timetable and plan for conducting the principal photography of a motion picture. Such a schedule would include a start date and may be set out in the production-financing agreement, e.g., approximately eleven weeks, comprised of five-day work weeks with two holidays off, for a total of fifty-three production days (see "Principal Photography").

PRODUCTION SLOWDOWN. A reduction in the normal work pace of persons involved in the production of a motion picture. Sometimes in the context of employer/employee negotiations unions or guilds use the tactic of a production slowdown to force employers to meet their demands instead of a full scale strike (see "De Facto Strike" and "Strike").

PRODUCTION SOUND EFFECTS (see "Sound Effects").

PRODUCTION SPECIFICATIONS. The contractual requirements of a film financier with respect to the production of a motion picture being financed. Such specifications may include agreed upon requirements relating to a start date, production schedule and locations along with the identities of the production company counsel and the studio's production executive (see "Basic Elements," "Deal Terms," "Picture Specifications" and "Production Schedule").

PRODUCTION STAFF. All of the persons working on a given film shooting assignment who work directly for the studio or production company, i.e., producer, line producer, production manager, production associate, director (in some cases), production secretary and others (see "Cast," "Crew," "Operational Staff" and "Staff").

PRODUCTION STILL. A photograph taken during a film's production which is shot with a still camera as opposed to a motion picture camera. A still is usually printed as an 8 x 10 inch black and white glossy or color photograph of an actor or a scene from a film and is used for matching continuity in later shots and for advertising or publicity purposes (see "Still Photographer").

PRODUCTION UNIT. A self-contained group consisting of director, camera crew, sound crew, electricians, etc. that works on a soundstage or on location to shoot an assigned motion picture or section of the film (see "Unit Production Manager").

PRODUCTION VALUE. The general appeal of a film due to a certain favorable combination of the film's elements or the appeal of a specific element in such film. Also a reference to the quality of certain aspects of a feature film production (see "Audience" and "Elements").

PRODUCT PLACEMENT. The activities of feature film producers, distributors or their representatives (e.g., product-placement firms) in arranging for the appearance of a commercial product in a film for a fee, products or promotional considerations. The practice raises ethical questions with regard to subjecting unsuspecting moviegoers to commercial messages without some form of pre-exhibition disclosure or disclaimer. Notwithstanding the ethical considerations, some studios and producers are able to raise a certain portion of the production or enhancement funds for producing their movies through product placements (see "Advertising Tie-Ins," "Commercials," "Distributor Commercials" and "Promotional Tie-Ins").

PRODUCT SHORTAGE. A subjective term referring to a significant reduction in the number of feature films produced or distributed in a given year. All other factors being equal, a product shortage tends to improve the bargaining position of feature film producers in relation to distributors, but may also improve the bargaining position of the distributors in relation to exhibitors (see "Bargaining Position," "Bargaining Power," "Inferior Bargaining Position," "Law of Supply and Demand" and "Product Glut").

PRODUCT SOURCE. For distributors, movie production companies are sources of product, i.e., motion pictures. For exhibitors, the distributors are their product source (see "Product Flow").

PRODUCT SPLITTING. A film industry practice in which exhibitors allocate among themselves the rights to negotiate for the exhibition of films distributed by motion picture distributors, i.e., a film exhibition practice in which several theatres in a territory informally agree not to bid aggressively against each other for certain films offered by a distributor with the intent of increasing the likelihood that the distributor terms ultimately agreed to by the distributor will be more favorable to the exhibitors. Each theatre in a given territory thus would get the chance to license highly desirable films on more favorable terms on a regular rotating basis. Thus, the practice is designed to create a more fair allocation of films among the existing theatres in a given area, to reduce the prices exhibitors have to pay to distributors for the right to exhibit films and as a counter-measure to the distributor practice of blind bidding (same as "Film Splitting" or "Splitting;" see "Anti-Competitive Practices").

PROFESSIONAL ASSOCIATION. A membership organization made up of persons engaged in a specific profession who have joined together to promote their mutual interests, through educational programs for members, lobbying activities and public-information programs (see "Industry Groups," "Lobbyists" and "Trade Association;" contrast with "Guild" and "PGA;" also called "Professional and Trade Associations").

PROFESSIONAL BUDGET. A film budget prepared for a fee by a specialist in film budgeting as opposed to the film's producer who may or may not have bona fide expertise in the preparation of film budgets (see "Budget").

PROFILE. A description of a specific segment of the movie-going public in terms of their demographic and psychographic characteristics, including such factors as age, sex, income, education and life style (see "Demographics" and "Psychographic").

PROFIT. Generally, the positive difference that results from selling products and services for more than the cost of producing such goods. In film, the amount left over after an exhibitor, distributor, producer or financing entity or group has paid all its bills or expenses. Depending on the deal between each entity, one participant in a movie project will reach profits before others who are participating in the revenue stream at a different level. The definitions of net and gross profits will vary from deal to deal depending on what income is included and to be accounted for and what deductions are to be taken against that income before applying a profit participant's percentage to the balance (see "Actual Breakeven," "Artificial Breakeven," "Breakeven," "Most Favored Nations Clause" and "Pari Passu").

PROFITABILITY. The quality or state of having an excess of returns over expenditures in a transaction or in a business entity's transactions. The lack of consistent profitability in a business or industry tends to make it difficult to attract capital (see "Profit" and "Profit Margin").

PROFIT AND LOSS STATEMENT (see "Income Statement").

PROFIT CENTER. A department or area of business within a company or business entity which produces a profit if considered as an independent operation. The most significant profit center for film studios has traditionally been their distribution activities (see "Creative Accounting," "Distribution" and "Profit").

PROFIT MARGIN. The difference between a business' gross sales and net profits (see "Operating Profit" and "Profitability").

PROFIT MOTIVE. A reason for conducting a business activity. For tax purposes, an essential element in the analysis of whether a trade or business expense is deductible, i.e., to be deductible as a trade or business expense, an expenditure must be paid or incurred in connection with a trade or business and that trade or business must be carried on primarily for profit (as opposed to a hobby for recreation and pleasure). Profit motive is determined by an examination of all the circumstances in the case. There need not be a reasonable expectation that the activity will yield a profit. It is sufficient if it is entered into in good faith with the purpose of making a profit (see "Limited Partnership" and "Tax Opinion").

PROFIT PARTICIPATION. Percentage participations typically based on net profits as defined in the distribution agreement; payments to talent or others computed as a percentage of the profits generated by a film or fixed sums to be paid if a movie's profits reach a certain level. Such participations are negotiable and thus may be based on gross receipts, net profits or other stages in a movie's revenue stream. If reasonable controls and/or limitations are not imposed on the distributor's claimed distribution expenses, the distribution fees are not reasonable and other parties are allowed to participate in the distributor's gross receipts, net profit participations are not likely to occur. Such practices could impact adversely on the financial interests of investors, producers, executive producers, directors, screenwriters, actors or others who have negotiated a profit participation interest in a given motion picture (see "Association of Net Profit Participants," "Net Profit Participant," "Percentage Participation" and "Points").

PROFIT PROJECTIONS. A prospective financial forecast which implies that a profit, at some level, will occur, a risky implication at best in motion picture finance (see "Financial Forecasts" and "Projections" and "Financial Projections").

PROFIT POTENTIAL. The highest level of earnings for a business transaction that can be reasonably anticipated (see "Maximum Exploitation" and "Profit").

PROFIT-SHARING RATIO. The ratio in which partners in limited partnerships have agreed to share profits and losses. Profit-sharing and loss-sharing ratios, however, sometimes differ (see "Post-Payout Sharing Ratio").

PROFITS, LOSSES OR CREDITS. IRS terminology for the net income, net loss or credits of a limited partnership, as determined for federal income tax purposes (see "Income Tax").

PRO FORMA (see "Pro Forma Financial Statements").

PRO FORMA CASH FLOW SCHEDULE. A prospective financial report prepared by or on behalf of a film's producer, typically at the request of and for the benefit of a bank in a production loan situation, setting out on a weekly basis the amount of money needed to pay for the anticipated production expenses of a film (see "Cash Flow," "Cash Flow Chart" and "Cash Flow Schedule").

PRO FORMA FINANCIAL STATEMENTS. Financial presentations that are designed to demonstrate the effect of a future or hypothetical transaction or event by showing how it might have affected the historical financial statements if it had been consummated during the period covered by those statements, i.e., financial statements that represent proposed events in the form in which they will appear if or when the event actually occurs (see "Financial Forecasts," "Financial Projections," "Partial Presentations" and "Prospective Financial Statements").

PROGRAM HIGHLIGHTS. A non-required section of a securities disclosure document which typically takes the form of a one-page point-by-point abstract of the summary of the offering, i.e., listing the main points of the securities offering of interest to an investor (see "Disclosure Document" and "Summary of Offering").

PROGRAMMED MUSIC. The generation of music by means of automatic high-speed digital computers (see "Music").

PROGRESS TO PRODUCTION SCHEDULE. A feature film development-stage planning device which amounts to a projected timetable setting out when the various development steps are expected to be completed (see "Development").

PROJECTED AUDIENCE. The total number of persons who are expected to see a given movie in a specific market (see "Target Audience").

PROJECTED CASH FLOW SCHEDULE. A prospective financial report prepared by or on behalf of a film production company or producer, at the request of and for the benefit of a studio financier, which sets out on a weekly basis the amount of money needed to pay for the anticipated production expenses of a film (see "Cash Flow" and "Pro Forma Cash Flow Schedule").

PROJECTED OVERAGE. A forecast made during the production of a motion picture which estimates how much the actual production costs of the film will exceed the approved production budget and contingency. Studio production-financing/distribution agreements typically contain provisions that allow the studio to take over the production of a motion picture if, based on the information available (including, but not limited to, the weekly reporting papers furnished by the production company), the studio reasonably believes that the estimated cost of production of the picture will exceed the contingency. In such instances, the studio and production company may engage in efforts to reduce the projected overage by conferring for a stated period, e.g., three days, on a method to reduce the projected overage to a point which will not exceed the contingency. If the studio and production company agree to a reduction plan that will ensure that the contingency will not be exceeded, such reductions may then become part of the approved production budget for the picture. However, if the parties are unable to agree on a reduction plan within the stated period, the studio usually has the right to take over the picture (see "Approved Production Budget," "Contingency" and "Overages").

PROJECT FINANCING (same as "Single-Picture Financing").

PROJECTION OF REVENUES. An estimated forecast of earnings from a proposed business activity. Most feature film producers and/or production companies do some sort of projection of revenues from a film before committing to do a project (see "Computer Model," "Financial Management," "Financial Projections" and "Mental Modeling").

PROJECTIONS (see "Financial Projections" and "Profit Projections").

PROMINENCE. The style, size and other factors which make a screen credit appear more prestigious (see "Billing" and "Credits").

PROMISE. A declaration of one's intention to do or to refrain from doing something (see "Contract").

PROMISSORY NOTE. A written promise committing the maker to pay the payee a specified sum of money either on demand or at a fixed or determinable future date, with or without interest (also called "Note;" see "Debt" and "Lender Financing").

PROMOTER. In corporate law, generally anyone who undertakes to form a corporation and to procure for it the rights, instrumentalities, and capital by which it is to carry out the purposes set forth in its charter. The SEC defines a promoter as any person who, acting alone or in conjunction with one or more persons, directly or indirectly takes the initiative in founding or organizing the business or enterprise of an issuer of securities or any person who receives 10% or more of any class of securities of an issuer on the proceeds therefrom in consideration for services or property. However, a person who receives such securities or proceeds either solely as underwriting commissions or solely in consideration of property will not be deemed a promoter if such person does not otherwise take part in founding and organizing the enterprise (also called "Sponsor;" see "Corporation").

PROMOTIONAL ACTIVITIES. Film publicity activities geared towards gaining media attention and public interest such as interviews, special screenings for critics, opinion-makers or specific interest groups, public appearances by the director, actors or others involved in the film, sandwich-board advertising, T-shirts, comic books, sneak previews and flyers (see "Advertising" and "Publicity").

PROMOTIONAL CAMPAIGN. The strategy and planned activities designed to publicize a movie (see "Promotional Activities").

PROMOTIONAL CONCEPT. The primary element of a film that will be utilized in advertising and promoting its exhibition (see "Concept").

PROMOTIONAL MATERIALS. All of the documents and other items that can be used to obtain publicity for a motion picture including press releases, a description of the film, biographies of key personnel, a list of screening sites, press clippings, recommendations, quotes and flyers. Such materials may be helpful in stimulating the interest of a distributor in distributing a film or in persuading a potential distributor to at least attend a screening of the film (see "Press Kit").

PROMOTIONAL QUOTES. Excerpts from the critical reviews by motion picture critics which are used in the advertising of feature films (see "Blurbs," "Body Copy," "Critic's Review," "Cross Plugs," "Display Advertising," "Press Kit," "Publicity Articles" and "Puffery").

PROMOTIONAL TIE-INS. Advertising campaigns which combine the promotion of a motion picture with a product, such as a soft drink or pizza. Sometimes such products may be subtly or even prominently displayed within the movie for a fee or as part of the tie-in arrangement (contrast with "Product Placement;" see "Promotional Campaign").

PROMPT PAYMENT. The timely remittance of amounts due. It is not uncommon for studios or other distributors to hold payments from television and cable sales until actual play dates, even though the funds have been received one or two (or more) years in advance. Producers may want to negotiate for the prompt payment of all funds due the producer and attempt to define what is reasonably prompt in the case of each type of payment (see "Unethical Business Practices").

PROPAGANDA. Ideas, facts or allegations disseminated with the expressed intent of furthering one's cause or of damaging an opposing cause (see "Communication," "Communications Industry," "Entertainment," "Entertainment Industry," "Favorable Portrayal," "Idea," "Marketplace of Ideas," "Movies With a Message," "Multi-Cultural Society," "Pattern of Bias" and "Unfavorable Portrayal").

PROPER TITLE. Appropriate or suitable ownership (see "Clear Title," "Good Title" and "Just Title").

PROPERTY. In general, every species of valuable right or interest that is subject to ownership, has an exchangeable value or adds to one's wealth. Property describes one's exclusive right to possess, use and dispose of a thing. With respect to film, the word "property" usually refers to an idea, concept, outline, synopsis, treatment, short story, magazine article, novel, screenplay or other literary form that someone has a legal right to develop to the exclusion of others and which may form the basis for a motion picture. Recognize that some of the above set out property forms, i.e., idea and concept, may be more difficult to protect than others (see "Literary Materials" or "Literary Works").

PROPERTY DAMAGE LIABILITY INSURANCE. A type of insurance that pays for damage or destruction of property of others (including loss of use of the property) while the property is in the care, custody or control of the film production company and is used or to be used in an insured production (see "Liability Insurance").

PROPORTIONATE SHARE OF DEDUCTIONS. A reference to the allocation of tax deductions generated by film production activities among equity owners. In a joint-venture context, both venturers would receive their proportionate share of such deductions and in a limited partnership, each limited partner would be allocated his or her proportionate share of tax deductions (see "Deductions").

PROPRIETORSHIP (see "Sole Proprietorship").

PROPS. Any movable items seen or used on a motion picture set and used in a particular scene (see "Set Dressing").

PROPS, SETS AND WARDROBE INSURANCE. A type of insurance policy that covers props, sets, scenery, costumes, wardrobe and similar theatrical property against all risks of direct physical loss, damage or destruction during a film's production (see "Insurance").

PRO RATA. Proportionately allocated in accordance with some standard, e.g., the interests held by investors in a limited partnership (see "Pari Passu").

PROSPECTIVE FINANCIAL STATEMENTS. Either financial forecasts or financial projections including the summaries of significant assumptions and accounting policies. Although prospective financial statements may cover a period that has partially expired, statements for periods that have completely expired are not considered to be prospective financial statements. Thus, pro forma financial statements and partial presentations are not considered to be prospective financial statements (see "Financial Forecasts," "Financial Projections," "Limited Use," "Partial Presentations" and "Pro Forma Financial Statements").

PROSPECTIVE PURCHASERS. This term is often used in limited partnership offerings to describe those persons or entities who are offered units in the partnership or receive copies of the offering memorandum and are considering investing in the offering (see "Limited Partnership").

PROSPECTUS. A document that discloses financial information about an issuer of securities to prospective purchasers and explains the plans and objectives of the business' undertakings in a public/registered securities offering; also any communication, either written or broadcast by radio or television, that offers a security for sale. The Securities Act of 1933 requires the filing of a prospectus, as part of the registration statement, with the SEC and that a copy of the prospectus be provided to each buyer of the securities. The prospectus contains the most important parts of the securities registration statement in a public offering and such document must provide all information relevant to the issue. A prospectus must be written in a clear, unambiguous manner since any injurious misrepresentation constitutes fraud and the complaining party may sue for damage or rescission (see "Anti-Fraud," "Disclosure Document," "Final Prospectus," "Offering Memorandum," "Preliminary Offering Circular," "Registration Statement," "Rescission" and "Waiting Period").

PROVISION FOR ARBITRATION. A clause in an agreement which sets out the circumstances under which the parties to the contract will be obligated to take a dispute to an arbitrator for resolution (see "Arbitration Clause").

PROXY. A written authorization signed by one who holds the right to vote on matters to be decided by the ownership of a business entity, such as a corporation or partnership, which authorizes the holder of the proxy right to exercise the power to vote with respect to the interest of the person who signed the document and had the right to grant such power (see "Power of Attorney" and "Voting Stock").

PROXY HOLDER. One who has been authorized to cast a vote for another (see "Proxy" above).

PRURIENT. Shameful and morbid interest in nudity, sex or excretion. It is one criteria in determining whether or not something is obscene (see "Obscene Material").

PSYCHOGRAPHIC. Of or relating to a graph representing the extent to which an individual exhibits traits or abilities as determined by tests or ratings (see "Profile" and "Target Audience").

PUBLIC ACCOUNTANT (PA). A person who meets the educational, training, exam and licensing requirements of the state in which he or she practices the profession of accounting, i.e., the recording and summarizing of business and financial transactions along with analyzing, verifying and reporting the results of such transactions, but who was not required to pass the Uniform Certified Public Exam, typically because such accountant had already been practicing for a number of years before such exam and certification program was adopted in that state (see "Certified Public Accountant").

PUBLICATION RIGHTS. The authority to reduce certain information to writing and to make such information known to the general public. Certain publication rights are often granted or reserved in conjunction with a motion picture production, e.g., for the publication of a book about the making of the movie or for the novelization of the screenplay (see "Novelization").

PUBLIC BROADCASTING SYSTEM (PBS). A group of some 300-plus television stations that are loosely affiliated in a relationship somewhat akin to a network (i.e., they share programming) and that carry special educational, documentary, in-depth news and other programs not generally carried by the major TV networks (see "Network" and "Network Television").

PUBLIC CORPORATION (see "Publicly Held").

PUBLIC DOMAIN. Information or a literary, artistic or musical work which is available for anyone to use and not subject to copyright protection, e.g., the information or work was not copyrighted or the term of copyright protection has expired (see "Copyright").

PUBLIC EXHIBITION. The showing of a film to a general audience irrespective of whether the audience paid to view the film (also see "Commercial Public Exhibition").

PUBLIC FIGURE. In libel and privacy law, a person of general fame and notoriety in the community and pervasive involvement in the affairs of society. Under the First Amendment, a public figure is required to show a defendant acted with actual malice before recovering damages for libel (see "Libel" and "Tort").

PUBLICIST. The person responsible for promotion and publicity of a person or film through all media including radio, television, newspapers, magazines, etc. A publicist on a film project is referred to as the unit publicist (see "Unit Publicist").

PUBLICITY. Any act or device designed to attract public interest, e.g., information with news value issued as a means of gaining public attention or support, i.e., editorial content as opposed to paid advertising. Publicity is used to exploit a motion picture beyond its advertising (see "Advertising," "Buzz," "Hype," "Junket," "Marketing" and "Promotional Activities").

PUBLICITY ARTICLES. Articles relating to a film which are prepared by the producer or distributor and provided as part of the press kit presented to the media (see "Press Kit").

PUBLICITY MATERIAL. The physical items utilized in attracting public attention to a given movie, including such things as the final set of cast and production credits, a detailed synopsis of the picture, detailed production notes about making the picture, complete biographies of starring and key feature players, feature stories on key stars and filmmakers and column items or "shorts" (see "Column Item" and "Shorts").

PUBLICITY RIGHTS. The legal power and authority to publicize a movie, literary property or individual. Also, in privacy law, the right to use or prevent the use of an individual's name, voice or likeness (see "Publicity").

PUBLICITY STILL. A still photograph relating to a motion picture and used in promoting the movie (see "Photograph").

PUBLIC LIMITED PARTNERSHIP. A limited partnership whose limited partnership interests are registered for sale with the SEC and in each state in which such interests are offered (contrast with "Private Placement").

PUBLICLY HELD. A corporation whose shares are available to the public at large and whose activities are regulated by the SEC and the appropriate state securities regulatory authorities (see "Public Offering" and "Securities").

PUBLICLY TRADED. Corporations whose securities are registered with the Securities and Exchange Commission and bought and sold by the general public either through the facilities of an organized stock market or over the counter (see "Over-the-Counter Market," "Public Offering" and "Securities").

PUBLICLY TRADED PARTNERSHIP (same as "Master Limited Partnership").

PUBLIC OFFERING. A securities offering which has been registered with the state and federal securities regulatory authorities and which allows the issuer of such securities to advertise and generally solicit prospective investors (also called "Registered Offering;" contrast with "Private Offering;" see "Cold Call," "Limitations on Manner of Offering" and "Registration").

PUBLIC OFFERING PRICE (same as "Offering Price").

PUBLISH. To make known to the general public; to inform one or more persons of a fact or matter that they would not otherwise have reason to know of. In the law of torts, a statement does not constitute defamation unless it is published, i.e., unless it is made known to some third party other than the party making the statement or the party defamed. The act of publishing can involve any form of communication, including motion pictures (see "Copyright").

PUBLISHER. A person or entity that issues and offers for sale books, sheet music or other printed material. Also, in music, the person or entity holding the legal right to record or otherwise exploit a musical work or to license others to do so (see "Book," "Publication Rights" and "Publish").

PUBLISHING RIGHTS (see "Publication Rights").

PUBLISHING ROYALTY (see "Merchandise and Publishing Royalty").

PUFFED NUMBERS. The inflated reports of the performance of a motion picture at the box office. Exhibitor's sometimes exaggerate the box office performance of a film at a specific theatre when responding to the inquiries of the trades or various box-office reporting services in order to create the impression in the industry that a film is doing better at that theatre than it actually is. Distributor's also may "puff" their numbers for industry consumption in order to encourage exhibitors to increase their bids for subsequent runs. Such reports then mislead prospective net profit participants into thinking that a film may achieve net profits when it actually will not (see "Settlement Transaction").

PUFFERY. Flattering publicity or extravagant commendation (see "Blurbs," "Body Copy," "Critic's Review," "Cross Plugs," "Display Advertising," "Press Kit," "Publicity Articles" and the back cover of this book).

PURCHASE. The acquisition of a literary property in exchange for valuable consideration (see "Consideration" and "Literary Property").

PURCHASE AGREEMENT (same as "Acquisition Agreement" and "Rights Agreement").

PURCHASE GROUP. A group of investment bankers that, operating under an agreement among underwriters, agrees to purchase a new issue of securities from the issuer for resale to the investing public (same as "Underwriting Group" or "Syndicate;" see "Selling Group of Broker/Dealers" and "Negotiated Underwriting").

PURCHASER COUNTING RULES (see "Counting Rules").

PURCHASER REPRESENTATIONS. Written statements made by a prospective purchaser of a security to the issuer of such security and made for the purpose of meeting investor suitability requirements for the offering, e.g., regarding the purchaser's intention to purchase such security for his, her or its own investment, the purchaser's state of residence and the purchaser's income or net worth. Such statements generally are made in response to inquiries in the offering subscription agreement. Many state limited offering exemptions require specific purchaser representations as a condition to qualifying for such exemption from that state's securities registration requirement (see "Investor Suitability Standards" and "Legend").

PURCHASER REPRESENTATIVE. Any person who has such knowledge and experience in financial and business matters that he or she is capable of evaluating, alone or together with other representatives of the purchaser (or together with the purchaser), the merits and risks of a prospective investment and meets other requirements set out in Rule 501 of the SEC's Regulation D. Such purchaser representatives function as financial advisors to the prospective purchaser in a limited partnership or other securities offerings and may help the prospective purchaser meet the offering's investor suitability standards for such offerings (see "Investor Suitability Standards").

PURE GROSS. The gross receipts received by a feature film distributor prior to any deductions whatsoever, including off-the-top deductions (see "Gross Receipts" and "Off-the-Top Deductions").

PURE GROSS PARTICIPATIONS. Percentage contingent compensation based on and paid out of a feature film distributor's gross receipts prior to any other deductions. Such participations are rarely granted (see "Contingent Compensation," "First Dollar Gross," "Gross Receipts" and "Off-the-Top Deductions").

— Q —

QUALIFIED OPINION. An auditor's opinion which accompanies financial statements and calls attention to certain limitations of the audit or exceptions the auditor takes to the statements (see "Audit").

QUARTERLY FINANCIAL RESULTS. The fiscal consequences of the operations of a business reported for a three-month period of the company's operations (see "Financial Standings").

QUARTERLY REPORTS. Prepared statements relating to a company's operations and financial results for a three-month period. Generally, earnings reports to shareholders of publicly held corporations are made on a quarterly basis and stock dividends are also paid on the same basis (see "Annual Report").

QUIET AND PEACEFUL ENJOYMENT. The right to unimpaired use and enjoyment of property leased or conveyed (see "Covenant of Good Faith and Fair Dealing," "Warranties and Representations" and "Warranty").

QUIET PERIOD. The period of time during which an issuer of securities in the process of being registered for public offering is restricted by the SEC from putting out promotional publicity. The period generally dates from the pre-underwriting decision to forty or ninety days after the effective date (see "Effective Date," "Prospectus" and "Waiting Period").

QUOTA BARRIERS (see "Quotas").

QUOTAS. Limits imposed on the number of products which may be imported into a given country, e.g., limits imposed on the number of American-made feature film productions which may be broadcast on European television or exhibited theatrically (see "Foreign Market").

QUOTES. Excerpts from critical film reviews that are used in advertising a film. Such excerpts are supposed to be specifically approved by the critic prior to use in any advertisement (see "Critic").

— R —

RACKETEERING. Originally, an organized conspiracy to commit extortion, but the concept has, in more recent times, been superseded by RICO (acronym for Racketeer Influenced and Corrupt Organizations act), a federal statute which provides for four punishable racketeering offenses: (1) for directly or indirectly investing income derived from a pattern of racketeering activity or through collection of an unlawful debt in any enterprise affecting trade or commerce; (2) for acquiring or maintaining any interest in an enterprise through a pattern of racketeering activity or collection of an unlawful debt; (3) for conducting or participating in the affairs of the enterprise through a pattern of racketeering activity or collection of an unlawful debt; or (4) for conspiring to violate the racketeering provisions.

A "pattern of racketeering activity" requires engaging in at least two incidents of racketeering conduct within ten years of each other. Racketeering activity includes, among other acts, certain indictable acts under federal and state laws including bribery, embezzlement from pension and welfare funds, extortionate credit transactions, mail fraud, wire fraud, interference with commerce and fraud in the sale of securities. The term "enterprise" in the federal act includes any individual, partnership, corporation or any union or group of individuals associated in fact though not a legal entity. RICO also makes it unlawful for any person employed by or associated with any enterprise engaged in, or the activities of which affect, interstate commerce to conduct or participate in the conduct of the enterprise's affairs through a pattern of racketeering activity.

Criminal violations may result in fines of $25,000 and/or a twenty-year prison term and the forfeiture to the United States of any interest or security or contractual right of any kind affording a source of influence over the enterprise. RICO also provides for civil remedies. Any person injured in his business or property by reason of a violation may sue in any federal district court and may recover triple the substantial damages, cost of the suit, including a reasonable attorney's fees.

The principal purpose of the act is to strengthen means of preventing money and power obtained from illegal endeavors to corrupt democratic business practices so as to interfere with free competition and to burden interstate and foreign commerce. Essentially, Congress is seeking to halt a pattern of infiltration of business by organized crime.

Although most profit participants, including investors in film corporations and film limited partnerships, do not think of film distributors as a branch of "organized crime," if, in fact, a given distributor engages in a number of the practices described herein, and raises production and/or distribution funds through the sale of corporate stock or limited partnership interests (both of which are securities), such distributors may have committed securities fraud since the disclosure of such practices would almost certainly be considered material to prospective investors and issuers of securities are under an obligation to disclose all material aspects of any such securities transaction. Thus, a disgruntled investor or other person "wronged" by the activities of a film distributor may be able to establish that the film distributor engaged in numerous instances of racketeering activity, i.e., securities fraud by selling its stock or limited partnership interests without disclosing that it engaged in anti-competitive business practices, questionable or unethical conduct, creative accounting or sharp negotiating tactics, all of which may have an adverse impact on the interests of the investor and/or other profit participants (see "Extortion," "Mafia," "Money Laundering," "Mob Controlled Distribution Company," "RICO," "Theft" and "White Collar Crime").

RADIO. The broadcasting industry which uses electric waves for the wireless transmission of electric impulses, which are converted into sound (see "Broadcast" and "Television").

RADIO SPOTS. Film ads for use on radio; running times for radio spots are usually ten, thirty and sixty seconds. Radio spots are sent to sub-distributors, exhibitors and licensees on cassettes as part of the initial sales package prepared by the distributor of a film (see "Advertising").

RATE OF RETURN. The earnings or profit levels from owning assets or equity positions, expressed as a percentage of the original investment, i.e., the return on the investment. For common stock, the rate of return is the dividend yield, i.e., the annual amount paid through dividends divided by the purchase price of the stock (also called "Return on Equity" or "Return On Invested Capital;" see "Interest," "Real Rate of Return" and "Return On Investment").

RATE SHEET. A photocopied or printed page or brochure showing the costs of various services provided by film production-service companies such as equipment-rental houses, soundstage facilities, labs, graphics shops and sound-recording studios (also called "Price List").

RATING (see "Motion Picture Association of America," "MPAA Rating Administration" and "Ratings").

RATING APPEALS BOARD. An organization made up of twenty-two members from the MPAA and NATO (and formerly from the IFIDA), to which a producer who is for any reason displeased with the rating given his or her movie by CARA may appeal. The Rating Appeals Board sits as the final industry arbiter of movie ratings. Producers still dissatisfied with their movie's rating, however, may bring suit in a proper court of law (see "Rating Board").

RATING BOARD. A full-time board of seven individuals who are employed by the MPAA and its Classification and Rating Administration to rate movies submitted for rating. Since many of the movies submitted for rating have not been produced by MPAA members, an obvious and built-in potential conflict of interest exists between the MPAA and independent producers (who are not members of the MPAA) in the outcome of such ratings. The MPAA reports that some 614 films were submitted to the rating board in 1991 as opposed to 570 in 1990. The 1991 figure is a record high for the twenty-three years of the board. Some of the films which sought ratings, however, went straight to video, thus were not theatrical releases (see "MPAA" and "Ratings").

RATINGS. A very general system of movie classification provided by the MPAA for films to be released, utilizing the following letter designations: "G" for general audience (all ages, i.e., a family film), "PG" for parental guidance (i.e., some of the material might not be suitable for children), "PG-13" (some material may be inappropriate for pre-teenagers), "R" for restricted to those of a certain age (this age varies from sixteen to twenty-one, with eighteen being the Motion Picture Association of America's suggested age) and "NC-17" for adults only. The stated purpose of the rating system is to provide advance information to enable parents to make judgments as to whether they want their children to see certain movies. A full-time rating board (employees of the MPAA), composed of seven persons (all of whom have shared the parenthood experience), and headed by a chairman decide on the rating for a given movie by a majority vote. The rating board does not rate films for quality or the lack thereof. The rating board's criteria include theme, language, nudity, sex and violence. The rating assigned can in some cases significantly increase or decrease the potential audience for a movie and thus impact a movie's potential revenue, e.g., the difference in revenue potential between an "R" rated movie and the previously used "X" rating was substantial. Producers who are not satisfied with the MPAA rating assigned to their film have the right to re-edit the film and re-submit to the ratings board, or they can release the film without an MPAA rating. Producers also have a right to appeal a rating board decision to the Rating Appeals Board and can of course litigate the question in court. A number of lawsuits were filed in 1989 and 1990 by independent producers challenging the ratings assigned to their movies, particularly the former "X" rating. This prompted the MPAA to adopt the "NC-17" rating, even though some members of the public and exhibitors contend that such a change is merely a substitution of labels and makes no substantive change. Such lawsuits and criticism have also raised the basic question relating to the inherent conflict of interest in a system which allows an MPAA sponsored organization to rate movies produced by its members as well as the movies produced by non-members of the MPAA, although this issue has yet to be resolved. The MPAA has traditionally been opposed to attempts by any governmental entity (or other organization) which tries to set up a system for rating motion pictures as to their content and has used the existence of the MPAA ratings systems (controlled by the MPAA) as an argument against such efforts (see "CARA," "Minimum Rating," "MPAA," "NC-17," "Rating Appeals Board" and "Trailer Tags").

RATIO (see "Aspect Ratio").

RAW STOCK. Film that has not been exposed or processed (see "Film").

READER. An agency, film studio or production company story department employee (or freelance reader) who is responsible for reading, summarizing and writing an opinion on literary material submitted to such agency, studio or production company for consideration. The resulting analysis is referred to as coverage or development notes (see "Coverage" and "Development Notes").

REAL INCOME. Income of an individual, group or country adjusted for changes in purchasing power caused by inflation (see "Income").

REAL INTEREST RATE. The current interest rate minus the inflation rate (see "Inflation").

REALIZED PROFIT (OR LOSS). Profit or loss resulting from the sale or other disposal of a security. Capital gains taxes may be due when profits are realized. Realized losses can be used to offset realized gains for tax purposes [see "Paper Profit (or Loss)"].

REAL MODEL. A reference to computer-based financial forecasting or modeling which is done on an ongoing basis and which suggests that such techniques are superior to hard-copy-based pro forma financial forecasts, which may be done and then forgotten as the business progresses during the forecast period (see "Mental Modeling" and "Financial Forecasts").

REAL RATE OF RETURN. The return on an investment adjusted for inflation (see "Investor Financing" and "Rate of Return").

REASONABLE AND CUSTOMARY. A general standard of conduct for commercial affairs which may only be ascertained on a case by case basis, after the fact, by testimony provided in the context of litigation. A negotiated and more concrete standard of conduct is generally more useful to the parties to a contract and may help to prevent litigation. Such standards are also difficult to establish in the film industry (see "Subjective Terms").

REASONABLE DILIGENCE (see "Due Diligence").

REASONABLE EFFORTS CLAUSE. A provision in film distribution contracts which merely obligates the distributor to put forth reasonable efforts in distributing the film. Less effort is required of the distributor pursuant to a reasonable efforts clause than a best efforts clause. If no higher standard of conduct can be negotiated, the producer should prefer the best efforts standard over reasonable efforts (see "Best Efforts Clause").

REBATE. In lending, the unearned interest refunded to a borrower if the loan is paid off before maturity. In other commercial transactions, the return by a purchaser to a seller of goods (or provider of services) of a portion of the payment for such goods or services. If a film lab, advertising agency or exhibitor gives a rebate to a distributor because of the volume of business the distributor gives the lab, agency or exhibitor a question may arise as to whether the distributor is obligated to credit a portion of that rebate to the gross receipts of each of the films involved so that the producers and other net profit participants share in the benefits of the rebate. Rebates, like discounts, are often negotiated and/or awarded by exhibitors and other feature film licensees to distributors on a given picture or they are also sometimes based on the volume of pictures provided by the distributor. Distributors often seek to exclude the value of such rebates in profit participation calculations, arguing that the distributor's activities are solely responsible for earning them. However, as with discounts, without the feature film or films made available to the distributor by the producer and other profit participants, the distributor would not be in a position to either negotiate or receive such rebates. Producers should seek to negotiate a fair provision in the distribution agreement which includes the value of such rebates in the profit participation calculations. Even if a producer is successful in negotiating such a provision, it is not unthinkable for a distributor who has a particularly close relationship with a given exhibitor or other film licensee to have the rebate shifted (on paper) to another producer's film and/or included as part of an overall settlement as between the distributor and the licensee, in which case the distributor may have the discretion to allocate the amount of the settlement among various films distributed by the distributor on behalf of several different producers. Also, it may be difficult for an auditor to distinguish between such a rebate and an impermissible kickback (see "Discount," "Insider's Game," "Kickback," "Reciprocal Preferences" and "Relationship-Driven Business").

RECAPTURE. Tax terminology referring to the forfeiture (or recognition as ordinary income) of tax benefits previously allowed (see "Income Tax").

RECEIPTS. A term defined in some distribution agreements as the rentals, license fees, royalties or other charges received for the license or privilege to exhibit a film (including reissues of the film, but excluding remakes and sequels) or trailers of the film in any way, including theatrical and non-theatrical exhibitions, and exhibitions on or by means of television and including exhibitions by any other process now known or hereafter devised, whether on film or by means of magnetic tape, wire, cassettes, discs or any other devices now known or hereafter devised, but excluding any amounts received from outright sales (see "Outright Sale").

RECEIVER. Court-appointed person who takes possession of, but not title to, the assets and affairs of a business or estate that is in a form of bankruptcy called receivership or is involved in litigation. The receiver collects rents and other income and generally manages the affairs of the entity for the benefit of its owners and creditors until a disposition of the matter is made by the court (see "Receivership").

RECEIVERSHIP. An equitable remedy used by a court to place property under the control of a receiver so that it may be preserved for the benefit of affected parties (see "Bankruptcy," "Receiver" and "Reorganization").

RECESSION. A downturn in economic activity, defined by many economists as at least two consecutive quarters of decline in a country's gross national product (see "Recession-Proof" and "Recession-Resistent").

RECESSION-PROOF. A phrase which used to be applied to the film business since, historically, the demand for movies had remained fairly constant regardless of the state of the economy (see "Recession" and "Recession-Resistent").

RECESSION-RESISTENT. The phrase suggesting that a general downtown in the economy will not significantly impact motion picture ticket sales. This phrase has until recent years more accurately described the film business (as opposed to phrase "recession-proof") but since the 1991 U.S. recession demonstrated that a general downturn in the economy may in fact have an adverse impact on motion picture ticket sales, even "recession-resistent" does not accurately described the movie business. In today's marketplace, there are apparently too many other entertainment options available which were not available in the Great Depression when the myth about the film business being either "recession-proof" or "recession-resistent" was first created (see "Recession-Proof").

RECIPROCAL PREFERENCES. Mutual partiality among competing businesses, an illegal trade practice which violates Section 1 of the Sherman Anti-Trust Act. In the context of a vertically integrated motion picture industry, a reciprocal preference might take the form of a group of competing distributors/exhibitors, such as the major studio/distributors providing the other major studio/distributor/exhibitors selective contracts for exclusive first runs in their best theatres or at just the exhibitor level with the competing major exhibition chains, each giving some preference to the other's films by organizing splitting arrangements which can help to guarantee the distribution of the best films in their theatres as opposed to the theatres of the smaller independent exhibitors. The concept of reciprocal preferences may also apply to the exhibitor practice of bidding aggressively on films that are distributed by distributors who are fairly lenient when it comes time to settle with the exhibitor, i.e., accept a lesser round-dollar amount for the exhibition of a certain film in exchange for the exhibitor's showing a less desirable film in the past or in the future. At least one major studio/ distributor reportedly does not engage in these kinds of settlement transactions and thus does not benefit from this form of reciprocal preference, i.e., it's films are not typically exhibited in the best theatres (see "Blind Bidding," "Major Exhibition Chains," "Major Studio/Distributors," "Paramount Consent Decree of 1948," "Predatory Practices," "Selling Subject to Review," "Settlement Transaction," "Split Agreement" and "Vertical Integration").

RECISION (alternative spelling for "Rescission").

RECOGNIZABLE NAMES. Names of actors and/or directors who are recognized by a sufficiently large segment of the movie-going public (see "Recognizable Stars").

RECOGNIZABLE STARS. A somewhat redundant phrase referring to actors or actresses whose names are recognized by a sufficiently large segment of the movie-going public and who are also considered movie stars. Being a star probably includes being a recognizable name (see "Recognizable Name").

RECORD. A disc with a spiral groove carrying recorded sound for phonograph reproduction (see "Laser Disc").

RECORD ADVANCE (see "Sound Track Album Advance").

RECORDING. The process of affixing live or previously recorded sounds or images on magnetic tape (also see "Phonograph").

RECORD OF ABSENTEEISM. The history or reputation of an actor for being absent from the set of a movie production when his or her services are required, thus slowing the production. Lenders and completion guarantors are wary of actors who have had such problems in the past (see "Completion Guarantor" and "Lender Financing").

RECORD ROYALTIES. In the context of the film business, percentage payments paid for the rights relating to and based on the sale of motion picture soundtrack albums (see "Sound Track Albums").

RECOUPMENT. The point at which revenues equal contractually defined expenses, i.e., when the costs and expenses incurred in the production of a film are recovered from the film's revenues. In the context of a film limited partnership, the point at which an investor recovers at least 100% of such investor's investment. In such partnerships, recoupment is a defined term which is generally that point at which 100% of distributable cash paid or credited to the unit holders equals all capital contributions made to the partnership; however, in a so-called "investor oriented" film limited partnership, recoupment may be defined as more than 100%, i.e., 110%, 115% or 125% of original invested capital (see "Advance" or "Advances," "Breakeven," "Payout," "Post-Payout Sharing Ratio," "Pre-Payout Sharing Ratio" and "Non-Returnable Advance").

RECOURSE. The act of satisfying a claim (see "Recourse Debt" and "Remedy").

RECOURSE DEBT. A note, loan, liability or obligation in which the person or entity to whom the debt is owed has the ability to pursue a judgment for a default not only against the property used as collateral but also against the party or parties signing the debt instrument (see "Non-Recourse Debt").

RECOURSE LOAN. A loan for which an endorser or guarantor is liable for payment in the event the borrower defaults. Also a loan made to a direct participation program or limited partnership whereby the lender, in addition to being secured by specific assets, has recourse against the general assets of the partnership (see "Non-Recourse Loan" and "Personal Security").

RED BAND TRAILER. A movie trailer that can only be shown to an audience that is in the theatre to see an "R" rated film, since the trailer itself may contain subject matter unsuitable for general audiences (see "Green Band Trailer" and "Trailer").

REDEEMABLE SECURITY. Any security, other than short-term paper, under the terms of which the holder upon its presentation to the issuer or to a person designated by the issuer is entitled (whether absolutely or only out of surplus) to receive approximately his, her or its proportionate share of the issuer's current net assets, or the cash equivalent thereof (see "Redemption" and "Stock Redemption Agreement").

REDEMPTION. To regain possession by paying a stipulated price. Some corporations may have a right of redemption with respect to the repurchase of such corporations' outstanding corporate debt or equity securities (see "Redeemable Security" and "Stock Redemption Agreement").

RED HERRING. A preliminary prospectus (securities disclosure document used in a public/registered offering) relating to the future securities issue and distributed to broker/dealers and prospective purchasers during the waiting period. This disclosure document is called a "red herring" because a required legend regarding the incompleteness of the information is printed on the cover page in red ink (see "Disclosure Document," "Effective Date," "Preliminary Prospectus" and "Waiting Period").

REDUCED DISTRIBUTION FEE. A lower-than-customary charge for providing the services associated with the release of a motion picture. Distribution fees relating to feature films have traditionally ranged from 15% to 40% depending on the market, media and financial risk undertaken by the distributor. The lower-end 15% fees have generally been reserved for the rent-a-distributor situations where the distributor has not been asked either to put up production or distribution funds (see "Rent-A-Distributor").

REDUCTION. In music, a small version of the original, such as a reduced score. Also, the arrangement of a composition for a smaller number of instruments (see "Orchestra").

REDUCTION NEGATIVE. A negative made from a wider-gauge original, e.g., a 16mm negative made from a 35mm original (see "Blow-Up").

REDUCTION PLAN. A strategy developed by a studio/distributor financier of a film project and the production company to lower the actual production costs of a motion picture in progress in order to avoid going over-budget and beyond the contingency (see "Projected Overage" and "Take-Over").

REEL. Metal or plastic wheels on which film is wound for projection and storage purposes. A standard size 35mm reel holds 1,000 feet or approximately ten minutes of film (see "Can," "In the Can" and "Running Time").

REFUNDABLE DEPOSIT. Refundable payments made to secure the payor's (e.g., a film distributor's) performance of its legal obligations under a contract, including its obligation to make payments under the contract. Courts have held in some cases that refundable deposits, unlike advance payments, are not taxable when received (see "Advance Payments" and "Deferral Structures").

REGIONAL INVESTMENT BANKING HOUSE. A broker/dealer firm which provides investment banking services in only a limited number of states as opposed to nationally (see "Investment Bank" or "Investment Banker").

REGIONAL PREJUDICE. A preconceived judgment or opinion about persons, groups or things based on the geographical area from which they originate, i.e., an irrational attitude of hostility directed against an individual or group because of the supposed characteristics of the people and items from a given area of a country. Regional prejudice is sometimes used as a theme or sub-theme in motion pictures and appears to be a commonly held attitude of many people in the film industry. Regional prejudice can be just as devastating and/or debilitating as any other form of prejudice and is just as wrong (see "Bias," "Discrimination," "Favorable Portrayal," "Pattern of Bias," "Prejudice" and "Unfavorable Portrayal").

REGIONAL RELEASE PATTERN. A method of film distribution in which a film is opened in one or more but a limited number of territories with the expectation that the film will later be opened in additional territories, in a pre-set or ad hoc pattern, over a period of time. A regional release is generally less expensive than a simultaneous national release due to the fewer number of prints required (see "National Release," "Release Pattern," "Selective Release," "Special Distribution" and "Wide Release").

REGIONAL STOCK EXCHANGES. Organized securities exchanges located outside New York City and registered with the SEC, including Boston, Cincinnati, Intermountain (Salt Lake City), Midwest (Chicago), Pacific (Los Angeles and San Francisco), Philadelphia (Philadelphia and Miami) and Spokane.

REGISTERED OFFERING (see "Public Offering").

REGISTERED REPRESENTATIVE. A selling agent of a securities broker/dealer firm; commissioned salespersons qualified to take orders for securities from the general public. Such agents must be licensed and in good standing with the SEC, NASD and in each state in which such agents may sell securities such as units in a limited partnership. Registered representatives are often referred to as account executives by the broker/dealer firm employer (see "NASD" and "Private Securities Transaction").

REGISTRAR AND TRANSFER AGENT (see "Transfer Agent").

REGISTRATION. In securities law, the process by which an issuer of securities (e.g., corporate stock or limited partnership interests) submits data to the SEC and the securities regulators in each state in which such securities are to be offered and seeks approval for the sale of such securities to the public in such jurisdictions (contrast with "Notice Filing;" see "Copyright Registration," "Private Offering" and "Public Offering").

REGISTRATION FEE. A charge required by the SEC and the securities regulatory authority in each state and paid by the issuer of securities in a public/registered offering (see "Registration" and "Registration Filing Fee").

REGISTRATION FILING FEE. An amount required by the SEC and the applicable state securities regulatory authorities to be paid to such securities regulators in conjunction with the registration of a securities offering. Typically, such fees are equal to one-tenth of one percent of the total amount of the offering (see "Public Offering").

REGISTRATION STATEMENT. A document required by the Securities Act of 1934 that must be submitted to and approved by the SEC prior to a public/registered offering of securities through the mails or in interstate commerce. The registration statement must describe the securities offered and must disclose, in detail, information on the nature of the business including accounting statements, the identity of management and key owners and the purpose of the offering, including the use to be made of the proceeds (see "Prospectus, Private Offering," "Registration" and "Waiting Period").

REGULAR CORPORATION (same as "C-Corporation").

REGULAR EMPLOYEE. All film employees except those who are hired as freelance employees (see "Freelance Employee").

REGULATION A. A federal regulation for small public offerings (promulgated pursuant to Section 3(b) of the Securities Act of 1933) which permits the public offering of securities not to exceed $1.5 million in proceeds to the issuer over a twelve-month period and requires the filing of an offering statement (Form 1-A), notification, offering circular and exhibits. Regulation A offerings require less disclosure, however, than S-1 or S-18 offerings (see "Offering Circular" and "Preliminary Offering Circular").

REGULATION D. A federal exemption from the securities registration requirements, promulgated by the Securities and Exchange Commission pursuant to the Securities Act of 1933, which permits the offer and sale of securities without registration so long as the offering is in compliance with a number of conditions and limitations, such as limitations on the amount of money that can be raised, on the number of investors and on the manner of conducting the offering (no general solicitation or advertising), required disclosure of information to prospective investors and notice of sale filing requirements (see "Investor Numerical Limitations," "Investor Sophistication Requirements," "Limitations on Manner of Offering," "Limited Offering Exemptions," "Private Limited Partnership" and "Private Offering").

REGULATION S-K. The integrated disclosure rules governing the non-financial portions of forms and reports filed under the Securities

Acts. Regulation S-K governs the content of an issuer's disclosure document for both public and private offerings (see "Private Offering" and "Public Offering").

REGULATION S-X. The SEC's accounting standards to be used in the preparation of financial statements for inclusion in a registration statement for a public offering of securities (see "GAAP").

REINSURANCE. A financial transaction which provides for the sharing of risk among insurance companies, i.e., a portion of an insurer's risk is assumed by other insurance carriers in return for a part of the premium fee paid by the insured. By spreading the risk, reinsurance allows an individual insurance company to insure clients whose coverage would otherwise be too great a burden for the one insurer to carry alone (see "Cut Through Endorsement," "Excess Insurance Coverage," "Insurance" and "Primary Insurance").

REISSUE. The re-release of a motion picture. The circumstances under which a film may be reissued are sometimes set out in the original distribution agreement, e.g., the film will be re-released in a minimum number of theatres which represents a certain agreed upon percentage of the maximum number of theatres that were used in the original release of the picture, plus a suitable hiatus between the initial release and reissue during which the film was not exhibited in theatres (see "Hiatus" and "Re-Issuing Costs").

RE-ISSUING COSTS. The expenses associated with re-issuing or re-releasing a film (see "Initial Distribution" and "Re-Release").

REJECTION. In banking, the refusal to grant credit to an applicant because of inadequate financial strength, a poor credit history or some other reason (see "Lender Financing").

RELATIONSHIP-DRIVEN BUSINESS. An industry in which business choices and decisions relating to whether business should be conducted with certain other individuals or entities are based to a great extent on some affinity, link, affiliation or association which may or may not be directly related to the nature of the business. In this sense, such relationship choices might be viewed as another barrier to entry in any of the production, distribution and/or exhibition levels of the motion picture business (see "Barriers to Entry," "Insider's Game," "Level Playing Field," "Member of the Club," "Movies With a Message," "Nepotism," "Reciprocal Preferences" and "Role of Government").

RELEASE (Film). The completed film used for general distribution or exhibition; also the act and activities associated with the exhibition of a film, e.g., once a motion picture is being exhibited to the public it is considered to be in release or it has been released or it is being exhibited in a certain release pattern (see "Launch").

RELEASE (Law). The act or writing by which, or a written document whereby, some claim, right or interest is given up to the person against whom the claim, right or interest could have been enforced. The release clears for use individuals who appear on film, i.e., it may not be safe to use the names, faces or likenesses of any recognizable living persons unless written releases have been obtained and/or other arrangements have been made. A release is not necessary, however, if the person is part of a crowd scene or shown in a fleeting background (see "Submission Release").

RELEASE BUDGET. The film distributor's plan for the coordination of resources and expenditures relating to the distribution of a specific film (see "Budget" and "Prints and Ads Budget").

RELEASE CAMPAIGN (see "Distributor's Release Campaign").

RELEASE COMMITMENT. The pledges, promises or guarantees of a film distributor relating to the distribution of a given film, e.g., agreements by a distributor to spend a certain amount of money on prints and advertising and/or to release a film in the major population centers in the U.S. Such commitments are usually required by home video companies before such companies will provide a home video advance or guarantee. The producer should check with video companies in advance to determine what level of release commitment from the distributor in the domestic theatrical release will create value in the property from the video company's point of view. At a minimum, the producer should see that the distribution agreement guarantees a theatrical release. However, distributors will generally resist guaranteeing the type or pattern of release of a picture. They feel that even the use of a broad standard such as "reasonable business judgment" or "best efforts" may invite litigation if the distributor uses incorrect judgment in its selection of a distribution pattern. The producer should, however, seek minimum specific commitments for prints and advertising, particularly for theatrical distribution, since such amounts demonstrate the distributor's commitment to exploitation of the film. For low-to medium-budget pictures, it is not unusual for P&A commitments to equal to 50% to 100% of the film's budget. In addition, to the guarantee of a theatrical release, the producer may seek distributor commitments for producer consultation and approval rights relating to the release pattern, a theatrical release in certain cities and specified limits on distribution expenses. It would seem that if the distributor would work with the producer on such issues and obtain producer approvals of its release plan, there would be no grounds for litigation (see "Advance" or "Advances," "Guarantees" and "Video Rights Agreement").

RELEASE DATE. The date on which a film first opens, in a given market or nationally (see "Blind Bidding," "Opening Date" and "Run").

RELEASED PRODUCTION. A film which is currently being shown in theatres or on television during its initial distribution (see "Release").

RELEASE NEGATIVE. A complete master negative prepared specifically for printing release prints (see "Print").

RELEASE PATTERN. The general exhibition plan, strategy or manner in which a certain film is exhibited in a single territory or nationally. The goal of such a plan is generally to maximize the number of moviegoers who will pay to see the movie. Factors considered in formulating a release pattern may include the film genre, its MPAA rating, the quality of the film, the most efficient advertising and publicity, the costs of prints, the availability of theatres, the optimum playing time, the anticipated gross potential and expected word-of-mouth (contrast with "Release Sequence;" see "General Release," "Limited Release," "Platformed," "Regional Release Pattern," "Rollout," "Saturation Release" and "Wide Release").

RELEASE PRINT. The final version of a film made from the color-reversal negative and ready for distribution to exhibitors, i.e., a composite print made for general distribution. The release print is prepared after the final trial composite or sample print has been approved (see "Print Costs" and "Release Negative").

RELEASE SCHEDULE. A phrase used primarily to refer to the timetable established by each feature film distributor for beginning the domestic theatrical exhibition of each of its films, although the term may also be used to describe the similar plans relating to other territories and media. Motion picture distributors often consider the release plans of the films being released by other competing distributors when selecting the optimum time to release a given film (see "Release Sequence").

RELEASE SEQUENCE. The planned order in which a motion picture is exhibited in the various media and territories worldwide. For example, a U.S.-made film may be first released for domestic theatrical distribution, then for pay-per-view, followed by foreign theatrical, home video, pay television, foreign television, network television and TV syndications. Distributors are constantly changing such release patterns in a continuing effort to maximize the potential revenues generated by a motion picture in all markets (contrast with "Release Pattern" and "Window").

RELEASE SLOTS. A limited measure of time or distributor resources that a feature film distributor is able to commit to the distribution of a film. In any one year, most major studio/distributors will not commit to release more than twenty-four or so motion pictures, i.e., they have approximately twenty-four release slots to fill each year or an average of one film released each two weeks or so. On the other hand, the production side of the major studio/distributors is seldom able to produce more than fifteen quality films a year (as either in-house product, on a production-financing/distribution basis or as negative pickups where the studio has significant controls and approvals). Thus, in order to be able to amortize the studio/distributor's ongoing operating costs, many will take in other product to fill those release slots and to maintain their relationships and leverage with the exhibitors as consistent suppliers of quality film product. The additional films will be distributed either on a pure acquisition or rent-a-system basis (see "Acquisition Distribution Agreement," "In-House Product," "Negative Pickup," "Production-Financing/Distribution Agreement" and "Rent-A-Distributor").

RELEASE STRATEGIES (see "Marketing Strategy").

RELEASE TITLE. The actual name of the film used during its public exhibition. A film may be developed using a working title or tentative title (see "Working Title").

RELEASING COST RISK. The danger associated with distributing motion pictures and funding the accompanying expenses that such costs will not be recouped by the distributor or whoever provides such funds (see "Lender Risk Elimination").

RELEASING COSTS. Expenses incurred in putting a motion picture into general or limited distribution. The MPAA reports that the average cost for marketing a major studio release rose less than 1% in 1991 to $12.1 million per picture from $11.9 million in 1990 (see "Rising Production Costs").

RELIEF. The remedy, assistance or compensation awarded to a complainant by a court, particularly a court of equity, including such remedies as rescission of a contract, specific performance and injunction. The term, however, generally does not mean an award of money damages. Thus, "affirmative relief" is more commonly associated with protection from future harm rather than compensation for past injury (see "Damages," "Interim Relief," "Remedy," "Rescission" and "TriStar Case").

REMAKE. A new production and release of a previously made film (see "Prequel" and "Sequel").

REMAKE AND SEQUEL PROVISION. A clause in a feature film distribution agreement which sets forth the circumstances under which the distributor and the other party or parties may participate in a remake of the same motion picture or the production and release of a sequel to the picture. For example, the parties may negotiate language similar to the following: "If the distributor determines at any time hereafter to exercise its theatrical derivative distribution rights granted pursuant to this distribution agreement, the distributor, the production company and the producer shall then negotiate with each other in good faith for their mutual participation in a theatrical production based on such rights on terms no less favorable to the production company and the producer than those contained in this agreement. If no agreement is reached within thirty days after such negotiations have commenced, all such rights shall be frozen (see "Frozen," "Prequel," "Remake," "Sequel" and "Theatrical Derivative Distribution Rights").

REMEDY OR REMEDIES. The means employed to enforce or redress an injury. The most common remedy at law consists of money damages. Other court imposed remedies include specific performance, restraining orders including injunctions, appointment of a receiver and attachment. Other remedies that do not involve litigation, including lobbying for legislation or taking your arguments to the public, e.g., by advocating an economic boycott or other action by the public (see "Damages," "Lobbyists," "Professional Association," "Trade Association" and "Sue Us").

REMIT. To send back (see "Remitted or Remittable").

REMITTANCE TAX. A sum of money paid to a foreign government as an assessment on the conduct of business in that country. In feature film distribution, remittance taxes are typically deducted from distributor gross receipts as a distributor expense (see "Foreign Tax Credit").

REMITTED OR REMITTABLE. Already sent back or that which is able to be sent back. With respect to foreign receipts for the exploitation of a motion picture in international territories, the question often arises as to whether a net profit participant should receive the benefit of monies collected in the foreign territory and that could be remitted back to the United States but which have not yet been sent back. The typical major studio/distributor definition of the term gross receipts excludes foreign receipts until they are collected and converted into dollars here in the U. S. When the distribution agreement is negotiated, net profit participants should take the position that foreign receipts which have been remitted or which are remittable be included in gross receipts (see "Foreign Receipts" and "Net Profit").

REMUNERATION. Compensation or payment for a service, loss or expense (see "Bonus," "Compensation," "Contingent Compensation," "Profit Participation," "Royalties" and "Salaries").

RENT. Compensation for the right to use property; it is fixed and certain in amount and payable over a fixed period regardless of the extent of the use of the property (contrast with "Royalties;" see "Lease").

RENT-A-DISTRIBUTOR. A method for distributing independently produced films in which the producer provides the production and releasing costs but contracts with a distributor to handle the distribution of the film. This form of distribution involves the least amount of risk for the distributor since the decision relating to whether or not to distribute is made after the film is in the can and the distributor is not being asked to risk any of its capital on production or distribution. A producer may thus expect the distributor's fee to be at the low end of the spectrum, i.e., about 15% using this arrangement. This distribution method is often criticized on the assumption that such distributors are not likely to make their best efforts on behalf of product in which they have little of their own money invested, particularly when in competition with their own films. Distributors themselves deny that the source of a film has any impact on their level of support. This potential conflict, however, requires an even more careful review of numerous distribution agreement provisions which are effected by the changed circumstances relating to this form of distribution (compare with "Acquisition Distribution Agreement" and "Negative Pickup;" see "Decision-Making Continuum," "Release Slots," "Releasing Cost Risk" and "Up-Front Financing").

RENTALS. That portion of box office receipts owed by the exhibitor to the distributor; sometimes defined as the amount paid to the distributor after the exhibitor has received its share, a concept similar to the distributor's gross receipts, except that the term "gross receipts" is much broader, i.e., rentals only applies to theatrical exhibition, whereas gross receipts applies to all markets and media. Various authorities seem to disagree as to whether the term "film rentals" means monies owed and received or only monies actually received. In addition, producers may want to indicate in the distribution agreement whether monies received and under the control of the distributor, but still in a foreign territory, should be included as distributor rentals. Some industry analysts estimate that as an average the major studio/distributors are paid approximately 45% of the exhibitors' box office revenues as distributor rentals. If that average percentage is approximately correct, then any financial forecasts projecting prospective revenues from the exploitation of a motion picture should not assume a higher percentage for film rentals and should assume an even lower percentage if the distributor is not going to be a major studio/distributor (see "Assumptions," "Box Office Gross," "Distributor Rentals," "Financial Projections," "Foreign Receipts," "Gross Receipts," "House Nut" and "Remitted or Remittable").

RENT-A-MAJOR (see "Rent-A-Distributor").

RENT-A-RELEASE (see "Rent-A-Distributor").

RENT-A-SYSTEM DEAL (see "Rent-A-Distributor").

RENT-A-SYSTEM TRANSACTION (see "Rent-A-Distributor").

REORGANIZATION. In corporate income tax law, a group of transactions including mergers, consolidations, recapitalizations, acquisitions of the stock or assets of another corporation and changes in form or place of organization. The common element in each of these transactions is that if various technical requirements are met, the corporations or shareholders involved may not recognize any gain for income tax purposes and the transaction may take place without generating tax liability (also see "Bankruptcy" and "Receivership").

REPACKAGING. The development of a new marketing strategy, advertising campaign and title for a previously released motion picture. Repackaging generally occurs only when a film, in its initial release, performs poorly at the box office and the distributor decides to withdraw it from exhibition and re-release it later as a new film (see "Advertising" and "Marketing").

REPAYMENT SOURCES. The funds, revenue stream or collateral from which a production lender looks to recover its loaned funds, interest and fees. Lenders typically require at least two sources of repayment, i.e., primary and secondary sources, with the primary source of repayment being the guarantee of the distributor of the film and secondary sources being collateral which may include pre-sale contracts, letters of credit or asset collateral (see "Revenue Sources").

REPORT SHEETS. Logs or data sheets completed on a daily basis by the camera and sound professionals working on a film shoot. Such reports list each take and note which shots are to be printed and which ones are no good (see "Production Reports").

REPRESENTATION. A statement; something short of a warranty but sufficient to create a distinct impression of fact conducive to action. Federal and state securities laws often require that prospective purchasers provide certain representations to issuers prior to the purchase of securities (see "Warranty").

REPRESENTATION OF MULTIPLE CLIENTS. The practice among some attorneys, particularly entertainment attorneys serving as the lawyer for more than one client on the same transaction. Such a situation inevitably raises questions of attorney conflicts of interest (see "Conflicts of Interest," "Conflict Waivers" and "Ethics").

REQUIRED RATE OF RETURN. The return on investment required by sophisticated investors before they will commit money to an investment at a given level of risk. Unless the expected return exceeds this level of required return, the investment will generally be considered unacceptable (see "Internal Rate of Return").

RE-RECORDING. The transferring of sound records from one or more films or discs to other films or discs using electrical processes; also the combining of all tracks, i.e., sound effects, dialogue and music, onto one final release-track (see "Mix").

RE-RELEASE. Release of a film for theatrical or television exhibition at any time after its initial distribution has been completed. A re-released film does not require newly incurred production costs, i.e., the primary expense of a re-release is advertising, thus re-releasing a popular film may offer significant profit possibilities. Net profit participants must be sure that revenues generated from the re-release of a film are not excluded from gross receipts. The term "re-release" may also apply to a second release of films on videocassette. As a strategy to stimulate secondary sales, the video industry has developed a two-tiered sequential pricing structure. New feature film videos will typically enter the home video market at a suggested retail price in the $60 to $90 range. Consequently, nearly all of the videocassettes sold during this initial release are purchased by video retailers for rental purposes. As certain titles are then re-released months after the initial home video release, they are priced at wholesale prices designed to permit much lower retail prices (typically in the $15 to $30 range), which in turn stimulates more consumer purchases in this sell-through market (see "Re-Issuing Costs" and "Sell-Through Market," "Twenty-Percent Rule" and "Videocassette Revenue Reporting").

RE-RELEASE SHOWING (see "Re-Release").

RERUN. The subsequent televising of a specific film or program in a specific market as defined by union or distribution agreements (see "Residuals").

RERUN FEES. Payments made for the exploitation of a film after its initial showing on television (see "Rerun" and "Residuals").

RESCIND. To abrogate a contract, release the parties from further obligations to each other and restore the parties to their status quo ante (prior positions) or the positions they would have occupied if the contract had never been made (see "Rescission").

RESCISSION. The cancellation of a contract and the return of the parties to the positions they would have occupied if the contract had not been made (see "Prospectus").

RESCISSION OFFER. An invitation by an issuer of securities to a purchaser to cancel the investment contract and return the amount invested to the purchaser. Rescission offers are sometimes mandated by state or federal securities laws as a civil remedy to correct non-compliance with a securities law or regulation. Many states have explicit rescission offer statutes (see "Security" or "Securities").

RESERVATION OF BOOK PUBLISHING RIGHTS. A clause in a film distribution agreement which permits the person granting distribution rights to a distributor to retain rights relating to the publication of books or specific kinds of books, e.g., book about the making of the motion picture (see "Publishing Rights").

RESERVATION OF RIGHTS PROVISION. A clause in a film distribution agreement that permits the person granting distribution rights to a distributor to retain all rights not specifically granted to the distributor (see "Reservation of Book Publishing Rights").

RESERVE. Funds kept available to meet future contingencies (see "Contingency").

RESERVED ADMISSION ENGAGEMENTS. Film exhibitions in which all of the theatre seating has been set aside for specific groups or individuals (see "Premiere" and "Premiere Benefit").

RESERVED RIGHTS. Those licensing authorizations that are held back or retained by a person or entity which grants rights relating to the distribution of a motion picture to a distributor. For example, the producer may want to retain all rights not expressly granted to the distributor, including without limitation all remake and sequel rights, the right to license and/or produce television productions (e.g., television series, mini-series, movies for television) based on the picture, all live-stage and radio rights and theme-park attraction rights, as well as all rights outside the licensed territory and all rights in the licensed territory after the expiration of the licensed term. The producer may also want to add that, without limiting the generality of the foregoing, the producer will reserve all publishing rights including, without limitation, all screenplay publication, novelization, calendar and comic-book rights (see "Reservation of Rights Provision").

RESERVE FOR RETURNS. A deduction by the distributor from video gross receipts to account for the estimated dollar value of videocassettes sent back to the distributor from the video wholesaler because they were defective or for other reasons. The distributor may want to hold back as much as 25% of the video gross receipts as reserves for video returns. The film producer may want to ask for statistics on such returns to determine whether the percentage is reasonable (see "Videocassette Revenue Reporting").

RESERVE FOR STEP PAYMENTS. Funds set aside by a production company for the purpose of periodically compensating producers, writers or directors who have development deals with the production company (see "Development Deal" and "Development Stages").

RESIDENCE SHARING RELATIVE. Securities law concept which pursuant to Regulation D Rule 501(e) excludes from the numerical count of investors any relative, spouse or relative of the spouse of a purchaser who has the same principal residence as the purchaser (see "Counting Rules" and "Regulation D").

RESIDUAL PACKAGE. That collection of policies and procedures of a given union or guild applied toward the various residuals called for by their respective collective bargaining agreements (see "Flat Dollar Payments").

RESIDUALS (OR RESIDUAL PAYMENTS). Generally, residuals are percentage participations for the exhibition of films or other programs on television, i.e., payments (as to an actor or writer) for each re-run after the initial showing and pursuant to a union agreement. Residuals are generally based on the number of times a film is exhibited on television or as a percentage of revenues from television exhibition and is generally considered a distribution expense for the film's distributor. Thus, from the point of view of the distributor, residuals are costs incurred and payments required under applicable collective bargaining agreements by reason of or as a condition to the use of or the exhibition of a film on television or any other media. The film distribution agreement may provide that any payments made to or on behalf of a participant, may be deemed to be a credit against any percentage compensation payable to the participant to the extent not prohibited by the applicable collective bargaining agreement. The participant should see that this provision states that such a credit cannot be deducted a second time against the participant (see "Distribution Expense," "Flat Dollar Payments," "Participant" and "Royalties").

RESIDUALS AND ROYALTIES PROVISION. Language or a paragraph typically found in a film distribution agreement which provides for the payment of residuals and royalties associated with the picture, e.g., that the distribution company agrees to make all residual and supplemental payments required to be made in the distribution of the picture. Residuals (or residual payments) are percentage participations for television, i.e., payments (as to an actor or writer) for each rerun after the initial showing and pursuant to a union agreement. Residuals are generally based on the number of times the film is exhibited on television, or as a percentage of revenues from television exhibition. Royalties, on the other hand, are payments to the holder for the right to use property such as copyrighted material, i.e., a negotiated percentage of income paid to an author or composer for each copy of the work sold. A royalty is a share of the product or of the proceeds therefrom reserved by an owner for permitting another to exploit and use his or her property, i.e., the rental that is paid to the original owner of property based on a percentage of profit or production. Royalty is compensation for the use of property, but it is based as to amount entirely upon the use actually made of the property. If residual and royalty payments are defined as a distribution expense, they are typically paid prior to net profit participation payments and, in certain transactions, prior to the recoupment of the film's negative costs, which stops interest from accruing. On the other hand, if they are not paid as a distribution expense, they may have to be paid out of the producer's share. Producers may want to watch for language in a distribution agreement which tries to shift the burden of making such payments to the producer and asks the producer to make such payments out of the producer's share, a tactic which would tend to reduce the producer's profit participation in relation to other profit participants (see "Dues and Assessments").

RESPONSIBLE PARTY. Accounting terminology for the person or persons who are responsible for the assumptions underlying prospective financial statements. The responsible party usually is management but it can be persons outside of the entity who do not currently have the authority to direct operations, e.g., a party considering acquiring an entity (see "Financial Projections" and "Limited Use").

RESTITUTION. The act of making good, or of giving the equivalent for, any loss, damage or injury (see "Indemnification" and "In Kind").

RESTRAINING ORDER. A court order granted without notice or hearing, requiring the preservation of the status quo until a hearing can be had to determine the propriety of any injunctive relief, temporary or permanent (see "Equitable Remedy" and "Remedy or Remedies").

RESTRAINT OF TRADE. Illegal restraints interfering with free competition in business and commercial transactions which tend to restrict production, affect prices or otherwise control the market to the detriment of purchasers or consumers of goods and services. What would otherwise be considered a reasonable restraint of trade may be made unreasonable if they are intended to accomplish the equivalent of an illegal restraint (see "Anti-Trust Laws," "Conspiracy," "Paramount Consent Decree of 1948" and "Sherman Anti-Trust Act").

RESTRICTED CURRENCIES. A foreign currency which is or becomes subject to moratorium, embargo, banking or exchange restrictions, or impediments against remittances to the United States. A producer and other net profit participants may want to clarify in the distribution agreement for a film, whether such funds will be included in the distributor's definition of gross receipts (see "Blocked Currencies," "Embargo" and "Moratorium Statutes").

RESTRICTED FUNDS (see "Restricted Currencies").

RESTRICTED SECURITIES. Securities acquired from an issuer in a non-public transfer, that is, on terms and at a price not offered to the general public through an underwriter. Since the securities were not part of a public/registered offering and thus not subject to the safeguards of the Securities Act of 1933, such as the registration of the securities and the issuing of a prospectus, their sale to the public is restricted. Under the SEC's Rule 144, restricted securities must be held at least two years prior to their re-sale and may only be sold in small amounts (see "Private Offering").

RETAINED EARNINGS. Net profits kept to accumulate in a business after dividends are paid (also called "Undistributed Profits" or "Earned Surplus;" contrast with "Capital").

RETROACTIVE BASIS. The doing of some act in a manner which extends its effect back to a prior time. For example, if a producer of a feature film is also an established producer of soundtrack albums, he or she may be able to negotiate a separate deal for a royalty on the soundtrack recording. If the film distributor is amenable, it is not likely to agree to make such payments until after the motion picture has reached some specified level of breakeven, at which time the participation may be awarded on a retroactive basis. Of course, when a participant shares on a separate basis, as described above, the revenue from such a separate source will generally be excluded from the distributor's gross receipts in computing that participant's share of net profits, since, if it were included, the participant would be sharing twice in the same revenue. It might not be unreasonable to ask those distributors who have an ownership interest in video wholesalers to use the same reasoning to avoid their double dip in the video revenue stream (see "Outside the Pot" and "Videocassette Revenue Reporting").

RETROACTIVE ESCALATION OF FEES (see "Retroactive Increase").

RETROACTIVE INCREASE. A larger payment which is not triggered until a certain event occurs, but which, when triggered, permits the recipient to go back to the first revenue dollars relating to the transaction and recoup at the higher rate. Some film distribution agreements provide for distribution fees that escalate retroactively. In such instances, it is important to limit or segregate the revenues from which the retroactive recoupment can be extracted. If the distribution agreement does not address this point, the distributor will most likely take its retroactive increase from 100% of the subsequently accruing revenues (i.e., after the triggering event occurs, the distributor will take all of the next revenues to pay for the increase in its distribution fees back to the first dollar). Thus, the susceptible payment corridor from which the retroactive increase is paid should be limited in some reasonable manner (e.g., 50% of gross receipts), which allows the production company and other participants to continue receiving their percentage participations while the distributor is recouping retroactively (see "Rent-A-Distributor").

RETURN. Profit on a securities or capital investment, usually expressed as an annual percentage rate (see "Rate of Return," "Return on Equity" and "Return on Invested Capital").

RETURN OF CAPITAL. The recoupment by an investor of 100% of the money invested in a venture. Distributions of cash resulting from the sale of a capital asset or of securities in a portfolio, depreciation tax savings or any other transaction unrelated to retained earnings. Returns of capital are not directly taxable but may result in higher capital gains taxes later if they reduce the acquisition cost base of the property involved. In the context of a limited partnership, unless otherwise provided in the partnership agreement, a return of capital is considered any distribution to a partner to the extent that the partner's capital account, immediately after the distribution, is less than the amount of that partner's contributions to the partnership as reduced by prior distributions which were a return of capital (see "Basis," "Capital," "Capital Account" and "Return on Capital").

RETURN OF EQUITY. The replacement of an investor's original investment (see "Equity").

RETURN ON CAPITAL. The amount of money recouped, expressed as a percentage of the money originally invested, over and above that original investment, e.g., a 110% return of capital would equal a 10% return on capital (see "Return Of Capital").

RETURN ON EQUITY. Amount, expressed as a percentage, earned on an investor's original investment, e.g., a company's common stock investment for a given period (see "Equity" and "Rate of Return").

RETURN ON INVESTED CAPITAL. Amount, expressed as a percentage, earned on a company's total capital, e.g., in a corporate context, its common and preferred stock equity plus its long-term funded debt, calculated by dividing total capital into earnings before interest, taxes and dividends (also called "Return on Investment" or "ROI;" see "Rate of Return" and "Yield").

RETURN ON INVESTMENT (ROI) (see "Return on Invested Capital" and "Rate of Return").

RETURN RATIO. The relationship between investment and return expressed as a percentage (see "Rate of Return").

RETURNS TO INVESTORS. The money paid to or paid back to investors in a film deal or other investment (see "Return of Capital" and "Return On Capital").

REVENUE. Income from whatever source; that which returns or comes back from an investment (see "Income").

REVENUE CHAIN (same as "Revenue Stream").

REVENUE CORRIDOR. A segregated portion of the earnings flowing back from the retail sales source to the various levels of distribution and production (see "Outside the Pot," "Revenue Stream" and "Video Corridor").

REVENUE PARTICIPATIONS. Percentage participations based on distributor gross revenues as defined in the distribution agreement. Sometimes, revenue participations begin after the film's breakeven (see "Profit Participation").

REVENUE RECOGNITION AND REPORTING. An accounting concept which, as applied to the film industry, means that film producers and distributors cannot recognize revenue from any market or deal until the product is legally made available to the licensee for telecast, exhibition or sub-distribution, e.g., a distributor is not allowed to recognize or record revenue from a fixed, non-cancelable pay-TV license during the theatrical run of the movie, since the film will not be available for exhibition in the pay-TV market until some point in the future (see "Accounting Principles and Practices," "GAAP" and "FASB Statement No. 53").

REVENUE SHARING. In limited partnerships, the percentage split between the general partner and limited partners of profits, losses, cash distributions and other income or losses which result from the operation of the partnership (see "Limited Partnership" and "Profit Sharing Ratio").

REVENUE SOURCES. The various markets in which a feature film may be exploited and which may in turn generate income. Such sources include domestic theatrical, foreign theatrical, domestic home video, foreign home video, pay-per-view, pay television, foreign television, network television, syndication, non-theatrical, merchandising and soundtrack albums. As of 1986, feature film distributors generated more in domestic wholesale gross revenues from home video than from theatrical sources, and this pattern has continued since (see "Domestic Theatrical," "Fractured Rights," "Split-Rights Deal" and "Videocassette Revenue Reporting").

REVENUE STREAM. The income generated by the sale of any product which begins with retail sales and returns through various levels of distribution back to the product source. In the film industry, monies sometimes flow back from the exhibition of a given film, from the exhibitor to the sub-distributors and/or distributor, then to the producer, participants and financier/investors (same as "Revenue Chain;" see "Adjusted Gross," "Gross Receipts," "Net Profits," "Off-the-Top," "Revenue Corridor" and "Video Corridor").

REVERSAL FILM STOCK. A type of motion picture film which, after it is exposed, is processed to produce a positive image on the same film rather than the customary negative image. If exposure is made by printing from a negative, a negative image is produced directly (see "Internegative").

REVERSAL OPTICAL. A method of reversing the direction of motion in a movie scene effected by turning the film over and re-photographing it in an optical printer, so that the emulsion side becomes the base side and vice versa (see "Optical Effects").

REVERSAL PRINT. A print-to-print duplication of a film which is made on special reversal film that transfers a positive to positive image without the use of an intermediate negative (see "Print").

REVERSION PROVISION OR AGREEMENT. A contractual clause commonly found in option agreements or a separate agreement which provides that rights to the literary property which is the subject of the option agreement may automatically revert or be reacquired by the author or owner under specific conditions, e.g., if the option is not exercised within a stated period of time or if exercised, the commencement of principal photography has not begun as of a stated time. The reversion provision is typically associated with the option agreement whereas the turnaround provision is more commonly found in the acquisition agreement (see "Substitution Clause or Agreement," "Turnaround Provision or Agreement" and "Reversion Right").

REVERSION RIGHT. The power to reacquire the rights to develop, produce, distribute or otherwise exploit a particular literary property under specified circumstances (see "Reversion Provision or Agreement" and "Turnaround Provision or Agreement").

REVERSIONARY RIGHTS. The interest created by operation of law by a conveyance of property but not transferred by that conveyance, thus reversionary rights remain in the grantor. The reversion of rights to a screenplay provided for in an option agreement depends on the occurrence or non-occurrence of a specific event, e.g., failure to pay a subsequent option payment (contrast with "Turnaround Provision or Agreement").

REVIEW. A critical examination of a movie (see "Blurbs," "Critic," "Industry Critic" and "Positive Review").

REVISION. The script re-writing step beyond a polish but not yet rising to the level of the next draft. Like the polish, the revision is another special stage in the scriptwriting process recognized by the Writers Guild of America for a separate pay scale (same as "Rewrite;" see "Draft," "Final Draft," "Polish" and "Script" or "Screenplay").

REVIVAL HOUSE. A motion picture theatre which specializes in showing films that are no longer in current release (see "Calendar House").

REVOLVING LINE OF CREDIT (see "Revolving Credit Facility").

REVOLVING CREDIT FACILITY. A contractual agreement between a bank and a studio or production company customer whereby the bank agrees to make loans up to a specified maximum for a specified period, usually a year or more. As the studio/production company (borrower) repays a portion of the loan, an amount equal to the repayment can be borrowed again under the terms of the agreement. In addition to interest, the bank charges a fee for the commitment to hold the funds available (see "Credit" and "Lender Financing").

REVOLVING DOOR. A concept more commonly applied to government and which refers to the practice of private citizens, such as attorneys, who go into the service of the government, typically in some regulatory capacity, only to return to private practice following government service and in a position to utilize the expertise and/or contacts gained in government service to enhance their abilities and economic prospects in the commercial marketplace. The problem with this practice typically occurs in the form of conflicts of interest, i.e., the government official makes a government decision influenced by a possible private benefit which might accrue to such individual when he or she becomes a private citizen again. Generally speaking, in a private industry such as the film business, the revolving door concept is not a problem. However, when a relatively small but highly visible industry like film, with a high concentration of its participating companies primarily based in one city, like Los Angeles, is dominated by a small number of corporate entities and individual executives with large monetary rewards floating around, it is not unusual to see people in that industry, entertainment attorneys, in particular, move from private practice into the corporate structure of major studio/distributor and back, creating similar opportunities for conflicts of interest. In addition, any independent producer utilizing the services of an entertainment attorney must have to wonder whether that attorney is going to be a film producer or a studio executive next year and thus effectively compete with his or her former client or whether that attorney, who may be hoping to move over and accept a position with a major studio/distributor in the near future, can really vigorously represent the interests of the producer in negotiating a distribution deal with that same distributor. This constant movement back and forth between and among the studios and other segments of the industry does create numerous conflict-of-interest opportunities, which many in the industry are not even aware of or seem to completely disregard in their blind quest for fame and fortune (see "Code of Professional Responsibility," "Conflicts of Interest," "Ethics" and "Greed").

REWRITE. The writing of significant changes in plot, story line or interrelationship of characters in a screenplay or teleplay (see "Polish" and "Revision").

RICO. Acronym for Racketeer Influenced and Corrupt Organizations, a federal statute which provides for four punishable racketeering offenses (1) directly or indirectly investing income derived from a pattern of racketeering activity or through collection of an unlawful debt in any enterprise affecting trade or commerce; (2) acquiring or maintaining any interest in an enterprise through a pattern of racketeering activity or collection of an unlawful debt; (3) conducting or participating in the affairs of the enterprise through a pattern of racketeering activity or collection of an unlawful debt; or (4) conspiring to violate the racketeering provisions. A "pattern of racketeering activity" requires engaging in at least two incidents of racketeering conduct within ten years of each other. Specified offenses involved in racketeering include criminal usury, theft and forgery. Theft may include larceny (i.e., the taking of another's property unlawfully with the intention of depriving the owner of its use). The term "enterprise" in the federal act includes any individual, partnership, corporation or any union or group of individuals associated in fact though not a legal entity. Many states have also passed RICO statutes (see "Anti-Trust Laws," "Fraud," "Mob-Controlled Distribution Company," "Money Laundering," "Racketeering," "Self-Dealing," "Usurious Contract" and "White Collar Crime").

RIDER. An amendment or addition attached to another document which makes changes to the original document (see "Nudity Rider").

RIGHT. A claim or title to or an interest in anything that is enforceable by law (see "Power" and "Title").

RIGHT OF CONSULTATION (see "Consultation Rights").

RIGHT OF FIRST NEGOTIATION. The requirement that a prospective transferor (seller) and holder of a right will first negotiate in good faith concerning the purchase of the interest to be transferred with a specified party. If they fail to reach agreement, the transferor can sell his or her interest within a specified period, but at a price no less than the last offer by the specified party. Thus, a right of first negotiation is an agreement which contractually provides one party with the first opportunity to enter into a subsequent transaction. As an example, a film distributor may want a right of first negotiation to acquire the publication rights to a book (the publishing rights to which have been reserved by a producer), and the distributor may provide in the distribution agreement that if pursuant to such right of first negotiation, the parties cannot agree on terms, then the distributor will have a continuing right of first refusal with respect to any terms less favorable to the producer which the producer is thereafter willing to accept. Also, motion picture exhibitors may enter into agreements which allocate among them the right of first negotiation for films. Under some circumstances, a right of first negotiation may be considered an impediment to price competition in the market (see "Anti-Trust Laws," "Restraint of Trade" and "Right of First Refusal").

RIGHT OF FIRST REFUSAL. The right of first refusal typically requires a prospective transferring party to secure a bona fide offer for his or her interest and then first offer such interest to another specified party, i.e., the holder of the right on similar terms. If the right is not exercised, then during a specified window period, the transferor can sell for the same or greater purchase price as that offered to the holder of the right of first refusal. Thus, in a feature film context, a right of first refusal may be seen as a contractual provision which gives one party to the agreement the power to exercise its right to develop, produce or distribute a film project under certain circumstances and to the exclusion of all others. Such provisions may be found in literary purchase agreements and in studio development deals or so-called overall deals (same as "First Look Deal;" see "Overall Deal" and "Right of First Negotiation").

RIGHT OF PREPAYMENT. In lending, a negotiated right to pay off the entire amount of the loan without a penalty (see "Prepayment Penalty").

RIGHT OF PRIVACY (see "Privacy, Right of").

RIGHT OF PUBLICITY (see "Publicity Rights").

RIGHT OF RECISION (see "Recision").

RIGHTS. Power or privilege to which one is justly entitled. In a motion picture context, rights refer to the power or privilege of developing, producing and exploiting a literary property, screenplay and/or movie (see "Discretion," "Power" and "Title").

RIGHTS AGREEMENT (same as "Acquisition Agreement" and "Purchase Agreement").

RIGHTS GRANTED (see "Grant of Rights").

RIGHTS GRANTED/RESERVED. A common heading in a feature film distribution agreement for the provision that sets forth the motion picture rights being granted to the distributor as well as any reservation of rights being made by the person or entity making the grant to the distributor, e.g., a producer (see "Grant of Rights," "Reservation of Rights Provision" and "Reserved Rights").

RIGHTS OFFERING. Offering of common stock to existing shareholders who hold rights that entitle them to buy newly issued shares at a discount from the price at which shares will later be offered to the public (see "Preemptive Right" and "Subscription Right").

RIGHT TO AUDIT (see "Audit Rights").

RIPOFF. Acronym for Recalcitrant Independent Producers of Feature Film, a secret society of independent feature-film producers operating in Hollywood today. Also, a reference to the way home video revenues are often handled (see "Videocassette Revenue Reporting" and "Twenty-Percent Rule").

RISK. The possibility of losing or not gaining value (see "Interest Rate Risk," "Lender Risk Elimination," "Speculation" and "Underwriting Risk").

RISK CAPITAL. The money invested in a business venture where such funds are subject to the risks of the enterprise, i.e., risk of loss. Generally, if the investor is passive, i.e., does not participate in the management of the enterprise, such an investment involves the offer and sale of a security (see "Capital Investment," "Equity Financing," "Security or Securities" and "Venture Capital").

RISK DISCLOSURE. The act of informing prospective investors of a securities offering, in writing, about all of the material dangers of an investment in such offering. In securities offerings, certain risks are required to be disclosed and the "risk factors" section is required to be placed in a specific location within the disclosure document (see "Risk Factors").

RISING PRODUCTION COSTS. The seemingly ever-increasing expense involved in the making of a motion picture. Many in the film industry have complained for the last several years about the rising production costs (reportedly down 3% in 1991 for MPAA movies to $26.1 million) which have been occurring during a period that has witnessed declining theatrical admissions, a slowing of home video cassette sales worldwide, a leveling off of U.S.-made programming sales to Europe and reduced margins of profit. The warning has gone out that this lack of profitability in the film business will make it more and more difficult to attract capital. But it appears that the only thing the business leaders in various segments of the film industry can suggest to lower production costs is for the other guy to quit being so greedy. For example, the studio/distributors complain that the agents and their actor clients need to reduce their up-front and gross participation demands. In response, the high-priced talent attorneys counter that they will consider such a proposal if the studio/distributors will handle net profit participations more fairly, particularly in the area of home video. This inter-industry economic warfare is unfortunate, in light of what has happened in recent years to other great American industries which could not downshift across the board as the rest of the world became increasingly more competitive and globally integrated (see "Budget," "Budget Categories," "Economic War Zone," "Global Integration" and "Perks").

RISK FACTORS. In securities offerings, a required discussion of the principal factors that make the offering speculative or one of high risk which must be set forth in the forepart of the disclosure document (see "Investor Financing," "Limited Partnership" and "Securities").

ROAD SHOW. A feature film theatrical exhibition in which the distributor takes over the operation of the theatre. A road show is a public exhibition of a feature in a limited number of theatres, in advance of its general release, at admission prices higher than those customarily charged in first-run theatres in those areas (see "Four-Wall"). In the context of a securities offering, a road show refers to a multi-city trip by a company's executives, with the broker/dealer, for the purpose of selling the issue through presentations to prospective purchasers and underwriters (see "Dog and Pony Show").

ROAD SHOW EXHIBITION (see "Road Show").

ROBINSON-PATMAN ACT. A federal statute (section 2(a) of the Clayton Act) which prohibits price discrimination between purchasers of commodities of like grade and quality where the effect of the discrimination may be to substantially lessen competition or tend to create a monopoly in any line of commerce. The illegal discrimination may include payment or acceptance of commissions, brokerage fees or other compensation, payment for services or facilities for processing or sale, furnishing services or facilities for processing or handling, knowingly inducing or receiving discriminatory prices, the discriminatory use of rebates, discounts or advertising service charges or underselling particular localities (see "Anti-Trust Laws," "Clayton Act," "Kickbacks," "Rebates" and Sherman Anti-Trust Act").

ROLE. The part played in a film by an actor or an actress as an individual characterization (see "Actor").

ROLE OF GOVERNMENT. The function and activities of the sovereign ruling agency in any given jurisdiction. In a country like the United States where an essentially free-enterprise economy is part of the national fabric, the role of the federal government is generally minimized, except in situations where private enterprise engages in business practices which reduce or tend to reduce the competitiveness within an industry, i.e., businesses engage in unreasonable restraints of trade, or other civil or criminal violations of the U.S. laws. In the current economic environment, one of the government's regulatory dilemma's relating to the balancing of competitive interests in an industry like the motion picture industry is how to permit combinations of businesses to grow large enough to compete in an increasingly international economy without stifling the small-business interests within the domestic industry. However, so long as no organized interest group speaks up for the interests of the small businesses in such an industry, the government is very likely to respond favorably to requests from the larger entities in that industry to allow them the freedom to grow and compete effectively on an international scale. On the other hand, it may be possible to allow business combinations for the purpose of international trade without permitting the same combinations in the domestic marketplace (see "Anti-Trust Laws," "Fair Competition," "Free Enterprise," "Industry Groups," "Global Integration," "Predatory Practices," "Money Laundering," "Movies With a Message," "MPAA," "Political Influence," "Restraint of Trade," "Unfair Competition" and "Vertical Integration").

ROLLBACK. A retroactive gross participation that may be negotiated for a top actor, director, producer or writer if the motion picture he or she is involved with earns a certain high level of distributor gross receipts (see "Gross Receipts," "Net Profits," "Retroactive Escalation of Fees" and "Rising Production Costs").

ROLLING BREAKEVEN. A point at which a film's revenues are equal to expenses on a continuing basis, i.e., after all appropriate deductions are taken from film rentals in each accounting period, those persons who have been able to negotiate a percentage or fixed participation at such accounting stages may be paid if the film is in a profit position. Too much discretion, latitude, flexibility in the standards of conduct, lack of definition and too little auditing leeway, etc. in the distribution deal creates an opportunity for the distributor to keep delaying breakeven, i.e., rolling it back so that actual breakeven is never achieved and, thus, net profit participants quite often do not receive any money for their net profit participation interests (see "Actual Breakeven," "Artificial Breakeven," "Breakeven," "Cash Breakeven" and "Creative Accounting").

ROLLING TITLES. Film credits that move from the bottom to the top of the movie screen; a technique more commonly used for end credits than the main credits (see "Crawl").

ROLLOUT. A release pattern with scheduled, usually weekly, phases of expanding theatrical exhibition, e.g., a film may open in several key cities or in only one (usually New York), followed one or two weeks later by a number of additional smaller markets, and shortly thereafter by more smaller markets or perhaps the rest of the country (see "Platformed" and "Release Pattern").

ROLLOVER. The movement of funds from one investment to another; also a term often used by banks when they allow a borrower to delay making a principal payment on a loan (see "Debt" and "Lender Financing").

ROOM TONE. A recording of the existing presence or ambience of a quiet room. The recording is later mixed in with a film's dialogue track, making the scenes sound more realistic. Room tone may also be used to hide edits, cuts or breaks in the dialogue track (see "Mix").

ROSTERS. Lists of union and guild members maintained by the various unions and guilds of their respective members who are available for work (see "Guild" and "Union").

ROUGH CUT. An early stage of editing a film; the version of the workprint of a film that follows assembly in the film's progress toward the fine-cut stage and completion, i.e., the point at which all the film's scenes are edited together in the desired order for telling the story (see "Editor" and "Final Cut").

ROUND LOT. A generally accepted unit of trading on a securities exchange (see "Securities" and "Stock Exchange").

ROYALTIES. Payments to the holder for the right to use property such as copyrighted material; negotiated percentages of income paid to an author or composer for each copy of the work sold; a share of the product or of the proceeds therefrom reserved by an owner for permitting another to exploit and use his, her or its property; the rental that is paid to the original owner of property based on a percentage of profit or production. Royalty is compensation for the use of property, but it is based as to amount entirely upon the use actually made of the property (see "Commission," "Rent," "Residuals" or "Residual Payments," "Residuals and Royalties Provision" and "Videocassette Revenue Reporting").

ROYALTY BASIS. The payment of percentage compensation based on the use of property or rights as a royalty as opposed to making such payments in the form of a distribution fee. Unlike other areas of the feature film business, home-video revenue percentage participations have been handled on a royalty basis (similar to the record industry) rather than on a distribution fee basis. Royalty payments are traditionally much lower than distribution fees. Also, although the royalty approach is used for determining what goes into the film distributor's gross, the film distributors have, not surprisingly, generally opted for the distribution fee approach with regard to home video revenue once it reaches the distributor's gross receipts pool (see "Distribution Fee Basis," "Royalty" and "Videocassette Revenue Reporting").

ROYALTY ON HOME VIDEO (see "Home Video Royalty").

"R" RATING. An MPAA rating indicating that a motion picture has been reviewed by the MPAA's Classification and Rating Administration, that the film contains some adult material, and attendance is restricted, i.e., parents are urged to learn more about the film before taking their young children with them (see "Ratings").

RULES. Another term with different levels of meanings, i.e., (1) a prescribed guide for conduct or action, (2) an accepted procedure, custom or habit and (3) a law or regulation governing procedure or conduct. One of the more common statements made by film industry "insiders" who participate in discussions regarding film finance is "There are no rules." In at least a couple of ways, this may be true, i.e., there is no overall best way to go about financing a motion picture (it really depends on the project) and there are no prescribed guidelines for what works at the box office. But in other ways, this can be an extremely misleading and dangerous statement in that there certainly are a great number of rules when it comes to forming a corporation, creating a limited partnership, running a business, contracting with others, structuring a deal with tax considerations in mind, etc. In that sense, the people who are making the statement "There are no rules" may in reality be saying, "We know there are rules, but we are not going to abide by them because we know that no one who wants to stay in this business will complain and, even if they do, their remedies are woefully inadequate." (see "Anti-Trust Laws," "Blacklist," "Code," "Conduct Restrictions," "Conflicts of Interest," "Crime," "Ethics," "Extortion," "Insider's Game," "Internal Revenue Service," "Larceny," "Merger

Guidelines," "Pro and Con Analysis," "Remedy," "Securities Acts," "Sue Us," "U.S. Justice Department" and "Usury").

RUN. As a verb in the film industry, "run" means to exhibit a film. As a noun, the term refers to the continuous exhibition of a motion picture in a defined geographic area for a specified period of time or the length of time feature films play in a movie theatre, theatres or territory, i.e., successive exhibition of a feature in a given area, first-run being the first exhibition in that area, second-run being the next subsequent, and so on, including successive exhibitions in different theatres, even though such theatres may be under a common ownership or management. Certain distributors have been known to require an exhibitor commitment of a twelve-week run for a particularly strong motion picture (e.g., "Hook"), and certain films have been known to continue in a run at certain theatres for as much as fifty weeks, e.g., "Arthur" (see "Break," "Playtime," "Release Date" and "Two-Run Break;" contrast with "Runs").

RUNNING TIME. The total length of time needed to project a film at its normal speed. Feature films usually require a running time of 90 to 120 minutes. Exhibitors prefer the short running times since that may allow them to bring in one more audience during the course of a day thus increasing their concession sales. Many distribution agreements specify a range in which the running time must fall and may make compliance a condition of delivery. Thus, if the producer comes close but fails to come within the prescribed running time, the distributor may be able to use this technical default to avoid its obligations to make payments to the producer pursuant to pre-sale or negative pickup agreements and avoid its obligation to distribute the picture (see "Feature Length" and "Negative Pickup").

RUNNING TIME REQUIREMENTS. The outside limit specified by the distributor for the length of a film to be delivered to the distributor. The producer must be certain that he or she can comply with such specific time limits; otherwise the producer runs the risk that the distributor will use the excessive running time of the film as an excuse not to comply with its obligations to distribute the film (see "Running Time").

RUNS. The number of continuous, sequential exhibitions of a motion picture in a defined geographic area for a specified period of time or the number of contemporaneous exhibitions of a film within a defined geographic area (contrast with "Run;" see "Clearances," "Licensing Terms" and "Minimum Admission Prices").

RUSHES (see "Dailies").

— S —

SAFE HARBOR. A provision in a law that excuses liability if the attempt to comply with the requirements of the law (in good faith) can be demonstrated (see "Integration," "Regulation D" and "Securities").

SAFETY HEDGES. Steps taken by a producer or elements added to a film which help to reduce the downside risk of investing in the film. The more safety hedges a producer can offer a prospective investor, the easier it will be, theoretically, to get a person to invest in a film project. On the other hand, it may be just as effective to sell based on the theory that the higher the risk, the greater the potential reward. For example, although it is riskier to finance and produce a motion picture without a distribution agreement in place, industry analysts generally agree that a producer is more likely to be able to negotiate more favorable distribution terms for a completed motion picture, as opposed to the terms that may be available for the same movie when the distribution agreement is negotiated prior to completion of the picture (see "Downside Protection," "Downside Risk," "Negative Pickup" and "Upside Potential").

SAG (see "Screen Actors Guild").

SAG FINAL CAST LIST. The list provided to SAG by a film's producer listing the final cast members selected for a film (see "Director's Cast List" and "Screen Actor's Guild").

SAG NUDITY WAIVER (see "Nudity Waiver").

SAG PRODUCER'S AGREEMENT. The union agreement which movie producers who use actors who are members of the Screen Actors Guild must sign in order to comply with union rules (see "Screen Actor's Guild").

SALABLE (see "Merchantable").

SALARY. A fixed and periodic payment for services performed without regard to actual results achieved (see "Commission" and "Issuer Sales").

SALE. A contract or agreement by which property is transferred from the seller to the buyer for a fixed price in money, paid or agreed to be paid by the buyer. A sale contemplates a free offer and acceptance, a seller and purchaser dealing at arm's length, and the fixing and payment of a purchase price (see "Sell").

SALE/LEASE-BACK DEAL. A film investment arrangement in which the film's producer sells the negative to a group of investors and then leases it back over a period of years. If structured properly, such arrangements may provide tax benefits to the investors and the producer can realize an up-front cash benefit (see "Financing").

SALES (see "Distribution").

SALES AGENT. A movie distributor's representative who markets films to foreign territories (same as "Foreign Sales Representative").

SALES AGENT FEES. Compensation for the activities of a sales agent (see "Distribution Fee" or "Distributor's Fee").

SAME AVAILABILITY. A manner of making a film available for exhibition so that two or more theatres may not exhibit a certain film before a date certain, on and after which the theatres so tied may exhibit that film regardless of whether all of the others so tied (due to prior commitments or holdovers) can then exhibit that film (see "Availability").

SAME PERCENTAGE AS FILM RENTAL EARNED (SPFRE). A financial arrangement negotiated between a film distributor and exhibitor in which the exhibitor agrees to pay the same percentage of the week's advertising cost for the movie as the exhibitor's percentage of the box office receipts received by the exhibitor in that same week. A similar concept might be used in negotiating a feature film distribution deal with a distributor, i.e., using the SPFRE concept in place of the distributor's "discretion" to make allocations among films licensed as a package (see "Allocation").

SAMPLE ADVERTISING CAMPAIGN MOCK-UP. A full-size presentation, prepared by or on behalf of a film producer, of a suggested movie promotional concept that can often be used to solicit the interest of a studio in producing a film (see "Producer's Package").

SATELLITE TELEVISION. Television programming transmitted via satellite (see "Cable Television" and "Free Television").

SATURATION BOOKING. Scheduling a motion picture for exhibition in a limited market or area at a large number of theatres and supporting it with a strong advertising and publicity campaign (see "Release Pattern").

SATURATION RELEASE (see "Saturation Booking").

SAVE HARMLESS (see "Hold Harmless").

SCALE. The minimum wage set by the respective film-industry unions and guilds for each individual job category that is performed on a film by union and guild members, i.e., the payment of the minimum salary for a film cast or crew member as specified by the applicable union or guild (see "Double Scale" and "Guild").

SCALE-PLUS-TEN. Payment of the minimum wage plus 10%. A common practice in the film industry for actors in order to cover the fees of their agents (see "Scale").

SCAM. A planned deception in which persons pretending to be engaged in some form of business transaction are actually involved in a ruse designed to separate a victim from his or her money. Among independent feature-film producers who are desperately seeking financing for their latest project, the typical pattern is to promise full production money funding of the motion picture if the producer will provide a certain amount of up-front money to demonstrate to the supposed financing source that the producer is serious. In some instances, it is extremely difficult to distinguish between a legitimate operation and a total fraud until after the fact. It may help to get an attorney involved and create a substantial paper trail relating to the transaction while checking to confirm as much information about the parties as possible, e.g., calling the Secretary of State's office to determine whether an entity which is purported to be incorporated, is in fact, a corporation in good standing (see "Due Diligence," "Fraud" and "White Collar Crime").

SCENARIO. An outline or synopsis of a screenplay (see "Screenplay").

SCENE. A single shot or a series of shots that presents some important segment of a screenplay's action or activity. A scene may be filmed with one basic number from end to end, then broken down for coverage into scene numbers, with each sequential number moving up. For example, a full dramatic scene may be composed of several scene numbers and slated and filmed as such in the master scene. Afterwards, coverage shots or cover shots are filmed separately. Thus, a director, or distributor with editing rights, may be able to insert a cover shot at a later time. Scene number and slate numbers are the same (see "Final Cut," "Shot and Take").

SCHEDULE FOR PRODUCTION (see "Production Schedule").

SCHEDULE K-1. An IRS form which must be filed annually on behalf of a limited partnership and which lists each partner's share of income, deductions, credits, etc. (see "Internal Revenue Service" and "Limited Partnership").

SCHEDULE OF NET PROFIT PARTICIPATIONS (see "Net Profit Participation Schedule").

SCOPE OF RELEASE. How wide a geographical area or how many cities the initial release of a motion picture covers (see "Release Pattern").

SCORE. As a noun, the written arrangement of music for a specific performance and medium, e.g., film. As a verb, to compose or to select music to go with a film (see "Composer's Original Score").

SCORING. The activity involved in composing, arranging, orchestrating, copying and recording music for a film (see "Composer's Original Score").

S CORP. A corporation that has gained, by election, a special status for tax purposes. It is treated somewhat (but not in all respects) as a partnership since the results of its operations generally are reported by its shareholders and no tax is paid by the corporation. Qualification for such status is limited and accordingly not available or advisable for all corporations. For example, only a small business can elect S status; the corporation must be a domestic corporation; it must not have more than thirty-five shareholders; only individuals, estates and certain trusts are eligible to hold stock; non-resident aliens may not hold stock; with respect to assets and distribution of profits, only one class of stock may be issued; timely filings must be effected to gain the status and the status may be terminated for non-compliance with the rules. Such corporations were formerly called "Sub-S" or "Subchapter S Corporations" (see "Corporation").

SCRAPPING PRINTS. The selling of used feature-film prints for their salvage value. Although only a relatively small amount of distributor revenues may be generated through such sales, a producer and other net profit participants may be interested in seeing that the distribution agreement includes such revenue in the definition of gross receipts (see "Junking Costs").

SCREEN. A whitish, matte, beaded or metallic surface on which the photographic image of a film is projected. A film screen is often perforated in order to transmit sound freely from loudspeakers mounted to the rear of the screen (see "Number of Screens").

SCREEN ACTORS GUILD (SAG). The union which represents actors (principal performers), sets standards for wages, working conditions and other issues of interest to members and negotiates industry contracts on behalf of its members (see "Guild").

SCREEN CREDITS (see "Credits").

SCREEN EXTRAS GUILD. The union which represents film extras (see "Extra").

SCREENING. A private showing of all or part of a film, for a selected audience. Generally, no admission is charged (see "Preview" and "Sneak Preview").

SCREENING EXPENSE. A cost which may be incurred by the distributor and which is often included as a deductible distributor expense in the distribution agreement (see "Distribution Expenses").

SCREENING ROOM. A theatre with limited seating but equipped with projection equipment and used for showing completed films or films in progress (see "Trade Screening").

SCREENPLAY. The working manuscript for a film, i.e., written dialogue and scene descriptions. The screenplay generally evolves from concept through outline, synopsis, treatment, first draft, other drafts to shooting script (see "Original Screenplay").

SCREENPLAY BY. The screen credit provided for the writer or writers of a screenplay (see "Written By").

SCREENPLAY LOG. A record maintained in film studios or production companies with a significant number of screenplays under development in which the dates and descriptions of all activities relating to the screenplay are noted along with the name of the responsible person, e.g., who receives copies, when synopses are prepared, by whom and when distributed and when various stages of the drafts are received (see "Coverage," "Development" and "Screenplay").

SCREENS. The plural of screen; also the same as theatre in some situations, except that some theatres may have more than one screen (see "Multiplex" and "Number of Screens").

SCREEN SPLITTING. The exhibitor practice of double-booking for a single theatre screen and exhibiting both of such booked films so that the same film is not exhibited at every one of a theatre's daily performances. A separate ticket price is charged to the public for each film's exhibition so that the films are not exhibited as a single-charge double feature. Screen splitting is not to be confused with the splitting of films (same as "Splitting the Screen;" see "Product Splitting" and "Unethical Business Practices").

SCREEN TEST. The performance of a scene by an actor being considered for a part in a film; the scene is from the producer's script, usually in full costume and makeup and recorded on film (see "Audition").

SCREEN TREATMENT (see "Treatment").

SCREENWRITER. The person who writes a film's screenplay and may have also been involved in writing the story outline, synopsis and treatment (see "Screenplay," "Spec Script," "Writer for Hire" and "Writers Guild of America").

SCREEN WRITERS GUILD (see "Writers Guild of America").

SCRIPT (see "Screenplay").

SCRIPT BREAKDOWN (see "Production Breakdown").

SCRIPT CHANGES. Modifications to a screenplay. Such changes will almost inevitably occur during production of a picture and may create problems with a distributor and/or the completion guarantor. In the event that a distribution agreement was negotiated and signed prior to principal photography, the distributor typically includes a provision providing for script approval. The producer should also include a mechanism for approving subsequent changes and for determining which changes during production require distributor approval, otherwise, the producer risks creating a situation in which the distributor may avoid its obligations under the distribution agreement because of what it considers substantial script changes that have not been approved by the distributor. In addition, when a completion guarantee has been provided, it typically does not cover budget overruns caused by script changes. The producer, however, should at least insist on a provision in the completion guarantee that covers script changes prompted by uninsured events that are beyond the control of either the producer or the director ("Approvals").

SCRIPT CLEARANCE (see "Clearance" and "Clearance Procedure").

SCRIPT LOG. A record-keeping system (either manual or computerized) for keeping track of the screenplays submitted to a production company or studio and what happens to such scripts, e.g., when they first arrive, who checks them out, etc. (see "Clearance" and "Development Notes").

SCRIPT SUPERVISOR (OR SCRIPT CLERK). A member of the film production crew and the person responsible on a set or on location for taking detailed notes during production, keeping a record of all scenes and takes, recording such information on the shooting script as scene and take number, camera position, performance continuity, dialogue changes and running time of each shot, and presenting this information in a useful form for the film's editor. The script supervisor is also responsible for recording such information relating to later retakes of the same scene and for bringing continuity discrepancies in an actor's action and/or dialogue to the attention of the director.

These notes will be an aid to the director during production and to the editor during post-production (see "Screenplay").

SCRIPTWRITER'S COST. The feature film development and production expenses associated with the compensation paid to a screenwriter (see "Rising Production Costs" and "Spec Script").

SEC (see "Securities and Exchange Commission").

SEC ATTORNEY. A lawyer who practices securities law (see "Securities Attorney").

SECONDARY ANCILLARY RIGHTS. The power, privileges and authority associated with a motion picture which is additional to the theatrical exhibition right but not a primary ancillary right such as the right to produce a remake, sequel or television series, but rather the typically less important ancillary rights such as merchandising, soundtrack album, music publishing and live stage play (see "Ancillary Rights").

SECONDARY AUDIENCE. A specific demographic population which may be interested in a given movie but which is not necessarily the movie's primary target group (see "Appeal" and "Audience").

SECONDARY CAMPAIGN (see "Alternate Campaign").

SECONDARY CITIES. Smaller, less lucrative markets, often satellites of key cities (see "Major Markets").

SECONDARY DISTRIBUTION. Public sale of previously issued securities held by large investors, usually corporations, institutions or other affiliated persons, as distinguished from a new issue or primary distribution, where the seller is the issuing entity (see "Publicly Held" and "Securities").

SECONDARY LOCATIONS. The less important locations for a film. In scouting locations, generally the primary locations are sought first and then nearby secondary locations are acquired (see "Location").

SECONDARY OFFERING. An offering of securities by the holder thereof and not the issuer (see "Restricted Securities").

SECONDARY PLAYERS. Non-major speaking parts (see "Principals" or "Principal Players").

SECONDARY SALES. Reorders of pre-recorded videocassettes (see "Re-Release" and "Sell-Through Market").

SECOND ASSISTANT CAMERAPERSON. The film production person responsible for loading and unloading film, maintaining all camera department paperwork such as camera reports and shipping labels, preparing the slate for each take, and aiding the first assistant cameraperson (see "Cinematographer").

SECOND ASSISTANT DIRECTOR. The person involved in the production of a film who assists the first assistant director in conducting the business of the movie set or the location site [see "Director (Film)" and "First Assistant Director"].

SECOND BREAKEVEN. A contractually defined point in a motion picture's revenue stream when revenues equal costs again, i.e., following the first such occurrence (see "Actual Breakeven," "Artificial Breakeven," "Cash Breakeven," "First Breakeven," "Gross Proceeds at First Breakeven" and "Rolling Breakeven").

SECOND FEATURE. The second film when two features are playing on the same bill at a theatre (see "Double Feature").

SECOND DRAFT. A rewrite of the first draft (contrast with "Polish" and "Revision").

SECOND ROUND. Intermediate stage of venture capital financing, coming after the seed money (or start-up) and first-round stages and before the mezzanine level, when the company has matured to the point where it might consider an initial public offering (see "IPO," "Mezzanine Level" and "Venture Capital").

SECOND RUN. The next continuous exhibition of a motion picture in a designated geographic area for a specified period of time after the conclusion of the film's first run (see "Run").

SECOND TAKE. A second filming of the same or similar scene (see "Cutouts").

SECOND UNIT. An additional film production crew (other than the main photographic unit) used for shooting sequences that do not involve principal players but still may require the services of persons whose actions before the camera require direction. Second unit shooting may occur before, during or after principal photography (see "Principal Photography").

SECURED CREDITOR. A creditor who holds security that will cover the amount the debtor owes, i.e., persons or entities which have made loans or extended credit the repayment of which has been guaranteed by the pledge of assets or other collateral. For example, a bank which lends money for the production of a film will almost always insist on being a secured creditor, i.e., will not take an equity position or be at risk with respect to the money it has lent (see "Bankable Pre-Sales Commitments" and "Collateral").

SECURED DEBT. Debt guaranteed by the pledge of assets or other collateral (see "Assign" and "Hypothecation").

SECURITIES ACTS. The popular name given to the two major federal statues regulating the issue of and marketing trade in securities. The Securities Act of 1933 deals primarily with the initial distribution of securities by the issuer, and its objective is to provide full disclosure of facts material to the securities for sale so that investors are able to make informed investment decisions. The Securities Exchange Act of 1934 is designed to regulate post-distribution trading in securities and provides for the registration and regulation of securities exchanges, including disclosure of information about the issue for the purpose of prohibiting fraud and manipulation in connection with the sale or purchase of securities (contrast with "Blue Sky Laws").

SECURITIES ANALYST. An individual, usually employed by a stock brokerage house, bank or investment institution, who performs investment research and examines the financial condition of a company or group of companies in an industry and in the context of the securities markets (see "Industry Analysts" and "Securities").

SECURITIES AND EXCHANGE COMMISSION (SEC). The federal agency empowered to administer the Securities Act and to regulate and supervise the offer and sales of securities (see "NASD" and "Securities").

SECURITIES ATTORNEY. A lawyer who has expertise relating to the federal and state securities laws (see "Entertainment Attorney," "Securities Acts" and "Blue Sky Laws").

SECURITIES DISCLOSURE DOCUMENT (see "Disclosure Document," "Offering Circular," "Offering Memorandum" and "Prospectus").

SECURITIES LOAN. A loan collateralized by marketable securities (see "Lender Financing").

SECURITY. Collateral offered by a debtor to a lender to secure a loan. For example, in a production-financing/distribution agreement, the distributor will generally take a security interest in certain items relating to the film in order to secure its advance of production funds to the production company. In other words, the distributor will ask the production company to assign to the distributor as security all of the production company's right, title and interest in and to the picture (including without limitation, all interest in the results and proceeds of the services of all persons engaged in connection with the picture), whether now owned or hereafter acquired, including, but not limited to, the copyright, all negatives, film, tape and other physical properties created or acquired for the picture (same as "Collateral Security;" see "Equity Security").

SECURITY (OR SECURITIES). Any financial investment, instrument, arrangement or obligation in which the investors in an enterprise engaged in for profit are passive and have a right to participate in profits; also evidence of a right created in the holder of the security to participate in profits or assets distribution of a profit-making enterprise primarily managed by others. The offer and sale of securities are regulated by both the federal and state governments. One of the primary purposes of the sale of a security is to raise capital for businesses. Common examples of securities utilized for funding film projects are corporate stocks, interests in limited partnerships and investment contracts. Other securities include notes, stocks, treasury stock, bonds, debentures, certificates of interest or participation in any profit-sharing agreement, collateral-trust certificates, pre-organization certificates or subscriptions, transferable shares, voting-trust certificates, certificates of deposit, or in general, any instrument commonly known as a "security;" or certificates of interest or participations therein, temporary or interim certificates for, receipts for, or warrants or rights to subscribe to or purchase, any of the foregoing; but not currency or any note, draft, bill of exchange, or banker's acceptance which has a maturity at the time of issuance not exceeding nine months, exclusive of days of grace, or a renewal thereof the maturity of which is likewise limited (contrast with "Loan;" see "Investment Contract," "Limited Partnership," "Participatory Debt Instrument," "Penny Stock," "Stock" and "Subscription Application and Agreement").

SECURITY AGREEMENT. The written contract between a feature film producer and a lender providing financing for the producer's motion picture which identifies the collateral offered by the debtor/producer to the lending entity as security for the loan and grants such lender certain rights with respect to the collateral in the event the loan is not repaid by or on behalf of the producer in a timely manner (see "Collateral," "Notice of Assignment" and "Studio Security Agreement").

SECURITY DEALERS OF NORTH AMERICA. A directory of investment banking and brokerage firms in North America published by Standard & Poor's (see "Broker/Dealer" and "NASD") .

SECURITY INTEREST. An interest in real or personal property which secures the payment of an obligation. In the context of a production-financing/distribution agreement, the distributor will generally provide that the security interest granted to the distributor will be prior to all other security interests, other than any security interests in favor of guilds, unions and film laboratories. Also, the distributor will ask the production company to promise to execute and deliver to the distributor all documents the distributor deems necessary or appropriate to perfect its security interest (see "Collateral," "Debt" and "Security").

SEED MONEY. The earliest funds required for the activities undertaken during the development stage of a business or firm; more often referred to as preliminary or developmental monies in the context of feature films. The term "seed money" is more typically associated with venture capital fundings, i.e., it is the venture capitalist's first contribution toward the financing or capital requirements of a start-up business. It frequently takes the form of a loan, often subordinated, or an investment in convertible bonds or preferred stock for a start-up corporation (see "Development Funds," "Preliminary Investors" and "Venture Capital").

SEG (see "Screen Extras Guild").

SEGREGATED BANK ACCOUNT. A separate bank record of financial transactions relating to a given film (see "Bank" and "Production Account").

SELECTIVE RELEASING. A method of distributing films, typically utilized by low-budget independent producers or distributors in which a movie receives a limited release in selected cities, i.e., key smaller markets in the U.S. and then rotated around to other markets (see "Regional Release Pattern").

SELF-DEALING. Transactions in which a fiduciary uses or appropriates the property held in his or her fiduciary capacity for his or her own benefit. Many federal and state statutes prohibit self-dealing (see "Arm's Length," "Conflicts of Interest," "RICO" and "Videocassette Revenue Reporting").

SELF-DISTRIBUTION. The booking of a motion picture into theatres directly by its producer. Traditionally, "self-distribution" is considered to be the same as four-walling, although technically it is possible to self-distribute a film without four-walling (see "Four-Wall").

SELF-FINANCING. The funding of the development and/or production costs of a motion picture with personal funds (see "Financing").

SELF-INSURE. To either go without insurance or to set aside a specified amount of money to protect against the risk of loss (see "Insurance").

SELL. In securities terminology, the terms "sell," "sale" and "offer for sale" include every disposition or attempt to dispose of a security for value (see "Securities").

SELLER'S MARKET. A market situation in which there are more buyers than sellers; the opposite of a buyer's market. Generally speaking, the film distribution arena is a buyer's market (see "Buyer's Market," "Law of Supply and Demand" and "Leverage").

SELLING AGREEMENT (see "Broker/Dealer Selling Agreement" and "Selling Broker/Dealer").

SELLING BROKER/DEALER. Securities terminology for a broker/dealer firm which has agreed to sell securities on behalf of an issuer of such securities (see "Broker/Dealer Selling Agreement," "Managing Broker/Dealer" and "Underwriting Group").

SELLING COMMISSIONS. The transaction-related compensation paid to selling broker/dealers for sales of securities. Such commissions are based on a percentage of the sales price of the investment unit, e.g., 10% of the price of a limited partnership unit may be paid to selling broker/dealers out of the offering proceeds once the escrow account has closed, i.e., broken escrow (see "Broker/Dealer," "Finder's Fee," "NASD" and "Securities").

SELLING CONCESSION. The discount at which securities in a new issue offering (or a secondary distribution) are allocated to members of a selling group by the underwriters. Since the selling group cannot sell to the public at a price higher than the public offering price, its compensation comes out of the difference between the price paid to the issuer by the underwriters and the public offering price, called the "spread." The selling group's portion, called the "concession," is normally one half or more of the gross spread, expressed as a discount off the public offering price (see "Underwriting Spread").

SELLING EXPENSES. Costs incurred in marketing a limited partnership investment or other securities offering. Because such costs generally are paid from the investors' capital, their status for tax purposes is important. Certain costs, such as syndication costs, are not deductible for tax purposes (see "Syndication Expenses").

SELLING GROUP. Group of investment bankers or securities broker/dealer firms organized by the purchase group, including members of the purchase group, whose purpose is to distribute a new issue of securities (also called "Selling Syndicate;" see "Broker/Dealer," "Investment Bank" or "Investment Banker," "Purchase Group" and "Underwriter").

SELLING POINT. A positive element or factor relating to an investment deal which is considered helpful in marketing the program; something about an offering which might encourage an investor to invest (see "Investment Tax Credit," "Offering Expenses" and "Tax Benefits").

SELLING SUBJECT TO REVIEW. A film industry practice, as between exhibitors and distributors, in which these parties renegotiate the film rental due the distributor after the film's theatrical engagement has been completed. From the distributor's point of view, such a practice may be considered necessary because the film performance at the box office was poorer than expected and the distributor wants to book its next film at the same theatre under the best available terms. Unfortunately, for the other gross and/or net profit participants on the first movie, who are not likely to be affiliated in any way with the distributor's next movie in release, this practice is blatantly unfair, because, if the distributor accepts a smaller amount of film rentals from the exhibitor on the first film just so it can get better terms on a second film, the financial interests of the participants in the first film have been sacrificed for the benefit of the distributor. In the context of a so-called "Relationship-Driven Business," it would appear that the relationship that means the most to the distributor is the distributor's relationships with the exhibitors as opposed to its relationship with other gross or net profit participants. This is also a business practice that, even if addressed at the negotiating stage of the distribution agreement, is most likely to be presented on a take-it-or-leave-it basis and, if the distributor is confronted by an auditor who questions the practice, the auditor is likely to get the "sue us" response. Thus, instead of "our films did not do well at the box office," this practice and others discussed herein may be the real reasons the major distributors and exhibitors seem to do so well in the business while the smaller production companies and distributors fall by the way side (see "Adhesion Contract," "Creative Accounting," "Conflict of Interest," "Predatory Practices," "Reciprocal Preferences," "Relationship-Driven Business," "Settlement Transactions," "Sue Us" and "Unethical Business Practices").

SELL-SHEET. An 8 1/2" x 11" reduction and reproduction of a movie one-sheet used in promoting and selling a film to investors and distributors (see "Lobby Card," "One-Sheet" and "Poster").

SELL-THROUGH MARKET. The aggregate film viewers who will purchase a videocassette if the price is attractive enough, as opposed to renting a video at a rental location. Once the number of movie retail locations peaked in the mid-'80s, the major studio/distributors focused on developing a sell-through rather than a rental market for their motion picture videocassettes (see "Videocassette Revenue Reporting").

SEMI-ANNUAL PAYMENTS. Compensation paid by a feature film distributor to gross and/or net profit participants twice a year. Most distribution companies make semi-annual payments. Some will seek to limit their payment and reporting obligations to once a year. Fewer still are willing to report and pay on a quarterly basis (see "Accounting Period" and "Audit").

SEPARATION OF RIGHTS. A Writers Guild basic agreement provision (Article 16) which sets forth the circumstances under which the writer of an original story (or an original story and screenplay) is permitted to retain the rights to certain separable material (e.g., dramatic rights, publication rights and sequel rights) even though the story and/or screenplay was written while the writer was in the employment of a production company, which has the rights to exploit the story and/or screenplay (see "Writers Guild of America").

SEQUEL. A literary work continuing the course of a narrative begun in a preceding one; a feature film that is released after the original and tells a related story that occurred after the story depicted in the earlier released film (see "Prequel").

SEQUENCE. A series of shots with a continuity of location, action, time or story and usually with a beginning, middle and end (see "Continuity," "Location" and "Shot").

SERIES (see "Television Series").

SERIES RIGHTS. The power and privilege to produce a television series based on the same story (see "Television Series").

SERVICE. Useful labor that does not produce a tangible commodity. The term "service" is also used as a short form of service of process (see "Service of Process" below).

SERVICE MARK. A mark used in the sale or advertising of services to identify the services of one person and distinguish them from the services of others. Like a trademark, a service mark should be searched, cleared and registered with the Secretary of State in the state in which it is being used and with the U.S. Patent and Trademark Office so as to provide constructive notice to subsequent users of the same marks that the marks are no longer available for use (see "Trademark" and "Trade Name").

SERVICE OF PROCESS. In law, "service" or "service of process" refers to the delivery of a pleading, notice or other paper in a lawsuit to the opposite party, so as to charge the party with the receipt of it and subject the party to its legal effect (see "Consent to Service of Process").

SERVICES CLAUSE. A provision in the employment agreements of actors, producers, directors and writers which sets out the duties to be undertaken by the employee on behalf of an employer production company (see "Employment Agreement").

SET. The place where a film is shot. Sets may be exterior or interior (see "Location," "Set Dressing" and "Studio").

SET CONSTRUCTION FOREPERSON. A film production's key carpenter who is responsible for supervising all construction associated with the production including sets, set dressings and scaffolding (see "Set").

SET DESIGN. The plan and overall look of the place and places where scenes for a film are shot (see "Set Designer" and "Set Dressing").

SET DESIGNER. The film production person responsible for the supervision and preparation of all sets and shooting locations as required by the production, as well as the supervision of all set dressings and properties (see "Set Design").

SET DRESSING. The furnishings that are used to decorate a film set (see "Props").

SETTLEMENT. A conclusive fixing or resolution, usually a compromise, between the distributor and exhibitor or distributor and subdistributors relating to the amount of monies due to be paid to the distributor for a film's exploitation. Generally, settlements are calculated or negotiated on a weekly basis, at least initially between the individual theatre and the branch office of the distributor. As between the distributor and exhibitor, settlement is sometimes used to refer to the percentage retained by the exhibitor. The amount actually settled upon may be 10% to 30% below what the contractual amount due to be paid to the distributor would have been. There is almost never any written communication between the distributor and exhibitor relating to such settlement negotiations, i.e., it's all oral, thus the net profit participation auditor can only compare what was paid with what should have been paid pursuant to the contract between the distributor and exhibitor. These settlements may significantly reduce the chances that a given film will ever reach net profits, thus such negotiations impact on the financial interests of a film's producer and its other profit participants. For example, a distributor may be willing to settle for less than the money actually owed by an exhibitor on a given film in order to help the distributor obtain more favorable exhibition terms on its next film. Some entertainment attorneys have suggested that these settlement transactions would not hold up in court if challenged because the distributor, in its distribution agreement, generally has contracted to maximize its distribution revenue on the film on behalf of all gross and net profit participants. Few if any producers or other profit participants, however, have chosen to litigate this issue and even when confronted by profit participation auditors, this appears to be one of those issues the distributors routinely respond to by saying "sue us" (see "Black-listing," "Contract of Adhesion," "Creative Accounting," "Net Profit Participant Association," "Outstandings," "Problem Producer," "Selling Subject to Review" and "Sue Us").

SETTLEMENT TRANSACTIONS. Agreements between exhibitors and distributors (or distributors and sub-distributors) which settle their respective accounts and which often cover the receipts, deductions, fees etc. for several movies exhibited by such exhibitor and distributed by such distributor (or sub-distributor). The actual numbers in such transactions are typically rounded off, averaged or compromised, thus making it difficult for a producer of a movie involved in such a transaction to determine what amount paid to the distributor should be properly allocated to such producer's motion picture. This is a form of cross-collateralization which producers should object to. To prevent this problem, the producer should require that the distributor insert "floors" in its agreements with sub-distributors and exhibitors. A "floor" is a minimum percentage of the box office gross receipts, with the floors or percentages varying from territory to territory on a sliding scale over time. In addition, the producer should see that a "good faith" standard is inserted as part of the distributor's obligations relating to such settlements (see "Audit," "Creative Accounting," "Cross-Collateralization," "Selling Subject to Review" and "Sue Us").

SEVEN SHEET. Pre-printed paper containing motion picture advertising which is posted on junior panels or mini (outdoor) posters measuring approximately eight feet in width by nine feet in height (see "One Sheet," "Poster" and "Sell-Sheet").

SEVENTY/THIRTY SPLIT. One of the possible divisions of revenue between a film's producer and distributor in which the distributor receives a 30% distribution fee on all revenues (i.e., gross film rentals) and the producer receives the remaining 70%, minus all distribution costs. That is the same as saying the distributor first deducts a 30% distribution fee across the board, then deducts its distribution expenses and the producer group receives what is left, if any (see "Net Profit Participation Schedule").

SEVERABILITY CLAUSE. A contractual provision usually found in the miscellaneous provisions section of an agreement which provides that, if any provision of the agreement as applied to either party or any circumstance is adjudged by a court to be void and unenforceable, such provision will in no way affect any other provision of the agreement, the application of such provision in any other circumstance or the validity or enforceability of the agreement as a whole (see "Contract").

SFX (see "Sound Effects").

SHAM TRANSACTION. A transaction that will be ignored for tax purposes because it is deemed to have no substance (see "Transaction").

SHARE. A unit of equity ownership in a corporation. This ownership is represented by a stock certificate, which names the company and the shareholder (see "Corporate Stock" and Equity").

SHARED EMPLOYEE SALARIES. A movie studio accounting concept in which the compensation paid to certain employees of the studio is allocated among the various movies that are being produced at the studio, even though such employees may not actually perform any services that directly benefit a given motion picture (see "Overhead" or "Overhead Costs").

SHARED TALENT POOL. A reference to the fact that many of the people who are involved in the production of television shows are also some of the same people involved in the production of feature films (see "Television and Film Inter-Relationship").

SHAREHOLDERS. The equity owners of a corporation. Shareholders have ultimate control over the existence of a corporation and such control is exerted by voting in elections of directors and on certain major transactions proposed by the directors and management. Shareholders generally do not participate directly in the day-to-day management of the corporation or approve ordinary contracts (see "Equity" and "Stock").

SHARE OF STOCK (same as "Share").

SHARE TURNOVER. A measure of the rate at which corporate stock is bought and sold (see "Corporation" and "Corporate Stock").

SHARES AUTHORIZED. The number of corporate shares authorized to be issued by a corporation's articles of incorporation [see "Articles of Incorporation," "Charter," "Director (Corporate)," "Officers" and "Management"].**SHARES OUTSTANDING** (see "Issued and Outstanding").

SHEET MUSIC. The score of a musical composition printed on large unbound sheets of paper (see "Music").

SHELL CORPORATION. A corporation that is formed without significant assets or ongoing operations. Some banks require that a feature film producer seeking a production money loan as part of a negative pickup or split-rights transaction incorporate a shell corporation for the sole purpose of holding the single film being financed as its only asset and to start operations with no liabilities. This helps to insure that the bank will have a first-priority claim against all of the assets of the newly formed company (as opposed to any other prospective creditor) as the corporation begins operations. The term "shell corporation" is also sometimes used to describe companies set up for fraudulent purposes, e.g., as fronts to conceal money laundering or tax evasion schemes (see "Corporate Stock," "Lender Financing," "Mafia," "Mob-Controlled Distribution Company," "Money Laundering," "Negative Pickup," "Securities" and "Split-Rights Deal").

SHELTER (see "Tax Shelter").

SHERMAN ANTI-TRUST ACT. Federal anti-trust statute which, among other things, prohibits monopolies, attempts to monopolize and unreasonable restraints of trade. Film industry practices which raise anti-trust questions include tying arrangements, discrimination, clearances, block booking, pooling agreements, price fixing, formula deals, master agreements and franchises (see "Anti-Trust Laws" and "Clayton Act").

SHOOT. To photograph a scene, a sequence or an entire film with a motion picture camera (see "Shot").

SHOOTING (see "Principal Photography").

SHOOTING COMPANY. The organization working on a particular motion picture (see "Production Company").

SHOOTING OUTLINE. A sketchily written list of actions and objects to be filmed when a shooting script is not available (see "Shooting Script").

SHOOTING RATIO. The ratio of the length of raw film exposed in shooting a film to the footage actually used in the completed motion picture. A 4:1 ratio would be considered very economical while a 10:1 ratio would be somewhat wasteful (see "Principal Photography").

SHOOTING SCHEDULE. The breakdown and organization of a script or storyboard into minutes, hours, and days for the shooting time allocated by page, scene, or locale for a production to be filmed or taped. The objective is to plan the shooting so as to most efficiently utilize all of the elements involved (see "Production Board").

SHOOTING SCRIPT. The final, completely detailed version of a motion-picture script in which scenes are grouped in the order most convenient for shooting and without regard to plot sequence; the final working script for a motion picture. It details the film's shots one-by-one in relation to corresponding dialogue and/or other sound (see "First Draft," "Final Screenplay," "Master Script," "Polish" and "Revision").

SHORT (see "Film Short").

SHORT FORM AGREEMENT. An abbreviated contract, often drafted in letter form, which contains only the most important terms and provisions and usually provides that it is the intention of the parties to negotiate a more complete agreement at some time in the future to take the place of the short form agreement (see "Contract," "Deal Memo," "Fully Negotiated Agreement," "Letter Agreement," "Long Form Agreement," "Player Agreement" and "Standard Contract").

SHORTS. A brief written statement of information relating to the promotion of a film (see "Pre-Feature Entertainment" and "Publicity Material").

SHORT STAR LIST. A very limited number of actors who currently have the recognized ability to attract significant numbers of movie-goers into the theatres that are playing motion pictures in which such stars are featured (see "Star").

SHORT SUBJECT (see "Film Short").

SHORT TERM. In accounting terminology, assets expected to be converted into cash within the normal operating cycle (usually one year); or liabilities coming due in one year or less. In investment terminology, an investment with a maturity of one year or less (see "Asset").

SHORT-TERM SECURITY. A bond or note which matures in and is payable within a short span of time. Such securities are purchased by institutional investors for income rather than for growth potential (see "Short-Term").

SHOT. One continuous take in motion picture filming; the basic component of a motion picture (see "Scene," "Sequence" and "Take").

SHOW BIZ NEWS. A semi-monthly newsletter formerly published as a joint venture by Act II Publishing and Summit Media International in 1989 and 1990 and which focused specifically on the business side of the entertainment industry, looking at Hollywood from the studio executive's perspective. This publication was discontinued (see "Trades").

SIGNATORIES. Individual producers or film production companies that have signed union or guild collective bargaining agreements which obligate them to comply with such union's or guild's rules and regulations (see "Guild" and "Union").

SIGNIFICANT BARRIERS. Serious things that impede or separate. In an anti-trust law context, the phrase "significant barriers" refers to the serious things that may keep a business from either entering or continuing to do business in a particular field, e.g, feature film distribution or exhibition. Several of the U.S. Justice Department vertical merger guidelines relate to the issue of whether or not a feature film distributor or exhibitor must be vertically integrated in order to enter or continue in the distribution or exhibition business (i.e., to successfully compete in those levels of the motion picture business today). As a means of analyzing proposed vertical mergers in the motion picture business, these guidelines further ask how difficult is it to achieve such vertical integration (assuming it is necessary to succeed in today's marketplace), and, if vertical integration is required and there are significant barriers to such integration, is the market otherwise conducive to non-competitive performance. In other words, the U.S. Justice Department has apparently taken the position that in a market not otherwise conducive to single-firm market power or coordination among several firms, even significant increases in barriers to entry are unlikely to affect competitive market performance adversely (see "Barriers to Entry," "Merger Guidelines," "Paramount Consent Decree of 1948" and "TriStar Case").

SILENT BIT. An extra player performing pantomime of such significance that it portrays a point essential to the staging of the scene involved (see "Bit Player" and "Special-Ability Extra").

SILENT PARTNER. A limited partner in a direct participation program, in which cash flow and tax benefits are passed directly through to the equity owners. Such partners are called silent because, unlike general partners, they have no direct role in management and no liability beyond their individual investment (see "Direct Participation Program," "Limited Partners" and "Limited Partnership").

SILVER SCREEN (see "Screen").

SIMILAR PICTURES. Films that closely resemble each other in significant respects. The concept is most often used to help estimate the projected performance of a proposed film by comparing it to other similar films that have been produced and distributed in recent years (see "Box Office Comparables" and "Past Performance").

SIMPLE INTEREST. Interest calculation based only on the original principal amount (contrast with "Compound Interest").

SIMPLE VS. EXACT INTEREST (see "Interest").

SINGLE-PICTURE DOMESTIC DISTRIBUTION AGREEMENT. A contract between a producer and a feature film distributor which sets out the terms under which the distributor agrees to distribute one motion picture in the U.S. and Canada (see "Multiple Picture Distribution Agreement," "Output Deal" and "Output Distribution Agreement").

SINGLE-PICTURE FINANCING. All forms of film finance utilized in funding the production and/or distribution costs of one film, e.g., debt financed by banks against the collateral of distribution guarantees payable on delivery of the picture or single-picture limited partnerships. As a general rule, a production entity with a multiple slate of motion pictures will have more bargaining power with distributors than a producer who is only seeking distribution for a single picture (all other things being equal). The same general rule is also true for distributors seeking to book their motion pictures into theatres. Investors would also probably prefer to spread their investment out over a slate of pictures rather than put all of their investment into a single project (see "Corporate Financing," "Financing," "Multi-Picture Financing" and "Slate Cross-Collateralization").

SINGLE-PICTURE LICENSE. A feature-film licensing agreement authorizing the licensee to exploit a motion picture in one or more specific territories and media (see "Single-Picture Domestic Distribution Agreement").

SINGLE-PICTURE TRANSACTIONS (see "Single-Picture Financing").

SINKING FUND. Money accumulated by a corporation on a regular basis in a separate custodial account that is used to redeem debt securities or preferred stock issues. A bond indenture or preferred stock charter may specify that payments be made to a sinking fund, thus assuring investors that the issues are safer than bonds (or preferred stocks) for which the issuer must make payment all at once, without the benefit of a sinking fund (see "Bond").

SKIMMING. Stealing at various stages in a film's revenue stream, e.g., by a theatre's cashier and door person, the theatre owner under-reporting ticket sales to the sub-distributor, the sub-distributor taking a little off the top before reporting to the distributor or the distributor doing the same before reporting to the producer. It is important for the producer to inquire about and to see that the distributor has vigorous ongoing checking and collection programs (see "Audit," "Checking Services," "Insider's Game," "Reciprocal Preferences," "Relationship-Driven Business" and "Underreported Rentals").

SLANDER. A form of defamation, spoken words that tend to damage the reputation of another. Truth is an absolute defense to an action for slander (see "Defamation," "Defamation of Character," "Errors and Omissions Insurance," "Libel" and "Tort").

SLATE CROSS-COLLATERALIZATION. A feature-film distributor practice in which the distributor offsets the financial performance of one motion picture against the financial performance of other films produced by the same production company (see "Cross-Collateralization," "Cross-Collateralization of Movie Slates" and "Single-Picture Financing").

SLATE OF PICTURES. A feature film production company's list of proposed motion pictures which are being developed and are planned to be produced (see "Output Deal").

SLEEPER. A film that does surprisingly well at the box office, i.e., a motion picture, initially believed to have only limited audience appeal, that is able to "crossover" to a much broader audience because of positive word-of-mouth. A sleeper is a film which becomes a financial success although it had not been expected to be one, e.g., low-budget production brought out with little advance publicity (see "Crossover Film").

SLICKS. Standardized display ads for films, printed on glossy paper in various sizes and designed to receive local theatre information as needed. Slicks are prepared for use in newspapers and magazines (see "Advertising").

SLIDING SCALE. A financial arrangement, which, in the film business, often occurs in the deal between an exhibitor and distributor in which the exhibitor agrees to pay the distributor a different amount (percentage) of film rental depending on the level of box office gross for the week; typically, the greater the weekly box-office gross, the higher the percentage paid to the distributor as film rental (see "Ninety/Ten Deal").

SLOTS (see "Release Slots").

SMALL BUSINESS ADMINISTRATION (SBA). Federal agency created in 1953 to provide financial assistance (through direct loans and loan guarantees) as well as management assistance to businesses that lack the access to capital markets enjoyed by larger, more creditworthy corporations (see "Corporations," "Start-Up" and "Venture Capital").

SMALL OFFERING EXEMPTION. A term used in some states to describe a transactional exemption that may be available for smaller offerings than those relying on such state's limited offering exemption (see "Exempt Offering," "Limited Offering Exemption" and "Private Placement").

SMPTE (acronym for "Society of Motion Picture and Television Engineers").

SMPTE TIME CODE. A film, video and audio industries standardized code (a digital signal) used to enable audio and video playback equipment to lock together in synch. The code is also used in audio and videotape editing to define specific moments on a tape (see "Society of Motion Picture and Television Engineers").

SNEAK PREVIEW. An advance showing of a film in a theatre either free, by invitation or to a paying audience to test reaction or hopefully to generate favorable word-of-mouth (see "Director's Cut," "Preview," "Screening," "Sneak Preview Advertising," "Test Marketing," "Trade Sneak" and "Word-of-Mouth Sneak").

SNEAK PREVIEW ADVERTISING. Motion picture advertising designed to promote the various kinds of sneak previews (see "Director's Cut," "Preview," "Screening," "Sneak Preview," "Trade Sneak," "Word-of-Mouth Sneak").

SOCIETY OF MOTION PICTURE AND TELEVISION ENGINEERS (SMPTE). A professional association of sound, camera and film lab technicians who encourage the maintenance of high technical standards in film and television through the presentation of seminars and the publication of books and scientific papers (see "SMPTE Time Code").

SOFT FLOOR. In the context of percentage participations, a floor is a minimum percentage beyond which the participation will not fall. However, a "soft floor" refers to a floor situation in which the floor is subject to further reduction under certain circumstances. For example, once a floor is reached, additional participations may be taken off-the-top, thereby effectively further reducing the floor. Floors, both "soft floors" and "hard floors," may also be used in setting the lowest acceptable weekly rental payments to be paid by a movie exhibitor to the distributor. In that case, the floor is a percentage of the total box-office gross receipts for the exhibition of the motion picture (see "Floor" and "Hard Floor").

SOFT MARKET. Market characterized by an excess of supply over demand. The market for the distribution of U.S. feature films would have to be considered a soft market since there is a significantly larger number of feature films produced in the U.S. than there are capable film distributors available to distribute such films in any given year (also called a "Buyer's Market;" see "Law of Supply and Demand").

SOLE DISCRETION. Latitude of choice within the control of a solitary individual or entity. Certain issues relating to motion picture distribution agreements may specifically be determined in the sole discretion of the film distributor or other parties to the contract ("Consultation Rights," "Discretion" and "Mutual Approval").

SOLE PROPRIETORSHIP. An unincorporated business owned and managed by one person for the purpose of making a profit; a business or financial venture carried on by a single person which is not a trust or corporation. Unlike a corporation or a trust, a sole proprietorship is not a separate taxpaying entity. Instead, its income is taxed directly to the individual proprietor (same as "Proprietorship;" see "Entity").

SOLE SCREEN CREDIT. The acknowledgement on the motion picture screen that a single person performed a certain task relating to the production of the film, e.g., wrote the screenplay (see "Credits").

SOLE SHAREHOLDER. A single individual or entity who owns all of the shares of a corporation (see "Majority Shareholder" and "Principal Stockholder").

SOLICITATION. The process of offering and selling a security to a prospective investor (see "General Solicitation" and "Limitations on Manner of Offering").

SOLID WORD-OF-MOUTH. Favorable reactions from moviegoers to a particular movie that are passed along verbally to other potential moviegoers (see "Word-of-Mouth").

SOLVENCY. The ability to pay all debts and just claims as they come due (see "Bankruptcy").

SONG. A short poem presented within a musical setting (see "Lyrics" and "Music").

SONG WRITER. One who writes, composes, creates or conceives, alone or in collaboration with another or others, the words and/or music of any original composition. Also, one who creates original arrangements of musical compositions in the public domain or with the permission of the copyright owner (see "Lyrics").

SOUND. The recorded auditory portions of a motion picture including speaking, singing, music and noise (see "Sound Editor" and "Sound Effects").

SOUND ALBUM MATERIALS. All of those physical items associated with the production of a phonograph record of the music and songs heard as part of a motion picture (see "Album" and "Album Cover").

SOUND EDITOR. The film production person engaged in supervising the making or creating of sound effects and/or the creating or making of such effects and/or engaged in assembling and synchronizing sound effects tracks for the purpose of re-recording, including the synchronizing of re-recorded dialogue tracks to the action in a motion picture (see "Picture Editor").

SOUND EFFECT TRACK(S). The audio track(s) containing only sound effects. These tracks only exist as separate tracks until the final mix of music, sound effects and dialogue into a composite soundtrack (see "Sound Effects").

SOUND EFFECTS. All artificially created or natural sounds, other than synchronized voices, narration and music, which may be recorded on the soundtrack of a film. Prior to re-recording, these effects usually occupy a separate sound track or tracks called sound effects track(s) (often abbreviated "SFX;" see "Sound Tracks").

SOUND FACILITIES. Physical plants where movie sound is transferred, synced, looped, re-recorded and mixed (same as "Sound Laboratory").

SOUND LABORATORY (see "Sound Facilities").

SOUND LABORATORY AGREEMENTS. The contracts setting forth the terms under which a sound laboratory is to provide services relating to the production of a motion picture (see "Sound Facilities").

SOUND MIXER. The film production person responsible for selecting and operating all sound equipment. This person is called a mixer because, during film takes that require the use of more than one microphone, he or she mixes (balances level and equalization) between the microphones (level refers to volume; equalization refers to the relative intensity of various frequencies, e.g., treble, mid-range and bass). The mixer is also responsible for monitoring each recording and keeping accurate records on the sound reports (see "Mix").

SOUND, MUSIC, EFFECTS AND DUBBING EDITOR. A combined screen credit sometimes used to described a single individual who creates and/or selects, assembles and synchronizes music and all other sound tracks for the purpose of re-recording; times and cues the picture for scoring; prepares click, tempo and cueing tracks; edits sound and synchronizes the various tracks to the movie's action and dialogue; intercuts playback and dubbed music tracks; and creates or uses available sound effects tracks for the purpose of recording (see "Effects Editor," "Music Editor," "Sound Editor" and "Supervising Sound Editor").

SOUNDSTAGE. A large warehouse-type facility which is soundproof, contains rigging for lights and cables, provides a generous supply of electrical power, with a smooth floor surface and is available for rent and use in building film sets and producing films (see "Studio").

SOUND STOCK. Blank tapes for the recording of sound (see "Film Stock").

SOUNDTRACK. The physical portion of a film where either magnetically or optically recorded audio material is contained. Also, a recording of the musical score from a film (see "Dialogue Track," "Music Track," "Sound Effects Track" and "Soundtrack Albums").

SOUNDTRACK ALBUM ADVANCE. Up-front compensation paid to a motion picture or other person relating to the acquisition of rights to distribute a soundtrack album for a film (see "Soundtrack Album Right Approval").

SOUNDTRACK ALBUM RIGHT OF APPROVAL. The contractually granted authority to approve or disapprove of certain matters relating to the production of a motion picture soundtrack album. Such a provision may appear in a feature film distribution agreement, e.g., the distributor may want to have approval rights (not to be unreasonably withheld) of the record company with which the soundtrack album for the picture is placed and the terms of the agreement (see "Soundtrack Album Advance").

SOUNDTRACK ALBUMS. Phonograph records, tape recordings and compact discs which contain selected portions of a movie's musical score. Soundtrack albums represent another possible source of motion picture related revenue (see "Ancillary Rights").

SOUNDTRACK DISTRIBUTION RIGHTS (see "Soundtrack Rights").

SOUNDTRACK RIGHTS. The legal power and authority to exploit the soundtrack of a motion picture (see "Soundtrack Albums").

SOURCES OF REVENUE (see "Revenue Sources").

SPEC. Short for speculation; e.g., a film that is produced by an independent producer for marketing to distributors as a finished film is said to be produced on spec, i.e., the producer is speculating as to whether a distributor will be interested and as to how much such a producer will be paid for the film by a distributor. Many low-budget independent producers also try to persuade persons who provide all sorts of property and services in the production of movies to provide such property and services on spec, i.e., in exchange for a very speculative percentage participation in the movie's net profits (see "Net Profit Participant").

SPECIAL-ABILITY EXTRA. An extra who possesses special ability, such as horse riding, handling livestock, professional or collegiate-level athletic ability, skating and/or swimming (see "Extra" and "Silent Bit").

SPECIAL EFFECTS. Optical effects or tricks used to portray or suggest a spectacle or occurrence in a film that would ordinarily be impractical or impossible. The basis of such effects are typically artificially constructed, as a rule in a studio separate from the main shooting stages. Special effects may include split screens, matting, models and combination foregrounds and backgrounds (contrast with "Sound Effects").

SPECIAL EFFECTS TECHNICIAN. The film production person responsible to the director for safely and effectively planning and executing all special effects required for a film production (see "Special Effects").

SPECIAL HANDLING. Specific film marketing strategies for what may be quality films but which do not have obvious broad commercial appeal. Such strategies include exclusive runs in a limited number of selected theatres, advertising campaigns that appeal to more artistic sensibilities as opposed to a more "hard-sell" approach and keeping such a movie in the marketplace long enough for it to find its audience through word-of-mouth (see "Art Film" and "Exclusive Run").

SPECIALIZED DISTRIBUTION. Distribution of a film to a limited target audience, in a smaller number of theatres than a commercial distribution, with limited advertising expenditures and a strong emphasis on publicity and critical reviews to reach a discerning public (see "Regional Release Pattern" and "Wide Release").

SPECIFIC PERFORMANCE. An equitable remedy available to an aggrieved party when the party's remedy at law is inadequate, consisting of a requirement that the party responsible for a breach of contract undertake to perform or to complete performance of his or her obligations under the contract (see "Equity" and "Remedy or Remedies").

SPEC SCRIPT. A motion picture screenplay written by a screenwriter who is not writing such screenplay at the request of an employer production company and without any commitment from any prospective purchaser to purchase the screenplay (see "Bidding War," "Conscious Parallelism," "Rising Production Costs," "Spec," "Work Made for Hire" and "Writer for Hire").

SPECULATION. Assumption of risk in anticipation of gain but recognizing a higher than average possibility of loss (see "Risk" and "Spec").

SPFRE (see "Same Percentage as Film Rental Earned").

SPIN OFF. A motion picture based on a new television series and which incorporates any continuing character or substantial element from the series (see "Television Series").

SPLICE. The method used for joining together the ends of two pieces of film so that they do not overlap (see "Edit").

SPLIT. The increase in a corporation's number of outstanding shares of stock without any change in the shareholders' equity or the aggregate market value at the time of the split (see "Corporate Stock").

SPLIT AGREEMENT. An agreement reached by exhibitors which allocates among the exhibitors the rights to negotiate for the exhibition of films distributed by motion picture distributors. A split agreement may be either film-by-film (in which the exhibitors take turns selecting films for their theatres on a film-by-film basis so that no two theatres in the same competitive theatre area play the same film simultaneously) or distributor-by-distributor, in which the exhibitors allocate among themselves the rights to negotiate with particular distributors for the licensing of films at particular theatres (same as "Product Splitting;" see "Anti-Trust Laws," "Blind Bidding" and "Unethical Business Practices").

SPLIT OF PROCEEDS. A term which could apply to any division of revenues between business entities or individuals involved in a transaction, but which in the motion picture industry is most often used to described the percentage sharing between the distributor and exhibitor in the balance of gross box-office receipts after exhibitor deductions. For example, a fairly typical exhibitor's bid for a long-run engagement of a film may call for the distributor to receive 90% of the box office receipts for the first two weeks after a negotiated fixed sum is deducted for house expenses, then, after the third week, the distributor's share would begin to decline until the ninth week, when it reaches 25%. The distributor's share would remain at the 25% level through the balance of the engagement. Using this split of proceeds, the exhibitor benefits most if the film stays at the theatre for a long period of time (see "Concessions," "House Nut," "Ninety/Ten Deal," "Selling Subject to Review," "Settlement Transaction" and "Sliding Scale").

SPLIT-RIGHTS BASIS (see "Split-Rights Deal").

SPLIT-RIGHTS DEAL. A film finance and distribution transaction which has apparently replaced the "fractured-rights deals" of the 1980s in which the producer pre-sells domestic rights only to a distributor and retains international rights. By keeping the international rights on a promising film that is pre-packaged and financed, the producer may be able to sell these international rights on an auction basis to the highest bidder. The total price obtained may exceed the actual costs incurred in making the film. In addition, the domestic and international rights are not cross-collateralized (i.e., uncrossed) with respect to the producer. In the event that the film is well received at the box office either in the domestic marketplace or internationally, the producer may earn more overages than in a crossed situation, such as a worldwide pickup or production-financing/distribution deal. The producer may also be able to limit the studio/distributor's term of rights in split rights deals (see "Distribution Term," "Pre-Sales" and "Fractured-Rights Deals").

SPLIT-RIGHTS PICKUPS. A variation on the single negative pickup distribution agreement for worldwide rights in which at least two different distribution commitments are obtained from different entities prior to the production of a feature film with the distribution rights being split along domestic and international lines. These contractual commitments are then taken to a bank or other lending source, where the contracts are discounted and production funds are loaned to the producer (see "Negative Pickup" and "Split-Rights Deal").

SPLITTING (see "Product Splitting" and "Split Agreement").

SPLITTING ARRANGEMENTS (see "Product Splitting" and "Split Agreement").

SPLITTING THE SCREEN (see "Screen Splitting").

SPONSOR. In limited partnerships, the general partner who organizes and sells the limited partnership interests (also called "Promoter").

SPOT ANNOUNCEMENTS (see "Commercials").

SPOT MARKET. That portion of the buying and selling of radio and television advertising time for the promotion of motion pictures where purchases of time are made on a selective basis with a specific target audience in mind. Spot market purchases are generally more expensive per minute than the blanket network buys, but the purchase of significantly fewer properly targeted advertising slots can generate savings and may produce better results (see "Blanket Network Buys," "Media Mix" and "Rising Production Costs").

SPOTS (see "Commercials").

SPREADING RISK (see "Diversification").

SPREADSHEET. Ledger sheet on which a company's financial statements, such as balance sheets, income statements and sales reports, are laid out in columns and rows (see "Financial Statement").

SQUEAKY WHEEL GETS THE GREASE. An old saying meaning those who complain or make their positions known are more likely to get the desired attention and favorable treatment as opposed to those who suffer quietly. In the context of the film industry, for example, the major feature-film distributors have a well-organized trade group (the MPAA) that provides an aggressive lobbying service for its member firms. The MPAA is generally opposed to the passage of anti-blind bidding statutes by state legislatures and, to date, the interests of the major distributors have won out over the interests of the independent exhibitors on that question in most state jurisdictions. In addition, the MPAA has successfully lobbied the past two U.S. presidential administrations for relaxation of the U.S. Justice Department enforcement of federal anti-trust laws in the entertainment industry with the result that some of the major studio/distributors (MPAA member companies) have been able to vertically integrate by merging with or acquiring corporate affiliations with exhibition chains. In the meantime, the independent producers whose interests are significantly effected by both the practice of blind bidding and the ownership of theatres by the major studio/distributors have failed to organize any effective advocacy group to speak up in these various forums on behalf of their interests (see "AIVF," "Anti-Blind Bidding," "Anti-Trust Laws," "Blind Bidding," "IFP," "IFP/West," "Industry Groups," "Lobbyists," "Major Exhibition Chains," "Model Agreements," "MPAA," "Paramount Consent Decree of 1948," "Producers Guild of America," "TriStar Case" and "Vertical Integration").

SQUEEZE-OUT. In corporate law, any transaction engaged in by the parties in control of a corporation for the purpose of eliminating minority shareholders. In a more general business sense, the gradual elimination of smaller, less powerful competitors through the use of anti-competitive practices (see "Anti-Competitive Practices," "Anti-Trust Laws," "Cartel," "Independent Distributor" and "Major Studio/ Distributors").

STABILIZATION. The purchase of securities by the underwriters for their own account during the distribution of an issue, when the market price is at or below the public offering price, in order to keep the price up so purchasers will buy from the underwriters in the offering and not on the open market (see "Securities").

STAFF. The staff on a motion picture project includes everyone but the performers. The crew is regarded as operational staff and others as production staff, although these categories often overlap (see "Cast," "Crew," "Operational Staff" and "Production Staff").

STAGE AGREEMENT. A contract between a feature film production company and a studio that sets out the terms under which the production company may use the stage in the production of a film (see "Location Agreement").

STAGGERED BOARD OF DIRECTORS. Corporate board of directors a portion of which are elected each year, instead of all at once (see "Corporation").

STAGING. A phase of film rehearsal for the actors in which the action in a given scene is blocked out (see "Blocking").

STANDARD CONTRACT. An often abused and misused term; a document which does not exist in reality in any business transaction involving negotiations. Producers should avoid doing business with distributors who suggest that they have a standard contract or that there is a standard contract for the industry or a segment of the industry. Every material term of a contract should be considered negotiable. By contrast, in those segments of the film industry in which guilds are authorized to represent particular individuals, a standard guild contract actually exists, but no guild has been authorized to negotiate on behalf of feature film producers (see "Contract of Adhesion," "Creative Accounting," "Customary Terms," "Model Agreement," "Producers Guild of America," "Professional Association" and "Letter of Agreement").

STANDARD SPLIT. An outdated and/or mythical profit-sharing ratio between distributors and producers which was once believed to be 70/30 after the distributor deducted all of its distribution expenses. There is no such standard provision in an industry where each distribution deal is negotiated between the specific parties to each deal. Distributors who suggest that such a standard exists are probably hoping to lull a gullible producer into accepting onerous or burdensome provisions solely based on the suggestion that "everyone else is doing it;" whereas, if such a standard split actually existed, it might raise anti-trust or more specifically price-fixing concerns. Of course, some in the industry feel that any producer who accepts the notion of a standard split deserves the deal he or she gets (see "Minimum Film Rental," "Ninety/Ten Deal" and "Sliding Scale").

STANDARDS AND PRACTICES. The guidelines and procedures imposed by the Standards and Practices Departments of the major free-television networks on material presented for broadcast. For example, "R" rated feature films are generally not considered in compliance with these more restrictive free-television requirements. Film distribution agreements typically require that additional television cover shots be provided on such movies. If such cover shots are not provided and/or the movie does not meet the networks' standards, the film distributor may avoid its obligation to make payments to the producer, refuse to license the film in that market or (in some instances) may be authorized to edit the film itself. In a broader sense, the term "standards and practices" may also apply to the similar guidelines and procedures of newer networks and the cable media (see "Network" and "Other Versions").

STANDARD TERMS AND CONDITIONS. A major section of the typical studio/distributor feature-film distribution agreement which sets out the terms and provisions relating to the distribution of a feature film that the studio considers standard. It is important to recognize that what is considered standard for that studio may or may not be standard for another major studio/distributor or for an independent distributor, regardless of the fact that such provisions are often similar. For example, it would be a violation of the anti-trust laws for competitors like the major studio/distributors, even through the facilities of their trade association (the MPAA), to get together and agree on standard terms and conditions. Thus, the phrase "standard terms and conditions" does not necessarily mean that such terms and conditions are standard in the industry, nor should independent producers allow themselves to be led to believe that is the case. In other words, a distributor's standard terms and conditions should also be negotiable. Generally, the studio/distributor distribution agreement will also contain a provision which says "To the extent any terms or conditions of the Standard Terms and Conditions are inconsistent with the Deal Terms, the Deal Terms shall govern." Thus, the studio is setting out in the "Standard Terms and Conditions" section what it would prefer with respect to certain issues, and, if producers want something different, they need to speak up during the negotiations and ask that the language in the "Standard Terms and Conditions" section be crossed out, modified or otherwise altered or that different language be included in the "Deal Terms" section of the agreement which overrules the "Standard Terms and Conditions" section (see "Anti-Trust Laws," "Deal Terms," "Major Studio/Distributors," "MPAA" and "Squeaky Wheel Gets the Grease").

STANDBY COMMITMENT. In securities, an agreement between a corporation and an investment banking firm or group (the standby underwriter) whereby the latter contracts (for a fee) to purchase for resale, any portion of a stock issue offered to current shareholders in a rights offering that is not subscribed to during the two- to four-week standby period. In lending, a bank commitment to lend money up to a specified amount for a specific period, to be used only in a certain contingency (see "Lender Financing" and "Securities").

STANDBY LETTER OF CREDIT. A non-negotiable, non-transferable (except together with the evidence of indebtedness which it secures) letter of credit, issued by a bank or other financial institution which serves as a guarantor of the indebtedness which is secured by the letter of credit. A standby letter of credit is payable only if the payor defaults on its obligation to make payments under the contract (see "Letter of Credit").

STAR. A leading actor who is well-known and constantly publicized. The star has billing above the feature players and sometimes enjoys credit lettering which is larger than the credit of the director or producer, depending on the status of the star at the time (see "Marque Value," "Name Actors" and "Prima Donna").

STAR COMMITMENT. The pledge or promise of a proposed lead actor for a motion picture, either directly or through an agent, to appear in a specified role in the project, assuming certain conditions are met. Such commitments are often used by producers to help raise production funding for a film. Star commitments come in all "shapes and sizes," from oral commitments between friends to legally enforceable letters of intent and pay-or-play and pay-and-play contractual commitments (see "Director Commitment," "Letters of Intent," "Letters of Interest," "Nominal Payments," "Package," "Packaging," "Pay and Play" and "Pay or Play").

STAR DEFERMENTS. Any agreed-upon delayed compensation arrangement for a lead actor in a movie. Some actors have been known to delay all or a portion of their negotiated salaries to be paid out of first monies received by a studio/distributor or by the producer in order to help in making the limited available production funds for a special project cover the other costs of production (see "Contingent Compensation" and "Deferrals").

STAR PROPERTIES. Feature film projects that are considered excellent vehicles for certain high-profile lead actors. Some industry observers suggest that competition among the major studio/distributors for star properties has resulted in a studio give-away of most of the upside potential of such motion pictures to those stars or to the independently financed production companies that now simply rent the distribution systems of the major studio/distributors for distribution purposes (see "Bidding War," "Rent-A-Distributor" and "Star").

START-DATE. The projected calendar date on or about which the production of a planned motion picture will begin. A "start date" will almost always be included in production-financing/distribution agreements and negative pickup agreements and will, in both cases, signify the beginning of the specified production schedule and the time when production funds begin to flow from the financing source to the production company as per the projected cash flow schedule. Such dates are also important for obtaining the more formal star commitments (see "Delivery Date," "Production Schedule," "Projected Cash Flow Schedule" and "Star Commitment").

START-UP. A new business venture. In venture capital terminology, start-up is the earliest stage at which a venture capital investor or investment pool will provide funds to an enterprise, usually on the basis of a business plan detailing the background of the management group along with market and financial projections. Investments or loans made at this stage are called seed money (see "Business Plan," "Financial Projections," "Seed Money" and "Venture Capital").

START-UP COSTS. Expenses necessary to start a new business, incurred prior to commencement of active business operations. The extent of such costs and their status for tax purposes are important to an investor, since they may not be currently recoverable as tax deductions. However, if the taxpayer so elects, trade or business start-up expenses may be amortized (i.e., deducted ratably) over a period of at least sixty months beginning with the month the trade or business begins. There are three types of trade or business start-up expenditures: (1) investigatory expenses for seeking and investigating the feasibility of acquiring or establishing an active trade or business, (2) establishing an active trade or business and (3) activities engaged in for profit or for the production of income before the day on which the trade or business begins, in anticipation of such activities becoming an active trade or business (see "Organizational Expenses" and "Syndication Expenses").

STAR VEHICLES (see "Star Properties").

STATED VALUE. The assigned value given to a corporation's stock for accounting purposes in lieu of par value (see "No-Par Stock" and "Par").

STATE LEGISLATURES. The branch of state governments which passes state laws. The issue of blind bidding or anti-blind bidding statutes is a matter that is brought before the state legislatures as opposed to the U.S. Congress, thus those proponents and opponents of blind bidding must lobby with state legislators (see "Anti-Blind Bidding Statutes," "Blind Bidding," "Blue Sky Laws" and "Lobbying").

STATE SUPPORTED FUNDING (see "Government Subsidies").

STATUTE OF LIMITATIONS. A law that establishes a time within which parties to a contract or transaction must take judicial action to enforce their rights or else they will be forever barred from enforcing them (see "Audit," "Litigation" and "Remedy").

STATUTORY LIEN. A charge, hold, claim or encumbrance upon the property of another as security for some debt or charge which is imposed or created by statute (see "Lien").

STEP DEAL. A form of feature film development agreement between a producer (writer and/or director) and studio/distributor whereby the decisions to proceed are made and payments to the producer (writer and/or director) are made at each stage of development of the film's screenplay. The first step might involve developing an outline of the screenplay, the second step might involve developing a first draft of the script and so forth. The studio will have the right to decline to develop the project beyond any given stage, if it so chooses (see "Development" and "Turnaround").

STILL (see "Production Still").

STILL PHOTOGRAPHER. The film production person responsible to the producer and/or publicist for taking production stills on a movie set or in association with a film production (see "Production Still").

STOCK. Negative film that has not been exposed (see "Film").

STOCK (see "Corporate Stock").

STOCK CERTIFICATE. Written instrument evidencing a share in the ownership of a corporation and showing the number of shares owned, name of the issuer, amount of par or stated value represented or a declaration of no-par value, the rights of the shareholder and signature of the president and sometimes the secretary (see "Partnership Certificate").

STOCK DIVIDEND. Payment of corporate dividends in the form of stock rather than cash and as additional shares in either the corporation or a subsidiary (see "Corporate Stock").

STOCK EXCHANGE. A market maintained for the purpose of buying and selling securities (see "Publicly Held" and "Securities").

STOCK FOOTAGE. Exposed film of scenes or past events that can be duplicated and incorporated into a new production. Stock footage is used when needed shots are too expensive, difficult or impossible to recreate (see "Film").

STOCK FRAUD. In the sale or offer of corporate stocks, the intentional misrepresentation, concealment or omission of the truth, for the purpose of deception or manipulation to the detriment of an investor or prospective investor. It would appear that the failure of any feature film studio/distributor or independent distributor which is publicly or even privately owned by shareholders, to disclose that they engage in many of the practices described herein (if in fact such is the case) might constitute stock fraud. It is also possible that the publication of this list of distributor/industry practices might create a greater need for stock brokers who offer or sell the stocks of studio distributors, independent distributors or other film industry corporations, to conduct more thorough due diligence investigations of such entities before offering their stocks; otherwise, the stock brokers themselves may be exposed to greater liability based on their failure to discover and disclose such practices which tend to be detrimental to the interests of the investor clients of the stock brokers. This compilation may also encourage closer scrutiny by shareholders of the manner in which a film distributor operates and could conceivably prompt shareholder lawsuits in instances where such practices seem to be prevalent and harmful to such shareholders (see "Creative Accounting" and "Due Diligence").

STOCKHOLDER. Individual or organization with an equity ownership interest in a corporation. Stockholders must own at least one share. The shareholders of corporate entities may be individuals or other corporations. Some corporate conglomerates that have purchased equity ownership interests in motion picture production companies and/or distributors where a certain level of autonomy for the existing management remains intact as part of the deal have been somewhat disappointed in the financial results of their investment. In other words, even though the entertainment entity operates at an acceptable level of profitability, for various reasons the profits do not always seem to flow through to the equity shareholders (also called "Shareholder" or "Shareowner;" see "Corporate Stock," "Dividend," "Greed," "Mergers and Acquisitions," "Profitability" and "Rising Production Costs").

STOCKHOLDER OF RECORD. Common or preferred stockholder whose name is registered on the books of a corporation as owning shares as of a particular date. Dividends and other distributions are made only to shareholders of record (see "Corporate Stock").

STOCK MARKET. An organized market where stocks and bonds are actively traded such as stock exchanges or over-the-counter markets (see "Corporate Stock" and "Stock Exchange").

STOCK REDEMPTION AGREEMENT. A contract between a corporation and an investor for the repayment of a debt security or preferred stock issue at or before maturity, at par or at a premium price (see "Redeemable Security," "Redemption" and "Stock").

STONEWALL DEFENSE. A position taken by a prospective defendant in negotiations between parties designed to avoid litigation in which the defendant simply says "see you in court." The tort of "bad faith denial of contract" seeks to provide a recovery based on a defendant's bad faith conduct in asserting a stonewall defense to an ordinary commercial contract (see "Bad Faith Denial of Contract," "Probable Cause" and "Sue Us").

STORY. Literary or dramatic material setting forth the characterization of the principal characters and containing cohesive sequences and action constituting a plot or suitable for use in, or representing a substantial contribution to, a final script (see "Plot").

STORY ANALYST. An employee of a studio or film production company in the story department who reads and analyzes literary material such as screenplays, treatments, magazine articles and books submitted to the story department and who prepares synopses of such material for review by the story analyst's supervisor, who is usually called the "story editor." Stories that are to be selected and developed into screenplays by the studio or film production company are reviewed initially by the story analyst (see "Coverage," "Development Notes" and "Story Editor").

STORYBOARD. Sketches or drawings of key incidents in the action described by a movie screenplay which are arranged in order on a board and captioned. Storyboards often play an important role in preparing a shooting schedule and otherwise planning for principal photography. Some producers rely more heavily than others on storyboards (see "Pre-Production").

STORY BY. The screen credit awarded the person who developed a film's story but did not write the screenplay (see "Screenplay By" and "Written By").

STORY DEVELOPMENT (see "Development").

STORY DRIVEN. A motion picture or screenplay which has a well-developed story line as one of its strongest elements, as opposed to certain more exploitative fare which places less emphasis on the story and develops a motion picture centered more on violence, sex, nudity or other such factors (see "Elements").

STORY EDITOR. A supervisor of several story analysts in a movie studio or film production company's story department who reviews the synopses prepared by the story analysts and makes recommendations to the company's production vice presidents as to whether the literary property should be acquired and/or developed (see "Story Analyst").

STORY LINE. The basic points that form the continuity of a screenplay (see "Narrative").

STRAIGHT EMPLOYMENT AGREEMENT. The written contract made directly between an individual, e.g., a feature film director, and the motion picture production company that is hiring such individual without the intervention of a third entity such as a loan-out company (see "Lending Agreement" and "Three-Party Agreement").

STRAIGHT-LINE DEPRECIATION. Method of depreciating (recovering the cost through tax deductions) a fixed asset whereby the asset's useful life is divided into the total cost less the estimated salvage value. The resulting annual depreciation expense is charged against income before figuring income taxes (contrast with "Accelerated Cost Recovery;" also see "Income Forecast Method").

STRATEGIC PLANNING. The design of and activities relating to the critical components involved in the manner of operating of business (see "Financial Management").

STREET DATE. The date on which videocassette copies of a movie are made available for rental or purchase at the retail video stores (see "Videocassette Revenue Reporting").

STRIKE. The dismantling of a movie set after shooting has been completed. Also, a work stoppage by union members to enforce compliance with demands made on the employer. And, to create a print from a negative (see "De Facto Strike" and "No Strike, No Lockout Clause").

STRIPBOARD (see "Storyboard").

STRONG PACKAGE. A proposed film for which many of the elements have been developed and/or committed and the film's elements appear to be very commercial or of a high quality, including commitments from well-known actors and creative talent (see "Elements" and "Packaging").

STUDIO. Technically speaking, the term "studio" refers to the organization which owns and provides (for film production company use) the physical locations and other facilities including soundstages, sets, prop departments, offices, commissaries, etc. for development, pre-production, production and post-production of feature films. There are, in fact, studios that only provide such facilities and related services. On the other hand, some of the major studios also function as production companies, film distributors and, in some cases, have moved back into film exhibition (see "Lot," "Major Studio/Distributors," "Set" and "Studio Lots").

STUDIO ACCOUNTING PRACTICES. Various methods of accounting for motion picture revenues which have long been alleged to be unfair. Such methods include the practice of charging unauthorized and excessive expenses to a given film being produced at the studio; the rolling breakeven which keeps rolling just beyond net profits; and unfair overhead charges imposed by the studio on net profit participants. In other words, the studio has the books and records, it interprets the production/distribution agreement, it computes the profit and it decides how much should be paid. Industry insiders have long maintained that there is a certain amount of inadvertent and some intentional abusive or unconscionable accounting practices regularly occurring at the studios (see "Creative Accounting," "Improperly Claimed Expenses" and "Overreported Travel").

STUDIO APPROVALS. The negotiated items over which a major studio/distributor has the right to approve or disapprove in the context of a feature film distribution agreement. As a general rule, the more money a producer tries to get from a studio, the more approvals a studio is likely to impose. Such approvals typically relate to the screenplay, budget, producer, director, lead performers, start date, locations and production schedule (see "Negative Pickup" and "Production-Financing/Distribution Agreement").

STUDIO FINANCING. The funding of the production costs of a film by a major studio/distributor. As with any form of film finance, studio financing offers some advantages along with some disadvantages. Also, certain small films or low-budget films are generally not considered suitable for studio financing, regardless of the advantages or disadvantages. Projects generally accepted for studio financing must have a fairly broad commercial appeal (see "Financing," "In-House Product," "Investor Financing," "Lender Financing" and "Production-Financing/Distribution Agreement").

STUDIO GUARANTEED LOAN. A bank loan for the production of a motion picture which has been guaranteed by a major studio/distributor (see "Negative Pickup").

STUDIO LOTS. The physical locations and other facilities including soundstages, sets, prop departments, offices, commissaries, etc. which are available to be used by in-house or independent production companies or producers for development, pre-production, production and post-production of films (see "Major," "Mini-Majors" and "Studio/Distributors").

STUDIO OVERHEAD (see "Overhead," "Overhead Costs" and "Production Overhead").

STUDIO PRODUCER. A feature film producer who works as an employee of a studio on in-house productions (see "Associate Producer," "Creative Producer," "Executive Producer," "Independent Producer," "In-House Product," "Line Producer," "Producer," "Producers Guild of America" and "RIPOFF").

STUDIO PRODUCTION. A motion picture produced as an in-house production at a major studio/distributor, i.e., the studio has acquired the rights to the screenplay either from its inception or at an early stage in its development and has financed the production of the film (contrast with "Production-Financing/Distribution Agreement," "Negative Pickup" and "Acquisition").

STUDIO RENTAL. The payments made by a production company to a studio for the use of studio facilities in the production of a motion picture (see "Stage Agreement").

STUDIO SECURITY AGREEMENT. A written contract between a studio/distributor financier of a motion picture's development and production costs and the film's producer which provides, as consideration for the monetary advances made by the studio/distributor for the development of the project, that the studio/distributor has a security interest in the production company's script and the underlying literary property (see "Collateral" and "Security Agreement").

STUNT. The dangerous leaps and falls from tall buildings, car or boat chases and crashes, fast and trick horseback riding, fights, etc. performed during the production of a motion picture (see "Stunt Coordinator" and "Stunt Person").

STUNT COORDINATOR. The film production person responsible to a film's director for safely and effectively planning and executing all stunts required for a film production (see "Stunt").

STUNT PERSON. The performer who actually performs the stunts in place of the film's principal actors (also called "Stand-In;" see "Stunt").

STV (see "Subscription Television").

STYLE. In music, a distinctive or characteristic mode of presentation, construction or execution (see "Lyrics" and "Music").

SUBCHAPTER S CORPORATION (see "S Corp").

SUB-DISTRIBUTOR. In theatrical releases, distributors who handle a specific, limited geographic territory for a film, i.e., territorial distributors who have contracted to represent an independent distribution company. Sub-distributors sub-contract with the main distributor, who co-ordinates the distribution plans and marketing for all the sub-distributors of a film. Since sub-distributors handle a limited territory or "exchange," they generally have an excellent working knowledge of their markets. However, they are paid a commission for booking a film, and this system of sub-distribution often makes it difficult to audit the independent distributors. The use of sub-distributors also creates the possibility of double distribution fees (see "Audit," "Distributor," "Double Distribution Fees," "Film Exchanges," "Franchised Sub-Distributor," "Supervision Fee" and "Sub-Distribution").

SUB-DISTRIBUTOR FEES. The compensation paid out of a film's revenue stream to sub-contractors who distribute the film in a limited geographical area. Major studio/distributors do not generally use the services of sub-distributors. Independent distributors, on the other hand, do typically use the services of sub-distributors, and sometimes the sub-distributor for an independent distributor is a major studio/distributor. Sub-distributor fees may be computed in a variety of ways, depending upon the contractual provisions negotiated by the producer and the actual distributor as such provisions are expressed in the distribution agreement. Such fees may be included in the distributor's fee or be paid in addition to the distributor's fee, or may be computed based on some projected level of gross receipts (see "Absorption Arrangement," "Cap," "Double Distribution Fees," "Override," "Pass-Through Arrangement" and "Sub-Distributor").

SUB-DISTRIBUTION. The distribution of a film in limited markets or territories through the facilities of a distributor that has been sub-contracted by the film's primary distributor (see "Double Distribution Fee," "Override," "Pass-Through," "Sub-Distributor" and "Supervision Fee").

SUB-HEAD. A secondary headline in a motion picture advertisement utilized to stimulate additional reader interest and/or communicate more of the film's thematic appeal (see "Headline").

SUBJECTIVE TERMS. Words or expressions used in contracts that are subject to or likely to be interpreted differently by different individuals, as opposed to more objective terms whose meaning may be more readily agreed upon. Subjective terms should be clearly defined or eliminated in the negotiation of such contracts, e.g., usual and customary practices in the industry (see "Creative Accounting," "Ordinary Course of Business" and "Takeover").

SUB-KEY. A geographical area with a population of approximately 25,000 to 50,000, denoted by the geographical area's historical ability to produce film rental income for distributors; a sub-key's theatre or theatres break a film after the nearby keys have exhibited that film (see "Key," "Major Key" and "Ordinary Key").

SUBMISSION LETTER. A written communication that accompanies a screenplay that is being submitted to a production company or studio in search of development or production funding (see "Submission Release").

SUBMISSION RELEASE. A written agreement which producers and/or production companies sometimes require to be signed by screenwriter or others submitting literary material to the producer/production company for consideration as the basis for producing a motion picture. Typically in such submission releases, the screenwriter is asked to give up his or her rights to make certain claims against the producer/production company. Some of the submission releases drafted and used by the major studio/distributors and other distributors in the industry today are ridiculously one-sided (see "Contracts of Adhesion," "Non-Disclosure Agreement," "Overreaching," "Release," "Unconscionable Contract" and "Unsolicited Material").

SUBORDINATED. Junior in claim on assets to other debt, i.e., repayable only after other debts with a higher claim have been satisfied. A bank, for example, may agree to subordinate its interest in the repayment of a movie production loan to a principal talent's right to deferred compensation. More commonly, the distributor agrees to subordinate its claims to distributor rentals until after the lender is paid its principal, interest and fees (see "Asset," "Debt" and "Lender Financing").

SUBORDINATION. To give one claim or debt a lower priority in relation to another claim or debt (see "Subordinated").

SUB-PLOT. A subordinated or secondary storyline in a motion picture or screenplay (see "Favorable Portrayal," "Plot" and "Unfavorable Portrayal").

SUB-RUN (same as "Subsequent Run").

SUB-RUN MARKETS (see "Sub-Run Theatre").

SUB-RUN THEATRE. A theatre which primarily exhibits films on such film's subsequent runs and/or exhibits exploitation films (see "Subsequent Run").

SUB-S-CORPORATION (see "S Corp").

SUBSCRIBER. A person who has agreed to take and pay for the original unissued shares of a corporation or other securities (see "Subscription Application and Agreement").

SUBSCRIPTION APPLICATION AND AGREEMENT. A document included as part of the separate packet accompanying a limited partnership or corporate stock offering memorandum which each person desiring to become a unit holder must complete, execute, acknowledge and deliver to the general partner or other representative of the securities issuer before being accepted as a unit holder. This document serves as both the subscriber (investor/purchaser) application to purchase the security and his/her/its agreement with the issuer (see "Security" or "Securities").

SUBSCRIPTION DOCUMENTS (see "Subscription Application and Agreement" and "Subscription Materials").

SUBSCRIPTION MATERIALS. In a limited partnership offering, the documents included in a separate packet accompanying the offering memorandum (sometimes re-printed as an exhibit and bound up in the memorandum, as a sample). For private offerings, the subscription materials generally include a purchaser questionnaire, purchaser representative questionnaire, subscription application and corporate resolution. The subscription materials for a private offering may be twenty or thirty pages in length, whereas the subscription application for a public offering is generally only one or two pages (also called "Subscription Documents;" see "Limited Partnership" and "Securities").

SUBSCRIPTION PRICE. The price at which existing shareholders of a corporation are entitled to purchase common shares in a rights offering or at which subscription warrants are exercisable (see "Subscription Right").

SUBSCRIPTION RIGHT. Privilege granted existing shareholders of a corporation to subscribe to shares of a new issue of common stock before it is offered to the public (see "Rights Offering").

SUBSCRIPTION TELEVISION. A pay-television program service which, for a fee, transmits scrambled television signals from a television station to television sets in a limited geographical area, and only those sets which have a device that can decode the scrambled signal are able to view the programming. The television signal utilized may be UHF or VHF (see "Cable Television" and "Pay-Per-View").

SUBSCRIPTION WARRANT. A type of security, usually issued together with a bond or preferred stock, that entitles the holder to buy a proportionate amount of common stock at a specified price, usually higher than the market price at the time of issuance, for a period of years or in perpetuity (also called "Warrant").

SUBSEQUENT RUN. Any continuous exhibition of a motion picture in a designated geographic area for a specified period of time after the film's first run (see "Sub-Run Theatre").

SUBSIDIARIES. Companies of which more than 50% of the voting shares are owned by another corporation, called the parent corporation (see "Affiliate" and "Parent Corporation").

SUBSIDIARY CORPORATION. A corporation in which another corporation owns at least a majority of the shares and thus has control (see "Holding Company" and "Parent Corporation").

SUBSIDIES (see "Film Subsidies," "Foreign Subsidies," "Grants" and "Government Subsidies").

SUBSTANTIAL PERFORMANCE. The performance of all the essential terms of a contract so that the purpose of the contract is accomplished. However, unimportant omissions and technical defects may exist in the strict performance of the contract (see "Contract" and "Material").

SUBSTITUTION CLAUSE OR AGREEMENT. A provision in a movie distribution agreement in which the distributor agrees to allow the producer to substitute another distributor under certain circumstances, including the payment of a substitution fee and the reimbursement of the distributor's expenses to date. Such provisions are more likely to appear in distribution agreements with small distributors and are included so as to protect the producer who may produce a movie that is desired by a much stronger distributor who can provide a wider release and more distributor support. Usually, such provision will require that the original distributor's expenses be reimbursed, that a substitution fee be paid, and sometimes a percentage participation is retained. To some extent, the substitution clause serves a purpose similar to the turnaround provision in a studio deal, except that the size of the distributor's involved are typically reversed (see "Reversion Provision and Agreement," "Substitution Fee" and "Turnaround Provision and Agreement").

SUBSTITUTION FEE. A sum charged by a distributor for the producer's privilege of substituting another distributor pursuant to a substitution clause in a film distribution agreement (see "Substitution Clause or Agreement").

SUBTITLE. A written presentation of the translation from one language to another of the movie characters' dialogue which appears on the lower part of the screen (see "Dialogue Replacement").

SUBURBAN VENUE. A theatre located in an outlying part of a city (see "Major Markets").

SUCCESSFUL FILM. A subjective term which generally refers to the financial success of a motion picture and at least implies that the film's distributor made a profit on the film. A film may be financially successful for a distributor but not for the producer (aside from the producer's fee paid out of the film's budget) or other net profit participants, including investors or other financiers, who must look to their possible participation in net profits for their return on investment (see "Blockbuster," "Bomb," "Hit" and "Sleeper").

SUCCESSOR. One who assumes the place of another and fulfills his, her or its role or continues in the position. A corporate successor is a corporation that takes on the burdens and assumes the rights of a predecessor corporation by merger, acquisition or other valid legal succession (also see "Assigns," "Personal Representative" and "Remedy or Remedies").

SUE US. A phrase which is descriptive of the attitude and "business as usual" tactic of some film studio/distributors and other distributors in their dealings with producers, particularly with independent producers, and which is used when the producer inquires about his or her share of net profits following the distribution of a film. Such distributors take the position that any net profits due the producer will not be voluntarily paid to the producer, thus the producer must audit, make demand and ultimately sue in order to be paid. Even then the distributor will generally settle out of court for less than was originally owed. In many instances, the producer (or other profit participant) will choose not to sue for fear of being blacklisted among Hollywood distributors. So what's to keep a distributor from using this tactic? Among other things, an association of independent feature-film producers must be created to monitor such unfair business tactics, make its members more aware of the practice and contractual provisions which improve the producer's position, publicly expose the consistent use of such tactics on the part of any distributor and/ or pursue legislative, regulatory and other remedies to help level the playing field (see "Blacklist," "Creative Accounting," "Leverage" "Lobbyists," "Overreaching" and "Stonewall Defense").

SUFFICIENT DETAIL. Enough information to permit a full understanding. A concept that relates to the negotiation of the audit rights provision in a feature film distribution agreement. The producer should seek to insert language in the audit rights provision requiring the distributor to provide accounting statements with sufficient detail to permit a full understanding of how the accompanying payment was determined (see "Audit Rights").

SUIT. Any proceeding in a court of justice by which an individual pursues a remedy which the law affords (see "Action" and "Remedy or Remedies").

SUITABILITY QUESTIONNAIRES. Questionnaires used by issuers and broker/dealers in securities offerings to elicit information from prospective investors so that such issuers and/or broker/dealers can determine whether such prospective investors meet the investor suitability standards established for such securities offering (see "Investor Suitability Standards").

SUITABILITY RULES (see "Investor Suitability Standards").

SUM CERTAIN. Any amount that is fixed, settled, stated or exact (see "Debt" and "Lender Financing").

SUMMARY OF THE OFFERING. A synopsis of the disclosures in a securities offering, typically set out in a three- or four-page presentation at the beginning of the disclosure document. Pursuant to SEC interpretations of Regulation D, a summary of the offering may be circulated to prospective investors prior to the actual start of the offering (see "Program Highlights" and "Regulation D").

SUMMER SEASON. The most important season for the theatrical exhibition of feature films. The Christmas Holidays is the second most desirable release time. Most independent distributors will avoid these two most important release periods because the major studio/distributors usually tie up all of the best playdates at the most desirable theatres during these times (see "Anti-Competitive Practices," "Anti-Trust Laws" and "Prime Release Dates").

SUNDANCE INSTITUTE. A film organization founded partly through the efforts of Robert Redford, with offices in Los Angeles and facilities in Utah, and supported by contributions from industry entities. The institute has an excellent script-development program, in which an experienced screenwriter or story editor will work with a producer on polishing the producer's script, and a production-assistance program through which funds are available for completion guarantees, short-term pre-production loans, and co-producer services. Sundance also sponsors an annual producer's conference at its Utah facility (see "Independent Producer").

SUPERIMPOSING. The act of preparing movie titles so that they appear over stationary or moving backgrounds (see "Supered Titles").

SUPERED TITLES (SUPERIMPOSED TITLES). Titles which appear over stationary or moving backgrounds (see "Superimposing").

SUPERVISING EDITOR. The person engaged in any or all of the defined duties of a film's editor in addition to being responsible for the work of any other editor or editors working on a given production (see "Editor").

SUPERVISING SOUND EDITOR. The person responsible for overseeing the editors who work on all audio material other than music (see "Sound Editor").

SUPERVISION FEE. The difference between the distribution fees charged by a primary distributor and a sub-distributor, which the primary distributor retains as its distribution fee for the market or territories handled by the sub-distributor (see "Double Distribution Fees," "Override," "Pass-Through," "Sub-Distributor" and Sub-Distribution").

SUPPLEMENTARY COLLATERAL. Security for a loan which is supplementary to primary collateral, i.e. an additional pledge of asset collateral, such as raw land, home equity, automobiles, stocks, bonds, coin collections, interests in other films or literary properties. Some banks will accept the producer's share of gross receipts as supplementary collateral to foreign and cable pre-sales if the distribution contract guarantees a sufficient number of prints, ads and quality theatres (see "Collateral" and "Negative Pickup").

SUPPLEMENTARY MARKETS. Certain media for the exploitation of a motion picture, sometimes defined in a feature film distribution agreement as pay, cable, and subscription television, as well as audio-visual cassettes, discs and similar devices for transmission of audio and visual images, whether now known or hereafter devised (see "Ancillary Markets" and "Secondary Ancillary Rights").

SUPPLY AND DEMAND (see "Law of Supply and Demand").

SUPPORT. When used as a verb, to maintain or provide backing for. In the film industry, the term is commonly used to describe the prints and ads commitment made by the film's distributor, i.e., a reference to the level of support the distributor is providing for a given film (see "Prints and Ads Commitment").

SUPPORT ADVERTISING. The promotional activities designed to increase the awareness and desire in a potential audience group to see a given movie (see "Advertising" and "Support").

SUPPORTING PLAYER. A secondary leading actor in a film (see "Actor" and "Bit Player").

SUPPORT MATERIALS. The items developed by a film distributor with the film's producer which are used to promote the film prior to and during its release. Such materials may include a press kit, cast photos, production stills, biographical information on the principals, favorable reviews or feature articles about the film, a one-sheet or poster, print ads, theatre lobby displays and the trailer (see "Press Kit" and "Trailer").

SURETY. One who undertakes to pay money or perform other acts in the event that the involved principal fails to do so. The surety is directly and immediately liable for the debt or performance (see "Completion Bond," "Completion Guarantor" and "Guaranty").

SURETY BOND. A bond issued by one party, the surety, guaranteeing that he, she or it will perform certain acts promised by another (the principal) or pay a stipulated sum, up to the bond limit, in lieu of performance should the principal fail to perform (see "Completion Bond" and "Completion Guarantor").

SWEETENER. A feature added to a securities offering to make it more attractive to prospective purchasers; also an inducement to a brokerage firm to enter into an underwriting arrangement with an issuer (see "Equity Kicker").

SYMPHONY. An orchestral composition which today usually contains four movements and is played by a symphony orchestra (see "Symphony Orchestra").

SYMPHONY ORCHESTRA. A large orchestra of winds, strings and percussion that plays symphonic works (see "Orchestra").

SYNC OR SYNCH (see "Synchronism" and "In Synch").

SYNCHRONISM. The relation between picture and sound on film with respect either to the physical location on the film or to the time at which corresponding picture and sound are seen and heard, i.e., picture and sound are in sync or out of sync (see "Composite" and "In Synch").

SYNCHRONIZATION. The timing of the picture and sound on a feature film so that they coincide properly (see "Looping").

SYNCHRONIZATION LICENSE. The right expressed in a written agreement to use musical compositions as part of the soundtrack of a motion picture or television film in synchronization with visual images (see "Synchronization").

SYNCHRONIZATION RIGHTS. The legal power and authority to use musical compositions as part of the soundtrack of a motion picture or television film (see "Synchronization").

SYNCHRONOUS SOUND. Sound in a motion picture that directly corresponds to the proper image on the film (see "Asynchronous Sound").

SYNC PULSE. A timing device; a sixty-second pulse used to keep the sound and image on motion picture film in sync (see "SMPTE Time Code").

SYNDICATE. The investment bankers who together underwrite and distribute an offering of securities (see "Purchase Group").

SYNDICATED FILMS. Motion pictures which are licensed for use by individual television stations or cable systems for exhibition in their own local markets. Films are usually packaged as a group for television syndication. There are some 200-plus television syndication markets in the U.S. The syndication of films may create an allocation issue with respect to how the fee paid for syndication rights is allocated among the various films in the syndication package. Generally, a rather arbitrary syndication formula is imposed on the producers of the various films in the package by the distributor, and the application of this formula does not vary from market to market. Producers may want to negotiate for an approval right over any such syndication formula used by a distributor on that producer's film when and if it is included in a syndicated package (see "Allocation," "Package" and "Syndication").

SYNDICATED TELEVISION (see "Film Package," "Syndication" and "Television Syndication").

SYNDICATE MANAGER (see "Managing Underwriter").

SYNDICATION. In the film and television industry, the process whereby previously exhibited or recorded material is reused by or licensed to a collection of buyers such as independent television stations usually on a regional basis. In film finance, a joint venture or limited partnership, usually formed to finance only one or a few films and generally managed by one or a few of its members (see "Film Package," "Joint Venture" and "Limited Partnership").

SYNDICATION AGREEMENT. A contract between a film's producer or distributor for the licensing of motion pictures (generally a group of movies) to non-network, or independent, free-television stations for broadcast to the general public (see "Syndicated Films").

SYNDICATION EXPENSES. In a limited partnership context, expenses paid or incurred in connection with the issuing and marketing of interests in the partnership, including brokerage fees, selling commissions, state ("Blue Sky") filing fees, legal fees of the issuer for consultations relating to the requirements of the applicable federal and state securities laws and for tax advice pertaining to the adequacy of tax disclosures in the offering memorandum, accounting fees, if any, for preparation of financial projections to be included in the offering materials, and printing/binding costs of such offering materials. Unlike other expenses, syndication expenses may not be deducted currently or amortized over a period of time, as in the case of partnership organizational expenses (see "Offering Expenses," "Organizational Expenses," "Partnership Expenses," "Selling Expenses" and "Start-Up Costs").

SYNDICATION REVENUE. Income generated through the packaging and selling of motion picture rights to independent television stations (see "Syndication").

SYNDICATION VERSION. A copy of a film that is suitable for exploitation on independent free-television (see "Other Versions" and "U.S. Theatrical Cut").

SYNOPSIS. A short narrative or preliminary version of a motion picture script or a summary of a completed film (see "One-Line Description," "Basic Story Outline," "Outline" and "Treatment").

SYNTHETIC MUSIC. Electronic music (see "Programmed Music").

SYSTEMATIC RISK. That part of a security's risk that is common to all securities of the same general class and thus cannot be eliminated by diversification (also called "Market Risk").

— T —

TAG LINE. The audio and/or video information provided at the conclusion of a radio or television spot announcement advertising a movie that tells the audience in what theatres the movie is or will be showing (see "Body Copy").

TAKE. A single, continuous exposure of film made by a motion picture camera. A director may require several takes of a given shot (see "Cover Shot," "Shot" and "Scene").

TAKEOVER. The assumption of control over the production of a motion picture by a financier (i.e., studio) or a representative of a lender (i.e., completion guarantor). A production-financing/distribution agreement will typically set out the studio's takeover rights, e.g., if, based on the information available (including, but not limited to, the weekly reporting papers furnished by the production company), the distributor reasonably believes that the estimated cost of production of the picture will exceed the contingency, the studio may enter into negotiations with the production company in an effort to come up with a plan designed to reduce the projected negative costs, but if not successful, the studio may take over primary responsibility for the continued production of the picture. With respect to a completion guarantor takeover, the completion bond company may assert its contractual rights to assume responsibility for completing the film since the producer defaulted in some way, e.g., went over-budget or did not complete the film on time. Generally, the event which triggers the takeover rights of the completion guarantor is the subjective judgment of its on site representative that the film is going overbudget (see "Completion Bond," "Reduction Plan" and "Subjective Terms").

TAKEOVER RIGHTS. The power and authority of the completion bond company to assume responsibility for completing a motion picture in accordance with the completion guarantee (see "Completion Bond" and "Takeover").

TALENT. As opposed to the crew on a film, any person or animal working as an on-camera performer. Some definitions of this term include off-camera performers and others are so broad as to include all of those involved in the artistic aspects of filmmaking (i.e., writers, actors, directors, etc.) as opposed to the people involved on the business end of film (see "Actor," "Actress," "Director" and "Screenwriter").

TALENT PARTICIPATION DEALS (see "Talent Participations").

TALENT PARTICIPATIONS. Financial interests of writers, directors and/or actors who negotiate percentage participations based on a film's earnings at some specific level of the film's revenue stream. Such participations are often expressed as points, i.e., a percentage of the revenue at a given level, e.g., "gross points" which can be defined in relation to a number of different types of gross, such as distributor's gross, gross receipts, adjusted gross or film rentals. Net points may also be defined at different levels of return, such as the producer's net or partnership net for films financed by means of a limited partnership (see "Adjusted Gross," "Gross," "Net Points," "Net Profits" and "Percentage Participation" or "Points").

TANGIBLE ASSET. Assets having physical existence, plus others, like accounts receivable, which accountant's have determined to be tangible (contrast with "Intangible Assets").

TAPE. A thin strip of plastic film coated with iron oxide or more a sophisticated coating which is used in reproducing sound by means of the magnetic arrangement of sound patterns on the tape and in recording and playing back audio and video materials (see "Video Tape").

TARGET AUDIENCE (same as "Primary Audience;" see "Projected Audience").

TARGET MARKET. A specific audience segment a producer and/or distributor seeks to reach with a film and its advertising and promotion campaign, e.g., teenagers (see "Primary Audience" and "Target Marketing").

TARGET MARKETING. A marketing technique used in film marketing which is designed to be implemented after a movie has been analyzed and its various target markets have been identified. As part of the analysis, the distributor or marketing entity must answer whether: (1) each target group is of sufficient size (2) a reasonable percentage of the group will be likely to respond to the marketing campaign (3) advertising vehicles are available to reach each such group and (4) their projected attendance level at the theatre where the motion picture is to be exhibited will be sufficient to generate enough revenue to justify the expense of that particular marketing campaign (see "Marketing," "Primary Audience" and "Target Audience").

TARIFF. Tax on imported and exported goods; a customs duty (see "Custom Duties" and "Tax").

TAX. A rate or sum of money assessed on a person or property for the support of the government. Certain taxes and associated costs are paid by a film distributor as a category of distribution expenses and this category as defined in the typical film distribution deal is rather broad. Included are taxes and governmental fees of any nature and however characterized, including costs of contesting, interest and penalties thereon (other than the distributor's or any sub-distributor's corporate income taxes), imposed directly or indirectly on the picture of any part thereof (including without limitation, the employer's share of payroll taxes with respect to deferred or contingent compensation) or on the gross receipts or the license, distribution or exhibition of the picture or collection, conversion or remittance of monies connected therewith (see "Foreign Tax Credits," "Income Tax" and "Tax Opinion").

TAXABLE INCOME. The amount of income (after all allowable deductions and adjustments to income) subject to tax; the amount applied to the rate of income tax in order to determine the income tax payable (see "Income Tax").

TAXABLE YEAR. The period during which the income tax liability of an individual or entity is incurred, or, in the case of certain non-taxable entities, such as limited partnerships, the period for which tax information is provided (see "K-1").

TAX ADVANTAGES (see "Tax Benefits").

TAX ASPECTS. The discussion of the material federal income tax issues and/or consequences of investing in a securities offering such as a limited partnership which makes up a major section of the partnership disclosure document (same as "Tax Discussion;" see "Tax Opinion").

TAX BASIS. The original cost of an asset, less accumulated depreciation, that goes into the calculation of a gain or loss for tax purposes (see "Basis" and "Income Tax").

TAX BENEFITS. Various useful or profitable tax provisions made available by governments in order to encourage certain types of investments. Such provisions may come in the form of immediate deductions of certain costs, the rapid recovery of others, tax credits, deferrals or preferences. Tax benefits can only enhance the economic viability of an investment. They cannot provide economic substance to a transaction that otherwise lacks such viability. With passage of the Tax Reform Act of 1986, the U.S. government eliminated the investment tax credit which had been successfully utilized by film limited partnerships as an extra incentive for investors and also limited the use of limited partnership deductions by virtue of the passive loss rules. However, the fact that the limited partnership is not a taxable entity itself is still a significant tax advantage in favor of the limited partnership as compared to the regular "C" corporation and some portion of the production costs of the film will still be available to investors in the limited partnership vehicle as deductible expenses (also called "Tax Advantages" and "Tax Incentives;" see "Depreciation," "Income Forecast Method," "Ordinary Expense," "Necessary Expense," "Selling Point" and "Tax Deduction").

TAX CONSEQUENCES. The effects an investment in a security may have on an individual investor's federal income tax; a major section of disclosure in a film limited partnership offering disclosure document which discusses all of the material tax issues relating to the offering (see "Tax Aspects" and "Tax Opinion").

TAX CREDIT. A direct, dollar-for-dollar reduction in a taxpayer's tax liability. The Tax Reform Act of 1986 repealed many tax credits including the investment tax credit (contrast with "Tax Deduction;" see "Foreign Tax Credit" and "Investment Tax Credit").

TAX DEDUCTION. A tax provision which permits taxpayers in a jurisdiction to deduct specified expenditures from their taxable income and/or reduce their taxes by a percentage applicable to such taxpayer's tax bracket (contrast with "Tax Credit"). Also, in the context of a film distribution agreement, an amount which the distributor is allowed to deduct from monies paid to the producer and which are required to pay tax liabilities to various governmental entities based on the exploitation of the film (also called "Withholdings;" see "Foreign Tax Shelter").

TAX DEFERRALS. The postponement of tax payments from the current year to a later year. Most countries have substituted tax deferrals for tax shelters and have adopted the U.S. "at-risk" provision as well as its requirement for capitalizing film costs (see "Tax Shelters").

TAX DISCUSSION (see "Tax Aspects" and "Tax Opinion").

TAX-DRIVEN MOVIE FINANCING. Motion picture investments which are significantly influenced by prospective tax benefits for the investors (see "Foreign Tax Shelter" and "Tax Benefits").

TAX EVASION. The fraudulent and willful underpayment or nonpayment of taxes (see "Foreign Tax Credit" and "Income Tax").

TAX INCENTIVES (see "Tax Benefits").

TAX MATTERS PARTNER. In a limited partnership context, the designated partner who, as required by the Tax Equity and Fiscal Responsibility Act of 1982, is to serve as the primary liaison between the partnership and the IRS with regard to partnership tax matters and proceedings before the IRS (see "Limited Partnership").

TAX OPINION. The information and belief provided by a practitioner (attorney or accountant) concerning the federal tax aspects of a tax shelter or other securities offering either appearing or referred to in the investment offering materials, or used or referred to in connection with sales promotion efforts, and directed to persons other than the client who engaged the practitioner to give the advice. The term includes the tax aspects or tax risks portion of the offering materials prepared by or at the direction of a practitioner, whether or not a separate opinion letter is issued or whether or not the practitioner's name is referred to in the offering materials or in connection with the sales promotion efforts. In addition, a financial forecast or projection prepared by a practitioner is a tax shelter opinion if it is predicated on assumptions regarding federal tax aspects of the investment, and it meets the other requirements above. The term does not, however, include rendering advice solely to the offeror or reviewing parts of the offering material, so long as neither the name of the practitioner nor the fact that a practitioner has rendered advice concerning the tax aspects is referred to in the offering material or in connection with the sales-promotion efforts (see "Limited Partnership," "Material Tax Issuer," "Tax Aspects" and "Tax Shelter").

TAXPAYER. The person who is determined to bear the tax liability for a given transaction (see "Income Tax").

TAX SHELTER. A transaction through which a taxpayer reduces his, her or its tax liability by engaging in activities that provide tax deductions or tax credits to apply against his or her tax liability; i.e., method used by investors to legally avoid or reduce tax liabilities. Also an investment which has as a significant and intended feature for federal income tax purposes either (1) deductions in excess of income from the investment being available in any year to reduce income from other sources in that year, or (2) credits in excess of the tax attributable to the income from the investment being available in any year to offset taxes on income from other sources in that year. For tax shelter registration purposes, the IRS defines a tax shelter as any investment that meets the following two requirements (1) the investment is one with respect to which a person could reasonably infer from representations made or to be made in connection with the offering for sale of an interest in the investment that the tax-shelter ratio may be greater than 2:1 for any investor at the close of any of the first five years ending after the date on which the investment is offered for sale; and (2) the investment is one that is required to be registered under a Federal or state law regulating securities, or that is sold pursuant to an exemption from registration requiring the filing of a notice with a Federal or state agency regulating the offering or sale of securities, or that is a substantial investment (contrast with "Abusive Tax Shelter;" see "Material Tax Issue," "Tax Aspects," "Tax Credit," "Tax Deduction," "Tax Opinion" and "Tax Shelter Registration").

TAX SHELTER REGISTRATION. The IRS requirement that certain investment programs meeting the very broad definition of a tax shelter provided by the IRS must register the program with the IRS or certain penalties may be imposed on several of the parties involved (see "Tax Shelter").

TEAMSTERS. The union concerned with pickup and/or delivery or hauling of any description, including all vehicles on, to, or from location work and studios, buses, limousines, motorcycles, picture cars, Hi-Lo's, camera cars, cherry-pickers, Cinemobiles, trailers (loaded and unloaded), combination-type vehicles of any description, and all other types of vehicles in or upon which cargo or personnel of any description is carried or which are to be photographed, whether such vehicles are rented, leased, owned or in any way made available or used by a film production company (see "Captain" and "Union").

TEASERS. Film trailers prepared for theatrical presentation in advance of the regular theatrical trailer. Such trailers typically have running times of only one minute or slightly more (see "Trailers").

TECHNICAL PERSONNEL. Film production employees or advisors who have specialized knowledge, experience and/or training (see "Production Staff").

TECHNOLOGICAL DEVELOPMENTS. Improvements relating to a specialized mechanical or scientific method of achieving a practical purpose, e.g., projecting a motion picture image on a screen or improving the sound systems associated with motion pictures (see "Laser Disc" and "New Delivery Technologies").

TELECAST. To broadcast by television (see "Television").

TELEFILM CANADA. A Canadian feature film fund created in 1986 with an annual budget of $30 million and designed to promote the production and theatrical distribution of high-quality dramatic films with a high level of Canadian content (see "Feature Film Fund").

TELEVISION. The broadcasting industry which utilizes an electronic system for transmitting transient images of fixed or moving objects together with sound over a wire or through space by apparatus that converts light and sound into electrical waves and reconverts them into visible light rays and audible sound (see "Cable Television" and "Radio").

TELEVISION ADS. Film advertising prepared for and carried on television; similar to trailers, only shorter, usually thirty seconds. Release prints for television spots are distributed in a 16mm format as opposed to 35mm (see "Advertising").

TELEVISION AND FILM INTER-RELATIONSHIP. The manner and effect of the common interests of the film and television industries. The television and film industries are significantly inter-related. They share a talent pool of producers, actors, directors and others, and many motion pictures are exploited on television. During the past several decades, the financial highs and lows of the film business have been evened out by the production of a relatively safe and predictable television product. Today, however, the television business is less stable and this development in turn places added financial pressure and uncertainty on the motion picture business (see "Financial Management" and "Strategic Planning").

TELEVISION COVER SHOT (see "Coverage" or "Cover Shot").

TELEVISION DERIVATIVE DISTRIBUTION RIGHTS. The legal power and authority granted to a feature film distributor in a distribution agreement to exploit television programming derived from a feature film in the television marketplace, including television specials, movies-of-the-week, pilots, multi-part series or television series (see "Derivative Distribution Rights" and "Theatrical Derivative Distribution Rights").

TELEVISION NETWORK (see "Network").

TELEVISION PRE-SALE. A contractual arrangement negotiated and consummated before a feature film is produced in which a television network commits to purchase a feature film. Although no actual cash is paid by the network, such contracts or the network's letter of commitment may be "bankable" if supported by a completion bond. This arrangement is similar to a studio negative pickup deal, although no longer very common (see "Fractionalizing," "Negative Pickup" and "Split-Rights Basis").

TELEVISION PROGRAM. A performance broadcast on television (see "Television Series").

TELEVISION REMAKES AND SEQUELS. A heading sometimes used in feature film distribution agreements wherein certain rights of the distributor relating to television distribution rights for programming derived from the motion picture are set out (see "Theatrical Remakes and Sequels" and "Television Derivative Distribution Rights").

TELEVISION SALES (see "TV Sales").

TELEVISION SERIES. A weekly or daily program on television, usually one half hour or one hour in length (see "Pilot").

TELEVISION SPOTS (see "Commercials").

TELEVISION SYNDICATION (see "Syndication").

TEMPORARY RESTRAINING ORDER. A court order granted without notice or hearing, demanding the preservation of the status quo until a hearing can be had to determine the propriety of injunctive relief, temporary or permanent (see "Equitable Remedy" and "Injunction").

TENTATIVE BUDGET. The preliminary statement of the projected costs of producing a motion picture. Obviously, a budget may change dramatically depending upon which actors become attached, and, since it is not always possible to get commitments from the lead performers (the ones ultimately selected) in advance of financing, reasonable estimates must be made (see "Budget" and "Packaging").

TENTATIVE SHOOTING SCHEDULE. The initial and temporary (at least until further modifications are required) list of when each shot and scene called for by a feature film screenplay is to be shot, including a detailed list of all of the people and things need to conduct such shoots (see "Shooting Schedule").

TERM. In contracts generally, the period of time during which the conditions of the contract will be carried out. In film distribution, the period of time expressed in years that a distributor has to distribute a picture, i.e., a limited number of years or infinity. If limited, the term is typically a minimum of five years but seldom more than fifteen. In a limited partnership context, "term" also refers to the number of years the partnership will operate and exist (see "Distribution Term").

TERM DEAL (see "Overall Deal").

TERM LOAN. Intermediate to long-term (typically, two to ten years) secured credit granted to a company by a commercial bank, insurance company or commercial finance company, usually to finance capital equipment or provide working capital. The loan is amortized over a fixed period, sometimes ending with a balloon payment. Borrowers under term loan agreements are normally required to meet minimum working capital and debt to net worth tests, to limit dividends and to maintain continuity of management (see "Debt," "Interest" and "Lender Financing").

TERM OF ART. Words or phrases that have a particular meaning within a given area of study or business activity. Such terms may have no meaning or a different meaning outside the context in which such terms are used in a given industry (see "Contractually Defined Terms").

TERMS. In contract law generally, the provisions stated or offered for acceptance which determine the essential nature and scope of the agreement. With respect to a distributor/exhibitor agreement for example, the terms are the conditions under which the distributor agrees to allow the exhibitor to show its product in a given theatre, and whereby the exhibitor agrees to show the product. Such terms typically include the basis on which film rentals will be paid (as a percentage of weekly gross box-office receipts or flat fee), playing time (number of weeks), choice of theatre, dollar participation in cooperative advertising expenditure, and clearance over other theatres (see "Clearance" and "Contract").

TERRITORIAL DISTRIBUTORS. Feature film distribution companies who handle film distribution for U.S. films in foreign countries (see "Foreign Distribution" and "Foreign Sales Representatives").

TERRITORIAL PRE-SALES (see "Pre-Sales").

TERRITORIAL SALES. The licensing of motion pictures in foreign markets (see "Outright Sale").

TERRITORY. A geographical area belonging to or under the jurisdiction of a governmental authority. Most commonly used in the film business to describe foreign countries as film markets (see "Foreign Market").

TEST MARKETING. The pre-releasing of a film in one or more small, representative markets before committing to an advertising campaign. The effectiveness of the initial marketing plan can thus be evaluated and modified, if necessary, prior to the subsequent release (see "Preview" and "Sneak Preview").

TEST MARKETING BUDGET. The projected expenses set out by category which are anticipated to be incurred in conducting a prerelease exhibition of a movie for the purpose of gauging an audience's reaction to the film (see "Test Marketing").

TEXT. The original written or printed words and form of a literary work or the main body of printed or written matter on a page or in an advertisement (see "Book" and "Novel").

THEATRE (OR THEATER). Any establishment in which motion pictures are exhibited regularly to the public for a charge, i.e., the commercial viewing center for the presentation of a motion picture to the public. Theatres are owned and operated by exhibitors (see "Exhibitor" and "Theatre Chains").

THEATRE-BY-THEATRE BASIS. The prescribed manner in which theatrical distributors were supposed to license their film product to exhibitors in the U.S. theatrical marketplace, pursuant to the Paramount Consent Decrees, i.e., without discrimination in favor of affiliated theatres (see "Paramount Consent Decree of 1948," "TriStar Case" and "Vertical Integration").

THEATRE CHAINS. An affiliated group of theatres operating under common ownership. Examples include American Multi-Cinema, General Cinema and Cineplex Odeon (also called "Theatre Circuits;" see "Exhibitor" and "Major Exhibition Chains").

THEATRE CHAIN VALUES. The amount that may be paid in an arm's-length transaction by a willing buyer to a willing seller for a theatrical exhibition circuit (see "Theatre Chains").

THEATRE HOLDINGS. The assets of a corporate conglomerate relating to motion picture exhibition. The Paramount consent decrees required the vertically integrated major studio/distributors of the time to divest themselves of their theatre holdings ("Anti-Trust Laws," "Major Studio/Distributors," "Original Paramount Defendants" and "Vertical Integration").

THEATRE STOCKS. Corporate shares in the publicly held exhibition chains (see "Major Exhibition Chains" and "Publicly Held").

THEATRICAL. Of or relating to motion picture theatres where full-length feature films are exhibited to the public for a charge. It is extremely important that this word be used as a modifier of the word "release" in a film distribution deal since, without the word "theatrical," the film distributor may be free to merely license the motion picture to video companies and cable television without its being exhibited at theatres (see "Non-Theatrical").

THEATRICAL ADMISSIONS. A statistical measurement of the number of people who buy movie tickets at the box office during any given period, e.g., in 1990 there were an estimated 1.06 billion moviegoers in the U.S., while 1991 apparently saw a 7% drop in admissions to 981.9 million (see "Box Office Gross" and "Domestic Theatrical Admissions").

THEATRICAL AGENTS. Independent contractors who negotiate contracts and solicit employment for their clients (see "Agent").

THEATRICAL AND TELEVISION FILM BASIC AGREEMENT (see "WGA Agreement").

THEATRICAL DERIVATIVE DISTRIBUTION RIGHTS. The term used in some feature film distribution agreements to refer to the legal power and authority to exploit a subsequently produced motion picture based on a preceding film, i.e., remakes and sequels (see "Prequel," "Remake" and "Sequel").

THEATRICAL DISTRIBUTION. The exploitation of motion pictures by means of exhibition in motion picture cinemas, in contrast to the exploitation of motion pictures in other media (see "Ancillary Rights").

THEATRICAL DISTRIBUTION CONTRACT. The agreement between a distributor and producer pursuant to which the distributor commits to provide a theatrical release for a motion picture or pictures (see "Production-Financing/Distribution Agreement," "Negative Pickup Distribution Agreement" and "Acquisition Distribution Agreement").

THEATRICAL EXPOSURE. The release and exhibition of a motion picture in theatres. Such exposure, i.e., viewing by a significant number of moviegoers, is considered an important element in determining the value of the movie in ancillary markets (see "Ancillary Markets").

THEATRICAL FILM RENTAL (see "Film Rental").

THEATRICAL MARKET. The exhibition of movies in theatres as opposed to other markets such as cable and videocassettes (see "Allied Rights," "Ancillary Markets" and "Non-Theatrical").

THEATRICAL MOTION PICTURE ACQUISITION/DISTRIBUTION AGREEMENT (see "Acquisition/Distribution Agreement").

THEATRICAL RELEASE. The exhibition of a feature film in theatres as opposed to licensing to home video, pay-cable, syndication, network and other ancillary markets. The theatrical release has traditionally been the only area of film distribution where it is possible to generate a negative cash flow, i.e., where releasing costs exceed income produced by a given film in that market (see "Allied Rights," "Ancillary Rights" and "Non-Theatrical").

THEATRICAL RELEASE COMMITMENT. A contractual promise by a feature film distributor relating to the distribution of a film in the theatrical marketplace (see "Release Commitment").

THEATRICAL RELEASING COSTS. The expenses associated with distributing a film for theatrical exhibition, primarily prints and advertising (see "Distribution Expenses").

THEATRICAL REMAKES AND SEQUELS. A common heading in a feature film distribution agreement which sets out the terms and circumstances under which the film distributor will exploit any films to be produced in the future which are based on the previous version (see "Prequel," "Remakes" and "Sequels").

THEATRICAL SELF-DISTRIBUTION (see "Four-Wall" and "Self-Distribution").

THEATRICAL TEAMSTERS (see "Teamsters").

THEFT (same as "Larceny;" see "Mafia," "Organized Crime," "Racketeering," "RICO" and "White Collar Crime").

THEME. The subject, i.e., the idea or concept which forms the basis of a screenplay or feature film. In music, the theme is the musical motto which serves as the basis of the composition or movement. In motion picture advertising, the theme is the promotional campaign's central concept, which is used in ads and/or commercials. Ad themes seek to distinguish the film advertised from others competing for the movie-going audience (see "Concept" and "Idea").

THEME SONG. The title song for a motion picture (see "Music").

THERE ARE NO RULES (see "Rules").

THIRD DECADE COUNCIL. A film industry membership organization whose membership is made up of the younger working members of the industry and which serves as a support group for the American Film Institute (now in its third decade). With the AFI, the Third Decade Council sponsors an annual conference which is structured as an informal, off-the-record series of discussions with established members of the entertainment community (see "American Film Institute" and "Industry Groups").

THIRD PARTIES. Persons who are not directly involved as decision makers to a transaction or agreement (see "Contract").

THIRD-PARTY BENEFICIARY. Persons who are recognized as having enforceable rights created in them by a contract to which they are not parties and for which they give no consideration (see "Contract" and "Parties").

THIRD-PARTY ESCROW. An escrow account set up and maintained by an entity not a party to the investment transaction, usually a bank or escrow company (see "Escrow").

THIRD-PARTY PARTICIPATION. A percentage interest in a specified level of a movie's revenue stream held by a person or entity who was not a party to the contract granting the interest, e.g., the feature film distribution agreement which is a contract between the distributor and the film's producer. Third-party participations may occur at gross or net levels. Feature film distributors routinely provide in their distribution agreements that third-party participations are to be paid out of net profits or the producer's share of net profits (see "Floor," "Percentage Participation" and "Points").

THIRTY-FIVE MILLIMETER (35MM). The standard gauge of film and equipment used in professional motion picture making and commercials. Sometimes 35mm is replaced by wider-gauge film (65 or 70mm), or by 16mm, which is then blown up to 35mm. Thirty-five millimeter film is 35 millimeters wide, has sixteen frames per foot, and four perforations per frame (see "Film").

THIRTY-THREE ACT ('33 ACT). The federal Securities Act of 1933, as amended. The federal legislation that regulates the sale of securities in the U.S. Federal securities law does not pre-empt state securities law, thus both federal and states securities laws and regulations must be complied with in any securities offering (see "Dual Regulation").

THREAT. A declaration of an intention or determination to inflict punishment, loss or pain on another, or to injure another by some wrongful act (see "Extortion," "Racketeering" and "RICO").

THREE-PARTY AGREEMENT. A written contract between a loan-out company and a feature film production company through which the loan-out company makes available for employment the services of the individual artist/performer who owns the loan-out company (see

"Borrowing Agreement," "Lending Agreement" and "Straight Employ-ment Agreement").

THREE-RUN BREAK. A film's break being available for no more than three theatres within the break's geographical area (see "Two-Run Break" and "Four-Run Break").

THREE SETS OF BOOKS. A reference to the alleged practice that distributors maintain several different versions of their business records, one for their own records, one for the producer and net profit participant group and another for the IRS (see "Creative Accounting," "Net Profit Participant Association" and "Unethical Business Practices").

TICKET PRE-SALES. The advance sales of blocks of motion picture theatre tickets to groups which have an interest in seeing a particular type of movie produced and exhibited. Ticket pre-sales can some-times play a role in financing the production costs of certain movies, e.g., by means of ticket pre-sales to religious groups (see "Pre-Sale Financing").

TICKET REVENUE (same as "Box Office Gross; see "Concession Sales" and "House Nut").

TIE-INS. Promotional campaigns for commercial products that are coordinated and otherwise related in some way to the release of a motion picture, e.g., the sale of cups with pictures of characters from a motion picture on sale at outlets of a fast-food chain (contrast with "Product Placement;" see "Promotional Tie-Ins").

TIER RELEASING (same as "First-Run Zoning").

TIME IS OF THE ESSENCE. A term used in contracts that fixes time of performance as a vital term of the contract, the breach of which may operate as a discharge of the entire contract (see "Contract").

TIME VALUE OF MONEY (see "Present Value").

TITLE. With respect to ownership, a shorthand term used to denote the facts which, if proved, will enable a plaintiff to recover posses-sion or a defendant to retain possession of property. Having title to something means having the right to possess, use and exploit it. In another sense and in relation to film, any written material that ap-pears on a film and is not a part of an original scene. Also the registered name of the screenplay or teleplay. The person in whose name it is registered, or to whom it is transferred by sale, lease or power of attorney, is said to "have title" to the script (see "Credit Titles," "Creeper Titles" and "Title Opinion").

TITLE CLEARANCE REPORT (see "Title Report and Opinion").

TITLE REPORT. A report consisting of a listing of all prior uses of a particular title in the literary, dramatic, motion picture, radio and television fields (see "Title Report," "Opinion" and "Working Title").

TITLE REPORT AND OPINION. A report prepared by entertainment attorneys which advises a producer as to whether a proposed film title has been used before, whether the use of a particular title is likely to cause confusion among the public and whether a court injunction preventing the use of such title may be successfully pursued (see "Title Report" and "Title Search").

TITLE SEARCH. A search made through the records maintained in public record offices to determine the state of a title, including all liens, encumbrances, mortgages, future interests, etc., affecting the property; the means by which a chain of title is ascertained (see "Title" and "Chain of Title").

TITLE SEARCH REPORT (same as "Title Report").

TITLE SONG. A song written for a movie that includes the title in its lyrics or is somewhat descriptive of what the movie is about (see "Music").

TITLE TREATMENT. A distinctive logo of a film's title used consistently in an advertising campaign, i.e., the graphic design of a film's title. Movie title treatments should be captivating and consistent with the film's theme. Techniques used to accomplish this include choice of typeface, hand lettering and/or visual imagery (see "Main and End Titles").

TOMBSTONE AD. A formal advertisement usually in the financial press announcing the commencement of an offering of securities, and listing the underwriting manager and members of the syndicate. The term derives from the fact that such advertisements usually consist of all copy and no illustrations, and thus look like a tombstone. A tombstone ad is merely a pubic announcement concerning such transactions and does not constitute either an offer to sell or to buy the securities (see "Private Offering," "Public Offering" and "Securities").

TOP BILLING. The first and/or most prominent credits on the screen, i.e., the credits placed in the most advantageous position in relation to the main title of the film. Top billing is a negotiable item in star contracts, but also may be negotiated for some producers, directors, writers, cinematographers and composers (see "Credits").

TOPICAL HOOK. A movie concept or theme which is likely to catch the attention of the movie's target audience and which can be easily promoted (see "Hook").

TOP SHEET. The first page of a detailed motion picture budget which provides a summary of the budget (see "Budget" and "Tentative Budget").

TORT. The French word for "wrong;" a private or civil wrong or injury resulting from a breach of a legal duty that exists by virtue of society's expectations regarding interpersonal conduct, rather than by contract or other private relationship, e.g., defamation, libel and invasion of privacy (see "Clearance," "Errors and Omissions Insurance," "Privacy, Right of," "Public Figure," "Droit Moral," "Editing Rights," "Moral Rights," "Negligence" and "Unfair Competition").

TOTAL CAPITALIZATION. The capital structure of a company, including long-term debt and all forms of equity (see "Capital," "Debt" and "Equity").

TOTAL RETURN. Return on investment, taking into account capital appreciation, dividends or interest and individual tax considerations adjusted for present value and expressed on an annual basis (see "Rate of Return").

TOTAL REVENUE. A general reference to all of the income generated by the exploitation of a motion picture in all markets and media or in specified markets and media (see "Film Rental" and "Gross Receipts").

TRACK. The physical area on a magnetic tape or optical film stock that stores audio information ("Sound Tracks").

TRACK RECORD. The prior performance of an individual or a film, i.e., the history of an individual or company involved in the production or distribution of films, e.g., of a director for a film that a bank is considering for a loan (see "Choosing A Distributor," "Lending Standards" and "Past Performance").

TRACKS. The relatively fixed constellations of theatres that play a given distributor's product, the existence of which confirm that feature films are rarely, if ever, sold theatre by theatre, without discrimination, solely on the merits (see "Anti-Trust Laws," "Block Booking" and "Paramount Consent Decree of 1948").

TRACK SYSTEM. An arrangement under which most of a distributor's films are customarily exhibited at a certain exhibitor's theatres; additionally, "track system" and "track" means a group of theatres within a major key, which may be operated by different exhibitors, chosen by a distributor (through negotiations with the exhibitors) to play a film simultaneously (see "Tracks").

TRADE ADVERTISING. Movie advertisements that are carried in the trade publications and, thus, are directed to distributors or exhibitors as opposed to a movie's potential general audience (see "Advertising" and "Trades").

TRADE ASSOCIATION. An organization created for the purpose of promoting and protecting the common interests of a given industry or segment of an industry (contrast with "Guild;" see "Association Projects," "Industry Groups," "MPAA" and "Professional Association").

TRADE ASSOCIATION AND GUILD FEES. Membership fees paid by members of professional and trade associations and unions (see "Dues and Assessments" and "Trade Association Dues and Fees").

TRADE ASSOCIATION DUES AND FEES. A category of distributor expenses that are deducted from gross receipts (sometimes off-the-top) and paid as the distributor company's allocable portion of the dues and assessments of the trade association or associations to which the distributor belongs, e.g., the MPAA and AMPTP or similarly constituted or substitute organizations throughout the world. This category of distributor expense may include legal fees to such association's outside counsel (not its in-house counsel) relating to anti-trust matters, which means the major distributors are deducting from gross receipts, i.e., reducing the amount of funds that other participants may share in, to pay for activities which help to continue or improve their position of market dominance. Thus, most independent producers who have to wait until a film's revenue stream reaches net profits (since most producers are relegated to a net profit's position) are contributing to the payment of the distributor association's costs incurred in conjunction with fighting anti-trust claims or taking positions on issues most of which would be opposed by the independent producer whose funds are being used. That being the case, it would seem only fair that if an association of independent feature film producers were formed, then each film produced by a member production company and distributed by an MPAA distributor would contribute a portion of its gross receipts to the independent producer's association as association dues at the same time that the MPAA and other distributor trade organization dues were being deducted and paid. In addition, independently produced films that were distributed by AFMA member distributors would also contribute an allocable portion to the support of such an organization. In any case, a producer is able to negotiate a flat-dollar cap on the amount of gross receipts that may be deducted for association dues, e.g., $75,000 (see "AFMA," "AMPTP," "Association Projects," "Blind Bidding," "Industry Groups," "Gross Receipts," "Lobbying," "MPAA," "Off-the-Top," "Piracy," "RIPOFF" and "TriStar Case").

TRADE ASSOCIATION RELATED SERVICES (see "Association Projects").

TRADE DUES (see "Trade Association Dues and Fees").

TRADEMARK. Any word, name, symbol or device used by a manufacturer or merchant to identify his, her or its goods and to distinguish them from goods made or sold by others. The basis for trademark law lies in the tort of unfair competition, under which a seller using a mark similar to one already in use could be liable for the buyer's likely confusion between two products or services due to the seller's efforts considered as a whole (see "Logo," "Patent," "Service Mark," "Trade Name" and "Unfair Competition").

TRADEMARK REPORT. A report covering a search of the trademark records of the U.S. Patent and Trademark Office provided for persons who wish to use a particular mark for a product or service (see "Trademark").

TRADE NAME. A word, name, symbol, device or any combination thereof used by a person to identify that person's business, vocation or occupation. Unlike the trademark or service mark, a trade name does not have to be registered, although the first user of a trade name can still sue subsequent users for trade-name infringement under common-law principles, and the unlawful use of a trade name may be enjoined (see "Service Mark" and "Trademark").

TRADE PRACTICES (same as "Business Practices").

TRADE PUBLICATIONS (see "Trades").

TRADES. The daily, weekly or monthly newspapers and magazines that specialize in reporting news and information relating to the entertainment industry, e.g., "American Cinematographer," "Boxoffice," "The Business of Film," "Daily Variety," "The Film Journal," "Hollywood Reporter," "Millimeter," "Montage," "Movie/TV Marketing," "Screen International," "Show Biz News" (now defunct), the weekly "SMPTE Journal" and "Variety" (see "Press Release").

TRADE SCREENING. The showing of a motion picture by a distributor which is open to any exhibitor interested in exhibiting the motion picture (see "Anti-Blind Bidding Statutes" and "Blind Bidding").

TRADE SCREENING REQUIREMENT. An implicit element of anti-blind bidding legislation which provides that distributors must allow exhibitors the opportunity to view an upcoming film before contractually committing to exhibit the film. A trade screening requirement would seem to help the exhibitors make more accurate predictions about the performance of a particular film in the exhibitor's theatres, at least more accurate than those judgments based on the very small amount of information now provided by certain distributors in states which do not have the trade screening requirement (see "Anti-Blind Bidding Statutes" and "Blind Bidding").

TRADE SECRET. Any process, pattern, formula or machine used in someone's business during the manufacture or production of a product which may give the user the opportunity to obtain an advantage over his, her or its competitors. When trade secrets are acquired and used without the rightful owner's authorization, the owner may be able to seek money damages and, in some instances, a court-ordered injunction to stop and/or prevent the unauthorized use of the trade secret. In order to recover in court, the owner of the trade secret must establish that the idea or item was held in the strictest of confidence, and that it was obtained by the other party through fraud or other unfair means. Once a trade secret is discovered either by analysis of the product or by any other proper method, it is then permissible for the discoverer to use it for his, her or its own advantage (see "Anti-Trust Laws," "Covenant not to Compete" and "Non-Disclosure Provisions").

TRADE SNEAK. A sneak preview, usually scheduled by a film's distributor several months prior to a film's release and designed to secure distribution for the film in given markets. Exhibitors are invited to view the movie at a trade sneak along with the public and after viewing the motion picture and making a judgment regarding the audience's reaction, the exhibitors are asked to bid on the film. All expenditures incurred in the conduct of a trade sneak would generally be considered distribution costs by the distributor (see "Director's Cut," "Sneak Preview," "Sneak Preview Advertising" and "Word-of-Mouth Sneak").

TRADE UNION (see "Guild" and "Union").

TRADE USAGE. Specialized meanings given to certain terms due to their general acceptance in a trade or industry and the reasonable reliance of the persons involved in that trade or industry on those meanings. Trade usage also refers to business practices that are generally accepted and relied on in many transactions in a specific trade or industry (see "Business Practices," "Customary Terms" and "Term of Art").

TRAFFIC IN. To carry on commercial activity relating to a given commodity, e.g., feature films, videocassettes or pornography (see "Exploit").

TRAILER. A short promotional film exhibited in theatres (usually beginning two to three weeks prior to the release of the subject film) as a preview of coming attractions. A trailer usually runs less than three minutes (see "Green Band Trailer," "Pre-Feature Entertainment," "Red Band Trailer," "Teasers" and "Trailer Tags").

TRAILER CROSSPLUG. A teaser trailer shown by an exhibitor to movie patrons in one theatre which advertises a movie showing in another theatre, in the same complex or otherwise (see "Teasers" and "Trailer").

TRAILER REVENUES. Income allocated by an exhibitor and paid to the distributor for the exhibition of a trailer. A distributor may incur substantial expense in preparing trailers and advertising accessories. If such expenses are charged against the distributor's proceeds as expenses of distribution, then any amounts of revenues derived from trailers and advertising accessories should be included in gross receipts to the distributor for purposes of calculating profit participations. Such payments may be made by exhibitors in certain territories. Legal requirements in many countries provide that a short or trailer be included with any film sent into such country, thus allocation issues arise with respect to what portion of a film's rentals should be allocated to the costs associated with producing the shorts or trailers. If the distributor wants to keep its revenues from trailers and accessories, it should not be able to deduct costs associated with the preparation of such items as distribution expenses (see "Allocations" and "Trailer").

TRAILER TAGS. A distinctive or identifying word or phrase, such as "for general audiences," assigned by the MPAA Ratings Board that provides the rating designation for a film. Such tags are required to be included on all movie trailers for MPAA-rated films (see "Ratings" and "Trailers").

TRANSACTION. Generally, the doing or performance of some matter of business between two or more persons. In accounting, an event or condition recognized by an entry in the books of account. In securities, the execution of an order to buy or sell a security. For tax purposes, any sale, exchange, or other disposition; any lease or rental; and any furnishing of services (see "Sham Transaction").

TRANSACTIONAL EXEMPTION (same as "Exempt Transaction").

TRANSCRIPTION. In music, an arrangement of a piece for some voice or instrument, or combination thereof, other than that for which it was originally intended (see "Music").

TRANSFER AGENT. An agent, usually a commercial bank, appointed by a corporation to maintain records of the corporation's stock and bond owners, to cancel and issue certificates, and to resolve problems arising from lost, destroyed, or stolen stock certificates. A corporation may also serve as its own transfer agent (see "Corporate Stock").

TRANSFER OF COPYRIGHT OWNERSHIP. An assignment, mortgage, grant of exclusive license, transfer by will or intestate succession, or any other change in the ownership of any or all of the exclusive rights in the copyrights associated with a property whether or not it is limited in time or place of effect, but not including a nonexclusive license. A transfer of exclusive rights, other than by operation of law, is not valid unless an instrument of conveyance (for example, contract, bond, deed), or a note or memorandum of the transfer, is in writing and signed by the owner of the rights conveyed or the owner's duly authorized agent. The U.S. Copyright Office does not make transfers of copyright ownership, but rather records a document of transfer after it has been executed by the parties (see "Copyright Assignment").

TRANSNATIONAL CARTELIZATION. The combining of independent commercial enterprises beyond national boundaries in an effort to limit competition (see "Cartel").

TRANSPORTATION COSTS. The expenses associated with moving people, animals or equipment from one point to another. Transportation costs may be a significant cost of producing a motion picture on location (see "Budget," "Budget Categories," "Living Expenses" and "Rising Production Costs").

TREASURY STOCK. Corporate stock reacquired by the issuing company and available for retirement or resale, i.e., it is issued but not outstanding (see "Corporate Stock").

TREATMENT. An intermediate stage between the movie script idea and the shooting script, i.e., an essay style description of the story and characters. There is no specific length, but a treatment generally runs twenty-five to thirty pages. It tells the story of the motion picture in sequence, showing in more or less detail the form the final film will take, with specific examples of the dialogue, setting, camera angles, etc. It is more than a bare statement of an idea or concept and it can be copyrighted and may meet WGA requirements for registration. Copyright registration, however, only covers the creative expression in the treatment itself; it does not give any protection for the general ideas revealed in the treatment, and is not a substitute for registration of the finished motion picture. The WGA defines treatment as an adaptation of a story, book, play, or other literary, dramatic, or dramatic-musical material for motion picture purposes in a form suitable for use as the basis of a screenplay (see "One Line Description," "Basic Story Outline," "Outline" and "Synopsis").

TREND. A prevailing tendency or inclination, i.e, a general movement or swing in current preferences. In the financing of independent films, a number of factors may contribute to the appearance of trends: changing economic and tax considerations, the over-eagerness for the trade press to identify and report on such trends (whether real or not), the prevailing lack of knowledge and expertise in the area of film finance among independent producers and the self-serving promotion of such trends by those who may have expertise in a limited area of film finance (see "Financing," "Scam" and "Trades").

TRIMS. Unused portions of film cut from a scene (see "Cutouts" and "Editor").

TRISTAR CASE. A series of court hearings relating to the application of the Paramount Consent Decree to the motion picture distributor TriStar. In 1980, Loew's Theatres petitioned the judge who had been supervising the implementation of the Paramount Consent Decrees for slightly more than three decades for relief that would allow Loew's to enter the motion picture distribution business in addition to its activities as an exhibitor. The motion was granted subject to several conditions including (1) Loew's could not exhibit any films it distributed or any films in which it had a financial interest and (2) as a distributor, Loew's had to abide by the same conduct restrictions imposed by the original Paramount decree. After TriStar acquired Loew's in 1986, those two entities applied to the court for interim relief (1) to allow the exhibition of TriStar films in Loews theatres during the important Christmas holiday season and (2) for removal of the trade practice injunctions prohibiting TriStar from conducting business as a distributor with any other exhibitors except Loews. This relief was also granted, but on an interim basis. In 1987, TriStar and Loews went back to the court and asked for permanent relief from the Paramount Consent Decree and from the 1980 order. At that point, the U.S. Justice Department offered its vigorous support for the TriStar application (based on its 1984 merger guidelines for vertical mergers), and again the TriStar/Loews motion was granted (see "Conduct Restrictions," "Merger Guidelines," "Paramount Consent Decree of 1948," "Relief" and "Vertical Merger").

TRUE AVAILABILITY. A condition whereby a film becomes available to an exhibitor either for a first run immediately upon that film's national break or for a subsequent run immediately upon the film's prior run's conclusion (see "Availability").

TRUST. A combination of business firms or corporations formed by a legal agreement, particularly a combination that reduces or threatens to reduce competition (see "Anti-Trust Laws," "Cartel," "Monopoly," "Oligopoly" and "Transnational Cartelization").

TRUSTEE. One who holds legal title to property "in trust" for the benefit of another person and who is required to carry out specific duties with regard to the property or who has been given power affecting the disposition of property for another's benefit. The term is also sometimes used to describe anyone who acts as a guardian or fiduciary in a relationship to another, e.g., a partner to co-partner (see "Fiduciary").

TRUST ME. A request made to someone who may be doubting a statement or proposed course of action indicating that the doubting person can rely on the party offering the statement or proposal. During the course of negotiating an important contract, such as a feature film distribution agreement, there should be no need to accept any oral representations of this sort so long as language may be drafted to cover the subject contingency. Also, in less formal business relations (i.e., non-contractual), trust should be reserved for emergencies, i.e., those situations in which the parties are not be able to communicate (see "Entire Agreement Clause" and "Sue Us").

TV ADS (see "Commercials").

TV PRINT. A composite color-film print that has been balanced for xenon projection, i.e., for television (see "Other Versions").

TV SALES. In film distribution, the licensing of films for exhibition on network and for syndication, cable, pay-TV, video-cassette, video-disc and other new television technologies (see "Cable Television," "Free Television" and "Syndication").

TV SPECIAL (see "Television Special").

TURNAROUND. A screenplay development situation in which the original studio/purchaser of a property has declined to go forward with the project beyond a certain point, has provided a turnaround notice to the original producer/seller and the project is available to be picked up by another studio or production company. The project is in turnaround (see "Step Deal," "Turnaround Provision or Agreement" and "Venture Capital").

TURNAROUND AGREEMENT OR CLAUSE (same as "Turnaround Provision or Agreement").

TURNAROUND PROVISION OR AGREEMENT. A clause commonly found in literary purchase agreements or production-financing/distribution agreements with studios or distributors and in studio development deals (or a separate agreement) which provides the right to a producer or screenwriter to submit a film project to another production company or studio if the original developing production company at which the project was being acquired or developed elects not to proceed with the production of the film, e.g., ". . . film project will be turned back to the producer for twelve months if the studio does not begin production within six months after the 120-day development period." If there is a turnaround, it does not depend upon the occurrence of a specific event as does the reversion in an option agreement (i.e., the failure to make an option payment in a timely manner); rather, it is a right which may be exercised by the owner, at its election, to reacquire the property after notice by the purchaser/studio of its decision not to proceed with production. Such right is often contingent upon the original developing production company's development expenses to date being repaid and sometimes the original development company may retain an interest in the film's earnings (see "Reversion Provision or Agreement" and "Substitution Clause or Agreement").

TURNAROUND HELL. The circumstances in which a producer is not able to reacquire the rights to produce a screenplay from a studio/production company and the screenplay thus gathers dust at the studio/production company in some repository of incomplete projects (see "Turnaround Provision").

TURNAROUND NOTICE. A written notification provided by a purchaser of a literary property upon which a motion picture is to be based that such purchaser will not proceed with further development of the screenplay or production of the motion picture and that the author or owner may want to exercise its rights to reacquire the property or interest another production company in acquiring the property (see "Turnaround").

TURNAROUND TIME. The minimum and specific number of hours that must be provided to a union member in accordance with union contracts before that union member may be required to return to work. Also, the amount of time it takes a securities attorney to produce the first draft of a disclosure document for a film limited partnership once the producer has provided sufficient information for the draft to be prepared (see "Securities" and "Union").

TWENTY-PERCENT RULE. An informal guideline allegedly used by many of the major-studio owned or controlled video companies when dividing up the monies received from home video (and laser video disc) retail sales and rentals. Pursuant to such rule, an arbitrary share of 20% of the total of video-company wholesale revenues is designated as a royalty to be paid to the distributor. The twenty-percent rule is based on an early estimate of what video profits would be and may have no relationship to the actual current numbers. Initially, the marketing and manufacturing costs associated with the new video technology was significant; thus, the initial 20% royalty payment to film distributors may have made sense. Now, however, both the marketing and manufacturing costs relating to video-cassettes have dropped drastically (per unit), and the 20% royalty is significantly out of line. Some in the industry have alleged that by uniformly applying this twenty-percent rule, the studios are conspiring to deny profit participants in movies and television shows their fair share from the sale of videocassettes. Other industry observers suggest that arm's length home-video deals can be negotiated in the current marketplace either on a royalty or distribution fee basis (see "Conscious Parallelism," "Distribution Fee Basis," "RIPOFF," "Royalty Basis," "Videocassette Revenue Reporting" and "Video Companies").

TWO-RUN BREAK. A film's break being available for no more than two theatres within the break's geographical area (see "Three-Run Break" and "Four-Run Break").

TWO-TIERED SEQUENTIAL PRICING STRUCTURES. The traditional policy with regard to setting the retail price for a motion picture on videocassette, i.e., the initial release is priced somewhat higher (in the $60 to $90 range) with the result that most purchases are made for video rental purposes and a later secondary sale at a much lower price (in the $15 to $30 range), which encourages more consumer purchasers of the videos at that time (see "Re-Release," "Sell-Through Market" and "Videocassette Revenue Reporting").

TYING ARRANGEMENT. The sale of one product on the condition that the purchaser also buy another product, or agree to not buy the other product from anyone else. A tying arrangement is a per-se violation of the Sherman Anti-trust Act in that it allows the seller to exploit his, her or its control over the tying product to force the buyer into the purchase of a tied product that the buyer either did not want at all or might have preferred to purchase elsewhere on different terms. If a seller does not possess sufficient market power to cause an actual adverse effect on competition, a court will not find a tying arrangement, and therefore the per-se rule will not apply (see "Antitrust Laws" and "Block Booking").

TYPECAST. The selecting of actors for film roles because they have played similar parts before or because they are very much like the characters to be played (see "Actor").

— U —

U.K. VERSION. A copy of a motion picture produced outside of the United Kingdom but specifically edited in a manner that is suitable for exhibition in the U.K. (see "Other Versions" and "U.S. Theatrical Cut").

ULOE. Acronym for uniform limited offering exemption (see "Uniform Limited Offering Exemption" below).

ULTRA-LOW BUDGET. A subjective term whose meaning may change from year to year, but which currently refers to feature films that are produced for less than a million dollars (see "Big-Budget Films," "Low-Budget Films" and "Medium-Budget Films").

ULTRA VIRES ACTIVITIES. Actions of a corporation or its officers and directors that are not authorized by its charter and that may therefore lead to shareholder or third-party lawsuits and personal liability of the corporation's officers and/or directors (see "Articles of Incorporation," "Charter" and "Piercing the Corporate Veil").

UNAUTHORIZED CROSS-COLLATERALIZATION. A feature film distributor's unauthorized offsetting of the profits of a movie against the same movie's profits in another market, against the profits of one movie against the profits of another movie produced by the same production company or against the profits of another movie produced by a different production company. A cross-collateralization provision may authorize one but not the other (see "Allocation," "Creative Accounting," "Cross-Collateralization," "Cross-Collateralization of Markets," "Cross-Collateralization of Slates," "De Facto Cross-Collateralization," "Discretionary Cross-Collateralization," "Overage" and "Unrecouped Expenses").

UNAUTHORIZED DISTRIBUTION. The sale, rental or other exploitation of a film without a grant of distribution rights; an activity which the distributor may seek to prevent and in the process incur costs which are typically defined as deductible distribution expenses. Distributor association dues, fees, assessments or other levies are typically made to cover the costs of such activities conducted on behalf of its distributor members. Individual distributors may also incur such costs, but as with any distribution expense, such costs must be carefully reviewed, confirmed and adjudged reasonable to prevent overstated expenses. The producer may want to ask the distributor if it anticipates any such costs beyond industry assessments for such activities (see "Distribution Expenses").

UNCOLLECTIBLE INDEBTEDNESS. Debts owed to a debtor or creditor which are determined to be impossible or impractical to collect, e.g., debts owed by a sub-distributor, exhibitors or licensees to a film's distributor, which the distributor has determined to be uncollectible. Independent producers must be wary of unscrupulous distributors who may fraudulently claim that such debts cannot be collected when in fact they have been or will be in the future (see "Bad Debt").

UNCONSCIONABLE CONTRACT. A contract that is so unfair or unreasonably detrimental to the interests of a contracting party as to render the contract legally unenforceable. The basic test is whether, in the light of the general commercial background and the commercial needs of the particular trade or case, the clauses involved are so one-sided as to be unfair or intolerable under the circumstances existing at the time of the making of the contract. This term refers to a bargain so one-sided as to amount to an "absence of meaningful choice" on the part of one of the parties together with contract terms which are unreasonably favorable to the other party. Ordinarily, one who signs an agreement without full knowledge or understanding of its terms might be held to assume the risk that he or she has entered into a one-sided bargain. But when a party of little bargaining power and, hence, little real choice signs a commercially unreasonable contract with little or no knowledge or understanding of its terms, it is hardly likely that his or her consent was ever given to all the terms. In such a case, the usual rule that the terms of an agreement are not to be questioned may be abandoned, and a court may consider whether the terms of the contract are so unfair that enforcement should be withheld (see "Contract of Adhesion," "Overreaching" and "Submission Release").

UNCONTROLLED DISTRIBUTION. Securities terminology for an offering of securities by selling stockholders (as opposed to the issuer

of the securities) on a random basis through any number of broker/
dealers who are willing to assist such persons or an offering by such
persons without the use of a broker (see "Controlled Distribution"
and "Distribution").

UNCROSSED. Not cross-collateralized (see "Cross-Collateralization,"
"Cross-Collateralization of Slates" and "De Facto Cross
Collateralization").

UNDERAGE. An amount an exhibitor falls short in meeting a film
rental commitment to a distributor on a given film. Exhibitors sometimes use excess film rental earned in one circuit theatre to fulfill a
rental commitment defaulted by another. This practice effectively
cross-collateralizes the financial results of several unrelated films
(see "Cross-Collateralization" and "Overage").

UNDERBUDGETING ERRORS. Mistakes in estimating the production
costs of a movie, i.e., not enough money is allocated for certain
budget items (see "Budget").

UNDERCAPITALIZATION. The failure to provide sufficient cash capital
to give a corporation or other business a reasonable chance of
survival. Undercapitalization is one of several operational defects
which may cause the loss of a corporation's separate identity from its
owners (see "Piercing the Corporate Veil").

UNDERLYING MATERIAL (see "Underlying Property").

UNDERLYING PROPERTY. The literary or other work upon which
rights to produce and distribute a motion picture are based. Such works
may include a book, play, treatment, synopsis, outline or original
screenplay (see "Literary Materials" or Literary Works" and "Property").

UNDERLYING RIGHTS. The legal privilege, power and authority
upon which the licenses to produce and distribute a motion picture
are based (see "Clearance" and "Underlying Property").

UNDERLYING RIGHTS AGREEMENTS. The contracts between a
writer or producer and the author, owner or publisher of a literary or
other work upon which rights to produce and distribute a motion
picture are based (see "Clearance" and "Underlying Property").

UNDERREPORTED RENTALS. The false and understated totals relating to the revenues earned by a given film as prepared and reported
by the film's distributor to the film's producer and other net profit
participants. This is less likely to occur if the distribution fee is a
percentage of the distributor's gross receipts, but if the distributor fee
is based on some form of adjusted gross, i.e., not calculated until

after certain deductions are made from gross receipts it would make more sense for the unscrupulous distributor (see "Audit," "Creative Accounting" and "Skimming").

UNDERWRITE. To ensure the sale of stocks or bonds by agreeing to buy, before a certain date, the entire issue if they are not sold to the public, or any part of the issue remaining after the sale. Underwriting is one method used by corporations to raise capital. A conventional underwriting is handled by an investment banker who agrees to buy the issue from the seller and who forms a syndicate to provide the necessary capital and distribution network. The syndicate then sells the issue to investors and the proceeds of that sale, less an underwriting fee, are paid to the client company (see "Underwriter" and "Primary Distribution").

UNDERWRITER. An investment banker who, singly or as a member of an underwriting group or syndicate, agrees with an issuer or other person on whose behalf a distribution is to be made (a) to purchase securities for distribution to investors or (b) to distribute securities to investors for or on behalf of such issuer or other person or (c) to manage or supervise a distribution of securities for or on behalf of such issuer or other person, hoping in the process to make a profit on the underwriting spread. Also defined as any person, group or firm that assumes a risk in relation to the offer or sales of securities in return for a fee, usually called a premium or commission (see "Issuer Sales," "Selling Group" and "Underwrite").

UNDERWRITER RISK. The risk taken by an investment banker that a new issue of securities purchased outright will not be bought by the public and/or that the market price will drop during the offering period (see "Risk").

UNDERWRITER'S QUESTIONNAIRE. A questionnaire circulated by the underwriting manager to all prospective members of the underwriting syndicate to obtain information to be used in a securities offering, including the names and addresses of the underwriters, any relationships with the issuer and stock ownership (see "Due Diligence").

UNDERWRITING AGREEMENT. An agreement between a corporation issuing new securities to be offered to the public and the managing underwriter as agent for the underwriting group. The agreement sets out the underwriter's commitment to purchase the securities, the public offering price, the underwriting spread (including all discounts and commissions), the net proceeds to the issuer and the settlement date (see "Managing Broker/Dealer Agreement").

UNDERWRITING GROUP. A temporary association of investment bankers, organized by the originating investment bank in a new issue of securities (see "Purchase Group" and "Selling Broker/Dealers").

UNDERWRITING SPREAD. The difference between the amount paid to an issuer of securities in a primary distribution and the public offering price (see "Firm Commitment" and "Selling Concession").

UNEARNED INCOME (REVENUE). In accounting, income received but not yet earned, such as advances from customers. For income tax purposes, income from sources other than wages, salaries, tips, and other employee compensation, e.g., dividends, interest and rent (see "Income").

UNEARNED INTEREST. Interest that has already been collected on a loan by a financial institution, but that cannot yet be counted as part of earnings because the principal of the loan has not been outstanding long enough (also called "Discount;" see "Interest").

UNENCUMBERED ASSETS. Property which is free and clear of all liens, i.e., creditor claims (see "Asset," "Debt" and "Liquid Asset").

UNETHICAL. Not in conformance with accepted or prescribed professional standards of conduct (see "Conflicts of Interest," "Ethics" and "Professional Code of Responsibility").

UNETHICAL BUSINESS PRACTICES. Procedures and activities engaged in by commercial enterprises that are not in conformance with accepted standards (see "Anti-Trust Laws," "Anti-Competitive Practices," "Blind Bidding," "Closed Bidding," "Creative Accounting," "Five "O'Clock Look," "Franchise Agreements," "Predatory Practices," "Price Fixing," "Product Splitting" and "Reciprocal Preferences").

UNFAIR COMPETITION. A tort (private or civil wrong or injury resulting from a breach of a legal duty that exits by virtue of society's expectations regarding interpersonal conduct rather than by contract or other private relationship) consisting of representations or conduct that deceives the public into believing that the business name, reputation or good will of one person is that of another; unfair, untrue or misleading advertising that is likely to lead the public into believing that certain goods are associated with another entity; imitation of a competitor's product, package or trademark in circumstances where the consumer might be misled (see "Fair Competition," "Predatory Practices," "Reciprocal Preferences," "Tort," "Trademark" and "Unethical Business Practices").

UNFAIR NEGOTIATING TACTICS. Inequitable, unethical or unjust bargaining methods (see "Anti-Competitive Practices" and "Negotiation").

UNFAVORABLE PORTRAYAL. The negative depiction of someone or something in a motion picture (see "Favorable Portrayal" and "Hidden Agenda").

UNIFORM LIMITED OFFERING EXEMPTION (ULOE). A model statute promulgated by the North American Securities Administrators Association which most states have adopted in some form or another to provide a state transactional exemption from the securities registration requirement. TheULOE is somewhat compatible with the federal Regulation D exemption (see "Regulation D," "Limited Offering Exemption" and "NASAA").

UNIFORM LIMITED PARTNERSHIP ACT. A model statute promulgated by the North American Securities Administrators Association which most states have adopted in some form or another to govern the creation and activities of limited partnerships in their respective states (see "Limited Partnership" and "NASAA").

UNINTEGRATED EXHIBITION AND DISTRIBUTION CAPACITY. In the context of the U.S. Justice Department merger guidelines, a phrase which refers to the number of motion picture distribution and exhibition companies that are not vertically integrated. The stated policy suggests that if there are a substantial number of such firms at either or both of the distribution and exhibition levels of the motion picture business, the fact that another firm (TriStar in this case) had become vertically integrated does not necessarily mean that competition in distribution or exhibition would be unreasonably restrained (see "Business Practices," "Conduct Restrictions," "Market Power," "Merger Guidelines," "Restraint of Trade," "TriStar Case," "Vertical Integration" and "Vertical Merger").

UNION. An association of workers whose main purpose is to bargain on behalf of such workers with employers about the terms and conditions of employment (see "Guild" and "Teamsters").

UNION LABOR. Film crew made up of union members. Typically, union film crews are more expensive than non-union crews but presumably more experienced (see "Artificial Pickup" and "Union").

UNION LIST. A list prepared by a union or guild and made available to its members which provides the names of film production companies that have become signatories to the union or guild's contract and have agreed to abide by the union's fair-practice standards. The list may also include the names of production companies which are not signatories to the union contract or whose labor practices are deemed to be unfair by the union. The phrase "union list" may also refer to a listing of union members who are active members of the union and are thus available for employment on a union job (see "Union").

UNIONS AND GUILDS FLIGHT ACCIDENT INSURANCE. Insurance which provides aircraft accidental-death insurance to all performers and production crew members, according to the union or guild contract requirements (see "Insurance").

UNISSUED STOCK. Shares of a corporation's stock authorized in its charter to be issued, but not yet issued (see "Corporate Stock" and "Issuer").

UNIT. A commonly used term in a limited partnership context to describe a ratable interest in the limited partnership of a unit holder or purchaser, i.e., the measure of participation in the ownership of the limited partnership (a partnership interest). Often the minimum purchase is limited to one (1) Unit, or, in the discretion of the general partner, half units or fractional units (see "Limited Partnership" and "Majority-In-Interest").

UNITED STATES COPYRIGHT OFFICE. The federal administrative agency responsible for implementing the copyright laws (see "Copyright").

UNIT HOLDER OR UNIT PURCHASER. A term commonly used in limited partnerships to identify the investors in such partnerships, i.e., one who purchases one or more units (or an approved purchase of a fraction of a unit) and has thereby obtained a pro rata share in the partnership (see "Limited Partner").

UNIT PRODUCTION MANAGER. The producer's executive assigned to a motion picture production and responsible for coordinating and supervising all administrative, financial and technical details of the production, and overseeing the activities of the entire crew on a given film or production unit. The unit production manager coordinates, facilitates and oversees the preparation of the production unit, all off-set logistics, day-to-day production decisions, locations, budget schedules and personnel (see "Line Producer," "Production Manager" and "Production Unit").

UNIT PUBLICIST. The publicist assigned to a film during pre-production and production for the purpose of generating publicity (see "Publicist").

UNIVERSE. A term often used in film distribution agreements to indicate that the distributor has the right to distribute the film in all markets, i.e., throughout the world or everywhere (see "Distribution Territories").

UNLISTED SECURITY. An over-the-counter security which is not listed on a stock exchange (see "Securities" and "Stock Exchange").

UNPAID DIVIDEND. Dividend that has been declared by the board of directors of a corporation but has not reached its payment date (see "Corporate Stock").

UNQUALIFIED AUDIT (see "Complete Audit").

UNRECOUPED EXPENSES. The expenses incurred in the production or distribution of a film that have not been recouped in distributing the film. Distributors may seek to offset such losses with profits on other films or in other markets (see "Allocation" and "Cross-Collateralization").

UNRETURNED CAPITAL CONTRIBUTION. In some limited partnerships, a term used to mean any partner's capital contribution minus the cash which has been distributed to that partner pursuant to the partnership agreement. Not all limited partnerships use this terminology (see "Capital").

UNSECURED DEBT. An obligation not backed by the pledge of specific collateral (see "Collateral" and "Debt").

UNSOLICITED MATERIAL. Literary works submitted to producers or production companies that were not requested (see "Submission Release").

UP FRONT. In a film context, before a production begins. The phrase may refer to a commitment to pay compensation to an executive producer, producer, director, etc. prior to the commencement of principal photography. In a limited partnership context, the phrase may refer to the expenses to be incurred by the general partner in organizing and selling the limited partnership and may include some legal, accounting, printing, binding, art and marketing costs including broker/dealer due diligence fees, if any (see "Frontend Load").

UP-FRONT DISTRIBUTION MONEY. Funds provided by a distributor to the producer of a film prior to the production of the film (see "Producer's Advance").

UP-FRONT EXPENDITURES. In a limited partnership context, the expenses of organizing and selling the partnership interests (see "Organizational Costs," "Start-Up Costs" and "Syndication Expenses").

UP-FRONT FINANCING. A significant financial contribution by a film's distributor to the production cost of the movie. Sometimes up-front financing is required by a lending bank of the distributor so that the distributor has a financial stake in the picture and the distributor will therefore be motivated to open the film in the better theatres and to provide adequate expenditures for prints and ads (see "Financing" and "Rent-A-Major").

UP-FRONT SALARY. Monies paid to film talent before the production begins or during production, as opposed to backend participations (see "Backend Participations" and "Contingent Compensation").

UPS AND DOWNS. In a business context, the rise and fall of the fortunes of various segments of an industry. In the motion picture business, the fortunes of individuals and entities can rise and fall with amazing swiftness. With such incredible compensation being paid to the top performers in each area of the motion picture business, i.e., studio executives, actors/actresses, directors, agents, etc., it is easy for the industry to attract more than enough top talent in all of these fields. On the other hand, if for any reason (justifiable or not) such persons suddenly become out of favor with the sources of such inflated compensation, the fall can be sudden and devastating. This phenomenon further amplifies the power of the individuals and entities at the top of the pecking order in the movie industry, skews the economic principle of supply and demand, and creates artificial barriers to entry for organizations that cannot pay the inflated costs (see "A-Title," "Barriers to Entry," "Law of Supply and Demand," "Leverage," "Pied Piper," "Polarization" and "Rising Production Costs").

UPSIDE POTENTIAL. The possible upward price movement an investor may enjoy in a particular investment or the prospective profits of an investor. Also, a speculative reference to the amount of money a motion picture may make (see "Downside Exposure").

U.S. BOX-OFFICE GROSS. The total amount of money paid by moviegoers for admission tickets to see motion pictures at theatres in the United States. The MPAA estimates that U.S. box office gross fell 4.4% to $4.8 billion in 1991, from $5.02 billion in 1990 (see "Box Office Gross").

U.S. DOLLAR DENOMINATED LETTERS OF CREDIT. Written guarantees issued by a foreign bank which state that, on delivery of the film, the bank will pay a specific amount in U.S. dollars (see "Letters of Credit").

USE OF PROCEEDS. A major required section in the disclosure document for a securities offering which sets out the principal purposes for which the net proceeds of the offering are intended to be used and the approximate amount intended to be used for each such purpose. Also, if less than all the securities to be offered may be sold and more than one use is listed for the proceeds, the order of priority of such purposes must be indicated (sometimes called "Estimated Use of Proceeds;" see "Disclosure Document" and "Mini-Maxi Offering").

U.S. FREE-TELEVISION VERSION. A copy of a motion picture that has been edited so that it is suitable for exhibition on the broadcast television networks in the United States (see "Other Versions" and "U.S. Theatrical Cut").

U.S. JUSTICE DEPARTMENT. The federal agency responsible for, among other things, enforcing criminal provisions of the U.S. antitrust laws (see "Federal Trade Commission," "Merger Guidelines," "Paramount Consent Decree of 1948" and "TriStar Case").

U.S. NETWORK BROADCAST. Television programming telecast by one of the television networks based in the U.S. (see "Network" and "Network Broadcast").

U.S. THEATRICAL. The feature film market in theatres located within the United States or in areas under U.S. control (see "Domestic Theatrical Market").

U.S. THEATRICAL ADMISSIONS. The number of moviegoers who purchase tickets to see motion pictures at U.S. theatres (see "Theatrical Admissions").

U.S. THEATRICAL CUT. Generally, the first version of a motion picture released for exhibition in the domestic theatrical marketplace, i.e., that version of a film that is shown in the U.S. theatres (see "Cutting Rights," "Final Cut," "Other Versions" and "U.S. Free Television Version").

USURIOUS CONTRACT. A contract that imposes interest on a debt at a rate in excess of that permitted by law (see "Loan Sharking," "RICO" and "Usury").

USURY. An unconscionable or exorbitant rate of interest; an excessive and illegal requirement of compensation for forbearance on a debt (interest). Each state's legislature determines the maximum allowable rates of interest that may be demanded in any financial transaction, however, usury laws generally do not apply to corporate borrowers. Individual independent producers whose films are being financed by a studio which charges interest on the production monies provided may want to consider whether usury laws apply to the transaction (see "Creative Accounting," "Loan Sharking" and "Usurious Contract").

—V—

VALUE. The monetary worth of a thing; marketable price; estimated or assessed worth (see "Asset Value").

VANITY SCREENING. A preview of a completed motion picture sponsored by the producers or actors of the film as opposed to a distributor, i.e., the film does not yet have a distributor. Vanity screening is a form of self-distribution (see "Four-Walling" and "Self-Distribution").

VARIETY. An entertainment-oriented newspaper published weekly in New York for international distribution and daily in Los Angeles. "Variety" is owned by Cahners, a division of the British publishing company Reed International (see "Daily Variety" and "Trades").

VCR (see "Videocassette Recorder").

VENTURE CAPITAL. A source of financing for start-up companies or others embarking on new or turnaround ventures that entail some investment risk but offer the potential for above-average future profits. Sources of venture capital include wealthy individual investors; subsidiaries of banks and other corporations organized as small-business investment companies (SBICs); groups of investment banks and other financing sources who pool investments in venture capital funds or venture capital limited partnerships. The Small Business Administration promotes venture capital programs through the licensing and financing of SBICs. Venture capital financing supplements other personal or external funds that an entrepreneur is able to tap, or takes the place of loans or other funds that conventional financial institutions are unable or unwilling to risk. Some venture capital sources invest only at certain stages of entrepreneurship, such as the start-up or seed-money stage, the first-round or second-round phases that follow, or the mezzanine level immediately preceding an initial public offering. In return for taking an investment risk, venture capitalists are usually rewarded with some combination of profits, preferred stock, royalties on sales and/or capital appreciation of common shares (see "Development Funds," "Entrepreneur," "IPO," "Plan of Business," "Preliminary/ Development Funding," "Risk Capital," "Second Round," "Seed Money" and "Turnaround").

VENTURE CAPITAL FINANCING. The funding of the production and/or distribution costs of a motion picture with infusions of cash from venture capital firms. Such companies usually invest in "going" concerns as opposed to a "one-shot" movie project and, more typically, in the high-tech arena. Venture capital funds will rarely invest in a film deal (see "Venture Capital").

VENTURE CAPITAL LIMITED PARTNERSHIP. An investment vehicle organized by a brokerage firm or entrepreneurial company to raise capital for start-up companies or those in the early processes of developing products and services. The partnership will usually take shares of stock in the company in return for capital supplied. Limited partners receive income from profits the company may earn. If the company is successful and goes public, limited partners' profits could be realized from the sale of formerly private stock to the public (see "Limited Partnership" and "Venture Capital").

VERTICAL INTEGRATION. The unified ownership of several different levels of production and distribution in the same industry, e.g., a film industry in which the same owner is allowed to own or control a studio facility, a production company, a distribution entity, exhibitor chain, or (technically) any two of the above which deal directly with each other, is vertically integrated. Following the issuance of the U.S. Justice Department merger guidelines and the TriStar Case, questions relating to whether film-industry companies are vertically integrated at the distributor/exhibitor levels, and, if so, whether such integration makes it more difficult for other companies to compete at those levels of the industry without being vertically integrated have been pivotal to the analysis regarding the anti-competitive effects of vertical mergers in that industry (see "Anti-Competitive Practices," "Arm's Length," "Anti-Trust Laws," "Blind Bidding," "Distributor," "Exhibitor," "Formula Deal," "Global Integration," "Major Exhibition Chains," "Merger Guidelines," "Number of Screens," "Paramount Consent Decree of 1948," "Producer," "Studio," "Transnational Cartelization," "TriStar Case" and "Vertical Merger").

VERTICAL PRICE FIXING. A combination or conspiracy formed for the purpose and with the effect of raising, depressing, fixing, pegging, or stabilizing the price of a product engaged in by members of different levels of an industry, e.g., in the film industry, at the production, distribution and/or exhibition levels (see "Horizontal Price Fixing" and "Price Fixing").

VIDEO. An electronic image-making system recorded on magnetic tape. The medium is primarily used for television, commercials and music videos, although some movie producers are beginning to experiment with the medium for feature-length presentations (see "HDTV").

VIDEOCASSETTE. A magnetic tape which is housed in a light-tight magazine and used to record and play back video images (see "Video" and "Videocassette Recorder").

VIDEOCASSETTE AFFILIATE. In the context of the motion picture industry, a company that is engaged in the manufacture, wholesale distribution or retail sales of feature-film home videos whose stock is partly owned (i.e., less than a majority of voting shares) by a feature film distribution company or both of such companies are subsidiaries of a third company (see "Videocassette Subsidiary").

VIDEOCASSETTE JACKET. The carton, covering or other packaging used to protect and market videocassette reproductions (see "Jacket").

VIDEOCASSETTE LICENSE AGREEMENT (see "Video Rights Agreement").

VIDEOCASSETTE RECORDER (VCR). Any videotape device that both records and/or plays back a magnetic tape. The video tape formats include 1/2-inch, 3/4-inch and 1-inch. These formats may be for both professional and/or home use, but the 1" format is typically used for professional video recording and replaces the standard 2-inch tapes used originally for television broadcasting. Also, the 1-inch system does not operate with self-contained cassettes but with reel to reel recording tape, i.e., the tape moves from feed roll to take-up roll (see "Videocassettes").

VIDEOCASSETTE REVENUE REPORTING. In recent years, the videocassette market has been one of the fastest-growing revenue sources for films; thus, some of the major studios have created wholly owned subsidiaries or joint ventures to manufacture and distribute videocassettes, and these entities typically only pay 20% of wholesale receipts as a royalty fee to the parent company. In other words, unlike other areas of motion picture revenue reporting, home video is handled on a royalty basis (more like the record industry) rather than remitting the distributor's share of the wholesale revenues on a distribution fee basis. The system then switches back to the distribution fee basis at the distributor level, since the parent distributor, in turn, charges a distribution fee (usually about 30%), leaving only a very small percentage remaining for profit participants. In addition to allowing a studio/distributor to take a fee on a related company transaction, this structure and these calculations permit the distributor to keep a disproportionate share of videocassette revenues. In situations where the distributor is participating in the wholesale revenues of the video company, producers must address this issue in negotiations relating to the distribution agreement and seek to substitute a reasonable distribution fee for the typical 20% royalty at the wholesale level so that the distributor will include a higher percentage of the wholesale revenues in its gross. This, in turn, may allow the profit participants to participate in a larger net-profit pool. In addition, the producer should seek to reduce the distribution fees being taken by the distributor in recognition of the fact that the distributor is also sharing in the wholesale revenues of its wholly owned or subsidiary video company (see "Arm's Length," "Home Video Royalty," "Predatory Practices," "Royalties," "Royalty Basis," "Twenty-Percent Rule" and "Unethical Business Practices").

VIDEOCASSETTE SUBSIDIARY. In the context of the motion picture industry, a company that is engaged in the manufacture, wholesale distribution or retail sales of feature-film home videos whose voting corporate shares or more than 50% owned by a feature film distribution company or a common parent corporation (see "Arm's Length," "Conflicts of Interest," "Predatory Practices," "Twenty-Percent Rule," "Reciprocal Preferences," "RIPOFF," "Unethical Business Practices," "Videocassette Affiliate" and "Videocassette Revenue Reporting").

VIDEO COMPANIES. Entertainment industry businesses which operate at the wholesale level and market videocassettes to retail outlets who in turn sell or rent to the general public (see "Videocassette Revenue Reporting").

VIDEO CORRIDOR. The revenue stream generated by the sale of feature film videocassettes through a film distributor to a video wholesaler as distinct from the revenues generated by the exploitation of the same film in other media. Sometimes additional or separate percentage participations may be granted to certain individuals or entities in this video revenue corridor (see "Outside the Pot" and "Participant").

VIDEODISC. A disc or "record" on which digitized video images and audio signals are stored to be electronically reassembled for playback. In the U.S., originally a needle-in-groove system, similar to the audio records, the old phonograph system, was utilized, but, subsequently, a laser video system, is being used. This system is played by a light beam with no pickup device actually touching the disk. The Japanese videodisc system utilizes a magnetic field with a "needle" floating over it but not actually touching the disc (see "Compact Disc" and "Laser Disc").

VIDEO FORMAT. The number of lines a television picture utilizes in reproducing an image. There are three basic video-broadcasting formats in the world: the U.S. and Japan use a 525 line format (the

NTSC format) while the Russian and French system (the SECAM system) and the system used throughout the rest of Europe and Australia (the PAL system) both use over 600-line images (see "HDTV").

VIDEO RIGHTS AGREEMENT. The contract between a film's distributor or copyright owner and a video company which sets forth the terms pursuant to which a film may be distributed in the home video market (see "First Sale Doctrine" and "Release Commitment").

VIDEOTAPE. A magnetic tape on which visual images are electronically recorded. Such tapes typically have a side track for synchronized sound (see "Tape").

VIDEO TAPE RECORDER (VTR). An electronic device which permits the user to record visual images on magnetic tape (see "Videotape").

VIDEO TAPE RECORDING. The act of creating a visual record on magnetic tape using a video tape recorder (see "Video Tape Recorder" and "Videotape").

VIEWING RESTRICTIONS. Limitations placed on screenings of leased or purchased educational or informational films, e.g., no paid admissions, no subcontracting for live, theatrical or television screenings, or no direct optical projection for paying or nonpaying audiences (see "Unauthorized Distribution").

VISUAL EFFECTS. Special effects or techniques used to obtain a certain look for a feature film. Such effects may include sets being designed for light absorbency, pushed-stop filming, customized lab work, special lighting and creative utilization of standard camera filters, speeds and lenses (see "Optical Effects").

VOICE-OVER. A performer engaged to give off-camera voicing who is not involved in an on-camera performance (see "Dialogue Replacement").

VOIDABLE. A contract that can be annulled by either party after it is signed because of the existence of fraud, incompetence, another illegality or a right of rescission (see "Rescission").

VOLUME DISCOUNTS/REBATES. A reduction in price or the return of a portion of the price for a product sold in larger than usual numbers. In the film industry, feature film distributors sometimes receive discounts or rebates from the exhibitor retailers with whom they place their films because of the large number of films the distributor supplies to the exhibitor. If such transactions are not contemplated by the terms of the film distribution agreement, the distributor may (and usually does) choose not to credit a given film's gross receipts for an allocable portion of such discounts or rebates; thus, none of the participants who are supposed to be participating in all forms of valuable remuneration generated by the exploitation of their specific film will receive any benefit from such discounts or rebates. The distributors argue that they should be the sole benefactors of such discounts or rebates since such benefits are awarded because of the volume of business directed to an exhibitor by the distributor. Participants counter that the distributors would not have any volume where it not for the films produced by the participants. This is another issue that should be discussed during the negotiations of the film distribution agreement (see "Adhesion Contract," "Unethical Business Practices," "Predatory Practices," "Reciprocal Preferences" and "Settlement Transactions").

VOODOO ACCOUNTING. A slang reference to movie-studio accounting practices which are alleged to be unfair (see "Creative Accounting" and "Studio Accounting Practices").

VOTING SECURITY. Any security presently entitling the owner or holder thereof to vote for the election of directors of a company (see "Corporate Stock" and "Securities").

VOTING STOCK. Shares in a corporation that entitle the shareholder to voting and proxy rights (see "Proxy").

VOUCHER. A documentary record of a business transaction; a written affidavit or authorization (see "Corporate Stock").

VTR (see "Video Tape Recorder").

— W —

WAITING PERIOD. The period between the date the registration statement in a public securities offering is initially filed with the SEC and the date it is declared effective. This so-called "cooling-off" period may be extended if more time is needed to make corrections or add information to the registration statement and prospectus (see "Acceleration," "Effective Date," "Prospectus," "Public Offering," "Red Herring" and "Registration Statement").

WAIVER. An intentional and voluntary giving up, relinquishment or surrender of some known right. In general, a waiver may either result from an express agreement or be inferred from circumstances (see "Conflict Waiver," "Nudity Waiver," "Release" and "Waiver of Moral Rights").

WAIVER OF DROIT MORAL (see "Waiver of Moral Rights").

WAIVER OF MORAL RIGHTS. The intentional and voluntary giving up, relinquishment, or surrender of the rights known as droit moral (French for "moral right"). Moral rights refer to the right of an author or artist (such as a film producer or director) to object to any deformation, mutilation or other alteration of his or her work. Although the term is widely recognized in civil law countries, it is not mentioned in the U.S. Copyright Act. Nevertheless, a right analogous to moral right has been recognized in this country in several situations in which the integrity and reputation of an artistic creator was protected by the courts. The express grounds on which common-law protection has been given include libel, unfair competition, copyright and the right of privacy. The right of droit moral gives the author of a work certain power to prevent changes, notwithstanding the provisions of his or her contract, e.g., a director may be able to prevent cutting and editing of his or her picture (except for editing for television and censorship). Producers should be aware that film distribution agreements often contain such a waiver and, unless the producer is satisfied with the provisions of the distribution agreement with respect to the distributor's editing rights, the producer should consider deleting any attempted waiver of droit moral rights (see "Creative Control," "Editing Rights," "Final Cut" and Moral Rights").

WALK-ON. A small non-speaking part in a film (see "Bit Player").

WALL STREET. The popular name for the financial district at the lower end of Manhattan in New York City where the New York and American Stock Exchanges and numerous brokerage firms are headquartered. A reference to Wall Street interest in an industry, such as the film industry, alludes to whether or not such brokerage firms want to direct investor client funds into various film-industry investment vehicles (see "Corporate Stock," "Financing," "Investor Financing" and "Securities").

WARDROBE. Any clothes (personal, purchased or rented) worn before the camera and during rehearsals or used in connection with a film's production (see "Costumer and Wardrobe Supervisor").

WARRANTIES (see "Warranty").

WARRANTIES AND REPRESENTATIONS. A common heading in a contract (see "Representations" and "Warranty").

WARRANTY. An assurance by one party to a contract of the existence of a fact upon which the other party may rely, intended precisely to relieve the promisee of any duty to ascertain the fact, and amounting to a promise to indemnify the promisee for any loss if the fact warranted proves untrue. Such warranties are either made overtly i.e., express warranties, or by implication, i.e., implied warranties. In a film distribution agreement, producer warranties and representations are likely to be made regarding the quality of the picture, i.e, it will be fully edited, titled, synchronized with sound and of a quality, both artistic and technical, for general theatrical release, as well as for numerous other matters relating to content, ownership, the discharge of the producer's obligations, no infringements, no advertising matter, no impairment of rights granted, valid copyright and MPAA rating. On the other hand, film distributors seldom provide many warranties relating to their side of the bargain, if any (see "Covenant of Good Faith and Fair Dealing" and "Representation").

WARRANTY OF QUIET ENJOYMENT. A warranty given by the producer (i.e., the producer warrants that the distributor has the right to the unimpaired use and enjoyment of the film property) if it does not know of any actual, or potential, adverse claims which might be made against the distribution of the picture. If the distributor wants this warranty and representation included in the distribution agreement, the producer should seek language limiting the warranty to matters known as of the date the agreement was signed (see "Warranty").

WATERCRAFT LIABILITY INSURANCE. Insurance providing coverage when watercraft (such as boats, etc.) are used in connection with a production. Such policies are generally written on a case-by-case basis (see "Insurance").

WATERED STOCK. In corporate law, shares of stock that have been issued by the corporation for less than full lawful consideration; also stock representing ownership of overvalued assets, a condition of overcapitalized corporations, whose total worth is less than the invested capital (see "Corporate Stock").

WEALTHY PARTNER FINANCING. The funding of the production and/or distribution costs of a motion picture with an active partner who provides most if not all of the monies needed. Generally speaking, if such partner is not a "silent" partner, i.e., is active in the management of the project, such fundings will not be considered securities. In other words, if the financial arrangement is structured and actually operates as a general partnership, joint venture or investor financing agreement as opposed to a corporate stock offering, limited partnership offering or investment contract, the securities laws will not apply (see "Business Plan," "Investor Financing Agreement," "Joint Venture" and "Securities").

WEEKLY HOUSE ALLOWANCE (see "House Nut").

WEEKLY HOUSE EXPENSE (see "House Nut").

WEEKLY REPORTING PAPERS. Production and financial reports filed with a motion picture studio/financier by the production company (see "Production Reports").

WEEKLY VARIETY (see "Variety").

WE'RE DIFFERENT. An assertion that one party is not the same as another. Often distributors will make oral representations early in discussions with producers that their distribution organization is not typical of other feature film distributors, i.e., suggesting indirectly that they do not conduct their activities in a manner substantially characterized as described in this book. The proof of such self-serving descriptions should lie in the actual conduct of the distributor over a period of time and in a consistent pattern of behavior which avoids much of the above described business practices (see "Sue Us" and "Trust Me").

WGA AGREEMENT. The Writers Guild of America Theatrical and Television Film Basic Agreement which, among other things, sets out minimum credit and compensation requirements to be observed by motion picture production companies that are signatories to the agreement in their hiring of screenwriter members of the WGA. The WGA agreement minimums are also commonly used as guides for non-WGA member writer agreements (see "Compensation Schedules" and "Writers Guild of America").

WGA BASIC AGREEMENT (see "WGA Agreement").

WGA REGISTRATION. The filing of a treatment or screenplay with the Writers Guild of America for purposes of establishing evidence that the author reduced that specific expression of a proposed motion picture as of a certain date (see "Copyright Registration" and "Submission Release").

WELL-KNOWN TALENT. Motion picture actors or directors who are familiar to general movie-going audiences (see "Highest Leverage Position").

WHEN INTEREST CHARGES STOP (see "Interest").

WHEN THE MONEY'S PAID. A reference to one of the most critical concepts relating to film finance and the recoupment of invested funds which focuses on that point in a motion picture's revenue stream at which funds are deducted for purposes of compensating a specified party. For example, the term "gross receipts" is typically defined as an earlier stage in the revenue stream than "net profits;" thus, "gross receipts" is a larger pool of money than "net profits" and a percentage participation in gross receipts is a substantially larger interest than the same percentage interest in net profits. The same is true of the terms "net profits" and "producer's share." Typically, the "producer's share" is defined as a later stage in the film's revenue stream, thus it is a smaller pool of money (if any), and percentage participant's in the "producer's share" would be getting a smaller amount of funds than a participant in the "net profits" pool with the same percentage. This concept also becomes an important factor in the decision relating to how to finance a film, since, for example, the bank will insist on being paid its loan proceeds, interest and fees out of first monies back to the distributor in a negative pickup deal, whereas traditionally the investors in a limited partnership have had to wait until the revenue stream reaches net profits (if ever) before even recouping their investment (see "Adjusted Gross," "Accountable Gross," "Box Office Gross," "Breakeven," "Gross Receipts," "House Nut," "Net Profits," "Outside the Pot," "Producer's Share," "Reciprocal Preferences," "Revenue Corridor" and "Revenue Stream").

WHITE COLLAR CRIME. A phrase connoting a variety of frauds, schemes, corruptions and commercial offenses committed by business persons, con artists and public officials; a broad range of non-violent offenses that have cheating and dishonesty as their central element (see "Crime," "Fraud," "Mafia," "Organized Crime," "Racketeering," "RICO," "Rules," "Theft" and "Scam").

WHOLESALE RECEIPTS. The monies received for the sale of a product from the retail sellers of such product by a business operating as a middle-level distributor of the product (see "Videocassette Subsidiary" and "Videocassette Revenue Reporting").

WHOLESALE SELLING PRICE. The amount of money given or set as consideration for the sale of a product in quantity and for resale (see "Conscious Parallelism," "Distribution Fee Basis," "Predatory Practices," "Royalty Basis," "Twenty-Percent Rule," "Unethical Business Practices" and "Videocassette Revenue Reporting").

WIDE RELEASE. In the context of domestic theatrical exhibition for a motion picture, an extensive exhibition pattern including multiple bookings in most of the theatrical markets. In a period of ever-increasing movie screens, this phrase will inevitably involve larger numbers of prints and screens, although, at minimum, a domestic theatrical opening on at least 100 screens throughout the country is still considered a wide release by many in the industry. On the maximum end of the scale, during the early-'80s a simultaneous release in 1,000 or more screens was considered to be a wide release, whereas in the early-'90s something in excess of 2,000 would be considered a wide release (see "General Release," "Limited Engagement," "Mini-Multiple," "National Release," "Prints," "Regional Release Pattern," "Release Pattern" and "Specialized Distribution").

WIDE-SCREEN ASPECT RATIO. An aspect ratio of 2.35:1 (see "Aspect Ratio").

WILD LINES. Short words or phrases that are recorded wild, i.e., off camera in situations where the sync recording is questionable (see "Wild Picture").

WILD PICTURE. Film shot without sound (see "Wild Recording").

WILD RECORDING. A sound recording not made synchronously with the filmed picture. Sound effects, random voices, narration and music are generally recorded in this manner; also referred to as non-synchronous sound (see "In Synch").

WILD SOUND EFFECTS. Recordings of sound effects not made synchronously with a filmed picture. Common examples include footsteps, dog barks, shattering glass, body hits, tire squeals and gunshots (see "Wild Recording").

WINDING UP. The process of liquidating a corporation or partnership; the process of collecting the assets, paying the expenses involved, satisfying the creditors' claims and distributing whatever is left, the net assets, usually in cash but possibly in kind to the entity's owners in order of preference (see "Dissolution" and "Liquidation").

WINDOW. Generally, a limited time during which an opportunity should be seized or it may be lost. In film, the period of time in which a film is available in a given medium. Some windows may be open-ended, such as theatrical and home video, or limited, such as pay television or syndication. For U.S.-made films, domestic theatrical distribution is typically the first window (see "Direct to Video Release," "Made for Video" and "Release Sequence").

WITHHOLDING. Another form of over-budget penalty sometimes imposed by a studio which is financing the production of a film in which the studio will withhold a significant amount of the producer's fee until delivery of the film's answer print. If the picture is delivered within budget, the producer receives his or her complete fee, but if the film has gone over budget, the producer has to wait until first net profits to receive the balance as a deferment (see "Over-Budget Penalty," "Penalty-Free Cushion" and "Double Add-Back").

WITHHOLDINGS. The portion of wages earned that an employer, such as a motion picture production company, deducts, usually for income tax purposes, from each salary payment made to an employee. The amount deducted is then forwarded to the government to be credited against the total tax owed by the employee at the end of the taxable year. U.S. production companies involved in international co-productions must be careful to withhold for the foreign partner so as to avoid the joint and several liability which may apply to such withholdings in certain circumstances (see "International Co-Productions and Agreements" and "Tax Deductions").

WITHHOLDING TAXES (see "Withholdings").

WORD-OF-MOUTH. The opinions of moviegoers regarding a specific motion picture as expressed to potential moviegoers who have not yet seen the subject film. Word-of-mouth may be favorable or unfavorable and is considered a very significant factor in the success of a film beyond its opening period (see "Legs" and "Sneak Preview").

WORD-OF-MOUTH SNEAK. A motion-picture sneak preview designed to initiate word-of-mouth publicity for the film. Generally, a word-of-mouth sneak is scheduled approximately two weeks before the film's release. A cooperative local or national advertising campaign may be launched in support of such a sneak (see "Director's Cut," "Preview," "Sneak Preview," "Sneak Preview Advertising" and "Trade Sneak").

WORKER'S COMPENSATION INSURANCE. An insurance coverage required to be carried by state law which applies to all temporary or permanent cast or production crew members. The coverage provides medical, disability or death benefits to any cast or crew member who becomes injured in the course of his or her employment (see "Insurance").

WORKING CAPITAL. Funds invested in a company's cash, accounts receivable, inventory and other current assets. Working capital finances the cash-conversion cycle of a business, i.e., the time required to convert raw materials into finished goods, finished goods into sales, and accounts receivable into cash (same as "Net Current Assets").

WORKING CONTROL. Effective control of a corporation by a shareholder or shareholders with less than 51% voting interest. Working control by a minority shareholder, or by two or more minority shareholders acting together, is possible when share ownership of a firm is otherwise widely dispersed (see "Minority Interest").

WORKING TITLE. The tentative name given to a film until a final name has been chosen and cleared (see "Release Title" and "Title Report").

WORK MADE FOR HIRE. A copyright law concept which describes a literary work written by an employee, e.g., a writer hired by an employer to write a screenplay. The author and copyright owner of a work made for hire is the employer, not the employee. The U.S. Copyright Office Form TX, which is used to register textual works, and Form PA, used to register motion pictures, asks whether the contribution to the work was a "work made for hire" (see "Commissioned Work," "Copyright" and "Writer for Hire").

WORKPRINT. The film print that the editor assembles from the dailies and which will undergo any number of editings before finally reaching a version that is determined to be the final cut to which the negatives will be conformed. Also, a lab print from a developed original, which is used by the editor to first synch up to sound and then to put into a first assembly. More generally, the visual material used for film editing [see "Work Print (Picture)"].

WORK PRINT (PICTURE). A positive print that usually consists of, among other things, intercut daily prints, film library prints, prints of dissolves, montages and titles. A picture workprint constantly maintains synchronism with the corresponding sound workprint (same as "Locked Picture;" see "Workprint").

WORK PRINT (SOUND). A term (no longer in common use) which refers to a sound print that usually contains all of the sound tracks (including sound effects, original sound and dubbed sound), but commonly does not include the final musical score, which in many situations is added to the finished film (see "Editor's Worktrack").

WORLDWIDE PICKUP. The acquisition of rights to distribute a motion picture throughout the world (see "Acquisition Distribution Agreement," "Domestic Pickup" and "Negative Pickup").

WORLDWIDE RIGHTS. The right to exploit a film in all markets and throughout the world or universe (see "Distribution Territories").

WORLDWIDE THEATRICAL. The distribution of a motion picture in theatres throughout the world (see "Theatrical Distribution").

WRAP. An end to a given segment of filming relating to a motion picture. A "wrap" may refer to the end of a particular day's shooting, to the completion of a particular film assignment or location shoot or to the end of principal photography on a film (see "Second Unit").

WRINKLE. A novel feature that may attract a buyer for a new product or security (see "Selling Point").

WRITE-DOWNS (see "Write-Off").

WRITE-OFF. Charging an asset amount to expense or loss. The effect of a write-off is to reduce or eliminate the value of the asset and reduce profits. The term also refers to the practice of taking a tax deduction in the current year (same as "Write-Downs").

WRITTEN BY. The screen credit awarded to the writer or writers who developed the story and wrote the screenplay (see "Screenplay By" and "Story By").

WRITER. A person who is engaged by a film production company to write literary material, including making changes or revisions (see "Screenplay").

WRITER AGREEMENT (same as "Writer Employment Agreement").

WRITER EMPLOYMENT AGREEMENT (same as "Writing Services Agreement").

WRITER FOR HIRE. A screenwriter who writes for an employer and gives up all elements of ownership to the resulting screenplay. In copyright terminology, the phrase is "work-made-for-hire" (see "Copyright" and "Work Made For Hire").

WRITER'S CERTIFICATE (see "Certificate of Authorship").

WRITER'S DEVELOPMENT DEAL. A financial arrangement for a production company or studio to fund the expenses of developing a motion picture screenplay wherein such funds are paid to a screenwriter as opposed to a producer or director (see "Development," "Director's Development Deal" and "Producer's Development Deal").

WRITERS GUILD OF AMERICA (WGA). The film industry union for screen writers (see "WGA Agreement").

WRITING SERVICES AGREEMENT. The basic contract for the hiring of a screenwriter, usually by a producer or production company, setting forth the terms and conditions under which the screenwriter may write a screenplay or provide other specific services in connection with a particular literary work (e.g., writing a synopsis, treatment, outline, polish, revision, etc.), or render continuing services relating to more than one motion picture project (also called "Writer Employment Agreement;" see "WGA Agreement").

WRITTEN RELEASES (see "Release").

— X —

XENON PROJECTOR. A motion picture theatre projector which has been developed more recently and is replacing the arc projector in theatres. The xenon projector uses a bulb instead of a glowing element, and the bulb allows a longer period of use for the projector before the bulb has to be changed. It also does not require a full ventilation system to carry off the extreme heat generated by an arc projector (see "Film" and "Screen").

X-RATING (X-RATED). An MPAA rating discontinued in the fall of 1990 but which indicated that a motion picture had been reviewed by the MPAA's Classification and Rating Administration, and that no one under the age of seventeen was to be admitted to see the film, i.e., that the film's material was considered to be patently adult. In some states, an "X" rating meant that the material was for adults only—twenty-one and over. Often an "X" rating showed that the film dealt with explicit sex, but such rating may have in the alternative indicated the film contained graphic violence or language that could be offensive to some moviegoers. Some newspapers have refused to carry ads for "X" rated movies (see "MPAA," "NC-17" and "Ratings").

— Y —

YEAR END ADJUSTMENTS. Changes in the accounting statements on a motion picture made at the end of a given year. The authority to make such adjustments is commonly provided for in the film distribution agreement in relation to the net profits computation. Such adjustments are ostensibly made to make corrections and/or to report items overlooked (see "Selling Subject to Review" and "Settlement Transaction").

YIELD. The return on an investor's capital investment; the current return on a stock expressed as a percentage of the price (see "Return on Invested Capital"). In lending, the total money earned on a loan, i.e., the annual percentage rate of interest multiplied by the term of the loan (see "Debt," "Interest" and "Rate of Return").

YIELD SPREAD. The difference in yield among various issues of securities (see "Rate of Return" and "Securities").

— Z —

ZONE. Market areas in each city where a movie is shown at only one theatre. Movie theatre operators and the movie studios that provide them for divide each city into these market areas. In theory a movie only plays one theatre in any one zone (see "Competitive Theatre Area" and "First-Run Zoning").

Bibliography

Anti-Trust Developments in Sports and Entertainment Law, Paul J. Tagliabue, "Anti-Trust Law Journal," 1987.

Art Murphy's Box Office Register, 1990.

Bank Financing of a Motion Picture Production, Jill Mazirow Eshman, "Loyola of Los Angeles Entertainment Law Journal," 1992.

Blind Bidding: A Need For Change, Keith M. Gregory, "Beverly Hills Bar Journal," Winter 1982-1983.

Blue Sky Law Reporter, Commerce Clearing House, Inc., 1984.

Breaking Through, Selling Out, Dropping Dead and Other Notes on Filmmaking, William Bayer, Limelight Editions, 1989.

California Corporate Practice Guide—2nd Ed, Morgan D. King, Lawpress Corporation, 1989.

Commissions to Non-Broker/Dealers Under California Law, Elena R. Freshman, "Beverly Hills Bar Journal," Volume 22, Number 2.

Counseling Clients in the Entertainment Industry (seminar), Martin E. Silfen, Chairman, Practicing Law Institute, 1989.

Dark Victory (Ronald Reagan, MCA, and the Mob), Dan E. Moldea, Penguin Books, 1987.

Delson's Dictionary of Motion Picture Marketing Terms, Donn Delson and Stuart Jacob, Bradson Press, Inc., 1980.

Dictionary of Finance and Investment Terms—2nd Ed, John Downes and Jordan Elliot Goodman, Barron's Educational Series, Inc., 1987.

Dictionary of Media Terms, Edmund Penney, G.P. Putnam's Sons, 1984.

Defining Net Profits, Shares for a Motion Picture Deal, Edward E. Colton, "New York Law Journal," September 30, 1988.

Distributing Independent Films & Video, edited by Morrie Warshawski, The Media Project (Portland, Oregon) and Foundation for Independent Video and Filmmakers (New York), 1989.

Encyclopedia of Exhibition, National Association of Theatre Owners, 1990.

Entertainment Industry Contracts; Negotiating and Drafting Guide, Donald C. Farber-General Editor, Matthew Bender, 1990.

Entertainment Industry Economics, Harold L. Vogel, Cambridge University Press, 1986 & 1990.

Entertainment Law, Melvin Simensky and Thomas Selz, 1984.

Ernst & Young Business Plan Guide, Eric S. Siegel, Loren A. Schultz, Brian R. Ford and David C. Carney, John Wiley & Sons, 1987.

Feature Development: From Concept to Production, (seminar) Independent Feature Project/West, November, 1991.

Feature Film Limited Partnerships: A Practical Guide Focusing on Securities and Marketing for Independent Producers and Their Attorneys, John W. Cones, "Loyola of Los Angeles Entertainment Law Journal," 1992.

Federal Tax Coordinator 2d, Research Institute of America, Inc., 1990.

Filmmaker's Dictionary, Ralph S. Singleton, Lone Eagle Publishing Co., 1990.

Film Studios Threaten Retaliation Against States Banning Blind Bids, "Los Angeles Times," June 1, 1981.

Film-TV Law—3rd Ed., Walter E. Hurst, Johnny Minus and William Storm Hale, Seven Arts Press, Inc., 1976.

Financial Guidelines for Investing in Motion Picture Limited Partnerships, L. M. Farrell, "Loyola of Los Angeles Entertainment Law Journal," 1992.

Financing the Production of Theatrical Motion Pictures, Lionel S. Sobel, "Entertainment Law Reporter," May, 1984.

Financing Your Film, Trisha Curran, Praeger Publishers, 1985.

Hollywood Reporter (a world entertainment-news daily publication) published by Billboard Publications, Los Angeles, California (numerous issues from 1986 through early 1992).

Hollywood Reporter Blu-Book, Billboard Publications, 1990.

Hollywood's Hard Times, Jeffrey Goodell, "Premiere" magazine, January, 1992.

How Contracts Escalate into Torts, Kurt E. Wilson, "California Lawyer" magazine, January, 1992.

How to Draft Multi-Picture Deals, Nigel Sinclair, Entertainment Law & Finance, January, 1987.

How to Negotiate Contracts, Deals in the Movie Industry, Edward E. Colton, "New York Law Journal," September 23, 1988.

Independent Feature Film Production, Gregory Goodell, St. Martin's Press, 1982.

Law and Business of the Entertainment Industries, Biederman, Berry, Pierson, Silfen, and Glasser, Auburn House, 1987.

Law Dictionary—2nd Ed., Steven H. Gifis, Barron's Educational Series, Inc., 1984.

Legal Aspects of Film Financing, Barsky, Hertz, Ros & Vinnik, April, 1990.

Long-Term Contracts for Independent Producers, Nigel Sinclair, "Entertainment Law & Finance," November, 1986.

Making Millions and Going Broke, How Production Companies Make Fortunes and Bankrupt Themselves, David Royal, "American Premiere" magazine, November/December 1991.

Masters of the Deal, Cameron Stauth, "American Film" magazine, May, 1991.

Motion Picture Finance (seminar), Paul Kagan Associates, Inc., November, 1991.

Motion Picture Investor (newsletter), Paul Kagan Associates, Inc., June and December issues, 1990.

Movie Companies, TV Networks and Publishers Have Been Forced to Audition the Same Act: Cost Cutting, Kathryn Harris, "Forbes" magazine, January 6, 1992.

Movie Industry Update—1991, Goldman Sachs (Investment Research), 1991.

Music Theory Dictionary, Dr. William F. Lee, Hansen Publications, Ltd., 1966.

NASD Manual, National Association of Securities Dealers, Inc., September 1990.

Never Enough: The "A" Deal, Business, Legal and Ethical Realities, Sixteenth Annual UCLA Entertainment Symposium, February, 1992.

Off-Hollywood: The Making & Marketing of American Specialty Films, David Rosen and Peter Hamilton, The Sundance Institute and the Independent Feature Project, 1986.

One Producer's Inside View of Foreign and Domestic Pre-Sales in the Independent Financing of Motion Pictures, Arnold Kopelson, "Loyola of Los Angeles Entertainment Law Journal," 1992.

Opportunities Knock (Co-Production Possibilities with Japan and Britain, Kathryn Bowser, The Independent, November, 1991.

Pick-Ups, Pre-Sales and Co-Ventures, P.J. Abode, "Montage" (IFP/West publication), Winter 1991/1992.

Producer's Masterguide, Billboard Publications, Inc., 1989, 1990 & 1991.

Profit Participation In The Motion Picture Industry, Steven D. Sills and Ivan L. Axelrod, "Los Angeles Lawyer" magazine, April, 1989.

Projecting Profits from a Motion Picture (excerpts from an unpublished work), David J. Leedy, presented Fall 1991, for UCLA Extension class: "Contractual Aspects of Producing, Financing and Distributing Film."

Reel Power, The Struggle for Influence and Success in the New Hollywood, Mark Litwak, William Morrow and Company, Inc., 1986.

Representing Independent Motion Picture Producers, Sinclair and Gerse, "Los Angeles Lawyer" magazine, May, 1988.

Role of Completion Bonding Companies in Independent Productions, Mark C. Phillips, "Loyola of Los Angeles Entertainment Law Journal," 1992.

Role of Production Counsel in Feature Films, Beverly Hills Bar Association Education Publications.

Screenplay—The Foundations of Screenwriting, Syd Field, Dell Publishing Co., Inc., 1985.

Securities: Public and Private Offerings—(Rev. Ed.), William M. Prifti, Callaghan & Company, 1980.

Securities Regulation—3rd Ed., David L. Ratner, West Publishing Company, 1989.

Structuring Film Development Deals, Marc Jacobson, "Entertainment Law & Finance," September, 1990.

Successful Producing in the Entertainment Industry, Mark Litwak, UCLA Extension, 1990.

Tax Literacy for the Business Lawyer, Continuing Education of the Bar, California (seminar handout, September 1991).

Tax Shelters—The Basics, Arthur Andersen & Co., Harper & Row, Publishers, 1983.

Tax Shelters—The Bottom Line, Robert A. Stanger, Robert A. Stanger & Company, Publisher, 1982.

Television Writing (From Concept to Contract), Richard A. Blum, Focal Press, 1984.

Three Hundred Thirty-Seven Reported Practices of Feature Film Distributors (unpublished compilation), John W. Cones, 1992.

U.S./Foreign Film Funding (Co-Production Tips), Nigel Sinclair, "Entertainment Law & Finance," March, 1991.

Variety (Weekly and Daily Editions), Cahners Publishing Company (numerous issues: 1986 through early 1992).

Webster's Seventh New Collegiate Dictionary, G. & C. Merriam Company, Publishers, 1976.

What to Include in Pacts Between Author & Film Co., Edward E. Colton, "New York Law Journal," October 7, 1988.

Writers Guild of America Theatrical and Television Basic Agreement, 1988.

About the Author

John W. Cones is a Los Angeles-based securities/entertainment attorney who is licensed to practice law in the states of California and Texas. He currently maintains a private, solo practice advising independent feature film, video, television and theatrical producers regarding federal and state securities law compliance obligations in passive investor corporate, limited partnership and investment contract offerings, and related entertainment law matters. He prepares the "camera ready" offering disclosure documents for such offerings, serves as a liaison to managing and selling broker/dealers and prepares or assists in negotiating entertainment contracts, including film distribution agreements, for his clients.

Mr. Cones engaged in the private practice of law in Houston from 1981 through 1986. In that practice he supervised state securities compliance aspects of Regulation D (private placement) limited partnership and corporate offerings (including movie production/distribution, oil and gas, real estate, equipment leasing, night clubs, restaurants, cattle breeding/feeding, thorough-bred breeding and medical technology). In his securities law practice, Mr. Cones has participated in the preparation of disclosure documents and federal/state compliance for 135-plus public or private limited partnership, investment contract or corporate stock offerings. Mr. Cones moved his law practice to California in 1987 specifically to work with independent producers in the manner described above.

Mr. Cones is the author of state and national association magazine articles and his law journal article "Feature Film Limited Partnerships" appeared in the January 1992 symposium issue on independent productions published by the *Loyola of Los Angeles Entertainment Law Journal*. He has lectured extensively (in Los Angeles, Las Vegas, Dallas, Houston and San Francisco) on "Investor Financing of Entertainment Projects" for the American Film Institute, the University of

Southern California Cinema-Television Alumni Association, the Loyola Marymount Continuing Education Division, Cinetex '90 and UCLA Extension. He has also lectured for UCLA Extension and AFI on "The Film Distribution Deal" and currently serves as the Course Coordinator/Instructor for the UCLA Extension course "Contractual Aspects of Financing, Producing and Distributing Film."

In addition to being a member of the California and Texas state bar associations, he is a member of the Los Angeles County and Beverly Hills Bar Associations. He is also a member of the American Film Institute, the Independent Feature Project/West, the Association of Independent Video and Filmmakers and The Third Decade Council.

Prior to 1975, Mr. Cones was a Radio-Television News Reporter at KTBC (Channel 7) television, Austin, where he worked at varying times as a television news anchor, on general and film assignments, and as a sports or weather anchor. Mr. Cones worked at KTBC full-time while attending law school at UT Austin. He also had performed on-the-air news reporting duties previously at KRIS-TV, Corpus Christi, and KITE radio in San Antonio.

In 1975 and immediately following graduation from law school, he served as legislative counsel to the Texas House of Representatives. In that position, he drafted, edited and reviewed state legislation, counseled legislator sponsors with respect to state constitutional requirements applicable to such bills, and supervised union proof-readers who reviewed such legislation as it passed various legislative stages.

During the years 1976 through 1981, Mr. Cones worked as a lobbyist/association executive and in-house counsel for professional associations headquartered in Austin and Chicago. In those positions, along with his more general association management responsibilities, he prepared and delivered congressional testimony, drafted legislation and wrote and edited books, magazines, magazine articles, newsletters, speeches and press releases. His article "What Lobbyists Really Do" has been reprinted in four state association publications in three states. As an association executive he was also involved in long-term planning, board meetings, conventions, seminars, staff supervision and association membership activities.

Mr. Cones is a 1967 graduate of the University of Texas at Austin with a Bachelor of Science degree in Communications and a 1974 graduate of the UT Austin School of Law with a Doctor of Jurisprudence degree.